Designed for the Internal Medicine Clerkship

IM Essentials ☑

A Medical Knowledge Self-Assessment Program® (MKSAP®) for Students

Philip A. Masters, MD, FACP
Senior Physician Educator
American College of Physicians
Editor-in-Chief

American College of Physicians

Clerkship Directors in Internal Medicine

14 15 16 17 18 19 20 / 10 9 8 7 6 5 4 3 2 1

Foreword

Welcome to IM Essentials, an educational resource for learning internal medicine developed specifically for students!

IM Essentials is a suite of educational materials produced collaboratively by the American College of Physicians (ACP), the national practice society for internal medicine, and the Clerkship Directors in Internal Medicine (CDIM), the national organization of individuals responsible for teaching internal medicine to medical students.

The IM Essentials suite consists of IM Essentials Text, an abbreviated textbook of internal medicine organized by traditional topic areas, IM Essentials Questions, containing over 500 detailed self-assessment and study questions, and IM Essentials Online, a digital version available on multiple platforms that combines the textbook and self-assessment content and provides multiple additional features for use in learning internal medicine. Be sure to explore the special features of IM Essentials Online (available even if you are using the print version of either book) created specifically to optimize your studying, such as electronic flashcards and the ability to create custom quizzes.

The content in the IM Essentials suite has been developed by over 90 CDIM-member internal medicine clerkship directors and clerkship faculty representing 70 medical schools. Combined with the educational knowledge and expertise of the ACP, IM Essentials represents an authoritative, evidence-based resource that can be trusted to help you learn internal medicine.

As with the previous versions of these materials (Internal Medicine Essentials for Clerkship Students and MKSAP for Students), the content in IM Essentials is based on the Society of General Internal Medicine/CDIM core curriculum for the internal medicine clerkship, and focuses on the key internal medicine concepts and factual information that are evaluated on both the end-of-clerkship and USMLE Step 2 examinations.

As in the past, we hope to receive your feedback to help us improve future editions—please let us know your thoughts about IM Essentials and how it may best fit your learning needs.

Thank you for using IM Essentials, and enjoy learning internal medicine!

Philip A. Masters, MD, FACP
Editor-in-Chief
Senior Physician Educator
American College of Physicians

Editor-in-Chief

Philip A. Masters, MD, FACP
Senior Physician Educator
American College of Physicians
Philadelphia, Pennsylvania

Associate Editors

Jonathan S. Appelbaum, MD, FACP
Associate Professor, Clinical Sciences Department
Director, Internal Medicine Education
Florida State University College of Medicine
Tallahassee, Florida

Thomas M. De Fer, MD, FACP
Professor of Medicine
Director, Internal Medicine Clerkship
Washington University School of Medicine
Saint Louis, Missouri

Susan T. Hingle, MD, FACP
Associate Professor of Medicine
Internal Medicine Clerkship Director
Southern Illinois University School of Medicine
Springfield, Illinois

Robert Trowbridge, MD, FACP
Assistant Professor of Medicine
Tufts University School of Medicine
Director of Undergraduate Medical Education
Department of Medicine
Maine Medical Center
Portland, Maine

T. Robert Vu, MD, FACP
Associate Professor of Clinical Medicine
Director, Internal Medicine Clerkship
Indiana University School of Medicine
Indianapolis, Indiana

ACP Editorial Staff

Edward Warren
Project Manager

Lisa Levine
Editorial Production

Rosemarie Houton
Editorial Production

ACP Principal Staff

Patrick C. Alguire, MD, FACP
Senior Vice President, Medical Education

Sean McKinney
Vice President, Medical Education

CDIM Principal Staff

Sheila T. Costa
AAIM Director of Development and Communications
Alliance for Academic Internal Medicine

Acknowledgments

The American College of Physicians (ACP) gratefully acknowledges the special contributions to the development and production of the 1st edition of IM Essentials made by the following people:

Graphic Services: Michael Ripca (Graphics Technical Administrator/ Graphic Designer), Barry Moshinski (Art Director, Graphics Services), Thomas Malone (Graphics Production Supervisor)

Production/Systems: Dan Hoffmann (Director, Web Services & Systems Development), Scott Hurd (Manager, Content Systems), Neil Kohl (Senior Architect), Chris Patterson (Senior Architect) and Robert Guthy (Systems Analyst/Developer).

IM Essentials Online: Under the direction of Steven Spadt, Vice President, ACP Digital Products & Services, the online version of IM Essentials was developed within the ACP's Digital Product Development department, led by Brian Sweigard (Director). Other members of the team included Dan Barron (Senior Systems Analyst/Developer), Chris Forrest (Senior Software Developer/Design Lead), Kara Kronenwetter (Senior Web Developer), Brad Lord (Senior Web Application Developer), John McKnight (Senior Web Developer), and Nate Pershall (Senior Web Developer).

The College also wishes to acknowledge that many other persons, too numerous to mention, have contributed to the production of this program. Without their dedicated efforts, this program would not have been possible.

Disclosure Policy

It is the policy of the American College of Physicians (ACP) to ensure balance, independence, objectivity, and scientific rigor in all its educational activities. To this end, and consistent with the policies of the ACP and the Accreditation Council for Continuing Medical Education (ACCME), contributors to all ACP continuing medical education activities are required to disclose all relationships with any entity producing, marketing, re-selling, or distributing health care goods or services consumed by, or used on, patients. Contributors are required to use generic names in the discussion of therapeutic options and are required to identify any unapproved, off-label, or investigative use of commercial products or devices. Where a trade name is used, all available trade names for the same product type are also included. If trade-name products manufactured by companies with whom contributors have relationships are discussed, contributors are asked to provide evidence-based citations in support of the discussion. If necessary, adjustments to topics or contributors' roles in content development are made to balance the discussion. The editors of IM Essentials have ensured that content is based on best evidence and updated clinical care guidelines, when such evidence and guidelines were available. Contributors' disclosure information is reviewed by the editors and every effort was made to resolve any conflicts presented. Further, all readers of this text are asked to evaluate the content for evidence of commercial bias so that future decisions about content and contributors can be made in light of this information.

Educational Disclaimer

The editors and publisher of IM Essentials recognize that the development of new material offers many opportunities for error. Despite our best efforts, some errors may persist in print. Drug dosage schedules are, we believe, accurate and in accordance with current standards. Readers are advised, however, to ensure that the recommended dosages in IM Essentials concur with the information provided in the product information material. This is especially important in cases of new, infrequently used, or highly toxic drugs. Application of the information in IM Essentials remains the professional responsibility of the practitioner.

The primary purpose of IM Essentials is educational. Information presented, as well as publications, technologies, products, and/or services discussed, is intended to inform subscribers about the knowledge, techniques, and experiences of the contributors. A diversity of professional opinion exists, and the views of the contributors are their own and not those of the ACP. Inclusion of any material in the program does not constitute endorsement or recommendation by the ACP. The ACP does not warrant the safety, reliability, accuracy, completeness, or usefulness of and disclaims any and all liability for damages and claims that may result from the use of information, publications, technologies, products, and/or services discussed in this program.

Publisher's Information

Unauthorized Use of This Book Is Against the Law

ISBN: 978-1-938921-10-0

Printed in the United States of America

For order information in the U.S. or Canada call 800-523-1546, extension 2600. All other countries call 215-351-2600. Fax inquiries to 215-351-2799 or email to custserv@acponline.org.

Editorial Review Board

Contributing Authors

Gauri Agarwal, MD, FACP
Assistant Regional Dean for Medical Curriculum
Clerkship Director, Integrated Medicine
University of Miami Miller School of Medicine
Miami, Florida

Erik K. Alexander, MD, FACP
Director, Medical Student Education
Brigham and Women's Hospital
Associate Professor of Medicine
Harvard Medical School
Boston, Massachusetts

Irene Alexandraki, MD, MPH, FACP
Assistant Professor of Medicine
University of Central Florida College of Medicine
Orlando, Florida

Alpesh N. Amin, MD, MBA, FACP
Professor of Medicine
Medicine Clerkship Director
University of California, Irvine
Orange, California

Joel Appel, DO
Director, Ambulatory and Subinternship Programs
Section Chief Hematology/Oncology
Sinai-Grace Hospital
Wayne State University School of Medicine
Detroit, Michigan

Jonathan S. Appelbaum, MD, FACP
Education Director
Professor of Internal Medicine
Florida State University College of Medicine
Tallahassee, Florida

Mary Jane Barchman, MD, FACP, FASN
Professor of Medicine
Internal Medicine Clerkship Director
Section of Nephrology and Hypertension
Brody School of Medicine at East Carolina University
Greenville, North Carolina

Gonzalo Bearman, MD, MPH
Professor of Medicine
Associate Hospital Epidemiologist
Virginia Commonwealth University
Richmond, Virginia

Jennifer Bequette, MD, FACP
Assistant Professor, Department of Medicine
Continuing Care Clinic Clerkship Director
University of Missouri at Kansas City School of Medicine
Kansas City, Missouri

Jennifer Bierman, MD, FACP
Primary Care Clerkship Director
Northwestern University Feinberg School of Medicine
Chicago, Illinois

Matthew J. Burday, DO, FACP
Associate Program Director
Internal Medicine Residency Program Director
Medical Student Programs
Department of Medicine, Christiana Care Health System
Newark, Delaware

Cynthia A. Burns, MD, FACP
Assistant Professor
Internal Medicine Clerkship Director
Department of Internal Medicine
Section on Endocrinology & Metabolism
Wake Forest University School of Medicine
Winston-Salem, North Carolina

Danelle Cayea, MD, MS
Assistant Professor of Medicine
Johns Hopkins University School of Medicine
Baltimore, Maryland

Dennis T. Chang, MD
Assistant Professor, Department of Medicine
Co-Director, Medicine-Geriatrics Clerkship
Division of Hospital Medicine
Mount Sinai Health System
New York, New York

Joseph Charles, MD, FACP, FHM
Assistant Professor of Medicine
Division Education Coordinator
Department of Hospital Internal Medicine
4th year Clerkship Director
Mayo Clinic Hospital
Phoenix, Arizona

Mark D. Corriere, MD, FACP
Johns Hopkins University
Division of Endocrinology, Diabetes, and Metabolism
Baltimore, Maryland

Feroza Daroowalla, MD, MPH
Associate Professor, Department of Medicine
Stony Book University
Stony Brook, New York

Thomas M. DeFer, MD, FACP
Professor of Medicine
Clerkship Director
Washington University School of Medicine
Saint Louis, Missouri

Matthew J. Diamond, DO, MS, FACP
Associate Professor of Medicine, Section of Nephrology,
    Hypertension, and Transplant Medicine
The Medical College of Georgia at Georgia Regents University
Augusta, Georgia

Gretchen Diemer, MD, FACP
Assistant Professor of Internal Medicine
Director of Undergraduate Medical Education
Program Director, Internal Medicine Residency
Thomas Jefferson University
Philadelphia, Pennsylvania

Reed E. Drews, MD, FACP
Program Director, Hematology-Oncology
Beth Israel Deaconess Medical Center
Boston, Massachusetts

Maria Dungo, MD
Associate Professor
David Geffen School of Medicine, UCLA
Division of Medical Oncology and Hematology
Harbor-UCLA Medical Center
Torrance, California

Anne Eacker, MD, FACP
Associate Professor
Medicine Associate Dean, Student Affairs
University of Washington School of Medicine
Seattle, Washington

Richard S. Eisenstaedt, MD, MACP
Chair, Department of Medicine
Abington Memorial Hospital
Abington, Pennsylvania

D. Michael Elnicki, MD, FACP
Ambulatory Clerkship Director
University of Pittsburgh School of Medicine
Pittsburgh, Pennsylvania
Assistant Professor of Medicine
Clerkship Director, Medicine
Weill Cornell Medical College
New York, New York

Mark J. Fagan, MD, FACP
Internal Medicine Clerkship Director
Professor of Medicine
Alpert Medical School of Brown University
Providence, Rhode Island

Sara B. Fazio, MD, FACP
Associate Professor, Harvard Medical School
Division of General Internal Medicine
Beth Israel Deaconess Medical Center
Boston, Massachusetts

Jane P. Gagliardi, MD, MHS, FACP, FAPA
Assistant Professor of Psychiatry & Behavioral Sciences
Assistant Professor of Medicine
Duke University School of Medicine
Durham, North Carolina

Susan Glod MD, FACP
Assistant Professor of Medicine
Penn State College of Medicine
Hershey, Pennsylvania

Roderick Go, DO
Medicine Subinternship Director
Medicine Clerkship Co-Director
Stony Book University School of Medicine
Stony Brook, New York

Alda Maria R. Gonzaga, MD, MS, FACP, FAAP
Associate Professor of Internal Medicine and Pediatrics
Program Director, Internal Medicine-Pediatrics Residency
University of Pittsburgh School of Medicine
Pittsburgh, Pennsylvania

Eric Goren
Assistant Professor of Medicine
Perelman School of Medicine
University of Pennsylvania
Philadelphia, Pennsylvania

Eric H. Green, MD, MSc, FACP
Program Director, Internal Medicine
Clinical Associate Professor of Medicine
Mercy Catholic Medical Center
Drexel University College of Medicine
Philadelphia and Darby, Pennsylvania

David V. Gugliotti, MD, FACP, SFHM
Internal Medicine Discipline Leader/Clerkship Director
Clinical Assistant Professor of Medicine, Cleveland Clinic
Lerner College of Medicine of Case Western Reserve University
Cleveland, Ohio

Heather Harrell, MD, FACP
Clinical Associate Professor and Clerkship Director
Department of Medicine
University of Florida College of Medicine
Gainesville, Florida

Amy Hayton, MD, MPH
Assistant Professor of Medicine
Medicine Associate Clerkship Director
Loma Linda University School of Medicine
Loma Linda, California

Brian S. Heist, MD
Assistant Professor of Medicine
University of Pittsburgh School of Medicine
Pittsburgh, Pennsylvania

Scott Herrle, MD, MS, FACP
Assistant Professor of Medicine
University of Pittsburgh School of Medicine
VA Pittsburgh Healthcare System
Pittsburgh, Pennsylvania

Susan T. Hingle, MD, FACP
Professor of Medicine
Interim Chair, Department of Medicine
Medicine Clerkship Director
Southern Illinois University School of Medicine
Springfield, Illinois

Martha L. Hlafka, MD
Assistant Professor, Department of Internal Medicine
Associate Director, Internal Medicine Clerkship
Southern Illinois University School of Medicine
Springfield, Illinois

Eric Hsieh, MD, FACP
Program Director, Internal Medicine Residency
Assistant Professor of Clinical Medicine
Keck School of Medicine
University of Southern California
Los Angeles, California

Nadia Ismail, MD, MPH, MEd
Internal Medicine Clerkship Director
Baylor College of Medicine
Houston, Texas

Asra R. Khan, MD, FACP
Associate Professor of Clinical Medicine
Associate Program Director, Internal Medicine
Clerkship & Sub-I Director, Internal Medicine
Course Director, Essentials of Clinical Medicine
University of Illinois College of Medicine
Chicago, Illinois

Karen E. Kirkham, MD, FACP
Vice-Chair for Undergraduate Medical Education
Department of Internal Medicine
Boonshoft Wright State School of Medicine
Dayton, Ohio

Christopher A. Klipstein, MD
Professor of Medicine
Director, Medicine Inpatient Clerkship
University of North Carolina School of Medicine
Chapel Hill, North Carolina

Norra Kwong, MD
Endocrine Fellow
Brigham and Women's Hospital
Harvard Medical School
Boston, Massachusetts

Amalia M. Landa-Galindez, MD
Assistant Professor of Medicine
Assistant Clerkship Director, Internal Medicine
Florida International University
Herbert Wertheim College of Medicine
Miami, Florida

Valerie J. Lang, MD, FACP
Associate Professor of Medicine
Director, Inpatient Internal Medicine Clerkship
University of Rochester School of Medicine and Dentistry
Rochester, New York

Lawrence Loo, MD, MACP
Vice Chair for Education and Faculty Development
Professor of Medicine, Department of Medicine
Loma Linda University School of Medicine
Loma Linda, California

Fred A. Lopez, MD, MACP
Richard Vial Professor and Vice Chair
Department of Medicine
Louisiana State University Health Sciences Center
New Orleans, Louisiana

Merry Jennifer Markham, MD, FACP
Assistant Professor, Division of Hematology-Oncology
Co-Course Director, Medicine Clerkship
University of Florida College of Medicine
Gainesville, Florida

Lianne Marks, MD, PhD, FACP
Assistant Dean for Educational Development
Regional Chair of Internal Medicine
Texas A & M College of Medicine
Baylor Scott & White Health
Round Rock, Texas

Kevin M. McKown, MD, FACP
Professor of Medicine
University of Wisconsin School of Medicine and Public Health
Madison, Wisconsin

Alyssa C. McManamon, MD, FACP
Associate Clerkship Director, Department of Medicine
Uniformed Services University of the Health Sciences
Bethesda, Maryland

Chad S. Miller, MD, FACP
Director, Student Programs
Associate Program Director, Residency
Department of Internal Medicine
Tulane University Health Sciences Center
New Orleans, Louisiana

Nina Mingioni, MD, FACP, MD
Clerkship Director, Internal Medicine
Associate Program Director, Internal Medicine Residency
Jefferson Medical College
Thomas Jefferson University
Philadelphia, Pennsylvania

Lynda Misra, DO, FACP, MEd
Associate Dean, Undergraduate Clinical Education
Assistant Professor, Internal Medicine and Neurology
Oakland University William Beaumont School of Medicine
Rochester, Michigan

Liana Nikolaenko, MD
Fellow, Department of Hematology-Oncology
Harbor-UCLA Medical Center
Torrance, California

L. James Nixon, MD, MHPE
Professor of Medicine & Pediatrics
Vice Chair for Education, Department of Medicine
University of Minnesota Medical School
Minneapolis, Minnesota

Kendall Novoa-Takara, MD, FACP
Medicine Clerkship Site Director
University of Arizona College of Medicine
Phoenix, Arizona

Isaac O. Opole, MD, PhD, FACP
Associate Professor of Medicine
Assistant Dean for Student Affairs
Internal Medicine Clerkship Director
Department of Internal Medicine
University of Kansas School of Medicine
Kansas City, Kansas

Carlos Palacio, MD, MPH, FACP
Associate Professor of Medicine, Department of Medicine
University of Florida College of Medicine-Jacksonville
Jacksonville, Florida

Robert Pargament, MD, FACP
Program Director
Internal Medicine Residency Program
York Hospital
York, Pennsylvania

Michael Picchioni, MD
Assistant Professor of Medicine
Clerkship Site Director
Baystate Medical Center
Tufts University School of Medicine
Springfield, Massachusetts

Seth Politano, DO, FACP
Associate Program Director, Office of Educational Affairs
Assistant Professor of Clinical Medicine
Keck School of Medicine of the University of Southern California
Los Angeles, California

Nora L. Porter, MD, MPH, FACP
Professor of Medicine Co-Director, Internal Medicine Clerkship
Saint Louis University School of Medicine
Saint Louis, Missouri

Joseph Rencic, MD, FACP
Associate Professor of Medicine
Tufts Medical Center
Tufts University School of Medicine
Boston, Massachusetts

Juan Reyes, MD, MPH
Assistant Professor of Medicine
Clerkship Director Internal Medicine
George Washington University School of Medicine
Washington, DC

Robert Robinson, MD, FACP
Associate Professor of Clinical Medicine
Department of Internal Medicine
Southern Illinois University School of Medicine
Springfield, Illinois

Kathleen F. Ryan, MD, FACP
Associate Professor of Medicine
Department of Medicine
Drexel University College of Medicine
Philadelphia, Pennsylvania

Mysti D.W. Schott, MD, FACP
Clinical Associate Professor of Medicine
Department of Medicine, Division of General Medicine
University of Texas Health Science Center
San Antonio School of Medicine
San Antonio, Texas

Monica Ann Shaw, MD, FACP
Professor of Medicine
Associate Dean for Medical Education
University of Louisville School of Medicine
Louisville, Kentucky

Patricia Short, MD, FACP
Assistant Professor of Medicine
Program Director, Internal Medicine Residency
Uniformed Services University of the Health Sciences
Madigan Army Medical Center
Tacoma, Washington

Leigh Simmons, MD
Assistant Professor
Clerkship Director
Harvard Medical School
Massachusetts General Hospital
Boston, Massachusetts

Madhusree Singh, MD
Associate Clinical Professor
VA San Diego Health System
University of California, San Diego
San Diego, California

Karen Szauter, MD, FACP
Co-Director, Internal Medicine Clerkship
University of Texas Medical Branch
Galveston, Texas

Harold M. Szerlip, MD, FACP, FCCP, FASN, FNKF
Professor, Department of Medicine
University of North Texas Health Sciences Center
Fort Worth, Texas

Gary Tabas, MD, FACP
Transitional Year Program Director
University of Pittsburgh School of Medicine
UPMC Shadyside
Pittsburgh, Pennsylvania

Kimberly M. Tartaglia, MD, FACP
Assistant Professor – Clinical
Ohio State University College of Medicine
Ohio State University Wexner Medical Center
Columbus, Ohio

Bipin Thapa, MD, MS, FACP
Assistant Professor, Department of Medicine
Associate Clerkship Director, Internal Medicine Clerkship
Medical College of Wisconsin
Milwaukee, Wisconsin

David C. Tompkins, MD
Interim Chair, Department of Medicine
Director of Medical Education
Lutheran Medical Center
Brooklyn, New York

Robert L. Trowbridge, MD, FACP
Division Director, General Internal Medicine
Director of Student Education, Department of Medicine
Maine Medical Center
Portland, Maine

Corina Ungureanu, MD
Assistant Professor-Clinical, General Internal Medicine
Ambulatory Internal Medicine Clerkship Director
Ohio State University
Columbus, Ohio

John Varras, MD
Chairman
Department of Internal Medicine
University of Nevada School of Medicine
Las Vegas, Nevada

H. Douglas Walden, MD, MPH, FACP
Professor of Medicine
Co-Director, Internal Medicine Clerkship
Saint Louis University School of Medicine
Saint Louis, Missouri

John A. Walker, MD, FACP
Professor and Vice-Chair for Education
Department of Medicine
Medicine Clerkship Director
Rutgers Robert Wood Johnson Medical School
New Brunswick, New Jersey

Sarita Warrier, MD, FACP
Assistant Professor of Medicine
Division of General Internal Medicine
Warren Alpert Medical School of Brown University
Providence, Rhode Island

Joseph T. Wayne, MD, MPH, FACP
Internal Medicine Clerkship Director
Department of Internal Medicine
Albany Medical College
Albany, New York

Sean A. Whelton, MD
Associate Professor of Medicine (Rheumatology)
Clerkship Director, Internal Medicine
Georgetown University School of Medicine
Washington, DC

Jenny Wright, MD
Assistant Professor of Medicine
University of Washington School of Medicine
Seattle, Washington

Contents

Foreword iii

Cardiovascular Medicine Questions .... *Revisit # 47 & 48 - Mitral valve dx* 1
Cardiovascular Medicine Answers and Critiques .. *Revisit last 4 Questions on DVT* 20

Endocrinology and Metabolism Questions 43
Endocrinology and Metabolism Answers and Critiques 50

Gastroenterology and Hepatology Questions 63
Gastroenterology and Hepatology Answers and Critiques 75

General Internal Medicine Questions 95
General Internal Medicine Answers and Critiques 114

Hematology Questions 151
Hematology Answers and Critiques 160

Infectious Disease Medicine Questions 175
Infectious Disease Medicine Answers and Critiques 186

Nephrology Questions 207
Nephrology Answers and Critiques...216

Neurology Questions 231
Neurology Answers and Critiques 239

Oncology Questions 255
Oncology Answers and Critiques 262

Pulmonary Medicine Questions 275
Pulmonary Medicine Answers and Critiques 283

Rheumatology Questions..295
Rheumatology Answers and Critiques 304

Normal Laboratory Values 319

Color Plates .... back of book

Errata .... ime.acponline.org/errata

Section 1

Cardiovascular Medicine

Questions

Item 1 [Basic]

A 42-year-old woman is evaluated in the emergency department. She has a 2-day history of nonexertional chest pain. The pain is sharp, substernal, and worse when lying down or with deep breaths. She denies shortness of breath. Her symptoms were preceded by a recent upper respiratory tract infection.

On physical examination, temperature is 37.9°C (100.3°F), blood pressure is 165/90 mm Hg, pulse rate is 102/min, respiration rate is 18/min, and oxygen saturation is 96% on ambient air. The cardiopulmonary examination is normal as is the remainder of the physical examination.

An electrocardiogram is shown. Echocardiogram shows a small pericardial effusion.

Which of the following is the most appropriate initial therapy?

(A) Clopidogrel
(B) Heparin
(C) Ibuprofen
(D) Prednisone

Item 2 [Basic]

A 38-year-old man is evaluated in the emergency department. He has a 2-week history of nonpleuritic, sharp, anterior chest pain. Each episode of pain lasts 3 to 10 hours. He describes the pain as being located mostly to the left of the sternum, although at times it radiates across the entire chest but not to his shoulders, arms, or back.

The pain sometimes occurs at rest and is worsened with lateral movement of the trunk. It does not worsen with exertion. He has no other symptoms and no other medical problems. He does not use drugs and takes no medications.

On physical examination, temperature is 37.0°C (98.6°F), blood pressure is 132/70 mm Hg, pulse rate is 90/min, and respiration rate is 14/min. There is reproducible point tenderness along the left sternum. The remainder of the examination, including the cardiovascular examination, is normal.

Which of the following is the most likely diagnosis?

(A) Acute pericarditis
(B) Aortic dissection
(C) Costochondritis
(D) Unstable angina

Item 3 [Basic]

A 24-year-old man is evaluated for a 6-month history of episodic substernal chest pain. Episodes occur four to five times per week and are accompanied by palpitations and sweating. They resolve spontaneously after approximately 30 minutes. His symptoms are unrelieved with antacids, can occur at rest or with exertion, and are nonpositional. There are no specific precipitating factors. Lipid levels were obtained last year and were normal. The patient is a nonsmoker. He has no personal or family history of coronary artery disease, diabetes mellitus, hyperlipidemia, or hypertension. He is not taking any medications.

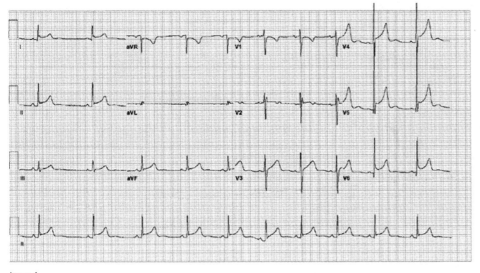

Item 1

On physical examination, vital signs are normal. He has no cardiac murmurs and no abdominal pain. Complete blood count, serum thyroid-stimulating hormone level, and electrocardiogram are all normal.

Which of the following is the most appropriate management of this patient?

(A) Cardiac event monitor
(B) Cardiac stress test
(C) Empiric trial of proton pump inhibitor
(D) Treatment with a selective serotonin reuptake inhibitor

Item 4 [Basic]

A 70-year-old man is evaluated for sharp left-sided pleuritic chest pain and shortness of breath that began suddenly 24 hours ago. The pain has been persistent over the last 24 hours and does not worsen or improve with exertion or position. The patient's history is significant for a 50-pack-year smoking history and severe chronic obstructive pulmonary disease, although he is currently a nonsmoker. Medications are ipratropium and albuterol.

On physical examination, temperature is normal, blood pressure is 128/80 mm Hg, pulse rate is 88/min, and respiration rate is 18/min. Oxygen saturation on ambient air is 89%. The trachea is midline. Lung examination shows hyperresonance, decreased chest wall expansion, and decreased breath sounds on the left. Cardiac examination shows distant heart sounds but no extra heart sounds.

Which of the following is the most appropriate diagnostic test to perform next?

(A) Chest CT
(B) Chest radiography
(C) Echocardiography
(D) Electrocardiography

Item 5 [Basic]

A 50-year-old woman is evaluated for a 1-year history of recurrent left-sided chest pain. The pain is poorly localized and nonexertional and occurs in 1-minute episodes. There is no dyspnea, nausea, or diaphoresis associated with these episodes. The patient has not had dysphagia, heartburn, weight change, or other gastrointestinal symptoms. She has no other medical problems and does not smoke cigarettes.

On physical examination, vital signs are normal. The patient's chest pain is not reproducible by palpation. The cardiac examination is unremarkable, as is the remainder of the physical examination.

Results of a lipid panel, a fasting plasma glucose test, and a chest radiograph are normal. An echocardiogram shows a normal ejection fraction, with no wall motion abnormalities. Results of an exercise stress test are normal.

Which of the following is the most appropriate next step in management?

(A) Ambulatory pH study
(B) Endoscopy
(C) Treatment with a nonsteroidal anti-inflammatory drug
(D) Trial of a proton pump inhibitor

Item 6 [Basic]

A 65-year-old man is evaluated because of chronic angina. He has a 10-year history of symptomatic coronary artery disease. The diagnosis was confirmed with an exercise stress test. Results of the test showed no high-risk features. His estimated left ventricular ejection fraction by echocardiography at that time was 56%. He occasionally has chest pain after walking four blocks. The pain is relieved by taking one sublingual nitroglycerin or by resting. His exercise capacity has not diminished, and the frequency, character, and duration of the pain have not changed. He denies shortness of breath, orthopnea, or paroxysmal nocturnal dyspnea. Current medications include simvastatin, aspirin, metoprolol, and sublingual nitroglycerin.

On examination, blood pressure is 122/82 mm Hg, pulse rate is 68/min, respiratory rate is 16/min, and body mass index is 27. There is no jugular venous distention, and there are no murmurs, gallops, rubs, or pulmonary crackles or peripheral edema.

Which of the following is the most appropriate management?

(A) Cardiac catheterization
(B) Current medical management
(C) Echocardiogram
(D) Exercise stress test

Item 7 [Basic]

A 60-year-old man is evaluated because of a 3-month history of intermittent chest pain. He has occasional substernal chest pressure when he exercises at the gym and occasionally after he eats a spicy meal. The pressure is not consistently relieved with rest and is occasionally relieved with antacid. He has no associated symptoms of shortness of breath, dizziness, or diaphoresis. His medical history includes hypertension and hyperlipidemia. Medications are lisinopril and pravastatin.

On physical examination, blood pressure is 128/80 mm hg, pulse rate is 84/min, and respiration rate is 16/min. Findings on cardiovascular examination are normal.

The electrocardiogram is shown.

Which of the following is the most appropriate diagnostic test to evaluate the patient's chest pain?

(A) Cardiac catheterization
(B) Dobutamine echocardiography
(C) Exercise echocardiography
(D) Exercise electrocardiography

Item 8 [Basic]

A 55-year-old woman is evaluated for symptoms of sharp, localized, left-sided chest pain for the last 3 weeks. The pain is unrelated to exertion and is associated with mild dyspnea and fatigue. Typically it lasts for 5 to 10 minutes and abates spontaneously. The pain is not pleuritic, positional, or related to eating. She has hypertension and hypercholesterolemia. Her father had a myocardial infarction at 54 years of age. Daily medications are hydrochlorothiazide, simvastatin, and aspirin.

On physical examination, blood pressure is 135/78 mm Hg, pulse rate is 78/min, and respiration rate is 14/min. Cardiac auscultation shows S_4 but is otherwise normal, as is the remainder of her physical examination.

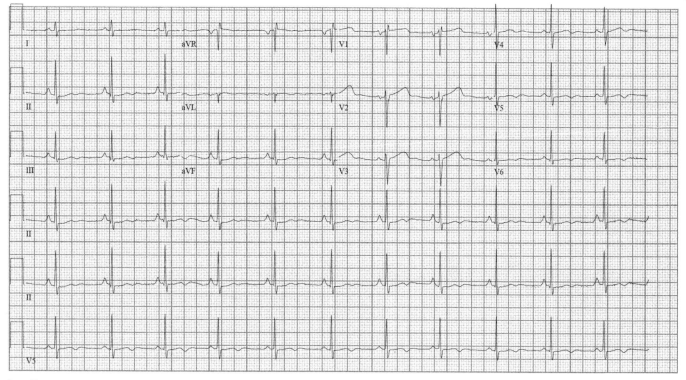

Item 7

Electrocardiogram shows sinus rhythm, with a heart rate of 75/min and no ST-segment or T-wave abnormalities.

Which of the following is the most appropriate diagnostic study?

(A) Coronary angiography
(B) Exercise echocardiography
(C) Exercise electrocardiography
(D) Pharmacologic stress test

Item 9 [Advanced]

A 68-year-old man is evaluated for exertional chest pain of 3 months' duration. He describes the chest pain as midsternal pressure without radiation that occurs with walking one to two blocks and resolves with rest or sublingual nitroglycerin. No symptoms have occurred at rest. His medical history is significant for myocardial infarction 3 years ago, hypertension, and hyperlipidemia. Medications are aspirin, metoprolol, simvastatin, isosorbide dinitrate, and sublingual nitroglycerin as needed for chest pain.

On physical examination, temperature is normal, blood pressure is 150/85 mm Hg, pulse rate is 80/min, and respiration rate is 12/min. The lungs are clear. Cardiac examination shows normal S_1 and S_2 with no extra heart sounds or murmurs. The remainder of the examination is unremarkable.

Electrocardiogram shows normal sinus rhythm, no left ventricular hypertrophy, no ST- or T-wave changes, and no Q waves.

Which of the following is the most appropriate management?

(A) Add diltiazem
(B) Add ranolazine
(C) Increase the metoprolol dosage
(D) Refer the patient for coronary angiography

Item 10 [Advanced]

A 62-year-old man with coronary artery disease is evaluated for angina. He was diagnosed 4 years ago, and since that time, his symptoms have been well controlled with metoprolol and isosorbide mononitrate. He had exertional angina 8 months ago. His dosages of metoprolol and isosorbide were increased and long-acting diltiazem was added, with improved control of his symptoms. He has had increasing symptoms over the last 2 months and now requires daily sublingual nitroglycerin for relief of angina during exercise. He has not had any episodes of angina at rest. His medical history is significant for hyperlipidemia treated with atorvastatin.

On physical examination, the patient is afebrile, blood pressure is 110/60 mm Hg, pulse rate is 55/min, and respiration rate is 12/min. Results of cardiopulmonary examination are unremarkable, as are the remainder of the findings of the physical examination.

Electrocardiogram shows no acute ischemic changes.

Which of the following should be the next step in this patient's management?

(A) Coronary angiography
(B) Exercise treadmill testing
(C) Increase β-blocker dosage
(D) Increase nitrate dosage

Item 11 [Basic]

A 68-year-old man is evaluated in the emergency department because of a 2-day history of intermittent chest pain. The pain is substernal, is not related to activity, and lasts less than 15 minutes. His medical history includes hypertension, hyperlipidemia, and type 2 diabetes. His medications include aspirin, metoprolol, lisinopril, simvastatin, and metformin. In the emergency department he received a dose of liquid antacid, and his chest pain partially resolved.

On physical examination, he is afebrile, blood pressure is 130/80 mm Hg, pulse rate is 70/min, respiration rate is 18/min, and oxygen saturation is 98% on ambient air. Results of cardiopulmonary examination are normal.

The electrocardiogram shows minor T-wave abnormalities. Troponin T measurement is less than 0.01 ng/mL (0.01 μg/L).

Which of the following is the most appropriate management of this patient's chest pain?

(A) Admission to the telemetry unit with serial electrocardiograms and troponin measurements
(B) Coronary angiography
(C) Discharge to home
(D) Esophageal pH probe
(E) Pharmacologic stress test with nuclear imaging

Item 12 [Advanced]

A 58-year-old woman is evaluated in the emergency department for chest pain, diaphoresis, and shortness of breath of 4 hours' duration. Three years ago she was diagnosed with a non–ST-elevation myocardial infarction and was treated medically. Additional medical history includes type 2 diabetes and hypertension. Her current medications are aspirin, lisinopril, atorvastatin, and glargine insulin.

On physical examination, she is afebrile, blood pressure is 125/60 mm Hg, pulse rate is 48/min, respiratory rate is 18/min, and oxygen saturation is 98% on ambient air. Cardiac examination shows no jugular venous distention, and the lungs are clear. An S_4 is present.

Electrocardiogram shows ST-segment elevation and T-wave inversions in leads II, III, and aVF. The initial troponin T measurement is elevated.

The nearest hospital capable of percutaneous coronary intervention is more than 2 hours away. The patient has no contraindication to thrombolytic therapy.

Which of the following is the most appropriate initial management for this patient?

(A) Aspirin, heparin, clopidogrel, intravenous nitroglycerin, and thrombolytic therapy
(B) Aspirin, heparin, intravenous nitroglycerin, metoprolol, and thrombolytic therapy
(C) Heparin, clopidogrel, pravastatin, and intravenous nitroglycerin
(D) Immediate transfer for percutaneous coronary intervention

Item 13 [Basic]

A 52-year-old woman was evaluated in the emergency department because of acute onset of dyspnea while shoveling snow this morning. The dyspnea resolved within 2 minutes of rest but recurred an hour later while she was watching television. Over the previous 10 days she has had several similar episodes of dyspnea with mild exertion, such as walking upstairs, and also at rest. She has no chest pain, palpitations, or orthopnea. She has a 15-year history of type 2 diabetes, hyperlipidemia, and hypertension treated with aspirin, metformin, chlorthalidone, ramipril, and rosuvastatin.

On physical examination, temperature was 37°C (98.6°F), blood pressure was 110/70 mm Hg, pulse rate was 80/min, respiratory rate was 18/min, and oxygen saturation was 96% on ambient air. There was no jugular distention, normal cardiac sounds were present without extra sounds or murmurs, and the lungs were clear to auscultation.

The initial electrocardiogram showed ST-segment changes. The first troponin I level was 0 ng/mL (0 μg/L).

An hour after admission to the emergency department, she had an episode of acute dyspnea. A repeat electrocardiogram at this time is shown. Repeat troponin level is 0.8 ng/mL (0.8 μg/L).

What of the following is the most appropriate next diagnostic test?

(A) Cardiac catheterization
(B) Echocardiogram
(C) Exercise stress test
(D) Repeat of troponin I level

Item 14 [Advanced]

A 78-year-old man is evaluated in the emergency department because of chest pain. He describes left substernal discomfort that began approximately 8 hours ago. He reports no similar episodes of chest pain. Medical history is significant for hypertension and a 30-pack-year history of ongoing tobacco use. His only medication is amlodipine.

On physical examination, the patient is afebrile, blood pressure is 130/80 mm Hg, pulse rate is 72/min, and respiration rate is 12/min. There is no jugular venous distention, the lung fields are clear, and cardiac examination shows a normal S_1 and S_2 without murmurs. No peripheral edema is present.

The initial troponin I level is 26 ng/mL (26 μg/L). Laboratory findings are otherwise normal.

Electrocardiogram shows sinus rhythm of 70/min and 2-mm ST-segment elevation in leads II, III, and aVF.

Which of the following is the most appropriate treatment approach?

(A) Coronary artery bypass surgery
(B) Intracoronary thrombolytic therapy
(C) Medical therapy
(D) Primary percutaneous coronary intervention

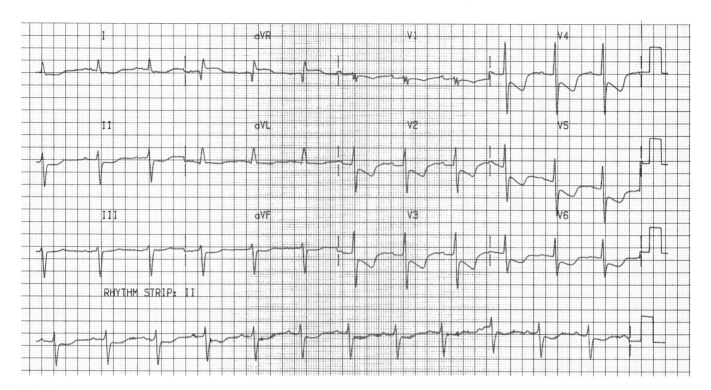

Item 13

Item 15 [Advanced]

A 70-year-old woman is hospitalized for an ST-elevation myocardial infarction involving the anterior wall. Her symptoms initially began 3 days before admission. The pain resolved spontaneously before she reached the hospital.

Two hours after presentation to the emergency department, she has acute onset of dyspnea and hypotension and requires emergent intubation. A portable chest radiograph shows cardiomegaly and pulmonary edema. Vasopressor therapy is initiated to support her blood pressure.

On physical examination, blood pressure is 90/60 mm Hg, pulse rate is 120/min, and respiration rate is 12/min. She has a grade 4/6 harsh holosystolic murmur at the right and left sternal borders associated with a palpable thrill. No S_3 or S_4 is heard. Crackles are heard bilaterally at the lung bases.

Which of the following is the most likely diagnosis?

(A) Aortic dissection
(B) Free wall rupture
(C) Right ventricular infarction
(D) Ventricular septal defect

Item 16 [Basic]

A 64-year-old man is evaluated in the emergency department because of chest pain. He describes the chest pain as nonradiating pressure in the midchest that began at rest 1 hour ago and is not associated with any symptoms. Medical history is remarkable for hypertension, type 2 diabetes mellitus, hyperlipidemia, and a 20-pack-year history of smoking. Medications are hydrochlorothiazide, metformin, and simvastatin.

On physical examination, he is afebrile, blood pressure is 140/80 mm Hg, pulse rate is 78/min, and respiration rate is 16/min. There is no jugular venous distention, the lungs are clear, and the findings on heart examination are normal.

Electrocardiogram shows a normal sinus rhythm and T-wave inversions in leads V_2 through V_6 without Q waves.

Initial cardiac biomarkers are within normal limits.

He is given aspirin, clopidogrel, low-molecular-weight heparin, and a nitrate, with resolution of his chest pain.

Which of the following is the most appropriate next step in management?

(A) Add metoprolol
(B) Add nifedipine
(C) Coronary angiography
(D) Thrombolysis

Item 17 [Basic]

A 54-year-old man is evaluated in the emergency department for an acute coronary syndrome that began 30 minutes ago. His medical history is significant for hypertension and type 2 diabetes mellitus. Medications are lisinopril and glipizide.

On physical examination, he is afebrile, blood pressure is 160/90 mm Hg, pulse rate is 80/min, and respiration rate is 12/min. Cardiovascular examination shows a normal S_1 and S_2 without an S_3 and no murmurs. Lung fields are clear.

An initial serum troponin level is pending. Electrocardiogram shows 3-mm ST-segment elevation in leads V$_2$ through V$_4$ and a 1-mm ST-segment depression in leads II, III, and aVF.

Treatment is initiated with aspirin, clopridogrel, a β-blocker, and unfractionated heparin. His symptoms of chest pain improve.

Which of the following is the most appropriate next step in management?

(A) Await troponin results

(B) Continue medical therapy

(C) Initiate thrombolytic therapy

(D) Percutaneous coronary intervention

Item 18 [Advanced]

A 77-year-old woman is admitted to the hospital for intermittent dizziness over the last few days. She reports no chest discomfort, dyspnea, palpitations, syncope, orthopnea, or edema. She underwent coronary artery bypass graft surgery 6 years ago after a myocardial infarction. She has hypertension and hyperlipidemia. Medications are hydrochlorothiazide, pravastatin, lisinopril, and aspirin.

On physical examination, blood pressure is 137/88 mm Hg and pulse rate is 52/min. The lungs are clear to auscultation. Cardiac auscultation shows bradycardia with regular S$_1$ and S$_2$ as well as an S$_4$. A grade 2/6 early systolic murmur is heard at the left upper sternal border. Edema is not present.

On telemetry, she has sinus bradycardia with rates between 40/min and 50/min, with two symptomatic sinus pauses of 3 to 5 seconds each.

Which of the following is the most likely cause of this patient's dizziness?

(A) Atrial fibrillation

(B) Complete heart block

(C) Nonsustained ventricular tachycardia

(D) Sick sinus syndrome

Item 19 [Basic]

A 73-year-old woman is evaluated during a routine examination. She has no symptoms and feels well. Her medications are levothyroxine for hypothyroidism and hydrochlorothiazide for hypertension. An electrocardiogram performed 2 years ago was normal.

On physical examination, heart rate is 42/min and regular. The remainder of the examination is normal. The thyroid-stimulating hormone level is normal. An electrocardiogram obtained as part of the current evaluation is shown.

Which of the following diagnoses is confirmed by the electrocardiogram?

(A) First-degree atrioventricular block

(B) Mobitz type I second-degree atrioventricular block

(C) Mobitz type II second-degree atrioventricular block

(D) Third-degree atrioventricular block (complete heart block)

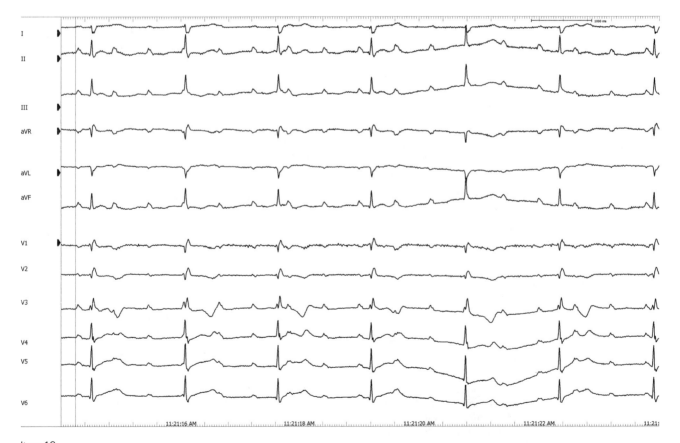

Item 19

Item 20 [Basic]

A 73-year-old man is evaluated in the emergency department for chest pressure with radiation to the arm, diaphoresis, and light-headedness of 4 hours' duration. His medical history includes a 20-year history of hypertension and type 2 diabetes mellitus. Medications are metformin, atenolol, and aspirin.

On physical examination, the patient is afebrile, blood pressure is 130/84 mm Hg in both arms, and pulse rate is 87/min and regular. The jugular vein is distended to 5 cm while the patient is upright. He has a faint left carotid bruit, bibasilar crackles to one-quarter up from the pulmonary bases, normal S_1 and S_2, and an S_4 and an S_3 with a grade 2/6 holosystolic murmur that is heard best at the apex to the axilla. Pulses are symmetric. The chest radiograph is consistent with heart failure. The electrocardiogram is shown. An electrocardiogram obtained 6 months ago was normal. The initial serum troponin measurement is elevated.

Which of the following is the most likely diagnosis?

(A) Acute myocardial infarction
(B) Aortic dissection
(C) Endocarditis
(D) Pericarditis

Item 21 [Basic]

A 67-year-old man is evaluated because of a 10-day history of light-headedness and increasing frequency of chest pain and palpitations for the last 3 days. He denies syncope. The medical history is significant for coronary artery disease and difficult-to-control hypertension. Medications are aspirin, nitroglycerin, atenolol, hydrochlorothiazide, and sustained release diltiazem.

On physical examination, blood pressure is 156/72 mm Hg; pulse rate is 60/min, with occasional irregularity; and respiration rate is 16/min. Jugular venous pressure is normal. The lungs are clear to auscultation. Cardiac examination shows a physiologically split S_2, an S_4, and no S_3. There is a grade 2/6 systolic murmur that is best heard in the second right intercostal space. The remainder of the physical examination is unremarkable.

The patient's electrocardiogram is shown.

Which of the following is the electrocardiographic diagnosis?

(A) Normal electrocardiogram
(B) First-degree atrioventricular block
(C) Second-degree atrioventricular block
(D) Third-degree (complete) atrioventricular block

Item 22 [Advanced]

A 32-year-old woman is evaluated in the emergency department because of intermittent palpitations and dizziness for the last week. She has not experienced chest pain, dyspnea, or orthopnea. She was ill 6 weeks ago with fever, fatigue and myalgias, and an associated erythematous rash on her abdomen that resolved over 2 weeks. She has no significant medical history. She works as a landscaper.

On physical examination, temperature is normal, blood pressure is 120/70 mm Hg, and pulse rate is 45/min. The cardiac examination shows bradycardia, but findings are otherwise unremarkable. The remainder of the physical examination is normal.

An electrocardiogram shows sinus rhythm with a heart rate of 90/min, with complete heart block and a junctional escape rate of 50/min.

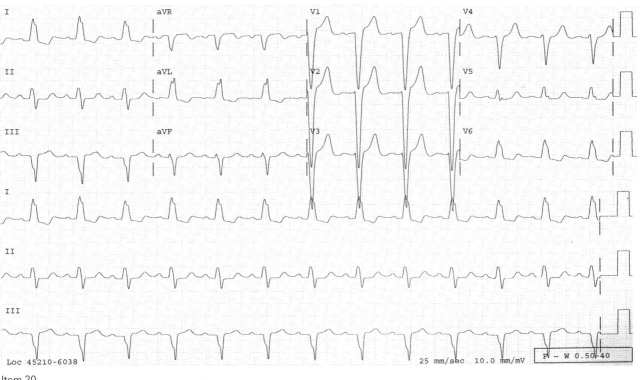

Loc 45210-6038   25 mm/sec 10.0 mm/mV F ~ W 0.50-40

Item 20

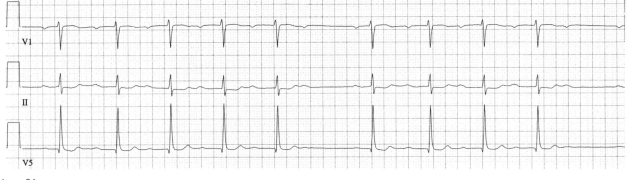

Item 21

In addition to hospitalization for cardiac monitoring, which of the following is the most appropriate management for this patient?

(A) Electrophysiology study
(B) Intravenous ceftriaxone
(C) Permanent pacemaker placement
(D) Temporary pacemaker placement

Item 23 [Basic]

A 62-year-old man is evaluated in the emergency department for a 2-day history of dyspnea and palpitations. His other medical problems include a 10-year history of hypertension and diabetes mellitus. Medications are lisinopril and metformin.

On physical examination, temperature is 37.0°C (98.6°F), blood pressure is 130/86 mm Hg, pulse rate is 132/min, respiration rate is 18/min, and oxygen saturation is 94% on ambient air. Cardiac examination shows a rapid heart rate but no other abnormalities.

Electrocardiogram is shown.

Which of the following is the most appropriate treatment?

(A) Adenosine given intravenously
(B) Digoxin given intravenously
(C) Diltiazem given intravenously
(D) Electrical cardioversion

Item 24 [Basic]

A 69-year-old man is evaluated in the emergency department for atrial fibrillation with a rapid ventricular response. His heart rate is controlled with intravenous diltiazem. Other medical problems include a myocardial infarction 5 years ago and hypertension. The

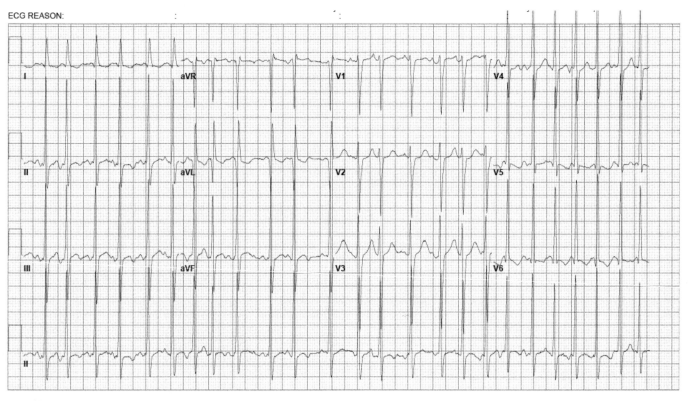

ECG REASON:

Item 23

patient had a transient ischemic attack 5 months ago. Medications are metoprolol, lisinopril, simvastatin, and aspirin.

On physical examination, the patient is afebrile, blood pressure is 165/90 mm Hg, pulse rate is 88/min and regular, respiratory rate is 20/min, and oxygen saturation is 97% on ambient air. Cardiac examination shows an irregular rhythm. There is no jugular venous distention or peripheral edema, and the lungs are clear to auscultation.

Echocardiogram shows a left ventricular ejection fraction of 55% and moderate dilation of the left atrium.

Which of the following should be included in the initial management of this patient's atrial fibrillation?

(A) Atrioventricular node ablation
(B) Clopidogrel
(C) Pulmonary vein radiofrequency ablation
(D) Warfarin

Item 25 [Advanced]

A 36-year-old woman is evaluated in the emergency department for an episode of chest pain, palpitations, and lightheadedness. The symptoms persisted for 1 hour and ceased shortly after she arrived at the hospital. She has no history of cardiac disease, but has a 6-month history of hypertension that is controlled with chlorthalidone 25 mg daily. She has occasional brief episodes of rapid palpitations provoked by exertion. She does not have exercise intolerance or exertional chest discomfort.

On physical examination, blood pressure is 154/94 mm Hg, without orthostatic change. Pulse rate is 60/min and regular. Findings on physical examination are remarkable only for a paradoxically split S$_2$. The patient's electrocardiogram is shown.

Which of the following best describes the electrocardiographic finding for this patient?

(A) Atrial fibrillation
(B) First-degree atrioventricular block
(C) Normal electrocardiogram
(D) Ventricular preexcitation syndrome (Wolff-Parkinson-White)

Item 26 [Basic]

A 71-year-old man is evaluated in the clinic for symptoms of palpitations, shortness of breath, and decreased exercise tolerance for the last 2 days. His medical history is significant for hypertension. His only medication is lisinopril.

On physical examination, blood pressure is 115/62 mm Hg and pulse rate is 152/min. The lungs are clear. Cardiac examination is significant for tachycardia, but no extra heart sounds or murmurs are noted.

The electrocardiogram is shown.

Which of the following is the most likely cause of this patient's symptoms?

(A) Atrial fibrillation
(B) Atrial flutter
(C) Multifocal atrial tachycardia
(D) Sinus tachycardia

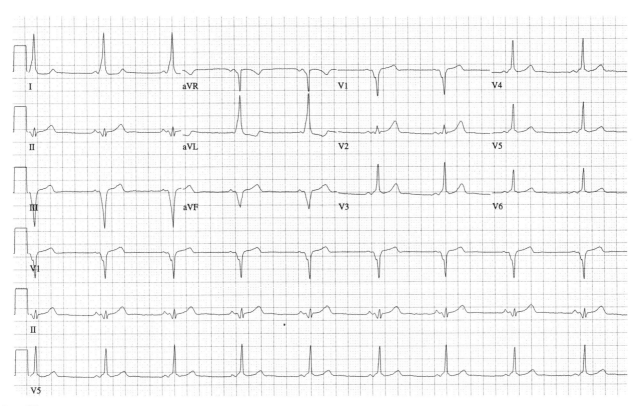

Item 25

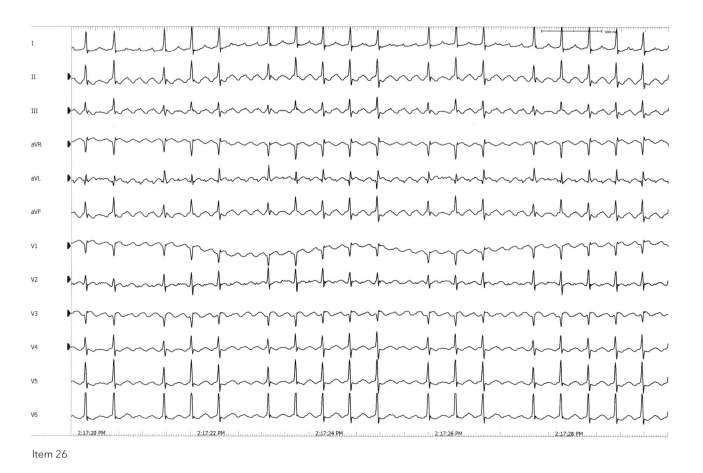

Item 26

Item 27 [Basic]

A 68-year-old man is evaluated in the emergency department for shortness of breath and palpitations that have worsened over the last 3 days. His medical history is significant for chronic obstructive pulmonary disease. He has a 50-pack-year smoking history and continues to smoke 1 pack of cigarettes daily. His medications include tiotropium and albuterol metered-dose inhalers.

On physical examination, temperature is 37.8°C (100°F) and pulse rate is 122/min. Oxygen saturation on ambient air is 89%. The patient is in moderate respiratory distress. Chest examination shows decreased airflow with diffuse expiratory wheezing. Cardiac examination shows distant heart sounds and an irregular rate with a loud S_2 and no murmurs.

Laboratory studies show normal electrolytes. The electrocardiogram is shown.

Which of the following is the most likely electrocardiographic diagnosis?

(A) Atrial fibrillation
(B) Atrioventricular nodal reentrant tachycardia
(C) Atrioventricular reentrant tachycardia
(D) Multifocal atrial tachycardia

Item 28 [Advanced]

A 34-year-old woman is evaluated in the emergency department after the acute onset of palpitations approximately 1 hour ago. She reports no shortness of breath, chest pain, presyncope, or syncope. The medical history is unremarkable, and there is no family history of sudden cardiac death. She takes no medications.

On physical examination, she is afebrile, blood pressure is 118/64 mm Hg, and pulse rate is 165/min. Other than a regular, rapid pulse, the cardiopulmonary examination is normal.

Baseline electrocardiogram shows a narrow complex tachycardia at 165/min. Adenosine is given as a rapid intravenous push, and the patient converts to normal sinus rhythm.

Which of the following is the most likely diagnosis?

(A) Atrial fibrillation
(B) Atrial tachycardia
(C) Atrioventricular nodal reentrant tachycardia
(D) Sinus tachycardia

Item 29 [Basic]

A 19-year-old man is evaluated after the recent sudden death of his father at 45 years of age. He reports no chest pain, shortness of breath, palpitations, dizziness, or syncope. He does not smoke or use drugs and is not hypertensive. He takes no medication. The patient has no siblings.

On physical examination, he is afebrile, blood pressure is 120/60 mm Hg, pulse rate is 60/min, and respiration rate is 14/min. A grade 2/6 midsystolic murmur that increases during the strain phase of the Valsalva maneuver is heard. The lungs are clear to auscultation.

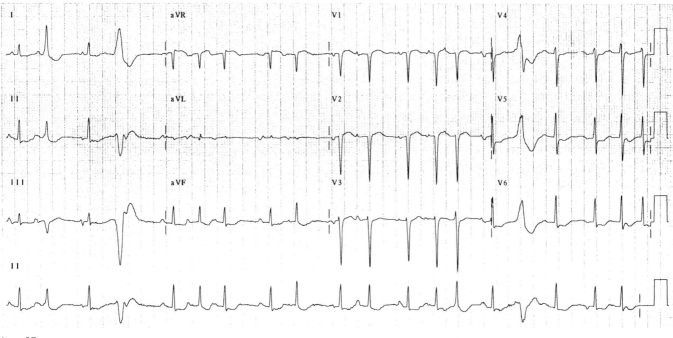

Item 27

Electrocardiogram shows sinus rhythm and increased QRS voltage in the precordial leads. Echocardiogram shows asymmetric basal and midseptal hypertrophy, a thickened septum, and increased left ventricular outflow tract gradient.

Which of the following is the most appropriate management?

(A) Electrophysiology testing
(B) Initiation of amiodarone
(C) Placement of an implantable cardioverter-defibrillator
(D) Septal ablation

Item 30 [Advanced]

A 54-year-old man is evaluated in the emergency department because of a 2-hour history of palpitations. He reports no syncope, presyncope, chest pain, or shortness of breath. He has had no previous episodes of palpitations. Medical history is significant for non-ischemic cardiomyopathy. The ejection fraction was most recently measured at 38%. Medications are carvedilol and candesartan.

On physical examination, the patient is afebrile, blood pressure is 125/86 mm Hg, and pulse rate is 110/min. Cardiac evaluation shows a regular rate and rhythm. The remainder of the findings on physical examination are unremarkable.

The electrocardiogram is shown.

Which of the following is the most appropriate treatment?

(A) Immediate cardioversion
(B) Intravenous adenosine
(C) Intravenous amiodarone
(D) Intravenous verapamil

Item 31 [Basic]

A 47-year-old woman is evaluated for a 4-month history of a sensation of "thumping" in her chest. She reports feeling as if her heart stops when these episodes occur. The symptoms occur frequently throughout the day but are more noticeable at night. She finds them bothersome and notes that her symptoms appear to decrease with exercise. She reports no chest pain, dyspnea, orthopnea, or edema. She is healthy and active and takes no medications.

On physical examination, the patient is afebrile, blood pressure is 110/67 mm Hg, and pulse is 72/min with occasional ectopy. Cardiac auscultation is normal except for occasional extra beats. There are no murmurs, gallops, or clicks. The remainder of her examination is unremarkable.

Electrocardiogram shows sinus rhythm with normal intervals and occasional premature ventricular contractions with varying morphologic patterns that correspond to her symptoms of palpitations. Echocardiogram shows a structurally normal heart.

Which of the following is the most appropriate treatment for this patient?

(A) Amiodarone
(B) Metoprolol
(C) Pacemaker implantation
(D) Radiofrequency ablation

Item 32 [Advanced]

A 19-year-old man is evaluated in the emergency department because of syncope. He was exercising when he lost consciousness. He had no previous symptoms. He recovered quickly and had no residual symptoms. He had three similar episodes in the past but did not seek evaluation. He did not consider these episodes significantly abnormal because his mother has similar symptoms periodically.

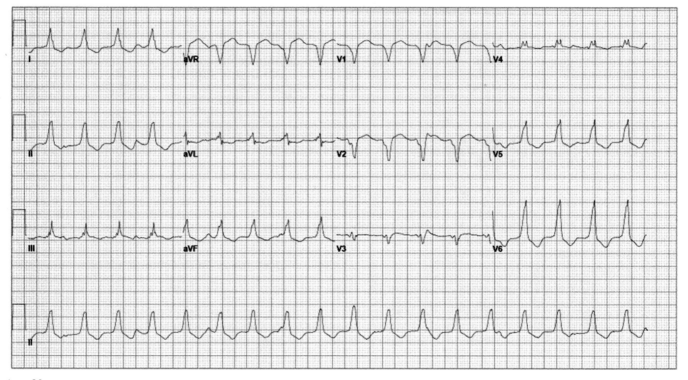

Item 30

He is physically active and has no other symptoms. He takes no medications. The medical history is otherwise unremarkable.

On physical examination, the patient is afebrile, blood pressure is 122/75 mm Hg, pulse rate is 67/min and regular, and respiration rate is 12/min. Findings of cardiac examination are normal, and the remainder of the physical examination is unremarkable.

An electrocardiogram is ordered.

Which of the following electrocardiographic findings is most likely to provide a diagnosis?

(A) Left bundle branch block
(B) Long P-R interval
(C) Long QT interval
(D) Right bundle branch block

Item 33 [Basic]

A 64-year-old man was admitted to the hospital 2 days ago with an acute ST-elevation myocardial infarction. At the time of presentation he became unresponsive because of ventricular fibrillation. He was resuscitated successfully and underwent stenting of a complete occlusion of his proximal left anterior descending artery in the cardiac catheterization laboratory. He has done well since that time. Current medications are aspirin, clopridogrel, metoprolol, lisinopril, and atorvastatin.

On physical examination, the patient is afebrile, blood pressure is 115/72 mm Hg, pulse rate is 65/min, and respiration rate is 12/min. There is no jugular venous distention, the lungs are clear, and findings of heart examination are unremarkable.

Electrocardiogram shows a resolving anterior myocardial infarction but is otherwise unremarkable. Echocardiogram shows mild hypokinesis of the anterior wall and left ventricular ejection fraction of 45%.

Which of the following is the most appropriate next step in management?

(A) Continuation of medical therapy
(B) Placement of an implantable cardioverter-defibrillator
(C) Placement of a pacemaker
(D) Treatment with amiodarone

Item 34 [Basic]

A 68-year-old man is evaluated during a routine appointment for stable heart failure. He has a 1-year history of New York Heart Association class III heart failure as a result of hypertensive cardiomyopathy. He has symptoms with minimal exertion, such as walking one block or climbing half a flight of stairs. Medications are furosemide, lisinopril, digoxin, and metoprolol. An implantable cardioverter-defibrillator was placed 6 months ago, after an echocardiogram showed left ventricular ejection fraction of 30%.

On physical examination, the patient is afebrile, blood pressure is 130/78 mm Hg, pulse rate is 78/min, respiration rate is 18/min, and oxygen saturation is 96% on ambient air. Cardiac examination shows a summation gallop but no murmurs. Estimated central venous pressure is 10 cm H_2O. Bilateral lower lobe crackles are present. There is trace ankle edema.

The serum creatinine level is 1.2 mg/dL (106.08 µmol/L), and the serum potassium level is 4.5 meq/L (4.50 mmol/L).

Which of the following is the most appropriate addition to this patient's heart failure medications?

(A) Amlodipine
(B) Nifedipine
(C) Spironolactone
(D) Valsartan

Item 35 [Advanced]

A 70-year-old woman is evaluated in the emergency department because of dyspnea. She has had progressive shortness of breath over the last 5 days associated with a nonproductive cough. Symptoms are greatest with exertion and possibly when lying down. She has no fever, chest pain, or increase in her chronic lower extremity edema. Her other medical problems are chronic venous insufficiency, chronic obstructive pulmonary disease, hypertension, and chronic kidney disease. Medications are chlorthalidone, amlodipine, lisinopril, and tiotropium inhaler.

On physical examination, she is afebrile, blood pressure is 144/88 mm Hg, pulse rate is 90/min, respiration rate is 22/min, and oxygen saturation is 94% on ambient air. Body mass index is 30. Because her neck is large, it is not possible to estimate central venous pressure. Breath sounds are distant, with occasional end-expiratory wheezing. Heart sounds are distant, and extra sounds or murmurs are not detected. There is 2+ ankle edema with hyperpigmentation localized to the medial aspect of the ankles.

Frontal chest radiograph shows increased radiolucency of the lung, flat diaphragms, and a narrow heart shadow. Electrocardiogram shows evidence of left ventricular hypertrophy. Laboratory tests, including serum creatinine, electrolytes, and B-type natriuretic peptide levels, are pending.

Which of the following factors increases the risk of a falsely low B-type natriuretic peptide level?

(A) Female sex
(B) Kidney failure
(C) Obesity
(D) Older age

Item 36 [Basic]

A 55-year-old man is evaluated because of a 2-month history of dyspnea on exertion without chest pain. Medical history is significant for type 2 diabetes mellitus, hypertension, and hyperlipidemia. He has a 30-pack-year smoking history but does not currently use tobacco products. Medications are metformin, lisinopril, pravastatin, and aspirin.

On physical examination, blood pressure is 110/75 mm Hg and pulse rate is 60/min. Jugular venous distention is noted, and trace lower extremity edema is present. The point of maximal impulse is normal in size and location. Cardiac examination shows regular rate and rhythm, and the chest is clear to auscultation.

Electrocardiogram is shown. Echocardiogram shows inferior wall hypokinesis and ejection fraction of 35%.

Which of the following is the most appropriate diagnostic test to perform next?

(A) Cardiac magnetic resonance imaging
(B) Coronary angiography
(C) Pharmacologic stress testing
(D) Pulmonary function testing

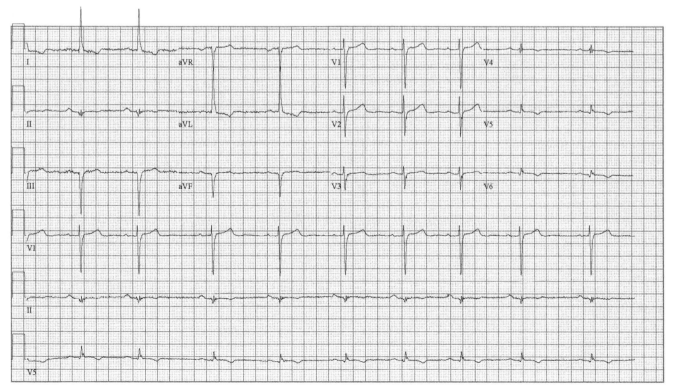

Item 36

Item 37 [Basic]

A 70-year-old man was admitted to the hospital 1 week ago with acute decompensated heart failure. Currently, he can walk about 200 yards before stopping because of fatigue and shortness of breath. Medical history is significant for nonischemic cardiomyopathy, with an implantable cardioverter-defibrillator placed 1 year ago. Medications are lisinopril, bumetanide, and spironolactone.

On physical examination, blood pressure is 90/70 mm Hg and pulse rate is 80/min. A grade 2/6 holosystolic murmur is heard at the left sternal border. No jugular venous distention is present, lungs are clear to auscultation, no S_3 is heard, and there is no peripheral edema.

Electrocardiogram shows normal sinus rhythm with a QRS complex duration of 110 msec. Echocardiogram shows left ventricular enlargement, ejection fraction of 20%, and moderate mitral regurgitation but a structurally normal valve.

Which of the following is the most appropriate treatment?

(A) Refer the patient for mitral valve repair
(B) Replace spironolactone with eplerenone
(C) Initiate treatment with metoprolol succinate
(D) Upgrade the cardioverter-defibrillator to a biventricular pacemaker

Item 38 [Advanced]

A 67-year-old woman is evaluated because of a 1-month history of shortness of breath and lower extremity edema. She has no chest pain, palpitations, or syncope. Medical history is notable for hypertension. Her only medication is hydrochlorothiazide.

On physical examination, blood pressure is 170/90 mm Hg and pulse rate is 65/min. Estimated central venous pressure is 12 cm H_2O. Cardiac examination shows a regular rhythm with no murmurs. Crackles are heard bilaterally in the lung bases. Pitting edema to the midshin is present bilaterally.

The electrocardiogram shows left ventricular hypertrophy by voltage criteria but no evidence of previous myocardial dysfunction. Echocardiogram shows moderate concentric left ventricular hypertrophy and no significant valvular abnormalities. Left ventricular ejection fraction is 60%.

Hydrochlorothiazide is discontinued, and treatment with furosemide is started.

Which of the following is the most appropriate additional therapy for this patient?

(A) Amlodipine
(B) Candesartan
(C) Digoxin
(D) Isosorbide mononitrate

Item 39 [Basic]

A 35-year-old woman is evaluated for follow-up of heart failure secondary to peripartum cardiomyopathy. Symptoms began in the third trimester, and therapy was initiated at that time. The patient gave birth to a healthy baby 3 weeks ago but remains symptomatic. She can walk approximately one block on level ground. Medical history is otherwise unremarkable. Medications are carvedilol, spironolactone, and hydrochlorothiazide.

On physical examination, the patient is afebrile, blood pressure is 100/70 mm Hg, and pulse rate is 50/min. No jugular venous distention is present. Lungs are clear to auscultation. Cardiac examination shows a regular rhythm and a normal S_1 and S_2, without an S_3. No peripheral edema is present.

Electrocardiogram shows normal sinus rhythm with a QRS complex duration of 110 msec and nonspecific ST-segment changes. Echocardiogram shows left ventricular ejection fraction of 25%.

Which of the following is the most appropriate management?

(A) Cardiac resynchronization therapy
(B) Endomyocardial biopsy
(C) Increase carvedilol
(D) Start enalapril

Item 40 [Advanced]

A 55-year-old man is evaluated during a routine examination. He has a 2-year history of nonischemic cardiomyopathy, with echocardiogram showing left ventricular ejection fraction of 35%. He is feeling well and reports no shortness of breath; he walks 2 miles daily without symptoms. Medical history is remarkable for hypertension. Medications are lisinopril, carvedilol, and chlorthalidone.

On physical examination, blood pressure is 150/90 mm Hg and pulse rate is 50/min. No jugular venous distention is present. Lungs are clear to auscultation. Cardiac examination shows a regular rhythm with no murmurs or gallops. No edema is present.

Laboratory studies show serum creatinine level of 1.5 mg/dL (133.0 μmol/L), sodium level of 138 meq/L (138 mmol/L), and potassium level of 4.0 meq/L (4.0 mmol/L).

Electrocardiogram shows a normal sinus rhythm and left ventricular hypertrophy.

Which of the following calcium channel blockers should be added to this patient's medical regimen?

(A) Amlodipine
(B) Diltiazem
(C) Nifedipine
(D) Verapamil

Item 41 [Basic]

A 63-year-old man is evaluated because of increased dyspnea and wheezing of 5 days' duration. New lower extremity edema has also developed over the last 6 weeks.

On physical examination, the patient is afebrile, blood pressure is 162/92 mm Hg, pulse rate is 116/min, respiration rate is 24/min, and oxygen saturation is 90% on ambient air. He has jugular venous distention and an early 2/6 systolic murmur isolated to the lower left sternal border. The murmur increases in intensity with inspiration. The liver is enlarged to palpation. Pedal edema is present bilaterally.

Which of the following is the most likely diagnosis?

(A) Aortic stenosis
(B) Mitral regurgitation
(C) Pulmonic stenosis
(D) Tricuspid regurgitation

Item 42 [Basic]

A 72-year-old man is evaluated because of progressive dyspnea that began 3 weeks ago. Six years ago, he underwent replacement of the aortic valve with a prosthetic value for treatment of calcific aortic stenosis. Until 3 weeks ago, he had been doing well. He has no other medical problems, and his only medication is warfarin.

On physical examination, he is afebrile, blood pressure is 134/68 mm Hg, pulse rate is 88/min, respiration rate is 20/min, and oxygen saturation is 96% on ambient air. Cardiac examination shows a laterally displaced apex beat, regular S_1 and S_2, a sharp aortic valve click, expiratory splitting of the S_2, a 2/6 systolic murmur that is loudest at the right second intercostal space without radiation, and a 1/6 blowing diastolic murmur that is loudest at the third left intercostal space. The remainder of the physical examination is normal.

Chest radiography shows cardiomegaly without interstitial edema or pulmonary vascular congestion. Electrocardiogram shows left bundle branch block.

Which of the following physical examination findings most strongly suggests dysfunction of the prosthetic heart value?

(A) Diastolic murmur
(B) Expiratory splitting of S_2
(C) Sharp valve click
(D) Systolic murmur

Item 43 [Basic]

A 38-year-old man is evaluated during a routine health examination. He exercises 2 or 3 days each week by jogging for 30 minutes without shortness of breath or chest discomfort. During stressful emotional situations, he occasionally feels "skipped heart beats" but has not had prolonged palpitations, presyncope, or syncope. He generally feels healthy. He has no history of medical problems and takes no medications. He has not had fever or chills.

Physical examination shows normal temperature, blood pressure of 124/68 mm Hg, pulse rate of 64/min and regular, and respiration rate of 14/min. Cardiac examination shows a grade 2/6 early systolic crescendo-decrescendo murmur heard at the lower left sternal border without radiation. The lungs are clear, and the peripheral pulses are normal.

Electrocardiogram shows normal results.

Which of the following is the most appropriate next test?

(A) Ambulatory electrocardiography
(B) Transesophageal echocardiography
(C) Transthoracic echocardiography
(D) No additional testing

Item 44 [Basic]

A 72-year-old man is evaluated in the emergency department because of worsening shortness of breath, orthopnea, and lower extremity edema. He has chest heaviness with exertion, but no presyncope or syncope.

On physical examination, blood pressure is 118/74 mm Hg, pulse rate is 96/min, and respiration rate is 20/min. Estimated central venous pressure is 10 cm H_2O. Cardiac examination shows a regular heart rate and S_2 that is diminished in intensity. A grade 3/6 systolic murmur at the left lower sternal border and an S_3 are present. Lung examination shows bibasilar crackles, and bilateral lower extremity edema of the knees is present.

Chest radiograph shows cardiomegaly and increased bilateral interstitial markings. Electrocardiogram shows sinus rhythm and left ventricular hypertrophy. Transthoracic echocardiogram shows concentric left ventricular dilation, with an ejection fraction of 30%. The aortic valve leaflets are calcified, with reduced mobility. The calculated valve area is 0.8 cm², and the estimated transvalvular pressure gradient is elevated.

In addition to diuresis, which of the following is the most appropriate treatment for this patient?

(A) Balloon aortic valvuloplasty
(B) Intravenous nitroprusside
(C) Surgical aortic valve replacement
(D) Transcatheter aortic valve implantation

Item 45 [Basic]

A 43-year-old woman is evaluated because of a 3-month history of substernal exertional chest pain and worsening dyspnea on exertion. Medical history is significant for Hodgkin lymphoma diagnosed 15 years ago that was treated with radiation therapy that involved the thorax.

On physical examination, temperature is normal, blood pressure is 148/41 mm Hg, pulse rate is 80/min, and respiration rate is 14/min. Carotid upstrokes are rapid and accentuated, with a rapid decline. She has no jugular venous distention. The S_2 is diminished in intensity, and there is no S_3 gallop present. A grade 2/6 high-pitched blowing diastolic decrescendo murmur is heard to the left of the sternum at the third intercostal space. The apical point of maximal impulse is displaced inferiorly and laterally. There is no hepatojugular reflux.

Which of the following is the most likely cause of the patient's symptoms?

(A) Aortic valve regurgitation
(B) Constrictive pericarditis
(C) Restrictive cardiomyopathy
(D) Severe tricuspid regurgitation

Item 46 [Advanced]

A 43-year-old man is evaluated during a routine examination. He is in good health and exercises regularly without difficulty. He has no history of presyncope, syncope, or palpitations. He is a nonsmoker and takes no medications.

On physical examination, he is afebrile, blood pressure is 120/64 mm Hg, pulse rate is 80/min and regular, and respiration rate is 16/min. Cardiac examination shows a normal S_1 and a physiologically split S_2. There is a grade 2/6 decrescendo diastolic murmur at the left sternal border. Distal pulses are normal, and there is no pedal edema.

Transthoracic echocardiogram shows normal ventricular size and function, with an ejection fraction of 65%. There is a bicuspid aortic valve with moderate regurgitation. The diameter of the proximal ascending aorta is normal, as are the estimated pulmonary arterial pressures.

Which of the following is the most appropriate next step in the management of this patient?

(A) Clinical follow-up in 1 year
(B) Magnetic resonance imaging of the aortic root
(C) Surgical aortic valve replacement
(D) Transesophageal echocardiography

Item 47 [Basic]

A 60-year-old woman is evaluated because of progressive exertional dyspnea and shortness of breath over the last 6 months. She has been healthy and has had no chest pain or other cardiovascular symptoms. Medical history is unremarkable. She is a nonsmoker and takes no medications.

On physical examination, the patient is afebrile, blood pressure is 122/85 mm Hg, and pulse rate is regular at 90/min. Estimated central venous pressure is 10 cm H_2O. Lungs are clear to auscultation. Cardiac examination shows a parasternal and prominent apical impulse, a loud S_1, a normal S_2, and an opening snap. There is a grade 2/6 holosystolic murmur at the cardiac apex radiating to the axilla and a low-pitched 3/6 middiastolic murmur after the opening snap that accentuates presystole. Trace bipedal edema is present.

Electrocardiogram shows sinus rhythm, left atrial enlargement, and right axis deviation.

Which of the following is the most likely cause of this patient's symptoms?

(A) Aortic regurgitation
(B) Atrial septal defect
(C) Mitral stenosis
(D) Patent ductus arteriosus

Item 48 [Basic]

A 54-year-old woman is evaluated because of progressive shortness of breath over the last 6 months. She has no chest pain. She has no history of cardiovascular disease or other medical problems. She is a nonsmoker and takes no medications. On physical examination, the patient is afebrile, blood pressure is 138/78 mm Hg, pulse rate is 95/min, and respiration rate is 14/min. Estimated central venous pressure is 8 cm H_2O. Lung examination shows bibasilar crackles. Cardiac examination shows a grade 2/6 holosystolic murmur at the apex that radiates to the axilla and does not vary with respiration, a loud pulmonic component of S_2, and an enlarged point of maximal impulse. Moderate bipedal edema is present.

Electrocardiogram shows normal sinus rhythm and left atrial and ventricular enlargement. Chest radiograph shows mild cardiomegaly and pulmonary congestion.

Which of the following is the most likely diagnosis?

(A) Aortic valve regurgitation
(B) Aortic valve stenosis
(C) Mitral valve regurgitation
(D) Mitral valve stenosis
(E) Tricuspid valve regurgitation

Item 49 [Basic]

A 19-year-old woman is evaluated because of palpitations. She describes the sensation of isolated "extra beats" that do not occur with any regularity. She has no personal or family history of cardiovascular disease, and she has not had either presyncope or syncope. She is a nonsmoker and takes no medications.

On physical examination, vital signs are normal. The lungs are clear. There are no extra heart sounds. There is a grade 2/6 late systolic murmur that is heard best at the cardiac apex and radiates toward the left axilla. A midsystolic click is heard. After a Valsalva maneuver and a squat-to-stand maneuver, the midsystolic click moves closer to the S_1, but the intensity of the murmur does not change. The remainder of the examination is unremarkable.

Which of the following is the most likely cause of the heart murmur?

(A) Benign (innocent) flow murmur
(B) Hypertrophic cardiomyopathy
(C) Mitral valve regurgitation
(D) Mitral valve prolapse

Item 50 [Advanced]

A 21-year-old man is evaluated during a routine medical examination. He feels well and is physically active. He plays sports and runs several times each week. He has no medical problems, does not smoke, and takes no medications or drugs.

On physical examination, blood pressure is 128/73 mm Hg, pulse rate is 56/min, and respiration rate is 16/min. There is no jugular venous distention. Carotid upstrokes are normal. There is a grade 2/6 early systolic murmur along the left lower sternal border that is accentuated by a Valsalva maneuver and is decreased with a handgrip maneuver. An S_4 is also noted.

Electrocardiogram shows sinus bradycardia and left ventricular hypertrophy by voltage. Echocardiogram shows left ventricular hypertrophy with septal hypertrophy, a small left ventricular cavity, normal systolic function with an ejection fraction of 65%, and left atrial enlargement.

Which of the following is the most likely diagnosis?

(A) Athlete's heart
(B) Dilated cardiomyopathy
(C) Hypertrophic cardiomyopathy
(D) Restrictive cardiomyopathy

Item 51 [Basic]

A 58-year-old man is evaluated for 3 to 4 months of progressive aching pain in the left buttock and hip. Pain occurs during walking and is relieved by rest. The patient has been experiencing erectile dysfunction over a similar period. He has a 30-pack-year history of smoking and quit 1 year ago. He has hypercholesterolemia and type 2 diabetes mellitus. Medications are aspirin, lisinopril, simvastatin, metformin, and metoprolol.

On physical examination, temperature is normal, blood pressure is 112/72 mm Hg, pulse rate is 68/min, and respiration rate is 16/min. Femoral, popliteal, and foot pulses are diminished. There is no distal ulceration or skin breakdown. Ankle-brachial index on the left side is 0.7.

Which of the following is the most likely site of this patient's arterial disease?

(A) Aortoiliac system
(B) Common femoral artery
(C) Popliteal artery
(D) Superficial femoral artery

Item 52 [Basic]

A 46-year-old man is evaluated in the emergency department because of acute onset of severe chest and back pain 1 hour ago. The pain has been unremitting. Medical history is significant for a bicuspid aortic valve that was detected in adolescence because of a murmur and also for hypertension. His only medication is valsartan.

On physical examination, the patient is conscious and in pain. He is afebrile, blood pressure is 90/50 mm Hg, pulse rate is 118/min and regular, and respiration rate is 18/min.

Pulse rate and blood pressure are equal in both arms. Heart sounds are distant, regular, and rapid. A very faint early diastolic murmur is heard at the right upper sternal border. Estimated central venous pressure is 12 cm H_2O.

Electrocardiogram indicates sinus tachycardia. A chest computed tomographic scan with intravenous contrast is shown.

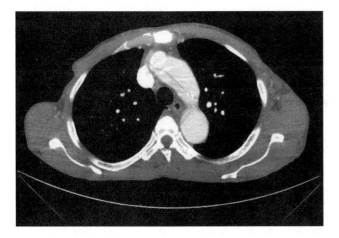

Which of the following is the most appropriate next step in management?

(A) Chest magnetic resonance imaging
(B) Emergency surgical intervention
(C) Endovascular stenting
(D) Transesophageal echocardiography

Item 53 [Advanced]

A 70-year-old man is evaluated in the emergency department for severe lower back pain that began suddenly 2 days ago and was associated with an episode of syncope. Since that time, he has had vague lower abdominal and back discomfort. He has had no change in bowel or urinary habits and no fever or chills. Medical history is significant for hypertension, hyperlipidemia, and a 40-pack-year smoking history. Medications are atorvastatin, aspirin, and lisinopril.

On physical examination, temperature is 37.7°C (99.8°F), blood pressure is 100/60 mm Hg, pulse rate is 98/min and regular, and respiration rate is 18/min. Results of cardiac and neurologic examinations are normal. Abdominal examination shows moderate tenderness to palpation in the infraumbilical and suprapubic regions, but without guarding or rebound tenderness. Findings on rectal examination are unremarkable, with guaiac-negative stool.

Laboratory results include hematocrit of 32% and leukocyte count of 12,000/µL (12.0 × 10⁹/L). Results of liver chemistry studies and urinalysis are normal. Electrocardiogram shows normal sinus rhythm and evidence of left ventricular hypertrophy. Plain abdominal radiograph shows no free air or air-fluid levels.

Which of the following is the most likely diagnosis?

(A) Acute myocardial infarction
(B) Diverticulitis
(C) Nephrolithiasis, or renal colic
(D) Ruptured abdominal aortic aneurysm

Item 54 [Basic]

A 76-year-old man is evaluated because of an episode of left-handed weakness involving all five digits that occurred yesterday and gradually subsided over 3 hours. He has had two similar episodes in the last 2 weeks. Medical history is unremarkable. His only medication is a daily low-dose aspirin.

On physical examination, blood pressure is 156/78 mm Hg and pulse rate is 76/min and regular. Cardiac examination shows a right carotid bruit. Other findings on physical examination, including a neurologic evaluation, are normal.

Electrocardiogram shows normal sinus rhythm with no evidence of ischemia. Carotid duplex ultrasound shows 80% to 99% stenosis of the right internal carotid artery, which is confirmed by computed tomographic angiography. Magnetic resonance imaging of the brain shows a 5-mm infarct in the right middle cerebral artery distribution.

Which of the following will have the greatest effect in reducing the risk of recurrent stroke in this patient?

(A) Carotid endarterectomy
(B) Carotid stenting
(C) Clopidogrel
(D) Warfarin

Item 55 [Advanced]

A 27-year-old woman is evaluated during a follow-up visit for high blood pressure that was diagnosed 4 months after she began taking an oral contraceptive pill. She has stopped using the oral contraceptive pill, but her blood pressure has remained high. She feels well and takes no medications. Medical history is otherwise unremarkable.

On physical examination, blood pressure is 166/108 mm Hg and the heart rate is 76/min. No orthostasis is present and the other vital signs are normal. There is a bruit noted in the right epigastric region. The remainder of the examination is unremarkable.

Kidney function is normal, and urinalysis is unremarkable.

A Doppler ultrasound study shows evidence of stenosis of the right renal artery. A kidney angiogram is shown.

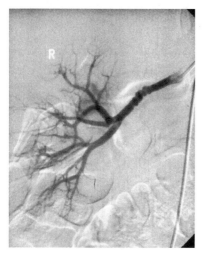

Which of the following is the most appropriate next step in management?

(A) Angiotensin-converting enzyme (ACE) inhibitor
(B) Combination of a calcium channel blocker and ACE inhibitor
(C) Percutaneous transluminal kidney angioplasty
(D) Surgical revascularization

Item 56 [Basic]

A 52-year-old man is evaluated in the emergency department for a 5-day history of pain and swelling in the right leg. He has no history of venous thromboembolism.

On physical examination, temperature is 36.5°C (97.7°F), blood pressure is 120/75 mm Hg, pulse rate is 85/min, and respiration rate is 22/min. The right lower extremity is swollen. Cardiopulmonary examination shows clear lungs and tachycardia.

A right popliteal vein deep venous thrombosis is confirmed by venous duplex compression ultrasonography. The patient is given low-molecular-weight heparin (LMWH).

Which of the following is the most appropriate management of this patient's transition to warfarin therapy?

(A) At least 3 days of LMWH plus warfarin with a target international normalized ratio (INR) of 1.5 or higher for 24 hours
(B) At least 3 days of LMWH plus warfarin with a target INR of 2 or higher for 24 hours
(C) At least 5 days of LMWH plus warfarin with a target INR of 2 or higher for 24 hours
(D) At least 5 days of LMWH plus warfarin with a target INR of 1.5 or higher for 24 hours

Item 57 [Basic]

A 75-year-old woman is evaluated in the hospital because of a 1-day history of swelling of the right leg. Three days ago, she underwent nephrectomy for renal cell carcinoma. Her only medication is unfractionated heparin, 5000 units subcutaneously twice daily.

On physical examination, blood pressure is 130/75 mm Hg, pulse rate is 85/min, and respiration rate is 20/min. Weight is 80 kg (176.3 lb). The right lower extremity is swollen, warm, and tender to palpation of the calf. The nephrectomy incision shows no erythema or bleeding. The remainder of the findings on examination are normal.

Laboratory studies:

Hematocrit	29%
Platelet count	275,000/µL (275 × 10⁹/L)
Creatinine	2.2 mg/dL (194.5 µmol/L)
Estimated glomerular filtration rate	23 mL/min/1.73 m²

Venous duplex ultrasonography shows a right lower extremity femoral and popliteal vein deep venous thrombosis.

In addition to cessation of subcutaneous unfractionated heparin administration, which of the following is the most appropriate treatment?

(A) Enoxaparin
(B) Fondaparinux
(C) Intravenous unfractionated heparin
(D) Warfarin

Item 58 [Basic]

A 55-year-old man is evaluated in the emergency department because of a 3-day history of swelling, pain, and erythema of the right leg. He is otherwise active and healthy and reports no recent immobilization, surgery, or cancer.

On physical examination, temperature is 38.2°C (100.8°F). Other vital signs are normal. Examination of the left leg shows warmth and circumscribed erythema and tenderness limited to the posterior tibial area. The circumference of the left leg is 1 cm greater than that of the right leg when measured 10 cm below the tibial tuberosity. There is no pitting edema.

Which of the following is the most appropriate next step in diagnosis?

(A) Computed tomography of the leg
(B) D-dimer assay
(C) Doppler ultrasound of the leg
(D) Venography

Item 59 [Advanced]

A 75-year-old man is evaluated in the hospital because of community-acquired pneumonia. He is bedbound. He has heart failure and hypertension. Medications are lisinopril and carvedilol.

On physical examination, temperature is 38.6°C (101.4°F), blood pressure is 110/65 mm Hg, pulse rate is 90/min, and respiration rate is 24/min. The patient has right lower lobe bronchial breathing and egophony.

Leukocyte count is 17,000/µL (17×10^9/L).

Chest radiograph shows right lower lobe consolidation.

Which of the following is the most appropriate venous thromboembolism prophylaxis in this patient?

(A) Aspirin, 325 mg/d
(B) Low-dose subcutaneous unfractionated heparin
(C) Pneumatic compression device
(D) Warfarin, 1 mg/d

Section 1

Cardiovascular Medicine

Answers and Critiques

Item 1 **Answer: C**
Educational Objective: *Treat pericarditis with an NSAID.*

The most appropriate initial therapy is ibuprofen. Acute pericarditis is the most likely diagnosis. Viral infection is the most common known cause of acute pericarditis. Diagnosis is most often made by confirming two of three classic findings: chest pain, often with a pleuritic component; friction rub; and diffuse ST-segment elevation on electrocardiography (ECG). This patient has chest pain and diffuse ST-segment elevation on ECG. A pericardial friction rub is virtually pathognomonic of acute pericarditis. It is best auscultated at the left lower sternal border during suspended respiration while the patient is leaning forward. The classic rub has three components and can be squeaky, scratchy, or swooshing. It is often transient. Although a pericardial friction rub is a highly specific sign of acute pericarditis, it is not very sensitive and its absence does not rule out the diagnosis. In acute pericarditis, epicardial inflammation causes upwardly concave ST-segment elevation in all leads except aVR. PR-segment depression in the limb leads (particularly lead II) or precordial leads and elevation in lead aVR may accompany ST-segment elevation. PR-segment shifts are highly specific but not sensitive findings for acute pericarditis. Echocardiography can detect very small pericardial effusions that may help with the diagnosis of pericarditis. More importantly, echocardiography can detect cardiac tamponade and heart failure that may complicate acute pericarditis.

Appropriate initial therapy for acute pericarditis is either aspirin or an a nonsteroidal anti-inflammatory drug (NSAID), such as ibuprofen. Chest pain resulting from acute pericarditis usually resolves within 24 hours of treatment with anti-inflammatory medications. Nonrandomized and nonblinded studies support the use of colchicine as an alternative first-line agent or an adjunctive treatment for acute pericarditis.

In the absence of a specific indication for their use, a glucocorticoid, such as prednisone, should only be used in refractory cases of acute pericarditis or in patients with contraindications to aspirin, NSAIDs, and colchicine. Glucocorticoids increase the risk of recurrent pericarditis.

The nature of the chest pain and the findings of PR-segment depression on ECG and a small effusion on echocardiography are most consistent with acute pericarditis and make acute coronary syndrome or pulmonary embolism unlikely. Therefore, heparin and clopidogrel are not indicated.

KEY POINT

Appropriate initial therapy for acute pericarditis is either aspirin or an NSAID, such as ibuprofen.

Bibliography

Lange RA, Hillis LD. Clinical practice. Acute pericarditis. N Engl J Med. 2004;351:2195-202. [PMID: 15548780]

Item 2 **Answer: C**
Educational Objective: *Diagnose costochondritis.*

This patient most likely has costochondritis. The cause of chest pain can be determined in most cases after a careful history and physical examination. Musculoskeletal chest pain has an insidious onset and may last for hours to weeks. It is most recognizable when it is sharp and localized to a specific area of the chest; however, it can also be poorly localized. The pain may be worsened by turning, deep breathing, or arm movement. Chest pain may or may not be reproducible by chest palpation (pain reproduced by palpation does not exclude ischemic heart disease), and the results of cardiovascular examination are often normal. Importantly, the patient's findings are not consistent with an alternative cause of chest pain. Treatment is typically rest and use of anti-inflammatory drugs.

The chest pain associated with acute pericarditis is typically pleuritic and is worsened when the patient lies down. A two- or three-component friction rub is often present. This patient does not have any risk factors for pericarditis. Specifically, he has no history of recent viral infection, myocardial infarction, trauma, malignancy, medication use, connective tissue disease, or uremia. Therefore, pericarditis is highly unlikely.

Aortic dissection is generally described as a tearing or ripping pain with radiation to the back. It is more commonly seen in patients with a history of hypertension. This patient's description of chest pain, the results of physical examination, and the absence of risk factors are inconsistent with aortic dissection.

This patient has no risk factors for cardiac disease. His history is inconsistent with descriptors that increase the probability of ischemic chest pain, including unstable angina. Specifically, there is no radiation to the arms, exertional component, relief with rest, diaphoresis, nausea, vomiting, or description of pressure. Considering the patient's age and description of his chest pain, the probability of unstable angina or an acute coronary syndrome is low.

KEY POINT

Musculoskeletal chest pain has an insidious onset and may last for hours to weeks. It is most recognizable when it is sharp and localized to a specific area of the chest. The pain may be worsened by turning, deep breathing, or arm movement.

Bibliography

Stochkendahl MJ, Christensen HW. Chest pain in focal musculoskeletal disorders. Med Clin North Am. 2010;94:259-73. [PMID: 20380955]

Item 3   Answer: D
Educational Objective: *Manage panic disorder.*

The most appropriate management of this patient is to prescribe a selective serotonin reuptake inhibitor. Panic disorder is a syndrome characterized by sudden panic attacks with acute onset of somatic symptoms that may include chest pain, palpitations, sweating, nausea, dizziness, dyspnea, and numbness. These symptoms usually last from 5 to 60 minutes. Approximately 50% of patients with panic disorder also have associated agoraphobia, with fears of being in crowds or in places from which escape would be difficult. Diagnosis is based on clinical descriptors and setting, but care should be taken to consider underlying medical disorders, such as cardiac disease, thyroid disease, or pheochromocytoma, particularly in patients who are at increased risk for one of these disorders. However, extensive testing is not necessary in most patients with a characteristic presentation and normal findings on physical examination and basic laboratory studies. Treatment options for panic disorder include medication and psychotherapy. Cognitive behavioral therapy (CBT) has been shown to be the most effective psychotherapeutic intervention in controlled trials. Selective serotonin reuptake inhibitors and serotonin-norepinephrine reuptake inhibitors have been shown to be effective. Panic disorder that is severe or refractory appears to be most amenable to a combination of CBT and pharmacotherapy compared with either treatment alone.

This patient has classic symptoms of panic disorder and no cardiac risk factors. It would be inappropriate to order further cardiac testing in the setting of a normal electrocardiogram and classic symptoms. This patient's symptoms are also atypical for gastroesophageal reflux disease, and so empiric proton pump inhibitor therapy would be inappropriate.

KEY POINT

Panic disorder is characterized by sudden panic attacks with acute onset of somatic symptoms that may include chest pain, palpitations, sweating, nausea, dizziness, dyspnea, and numbness.

Bibliography
McConaghy JR, Oza RS. Outpatient diagnosis of acute chest pain in adults. Am Fam Physician. 2013;87:177-82. [PMID: 23418761]

Item 4   Answer: B
Educational Objective: *Evaluate a patient with pleuritic chest pain.*

This patient should undergo chest radiography. He has severe chronic obstructive pulmonary disease (COPD) and findings that are consistent with spontaneous secondary pneumothorax. These findings include sudden, sharp, nonradiating pleuritic chest pain and shortness of breath with hyperresonance, decreased breath sounds, and decreased chest wall expansion on the side of the pneumothorax in a patient with underlying lung disease. Pneumothorax should be considered in any patient who has sudden onset of pleuritic chest pain and dyspnea. The diagnostic test of choice if pneumothorax is suspected is an upright chest radiograph. Findings on chest radiograph include separation of the parietal and visceral pleura by a collection of gas and the absence of vessels in this space. This patient is at increased risk for pneumothorax because of his COPD. Pneumothorax occurring in patients without known lung disease or a clear precipitating cause is termed primary spontaneous pneumothorax (PSP). PSP tends to occur more often in men, smokers, and those with a family history of PSP. The clinical presentation is similar in both primary or secondary pneumothorax.

Chest computed tomography (CT) also can be used to diagnose pneumothorax. Chest CT may be more sensitive than a chest radiograph in delineating smaller collections of gas in the pleural space and providing more information about the pulmonary parenchyma and pleura. However, plain film radiography remains the initial test of choice for most patients, and chest CT should be reserved for cases when the chest radiograph does not provide information to guide further treatment or evaluation.

The patient's history and physical examination are classic for pneumothorax, and his pain descriptors do not strongly suggest ischemia or other primary cardiovascular disease. Electrocardiogram and echocardiogram, which are the tests of choice to evaluate ischemic heart disease, valvular heart disease, or cardiomyopathy, would not be the first diagnostic tests of choice for suspected pneumothorax.

KEY POINT

Pneumothorax should be considered in any patient who has sudden onset of pleuritic chest pain and dyspnea. The diagnostic test of choice if pneumothorax is suspected is an upright chest radiograph.

Bibliography
Noppen M. Spontaneous pneumothorax: epidemiology, pathophysiology and cause. Eur Respir Rev. 2010;19:217-9. [PMID: 20956196]

Item 5   Answer: D
Educational Objective: *Manage noncardiac chest pain.*

This patient should receive twice-daily proton pump inhibitor (PPI) therapy for 8 to 10 weeks. Pain associated with gastroesophageal reflux can mimic ischemic chest pain. A cardiac cause should be carefully assessed and excluded in all patients with chest pain. This patient has nonanginal chest pain, no additional risk factors, and normal findings on exercise stress testing. Therefore, the likelihood of a cardiac cause of chest pain is low. Randomized controlled trials have shown that a therapeutic trial of twice-daily PPI treatment is effective in 50% to 60% of patients with noncardiac chest pain, indicating that gastroesophageal reflux disease is the underlying cause.

If the PPI trial is unsuccessful, further evaluation with endoscopy (to detect erosive esophagitis or achalasia), manometry (to detect esophageal motility disorders such as diffuse esophageal spasm), and ambulatory pH recording (to detect refractory reflux) would be reasonable.

Musculoskeletal chest pain has an insidious onset and may last for hours to weeks. It is most recognizable when it is sharp and localized to a specific area of the chest; however, it can also be poorly localized. The pain may be worsened by turning, deep breathing, or arm movement. Chest pain may or may not be reproducible by chest palpation (pain reproduced by palpation does not exclude ischemic heart disease), and findings on cardiovascular examination are often normal. This patient does not have the typical features of musculoskeletal chest pain. Therefore, treatment with an nonsteroidal anti-inflammatory drug is not the most appropriate first step in management.

KEY POINT

After cardiac causes have been excluded by comprehensive cardiac examination, an 8- to 10-week trial of proton pump inhibitor therapy is reasonable before further testing in patients with noncardiac chest pain who do not have concerning symptoms.

Bibliography
Fass R, Achem SR. Noncardiac chest pain: diagnostic evaluation. Dis Esophagus. 2012;25:89-101. [PMID: 21777340]

Item 6   Answer: B

Educational Objective: *Manage chronic stable angina.*

Continuing the current management is the most appropriate action. Several large trials have compared revascularization with optimal medical therapy. These studies found that revascularization combined with aggressive medical therapy was not superior to aggressive medical therapy alone in reducing death or myocardial infarction. Based on these studies, current guidelines recommend reserving coronary angiography and revascularization for patients who continue to have symptoms despite optimal medical therapy, patients who are unable to tolerate the side effects of medications, and those who have high-risk findings on noninvasive testing. This patient's pattern of angina is stable, he is tolerating his medications, and his original stress test showed no high-risk features. Therefore, a more aggressive intervention such as coronary angiography is not indicated as there would not be an expected improved outcome.

Routine follow-up electrocardiography, exercise stress testing (or other noninvasive imaging studies), and echocardiography are not indicated in patients with chronic stable angina. Although careful and frequent follow-up is indicated, disease assessment is conducted with a detailed history and physical examination. The history should focus on changes in physical activity and the frequency, severity, or pattern of chest pain. Reasonable laboratory monitoring includes periodic measurement of lipids and blood glucose levels. Follow-up electrocardiography should be considered when there are medication changes that could affect cardiac conduction; there is a change in the severity, frequency, or pattern of angina; symptoms that suggest dysthymia occur; or syncope develops. There are no indications for an electrocardiogram, an exercise stress test, or echocardiography.

KEY POINT

Routine follow-up electrocardiography, exercise stress testing (or other noninvasive imaging studies), and echocardiography are not indicated in patients with chronic stable angina.

Bibliography

Qaseem A, Fihn SD, Dallas P, et al. Management of stable ischemic heart disease: summary of a clinical practice guideline from the American College of Physicians/American College of Cardiology Foundation/American Heart Association/American Association for Thoracic Surgery/Preventive Cardiovascular Nurses Association/Society of Thoracic Surgeons. Ann Intern Med. 2012;157:735–43. [PMID: 23165665]

Item 7   Answer: D

Educational Objective: *Diagnose chronic angina with an exercise stress test.*

The most appropriate test to evaluate the patient's chest pain is exercise electrocardiography.

A variety of noninvasive stress tests are available to determine whether a patient with cardiovascular symptoms has coronary artery disease (CAD). The decision to perform a specific test is based on the pretest probability of CAD, the patient's ability to exercise, findings on resting electrocardiography (ECG), and comorbid conditions, such as reactive airways disease, that may influence the choice of a pharmacologic stress agent. Stress testing is most useful in patients with an intermediate pretest probability of CAD. For patients with a low pretest probability of CAD, stress testing is not useful because an abnormal test result is likely a false-positive finding and a normal test result only confirms the low pretest probabil-

ity of CAD. For patients with a high pretest probability of CAD, stress testing is not useful to diagnose CAD and empiric medical therapy should be initiated. In this setting, a normal stress test result would likely be a false-negative finding and an abnormal stress test result would only confirm a high pretest probability of CAD.

Exercise ECG testing is the standard stress test for the diagnosis of CAD in patients with normal baseline ECG findings. If abnormalities that limit ST-segment analysis are present (left bundle branch block, left ventricular hypertrophy, paced rhythm, Wolff-Parkinson-White pattern), the results may be difficult to interpret. In patients with abnormalities on resting ECG that impair the ability to interpret ST-segment changes, imaging increases diagnostic accuracy and ability to determine the site and extent of ischemia. Exercise is preferred to pharmacologic stressors because it provides a gauge of functional capacity and a contextual understanding of symptoms as well as a record of the hemodynamic response to exercise. For patients who cannot exercise because of physical limitations or physical deconditioning, pharmacologic stressors can be used. These agents, recommended if the patient cannot achieve at least 5 metabolic equivalents, increase myocardial contractility and oxygen demand (dobutamine) or induce regional hypoperfusion through coronary vasodilation (adenosine, dipyridamole, and regadenoson).

This patient has atypical chest pain (substernal pressure caused by exercise but not relieved with rest) and normal findings on ECG. The most appropriate diagnostic test to evaluate the patient's chest pain is exercise electrocardiography. Because he is a candidate for the preferred type of stress test, alternative methods, including imaging with echocardiography or pharmacologic stress testing with dobutamine, are not indicated.

Cardiac catheterization would not be an appropriate intervention given the patient's intermediate risk for cardiovascular disease. It might be appropriate if he had a high pretest probability of coronary artery disease or he had specific findings of coronary occlusion on stress testing.

KEY POINT

Exercise electrocardiography is the standard stress test used to diagnose coronary artery disease in patients who have normal findings on baseline electrocardiogram and are able to exercise.

Bibliography

Qaseem A, Fihn SD, Dallas P, et al. Clinical Guidelines Committee of the American College of Physicians. Management of stable ischemic heart disease: summary of a clinical practice guideline from the American College of Physicians/American College of Cardiology Foundation/American Heart Association/American Association for Thoracic Surgery/Preventive Cardiovascular Nurses Association/Society of Thoracic Surgeons. Ann Intern Med. 2012;157:735–43. [PMID: 23165665]

Item 8   Answer: C

Educational Objective: *Evaluate a woman with atypical chest pain.*

This patient should undergo exercise electrocardiography (ECG). She has several risk factors for coronary artery disease (CAD), including hypertension, hypercholesterolemia, and a family history of premature CAD. Her symptoms are not typical of angina (her chest discomfort is localized, sharp, and not reproducible with exertion), and the resting ECG is normal. Because this patient has multiple risk factors and atypical symptoms, the pretest probability that CAD is the cause of her symptoms is intermediate. The results of exercise ECG testing, whether normal or abnormal, will significantly affect the posttest probability of CAD. Exercise testing is recommended as the initial test in patients with an intermediate pretest probability of CAD based on age, sex, and symptoms, including patients with right bundle branch block or ST-segment depression of less than 1 mm at baseline. In addition, the results of the exercise ECG test will provide prognostic information about the risk of death and myocardial infarction on the basis of exercise duration, angina, and the magnitude of ST-segment depression.

Coronary angiography is not appropriate for this patient because the pretest probability of CAD is intermediate, which is too low to warrant immediate coronary angiography as the initial diagnostic test.

Although exercise ECG testing has been found to have lower specificity and a higher false-positive rate in women than in men, the routine use of exercise testing with echocardiography to assess left ventricular regional wall motion or perfusion imaging is not recommended for either women or men in the absence of baseline ECG abnormalities. Although echocardiography increases the sensitivity of the ECG results, the use of stress echocardiography as the initial test has not been found to reduce cardiovascular events compared with exercise ECG testing alone.

Pharmacologic stress testing is not indicated because this patient is physically able to exercise. Pharmacologic agents include dobutamine (which increases heart rate and myocardial contractility) and vasodilators (which cause relative increases in coronary blood flow in myocardial regions that are not supplied by stenotic vessels). Exercise is preferred over pharmacologic treatment because of the additional diagnostic and prognostic information provided by exercise testing.

KEY POINT

Although exercise electrocardiography is associated with a higher false-positive rate in women, it is the recommended modality for noninvasive diagnostic testing in women who are able to exercise and have interpretable electrocardiograms.

Bibliography

Shaw LJ, Bugiardini R, Merz CN. Women and ischemic heart disease: evolving knowledge. J Am Coll Cardiol. 2009;54:1561-75. [PMID: 19833255]

Item 9   Answer: C
Educational Objective: *Treat continuing angina in a patient with chronic stable coronary artery disease.*

In this patient with coronary artery disease and continuing angina, the medical therapy should be optimized by increasing the dosage of β-blocker. Physical examination is notable for blood pressure and heart rate that would allow further up-titration of the β-blocker dosage. Complete β-blockade typically results in a resting pulse rate of approximately 55 to 60/min. Therefore, the pulse rate of 80/min suggests that the dosage of metoprolol should be increased. β-Blockers are particularly effective antianginal medications because they decrease heart rate, myocardial contractility, and systemic blood pressure, thereby lowering myocardial oxygen demand.

Calcium channel blockers are first-line antianginal therapy in patients with contraindications to β-blockers. In patients with continuing angina despite optimal dosages of β-blocker and nitrates, a calcium channel blocker may be added. A calcium channel blocker such as diltiazem is not indicated in this patient because his dosage of metoprolol is not yet optimal.

Ranolazine should be considered only in patients who remain symptomatic despite optimal dosages of β-blockers, calcium channel blockers, and nitrates. Ranolazine decreases angina symptoms but is significantly more expensive and less effective than the usual antianginal medications.

Coronary angiography may be indicated in a patient who is receiving maximal medical therapy with continued symptoms of angina that affect quality of life. Referral for coronary angiography is not indicated for this patient because he is not currently receiving optimal medical therapy.

KEY POINT

In the treatment of chronic stable angina, the β-blocker dose is adjusted to achieve a resting pulse rate of approximately 55 to 60/min.

Bibliography

Boden WE, O'Rourke RA, Teo KK, et al. Optimal medical therapy with or without PCI for stable coronary disease. N Engl J Med. 2007;356:1503-16. [PMID: 17387127]

Item 10   Answer: A
Educational Objective: *Evaluate chronic stable angina.*

Coronary angiography is the most appropriate option in this patient who has had continued symptoms of angina despite optimal medical therapy. Although it has been shown that a routine strategy of coronary angiography and revascularization provides no benefit compared with optimal medical therapy in patients with chronic stable angina, coronary angiography may be of benefit in patients who are highly symptomatic despite optimal medical therapy, such as this patient. Coronary angiography allows direct evaluation of the coronary anatomy, with possible percutaneous coronary intervention or surgical revascularization if indicated. Coronary revascularization has been shown to be beneficial in patients with chronic stable angina and the following conditions: angina pectoris that is refractory to medical therapy; a large area of ischemic myocardium and high-risk criteria on stress testing; high-risk coronary anatomy, including left main coronary artery stenosis or three-vessel disease; and significant coronary artery disease with reduced left ventricular systolic function. In appropriately selected patients, revascularization, with either percutaneous coronary intervention or coronary artery bypass grafting surgery, has been shown to reduce angina, increase longevity, and improve left ventricular performance.

Exercise treadmill stress testing would not be useful in the management of this patient because it would only confirm the known diagnosis of coronary artery disease. Results of an exercise stress test would not influence therapeutic decisions.

Although β-blockers and nitrates are effective antianginal medications, the patient is receiving near-maximal doses of both drugs, as indicated by his pulse rate, which shows effective β-blockade, and his blood pressure, which likely would not tolerate an increase in the dosage of either medication.

KEY POINT

Coronary angiography is indicated in patients with chronic stable angina who have lifestyle-limiting angina despite optimal medical therapy.

Bibliography

Qaseem A, Fihn SD, Dallas P, et al. Management of stable ischemic heart disease: summary of a clinical practice guideline from the American College of Physicians/American College of Cardiology Foundation/American Heart Association/American Association for Thoracic Surgery/Preventive Cardiovascular Nurses Association/Society of Thoracic Surgeons. Ann Intern Med. 2012;157:735-43. [PMID: 23165665]

Item 11   Answer: A

Educational Objective: *Manage chest pain in the emergency department.*

The most appropriate management of this patient's chest pain is admission to the telemetry unit and ongoing assessment with serial electrocardiograms and troponin measurements. Based on this patient's age and the substernal nature of his chest pain, there is at least an intermediate likelihood of an acute coronary syndrome. The decision to hospitalize a patient with chest pain is challenging. The goal is to identify patients with life-threatening disease who require immediate attention while minimizing unnecessary evaluation and treatment in others. A rapid clinical determination of the likelihood of an acute coronary syndrome is the essential first task and should guide the admission decision. In addition, the physician should consider the likelihood of short-term adverse outcomes, including death and nonfatal myocardial infarction, in patients with acute coronary syndrome. When acute coronary syndrome is suspected, the patient should be admitted for evaluation and management. Low-risk patients can be further stratified with stress testing.

At this point, the patient does not have an indication for coronary angiography and acute intervention. If further chest pain develops in association with ST-segment or T-wave changes on electrocardiography or elevated cardiac enzyme levels and the patient is considered high risk according to his TIMI (Thrombolysis in Myocardial Infarction) score, cardiac angiography would be reasonable.

The most common gastrointestinal cause of chest pain is gastroesophageal reflux disease (GERD). Although the pain associated with GERD is often described as burning, it can mimic angina and may be relieved by nitroglycerin. It generally is worsened with bending over or recumbency and is relieved with antacids, histamine-2 blockers, or proton pump inhibitors. Because acute coronary syndrome is a life-threatening condition, this diagnosis must be addressed first. In addition, the preferred initial diagnostic test for GERD is a therapeutic trial of a proton pump inhibitor, not esophageal pH monitoring.

Cardiac stress testing can be highly valuable in identifying significant coronary insufficiency, and it would be the test of choice to diagnose stable angina. However, in the acute setting, stress testing is contraindicated in a patient with possible acute coronary syndrome. Once the patient is stabilized and acute coronary syndrome is excluded, stress testing can be used to further stratify risk in a low- or intermediate-risk patient. In this patient, the preferred cardiac stress test is an exercise stress test, not a pharmacologic stress test with nuclear imaging.

KEY POINT

The decision to hospitalize a patient with chest pain is based on the identification of potentially life-threatening disease that requires immediate assessment and stabilization.

Bibliography

Jneid H, Anderson JL, Wright RS, et al. 2012 ACCF/AHA Focused Update of the Guideline for the Management of Patients with Unstable Angina/Non-St-Elevation Myocardial Infarction (updating the 2007 Guideline and replacing the 2011 Focused Update): A Report of the American College of Cardiology Foundation/American Heart Association Task Force on Practice Guidelines. J Am Coll Cardiol. 2012;60:645-81. PMID: 22809746

Item 12   Answer: A

Educational Objective: *Treat an ST-elevation myocardial infarction with thrombolytic therapy.*

The most appropriate initial management of this patient consists of aspirin, heparin, intravenous nitroglycerin, and thrombolytic therapy. This patient has evidence of an ST-elevation myocardial infarction (STEMI) with acute ST-segment changes present in the inferior leads and an elevated troponin T level. The treatment of choice for STEMI is reperfusion therapy. Reperfusion for patients with STEMI can be achieved with thrombolytic therapy or primary percutaneous coronary intervention (PCI). Many patients with STEMI in the United States present to non–PCI-capable hospitals; as a result, thrombolytic therapy and transfer for primary PCI are the available treatment options. The time to achieve balloon inflation is a major determinant of the benefits of PCI versus thrombolytic therapy. If PCI must be delayed, then thrombolytic therapy should be considered. Observational data from community hospitals within the United States have found that fewer than 5% of patients achieve the guideline-suggested door-to-balloon time of less than 90 minutes. A projected 2-hour delay to a PCI facility makes thrombolytic therapy the best option for this patient.

β-Blockers reduce mortality and should be given to all patients with acute coronary syndrome except those with heart failure, systolic blood pressure of less than 90 mm Hg, bradycardia (<50/min), or second-degree atrioventricular block. Because this patient's heart rate is 48/min, metoprolol should not be administered. Treatment with heparin, clopidogrel, pravastatin, and intravenous nitroglycerin without thrombolytic therapy does not address the need for immediate myocardial reperfusion and is not adequate treatment for this patient.

KEY POINT

The time to achieve balloon inflation within 90 minutes is a major determinant of the benefits of percutaneous coronary intervention versus thrombolytic therapy.

Bibliography

Jneid H, Anderson JL, Wright RS, et al. 2012 ACCF/AHA Focused Update of the Guideline for the Management of Patients with Unstable Angina/Non-St-Elevation Myocardial Infarction (updating the 2007 Guideline and replacing the 2011 Focused Update): A Report of the American College of Cardiology Foundation/American Heart Association Task Force on Practice Guidelines. J Am Coll Cardiol. 2012;14;60:645-81. PMID: 22809746

Item 13   Answer: A

Educational Objective: *Manage non–ST-elevation myocardial infarction.*

The most appropriate next test is cardiac catheterization. Although chest pain is the most common presenting symptom for an acute coronary syndrome, women and patients with diabetes are more likely to have atypical angina symptoms, such as fatigue, dyspnea, and nausea. Acute coronary syndromes include unstable angina, non–ST-elevation myocardial infarction (NSTEMI), and ST-elevation myocardial infarction (STEMI). Patients with ischemic chest pain and STEMI benefit from reperfusion therapy, either thrombolytic therapy or primary angioplasty. Patients with NSTEMI or unstable angina are a heterogeneous group and require risk stratification (determination of their risk of death or nonfatal myocardial infection) to direct therapy. Although patients with unstable angina may have similar electrocardiographic findings to those with NSTEMI, they can be differentiated by the lack of elevation in serum cardiac biomarkers. This patient with recurrent unprovoked dyspnea, an evolving electrocardiogram showing ischemic changes in the anterolateral leads (ST-segment depression and T-wave inversion), and rising troponin level is at high risk for death or nonfatal myocardial infarction (5 points on the TIMI (Thrombolysis in Myocardial Infarction) risk stratification score). This patient will benefit from an early invasive approach that includes coronary angiography and subsequent revascularization (percutaneous coronary intervention or surgical revascularization). Most contemporary trials evaluating these two alternatives show a benefit for early angiography and revascularization (invasive approach).

An echocardiogram may show localized wall motion abnormalities associated with acute ischemia, but this finding does not alter the need for early intervention with cardiac catheterization and revascularization. An exercise stress test is contraindicated in patients with unstable ischemic heart disease. Repeating the troponin level will add no useful additional information to guide the management of this patient.

KEY POINT

Women and patients with diabetes are more likely to have atypical angina symptoms, such as fatigue, dyspnea, and nausea.

Bibliography

Makki N, Brennan TM, Girotra S. Acute coronary syndrome. J Intensive Care Med. 2013 Sep 18. [Epub ahead of print] [PMID: 24047692]

Item 14   Answer: D

Educational Objective: *Manage a patient presenting late with ST-elevation myocardial infarction using primary percutaneous coronary intervention.*

The patient should undergo primary percutaneous coronary intervention (PCI). He presents with evidence of ST-elevation myocardial infarction (STEMI). The goal of therapy in patients STEMI is to perform PCI within 90 minutes of presentation to a PCI-capable facility or within 120 minutes if the patient requires transfer from a non–PCI-capable hospital. However, patients may benefit from treatment up to 12 hours after the onset of symptoms and possibly even after this time, depending on clinical circumstances.

For patients with STEMI, including those presenting later than the optimal time frame, PCI is the preferred reperfusion strategy instead of treatment with thrombolytics. Thrombolytic therapy has not shown a clear benefit for patients with STEMI who present more than 12 hours after the onset of symptoms. It remains second-line treatment when PCI is not possible or is contraindicated.

Emergency coronary artery bypass graft surgery is not a routine method of revascularization in patients with STEMI. The reasons are logistical; it is nearly impossible to diagnose STEMI, perform cardiac catheterization, obtain access to an operating room, assemble a surgical team, and perform surgery within the necessary time frame to salvage the greatest amount of myocardium.

Compared with medical therapy alone, if performed promptly, coronary reperfusion (PCI or thrombolytic therapy) improves outcomes in nearly all groups of patients with acute STEMI.

KEY POINT

In patients presenting with ST-elevation myocardial infarction, primary percutaneous coronary intervention is the preferred therapy.

Bibliography

Armstrong PW, Westerhout CM, Welsh RC. Duration of symptoms is the key modulator of the choice of reperfusion for ST-elevation myocardial infarction. Circulation. 2009;119:1293-1303. [PMID: 19273730]

Item 15   Answer: D

Educational Objective: *Diagnose postinfarction ventricular septal defect.*

A postinfarction ventricular septal defect (VSD) is the most likely cause of this patient's symptoms. She initially presented with a delayed anterior wall ST-elevation myocardial infarction (STEMI). She then had acute respiratory distress and was found to have a new holosystolic murmur at the left sternal border on physical examination. These findings could be consistent with either a VSD or acute ischemic mitral regurgitation. However, given the location of the murmur and its association with a thrill, a VSD is more likely. With a postinfarction VSD, shunting of oxygenated blood from the left ventricle to the right ventricle occurs. This acute volume overload to the right ventricle results in cardiogenic shock and is rapidly fatal unless emergent surgical or possibly percutaneous intervention can be performed.

An acute aortic dissection associated with a myocardial infarction is more commonly associated with an inferior wall STEMI. Findings on physical examination may include asymmetric blood pressures and an early diastolic murmur of acute aortic insufficiency.

Rupture of the left ventricular free wall presents as hemopericardium with electromechanical dissociation and death. Risk factors include elderly age, female sex, first myocardial infarction, and anterior location of the infarction. The patient's loud holosystolic murmur and thrill are not compatible with a free wall rupture.

Physical examination findings of right ventricular infarction include hypotension, clear lung fields, and elevated jugular venous pulsations. It would be exceedingly unusual for a right ventricular infarction to develop in association with an anterior wall infarction.

Acute ischemic mitral regurgitation is another late complication of myocardial infarction and also presents with a new holosystolic murmur. Ischemia with subsequent rupture of a papillary muscle or chordae tendineae is the most likely cause of acute ischemic mitral regurgitation and may result in a "flail" mitral valve. Echocardiography can accurately distinguish acute ischemic mitral regurgitation from a postinfarction VSD.

KEY POINT

A postinfarction ventricular septal defect is characterized by a new holosystolic murmur at the left sternal border and usually presents several days after the initial infarct.

Bibliography

Poulsen SH, Praestholm M, Munk K, Wierup P, Egeblad H, Nielsen-Kudsk JE. Ventricular septal rupture complicating acute myocardial infarction: clinical characteristics and contemporary outcome. Ann Thorac Surg. 2008;85:1591-6. [PMID: 18442545]

Item 16   Answer: A

Educational Objective: *Treat unstable angina with appropriate medical therapy.*

A β-blocker, such as metoprolol, should be added to this patient's therapeutic regimen. He has acute-onset chest pain, normal cardiac biomarkers, and T-wave inversions shown on electrocardiogram. These findings are consistent with unstable angina. First-line therapies for patients with acute coronary syndromes, including unstable angina, include dual antiplatelet therapy with aspirin and a thienopyridine (e.g., clopidogrel, prasugrel, ticagrelor), a β-blocker, nitrates, and anticoagulation (e.g., heparin). Morphine may also be given in patients with active chest pain. These treatments attempt to minimize ischemia by addressing both the supply and demand of oxygen within myocardial cells.

When β-blockers are contraindicated for the treatment of unstable angina, as in a patient with severe bronchospastic lung disease that may be exacerbated by treatment, calcium channel blockers should be considered. However, the calcium channel blocker nifedipine causes an increase in heart rate and therefore myocardial oxygen demand and is contraindicated in patients with an acute coronary syndrome.

Reperfusion therapy, preferably with percutaneous coronary intervention or, alternatively, thrombolysis, is the mainstay of treatment for ST-elevation myocardial infarction. This patient has unstable angina based on his clinical presentation, findings on electrocardiogram, and normal cardiac biomarkers. Patients with unstable angina are usually treated initially with medical therapy, with further evaluation and treatment based on an assessment of the risk factors. Therefore, acute reperfusion therapy is not indicated in this patient.

KEY POINT

Medical therapy for most patients with acute coronary syndrome includes dual antiplatelet therapy, a β-blocker, anticoagulation, and nitrates and morphine for chest pain.

Bibliography

Jneid, H, Anderson JL, Wright RS, et al. 2012 ACCF/AHA Focused Update of the Guideline for the Management of Patients with Unstable angina/Non-ST-Elevation Myocardial Infarction (updating the 2007 Guideline and replacing the 2011 Focused Update). J Am Coll Cardiol. 2012;60:645-81. [PMID: 22809746]

Item 17   Answer: D

Educational Objective: *Understand the appropriate management in a patient with an acute ST-elevation myocardial infarction.*

This patient should undergo percutaneous coronary intervention (PCI). The electrocardiographic changes are consistent with acute anterior ST-elevation myocardial infarction (STEMI). Patients with STEMI who present within 12 hours of symptom onset should undergo either primary PCI or thrombolytic therapy. PCI is preferred because it is associated with a lower mortality rate compared with thrombolytic therapy. Ideally, it should be performed within 90 minutes of presentation to a facility with PCI capability or within 120 minutes if the patient requires transfer from a non–PCI-capable hospital. PCI also is indicated in patients with a contraindication to thrombolytic therapy and in patients with cardiogenic shock. PCI is most effective if completed within 12 hours of the onset of chest pain; the earlier the intervention, the better the outcome. Because this patient has no clear contraindication to PCI, this is the treatment of choice for STEMI.

Optimal management of patients with STEMI relies on timely recognition and rapid initiation of reperfusion therapy. Patients with an acute coronary syndrome and an electrocardiogram compatible with STEMI can be treated with reperfusion therapy without biomarker confirmation. Early biomarker results may be normal in patients with STEMI, and waiting for the results of the troponin level would delay appropriate treatment.

Medical therapy with further intervention based on risk stratification is indicated in patients with non–ST-elevation myocardial infarction or unstable angina, but would not be appropriate in this patient with STEMI.

KEY POINT

Reperfusion therapy, preferably with percutaneous coronary intervention or thrombolysis, is indicated in patients presenting with acute ST-elevation myocardial infarction.

Bibliography

O'Gara PT, Kushner FG, Ascheim DD, et al. 2013 ACCF/AHA Guideline for the Management of ST-Elevation Myocardial Infarction: Executive Summary: A Report of the American College of Cardiology Foundation/American Heart Associate Task Force on Practice Guidelines. Circulation. 2013;127:529-55. [PMID: 23247303]

Item 18   Answer: D

Educational Objective: *Diagnose sick sinus syndrome.*

This patient has symptomatic sick sinus syndrome (SSS) because her episodes of sinus bradycardia are correlated with dizziness. SSS comprises a collection of pathologic findings that result in bradycardia. These include sinus arrest, sinus exit block, and sinus bradycardia. SSS is common in the elderly, and because symptoms can be intermittent or nonspecific, misdiagnosis can occur.

Because there is no dissociation between atrial depolarization and conduction to the ventricles on telemetry, the patient does not have complete heart block (third-degree heart block).

Complete heart block (third-degree heart block) is characterized by complete absence of conduction from the atria to the ventricles; the P waves and the QRS complexes are completely independent of each other. This patient's P waves are followed by QRS complexes, and the pauses result from failure of the sinus node to fire (no P waves) and not from a failure of conduction from the atria to the ventricles.

The presence of P waves on telemetry excludes the diagnosis of atrial fibrillation, and the combination of conducted P waves and a narrow QRS complex makes nonsustained ventricular tachycardia unlikely.

KEY POINT

Sick sinus syndrome as a result of sinus node dysfunction may cause symptoms of dizziness that are correlated with episodes of bradycardia.

Bibliography

Semelka M, Gera J, Usman S. Sick sinus syndrome: a review. Am Fam Physician. 2013;87:691-6. [PMID: 23939447]

Item 19   Answer: D

Educational Objective: *Recognize complete heart block.*

Third-degree atrioventricular block, or complete heart block, refers to a lack of atrioventricular conduction (characterized by lack of conduction of all atrial impulses to the ventricles), as seen in this patient's electrocardiogram. This is an important diagnosis to make because pacemaker implantation may improve survival for patients with asymptomatic complete heart block; therefore, all patients with complete heart block should be treated with pacemaker implantation.

First-degree atrioventricular block is recognized electrocardiographically as a prolongation of the P-R interval; all P waves are conducted, and this condition requires no specific treatment. Second-degree atrioventricular block is characterized by intermittent nonconduction of P waves and subsequent "dropped" ventricular beats. Second-degree atrioventricular block is divided into two types, Mobitz type I and Mobitz type II. Mobitz type I second-degree atrioventricular block is characterized by progressive prolongation of the P-R interval until a dropped beat occurs. This type of heart block is characteristically transient and usually requires no specific treatment. Mobitz type II second-degree atrioventricular block is characterized by a regularly dropped beat (e.g., a nonconducted P wave every second or third beat), without progressive prolongation of the P-R interval. It is usually associated with evidence of additional disease in the conduction system, such as bundle branch block or bifascicular or trifascicular block. Mobitz type II atrioventricular block suddenly and unpredictably progresses to complete heart block and is usually treated with a pacemaker.

KEY POINT

A pacemaker is indicated in patients with acquired third-degree atrioventricular block.

Bibliography

Epstein AE, DiMarco JP, Ellenbogen KA, et al. American College of Cardiology Foundation; American Heart Association Task Force on Practice Guidelines; Heart Rhythm Society. 2012 ACCF/AHA/HRS Focused Update Incorporated into the ACCF/AHA/HRS 2008 Guidelines for Device-Based Therapy of Cardiac Rhythm Abnormalities: a Report of the American College of Cardiology Foundation/American Heart Association Task Force on Practice Guidelines and the Heart Rhythm Society. J Am Coll Cardiol. 2013;61(3):e6-75. [PMID: 23265327]

Item 20   Answer: A

Educational Objective: *Diagnose acute myocardial infarction in a patient with left bundle branch block on electrocardiogram.*

This patient is having an acute myocardial infarction manifesting as a new left bundle branch block on electrocardiogram and complicated by ischemic mitral regurgitation and heart failure. Electrocardiographically, left bundle branch block is associated with absent Q waves in leads I, aVL, and V_6; a large, wide, and positive R wave in leads I, aVL, and V_6; and prolongation of the QRS complex to greater than 0.12 seconds. Repolarization abnormalities are present and consist of ST-segment and T wave vectors directed opposite to the QRS complex. The presentation of acute coronary syndrome with new left bundle branch block should be considered equivalent to ST-elevation myocardial infarction and is an indication for acute reperfusion therapy. The diagnosis of acute aortic dissection should be considered in this patient, but the findings of symmetric blood pressures and pulse rates and normal mediastinum on chest radiograph are reassuring. Aortic dissection chest pain is often described as ripping and tends to radiate to the back. Although chest pain, left bundle branch block, mitral regurgitation, and heart failure may all be complications of endocarditis, the acute onset of this patient's symptoms and the fact that he is afebrile make this diagnosis much less likely than acute myocardial infarction. Pericarditis also generally has a more subacute presentation, and typical electrocardiographic findings include diffuse PR depressions or ST-segment elevations and not new left bundle branch block.

KEY POINTS

Left bundle branch block is associated with absent Q waves in leads I, aVL, and V_6; a large, wide, and positive R wave in leads I, aVL, and V_6 ("tombstone" R waves); and prolongation of the QRS complex to greater than 0.12 seconds.

The constellation of chest pain, elevated biomarkers, and new-onset left bundle branch block is considered equivalent to ST-elevation myocardial infarction.

Bibliography

Barold SS, Herweg B. Electrocardiographic diagnosis of myocardial infarction during left bundle branch block. Cardiol Clin. 2006;24:377-85. [PMID: 16939830]

Item 21   Answer: C

Educational Objective: *Diagnose second-degree atrioventricular block.*

This patient has second-degree atrioventricular block, diagnosed by the presence of isolated P waves that are not followed by a QRS complex. Second-degree atrioventricular block is divided into two types, Mobitz type I and Mobitz type II. This patient has second-degree atrioventricular block, Mobitz type I (Wenckebach), with progressive prolongation of the PR interval until the "dropped" beat. Additionally, in a Mobitz type I rhythm, the PP interval is constant but the PR interval decreases progressively until the dropped beat occurs. This patient's rhythm is most likely caused by the combination of atenolol and diltiazem, both of which can decrease conduction within the atrioventricular node. Mobitz type II atrioventricular block is much less common. It is usually associated with a right or left bundle branch block pattern, and the dropped beat is associated with an intermittent block of the remaining bundle branch, which indicates significant conduction system disease. A pacemaker is commonly required. In Mobitz type II atrioventricular block, the PR interval is constant in the conducted beats and the RR interval containing the nonconducted (dropped) beat is equal to two PP intervals.

First-degree atrioventricular block is characterized by a prolonged PR interval of more than 0.2 seconds. Complete heart block (third-degree atrioventricular block) is characterized by complete absence of conduction from the atria to the ventricles; the P waves and the QRS complexes are completely independent of each other. Careful analysis shows that the P wave rate and the QRS complex rate are different and that the PR interval is different for every QRS complex.

KEY POINT

Second-degree atrioventricular block is diagnosed by the presence of isolated P waves that are not followed by a QRS complex. There are two possible forms: Mobitz type I (Wenckebach), with progressive prolongation of the PR interval until the dropped beat, and Mobitz type II, with a constant PR interval and periodic dropped beats.

Bibliography

Ufberg JW, Clark JS. Bradydysrhythmias and atrioventricular conduction blocks. Emerg Med Clin North Am. 2006;24:1-9. [PMID: 16308110]

Item 22   Answer: B
Educational Objective: *Treat reversible heart block.*

This patient should be treated with intravenous ceftriaxone. She most likely has Lyme carditis manifested by acute-onset, high-grade atrioventricular conduction defects that occasionally may be associated with myocarditis. Carditis occurs in 5% to 10% of patients with Lyme disease, usually within a few weeks to months after infection. Atrioventricular block can present in any degree, and progression to complete heart block is often rapid. The prognosis is good, usually with resolution of atrioventricular block within days to weeks. The presence of the characteristic skin rash, erythema migrans, with or without a history of tick bite in an endemic region, has a greater than 80% probability of being caused by *Borrelia burgdorferi* infection and is sufficient to support a decision to treat Lyme disease empirically without laboratory confirmation of the diagnosis. The preferred antibiotic regimen is intravenous ceftriaxone until the heart block resolves, followed by a 21-day course of oral therapy.

An electrophysiology study is not indicated because it would not provide additional prognostic information. Atrioventricular block is usually within the node, but sinoatrial and His-Purkinje involvement has also been described.

Most cases of Lyme carditis resolve spontaneously, and neither temporary nor permanent pacemaker therapy is needed. Temporary pacing would be required if the patient were hemodynamically unstable with bradycardia. However, this rarely occurs in the setting of Lyme carditis. Indications for permanent pacemaker placement would include persistent high-grade atrioventricular block.

KEY POINT
Lyme carditis is manifested by acute-onset, high-grade atrioventricular conduction defects that occasionally may be associated with myocarditis.

Bibliography

Hu LT. In the clinic. Lyme disease. Ann Intern Med. 2012;157:ITC2-2-16. [PMID: 22868858]

Item 23   Answer: C
Educational Objective: *Treat atrial fibrillation with diltiazem.*

The most appropriate treatment for the patient is diltiazem given intravenously. He has atrial fibrillation with a rapid ventricular response. Atrial fibrillation is caused by rapid and uncoordinated electrical activation within the atria. The electrocardiogram shows an absence of P waves and an irregular ventricular response. Approximately 50% of episodes of atrial fibrillation convert to a normal rhythm spontaneously.

If the patient is symptomatic but hemodynamically stable, the initial goal is to reduce the heart rate to 60/min to 110/min with a rate control agent. Intravenous options include diltiazem, verapamil, metoprolol, and esmolol. Digoxin can be used as a second agent, especially in patients with heart failure or systolic dysfunction, but peak effect can take up to 6 hours. In those with rapid atrial fibrillation with minimal or mild symptoms, oral agents may be used.

Adenosine is an intravenous agent that transiently blocks atrioventricular nodal conduction; it is effective at terminating supraventricular tachycardia where the electrical circuit is dependent on the atrioventricular node. Intravenous adenosine may be used to break the reentrant rhythm in atrioventricular nodal reentrant tachycardia, or orthodromic atrioventricular reciprocating tachycardia. However, it is not an effective therapy for atrial fibrillation.

Patients with adverse or marginal hemodynamic status or acute coronary ischemia because of a rapid ventricular response should undergo immediate cardioversion. Cardioversion is also the treatment of choice for patients with wide complex tachycardia. This patient is hemodynamically stable, and immediate electrical cardioversion is not necessary.

KEY POINT
The acute management of atrial fibrillation in symptomatic but hemodynamically stable patients includes rate control with a β-blocking agent, such as metoprolol, or a calcium channel blocker, such as diltiazem.

Bibliography

Zimetbaum P. In the clinic. Atrial fibrillation. Ann Intern Med. 2010;153:ITC6-1-15, quiz ITC6-16. [PMID: 21135291]

Item 24   Answer: D
Educational Objective: *Treat atrial fibrillation with warfarin.*

The patient should receive long-term warfarin therapy to prevent cardiogenic thromboembolism related to the atrial fibrillation. In patients without significant valvular disease, the most commonly used method to determine the choice of thromboprophylaxis is the $CHADS_2$ score. One point each is given for congestive heart failure, hypertension (even if treated), age 75 years or older, and diabetes; 2 points are given for previous stroke or transient ischemic attack. Patients with zero points have a low stroke risk, and aspirin or no treatment is used. Those with a score of 1 have an intermediate stroke risk, and either warfarin or aspirin is used, based on physician and patient preference. A score of 2 or more on this scale indicates high risk, and therapeutic anticoagulation is preferred. Recently, the $CHADS_2$ score was updated to the CHA_2DS_2-VAS_c score, which better recognizes the influence of gender and the presence of established vascular disease as stroke risk factors. The CHA_2DS_2-VAS_c score also weights age more heavily as a risk factor. For a CHA_2DS_2-VAS_c score of 1, either anticoagulation or antiplatelet therapy is indicated. For a CHA_2DS_2-VAS_c score of 2 or greater, oral anticoagulation is recommended for prevention of stroke. This patient has a $CHADS_2$ score of 3 points (hypertension and transient ischemic attack), and a CHA_2DS_2-VAS_c score of 4 points (age range, gender, hypertension, and transient ischemic attack). Using either scoring system, therapeutic anticoagulation, such as with warfarin, is indicated.

A new class of anticoagulation agents is the direct thrombin inhibitors. These drugs, such as dabigatran, have been shown to be slightly superior to warfarin in preventing ischemic and hemorrhagic stroke, although their anticoagulant effect is not easily reversed and they are substantially more expensive than warfarin. These agents may be an alternative to warfarin in patients with nonvalvular atrial fibrillation.

In patients who are not candidates for warfarin treatment, adding clopidogrel to aspirin can reduce the risk of stroke more than aspirin alone, although the risk of major bleeding events is increased. In patients who are able to take warfarin, however, clopidogrel plus aspirin is inferior for preventing ischemic stroke.

Atrial fibrillation ablation is an option in patients who are symptomatic and have been treated unsuccessfully with at least one antiarrhythmic agent. The procedure entails electrical isolation of the pulmonary veins so that premature atrial contractions, which frequently originate in the pulmonary veins, cannot initiate atrial fibrillation. Atrioventricular node ablation is another option for patients who do not benefit from medical therapy. A pacemaker is inserted at the time of ablation, so the ventricular rate is controlled by the device. The patient does not meet the criteria for either of these procedures.

KEY POINT

Long-term anticoagulation therapy is indicated for patients with atrial fibrillation who are at increased risk for thromboembolism.

Bibliography

Zimetbaum P. In the clinic. Atrial fibrillation. Ann Intern Med. 2010;153:ITC6-1-15, quiz ITC616. [PMID: 21135291]

Item 25   Answer: D

Educational Objective: *Diagnose ventricular preexcitation syndrome.*

The electrocardiogram is diagnostic for ventricular preexcitation by an accessory atrioventricular connection, with a short P-R interval, prolonged QRS duration, and slurred onset of the QRS (delta wave) interval. With paroxysmal tachyarrhythmias, this pattern is diagnostic for Wolff-Parkinson-White syndrome and accounts for the paradoxically split S_2. In a symptomatic patient with recurrent palpitations or syncope, radiofrequency ablation of the accessory pathway is likely to provide the most definitive improvement.

The electrocardiogram does not show atrial fibrillation because it shows clearly discernible P waves and a regular rhythm. First-degree atrioventricular block is associated with a P-R interval of more than 0.20 seconds, not a shortened interval (<0.11 seconds), as seen in this case.

KEY POINT

An accessory atrioventricular conduction pathway not contained within the atrioventricular node may cause a short PR interval and a delta wave on electrocardiography; when present with symptomatic tachycardia is termed Wolff-Parkinson-White (WPW) syndrome.

Bibliography

Liu A, Pusalkar P. Asymptomatic Wolff-Parkinson-White syndrome: incidental ECG diagnosis and a review of literature regarding current treatment. BMJ Case Rep. 2011;2011. [PMCID: PMC3128358]

Item 26   Answer: B

Educational Objective: *Diagnose atrial flutter.*

The electrocardiogram shows atrial flutter, which is the likely cause of the patient's clinical symptoms. Atrial flutter is a rapid, regular atrial rhythm that appears as a "saw-tooth" pattern on an electrocardiogram, often best seen in the inferior leads. The atrial rate is characteristically approximately 300/min, with atrioventricular conduction occurring once every two flutter waves (2:1 atrioventricular conduction), a very typical pattern for atrial flutter.

Atrial fibrillation is more disorganized atrial activity at a rate of 350 to 600/min, with no discernible P waves. It is characteristically associated with an irregularly irregular rhythm, and the fibrillatory waves vary in amplitude, morphologic pattern, and interval, creating a rough, irregular baseline between QRS complexes. Multifocal atrial tachycardia is defined by the electrocardiographic finding of discrete P waves with at least three morphologic patterns with varying P-P, P-R, and R-R intervals. The morphologic features of P waves

are generally best seen in leads II, III, and V_1. In adults, multifocal atrial tachycardia is often associated with other disorders, often hypoxic chronic obstructive pulmonary disease or electrolyte abnormalities. Sinus tachycardia is a sinus rhythm with a ventricular rate greater than 100/min. The P waves have normal morphologic features but can become difficult to see with heart rates greater than 140/min because the P waves begin to merge with the preceding T waves. Slowing the heart rate with carotid sinus massage often shows the hidden P waves and establishes the diagnosis.

KEY POINT

Atrial flutter is characterized by a saw-tooth pattern on electrocardiogram that is most noticeable in the inferior leads.

Bibliography

Colucci RA, Silver MJ, Shubrook J. Common types of supraventricular tachycardia: diagnosis and management. Am Fam Physician. 2010;82:942-52. [PMID: 20949888]

Item 27   Answer: D

Educational Objective: *Diagnose multifocal atrial tachycardia.*

The electrocardiogram shows multifocal atrial tachycardia (MAT). MAT is most commonly seen in acutely ill patients, most often in the setting of pulmonary disease (such as the exacerbation of chronic obstructive pulmonary disease with associated hypoxia in this patient) and electrolyte abnormalities. The electrocardiogram in MAT is defined by the presence of discrete P waves with at least three different morphologic patterns with varying P-P, P-R, and R-R intervals. The morphologic features of P waves are generally best seen in leads II, III, and V_1. Therapy is directed at the underlying disease process because without treatment the arrhythmia is often refractory to therapy or may recur. In this patient, treatment should be directed toward the pulmonary disease and correction of electrolyte imbalances, especially magnesium. Therefore, the treatment of choice in this patient is oxygen, inhaled bronchodilators, antibiotics, and corticosteroids. Electrolyte levels should be corrected, and the heart rate may be controlled as needed by atrioventricular blocking agents.

Atrial fibrillation is characterized by disordered atrial electrical activity that leads to an irregular heart rate similar to MAT; however, P waves are not detectable, as in this patient's electrocardiogram. In atrioventricular nodal reentrant tachycardia, the atria and ventricles are activated simultaneously from a reentrant circuit within the atrioventricular node. The QRS complex is narrow, and no P waves are seen. Atrioventricular reciprocating tachycardia is a bypass tract–mediated reentrant tachycardia in which the anterograde conduction (atrium-to-ventricle) is typically via the atrioventricular node and retrograde conduction is via the bypass tract. Because bypass tract conduction is typically faster than conduction via the atrioventricular node, atrial activation occurs rapidly after the QRS complex, resulting in a "short R-P" tachycardia, and the P wave is usually located within the ST segment. Both atrioventricular reciprocating tachycardia and atrioventricular nodal reentrant tachycardia are regular rhythms.

KEY POINT

Multifocal atrial tachycardia is characterized on electrocardiograms by three or more P wave morphologic patterns and variable P-R intervals.

Bibliography

McCord J, Borzak S. Multifocal atrial tachycardia. Chest. 1998;113:203-9. [PMID: 9440591]

Item 28   Answer: C

Educational Objective: *Diagnose acute supraventricular tachycardia.*

The patient's arrhythmia is most likely atrioventricular nodal reentrant tachycardia (AVNRT). Supraventricular tachycardias (SVTs) are rapid heart rhythms that require atrial tissue or the atrioventricular node for initiation and maintenance. Although atrial fibrillation and atrial flutter are technically SVTs, the term is generally used to describe the most frequent paroxysmal SVTs: AVNRT, atrioventricular reciprocating tachycardia, and atrial tachycardia. The most common paroxysmal SVT is AVNRT, which involves a slow pathway and a fast pathway within the atrioventricular node. The slow pathway conducts slowly but repolarizes quickly, whereas the fast pathway conducts quickly but repolarizes slowly. Typical AVNRT (slow-fast) often has an R-P interval so short that the P wave is buried within the QRS complex. The QRS complex is usually narrow as long as conduction below the atrioventricular node is normal.

Adenosine, if pushed rapidly through an intravenous line, can be used to diagnose and treat supraventricular tachycardias. Up to 95% of reentrant atrioventricular node-dependent tachycardias, such as AVNRT and AVRT, terminate with adenosine if administered properly. Adenosine transiently blocks AV nodal conduction, interrupting the reentrant circuit and terminating the AV node-dependent arrhythmia.

Adenosine given in the presence of other supraventricular arrhythmias, including atrial tachycardia, atrial fibrillation, and sinus tachycardia, should only slow the ventricular rate; this may be useful in diagnosis because it may show the underlying rhythm.

KEY POINT

Adenosine can be used to diagnose or treat supraventricular tachycardias by transiently blocking atrioventricular nodal conduction and interrupting the reentrant circuit, thereby terminating atrioventricular nodal reentrant tachycardia and atrioventricular reciprocating tachycardia but not other supraventricular arrhythmias.

Bibliography

Colucci RA, Silver MJ, Shubrook J. Common types of supraventricular tachycardia: diagnosis and management. Am Fam Physician. 2010;82:942-52. [PMID: 20949888]

Item 29   Answer: C

Educational Objective: *Manage a patient with asymptomatic hypertrophic cardiomyopathy with risk factors for sudden cardiac death.*

This patient should undergo placement of an implantable cardioverter-defibrillator (ICD). Echocardiography is virtually diagnostic for hypertrophic cardiomyopathy (HCM). His current risk stratification shows two major risk factors for sudden cardiac death: family history of premature sudden death in a first-degree relative and significant left ventricular wall thickening. Management in this asymptomatic patient is predominantly focused on prevention of sudden cardiac death. ICD implantation is effective for primary prevention of sudden cardiac death in patients with HCM.

In patients with outflow tract obstruction and symptoms of heart failure that are refractory to medication, alleviation of the obstruction with septal myectomy or alcohol septal ablation may be indicated. The patient is asymptomatic; therefore, alcohol septal ablation is not indicated.

Electrophysiology testing is not a reliable method to stratify risk for sudden cardiac death in patients with HCM and is not an appropriate test for this patient.

Amiodarone may be used for primary prevention of sudden cardiac death in patients with HCM with one or more major risk factors, but its efficacy is not established. It may be considered when ICD implantation is not feasible.

American Heart Association consensus recommendations on physical activity in patients with HCM note that most low-level recreational activities, such as bowling or golf, are probably permissible. High-level recreational activities, such as basketball or bodybuilding, are not advised or are strongly discouraged. Recommendations on moderate-level recreational activities vary. Some activities, such as tennis, are deemed probably permissible, whereas others, including weightlifting, are strongly discouraged. Patients with HCM require formal counseling about acceptable levels of physical activity.

KEY POINT

Patients with hypertrophic cardiomyopathy who are at high risk for sudden cardiac death should have an implantable cardioverter-defibrillator placed.

Bibliography

Jacoby DL, DePasquale EC, McKenna WJ. Hypertrophic cardiomyopathy: diagnosis, risk stratification and treatment. CMAJ. 2013;185:127-34. [PMID: 23109605]

Item 30   Answer: C

Educational Objective: *Manage a patient with a hemodynamically stable wide-complex tachycardia.*

The most appropriate treatment for this patient is amiodarone. The electrocardiogram shows a regular, monomorphic wide-complex tachycardia. Although it is possible that the patient has supraventricular tachycardia with aberrancy or antidromic atrioventricular reciprocating tachycardia, in a patient with wide-complex tachycardia and a history of coronary artery disease or cardiomyopathy, ventricular tachycardia is the assumed diagnosis. Hemodynamic stability does not exclude a diagnosis of ventricular tachycardia. The first-line treatment for a hemodynamically stable ventricular tachycardia is an intravenous antiarrhythmic agent such as amiodarone. Procainamide and sotalol are also acceptable agents, and lidocaine can be used as a second-line agent.

Immediate cardioversion is not necessary because this patient does not have signs of instability. If an antiarrhythmic agent is not successful, then elective cardioversion with sedation can restore normal rhythm.

Adenosine may be given for a stable wide-complex rhythm to determine whether it is a supraventricular tachycardia with aberrant conduction or an antidromic atrioventricular reciprocating tachycardia. However, because of the patient's high risk of ventricular tachycardia given his known coronary artery disease, this would not be the most appropriate initial intervention.

The administration of verapamil or β-blockers is not indicated in patients with stable ventricular tachycardia. These drugs can cause severe hemodynamic deterioration and lead to ventricular fibrillation and cardiac arrest.

This patient should be offered an implanted cardioverter-defibrillator for long-term prevention of sudden cardiac death.

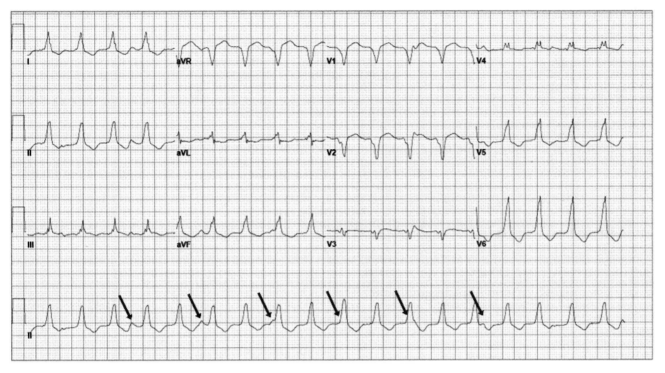

Item 30

In a patient with a wide-complex tachycardia with a history of coronary artery disease or cardiomyopathy, ventricular tachycardia is the most likely diagnosis.

Bibliography

Neumar RW, Otto CW, Link MS, et al. Part 8: Adult Advanced Cardiovascular Life Support: 2010 American Heart Association Guidelines for Cardiopulmonary Resuscitation and Emergency Cardiovascular Care. Circulation. 2010;122(18 suppl 3):S729-67. [PMID: 20956224]

Item 31   Answer: B

Educational Objective: *Treat symptomatic premature ventricular complexes.*

This patient has frequent symptomatic premature ventricular complexes. Premature ventricular complexes are spontaneous depolarizations originating from the ventricles. A premature complex may be single, may occur in pairs (couplets), or may alternate with sinus beats in a specific multiple, such as in bigeminy, in which premature ventricular complexes and sinus beats alternate in a 1:1 ratio. These beats are usually followed by a compensatory pause, and patients may feel as if their heart is stopping. In the absence of structural heart disease, the prognosis is benign. Treatment is based on ameliorating significant symptoms, which may include palpitations, fatigue, and lightheadedness. If the patient's symptoms are tolerable, no therapy is indicated. If not, β-blockers, such as metoprolol, are reasonably effective at suppressing premature ventricular complexes. In contrast, in patients with heart failure, hypertension, or left ventricular hypertrophy, ventricular ectopy has been described as a marker of increased risk of cardiovascular events.

The high incidence of side effects and organ system toxicity with amiodarone therapy proscribes its use as a first-line agent for suppression of premature ventricular complexes.

A pacemaker generally has no primary role in the treatment of symptomatic premature ventricular complexes.

Radiofrequency ablation is usually reserved for patients with severe symptoms that are refractory to drug therapy and those with more sustained ventricular arrhythmias, particularly those with ectopy originating from the right ventricular outflow tract. In the current patient, the multifocal nature of the patient's ectopy, as documented by the varying morphologic patterns of the premature ventricular complexes, would reduce the efficacy of the procedure.

Suppression of premature ventricular complexes is indicated only in patients with severe and disabling symptoms. In these patients, β-blockers are the safest initial therapy.

Bibliography

Cantillon DJ. Evaluation and management of premature ventricular complexes. Cleve Clin J Med. 2013;80:377-87. [PMID: 23733905]

Item 32   Answer: C

Educational Objective: *Diagnose familial long QT syndrome.*

This patient most likely has long QT syndrome (LQTS). Cardiac events in patients with LQTS include syncope and cardiac arrest as a result of torsade de pointes ventricular tachycardia. LQTS may be either congenital or acquired. This patient likely has congenital LQTS, suggested by recurrent syncope triggered by activity and a family history of similar symptoms. This diagnosis should be considered in patients who have family members with sudden death. Risk factors for acquired LQTS include female sex, hypokalemia, hypomagnesemia, structural heart disease, previous QT-interval prolongation, and a history of drug-induced arrhythmia. Other cardiac causes of syncope and sudden death in young patients include hypertrophic cardiomyopathy and arrhythmogenic right ventricular dysplasia.

Left bundle branch block (LBBB) and right bundle branch block (RBBB) are electrocardiographic patterns that increase in frequency with age. LBBB most often occurs in patients with underlying heart disease. In older patients, LBBB is associated with increased mortality. In younger patients, however, LBBB is not associated with syncope or sudden death and the prognosis is generally excellent. RBBB is similarly associated with increased mortality in older patients with underlying heart disease. When RBBB is not associated with underlying cardiac disease, patient outcomes are generally excellent. RBBB is an unlikely cause of this patient's symptoms.

First-degree atrioventricular block is characterized by prolongation of the P-R interval to more than 0.2 seconds. It usually is not associated with alterations in heart rate and has no association with syncope or sudden death.

KEY POINT

Cardiac events in patients with long QT syndrome include syncope and cardiac arrest as a result of torsade de pointes ventricular tachycardia.

Bibliography

Bennett MT, Sanatani S, Chakrabarti S, et al. Assessment of genetic causes of cardiac arrest. Can J Cardiol. 2013;29:100-10. [PMID: 23200097]

Item 33   Answer: A

Educational Objective: *Manage a patient with ventricular fibrillation arrest in the setting of acute myocardial infarction.*

The best option at this time is continued medical management. Ventricular tachyarrhythmias are common in the setting of acute myocardial infarction, occurring in up to 20% of patients. Despite a sixfold increase in the in-hospital mortality rate, the overall mortality rate at 1 year is not increased in patients with ventricular fibrillation that occurs early in this setting. Therefore, unlike sudden cardiac death occurring in other settings, cardiac arrest within the first 48 hours of transmural acute myocardial infarction does not require cardioverter-defibrillator placement.

Primary ventricular fibrillation should be distinguished from ventricular fibrillation that occurs later in the course of disease, usually as a result of heart failure. Before the advent of the implantable cardioverter-defibrillator, ventricular fibrillation occurring late in the hospital course was associated with a 1-year mortality rate of 85%. All patients, even those who have not had arrhythmia during myocardial infarction, should be reevaluated after myocardial infarction with echocardiography to further stratify risk. If the ejection fraction is reduced (<35%), the patient may be a candidate for cardioverter-defibrillator placement.

Amiodarone has not been shown to improve the overall mortality rate after myocardial infarction. In the general population of patients who have survived cardiac arrest, amiodarone does not improve the mortality rate.

Implantable cardioverter-defibrillator placement is not indicated for patients who experience ventricular arrhythmias less than 48 hours after an acute ST-elevation myocardial infarction. Implantable cardioverter-defibrillators have shown a mortality benefit for essentially all other groups of patients who have survived cardiac arrest.

Typical indications for pacemaker placement include symptomatic sinoatrial node dysfunction (sinus bradycardia, intra-atrial block, exit block) and symptomatic bradycardia as a result of advanced second- or third-degree heart block. The current patient, who is asymptomatic and has no evidence of bradycardia or advanced heart block on electrocardiogram, has no indication for pacemaker placement. Pacemaker placement does not prevent sudden death as a result of ventricular tachyarrhythmias.

KEY POINT

Cardiac arrest within the first 48 hours of an acute transmural myocardial infarction does not require secondary prevention therapy other than standard post-myocardial infarction care.

Bibliography

John RM, Tedrow UB, Albert CM, et al. Ventricular arrhythmias and sudden cardiac death. Lancet. 2012;380:1520-9. [PMID: 23101719]

Item 34   Answer: C

Educational Objective: *Treat New York Heart Association class III heart failure with spironolactone.*

The most appropriate addition to this patient's medications is spironolactone. Indications for specific medications for systolic heart failure are generally based on the patient's functional status as measured by New York Heart Association (NYHA) functional class. In the absence of contraindications or intolerance, treatment with an angiotensin converting enzyme (ACE) inhibitor (eg, lisinopril) and a β-blocker (eg, metoprolol) is indicated for all patients with systolic heart failure, regardless of functional status or symptom status. The addition of spironolactone to ACE inhibitor and β-blocker therapy is indicated for patients with severe systolic heart failure (NYHA class III-IV) and is associated with a 30% reduction in mortality rate (including sudden death and death as a result of progressive heart failure), reduction in hospitalizations, and improved NYHA functional class. Care should be taken to prescribe spironolactone according to evidence-based guidelines (NYHA class III-IV symptoms, serum potassium level <5 meq/L, and creatinine level <2.5 mg/dL), and should include close clinical and laboratory follow-up, with particular attention to serum potassium levels.

Routine combination of ACE inhibitor and angiotensin receptor blocker (ARB) therapy (eg, valsartan) is not recommended because of the increased risk of adverse effects, including acute kidney injury, hyperkalemia, and hypotension, without proven clinical benefit. Calcium channel blockers are not preferred agents for the treatment of systolic heart failure. These agents are not associated with improved outcomes and have been implicated in heart failure decompensation (13% in one study). These results are likely related to negative inotropic effects, particularly with the older-generation agents such as nifedipine. Amlodipine and felodipine are the only two calcium channel blockers that have been tested in large clinical trials to have neutral effects on mortality rates in patients with systolic heart failure. These agents would be acceptable to use for the treatment of conditions such as hypertension or angina that are not adequately controlled with the other evidence-based medications. They are not indicated for the treatment of systolic heart failure itself.

KEY POINT

The addition of spironolactone to ACE inhibitor and β-blocker therapy is indicated for patients with severe systolic heart failure (New York Heart Association (NYHA) class III-IV) and is associated with a 30% reduction in mortality rate, reduction in hospitalizations, and improved NYHA functional class.

Bibliography
Goldberg LR. Heart failure. Ann Intern Med. 2010;152:ITC6-1-15; quiz ITC6-16. [PMID: 20513825]

Item 35   Answer: C
Educational Objective: *Interpret the B-type natriuretic peptide level in an obese patient.*

Obesity increases the risk of a falsely low B-type natriuretic peptide (BNP) level. BNP, or *N*-terminal proBNP, levels should be assessed in patients suspected of having heart failure, particularly when the diagnosis or relative contribution of heart failure to symptoms is uncertain. BNP is especially helpful in differentiating dyspnea as a result of heart failure versus dyspnea as a result of pulmonary disease. Among patients presenting to the emergency department with dyspnea of undetermined cause, a BNP level of less than 100 pg/mL accurately excludes decompensated heart failure as a cause. However, among ambulatory patients with established heart failure, "normal" ranges for BNP during periods of clinical stability may be as high as 500 pg/mL. Factors other than heart failure that affect BNP levels include kidney failure, older age, and female sex, all of which increase BNP level. The BNP level is also elevated in pulmonary embolism, acute myocardial infarction, and acute tachycardia, which are conditions that increase ventricular strain. Obesity reduces BNP levels. Interpretation of BNP results should take these factors into account.

> **KEY POINT**
>
> Common factors other than ventricular wall stress that influence B-type natriuretic peptide levels include kidney failure, older age, and female sex, all of which increase B-type natriuretic peptide levels. Obesity reduces B-type natriuretic peptide levels.

Bibliography
Goldberg LR. Heart failure. Ann Intern Med. 2010;152(:ITC6-1-15; quiz ITC6-16. [PMID: 20513825]

Item 36   Answer: B
Educational Objective: *Evaluate for ischemia in a patient with new-onset heart failure and a high pretest probability of coronary artery disease.*

Coronary angiography is indicated to evaluate coronary artery disease (CAD) as a cause of newly diagnosed left ventricular systolic dysfunction. The patient has diabetes mellitus, which is a risk factor for CAD, and evidence of a previous inferior wall myocardial infarction on electrocardiogram (Q waves in leads II, III, and aVF). Indications for coronary angiography for evaluation of new-onset heart failure include angina or new-onset left ventricular dysfunction in the setting of a condition, such as diabetes, that may predispose to silent ischemia. Because revascularization may improve left ventricular function, some experts recommend a low threshold for evaluation for CAD.

Noninvasive stress testing, such as with an adenosine thallium test or a dobutamine echocardiographic stress test, would likely suggest CAD in this patient. However, given the relatively high pretest probability, a noninvasive stress test would not change that probability. The more relevant issue is whether the coronary anatomy is amenable to revascularization, which could improve function. Therefore, coronary angiography is the most appropriate diagnostic test.

Cardiac magnetic resonance imaging is useful for evaluating possible infiltrative or inflammatory cardiomyopathy. Given the significant evidence of CAD in this patient, the likelihood of an infiltrative or inflammatory cardiomyopathy is very low, and cardiac magnetic resonance imaging would not be an appropriate first diagnostic test.

Although this patient has some limiting symptoms (dyspnea on exertion) and a history of smoking, he has clinical evidence of heart failure. Pulmonary function testing would not aid in assessing the cause of new-onset heart failure nor would it be useful in diagnosing potential CAD.

> **KEY POINT**
>
> Coronary angiography is indicated in the evaluation of new-onset heart failure in patients with angina or new-onset left ventricular dysfunction in the setting of a condition that may predispose to silent ischemia.

Bibliography
McMurray JJ. Clinical practice. Systolic heart failure. N Engl J Med. 2010;362:228-38. [PMID: 20089973]

Item 37   Answer: C
Educational Objective: *Treat systolic heart failure with β-blocker therapy.*

Treatment should be started with a β-blocker, such as metoprolol succinate (long-acting form of metoprolol) or carvedilol. Patients with systolic heart failure should be treated with a β-blocker, regardless of symptom status, including heart failure that is asymptomatic or mildly symptomatic. However, β-blocker therapy generally should not be initiated in patients with decompensation, such as volume overload or a low-output state. Even patients with severe heart failure benefit from and tolerate β-blocker therapy. Even patients with significant pulmonary disease tolerate β-blocker therapy well, in particular, the more β$_1$-selective agents, such as metoprolol or bisoprolol. Initiation of β-blocker therapy is usually tolerated when patients are clinically stable, before hospital discharge.

This patient likely has functional mitral regurgitation secondary to tethering of the mitral valve leaflets as a result of ventricular dilation in the setting of cardiomyopathy. No definitive evidence suggests that surgically correcting functional mitral regurgitation in the setting of nonischemic cardiomyopathy improves survival rates.

Aldosterone antagonists block the deleterious effects of aldosterone on the heart and have been shown to improve survival, decrease symptoms, and improve functional level in patients with advanced heart failure (class III-IV symptoms and left ventricular ejection fraction of ≤35%). Spironolactone is usually the first-line therapy based on clinical experience and cost considerations, although eplerenone may be useful in those who have gynecomastia as a result of treatment with spironolactone. This patient has tolerated spironolactone without difficulty; therefore, no change in aldosterone antagonist therapy is indicated.

Biventricular pacing, together with an implantable cardioverter-defibrillator (cardiac resynchronization therapy), is indicated for patients with severe symptomatic heart failure (New York Heart Association [NYHA] class III-IV), ejection fraction of less than 35%, and ventricular dyssynchrony, as evidenced by a prolonged QRS complex on electrocardiogram (>120 msec) while taking optimal medical therapy. This patient does not have a prolonged QRS complex and therefore would not benefit from upgrading to a biventricular device.

KEY POINT

Patients with left ventricular dysfunction should be treated with a β-blocker, regardless of symptom status.

Bibliography

McMurry JJ. Clinical practice. Systolic heart failure. N Engl J Med. 2010;362:228-38. [PMID: 20089973]

Item 38   Answer: B

Educational Objective: *Treat heart failure with preserved ejection fraction.*

The most appropriate treatment for the patient is an angiotensin receptor blocker, such as candesartan. She has heart failure with preserved ejection fraction (HFPEF, or diastolic heart failure), as evidenced by signs and symptoms of heart failure (dyspnea, edema, examination findings consistent with volume overload) in the setting of a normal ejection fraction, as measured by echocardiography.

There is not a large body of evidence to guide the treatment of HFPEF. Therefore, treatment is primarily focused on managing the manifestations of heart failure (volume overload) and targeting risk factors for left ventricular hypertrophy (primarily hypertension), which is strongly associated with HFPEF. This patient's hypertension is not well controlled. In addition to reducing congestion by increasing the dose of diuretics, an antihypertensive agent should be added.

The angiotensin receptor blocker candesartan is an agent that has been studied in a large randomized controlled trial of HFPEF treatment and was associated with a reduction in hospitalizations. Other appropriate agents for use in HFPEF include angiotensin-converting enzyme inhibitors, nondihydropyridine calcium channel blockers (verapamil, diltiazem), and β-blockers.

Patients with HFPEF tend to have a small, stiff left ventricle that may be susceptible to excessive preload reduction that can lead to ventricular underfilling and decreased cardiac output. Therefore, medications that act primarily by decreasing preload are usually avoided, such as nitrates and dihydropyridine calcium channel blockers. Therefore, the preferred therapy would not include the calcium channel blocker amlodipine or the long-acting nitrate isosorbide mononitrate.

Although digoxin may be used in patients with severe systolic heart failure, there is no established role for digoxin in the treatment of HFPEF. This agent is generally avoided because of its positive inotropic effect.

KEY POINT

Treatment of heart failure with preserved ejection fraction is focused on managing the manifestations of heart failure and targeting risk factors for left ventricular hypertrophy, which is strongly associated with heart failure with preserved ejection fraction.

Bibliography

Paulus WJ, van Ballegoij JJ. Treatment of heart failure with normal ejection fraction: an inconvenient truth! J Am Coll Cardiol. 2010;55:526-37. [PMID: 20152557]

Item 39   Answer: D

Educational Objective: *Prescribe optimal medical therapy for severe systolic heart failure.*

The patient has systolic heart failure as a result of peripartum cardiomyopathy. Treatment with enalapril should be started. The patient appears euvolemic and reports symptoms of New York Heart Association (NYHA) functional class III heart failure. Medical therapy for heart failure during pregnancy should include standard therapy for heart failure with a β-blocker and diuretic. However, angiotensin-converting enzyme (ACE) inhibitors and angiotensin receptor blockers should be excluded until after delivery. Treatment with an ACE inhibitor, such as enalapril, should therefore be initiated. Because the patient has severe symptoms (NYHA class III), treatment with an aldosterone antagonist (spironolactone) is also indicated.

Cardiac resynchronization therapy is indicated in patients with heart failure (ejection fraction <35%) with persistent moderate to severe symptoms despite optimal medical therapy and a QRS interval of greater than 120 msec. However, the patient's medical therapy is not optimal because she is not taking an ACE inhibitor and her QRS interval is not prolonged.

Endomyocardial biopsy is generally indicated to assist in the diagnosis of suspected infiltrative or inflammatory cardiomyopathy in which a definitive diagnosis would affect treatment or prognosis, such as with amyloidosis, hemochromatosis, or sarcoidosis. The patient does not have significant evidence to suggest inflammatory cardiomyopathy, such as increased ventricular wall thickness; infiltrative cardiomyopathy, such as low voltage on electrocardiogram; or systemic manifestations of illness, such as fever.

Although, in general, it is desirable to titrate the β-blocker to target doses, increasing the dose of carvedilol in this patient would likely be limited by her relatively slow heart rate and significant fatigue.

KEY POINT

Optimal medical therapy for severe systolic heart failure includes an ACE inhibitor, a β-blocker, and spironolactone.

Bibliography

Goldberg LR. Heart failure. Ann Intern Med. 2010;152:ITC6-1-15. [PMID: 20513825]

Item 40   Answer: A

Educational Objective: *Treat resistant hypertension in a patient with systolic heart failure.*

A patient with resistant hypertension (blood pressure that is not at the target value with three-drug therapy with different classes of drugs, including a diuretic) and systolic heart failure should begin taking a newer-generation dihydropyridine calcium channel blocker, such as amlodipine, to improve control of blood pressure.

Although specific combinations of drugs have not been well studied in patients with resistant hypertension, many experts recommend adding a newer-generation dihydropine calcium channel blocker to an angiotensin-converting enzyme (ACE) inhibitor and a diuretic when blood pressure is not at the target value. Large-scale clinical trials have shown amlodipine and felodipine to have little or no negative inotropic effect and a neutral effect on morbidity and mortality rates. However, because they do not decrease morbidity or mortality rates, calcium channel blockers are not first-line treatment for systolic heart failure. Use of calcium channel blockers in systolic heart failure is generally reserved for treatment of conditions such as hypertension or angina that are not optimally managed with maximal doses of evidence-based medications such as ACE inhibitors and β-blockers.

Many calcium channel blockers are relatively contraindicated in patients with systolic heart failure because of an associated increased risk of exacerbation of heart failure. Older-generation calcium channel blockers, such as diltiazem, nifedipine, and verapamil, may precipitate exacerbation of heart failure because of their negative inotropic effects. Although this patient's symptoms are currently controlled (New York Heart Association class I), he would still be at risk for exacerbation of heart failure with one of these agents.

KEY POINT

The calcium channel blocker amlodipine is a reasonable option for additional blood pressure control in a patient with heart failure who is already receiving optimal multidrug therapy.

Bibliography

Tsuyuki RT, McKelvie RS, Arnold JM, et al. Acute precipitants of congestive heart failure exacerbations. Arch Intern Med. 2001;161:2337-42. [PMID: 11606149]

Item 41   Answer: D
Educational Objective: *Diagnose tricuspid insufficiency.*

The most likely diagnosis in this patient is tricuspid regurgitation. Tricuspid regurgitation is characterized by a systolic murmur at the lower left sternal border that may increase in intensity with inspiration. The murmur does not radiate well, although it can sometimes be heard at the upper left sternal border. A finding characteristic of right-sided murmurs is augmentation in intensity with inspiration. Tricuspid regurgitation most often is caused by left-sided heart disease that causes pulmonary hypertension, which leads to right ventricular enlargement and annular dilation. Primary pulmonary hypertension and elevated pulmonary pressure as a result of chronic lung disease also cause tricuspid regurgitation, with the term cor pulmonale describing right-sided heart failure as a result of pulmonary hypertension in the absence of left-sided heart disease. Other causes of tricuspid regurgitation include endocarditis, injury after pacer lead placement, carcinoid disease, mediastinal irradiation, and trauma. Carcinoid disease causes direct toxicity to the tricuspid valve, seen as leaflet thickening and retraction. In mild or moderate tricuspid regurgitation, most patients are asymptomatic. Severe tricuspid regurgitation may be associated with signs of advanced right-sided heart failure, including jugular venous distention, ascites, hepatomegaly (sometimes pulsatile), and lower extremity edema. Electrocardiography may show enlargement of the right atrium or the right ventricle.

Auscultatory features of aortic stenosis include a mid- to late-peaking systolic murmur that radiates to the carotid arteries, an S_4, a single S_2 as a result of loss of the aortic closure component, and delayed timing and decreased amplitude in the carotid pulses (pulsus parvus et tardus). Physical examination findings of chronic mitral regurgitation in patients with hyperdynamic systolic function include a prominent apical impulse with normal pulse pressure. The murmur is usually holosystolic, is heard best at the apex, and radiates laterally or posteriorly. The murmur of pulmonic regurgitation is diastolic murmur.

KEY POINT

Tricuspid regurgitation is most commonly the result of left-sided heart disease and is characterized by a systolic murmur at the lower left sternal border. The murmur may increase in intensity with inspiration.

Bibliography

Taramasso M, Vanermen H, Maisano F, Guidotti A, La Canna G, Alfieri O. The growing clinical importance of secondary tricuspid regurgitation. J Am Coll Cardiol. 2012; 59:703-10. [PMID: 22340261]

Item 42   Answer: A
Educational Objective: *Diagnose prosthetic aortic valve dysfunction.*

Development of a new diastolic murmur of aortic regurgitation is most closely associated with prosthetic value dysfunction. The murmur of aortic regurgitation is a soft, blowing diastolic murmur that is often heard best at the third left or second right intercostal space. It does not radiate well and may be confined to a very limited area of the chest wall. The murmur can be heard best with the patient leaning forward in end-expiration. A sharp valve click is often heard on auscultation of normal prosthetic valves. Dampening of a previously sharp valve click can suggest a thrombus or vegetation on the valve. Most individuals with prosthetic aortic valves have a systolic heart murmur because of turbulence across the prosthesis. This murmur is physiologic and does not indicate valvular dysfunction. Expiratory splitting of S_2 may be heard in patients with left bundle branch block or severe left ventricular hypertrophy as a result of delayed emptying of the left ventricle.

KEY POINT

Development of a new diastolic murmur of aortic regurgitation is most closely associated with prosthetic valve dysfunction.

Bibliography

Maganti K, Rigolin VH, Sarano ME, Bonow RO. Valvular heart disease: diagnosis and management. Mayo Clin Proc. 2010;85:483-500. [PMID: 20435842]

Item 43   Answer: D
Educational Objective: *Evaluate a low-intensity heart murmur.*

No additional testing is needed for this patient. He has an asymptomatic benign systolic ejection murmur. The benign characteristics of the murmur include its intensity or grade (<3/6), timing (early and brief systolic), lack of radiation, and absence of additional abnormal heart sounds. The remainder of the findings on physical examination and electrocardiogram are normal, without evidence of cardiac enlargement or dysfunction. In this common situation, the patient should be reassured. No additional diagnostic testing is indicated.

Ambulatory electrocardiography, obtained either continuously for 24 to 48 hours or as event-activated recordings, is not indicated. The patient's brief episodes of palpitations are sporadic and are not associated with hemodynamic abnormalities. In patients with repetitive, frequent palpitations, ambulatory electrocardiography may be diagnostically useful.

Transesophageal echocardiography may be useful in patients in whom a transthoracic study does not provide adequate diagnostic information or to evaluate the feasibility of surgical repair when surgery is planned. However, this testing is not indicated in this patient.

Transthoracic echocardiography is recommended for diagnosis of systolic murmurs that are grade 3/6 or greater in intensity, diastolic murmurs, continuous murmurs, holosystolic murmurs, late systolic murmurs, murmurs associated with ejection clicks, or murmurs that radiate to the neck or back. This patient's murmur does not have any of these characteristics.

KEY POINT

Echocardiography is not indicated for patients with brief, early systolic, low-intensity murmurs detected by physical examination without symptoms or associated findings of valvular or cardiac dysfunction.

Bibliography

Etchells E, Bell C, Robb K. Does this patient have an abnormal systolic murmur? JAMA. 1997;277:564-71. [PMID: 9032164]

Item 44   Answer: C

Educational Objective: *Treat aortic stenosis with left ventricular systolic dysfunction.*

Aortic valve replacement surgery is the appropriate treatment for the patient. He has decompensated heart failure caused by severe aortic stenosis. The aortic valve is calcified with a significantly decreased valve area. Despite severe left ventricular systolic dysfunction (as seen by the ejection fraction of 30%), the increased transvalvular pressure gradient suggests that his cardiac output is preserved and that the stenotic valve is the cause of the patient's heart failure. In patients with severe valve dysfunction with symptoms or abnormal ventricular function, surgical valve repair or replacement is the only definitive intervention.

Balloon aortic valvuloplasty is indicated only for patients with severe aortic stenosis with hemodynamic compromise or deterioration as a bridge to eventual aortic valve replacement. Although this patient has symptoms of heart failure, he is hemodynamically stable and has improved quickly with diuretic therapy. Balloon aortic valvuloplasty for calcific aortic stenosis results in only a small improvement in aortic valve area. It is associated with a high risk of stroke and has a high rate of restenosis 6 months after the procedure.

Patients with severe aortic stenosis complicated by decompensated heart failure and low cardiac output may benefit from intravenous nitroprusside. However, this patient does not have hemodynamic instability, and his response to intravenous diuretic therapy has not been assessed. Therefore, the use of nitroprusside is not indicated.

Transcatheter aortic valve implantation (TAVI) is a novel therapy for aortic valve replacement in patients with a very high predicted risk of operative mortality. Early studies of TAVI in patients with very high operative risk (approaching 50%) have shown improved survival compared with medical therapy, including balloon aortic valvuloplasty. However, this patient has an acceptable operative risk for aortic valve replacement and does not require TAVI.

KEY POINT

In patients with severe valve dysfunction with symptoms or abnormal ventricular function, surgical valve repair or replacement is the only definitive intervention.

Bibliography

Bonow RO, Carabello BA, Chatterjee K, et al. American College of Cardiology/American Heart Association Task Force on Practice Guidelines. 2008 Focused Update incorporated into the ACC/AHA 2006 Guidelines for the Management of Patients with Valvular Heart Disease: a Report of the American College of Cardiology/American Heart Association Task Force on Practice Guidelines (Writing Committee to revise the 1998 Guidelines for the Management of Patients with Valvular Heart Disease). Endorsed by the Society of Cardiovascular Anesthesiologists, Society for Cardiovascular Angiography and Interventions, and Society of Thoracic Surgeons. J Am Coll Cardiol. 2008;52:e1-142. [PMID: 18848134]

Item 45   Answer: A

Educational Objective: *Diagnose radiation-induced aortic valve regurgitation.*

The most likely cause of this patient's chest pain and worsening dyspnea is aortic valve regurgitation. On physical examination, the patient has a diastolic murmur, which is a key to diagnosis. Additionally, the carotid arteries have a rapid, accentuated upstroke, with a rapid decline (frequently referred to as a Corrigan pulse); the point of maximal impulse is displaced (suggesting left ventricular volume overload); and the pulse pressure is widened (systolic pressure minus diastolic pressure; normal is ≤40 mm Hg). These findings highly support a diagnosis of aortic regurgitation.

Aortic valve disease as a result of previous radiation therapy is the most likely cause of aortic regurgitation in this patient. The risk of cardiotoxicity, including valvular fibrosis and regurgitation, increases with higher total radiation dose. However, there is no single dose of radiation below which cardiotoxicity will not occur. The clinical onset of radiation-induced valvular regurgitation is variable and may occur 10 to 25 years or more after initial radiation therapy to the thorax. Clinically significant aortic valve regurgitation may occur in 25% or more of patients with previous radiation to the thorax. In this patient, dyspnea can be explained on the basis of elevation in left ventricular diastolic pressure as a result of hemodynamically significant aortic regurgitation. Chest pain occurs as a result of low coronary filling pressures and subsequent myocardial ischemia caused by low diastolic aortic pressure induced by aortic regurgitation.

Constrictive pericarditis should be considered in a patient with previous radiation of the thorax who presents with dyspnea on exertion. The right ventricle is more extensively involved, typically leading to right ventricular failure (jugular venous distention, hepatojugular reflux, peripheral edema). Physical examination in this patient showed no right ventricular involvement, making constrictive pericarditis unlikely.

Restrictive cardiomyopathy may occur as a result of previous radiation therapy but is unlikely in this patient. Findings on physical examination do not indicate right-sided pressure overload (jugular venous distention, hepatojugular reflux), which would be expected in a patient with symptomatic restrictive cardiomyopathy.

Tricuspid regurgitation also may occur as a result of previous radiation therapy to the thorax. However, findings on physical examination do not show evidence of hemodynamically significant tricuspid regurgitation, such as jugular venous distention, large retrograde v waves, or hepatojugular reflux. In severe tricuspid regurgitation, a systolic murmur is usually present but may be absent. When absent, however, a large jugular vein v wave would be expected.

KEY POINT

Clinically significant aortic valve regurgitation is common in patients with previous radiation to the thorax. It may occur 10 to 25 years or more after initial radiation therapy.

Bibliography

Walker CM, Saldaña DA, Gladish GW, et al. Cardiac complications of oncologic therapy. Radiographics. 2013;33:1801-15. [PMID: 24108563]

Item 46   Answer: A

Educational Objective: *Manage a patient with an asymptomatic bicuspid aortic valve.*

Clinical follow-up in 1 year is appropriate management for this patient. A bicuspid aortic valve is the most common congenital heart valve abnormality. It affects 1% of the population, with a male predominance. Because a bicuspid valve is subject to higher mechanical and shear stress than other valves, the disease process of progressive calcification is accelerated and clinical presentation tends to be earlier, in the fourth or fifth decade of life. A bicuspid aortic valve may have significant aortic regurgitation or stenosis and is at risk for infective endocarditis. A bicuspid aortic valve may also be associated with an underlying disorder of vascular connective tissue, with a loss of elastic tissue that leads to progressive dilation of the ascending aorta. Approximately 50% of patients have aortic root or ascending aortic dilation. This patient has a bicuspid aortic valve with moderate aortic regurgitation but normal left ventricular size and systolic function. Pulmonary pressures are in the normal range, and there is no evidence of adverse hemodynamic effects of valve regurgitation on the ventricle. Therefore, the patient needs no additional diagnostic studies or specific treatment at this time. However, because worsening of aortic regurgitation can be insidious, routine clinical follow-up is indicated at least yearly, typically with repeat transthoracic echocardiography to monitor for disease progression.

Aortic valve replacement surgery is recommended in patients with severe aortic regurgitation and cardiopulmonary symptoms. In asymptomatic patients with severe regurgitation, surgery is recommended when there are signs of adverse hemodynamic effects on the left ventricle, when there is left ventricular enlargement, or when the ejection fraction is less than 55%. This patient has moderate aortic regurgitation. He is asymptomatic and has normal left ventricular size and function. Valve replacement surgery is not indicated at this time. Patients with aortic root dilation should also be evaluated for surgery. If moderate dilation (diameter 4.0-4.9 cm) is noted, serial imaging is recommended to monitor for progressive dilation and dysfunction. Surgery is recommended when the aortic root or proximal ascending aorta exceeds 5 cm in diameter.

Transthoracic echocardiography is generally adequate for visualization of the proximal aortic root and routine evaluation and follow-up of a bicuspid aortic valve. However, transesophageal echocardiography or cardiac magnetic resonance imaging or computed tomography may be useful if inadequate visualization with transthoracic imaging is not possible.

KEY POINT

In patients with an asymptomatic congenital bicuspid aortic valve, monitoring for the development of significant aortic regurgitation and aortic root dilation is indicated.

Bibliography

Siu SC, Silversides CK. Bicuspid aortic valve disease. J Am Coll Cardiol. 2010;55:2789-2800. [PMID: 20579534]

Item 47   Answer: C

Educational Objective: *Diagnose mitral stenosis.*

This patient most likely has mitral stenosis as the cause of her progressive shortness of breath. Mitral stenosis should be suspected because of the opening snap followed by a diastolic murmur that is accentuated with atrial contraction. S_1 is usually loud; S_2 may be variable in intensity. The parasternal lift supports the presence of right ventricular hypertrophy. Electrocardiogram in patients with mitral stenosis typically shows features of left atrial enlargement and hypertrophy and right axis deviation.

Aortic regurgitation causes a diastolic murmur that is best heard at the second right and third left interspaces; there is no opening snap or associated left atrial enlargement or right ventricular hypertrophy. Aortic regurgitation is also associated with a widened pulse pressure (systolic pressure minus diastolic pressure; normal is ≤40 mm Hg). These findings are not present in this patient.

A significant atrial septal defect produces a systolic murmur without an opening snap. Because of left-to-right blood flow, fixed splitting of the S_2 and right-sided volume overload may result in right-sided chamber enlargement with a parasternal impulse. This patient's diastolic murmur and other findings are not consistent with this diagnosis.

Patent ductus arteriosus causes a continuous murmur in the left parasternal location. In moderate to severe cases, blood flow from the aorta to the pulmonary artery may lead to increased pulmonary blood flow and left ventricular volume overload, with associated findings. Similar to aortic regurgitation, the carotid pulses are brisk as a result of increased stroke volume. Pulse pressure may be increased as a result of diastolic runoff into the pulmonary artery.

KEY POINT

On physical examination, mitral stenosis is characterized by an opening snap followed by a diastolic murmur that is accentuated with atrial contraction. S_1 is usually loud, and S_2 may be variable in intensity.

Bibliography

Chandrashekhar Y, Westaby S, Narula J. Mitral stenosis. Lancet. 2009;374:1271-83. [PMID: 19747723]

Item 48   Answer: C

Educational Objective: *Diagnose mitral regurgitation.*

This patient has findings consistent with chronic mitral regurgitation with associated hemodynamic and structural effects, ultimately leading to symptomatic heart failure. The location of the murmur is characteristic of mitral valve regurgitation (holosystolic, loudest at the apex, and radiating to the axilla). The prominent pulmonic component of the S_2 suggests pulmonary hypertension secondary to chronic mitral valve regurgitation. The patient has evidence of left-sided heart failure, including left atrial and ventricular enlargement on electrocardiogram, crackles on lung examination, and pulmonary congestion on chest radiograph. The signs of right-sided heart failure (peripheral edema, jugular venous distention) result from elevation of the left-sided filling pressures.

Chronic aortic valve stenosis can also cause left-sided heart failure, but the murmur of aortic stenosis is diamond-shaped, is loudest at the right sternal border, and radiates to the carotid arteries.

Mitral valve stenosis is characterized by an opening snap after the S_2, followed by a low-frequency decrescendo murmur (diastolic "rumble"). Significant mitral valve stenosis causes elevated left atrial pressure, secondary pulmonary hypertension, and ultimately, right-sided heart failure. Because the left ventricle is protected from pressure or volume overload, mitral stenosis does not lead to left ventricular hypertrophy.

The murmur of aortic valve regurgitation is an early blowing diastolic murmur that is loudest at the left sternal border. Chronic aortic valve regurgitation may lead to left ventricular enlargement and left-sided heart failure.

The murmur of tricuspid valve regurgitation is systolic, is loudest at the lower left sternal border, and becomes louder with inspiration. Significant tricuspid valve regurgitation leads to right-sided heart failure but does not cause signs and symptoms of left-sided heart failure.

KEY POINT

Physical examination findings associated with mitral valve regurgitation include a holosystolic murmur at the apex that radiates to the axilla without respiratory variation.

Bibliography

Maganti K, Rigolin VH, Sarano ME, et al. Valvular heart disease. Mayo Clinic Proc. 2010;85:483-500. [PMID:20435842]

Item 49 **Answer: D**

Educational Objective: *Diagnose mitral valve prolapse.*

The patient's heart murmur is most likely caused by mitral valve prolapse. The auscultatory features of mitral valve prolapse include a "click-murmur" complex. This complex includes a midsystolic click, believed to be caused by sudden tensing of the mitral subvalvular apparatus as the leaflets prolapse into the left atrium, followed by a late systolic murmur. Performing the Valsalva maneuver and standing from a squatting position decrease end-diastolic volume and move the click-murmur complex closer to the S_1.

Mitral valve prolapse occurs in approximately 2% of the general population and is the most common cause of mitral regurgitation. In the absence of significant mitral regurgitation, primary mitral valve prolapse is usually asymptomatic but can present with palpitations or atypical chest discomfort. Palpitations are common and are usually associated with benign premature atrial or ventricular contractions. Sustained arrhythmias are exceedingly rare.

Hypertrophic cardiomyopathy is associated with a harsh crescendo-decrescendo systolic murmur that begins slightly after S_1 and is heard best at the apex and lower left sternal border. Performing the Valsalva maneuver and standing from a squatting position increase the intensity of the murmur. The murmur of hypertrophic cardiomyopathy is the only murmur that increases in intensity with the Valsalva maneuver.

Benign (innocent) flow murmurs are typically midsystolic grade 1 to 2/6 murmurs associated with normal heart sounds and no other findings. The presence of a click, an S_4, abnormal splitting of S_2, or increased intensity or duration of the murmur on performing the Valsalva maneuver or standing from a squatting position is not compatible with a benign (innocent) flow murmur.

The murmur of mitral valve regurgitation begins shortly after S_1 and ends just before S_2 (holosystolic murmur). It is not associated with clicks, and the intensity is not increased with standing from a squatting position or performing the Valsalva maneuver.

KEY POINT

The auscultatory feature of mitral valve prolapse is a midsystolic click followed by a late systolic murmur. Performing the Valsalva maneuver and standing from a squatting position move the click-murmur complex closer to S_1.

Bibliography

Guy TS, Hill AC. Mitral valve prolapse. Annu Rev Med. 2012;63:277-92. [PMID: 22248324]

Item 50 **Answer: C**

Educational Objective: *Diagnose hypertrophic cardiomyopathy.*

The most likely diagnosis is hypertrophic cardiomyopathy. The findings on cardiac examination are consistent with dynamic left ventricular outflow tract obstruction, with a systolic murmur that is accentuated during maneuvers that decrease preload (Valsalva maneuver) but is attenuated by increasing afterload (handgrip maneuver). Echocardiographic findings confirm asymmetric septal hypertrophy that is consistent with hypertrophic cardiomyopathy.

The echocardiographic features in hypertrophic cardiomyopathy are diverse but include left ventricular hypertrophy. The hypertrophy may be concentric (particularly if marked), but may also disproportionately involve the septal, anterior, lateral, or apical walls. Dynamic left ventricular outflow tract or midcavity obstruction is a feature of hypertrophic cardiomyopathy. However, it is not always seen nor is it a necessary finding to confirm the diagnosis. Additional echocardiographic features include a small left ventricular cavity and significant left atrial enlargement. Although patients with hypertrophic cardiomyopathy may present with symptoms such as dyspnea, chest pain, or dizziness, many are asymptomatic. However, because of the increased risk of associated mortality and the genetic basis of the disease, diagnosis is critical, even in asymptomatic patients.

Athlete's heart is concentric left ventricular hypertrophy that typically occurs in endurance athletes and sometimes in weightlifters. Concentric left ventricular hypertrophy may also be caused by long-standing hypertension, which is not present in this patient. Echocardiography is useful in differentiating hypertrophic cardiomyopathy from these other conditions. Compared with hypertrophic cardiomyopathy, athlete's heart is more likely to show less marked hypertrophy, hypertrophy that is concentric without significant asymmetry, an enlarged left ventricular cavity, a lack of marked left atrial enlargement, and normal diastolic function. Cardiovascular magnetic resonance imaging is helpful for diagnosis if hypertrophic cardiomyopathy cannot be confirmed or differentiated from other causes.

Dilated cardiomyopathy is easily excluded on the basis of echocardiography, which does not show an enlarged left ventricle with systolic dysfunction (ejection fraction <40%), as would be expected with this diagnosis.

Restrictive cardiomyopathy could explain the finding of left ventricular hypertrophy. However, an accentuated rate of early diastolic filling (restrictive filling) is characteristic of this entity, and not impaired early filling, as is present in this patient. Lack of this pattern of filling virtually excludes restrictive cardiomyopathy.

KEY POINT

Hypertrophic cardiomyopathy is characterized by dynamic left ventricular outflow tract obstruction evidenced by a systolic murmur that is accentuated during maneuvers that decrease preload (Valsalva maneuver) but attenuated by increasing afterload (handgrip maneuver).

Bibliography

Watkins H, Ashrafian H, Redwood C. Inherited cardiomyopathies. N Engl J Med. 2011;364:1643-56. [PMID: 21524215]

Item 51   Answer: A

Educational Objective: *Localize peripheral arterial disease.*

This patient most likely has aortoiliac disease. Symptoms often give important clues as to the likely site of peripheral arterial disease. The patient has buttock and hip claudication, diminished femoral pulses, and erectile dysfunction, sometimes referred to as Leriche syndrome. This presentation most commonly represents atherosclerotic disease within the aortoiliac system.

Claudication as a result of aortoiliac disease often results in greater disability compared with more distal disease. Additionally, aortoiliac disease increases the risk of distal embolization. Accordingly, a more aggressive approach to aortoiliac disease is typically taken that may include either endovascular intervention or aortoiliac surgery.

Common femoral arterial occlusive disease may cause thigh pain with effort, but it would not result in erectile dysfunction. Because of the location of the common femoral artery with respect to the hip joint, surgical therapy or angioplasty, but not stenting, would be considered as part of therapy.

Occlusive disease within the popliteal artery would produce pain within the lower calf. Disease in this location should be managed primarily with an exercise program and medical therapy. Patients who do not benefit from such conservative management should be considered for femoral-popliteal bypass.

Occlusive disease within the superficial femoral artery usually produces effort-related discomfort in the upper calf. Angioplasty may be appropriate for patients who have symptoms related to the superficial femoral artery and have not benefited from medical therapy or who are extremely limited in activity due to ischemia despite medical therapy.

KEY POINT

The combination of buttock and hip claudication, diminished femoral pulses, and erectile dysfunction (Leriche syndrome) suggests atherosclerotic disease within the aortoiliac system.

Bibliography

Mascarenhas JV, Albayati MA, Shearman CP, et al. Peripheral arterial disease. Endocrinol Metab Clin North Am. 2014;43:149-66. [PMID: 24582096]

Item 52   Answer: B

Educational Objective: *Treat type A acute aortic dissection.*

The computed tomographic scan with intravenous contrast shows a dissection plane (*arrows*) extending from the proximal aorta through the arch (AA) and into the descending aorta (DAo). This is a Stanford type A dissection (involving the ascending aorta), which requires emergency surgical intervention.

The patient has a long-standing history of a murmur associated with a documented bicuspid aortic valve. The most frequent cardiovascular finding associated with a bicuspid valve is dilation of the proximal ascending aorta, which is related to abnormalities of the aortic media. These changes in the aortic media are independent of the degree of functional stenosis of the valve and increase the risk of aneurysm formation and aortic dissection.

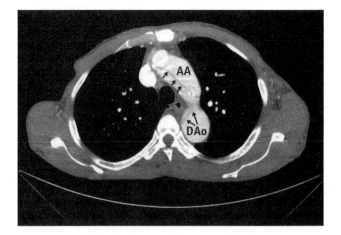

Abrupt onset of severe chest and back pain is typical of an acute aortic syndrome. A diastolic murmur consistent with aortic valvular insufficiency increases the clinical suspicion for a proximal aortic dissection that has disrupted normal valve function. Although marked asymmetry in upper extremity pulses and pressures are classic findings in aortic dissection, in many cases, these features may not be present. Syncope occurs in approximately 10% of patients with an acute aortic dissection and is more commonly associated with proximal dissection. Syncope is associated with a higher coincidence of pericardial tamponade and worse in-hospital survival rates.

Further diagnostic imaging with coronary angiography, magnetic resonance imaging, or transesophageal echocardiography is not necessary and would only delay necessary surgical repair.

There is no accepted role for endovascular treatment of an acute Stanford type A aortic dissection.

KEY POINT

A dissection originating within the ascending aorta or aortic arch (Stanford type A) is a surgical emergency.

Bibliography

Siu SC, Silversides CK. Bicuspid aortic valve disease. J Am Coll Cardiol. 2010;55:2789-00. [PMID: 20579534]

Item 53   Answer: D

Educational Objective: *Manage acute abdominal aortic aneurysm.*

The patient's clinical presentation of severe abdominal or back pain with syncope, followed by vague discomfort, is typical for a ruptured abdominal aortic aneurysm (AAA) that has been locally contained, preventing immediate death. The sentinel event of sudden, severe back pain associated with loss of consciousness marks the occurrence of rupture. Symptoms after that time are likely caused by either local irritation and inflammation related to the rupture and hemorrhage or expansion of the aneurysm against adjacent structures. Leukocytosis and anemia are common. CT scan should be performed for diagnosis, and the aneurysm should be repaired emergently.

This patient has several risk factors for AAA, including the major risk of cigarette smoking. The incidence of AAA is higher in men than in women and in whites versus blacks, and it increases with age. Hypertension and hyperlipidemia probably contribute to the risk of AAA development to a lesser degree.

Contained rupture of AAA, when misdiagnosed, is most often mistaken for renal colic, acute myocardial infarction, or diverticulitis. Renal colic may produce severe pain in the lower back, flank, or groin. Typically, the pain waxes and wanes. It is unlikely that renal colic would present with syncope, and the normal finding on urinalysis also makes this diagnosis unlikely.

Acute myocardial infarction can be associated with syncope, and electrocardiogram is not always diagnostic, particularly if there are findings such as left ventricular hypertrophy, which may obscure subtle abnormalities. However, the presence of abdominal and lower back pain rather than chest pain makes this diagnosis less likely.

Diverticulitis presents with crampy abdominal pain, most commonly in the left lower quadrant, often associated with a change in bowel habits. Leukocytosis may be present. Syncope associated with the onset of pain would be a very unusual presentation for this entity.

KEY POINT

Abdominal pain, back pain, and syncope often herald rupture of an abdominal aortic aneurysm.

Bibliography
Takayama T, Yamanouchi D. Aneurysmal disease: the abdominal aorta. Surg Clin North Am. 2013;93:877-91. [PMID: 23885935]

Item 54   Answer: A

Educational Objective: *Manage symptomatic internal carotid artery disease.*

This patient should be referred for immediate endarterectomy of the right internal carotid artery. He has had an acute ischemic stroke caused by symptomatic high-grade carotid stenosis. The risk of recurrent stroke is approximately 26% over the next 2 years. Carotid endarterectomy is highly effective in reducing the risk of recurrent stroke (number needed to treat = 17) in the immediate poststroke period. With symptomatic carotid stenosis, the risk of recurrent stroke is 1% per day for the first 2 weeks after a stroke or transient ischemic attack; therefore, the greatest benefit is gained when the procedure is performed early.

Carotid stenting would be inappropriate for this patient. Clinical trials have shown that for the primary outcomes of stroke, myocardial infarction, and death, stenting and endarterectomy are not significantly different. However, stenting poses a greater risk of perioperative stroke than endarterectomy. Therefore, it is not recommended as a primary intervention for symptomatic carotid artery stenosis.

Clopidogrel has a role in medical therapy for patients who are not able to take aspirin. However, antiplatelet agents generally provide only a marginal benefit compared with surgery in reducing the risk of stroke in the acute poststroke period in patients with symptomatic high-grade carotid stenosis.

Acute anticoagulation in the context of acute stroke has been associated with increased mortality rates and poorer neurologic outcomes. Similarly, long-term anticoagulation with warfarin or another oral anticoagulant is beneficial only in patients whose stroke is caused by atrial fibrillation or another source of cardiogenic embolism. Because this patient's stroke likely resulted from his high-grade carotid stenosis and he has no other indication for anticoagulation, treatment with warfarin would not be appropriate.

KEY POINT

Early carotid endarterectomy is indicated in patients with symptomatic high-grade carotid stenosis and is associated with a lower risk of perioperative stroke than stenting.

Bibliography
Brott TG, Hobson RW 2nd, Howard G, et al. Stenting versus endarterectomy for treatment of carotid-artery stenosis. N Engl J Med. 2010;363:11-23. [PMID: 20505173]

Item 55   Answer: C

Educational Objective: *Manage renovascular hypertension secondary to fibromuscular dysplasia.*

Percutaneous transluminal kidney angioplasty is indicated for this patient with renovascular hypertension secondary to fibromuscular dysplasia, a nonatherosclerotic, noninflammatory renovascular disease. Renovascular hypertension as a result of fibromuscular dysplasia is most commonly caused by medial fibroplasia of the renal artery. On angiogram, the characteristic finding of fibromuscular dysplasia is the "string of beads" appearance of the involved artery, which is apparent on this patient's angiogram. Fibromuscular dysplasia is a disease of unknown cause and usually involves the renal and carotid arteries. Hypertension caused by fibromuscular dysplasia is more common in women and usually affects patients between 15 and 30 years of age. Catheter-based kidney angiography is the most accurate method to diagnose this condition; revascularization with kidney angioplasty may be performed at the same time as diagnostic angiography. The young age of many patients with fibromuscular dysplasia, such as this 27-year-old woman, reduces the risk of complications from this procedure.

The high likelihood of both technical success and meaningful blood pressure improvement as a result of kidney angioplasty makes drug therapy in this young patient unnecessary at this time.

Surgical revascularization is not the first-line treatment for this patient, given the higher risk of morbidity. Surgery should be reserved for patients who do not respond to kidney angioplasty or who have arterial anatomy that is too complex for kidney angioplasty.

KEY POINT

Management of renovascular hypertension secondary to fibromuscular dysplasia may involve revascularization with kidney angioplasty.

Bibliography
Olin JW, Sealove BA. Diagnosis, management, and future developments of fibromuscular dysplasia. J Vasc Surg. 2011;53:826-36.e1. [PMID: 21236620]

Item 56   Answer: C

Educational Objective: *Manage anticoagulation in a patient with acute venous thromboembolism.*

The most appropriate management of this patient's transition from parenteral low-molecular-weight heparin (LMWH) to warfarin therapy requires at least 5 days of overlap with LMWH and warfarin therapy and an international normalized ratio of 2 or more for 24 hours. Randomized clinical trials show that 5 to 7 days of treatment with unfractionated heparin is as effective as 10 to 14 days of treatment when transitioning to warfarin therapy. Shorter durations of parenteral anticoagulation in the transition to vitamin K antagonists have not been tested and theoretically could confer a higher risk of recurrent thromboembolism. Warfarin acts as an anticoagulant by impairing hepatic synthesis of vitamin K-dependent coagulation factors rather than by directly inhibiting the function of already synthesized factors. Therefore, once an appropriate warfarin dose is initiated, the onset of therapeutic anticoagulation is dictated by the half-life of the coagulation factors. If a patient is receiving an adequate warfarin dose, it takes at least 5 days for vitamin K-dependent factor activity levels to decrease sufficiently for therapeutic anticoagulation (INR of 2-3) to occur. Consequently, parenteral anticoagulant therapy with LMWH should be continued along with warfarin for at least 5 days and until a therapeutic INR of 2 or more for 24 hours is achieved to avoid an increased risk of recurrent thromboembolism.

KEY POINT

In patients with acute venous thromboembolism, parenteral anticoagulation should be administered concomitantly with warfarin for at least 5 days and until an INR of 2 or more has been achieved for 24 hours.

Bibliography

Kearon C, Akl EA, Comerota AJ, et al. Antithrombotic therapy for VTE disease: Antithrombotic Therapy and Prevention of Thrombosis, 9th ed: American College of Chest Physicians Evidence-Based Clinical Practice Guidelines. Chest. 2012;141(2 Suppl):e419S-494S. [PMID: 22315268]

Item 57   Answer: C

Educational Objective: *Treat a patient with kidney insufficiency and acute venous thromboembolism in the postoperative period.*

Intravenous unfractionated heparin (UFH) adjusted to achieve a therapeutic activated partial thromboplastin time is the most appropriate treatment for this patient, who recently underwent a major surgical procedure and has chronic kidney disease. UFH is primarily cleared by the reticuloendothelial system rather than the kidneys. Therefore, it is preferable to the other choices for acute therapy for deep venous thrombosis (DVT). UFH also has a short half-life and is completely reversible with protamine.

Low-molecular-weight heparins are metabolized primarily by the kidneys, making dosing difficult in patients with a low glomerular filtration rate. The risk of underdosing may lead to inadequate therapy. Overdosing may lead to an increased risk of bleeding, and the ability to reverse anticoagulation with these agents is limited. Although anti-Xa levels may be helpful in monitoring the anticoagulant level, low-molecular-weight heparin is usually avoided in patients with advanced kidney disease.

Fondaparinux is cleared exclusively by the kidneys. Therefore, it is contraindicated in patients with poor renal function (estimated glomerular filtration rate <30 mL/min/1.73 m²). In addition, fondaparinux is not reversible with protamine. Consequently, potential bleeding is much more difficult to treat. Although the anticoagulant effects of fondaparinux can be treated with recombinant human factor VIIa, this factor concentrate has been associated with increased risk of thromboembolism, an important limitation in a patient with recent VTE.

Warfarin is metabolized by the liver and therefore does not accumulate in patients with worsening kidney function. However, its anticoagulant activity is delayed in onset by at least 5 to 7 days and is initially associated with transient hypercoagulability. Therefore, initial

anticoagulation with warfarin in patients with acute thromboembolism is always done concomitantly with a parenteral agent, such as UFH.

KEY POINT

Intravenous unfractionated heparin is the most appropriate treatment for deep venous thrombosis in patients who have undergone recent surgery and have chronic kidney disease.

Bibliography

Hirsh J, Bauer KA, Donati MB, et al. Parenteral anticoagulants: American College of Chest Physicians Evidence-Based Clinical Practice Guidelines (8th Edition). Chest. 2008;133(6 suppl):141S-59S. Erratum: Chest. 2008;134:473. [PMID: 18574264]

Item 58   Answer: B

Educational Objective: *Evaluate low-probability venous thrombosis with a D-dimer test.*

The most appropriate next diagnostic test is a D-dimer assay. Several imaging procedures can exclude deep venous thrombosis (DVT), but the diagnostic goal is to use the most efficient, least invasive, and least expensive method with the fewest side effects. A D-dimer assay is a simple, relatively noninvasive test that has been shown to have a high negative predictive value, especially if suspicion for DVT is low. A clinical prediction tool, the Wells score, has been established to help the clinician assess the likelihood of DVT. Studies have shown that when there is low clinical suspicion (as in this patient) and a negative finding on D-dimer assay, DVT can be reliably excluded without the need for more invasive or complex imaging.

According to the Wells criteria, the following clinical variables are assigned 1 point each: active cancer, paralysis or recent plaster cast, recent immobilization or major surgery, tenderness along the deep veins, swelling of the entire leg, a difference in calf circumference of more than 3 cm compared with the other leg, pitting edema, and collateral superficial veins. Clinical suspicion that an alternative diagnosis is likely is assigned -2 points. Based on this system, the pretest probability of DVT is considered high in patients with a score of 3 or higher, moderate in patients with a score of 1 to 2, and low in patients with a score of 0 or lower. This patient's Wells score is -2; therefore, the likelihood of DVT is low. This patient's low-grade fever, circumscribed area of warmth, and tenderness localized to the posterior calf could represent cellulitis, a reasonable alternative to the diagnosis of venous thrombosis.

Doppler ultrasonography is the most commonly used diagnostic study to evaluate for DVT and would be the test of choice for further evaluation, if indicated. Venography, the traditional gold standard for diagnosis of DVT, is rarely performed today because it is invasive, uncomfortable for the patient, expensive, and complex to perform. Computed tomography (or magnetic resonance imaging) scan of the leg has not been substantially validated as a reliable diagnostic test for DVT.

KEY POINT

Negative results on D-dimer assay and a low Wells score reliably exclude a diagnosis of deep venous thrombosis.

Bibliography

Hargett CW, Tapson VF. Clinical probability and D-dimer testing: how should we use them in clinical practice? Semin Respir Crit Care Med. 2008;29:15-24. [PMID: 18302083]

Item 59   Answer: B

Educational Objective: *Manage a medical inpatient who has risk factors for venous thromboembolism.*

The most appropriate treatment is low-dose subcutaneous unfractionated heparin. The patient is immobilized and has at least two major risk factors for venous thromboembolism (VTE). These are age older than 60 years and acute infectious illness. Therefore, he should receive pharmacologic VTE prophylaxis with low-dose unfractionated heparin for at least the duration of hospitalization.

Treatment with aspirin, 325 mg/d, is not appropriate prophylaxis in this medically ill patient who is at high risk for VTE. Aspirin, which is effective for prevention of stroke and myocardial infarction, has not been shown to be effective as prophylaxis for VTE. Appropriate options for this patient include low-dose subcutaneous unfractionated heparin, low-molecular-weight heparin, and fondaparinux.

Use of pneumatic compression devices would not be the optimal approach to VTE prophylaxis in this patient. The use of intermittent pneumatic compression devices is an effective form of VTE prophylaxis. However, data supporting their efficacy are almost exclusively limited to surgical patients, and these devices have not been shown to significantly reduce the incidence of pulmonary embolism. Furthermore, there are serious deficiencies with adherence to mechanical prophylaxis in routine care settings. Therefore, in patients without contraindications to its use, pharmacologic treatment is appropriate for VTE prophylaxis. Nonpneumatic graded external compression stockings have not been shown to be effective. They also increase the risk of skin complications and therefore should not be used for VTE prophylaxis.

Warfarin, 1 mg/d, is not appropriate VTE prophylaxis for this medical inpatient. Although an initial study of low-dose warfarin showed efficacy in preventing DVT in patients with central venous catheters, subsequent studies have not replicated these promising results. Low-intensity, fixed-dose warfarin has never been shown to be useful in VTE prophylaxis. In patients with total hip arthroplasty and knee arthroplasty, adjusted-dose warfarin (international normalized ratio 2-3) has been shown to be efficacious in preventing VTE. However, no studies of this regimen have been conducted in medical inpatients.

KEY POINT

Medical inpatients with two major risk factors for venous thromboembolism should receive pharmacologic prophylaxis for at least the duration of hospitalization.

Bibliography

Kahn SR, Lim W, Dunn AS, et al. Prevention of VTE in nonsurgical patients: Antithrombotic Therapy and Prevention of Thrombosis, 9th ed: American College of Chest Physicians Evidence-Based Clinical Practice Guidelines. Chest. 2012;141(2 suppl):e195S-226S. [PMID: 22315261]

Section 2

Endocrinology and Metabolism
Questions

Item 1 [Basic]

A 32-year-old woman is evaluated after missing several menstrual periods. She also reports vaginal dryness and several episodes of non-bloody bilateral breast discharge. The patient otherwise feels well. She has not had heat or cold intolerance or changes in appetite but does note decreased libido over the past several months. Medical history is unremarkable, and she takes no prescription or over-the-counter medications.

On physical examination, the patient appears healthy. Vital signs are normal. Body mass index is 25, which is a stable measurement. No skin rash or visual field defects are present. There is an expressible nonbloody discharge from both nipples. The remainder of the examination is normal.

A urine pregnancy test is negative.

Which of the following is the most appropriate next diagnostic study?

(A) Magnetic resonance imaging of the pituitary gland
(B) Serum estrogen and progesterone measurement
(C) Serum follicle-stimulating hormone–luteinizing hormone measurement
(D) Serum prolactin measurement

Item 2 [Basic]

An 82-year-old woman is evaluated in the emergency department for a 1-day history of nausea and vomiting. She was discharged from the hospital 4 weeks ago after an exacerbation of chronic obstructive pulmonary disease (COPD) and completed a glucocorticoid taper 1 week ago. The patient has had several exacerbations of COPD over the past year requiring similar treatment. Medical history is otherwise unremarkable, and her only medications are tiotropium and albuterol by metered-dose inhaler.

On physical examination, mental status is normal. Temperature is 35.6°C (96.1°F), blood pressure is 97/75 mm Hg, pulse rate is 120/min, and respiration rate is 12/min. Oxygen saturation is 92% (ambient air). Mucous membranes are dry. Decreased breath sounds and scattered wheezes are present. The abdomen is diffusely tender without guarding or rebound. The extremities are warm and dry. The remainder of the examination is unremarkable.

Laboratory studies:
Random glucose   87 mg/dL (4.8 mmol/L)
Sodium   126 mEq/L (126 mmol/L)
Potassium   3.9 mEq/L (3.9 mmol/L)
Urinalysis   >50 leukocytes/high-power field; positive leukocyte esterase

She is treated with 1.5 L of 0.9% saline intravenously and started on empiric broad-spectrum antibiotics. One hour later, her blood pressure is 79/50 mm Hg, pulse rate is 110/min, and plasma glucose level is 67 mg/dL (3.7 mmol/L).

Which of the following is the most appropriate next step in treatment?

(A) Dextrose 50% intravenous bolus
(B) Hydrocortisone intravenous bolus
(C) Hypertonic saline intravenous bolus
(D) Norepinephrine intravenous infusion

Item 3 [Advanced]

A 67-year-old man is evaluated in the emergency department for an explosive headache and blurred vision that began 4 hours ago. He reports a 3-month history of fatigue, weight gain (total, 4.5 kg [10 lb]), and erectile dysfunction. The patient has a 2-year history of atrial fibrillation treated with warfarin and metoprolol.

On physical examination, he is pale and appears uncomfortable. Blood pressure is 88/56 mm Hg, pulse rate is 88/min, and respiration rate is 18/min. Visual field examination reveals bitemporal hemianopia. The remainder of the examination is unremarkable.

Results of laboratory studies are significant for a serum sodium level of 128 mEq/L (128 mmol/L).

A noncontrast computed tomographic scan of the head shows a heterogeneous sellar mass with suprasellar extension and bowing of the optic chiasm.

In addition to neurosurgical consultation, which of the following is the most appropriate initial management?

(A) Glucocorticoid administration
(B) Levothyroxine administration
(C) Lumbar puncture
(D) Serum prolactin measurement

Item 4 [Basic]

A 28-year-old woman is evaluated for fatigue, a 2.3-kg (5-lb) weight gain, and occasional constipation. She does not have dizziness, nausea, vomiting, polyuria, or polydipsia. Her menstrual cycles are regular. Medical history is significant for a craniopharyngioma treated with resection and subsequent radiation therapy that resulted in hypopituitarism and diabetes insipidus. Medications are hydrocortisone, levothyroxine, desmopressin, and an oral contraceptive.

On physical examination, temperature is normal, blood pressure is 120/72 mm Hg and pulse rate is 70/min without orthostatic changes, and respiration rate is 12/min. There is no acne or striae. The examination is otherwise unremarkable.

Laboratory studies show normal serum electrolytes and kidney function tests. The serum thyroid-stimulating hormone level is 0.1 µU/mL (0.1 mU/L) and the serum free thyroxine level is 0.5 ng/dL (6.4 pmol/L).

Which of the following changes should be made to this patient's current therapy?

(A) Decrease the hydrocortisone dose
(B) Discontinue the oral contraceptive
(C) Increase the desmopressin dose
(D) Increase the levothyroxine dose

Item 5 [Basic]

A 56-year-old woman is evaluated for a 12-month history of slowly progressive fatigue, weight gain, and constipation. She has no other medical problems.

On physical examination, vital signs are normal. The thyroid is non-tender and diffusely enlarged to approximately twice normal size. The ankle deep tendon reflex recovery phase is delayed.

The serum thyroid-stimulating hormone level is 61.2 µU/mL (61.2 mU/L), and the serum free thyroxine level is 0.7 ng/dL (9.0 pmol/L). Thyroid peroxidase antibody titer is positive.

Which of the following is the most appropriate therapy for this patient?

(A) Combination levothyroxine and liothyronine
(B) Levothyroxine
(C) Liothyronine
(D) Prednisone

Item 6 [Advanced]

A 34-year-old woman is evaluated for a 2-month history of tremors and hot flushes. During this time she has unintentionally lost 6.8 kg (15 lb). Her menstrual cycles have been irregular for 3 months. She has no other medical problems and takes no medications.

On physical examination, temperature is normal, blood pressure is 140/90 mm Hg, pulse rate is 92/min, and respiration rate is 20/min. Body mass index is 19. A mild stare is present (white sclera is noted above the iris), but no proptosis or periorbital edema is evident. The thyroid is normal in size. A fine bilateral tremor is present.

The serum thyroid-stimulating hormone level is 0.11 µU/mL (0.11 mU/L) and the serum free thyroxine level is 1.9 ng/dL (24.5 pmol/L). A serum pregnancy test is negative. The radioactive iodine uptake is low.

Which of the following is the most likely diagnosis?

(A) Graves disease
(B) Lymphocytic thyroiditis
(C) Toxic adenoma
(D) Toxic multinodular goiter

Item 7 [Basic]

A 40-year-old man is evaluated during a routine examination. He reports feeling well with no nervousness, palpitations, neck discomfort, or dysphagia.

On physical examination, the patient appears healthy. Vital signs are normal. A 1.0-cm nodule is palpated in the right lobe of the thyroid gland; the thyroid is otherwise normal. There is no lymphadenopathy in the neck or cervical region. Lung, heart, and abdominal examination findings are unremarkable.

The serum thyroid-stimulating hormone level is 1.5 µU/mL (1.5 mU/L).

Ultrasound examination of the thyroid shows a 1.2-cm solid, hypo-echoic nodule.

Which of the following is the most appropriate management?

(A) Fine-needle aspiration biopsy
(B) Radioactive iodine uptake scan
(C) Repeat thyroid ultrasonography in 3 months
(D) Right thyroid lobectomy

Item 8 [Basic]

A 27-year-old woman is evaluated during a routine examination. She is in the fourth week of an uneventful pregnancy. The patient has a 3-year history of primary hypothyroidism due to Hashimoto thyroiditis (chronic autoimmune thyroiditis) that is treated with levothyroxine, 125 µg/d. She also takes prenatal vitamins and iron sulfate.

On physical examination, temperature is normal, blood pressure is 128/80 mm Hg, pulse rate is 95/min, and respiration rate is 18/min and regular. Body mass index is 25. The thyroid gland is smooth and slightly enlarged without a bruit or nodules. Lung, cardiac, skin, and neurologic examination findings are normal.

The serum thyroid-stimulating hormone level is 4.2 µU/mL (4.2 mU/L) and the serum free thyroxine level is 1.6 ng/dL (21 pmol/L).

Which of the following is the most appropriate management?

(A) Increase the levothyroxine dose by 10% now
(B) Increase the levothyroxine dose by 30% now
(C) Repeat thyroid function tests in 5 weeks
(D) Repeat thyroid function tests in the second trimester

Item 9 [Basic]

A 75-year-old woman is evaluated during a routine physical examination. She reports moderate fatigue that she believes has worsened over the past 6 months but has no other symptoms, such as nervousness, weight gain or loss, joint discomfort, constipation, palpitations, or dyspnea. The patient has a history of hypertension. Her only medication is daily lisinopril.

On physical examination, she appears healthy. Blood pressure is 132/75 mm Hg; all other vital signs are normal. The thyroid gland is not palpable; no cervical lymphadenopathy is noted. Cardiac and pulmonary examination findings are normal. Deep tendon reflexes are normal.

Laboratory studies:

Complete blood count	Normal
Comprehensive metabolic panel	Normal
Thyroid function tests (repeated and confirmed)	
Thyroid-stimulating hormone	6.8 µU/mL (6.8 mU/L)
Thyroxine, free	1.1 ng/dL (14 pmol/L)
Thyroid peroxidase antibody titer	Normal

Which of the following is the most appropriate management?

(A) Levothyroxine
(B) Liothyronine
(C) Radioactive iodine uptake study
(D) Repeat thyroid function testing in 6 months

Item 10 [Advanced]

An 18-year-old woman is evaluated for progressively worsening tachycardia, nervousness, decreased exercise tolerance, and weight loss over the past 6 months. Her medical history is otherwise unremarkable, and she takes no medications.

On physical examination, temperature is normal, blood pressure is 152/82 mm Hg, pulse rate is 122/min, and respiration rate is 16/min. Body mass index is 19. There is no proptosis. Examination of the thyroid gland shows symmetric, non-nodular enlargement to approximately twice normal size. Cardiac examination reveals regular tachycardia with a grade 2/6 systolic ejection murmur at the right upper sternal border. The remainder of the examination is unremarkable.

The serum thyroid-stimulating hormone level is less than 0.01 µU/mL (0.01 mU/L) and the serum free thyroxine level is 5.5 ng/dL (71.0 pmol/L). A urine pregnancy test is negative.

Which of the following is the most appropriate treatment for this patient?

(A) Atenolol
(B) Atenolol and methimazole
(C) Methimazole
(D) Radioactive iodine and methimazole

Item 11 [Basic]

A 68-year-old man is evaluated during a follow-up examination. He was recently hospitalized because of abdominal pain. During the hospitalization, an abdominal computed tomographic scan established the diagnosis of gallstone pancreatitis and also revealed a 2.5-cm left adrenal nodule with imaging characteristics consistent with an adenoma. The patient currently feels well and does not have headache, palpitations, or diaphoresis. He has a 9-year history of type 2 diabetes mellitus treated with metformin and a 15-year history of hypertension treated with lisinopril and chlorthalidone. Family history is unremarkable.

On physical examination, temperature is normal, blood pressure is 138/75 mm Hg, pulse rate is 82/min, and respiration rate is 12/min. Body mass index is 32. There is no evidence of abnormal fat distribution or striae. Abdominal examination shows no masses or tenderness to palpation. There is no peripheral edema. The remainder of the examination is normal.

At the time of hospital discharge, laboratory test results included a normal complete blood count, serum electrolyte and aminotransferase levels, and kidney function tests. Three months ago his hemoglobin A_{1c} value was 6.7%.

Which of the following laboratory tests should be done next to evaluate the adrenal mass?

(A) Overnight dexamethasone suppression test; 24-hour urine collection for metanephrines
(B) Overnight dexamethasone suppression test; 24-hour urine collection for metanephrines; measurement of plasma renin activity and serum aldosterone level
(C) 24-Hour urine collection for metanephrines; measurement of plasma renin activity and serum aldosterone level
(D) No additional testing is indicated

Item 12 [Advanced]

A 28-year-old woman is evaluated during a follow-up examination. She has an 18-month history of autoimmune hypophysitis that developed following her recent pregnancy. Other than occasional fatigue, she has been doing well and has no other medical problems. Current medications are hydrocortisone, estrogen, progesterone, growth hormone, and levothyroxine.

On physical examination, temperature is normal, blood pressure is 118/65 mm Hg, pulse rate is 82/min, and respiration rate is 14/min. Body mass index (BMI) is 25, which is unchanged from her BMI 18 months ago. There is no evidence of abnormal fat distribution or striae and no edema. The remainder of the physical examination is normal.

Results of a metabolic panel, including plasma glucose serum electrolyte levels, liver chemistry studies, and kidney function tests, are normal. The serum thyroxine level is also normal.

Which of the following is the most appropriate next step in the management of this patient's medication regimen?

(A) Add fludrocortisone
(B) Decrease the hydrocortisone dose
(C) Increase the hydrocortisone dose
(D) Measure serum thyroid-stimulating hormone level
(E) No changes are necessary

Item 13 [Basic]

A 59-year-old woman is evaluated for muscle cramps. She also has difficult-to-control hypertension. She reports no headaches or unexplained sweating. Hydrochlorothiazide was started 20 months ago when hypertension was initially diagnosed, but her medication was changed after she developed hypokalemia (serum potassium level, 1.9 mEq/L [1.9 mmol/L]). The subsequent addition of lisinopril, atenolol, amlodipine, and potassium chloride has not improved blood pressure control.

On physical examination, the patient has normal features. Temperature is normal, blood pressure is 186/102 mm Hg without orthostatic changes, pulse rate is 66/min without orthostatic changes, and respiration rate is 16/min. Body mass index is 29. Examination of the lungs, heart, and thyroid gland is normal.

Laboratory studies:

Electrolytes	
Sodium	143 mEq/L (143 mmol/L)
Potassium	2.9 mEq/L (2.9 mmol/L)
Chloride	96 mEq/L (96 mmol/L)
Bicarbonate	33 mEq/L (33 mmol/L)

Which of the following is the most appropriate next diagnostic test?

(A) Computed tomography of the abdomen

(B) Determination of plasma aldosterone to plasma renin activity ratio

(C) Dexamethasone suppression test

(D) Measurement of plasma catecholamine levels

(E) Measurement of 24-hour urine free cortisol excretion

Item 14 [Basic]

A 29-year-old woman is evaluated for a 2-day history of fever, cough, nasal congestion, myalgia, and fatigue. Primary adrenal insufficiency was diagnosed 3 months ago. Medications are replacement doses of hydrocortisone and fludrocortisone. She has been able to take her medications as scheduled and fluids as needed.

On physical examination, temperature is 38.2°C (100.8°F), blood pressure is 102/68 mm Hg without orthostatic changes, pulse rate is 88/min without orthostatic changes, and respiration rate is 21/min. Erythema is noted in the posterior pharynx, and bilateral small cervical lymph nodes are present. The remainder of the physical examination is unremarkable.

Which of the following is the most appropriate next step in management?

(A) Hospital admission for intravenous fluids and glucocorticoid therapy

(B) Increased fludrocortisone dose

(C) Increased hydrocortisone dose

(D) Symptomatic treatment only for upper respiratory tract infection

Item 15 [Advanced]

A 67-year-old woman is evaluated for muscle weakness that has developed over the past 6 months. The patient has gained significant weight and developed hypertension and type 2 diabetes mellitus 2 years ago. Her diabetes is not well controlled. Medications are metformin, hydrochlorothiazide, lisinopril, amlodipine, and metoprolol.

On physical examination she appears chronically ill. Blood pressure is 154/92 mm Hg, and other vital signs are normal. Body mass index is 40. Skin examination is notable for facial hirsutism. Central obesity, mild proximal muscle weakness, and 2+ peripheral edema are noted.

Results of recent laboratory studies show a serum creatinine level of 1.3 mg/dL (115 µmol/L), a fasting plasma glucose level of 144 mg/dL (8.0 mmol/L), and a serum potassium level of 2.9 mEq/L (2.9 mmol/L).

Which of the following tests should be performed to establish the cause of this patient's diabetes?

(A) Computed tomography of the adrenal glands

(B) Magnetic resonance imaging of the pancreas

(C) Serum C-peptide measurement

(D) Serum glutamic acid decarboxylase antibody titer

(E) 24-Hour urine free cortisol excretion

Item 16 [Basic]

A 36-year-old man is evaluated in the emergency department for headache and palpitations. He has had hypertension for the past 2 years, but his blood pressure has not been adequately controlled with a combination of medications. He frequently experiences episodes of headache and diaphoresis, during which his blood pressure is significantly increased. Medical history is otherwise unremarkable. Current medications are hydrochlorothiazide, lisinopril, and amlodipine.

On physical examination, he is anxious, tremulous, and diaphoretic. Temperature is normal, blood pressure is 198/106 mm Hg, pulse rate is 110/min, and respiration rate is 14/min. Cardiac examination is significant for tachycardia and a prominent point of maximal impulse. The remainder of the examination is unremarkable.

Results of baseline laboratory studies, including hemoglobin, kidney function tests, and serum electrolyte levels, are normal.

Which of the following is the most likely diagnosis?

(A) Carcinoid syndrome

(B) Hyperaldosteronism

(C) Hypercortisolism (Cushing syndrome)

(D) Pheochromocytoma

Item 17 [Advanced]

A 64-year-old man is admitted to the medical intensive care unit for treatment of pneumonia and sepsis. Intravenous cefepime and vancomycin are initiated. He has a 9-year history of type 2 diabetes mellitus treated with metformin.

On physical examination, temperature is 38.3°C (101.0°F), blood pressure is 160/95 mm Hg, pulse rate is 100/min, and respiration rate is 20/min. Arterial oxygen saturation (ambient air) is 92%. The plasma glucose level is 290 mg/dL (16.1 mmol/L).

Which of the following is the optimal glucose management for this patient?

(A) Insulin drip; target plasma glucose level of 80-110 mg/dL (4.4-6.1 mmol/L)

(B) Insulin drip; target plasma glucose level of 140-200 mg/dL (7.8-11.1 mmol/L)

(C) Metformin; target plasma glucose level of 80-110 mg/dL (4.4-6.1 mmol/L)

(D) Metformin; target plasma glucose level of 140-200 mg/dL (7.8-11.1 mmol/L)

(E) No therapy for hyperglycemia at this time

Item 18 [Basic]

An 18-year-old woman is evaluated during a routine office visit. She has a 2-year history of type 1 diabetes mellitus that is under excellent control with long-acting and bolus insulin. Her most recent hemoglobin A_{1c} value, measured 6 months ago, was 7.0%. She has not experienced any hypoglycemic episodes and has no symptoms, including visual changes or numbness or tingling. Medical history is otherwise unremarkable, and she has no family history of cardiovascular disease or diabetes.

On physical examination, vital signs are normal. Nondilated funduscopic examination is normal, and examination of the thyroid gland and feet is unremarkable.

Which of the following screening examinations are indicated?

(A) Dilated funduscopic examination
(B) Fasting lipid panel
(C) Urine albumin-creatinine ratio
(D) Urine albumin-creatinine ratio, fasting lipid panel, dilated funduscopic examination
(E) No further testing is needed

Item 19 [Advanced]

A 16-year-old boy is evaluated for excessive urination and thirst. He has been drinking almost 5 liters (169 ounces) of fluid daily for the past 2 months. The patient's mother has type 2 diabetes mellitus.

On physical examination, vital signs are normal. Body mass index is 35. Results of general physical and neurologic examinations are unremarkable. He is not dehydrated, and no ketones are detected on his breath.

Laboratory studies:
Hemoglobin A$_{1c}$ 8.7%
Glucose, random   324 mg/dL (18.0 mmol/L)
Electrolytes   Normal
Urine ketones   Negative

Which of the following diagnostic studies is most likely to identify the cause of this patient's findings?

(A) Measure fasting plasma C-peptide level
(B) Measure fasting plasma insulin level
(C) Measure stimulated plasma C-peptide level
(D) Obtain islet cell and glutamic acid decarboxylase antibody titers

Item 20 [Basic]

A 46-year-old woman is evaluated during a routine examination. She has a 6-year history of hypertension treated with amlodipine and atenolol and is currently asymptomatic. Her father had a myocardial infarction at age 50 years, and her mother developed type 2 diabetes mellitus at age 64 years.

On physical examination, blood pressure is 138/89 mm Hg, pulse rate is 76/min, and respiration rate is 18/min; Body mass index is 33. Central obesity is noted, but all other findings are unremarkable.

Results of laboratory studies show a hemoglobin A$_{1c}$ value of 6.6% and a fasting plasma glucose level of 114 mg/dL (6.3 mmol/L).

Which of the following diagnostic tests should be performed next?

(A) Oral glucose tolerance test
(B) Repeat measurement of fasting plasma glucose level
(C) Repeat measurement of hemoglobin A$_{1c}$ value
(D) No additional testing

Item 21 [Basic]

A 79-year-old woman is evaluated for the recent development of frequent episodes of confusion and forgetfulness. She has a 6-year his-

tory of type 2 diabetes mellitus. Medications are glyburide and metformin.

On physical examination, temperature is normal, blood pressure is 142/77 mm Hg, pulse rate is 87/min, and respiration rate is 16/min. Body mass index is 20. All other examination findings are unremarkable, including those from a mental status examination.

Results of laboratory studies show a serum creatinine level of 1.0 mg/dL (88 µmol/L) and a hemoglobin A$_{1c}$ value of 6.2%.

Which of the following is the most appropriate immediate next step in management?

(A) Change glyburide to glipizide
(B) Discontinue glyburide
(C) Discontinue metformin
(D) Discontinue oral medications and start a long-acting insulin

Item 22 [Advanced]

A 34-year-old man is evaluated after having three episodes of severe hypoglycemia in the past month. The patient has a 19-year history of type 1 diabetes mellitus. He states that he no longer experiences any warning symptoms before he becomes hypoglycemic. He has mild background diabetic retinopathy, mild peripheral neuropathy, and occasional orthostatic hypotension. Medications are insulin glargine, 24 units at bedtime, and insulin lispro, 6 to 10 units before meals based on pre-meal testing and what he is eating.

On physical examinations, vital signs are normal. Body mass index is 30. The remainder of the physical examination is unremarkable.

Laboratory studies are significant for a hemoglobin A$_{1c}$ value of 6.6% and no evidence of albuminuria.

Which of the following is the most appropriate treatment?

(A) Increase carbohydrate intake at meals
(B) Decrease exercise
(C) Decrease insulin doses
(D) Substitute insulin detemir for insulin glargine

Item 23 [Basic]

A 50-year-old man is evaluated during a routine health maintenance visit. He feels well and is asymptomatic, although he reports a steady weight gain over the past 5 years. He has no known medical problems and takes no medications. There is a family history of type 2 diabetes mellitus.

On physical examination, temperature is normal, blood pressure is 142/88 mm Hg, pulse rate is 80/min, and respiration rate is 12/min. Body mass index is 29. The remainder of the examination is unremarkable.

The fasting plasma glucose level is 113 mg/dL (6.3 mmol/L) and the hemoglobin A$_{1c}$ value is 6.2%.

Which of the following is the most appropriate treatment recommendation?

(A) Acarbose
(B) Diet and exercise
(C) Metformin
(D) Orlistat

Item 24 [Basic]

An 18-year-old man is evaluated in the emergency department for a 7-hour history of progressive abdominal pain, weakness, and confusion. The patient has no known medical conditions.

On physical examination, temperature is 36.0°C (96.8°F), blood pressure is 110/60 mm Hg, pulse rate is 110/min, and respiration rate is 28/min. The mouth is dry, and skin turgor is poor. The abdomen is tender to palpation without guarding or rebound.

Laboratory studies:

Bicarbonate	12 mEq/L (12 mmol/L)
Creatinine	3.1 mg/dL (274 µmol/L)
Glucose, random	596 mg/dL (33 mmol/L)
Serum ketones	Elevated
Urine ketones	Elevated

The patient receives 2 L of 0.9% (normal) saline over 30 minutes and an additional 2 L over the next 2 hours. Intravenous insulin is begun. No other therapy is given. Four hours later, the plasma glucose level is 201 mg/dL (11.2 mmol/L) and the serum bicarbonate level is 18 mEq/L (18 mmol/L)

Which of the following was the most likely serum potassium concentration at time of presentation, and 4 hours later?

(A) 2.7 mEq/L and 6.0 mEq/L (2.7 mmol/L and 6.0 mmol/L)
(B) 3.8 mEq/L and 5.1 mEq/L (3.8 mmol/L and 5.1 mmol/L)
(C) 4.3 mEq/L and 4.1 mEq/L (4.3 mmol/L and 4.1 mmol/L)
(D) 5.8 mEq/L and 4.8 mEq/L (5.8 mmol/L and 4.8 mmol/L)
(E) 6.1 mEq/L and 3.0 mEq/L (6.1 mmol/L and 3.0 mmol/L)

Item 25 [Basic]

A 64-year-old man is evaluated in the emergency department because of marked dehydration, tachypnea, and thirst. He has type 2 diabetes mellitus, which has been poorly controlled for 3 years. Medications are glyburide and metformin, although he has been only moderately compliant in taking these drugs.

On physical examination, blood pressure in the supine position is 160/95 mm Hg and pulse rate is 100/min, and when standing is 125/78 mm Hg with a pulse rate of 118/min. Respiration rate is 20/min. The mucus membranes are dry, but the remainder of the physical examination is unremarkable.

Laboratory studies:

Creatinine	2.9 mg/dL (256 µmol/L)
Glucose, random	1196 mg/dL (66.4 mmol/L)
Potassium	4.3 mEq/L (4.3 mmol/L)
Bicarbonate	24 mEq/L (24 mmol/L)
Serum ketones	Negative
Urine ketones	Negative

The patient receives 3 L of 0.9% (normal) saline over 3 hours.

Which of the following insulin regimens is most appropriate?

(A) Insulin lispro, by intravenous bolus
(B) Neutral protamine Hagedorn insulin, subcutaneously
(C) Regular insulin, by intravenous bolus
(D) Regular insulin, by intravenous infusion

Item 26 [Basic]

A 72-year-old man is evaluated for a change in mental status. He developed a fever 3 days ago and has become progressively lethargic and confused. Medical history is significant for type 2 diabetes mellitus. His only medication is metformin.

On physical examination, he is minimally responsive. Temperature is 38.8°C (101.8°F), blood pressure is 80/50 mm Hg, pulse rate is 120/min, and respiration rate is 14/min. Mucous membranes are dry. The lungs are clear. Cardiac examination discloses tachycardia and a grade 2/6 systolic ejection murmur at the right upper sternal border. The remainder of the examination is unremarkable.

Laboratory studies:

Glucose, random	1245 mg/dL (69.1 mmol/L)
Sodium	143 mEq/L (143 mmol/L)
Potassium	4.7 mEq/L (4.7 mmol/L)
Bicarbonate	25 mEq/L (25 mmol/L)
Urinalysis	Specific gravity 1.025; no ketones; >50 leukocytes/high-power field

Which of the following is the most appropriate initial intravenous fluid therapy for this patient?

(A) 5% dextrose with water
(B) 0.9% (normal) saline
(C) 0.45% saline
(D) 0.45% saline with 5% dextrose

Item 27 [Basic]

A 55-year-old woman undergoes a routine evaluation. She has no medical problems, and her family history is unremarkable. The patient engages in a regular exercise regimen and does not smoke cigarettes or drink alcoholic beverages. She consumes a diet rich in calcium and takes no medications or supplements other than vitamin D.

Which of the following should be done to manage her risk for osteoporosis?

(A) Begin alendronate
(B) Measure bone turnover markers
(C) Obtain a dual-energy x-ray absorptiometry scan
(D) Continue current lifestyle

Item 28 [Advanced]

A 69-year-old woman is evaluated following a routine dual-energy x-ray absorptiometry scan. The patient's T-score is -2.8, and a diagnosis of osteoporosis is established. Medical history is significant only for gastroesophageal reflux disease treated with omeprazole. Additional medications are calcium citrate and vitamin D. She does not smoke cigarettes or drink alcoholic beverages and does not have postmenopausal symptoms.

In addition to weight-bearing exercise, which of the following is the most appropriate therapy for this patient?

(A) Alendronate
(B) Calcitonin
(C) Oral estrogen and progesterone
(D) Teriparatide
(E) Zoledronic acid

Item 29 [Basic]

A 72-year-old woman is evaluated for a 1-week history of mid-thoracic back pain. She developed pain after doing routine housework but reports no trauma. Medical history is significant only for hypertension. She has never smoked cigarettes and rarely drinks alcoholic beverages. Medications are lisinopril and a multivitamin.

On physical examination, blood pressure is 128/78 mm Hg, pulse rate is 82/min, and respiration rate is 12/min. The lungs are clear, and the cardiac examination is normal. There is tenderness to palpation over the lower thoracic region.

Plain radiographs show a compression fracture at the T8 level.

Results of laboratory studies show normal kidney function tests and serum electrolyte, calcium, phosphorus, and alkaline phosphatase levels. A dual-energy x-ray absorptiometry scan shows T-scores of -2.6 at the spine and -1.9 at the hip.

Which of the following is the most likely diagnosis?

(A) Low bone mass
(B) Osteomalacia
(C) Osteoporosis
(D) Paget disease of bone

Item 30 [Basic]

A 54-year-old woman requests advice regarding maintaining bone health. She has no history of fracture. She underwent menopause at age 52 years and has persistent hot flushes. Her risk factors for osteoporosis include a slim body habitus, a mother who had a hip fracture at age 67 years, and a 25-pack-year history of cigarette smoking, although she is currently a nonsmoker.

Physical examination findings, including vital signs, are normal. Body mass index is 20.

Results of laboratory studies are normal. A dual-energy x-ray absorptiometry scan shows T-scores of -2.1 in the lumbar spine, -2.3 in the femoral neck, and -1.9 in the total hip. Her Fracture Risk Assessment Tool score indicates a 22% risk of major osteoporotic fracture and a 2.4% risk of hip fracture over the next 10 years. Optimal calcium and vitamin D supplementation and weight-bearing exercise are recommended.

Which of the following pharmacologic agents is the most appropriate to start in this patient?

(A) Alendronate
(B) Estrogen
(C) Raloxifene
(D) Teriparatide

Item 31 [Advanced]

A 55-year-old man is reevaluated during a follow-up examination. He slipped in his driveway 2 weeks ago and sustained a right wrist fracture. Radiographs showed evidence of cortical thinning of the bones of the wrist and forearm. Medical history is unremarkable, and he takes no medications. His age-appropriate preventive health interventions are current.

On physical examination, vital signs are normal. Body mass index is 19. Other than a cast on his right wrist, all other findings are normal.

Results of laboratory studies are significant for a hemoglobin level of 11.9 g/dL (119 g/L) and a serum 25-hydroxyvitamin D level of 17 ng/mL (42 nmol/L). Results of a comprehensive metabolic panel, urinalysis, and stool examination for occult blood are normal.

A dual-energy x-ray absorptiometry (DEXA) scan shows T-scores of -1.6 in the lumbar spine, -2.2 in the femoral neck, and -1.9 in the total hip.

Which of the following is the most appropriate next step in management?

(A) Begin alendronate
(B) Begin teriparatide
(C) Repeat DEXA scan in 1 year
(D) Screen for celiac disease

Section 2

Endocrinology and Metabolism
Answers and Critiques

Item 1   **Answer: D**

Educational Objective: *Diagnose central (secondary) hypogonadism secondary to a prolactinoma.*

Measurement of the serum prolactin level is the most appropriate next diagnostic step. Galactorrhea without evidence of an elevated serum human chorionic gonadotropin level is extremely suggestive of a prolactinoma. Missed menstrual periods, vaginal dryness, and decreased libido also suggest hypogonadism, which is likely due to decreased gonadotropin hormone secretion from the anterior pituitary gland (a frequent occurrence with a prolactinoma). Although prolactinomas may lead to classic bitemporal hemianopia, this finding only occurs if they enlarge adequately to compress the optic chiasm. An elevated serum prolactin level would confirm the clinical suspicion that a prolactinoma is inducing central secondary hypogonadism in this patient.

Magnetic resonance imaging of the pituitary gland would be a confirmatory test if the serum prolactin level is elevated; however, performing imaging studies before a biochemical diagnosis is established is not indicated and would not be a high-value initial intervention in the evaluation of this patient.

Serum estrogen and progesterone and follicle-stimulating hormone–luteinizing hormone measurements would likely be abnormal in this patient but would not explain the galactorrhea and would not identify the precise cause of her hypogonadism.

> **KEY POINT**
>
> Because prolactinomas in female patients often present with galactorrhea and signs and symptoms of secondary amenorrhea, a serum prolactin measurement is an appropriate initial study.

Bibliography

Klibanski A. Clinical practice. Prolactinomas. N Engl J Med. 2010 Apr 1;362(13):1219-26. [PMID: 20357284]

Item 2   **Answer: B**

Educational Objective: *Manage secondary adrenal insufficiency due to exogenous glucocorticoid administration.*

This patient should be given an intravenous bolus of hydrocortisone. Secondary adrenal insufficiency produced by decreased adrenocorticotropic hormone (ACTH) release is often caused by prolonged administration of exogenous glucocorticoids that suppress ACTH release and lead to decreased adrenal gland production of cortisol. Decreased cortisol release causes a number of effects, most often nausea, vomiting, and abdominal pain. Laboratory studies often show hyponatremia with or without hypokalemia. Of greatest concern is the presence of hypotension in the setting of infection (such as in this patient with a urinary tract infection) or other physiolog-

ic stressors in which cardiovascular collapse may occur if cortisol release is not adequate, given its key role in maintaining vascular tone. The hypotension is potentially fatal if not treated with hydrocortisone when initially suspected. Given this patient's recent, prolonged stay in an intensive care unit and her persistent hypotension despite administration of broad-spectrum antibiotics and intravenous fluids, adrenal insufficiency should be considered and empirically treated. Because the presentation of adrenal suppression may be difficult to differentiate from sepsis, a low threshold for considering an inadequate cortisol response to stress should be maintained in patients at risk for this occurrence.

Although this patient has mild hypoglycemia, this is likely secondary to adrenal insufficiency, and treatment of mild hypoglycemia with high concentrations of dextrose would not be indicated.

Hypertonic saline is typically reserved for patients with symptomatic hyponatremia and is used to rapidly increase the serum sodium concentration. Its use would be inappropriate in this patient.

Vasopressors are used when there is evidence of tissue hypoxia due to hypoperfusion caused by decreased cardiac output. Although this patient's blood pressure remains low despite fluid resuscitation, she is not showing evidence of tissue hypoperfusion (such as altered mental status or cool extremities). Treatment of her likely adrenal suppression is indicated, as this may be a primary contributor to her hypotension.

> **KEY POINT**
>
> Patients who recently received long-term glucocorticoid therapy and now present with hypotension may have adrenal insufficiency and require prompt treatment with intravenous hydrocortisone.

Bibliography

Charmandari E, Nicolaides NC, Chrousos GP. Adrenal insufficiency. Lancet. 2014;383: 2152-67 [PMID: 24503135]

Item 3   **Answer: A**

Educational Objective: *Manage pituitary tumor apoplexy.*

This patient has acute bleeding into the pituitary gland (pituitary tumor apoplexy) and should receive glucocorticoids in addition to undergoing surgical removal of the tumor. His history of fatigue, weight gain, and erectile dysfunction and the laboratory finding of hyponatremia suggest panhypopituitarism, and his acute headache is consistent with hemorrhage. Pituitary tumor apoplexy usually occurs in the setting of a preexisting pituitary adenoma, and thus a neuroimaging scan was appropriately obtained to confirm the diagnosis and show the pituitary anatomy. He also has evidence of bitemporal hemianopia caused by optic chiasmal compression by the mass. The anticoagulant taken by this patient may have predisposed him to hemorrhage.

Pituitary tumor apoplexy is generally a neurosurgical emergency. On occasion, hemorrhagic infarction of a pituitary adenoma may be less urgent, especially in the absence of associated mass effect, and can be managed with conservative follow-up monitoring. In the setting of local mass effect and severe headache, however, neurosurgical decompression of the pituitary gland is necessary. Urgent glucocorticoid administration is often required because of acute adrenocorticotropic hormone deficiency. The leading cause of death in patients with pituitary tumor apoplexy is adrenal insufficiency.

Levothyroxine is not indicated at this time. Although pituitary tumor apoplexy may result in the loss of thyroid-stimulating hormone with subsequent thyroid hormone deficiency requiring treatment, replacement of adrenal hormone with glucocorticoids is indicated acutely.

A lumbar puncture is useful in patients with suspected meningitis or in whom subarachnoid hemorrhage is suspected despite a negative imaging study. However, the imaging study already provides an explanation for this patient's stiff neck and headache, and a lumbar puncture is not only inappropriate but contraindicated in a patient with pituitary tumor apoplexy.

Measurement of the serum prolactin level typically is obtained after a diagnosis of pituitary adenoma is made to exclude prolactinoma. Because this patient's disorder is a neurosurgical emergency, this test is inappropriate before the apoplexy is addressed.

KEY POINT

In addition to neurosurgical decompression of the pituitary gland, urgent glucocorticoid administration is often necessary in patients with pituitary tumor apoplexy because of acute adrenocorticotropic hormone deficiency.

Bibliography

Nawar RN, AbdelMannan D, Selman WR, et al. Pituitary tumor apoplexy: a review. J Intensive Care Med. 2008;23:75-90. [PMID: 18372348]

Item 4   Answer: D
Educational Objective: *Treat central hypothyroidism.*

This patient has central hypothyroidism, and her thyroid hormone replacement therapy (levothyroxine) dose should be increased to normalize the serum free thyroxine (T_4) level and alleviate signs and symptoms of hypothyroidism. Although the serum thyroid-stimulating hormone (TSH) level is the most accurate indicator of thyroid function in patients with an intact hypothalamic-pituitary-thyroid axis, it cannot be used to monitor thyroid hormone replacement therapy in patients with central hypothyroidism. In these patients, the pituitary thyrotropes are absent, and the TSH level is always low, regardless of the level of circulating thyroid hormone. The goal of thyroid hormone replacement in these patients is to titrate the levothyroxine dose to normalize the free T_4 level (or total T_4 concentration and free T_4 index), not to normalize the TSH level.

The hydrocortisone dose does not need to be reduced because this patient does not have any clinical signs to suggest overreplacement (hypertension, acne, hirsutism). It is also important to maintain adequate adrenal hormone replacement when deficiency is due to loss of pituitary adrenocorticotropic hormone stimulation because of potential systemic adverse effects associated with underreplacement.

Oral contraceptives in this patient will help prevent the development of osteopenia or osteoporosis induced by hypogonadism and should therefore be continued.

The patient's desmopressin dose should not be altered because her symptoms are controlled on her current dose and she has normal serum electrolyte values.

KEY POINT

The serum thyroid-stimulating hormone level cannot be used to monitor thyroid hormone replacement therapy in patients with central hypothyroidism.

Bibliography

Persani L. Clinical review: Central hypothyroidism: pathogenic, diagnostic, and therapeutic challenges. J Clin Endocrinol Metab. 2012;97:3068-78. [PMID: 22851492]

Item 5   Answer: B
Educational Objective: *Treat hypothyroidism.*

The most appropriate treatment for this patient with Hashimoto thyroiditis (chronic autoimmune thyroiditis) and hypothyroidism is levothyroxine. Physical examination findings of hypothyroidism may include a reduced basal temperature, diastolic hypertension, an enlarged thyroid gland, bradycardia, pallor, dry and cold skin, brittle hair, hoarseness, and a delayed recovery phase of deep tendon reflexes, although not all of these findings may be present in a specific patient. Results of laboratory studies can confirm hypothyroidism; these include an elevated serum thyroid-stimulating hormone level and a normal or low serum free thyroxine level. Hashimoto thyroiditis is the most frequent cause of hypothyroidism and is associated with a positive thyroid peroxidase antibody measurement. Other less common causes of hypothyroidism include iatrogenic hypothyroidism, which can occur after radioactive iodine ablation for Graves disease, external-beam radiation to the thyroid bed, or surgical removal of the thyroid gland. The mainstay of thyroid hormone replacement is oral levothyroxine (T_4), which should always be taken on an empty stomach 1 hour before or 2 to 3 hours after intake of food or other medications.

Although much attention has recently been focused on therapy with liothyronine (T_3) or combination T_3/T_4 therapy using either thyroid hormone extract or synthetic T_3/T_4 combinations, most evidence to date shows no clinical advantage of combined T_3/T_4 therapy compared with traditional T_4 treatment. Available T_3 preparations have a short half-life and can be associated with acute spikes in serum T_3 levels, which are of particular concern in elderly patients or patients with cardiac abnormalities.

Although Hashimoto disease is an autoimmune condition, immunosuppression with agents such as prednisone are ineffective in addressing the underlying pathology and do not have a role in therapy.

KEY POINT

The mainstay of thyroid hormone replacement is oral levothyroxine (T_4) therapy.

Bibliography

McDermott MT. In the clinic. Hypothyroidism. Ann Intern Med. 2009;151:ITC61. [PMID: 19949140]

Item 6   Answer: B

Educational Objective: *Diagnose lymphocytic thyroiditis as a cause of hyperthyroidism.*

This patient most likely has silent lymphocytic thyroiditis (also known as chronic thyroiditis). Thyroiditis involves transient destruction of thyroid tissue, which disrupts follicles and causes the release of preformed thyroid hormone into the circulation. Forms of destructive thyroiditis include subacute (de Quervain), silent, and postpartum thyroiditis. Subacute thyroiditis most commonly occurs after a viral infection and usually involves severe thyroid and neck pain; fever, fatigue, malaise, anorexia, and myalgia are common. Silent thyroiditis is painless. Postpartum thyroiditis is a subset of painless autoimmune thyroiditis and can occur up to 12 months after parturition. It affects 5% to 8% of pregnant women in the United States and can recur with each pregnancy. Thyroiditis is associated with elevated serum free thyroxine (T_4) and triiodothyronine (T_3) levels and a low serum thyroid-stimulating hormone (TSH) level. The disorder usually follows a classic course of approximately 6 weeks of thyrotoxicosis, a shorter period of euthyroidism, 4 to 6 weeks of hypothyroidism, and then restoration of euthyroidism. In patients with subacute, silent, or postpartum thyroiditis or exposure to exogenous thyroid hormones, the radioactive iodine uptake (RAIU) will be very low (<5% at 24 hours), which indicates very little endogenous thyroid production.

Graves disease is an autoimmune disorder that can affect the thyroid gland, ocular muscles, orbital fat, and skin. Hyperthyroidism is by far the most common manifestation. Examination of the thyroid may reveal the classic smooth, rubbery, firm goiter, often associated with a bruit. Thyroid gland examination of patients with toxic adenoma or toxic multinodular goiter usually reveals one or more palpable nodule(s) or overall gland enlargement. Toxic multinodular goiter and toxic adenoma result from an activating somatic mutation in the TSH receptor gene, which leads to autonomy of function and secretion of excess T_4 and T_3 from the affected nodule(s). Patients with Graves disease, toxic adenoma, or toxic multinodular goiter have an elevated or high-normal RAIU, which indicates endogenous production of thyroid hormones. A thyroid scan will show diffuse uptake of radioactive iodine in patients with Graves disease or more focal uptake in those with toxic multinodular goiter or toxic adenoma.

KEY POINT

In patients with subacute, silent, or postpartum thyroiditis or exposure to exogenous thyroid hormones, the radioactive iodine uptake will be very low, which indicates very little endogenous thyroid production.

Bibliography

Samuels MH. Subacute, silent, and postpartum thyroiditis. Med Clin North Am. 2012; 96:223-33. [PMID: 22443972]

Item 7   Answer: A

Educational Objective: *Evaluate thyroid nodules with fine-needle aspiration biopsy.*

This patient should have a fine-needle aspiration (FNA) biopsy of the thyroid nodule. Most thyroid nodules are benign; only approximately 5% to 15% are malignant. FNA biopsy is the most accurate method to determine whether a nodule is benign or malignant. This is an outpatient procedure that allows cytologic categorization of the cells within a nodule as benign or suspicious for malignancy, follicular neoplasm, or papillary thyroid cancer. FNA biopsy is also the most sensitive and specific method to help diagnose the cause of a thyroid nodule.

Because thyroid nodules are extremely common (30% to 50% of healthy persons are estimated to have a thyroid nodule on thyroid ultrasonography), guidelines have been developed by the American Thyroid Association to maximize the effectiveness of thyroid FNA biopsy in diagnosing malignancy in a cost-effective manner. These guidelines take into account personal history and risk factors, family history, and ultrasound characteristics of the nodule to help predict the likelihood of malignancy and the need for thyroid FNA biopsy. FNA biopsy is recommended for any nodule greater than 1 cm in diameter that is solid and hypoechoic on ultrasonography and for any nodule 2 cm or greater that is mixed cystic-solid without worrisome sonographic characteristics. Biopsy may be appropriate for smaller nodules (at least 5 mm in diameter) in patients with risk factors, such as a history of radiation exposure, a family or personal history of thyroid cancer, cervical lymphadenopathy, or suspicious ultrasound characteristics. FNA biopsy is not routinely recommended for thyroid nodules less than 1 cm in diameter.

A radioactive iodine uptake scan is appropriate for patients with a suppressed serum thyroid-stimulating hormone level to evaluate for a possible toxic nodule (or toxic multinodular goiter), which is not applicable in this patient.

Because the size and characteristics of this patient's nodule meet the guideline criteria for biopsy, repeat thyroid ultrasonography would not be appropriate. However, ultrasound characteristics of thyroid nodules are very helpful in assessing malignant potential, and repeat ultrasonography for follow-up of lesions without clear indications for biopsy but with suspicious features may be helpful in selected patients.

Thyroid lobectomy is generally reserved for treatment of cancerous thyroid nodules but would be premature in this patient in whom a diagnosis of malignancy has not been established.

KEY POINT

A fine-needle aspiration biopsy is the most accurate way to determine if a thyroid nodule is benign or malignant.

Bibliography

American Thyroid Association (ATA) Guidelines Taskforce on Thyroid Nodules and Differentiated Thyroid Cancer; Cooper DS, Doherty GM, Haugen BR, et al. Revised American Thyroid Association management guidelines for patients with thyroid nodules and differentiated thyroid cancer [errata in Thyroid. 2010;20:674-675; and Thyroid. 2010;20:942]. Thyroid. 2009;19:1167-214. [PMID: 19860577]

Item 8   Answer: B

Educational Objective: *Manage hypothyroidism during pregnancy.*

This patient's levothyroxine (T_4) dose should be increased by 30% now, and the thyroid function tests should be repeated in 2 to 4 weeks. Pregnancy is known to increase levothyroxine requirements in most patients receiving thyroid replacement therapy, and this expected increase should be anticipated by increasing the levothyroxine dose. This is typically increased in the first (and sometimes in the second) trimester of pregnancy, with a possible total increase of 30% to 50%, and an increase in levothyroxine dose in this range to maintain the thyroid-stimulating hormone (TSH) level between approximately 0.1 and 2.5 µU/mL (0.1-2.5 mU/L) is associated with fewer maternal and fetal complications. The fetus is largely dependent on transplacental transfer of maternal thyroid hormones during the first 12 weeks of gestation, and the presence of maternal subclinical or overt hypothyroidism may be associated with subsequent fetal neurocognitive impairment, increased risk of premature birth, low birth weight, increased miscarriage rate, and even an increased risk of fetal death. In pregnant women with hypothyroidism, thyroid function testing should be frequent, preferably every 4 weeks, to protect the health of mother and fetus and to avoid pregnancy complications.

Continuing the current levothyroxine dose is inappropriate in this patient because her TSH level is already too high (4.2 μU/mL [4.2 mU/L]). TSH levels generally should range from 0.1 to 2.5 μU/mL (0.1-2.5 mU/L) in the first trimester, 0.2 to 3.0 μU/mL (0.2-3.0 mU/L) in the second trimester, and 0.3 to 3.0 μU/mL (0.3-3.0 mU/L) in the third trimester.

KEY POINT

Early in pregnancy, levothyroxine requirements are increased by 30% to 50% in most patients with hypothyroidism.

Bibliography

Yassa L, Marqusee E, Fawcett R, Alexander EK. Thyroid hormone early adjustment in pregnancy (the THERAPY) trial. J Clin Endocrinol Metab. 2010;95:3234-41. [PMID: 20463094]

Item 9   Answer: D
Educational Objective: *Manage subclinical hypothyroidism.*

This patient's thyroid function studies should be repeated in 6 months. She has subclinical hypothyroidism, defined as a serum thyroid-stimulating hormone (TSH) level greater than the reference range, with a concomitant serum free thyroxine (T_4) level in the reference range. Patients typically have mild or no symptoms of hypothyroidism. The causes of subclinical hypothyroidism are generally considered the same as for overt hypothyroidism. Patients with subclinical hypothyroidism may have mild elevations in serum total cholesterol, low-density lipoprotein cholesterol, and even C-reactive protein levels, and some meta-analyses have shown an increased risk for atherosclerosis and cardiac events. However, evidence is insufficient to conclude that treatment with levothyroxine minimizes risks or improves outcomes when the serum TSH level is 10 μU/mL (10 mU/L) or less. Treatment is recommended when serum TSH levels are greater than 10 μU/mL (10 mU/L). Levothyroxine also may be considered for patients who have marked symptoms, have a goiter, are pregnant or are planning to become pregnant, or have positive serum thyroid peroxidase antibody titers. This patient is asymptomatic (except for mild fatigue) and in good health. Her clinical examination findings are basically normal and thus support the concept that she does not require exogenous levothyroxine.

Most evidence to date has shown no clinical advantage of liothyronine compared with levothyroxine in patients requiring thyroid replacement therapy. Additionally, liothyronine and other tri-iodothyronine (T_3) preparations have a short half-life and have been associated with acute spikes in serum T_3 levels, which are of particular concern in older patients or patients with cardiac abnormalities.

A radioactive iodine uptake study is not useful in establishing the diagnosis of hypothyroidism and thus is inappropriate for this patient.

KEY POINT

Appropriate management of patients with subclinical hypothyroidism with a serum thyroid-stimulating hormone (TSH) level less than 10 μU/mL (10 mU/L) is repeat testing of thyroid function in 6 months without levothyroxine therapy except in certain clinical situations.

Bibliography

Surks MI, Ortiz E, Daniels GH, et al. Subclinical thyroid disease: scientific review and guidelines for diagnosis and management. JAMA. 2004;291:228-38. [PMID:14722150]

Item 10   Answer: B
Educational Objective: *Treat Graves disease.*

The most appropriate medical regimen for this patient with Graves disease is atenolol and methimazole. Graves disease can present with either subclinical or overt thyrotoxicosis. Physical examination findings may include tachycardia; an elevated systolic blood pressure with a widened pulse pressure; a palpable goiter, which is classically smooth; a thyrotoxic stare due to lid retraction; proptosis; and, infrequently, an infiltrative dermopathy. To control this patient's tachycardia, a β-blocker is indicated. Although all β-blockers are effective, atenolol is frequently used because of its β-1 selectivity and long half-life that allows once daily dosing in some patients. Given the clinical and laboratory findings, this patient also has moderate hyperthyroidism that can be treated with either methimazole or propylthiouracil. Methimazole, which generally has fewer side effects and results in quicker achievement of the euthyroid state than propylthiouracil, is preferred in most patients. Because of a presumed immunomodulatory effect, antithyroidal drugs result in drug-free remission rates of between 30% and 50% in patients with Graves disease who are treated for 1 year.

Atenolol alone would only address this patient's adrenergic symptoms and not reduce her thyroid hormone levels, and methimazole alone would not immediately address her tachycardia.

Radioactive iodine therapy preceded or followed by adjunctive therapy with an antithyroidal drug is occasionally used to treat Graves disease. An antithyroidal drug is given in an attempt to decrease the risk of a transient worsening of the thyrotoxicosis after thyroid ablation. Because antithyroidal drugs render the thyroid radioresistant, they must be stopped for several days before and after giving the radioactive iodine. Although an occasional patient becomes euthyroid after radioactive iodine administration, the expected outcome is hypothyroidism, which typically occurs within 2 to 3 months of therapy, at which time thyroid hormone replacement therapy is begun. Although this therapy might be a reasonable long term management option in this patient, it would not address her acute tachycardia and other hyperthyroid symptoms, which are more effectively treated with β-blockade.

KEY POINT

Acute therapy of symptomatic hyperthyroidism usually includes β-blockade and treatment with an antithyroid agent.

Bibliography

Nakamura H, Noh JY, Itoh K, et al. Comparison of methimazole and propylthiouracil in patients with hyperthyroidism caused by Graves' disease. J Clin Endocrinol Metab. 2007;92:2157-62. [PMID: 17389704]

Item 11   Answer: B

Educational Objective: *Evaluate an adrenal incidentaloma.*

This patient has an adrenal incidentaloma, and initial laboratory tests should include an overnight dexamethasone suppression test, 24-hour urine collection for metanephrines, and measurement of plasma renin activity and serum aldosterone level. The increasing use of imaging studies has revealed otherwise unrecognized adrenal masses in up to 7% of the population older than 70 years. Evaluating adrenal masses should address their potential for malignancy (whether primary or metastatic) and their functional status. Initial assessment should include a thorough history and physical examination to detect any clinical evidence of hormone hypersecretion. Nearly 10% of adrenal incidentalomas are functional, although most have no overt clinical manifestations. Therefore, testing is usually necessary to identify functional tumors secreting catecholamines, cortisol, or aldosterone. Measurements of urine excretion or plasma levels of catecholamine metabolites (fractionated metanephrines) are good initial tests for pheochromocytoma. Measurements of plasma adrenocorticotropic hormone and serum cortisol levels before and after the overnight administration of dexamethasone (1 mg) are appropriate initial tests to evaluate for possible cortisol production. Evaluation for aldosterone-secreting adenomas should be carried out in patients with hypertension, such as this patient, or those with spontaneous hypokalemia by determining the serum aldosterone level and plasma renin activity.

KEY POINT

Nearly 10% of adrenal incidentalomas are functional, and testing is usually necessary to identify functional tumors secreting catecholamines, cortisol, or aldosterone.

Bibliography

Arnaldi G, Boscaro M. Adrenal incidentaloma. Best Pract Res Clin Endocrinol Metab. 2012;26:405-19. [PMID: 22863384]

Item 12   Answer: E

Educational Objective: *Manage central adrenal insufficiency.*

No medications changes are necessary for this patient with central adrenal insufficiency. The hydrocortisone is appropriately dosed, as evidenced by the lack of signs or symptoms of Cushing syndrome such as weight gain, hyperglycemia, hypertension, striae, and abnormal fat distribution. Additionally, the patient has no evidence of hydrocortisone underreplacement, as she does not have nausea, vomiting, malaise, hypotension, weight loss, hyponatremia, or hypoglycemia.

In adrenocorticotropic hormone deficiency, adrenal production of mineralocorticoids and potassium homeostasis remain intact because production is controlled separately by the renin-angiotensin system. Therefore, this patient does not require replacement with a mineralocorticoid such as fludrocortisone. In patients with central hypothyroidism, thyroid-stimulating hormone (TSH) deficiency leads to reduced secretion of thyroxine (T_4), and measurement of the serum T_4 level is necessary to establish the diagnosis. Thyroid hormone dosing in patients with central hypothyroidism should be adjusted on the basis of clinical symptoms to maintain serum free T_4 levels within the middle of the reference range, unless doing so causes iatrogenic hyperthyroidism or hypothyroidism. Serum TSH values cannot be used as a measure of adequacy of replacement in these patients, although TSH values can be used in patients with an intact hypothalamic-pituitary axis.

KEY POINT

Patients with primary adrenal insufficiency, which is associated with both cortisol and aldosterone deficiencies, require daily glucocorticoid and mineralocorticoid replacement, whereas patients with central adrenal insufficiency have only cortisol deficiency and do not require mineralocorticoid replacement.

Bibliography

Chakera AJ, Vaidya B. Addison disease in adults: diagnosis and management. Am J Med. 2010;123:409-13.[PMID:20399314]

Item 13   Answer: B

Educational Objective: *Diagnose hyperaldosteronism.*

Determination of the plasma aldosterone to plasma renin activity ratio is most appropriate. This patient has biochemical features indicative of excessive mineralocorticoid secretion. Although several potential mineralocorticoids could be responsible for her symptoms, excessive aldosterone is the most likely cause. Hypertension and hypokalemia are two of the main manifestations of primary hyperaldosteronism. Increases in other mineralocorticoids occur in patients with unusually excessive cortisol secretion (Cushing syndrome), in whom the mineralocorticoid activity of cortisol becomes prominent, and in patients with congenital adrenal hyperplasia due to an enzyme deficiency. This patient's normal findings (except for blood pressure) on physical examination make the first possibility unlikely, and her less than 2-year history of hypertension makes a congenital enzyme deficiency also unlikely. The most appropriate screening test for hyperaldosteronism is the determination of the ratio of plasma aldosterone to plasma renin activity. The expected findings include an elevated plasma aldosterone level and suppressed plasma renin activity. Screening tests can be performed on random blood samples, even in patients taking antihypertensive medications (except the aldosterone receptor antagonists spironolactone and eplerenone). Confirmation of the biochemical diagnosis involves showing persistent elevation (poor suppressibility) of plasma aldosterone in response to a high salt load.

Imaging studies are inappropriate before a definite biochemical diagnosis is established. Therefore, computed tomography of the abdomen is premature at this time.

This patient did not exhibit any signs or symptoms that would warrant investigating the possibility of Cushing syndrome. Therefore, neither a dexamethasone suppression test nor a 24-hour measurement of urine free cortisol excretion is likely to be useful.

Nothing in the patient's history or clinical examination findings suggests the possibility of pheochromocytoma. Therefore, measurement of the plasma catecholamine levels is inappropriate as the next diagnostic test.

KEY POINT

The most appropriate screening test for hyperaldosteronism is the determination of the ratio of plasma aldosterone to plasma renin activity.

Bibliography

Funder JW, Carey RM, Fardella C, et al; Endocrine Society. Case detection, diagnosis, and treatment of patients with primary aldosteronism: an Endocrine Society clinical practice guideline. J Clin Endocrinol Metab. 2008;93:3266-81. [PMID: 18552288]

Item 14   Answer: C
Educational Objective: *Adjust hydrocortisone therapy during a minor illness.*

This patient's hydrocortisone dose should be increased. She has primary adrenal insufficiency (Addison disease) and now has an intercurrent upper respiratory tract infection. She has continued to take adequate amounts of fluids and her medications as scheduled. Except for findings related to an upper respiratory tract infection, vital signs and other physical examination findings are normal. Her hydrocortisone dose during her intercurrent illness should be increased approximately threefold over her baseline replacement dose, and the increase should be continued for 3 days. This step is necessary to minimize the possibility of adrenal crisis. Educating patients about the need to adjust (increase) their dose of hydrocortisone with even minor intercurrent illnesses is crucial in the successful management of adrenal insufficiency.

Because this patient is not hypotensive and is able to take fluids and her medications orally, hospitalization for intravenous administration of fluids and glucocorticoids is unnecessary.

In patients with adrenal insufficiency, fludrocortisone is typically given as mineralocorticoid therapy. The additional glucocorticoid (hydrocortisone) therapy that this patient requires because of her intercurrent illness also will result in additional mineralocorticoid activity. Therefore, adjusting mineralocorticoid doses during intercurrent medical illnesses is unnecessary.

Symptomatic treatment of her upper respiratory tract infection without adjustment of her hydrocortisone dose is inappropriate and likely to lead to prolongation and worsening of her symptoms of adrenal insufficiency

KEY POINT
Adjusting (increasing) the dose of hydrocortisone during even minor intercurrent illnesses is crucial to avoid adrenal crisis in patients with adrenal insufficiency.

Bibliography
Chakera AJ, Vaidya B. Addison disease in adults: diagnosis and management. Am J Med. 2010;123:409-13. [PMID: 20399314]

Item 15   Answer: E
Educational Objective: *Diagnose hypercortisolism (Cushing syndrome) as a secondary cause of diabetes mellitus.*

Measurement of the 24-hour excretion of urine free cortisol is the most appropriate next test in this patient to determine the cause of her diabetes mellitus. Various secondary causes of diabetes exist, most involving other endocrinopathies, effects of medications, pancreatic diseases, or genetic conditions. Hypercortisolism (Cushing syndrome) is one of these secondary causes. The most common cause of hypercortisolism is glucocorticoid therapy, followed by the secretion of adrenocorticotropic hormone (ACTH) by a pituitary adenoma (Cushing disease) and the hyperfunctioning of an adrenocortical adenoma. In this patient, the combination of diabetes, hypertension, central obesity, hypokalemia, proximal muscle weakness, and edema strongly suggests the presence of hypercortisolism. The diagnosis can be confirmed by several tests, including measurement of 24-hour excretion of urine free cortisol, an overnight dexamethasone suppression test, or a midnight salivary cortisol measurement.

Computed tomography of the adrenal glands is appropriate after hypercortisolism is diagnosed, especially when it is non–ACTH dependent, to identify the type of adrenal condition responsible. This test would be premature in this patient in whom the diagnosis has not been confirmed.

Pancreatic imaging could be considered when signs and symptoms (such as abdominal or back pain, jaundice, or chronic diarrhea) suggest that an underlying pancreatic disorder is the cause of diabetes. This patient has none of these signs or symptoms, and thus magnetic resonance imaging of the pancreas is unlikely to be revealing.

Residual β-cell function can be assessed by measuring the serum C-peptide level, which is often high-normal in patients with early type 2 diabetes because of insulin resistance. Similarly, measuring the serum glutamic acid decarboxylase antibody titer is useful to confirm the presence of autoimmune (type 1) diabetes when no other evidence exists. However, the serum C-peptide level will not indicate the cause of diabetes in this patient, and measuring the serum glutamic acid decarboxylase antibody titer also is unlikely to be helpful because she does not have type 1 diabetes.

KEY POINT
Hypercortisolism (Cushing syndrome) is a likely cause of secondary diabetes mellitus in a patient with hypertension, central obesity, and hypokalemia.

Bibliography
Reimondo G, Pia A, Allasino B, et al. Screening of Cushing's syndrome in adult patients with newly diagnosed diabetes mellitus. Clin Endocrinol (Oxf). 2007;67:225-9. [PMID: 17547690]

Item 16   Answer: D
Educational Objective: *Diagnose pheochromocytoma.*

This patient's clinical presentation is consistent with a diagnosis of pheochromocytoma. Although secondary causes of hypertension are uncommon, his young age and refractory hypertension warrant consideration of this possibility, particularly because of the presence of the classic triad of symptoms associated with pheochromocytoma–headaches, palpitations, and diaphoresis. These tumors are present in less than 1% of patients with hypertension, are derived from chromaffin cells, and elaborate norepinephrine, epinephrine, and dopamine. Tumors originating in the adrenal glands are referred to as pheochromocytomas, whereas those originating along the sympathetic paraganglia are referred to as paragangliomas. Hypertension is present in more than 90% of patients with pheochromocytoma: more than 50% of these patients have sustained elevations in blood pressure; 30% to 40% have episodic elevations; and up to 10% have no hypertension. Lability of blood pressure is due to episodic catecholamine release, volume depletion, and adrenergic receptor desensitization caused by chronic stimulation. Other symptoms include anxiety, tremor, and pallor. Chronic complications of excess catecholamine release include cardiac arrhythmias, both dilated and hypertrophic cardiomyopathy, and accelerated atherosclerosis related to hypertension.

Carcinoid syndrome is the term applied to symptoms mediated by humoral factors (for example, serotonin) released by some carcinoid tumors. Episodic flushing is most characteristic of the carcinoid syndrome; flushing begins suddenly and lasts up to 30 minutes. Severe flushes are accompanied by a fall in blood pressure and rise in heart rate. The patient does not have flushing or hypotension, making carcinoid syndrome an unlikely diagnosis.

Patients with primary hyperaldosteronism and hypercortisolism (Cushing syndrome) usually have decreased serum potassium levels, and neither condition is associated with headaches, palpitations, and diaphoresis.

KEY POINT

The classic symptoms of pheochromocytoma are hypertension, headaches, palpitations, and diaphoresis.

Bibliography

Meyer-Rochow GY, Sidhu SB. Pheochromocytoma and paraganglioma. Cancer Treat Res. 2010;153:135-62. [PMID: 19957224]

Item 17   Answer: B

Educational Objective: *Manage hyperglycemia in a patient in the medical intensive care unit.*

The optimal glucose management for this critically ill patient is an insulin drip with a target plasma glucose level of 140-200 mg/dL (7.8-11.1 mmol/L). Hyperglycemia in hospitalized patients, with or without diabetes mellitus, is associated with a poor outcome. The recommended glycemic goal in critically ill hospitalized patients has undergone important changes in the past decades. An early trial suggested that in patients in a surgical intensive care unit (ICU), intense glucose control to a target plasma glucose level of 80-110 mg/dL (4.4-6.1 mmol/L) resulted in reduced mortality rates when compared with patients managed with the conventional plasma glucose goal of 180-200 mg/dL (10.0-11.1 mmol/L). However, subsequent studies failed to reproduce these results, and some studies have reported increased mortality rates and severe hypoglycemia with stringent glycemic control. As the result of these studies, the current American Diabetes Association recommendation for critically ill hospitalized patients is to initiate insulin therapy for persistent hyperglycemia greater than 180 mg/dL (10.0 mmol/L) and aim for a target glycemic goal of 140-180 mg/dL (7.8-10.0 mmol/L). The American College of Physicians (ACP) recommendation is less stringent, with a target glycemic goal of 140-200 mg/dL (7.8-11.1 mmol/L). The authors of the ACP recommendation note that the evidence is not sufficient to provide a precise range for plasma glucose target values, and a goal of 140-200 mg/dL (7.8-11.1 mmol/L) is a reasonable option in patients in the ICU because it is associated with similar mortality outcomes as plasma glucose levels of 80-110 mg/dL (4.4-6.1 mmol/L) as well as with a lower risk for hypoglycemia.

Insulin is the mainstay therapy for the hyperglycemic state in critically ill patients, and oral antihyperglycemic agents, such as metformin, should be stopped. The use of oral antihyperglycemic agents is also limited in hospitalized patients who are not critically ill in order to avert the possibility of developing medication-related complications. Specifically, metformin should be stopped if intravenous contrast dye will be used or if the patient's condition on admission could cause lactic acidosis. This critically ill patient with pneumonia and sepsis is at risk for lactic acidosis, and metformin should be discontinued.

KEY POINT

The optimal glucose management for critically ill hospitalized patients is unknown, but an insulin drip with a glycemic target plasma glucose level of 140-200 mg/dL (7.8-11.1 mmol/L) is reasonable.

Bibliography

Qaseem A, Humphrey LL, Chou R, et al. Clinical Guidelines Committee of the American College of Physicians. Use of intensive insulin therapy for the management of glycemic control in hospitalized patients: a clinical practice guideline from the American College of Physicians. Ann Intern Med. 2011;154:260-7. [PMID:21320941]

Item 18   Answer: B

Educational Objective: *Screen for dyslipidemia in a patient with type 1 diabetes mellitus.*

The only screening test indicated for this patient is a fasting lipid panel. The recommended initial screening differs for patients with type 1 or type 2 diabetes mellitus. Patients with type 2 diabetes often experience a delay in diagnosis. As a result, these patients may already have diabetes-related complications at diagnosis. Therefore, screening for diabetic retinopathy, neuropathy, nephropathy, and dyslipidemia should be obtained once the diagnosis has been established. Patients with type 1 diabetes are typically diagnosed at the time of disease onset based on the occurrence of symptomatic hyperglycemia or ketoacidosis. Since microvascular complications in patients with type 1 diabetes typically occur after the onset of puberty and/or 5 to 10 years after the initial diagnosis, screening for these complications is delayed until that time. Because patients with type 1 diabetes have a higher risk of early cardiovascular disease, screening is typically done early in the disease course. The American Diabetes Association (ADA) recommends that such patients have a fasting lipid panel performed after puberty or at diagnosis if the diagnosis is established after puberty.

The ADA recommends screening for nephropathy (such as a urine albumin-creatinine ratio) once a patient with type 1 diabetes is 10 years of age or older and has been diagnosed with diabetes for 5 or more years. The first dilated funduscopic examination should be obtained once the child is 10 years of age or older and has been diagnosed with type 1 diabetes for 3 to 5 years. This patient only needs a fasting lipid profile since she was diagnosed with type 1 diabetes 2 years ago and is postpubertal.

KEY POINT

The American Diabetes Association recommends that patients with type 1 diabetes mellitus have a fasting lipid panel performed after puberty or at diagnosis if the diagnosis is established after puberty.

Bibliography

Executive summary: Standards of medical care in diabetes–2013. Diabetes Care.2013; 36 Suppl 1:S4-10. [PMID: 23264424]

Item 19   Answer: D

Educational Objective: *Differentiate type 1 from type 2 diabetes mellitus.*

This patient's blood should be checked for pancreatic autoantibodies, such as islet cell antibodies and glutamic acid decarboxylase antibodies. Although testing for autoantibodies is not always required for patients presenting with clinically apparent type 1 or type 2 diabetes mellitus, some patients may have clinical features consistent with either type, making differentiation difficult. This patient is obese and his mother has type 2 diabetes. Because of his age, however, type 1 diabetes is more likely to present. He may actually have type 1 diabetes presenting at an earlier stage of the disease process (when he still has significant endogenous insulin secretion) because of his obesity and insulin resistance. In young patients with probable diabetes, distinguishing between type 1 and type 2 diabetes is important, as patients with type 1 diabetes will require immediate insulin therapy. Insulin treatment in patients with type 1 diabetes helps preserve endogenous insulin secretion for a longer period of time, which makes it easier to achieve excellent glycemic control without development of hypoglycemia. If testing does not show pancreatic autoantibodies, this patient has type 2 diabetes and should be treated with lifestyle modifications and, possibly, metformin.

Checking this patient's plasma C-peptide level (whether fasting or stimulated) or fasting plasma insulin level may not help distinguish type 1 from type 2 diabetes. A patient who is obese and has hyperglycemia but no ketonuria or acidosis clearly has sufficient endogenous insulin secretion at present. Therefore, this patient's plasma C-peptide and insulin levels will both be high regardless of the type of diabetes present.

KEY POINT

In young patients with probable diabetes mellitus, the distinction between type 1 and type 2 diabetes should be made as soon as possible by checking for the presence of pancreatic autoantibodies, which indicate type 1 disease.

Bibliography
American Diabetes Association. Standards of medical care in diabetes–2013. Diabetes Care. 2013;36 Suppl 1:S11-66. [PMID: 23264422]

Item 20   Answer: C

Educational Objective: *Diagnose type 2 diabetes mellitus.*

This patient is at high risk for diabetes mellitus, and her hemoglobin A_{1c} value should be remeasured. She has a family history of type 2 diabetes and coronary artery disease, is obese, and has hypertension. According to the American Diabetes Association, in the absence of unequivocal symptomatic hyperglycemia, the diagnosis of diabetes must be confirmed on a subsequent day by repeating the same test suggestive of diabetes (in this patient, the hemoglobin A_{1c} measurement). If results of two different diagnostic tests are available and both are diagnostic for diabetes, additional testing is not needed. Although this patient's hemoglobin A_{1c} value is diagnostic of diabetes, her fasting plasma glucose level is only in the range of impaired fasting glucose. Because this patient had two different tests with discordant results, the test that is diagnostic of diabetes (the hemoglobin A_{1c} measurement) should be repeated to confirm the diagnosis.

In this patient without any hyperglycemic symptoms, remeasuring her hemoglobin A_{1c} value is a much simpler and less burdensome way of confirming the diagnosis of diabetes than performing an oral glucose tolerance test.

Because results of measurement of the hemoglobin A_{1c} value and fasting plasma glucose level were discordant, not performing any additional testing is inappropriate.

KEY POINT

If results of two different diagnostic tests for diabetes mellitus are discordant, the test that is diagnostic of diabetes should be repeated.

Bibliography
American Diabetes Association. Standards of medical care in diabetes–2013. Diabetes Care. 2013;36 Suppl 1:S11-66. [PMID: 23264422]

Item 21   Answer: B

Educational Objective: *Manage hypoglycemia in a patient taking a sulfonylurea.*

This patient should stop taking glyburide, as her presenting episodes may be related to hypoglycemia. A hemoglobin A_{1c} value of 6.2% may reflect a level of control in an older patient that may be causing episodes of hypoglycemia, which may be responsible for her recent episodes of confusion and forgetfulness. Because it may take several days after discontinuation for the glyburide to decrease to undetectable levels, checking her clinical symptoms and re-evaluating her plasma glucose level in 2 weeks would also be appropriate.

Although glipizide has fewer hypoglycemically active metabolites and has a shorter half-life than glyburide, it also frequently causes hypoglycemia, particularly in older patients. Additionally, insulin therapy is frequently associated with hypoglycemia, and it would be inappropriate to start a long-acting form of insulin before assessing her possible hypoglycemic episodes. No hypoglycemic agent (glipizide or insulin) should be given to this patient until glyburide is completely cleared from her body, which would then end the cycle of recurrent hypoglycemic episodes. Metformin is generally not associated with hypoglycemia, and it would be reasonable to continue this medication in this patient who has normal kidney function.

KEY POINT

Sulfonylureas, such as glyburide, should be discontinued in patients with suspected symptomatic hypoglycemia.

Bibliography
Greco D, Pisciotta M, Gambina F, Maggio F. Severe hypoglycaemia leading to hospital admission in type 2 diabetic patients aged 80 years or older. Exp Clin Endocrinol Diabetes. 2010;118:215-9. [PMID: 20072965]

Item 22   Answer: C

Educational Objective: *Treat hypoglycemic unawareness.*

This patient's doses of both long-acting and rapid-acting insulin should be decreased by approximately 20%. In some patients with type 1 diabetes mellitus or long-standing type 2 diabetes mellitus, glucose counterregulation may be altered by shifting the sympathoadrenal response to hypoglycemia to a lower blood glucose level, leading to episodes of severe hypoglycemia that may not be recognized by the patient (hypoglycemic unawareness). This effect appears to be exacerbated 48 to 72 hours after a severe episode of hypoglycemia, increasing the likelihood of a second severe episode of hypoglycemia, and thus a vicious circle develops. The best treatment is to reduce the dose of insulin and carefully monitor the blood glucose level for 1 week so that it does not become less than 100 mg/dL (5.6 mmol/L). This intervention allows the body to reset its adrenergic responses.

The options of increasing his carbohydrate intake at meals or decreasing exercise are both inappropriate because of the potential for weight gain.

Switching from insulin glargine to insulin detemir without reducing the dose of insulin is unlikely to be helpful in stopping or reducing this patient's hypoglycemic episodes.

Hypoglycemia is the major rate-limiting factor in attempting tight glycemic control, especially in patients with type 1 diabetes mellitus.

Bibliography

Cryer PE. The barrier of hypoglycemia in diabetes. Diabetes. 2008;57:3169-76. [PMID: 19033403]

Item 23   Answer: B

Educational Objective: *Treat prediabetes with diet and exercise.*

The most appropriate treatment recommendation for this patient with prediabetes is diet and exercise. Patients with glucose levels higher than normal but not meeting the criteria for a diagnosis of diabetes mellitus are considered to have prediabetes. Prediabetes may be diagnosed in the presence of a hemoglobin A_{1c} value of 5.7% to 6.4%, an impaired fasting glucose value (fasting plasma glucose level of 100 to 125 mg/dL [5.7 to 6.9 mmol/L]), or an impaired glucose tolerance test (2-hour postprandial plasma glucose level of 140 to 199 mg/dL [7.8 to 11.0 mmol/L]). Patients with these findings are at significant risk for developing diabetes, and lifestyle changes have been shown to decrease the risk of progression of disease. The relative risk reduction (RRR) in the incidence of diabetes in patients who make intensive lifestyle changes is approximately 60%. These changes include 30 minutes of exercise most days of the week and a calorie-restricted diet to achieve weight reduction of approximately 7% of body weight.

Pharmacologic therapy with glucose-lowering drugs is not indicated for this patient with prediabetes who has not attempted lifestyle changes, although they may be a reasonable alternative in patients who fail to make or are unable to sustain adequate changes.

Acarbose is an α-glucosidase inhibitor that impairs polysaccharide absorption in the intestine, does not cause hypoglycemia, and is relatively weight neutral. However, it has resulted in an approximately 25% RRR for development of diabetes, which is inferior to that obtained with diet and exercise.

Metformin is associated with a RRR of approximately 30% in the incidence of diabetes, which is also less effective than the change possible with diet and exercise.

Orlistat is an oral medication that alters fat digestion in the intestine by inhibiting pancreatic lipases; it is used primarily for weight loss, although it is only modestly effective and has notable gastrointestinal side effects. Although there is some evidence that orlistat may be helpful in decreasing progression to type 2 diabetes mellitus in obese patients, its use in these patients has not been established.

Patients with prediabetes should be advised to adopt a program of lifestyle changes to prevent progression to type 2 diabetes mellitus.

Bibliography

Vijan S. Type 2 diabetes. Ann Intern Med. 2010;152:ITC31-15. [PMID: 20194231]

Item 24   Answer: E

Educational Objective: *Predict potassium shifts during treatment for diabetic ketoacidosis.*

The serum potassium concentrations in this patient with diabetic ketoacidosis were most likely to have been 6.1 mEq/L and 3.0 mEq/L (6.1 mmol/L and 3.0 mmol/L). At the time of presentation, acidosis and dehydration contribute to hyperkalemia. This is compounded by a lack of circulating insulin, which is critical for intracellular potassium movement. Together, these changes frequently produce serum potassium values ranging from 6.0 to 7.0 mEq/L (6.0 to 7.0 mmol/L) at the time of presentation. Because of the presence of hyperkalemia, cardiac monitoring is required.

With hydration to correct volume contraction, the administration of insulin, and resolution of metabolic acidosis, the hyperkalemia will resolve and hypokalemia may develop. Hydration and improvement in the glomerular filtration rate facilitate urine potassium excretion. Insulin therapy will stimulate transfer of potassium from the extracellular to the intracellular space. Together, these cause a rapid drop in the serum potassium concentration within 2 to 6 hours of initial therapy. For almost all patients with diabetic ketoacidosis, effective therapy requires adding potassium to the intravenous fluid when serum potassium concentrations decline to 4.0 to 4.5 mEq/L (4.0 to 4.5 mmol/L). Without potassium supplementation, dangerous levels of hypokalemia may occur.

Diabetic ketoacidosis (DKA) is associated with hyperkalemia, and effective therapy of DKA results in hypokalemia.

Bibliography

Wilson JF. In clinic. Diabetic ketoacidosis. Ann Intern Med. 2010;152:ITC1-1-ITC1-15; quiz ITC1-16. [PMID:20048266]

Item 25   Answer: D

Educational Objective: *Select the appropriate type and route of insulin therapy in a patient with a hyperglycemic emergency.*

Regular insulin by intravenous infusion is the most appropriate therapy for this patient who has type 2 diabetes mellitus and presents with hyperglycemic hyperosmolar syndrome (HHS). He is being appropriately treated with rapid volume resuscitation, which will counteract several of the pathophysiologic processes that maintain and progressively worsen HHS. He also requires insulin to treat the underlying hyperglycemia.

In stable patients, insulin is most commonly delivered subcutaneously. When delivered by this route, insulin must move from the subcutaneous space into the intravascular space to be active. Insulin receptors are located in the muscles, liver, and pancreas – all of which require insulin to be circulated from place of entry via the arteriovenous system. There are many different types of insulin, and nearly all of them differ in the means by which they are absorbed from the subcutaneous space into the intravascular space. For example, neutral protamine Hagedorn insulin is a pentamer of the insulin molecule covalently bound to protamine, which inhibits free insulin release, leading to a long onset of action and prolonged duration of insulin release. In contrast, insulin lispro is a regular insulin molecule chemically modified to remove the disulfide bond between the amino acids lysine and proline, thus allowing for very rapid absorption from the subcutaneous space to the intravascular space.

In this patient who requires emergent rapid lowering of his blood glucose concentration, regular insulin administered intravenously, directly into the circulation, will interact with the insulin receptor almost immediately. As with almost all small peptides, the half-life of insulin is very short, with regular insulin having a half-life of 9 minutes. Therefore, it must be provided as a continuous infusion as opposed to bolus administration for a prolonged effect as would be needed in this patient.

KEY POINT

In patients who require emergent treatment of hyperglycemia, regular insulin by intravenous infusion, rather than subcutaneous insulin administration, is required because onset of action is immediate when the intravenous route is used.

Bibliography

Nucci G, Cobelli C. Models of subcutaneous insulin kinetics. A critical review. Comput Methods Programs Biomed. 2000;62:249-57. [PMID: 10837910]

Item 26   Answer: B

Educational Objective: *Treat hyperglycemic hyperosmolar syndrome with fluid resuscitation.*

The most appropriate initial intravenous fluid therapy for this patient with hyperglycemic hyperosmolar syndrome (HHS) is 0.9% (normal) saline. HHS develops primarily in patients with type 2 diabetes mellitus in the setting of a medical stressor, such as infection. In both diabetic ketoacidosis and HHS, the primary mechanism of disease is a relative deficiency of circulating insulin to adequately counteract hyperglycemia. This relative deficiency is more severe in patients with diabetic ketoacidosis and leads to ketone production, whereas in patients with HHS, insulin secretion is adequate to suppress ketosis but not hyperglycemia. This may lead to marked blood glucose elevation (plasma levels frequently >800 mg/dL [44.4 mmol/L]) due to progressive dehydration that further stimulates compensatory hormone secretion (such as catecholamines), leading to even greater hyperglycemia.

Patients with HHS are typically extremely volume contracted with severe free water and sodium losses, as in this patient who has dry mucous membranes, hypotension, and tachycardia. Intravenous insulin should be given to normalize his blood glucose concentration, but the most immediate concern is administration of intravenous fluids to correct hypotension and severe volume deficit, which is best achieved with 0.9% saline.

Crystalloid fluids are distributed across the extracellular space. Since 0.9% saline is almost isotonic with plasma, more volume stays within the intravascular space than when hypotonic solutions such as 0.45% saline are used, and volume deficit is more rapidly corrected. Therefore, even though this patient has hypernatremia, when his serum sodium concentration is corrected for the degree of hyperglycemia, initial hydration with 0.9% saline is indicated.

After the volume deficit is corrected, the free water deficit may be corrected with administration of 0.45% saline or 5% dextrose with water. Administration of dextrose-containing solutions would not be appropriate for this patient at this time.

KEY POINT

In patients with hyperglycemic hyperosmolar syndrome, the preservation of vascular volume is critical, and 0.9% (normal) saline is the initial intravenous fluid of choice, even before intravenous insulin is administered.

Bibliography

Kitabchi AE, Umpierrez GE, Miles JM, Fisher JN. Hyperglycemic crises in adult patients with diabetes. Diabetes Care. 2009;32:1335-43. [PMID: 19564476]

Item 27   Answer: D

Educational Objective: *Prevent osteoporosis.*

This patient should continue her current lifestyle without changes. Lifestyle modifications and adjustment of modifiable risk factors are the first steps in preventing or treating osteoporosis. Among the modifiable risk factors are adequate amounts of both calcium and vitamin D to maintain bone health. Regular exercise, with attention to weight-bearing exercise; cessation of cigarette smoking; and avoidance of alcohol abuse are other therapeutic lifestyle changes of benefit. This patient does not need any additional tests or therapeutic interventions at this time.

Bisphosphonates such as alendronate bind to the bone matrix and decrease osteoclast activity, thereby slowing bone resorption while new bone formation and mineralization continue. Alendronate has been studied most extensively; over a period of 2 to 3 years it produces a 6% increase in bone density and a 30% to 50% reduction in fracture risk at both vertebral and nonvertebral sites. Because of the cost and risks associated with bisphosphonates, therapy with these drugs should not be initiated until a diagnosis of osteoporosis has been established.

Biochemical markers that measure bone turnover are used in research to help identify the pathophysiology of osteoporosis. There is substantial overlap in these markers in patients with and without osteoporosis, and measurement is not helpful in evaluating an individual's risk of osteoporosis or determining if bone mineral density should be measured.

Measurement of bone mineral density is an essential tool to assess fracture risk. Of the available modalities, dual-energy x-ray absorptiometry (DEXA) has the highest accuracy and precision. The U.S. Preventive Services Task Force recommends screening for osteoporosis with DEXA in all women age 65 years or older and also in younger women with an elevated fracture risk. This patient is less than 65 years old and is not at increased risk for osteoporosis.

KEY POINT

Among the modifiable risk factors for osteoporosis are adequate amounts of both calcium and vitamin D, regular exercise, cessation of cigarette smoking, and avoidance of alcohol abuse.

Bibliography

Lewiecki EM. In the clinic. Osteoporosis. Ann Intern Med. 2011;155:ITC1-1-15; quiz ITC1-16. [PMID: 21727287]

Item 28   Answer: E

Educational Objective: *Treat osteoporosis with an intravenous bisphosphonate.*

The most appropriate therapy for this patient is the intravenous bisphosphonate zoledronic acid. Bisphosphonates bind to the bone matrix and decrease osteoclast activity, thereby slowing bone resorption while new bone formation and mineralization continue. Intravenous bisphosphonates, such as zoledronic acid, are preferred for women with postmenopausal osteoporosis who are unable to take oral bisphosphonates (such as this patient with gastroesophageal reflux disease) or who desire the convenience of less frequent dosing.

However, the costs associated with these drugs and their administration are significantly greater than those of available oral agents.

Esophagitis is a risk of oral bisphosphonate agents, such as alendronate, and these agents are contraindicated in patients with active esophageal disease or swallowing disorders.

The beneficial effects of calcitonin are much less pronounced than those of other antiresorptive agents. Calcitonin injections and nasal spray are approved for the treatment of established osteoporosis but not for its prevention. Calcitonin has been shown to prevent primarily vertebral fractures and is generally safe and well tolerated. However, because of the availability of other safe and more potent drugs, calcitonin is rarely used for osteoporosis treatment except when other options are lacking.

The use of estrogen and progesterone to maintain bone health has fallen out of favor because of data from the Women's Health Initiative indicating that estrogen increases the risk of cardiovascular disease and breast cancer.

Teriparatide (recombinant human parathyroid hormone [1-34]) is currently the only available anabolic agent for osteoporosis therapy in the United States and is generally used in patients with severe osteoporosis (T-score ≤ –3.5), recurrent fractures, or continuing bone loss while taking other medications. Teriparatide has a "black box" warning from the Food and Drug Administration concerning a risk of osteosarcoma, which is based on the increased incidence seen in rats.

KEY POINT

Esophagitis is a risk of oral bisphosphonate agents, such as alendronate, and intravenous bisphosphonate therapy is therefore preferred for patients with esophageal disorders.

Bibliography

Lewiecki EM. In the clinic. Osteoporosis. Ann Intern Med. 2011;155:ITC1-1-15; quiz ITC1-16. [PMID: 21727287]

Item 29   Answer: C

Educational Objective: *Diagnose osteoporosis.*

This patient most likely has osteoporosis. She had a recent vertebral compression fracture in response to minimal or no trauma and decreased bone mineral density on dual-energy x-ray absorptiometry (DEXA) scanning. Osteoporosis is diagnosed by a DEXA T-score of less than –2.5 or the presence of fragility fractures; a fragility fracture defines osteoporosis regardless of bone mineral density results.

Low bone mass is defined as a bone mineral density score that is between 1.0 and 2.5 SD below the young adult mean. Based on this patient's DEXA results and the presence of a vertebral fracture, she meets the criteria for the diagnosis of osteoporosis and not low bone mass.

Osteomalacia is a generalized disorder of bone resulting in decreased mineralization of newly formed osteoid at sites of bone turnover. Although it may be asymptomatic, osteomalacia may present with diffuse bone and joint pain, muscle weakness, and difficulty walking. It most commonly occurs in patients with low levels of vitamin D, hypophosphatemia, hypocalcemia, and increased serum parathyroid hormone and alkaline phosphatase levels. This patient has normal laboratory studies and a focal fragility fracture, making osteomalacia less likely.

Paget disease of bone is a focal disorder of bone metabolism characterized by an accelerated rate of bone remodeling that results in overgrowth of bone at a single or multiple sites and impaired integrity of affected bone. Although Paget disease is usually asymptomatic, if symptoms are present they are usually due to overgrowth of the affected bone, either in the bone itself or from bony overgrowth due to fracture or nerve impingement. The serum alkaline phosphatase level is typically elevated, and radiographs show increased bone density in involved areas, neither of which is present in this patient.

KEY POINT

Osteoporosis is diagnosed by the presence of fragility fractures or by a bone mineral density score less than –2.5 on dual-energy x-ray absorptiometry (DEXA) scanning.

Bibliography

Carriero FP, Christmas C. In the clinic. Hip fracture. Ann Intern Med. 2011;155:ITC6-1-ITC6-15. [PMID: 22147729]

Item 30   Answer: A

Educational Objective: *Treat a woman with low bone mass.*

The most appropriate medication for this patient is alendronate. Although she is younger than the recommended age for osteoporosis screening (age 65 years in average-risk women), her risk factors (family history, low body mass index, and smoking history) are indications for bone mineral density testing. She has low bone mass determined by dual-energy x-ray absorptiometry scan, and her major osteoporotic fracture risk of 22% by the Fracture Risk Assessment Tool (FRAX) is in a range for which the National Osteoporosis Foundation (NOF) guidelines favor treatment with antiosteoporotic therapy. The NOF recommends antiosteoporotic therapy for persons whose risk of major osteoporotic fracture over the next 10 years is 20% or greater or whose risk of hip fracture over the next 10 years is 3% or greater. Given her current FRAX score, it is reasonable to initiate therapy with a bisphosphonate such as alendronate now. Alendronate is approved for both osteoporosis prevention and treatment by the Food and Drug Administration (FDA).

Estrogen is effective in maintaining bone mass in postmenopausal women, and in the past was routinely prescribed for this purpose. However, it is no longer used for prevention or treatment of osteoporosis because of the potential negative effects in these women (thrombosis, breast and endometrial cancer) and the availability of other effective medications.

Raloxifene, a selective estrogen receptor modulator, is also approved for osteoporosis prevention by the FDA. However, vasomotor symptoms are highly associated with its use, and it may not be well tolerated in a patient already experiencing significant hot flushes.

Teriparatide, or recombinant human parathyroid hormone (1-34), is an anabolic agent that increases bone density and decreases fracture risk. However, it is considered second-line therapy to bisphosphonates, is expensive, and has been associated with an increased risk of osteosarcoma.

KEY POINT

Antiosteoporotic therapy should be considered in a patient with low bone mass whose Fracture Risk Assessment Tool (FRAX) risk of major osteoporotic fracture over the next 10 years is 20% or greater or whose risk of hip fracture over the next 10 years is 3% or greater.

Bibliography

Lecart MP, Reginster JY. Current options for the management of postmenopausal osteoporosis. Expert Opin Pharmacother. 2011:2533-52. [PMID: 21916810]

Item 31   Answer: D

Educational Objective: *Evaluate for secondary osteoporosis.*

The most appropriate next step in management is to screen this 55-year-old man for celiac disease as part of the evaluation for secondary causes of his low bone mass and fracture. This patient has a history of fragility fracture (fracture sustained in a fall from a standing height), and his bone density scan shows low bone mass. In an otherwise healthy 55-year-old man, these findings raise concern for a secondary cause of low bone mass and fragility fracture. Fifty percent of men with osteoporosis will have an identifiable cause. Therefore, screening guided by history and physical examination findings may include testing for hypogonadism, vitamin D deficiency, primary hyperparathyroidism, calcium malabsorption, and multiple myeloma. Calcium malabsorption may occur in patients with celiac disease and may cause secondary osteoporosis. Because of this patient's low body mass index, fragility fracture, and anemia (possibly representing iron deficiency), celiac disease is a concern, even if gastrointestinal symptoms are absent.

Initiation of therapy, such as the bisphosphonate alendronate, can be considered after the evaluation for secondary causes is completed and his fracture risk is assessed.

Teriparatide is considered second-line therapy for osteoporosis and would also not be appropriate treatment before evaluation for a secondary cause. All treatments for osteoporosis are more effective once the secondary cause of low bone mass has been corrected.

Repeating the dual-energy x-ray absorptiometry scan in 1 year without any intervention now would allow time for additional bone loss to occur and thus would not be the best management.

KEY POINT

A secondary cause for osteoporosis should be suspected in younger patients, in patients without clear risk factors, and in men.

Bibliography

Bours SP, van Geel TA, Geusens PP, et al. Contributors to secondary osteoporosis and metabolic bone diseases in patients presenting with a clinical fracture. J Clin Endocrinol Metab. 2011;96:1360-7. [PMID: 21411547]

Section 3

Gastroenterology and Hepatology

Questions

Item 1 [Basic]

A 21-year-old woman is evaluated for "gas pains" beginning 7 months ago. The pain has been increasing in frequency with episodes now occurring at least twice each week for the past 3 months. The pain is diffuse and nonradiating, lasts several hours, and is typically relieved with bowel movements. She has two bowel movements weekly, sometimes with lumpy stools and at other times with loose stools. She has not noted any blood in her bowel movements and does not have nocturnal pain or weight loss. Medical history is significant only for occasional episodes of mild depression. She takes no medications. There is no family history of colon cancer or other bowel-related diseases.

On physical examination, vital signs are normal. Body mass index is 26. Abdominal examination discloses normal bowel sounds and no evidence of guarding or rebound tenderness. There is firm stool present in the rectal vault.

Complete blood count is normal.

Which of the following is the most likely diagnosis?

(A) Celiac disease
(B) Crohn disease
(C) Irritable bowel syndrome
(D) Ischemic colitis
(E) Somatization disorder

Item 2 [Advanced]

A 59-year-old woman is evaluated in the emergency department for the acute onset of severe diffuse abdominal pain that began 1 hour ago. She has a history of coronary artery disease and underwent three-vessel coronary artery bypass graft surgery 2 years ago. Current medications are lisinopril, atenolol, simvastatin, and aspirin.

On physical examination, temperature is 36.8°C (98.2°F), blood pressure is 78/56 mm Hg, pulse rate is 142/min, and respiration rate is 29/min. Abdominal examination discloses diffuse mild abdominal tenderness to palpation with no guarding or rebound and no masses.

Laboratory studies reveal a leukocyte count of 14,000/µL (14×10^9/L), a serum bicarbonate level of 14 mEq/L (14 mmol/L), and an elevated serum lactate level.

Computed tomographic scan of the abdomen shows thickening of the small bowel wall and intestinal pneumatosis.

Which of the following is the most likely diagnosis?

(A) Acute mesenteric ischemia
(B) Crohn disease
(C) Intussusception
(D) Pancreatitis

Item 3 [Basic]

A 48-year-old man is evaluated for a 3-day history of left lower quadrant abdominal pain. He rates the pain as 6 on a scale of 1 to 10. His appetite is decreased, but he is able to tolerate oral intake. He is otherwise healthy and has had no previous gastrointestinal problems.

On physical examination, temperature is 38.2°C (100.8°F), blood pressure is 138/78 mm Hg, pulse rate is 103/min, and respiration rate is 14/min. Abdominal examination discloses focal tenderness in the left lower quadrant. There is perirectal fullness.

Laboratory studies reveal a hemoglobin level of 13.5 g/dL (135 g/L) and a leukocyte count of 14,000/µL (14×10^9/L). Urinalysis is normal. Computed tomographic scan of the abdomen and pelvis discloses moderately dense diverticula in the descending colon and proximal sigmoid colon; focal bowel wall thickening (5 mm) in the midsigmoid colon with associated inflammation of the pericolic fat; and no evidence of ileus, obstruction, abscess, or perforation.

Which of the following is the most appropriate initial management for this patient?

(A) Colonoscopy
(B) Intravenous metronidazole and ciprofloxacin
(C) Oral metronidazole and ciprofloxacin
(D) Surgical consultation for segmental colectomy

Item 4 [Basic]

A 25-year-old woman is evaluated for acute abdominal pain that began 6 hours ago. The pain was initially localized to the umbilical area but has now migrated to the right lower quadrant. After the onset of pain, she developed anorexia and vomited once. Medical history is unremarkable. The patient has regular menstrual periods, and her most recent period ended 2 days ago. She is sexually active with one male partner and uses oral contraceptives.

On physical examination, temperature is 39.0°C (102.3°F), blood pressure is 120/90 mm Hg, and pulse rate is 100/min. Abdominal examination reveals normal bowel sounds and tenderness in the right lower quadrant. Pelvic examination discloses tenderness on the right side but no adnexal enlargement or masses. There is no cervical or vaginal discharge or cervical motion tenderness.

The leukocyte count is 10,000/µL (10×10^9/L). Urinalysis shows 20 to 30 leukocytes/high-power field without bacteria. Urine pregnancy test is negative.

Which of the following is the most likely diagnosis?

(A) Acute appendicitis
(B) Pelvic inflammatory disease
(C) Pyelonephritis
(D) Ruptured ectopic pregnancy

Item 5 [Advanced]

A 56-year-old woman is evaluated for an 8-month history of abdominal pain and diarrhea. The pain is localized to the midepigastrium and is worse after eating. She has six to eight bowel movements each day, which usually occur after a meal, and has lost 6.8 kg (15 lb) over the past 6 months. The patient drinks six to eight glasses of vodka daily. Medical history is otherwise unremarkable, and she takes no medications.

On physical examination, the patient is afebrile and the other vital signs are normal. The patient is thin with a body mass index of 21. Abdominal examination discloses midepigastric tenderness but no evidence of hepatosplenomegaly or masses; bowel sounds are normal. Rectal examination reveals brown stool that is negative for occult blood. The remainder of the examination is normal.

Laboratory studies are significant for normal serum aspartate aminotransferase and alanine aminotransferase levels and a serum lipase level of 289 U/L.

Which of the following tests is most likely to establish the diagnosis in this patient?

(A) Colonoscopy
(B) Computed tomography of the abdomen
(C) Testing for celiac disease
(D) Stool for leukocytes, culture, and ova and parasites

Item 6 [Basic]

A 52-year-old man is evaluated for a 3-month history of postprandial fullness, early satiety, vomiting, and epigastric discomfort. He has had these symptoms intermittently for at least 6 months, but for the past 3 months they have occurred with nearly every meal. The symptoms tend to be much worse with large meals, especially dinner. The discomfort is described as a burning sensation that is located in the epigastrium. The patient does not have recent weight loss, dysphagia, odynophagia, or blood in his stool, although he has had several episodes of vomiting associated with his symptoms. He otherwise feels well. Medical history is unremarkable and he currently takes no medications.

Physical examination findings, including vital signs, are normal.

A complete blood count is normal.

Which of the following is the most appropriate management of this patient's symptoms?

(A) Abdominal Computed tomography
(B) Abdominal ultrasonography
(C) Empiric proton pump inhibitor therapy
(D) *Helicobacter pylori* fecal antigen testing
(E) Upper endoscopy

Item 7 [Basic]

A 27-year-old woman is evaluated for a 7-month history of abdominal discomfort after eating. Initially, her discomfort was intermittent, but during the last 4 months it has been present with every meal. The discomfort is described as a sense of fullness over the midepigastric region associated with bloating, and lasts for approximately 1 hour before resolving. Eating smaller meals decreases the intensity and duration of the discomfort. Calcium carbonate antacids and simethicone do not relieve her symptoms. She does not have heartburn, regurgitation, vomiting, belching, dysphagia, odynophagia, diarrhea, or constipation. The patient does not smoke cigarettes or drink alcoholic beverages. She has gained approximately 9 kg (20 lb) over the past year. Medical history is otherwise unremarkable, and she takes no medications.

On physical examination, vital signs are normal. Body mass index is 32. The remainder of the examination, including abdominal examination, is normal.

A complete blood count is normal. A urine pregnancy test is negative.

Which of the following is the most likely diagnosis?

(A) Biliary colic
(B) Dyspepsia
(C) Gastroesophageal reflux disease
(D) Peptic ulcer disease

Item 8 [Advanced]

A 55-year-old woman is evaluated for persistent acid reflux symptoms. Omeprazole daily for 1 month followed by pantoprazole daily for several weeks did not provide significant improvement. The patient does not have dysphagia, odynophagia, or unintentional weight loss. Upper endoscopy performed 4 months ago was normal and did not show evidence of *Helicobacter pylori* infection. A complete blood count done at the time of the upper endoscopy was normal.

Physical examination findings, including vital signs and general examination, are normal.

Which of the following studies should be done next to confirm this patient's most likely diagnosis?

(A) Ambulatory esophageal pH-impedance monitoring
(B) Barium swallow radiography
(C) Esophageal manometry
(D) Repeat *H. pylori* testing

Item 9 [Advanced]

A 60-year-old man is re-evaluated after undergoing upper endoscopy for acid reflux symptoms. The patient has a 15-year history of acid reflux symptoms that occur after meals and at night. He has a 30-pack-year history of smoking and continues to smoke one pack of cigarettes daily.

Proton pump inhibitor (PPI) therapy for reflux symptoms was started 6 weeks ago. His symptoms resolved while he was taking the PPI but returned when he discontinued therapy. He has since resumed taking the PPI. Because of continuing symptoms, upper endoscopy was performed. Endoscopic biopsy specimens showed Barrett esophagus without evidence of dysplasia.

Which of the following is the most appropriate management?

(A) Discontinuation of the PPI
(B) Endoscopic ablative therapy
(C) Fundoplication
(D) Partial esophagectomy
(E) Periodic upper endoscopy surveillance

Item 10 [Basic]

A 32-year-old man is evaluated for a 4-month history of an "upset stomach" that usually occurs after meals. He describes a sense of abdominal fullness and bloating associated with eating. He also has heartburn symptoms after meals at least four times each week. He has not had pain, difficulty swallowing, vomiting, weight loss, altered stool habits, or blood in the stool. There is no family history of gastrointestinal malignancy. He occasionally takes an over-the-counter H_2 receptor antagonist antacid that temporarily improves his symptoms.

On physical examination, vital signs are normal. Abdominal examination discloses a nontender epigastrium and no masses or lymphadenopathy.

A complete blood count is normal.

Which of the following is the most appropriate management?

(A) H_2 receptor antagonist therapy
(B) Proton pump inhibitor therapy
(C) Test for *Helicobacter pylori* and treat if positive
(D) Upper endoscopy

Item 11 [Basic]

A 40-year-old woman is evaluated for a 1-year history of reflux symptoms. She has heartburn and regurgitation of gastric contents several times each week. Lifestyle modification and an empiric trial of once-daily proton pump inhibitor (PPI) therapy were begun 12 weeks ago with minimal relief of symptoms. For the past 6 weeks she has taken the PPI twice daily, also with minimal symptom relief. The patient also has had intermittent solid-food dysphagia. She appears to be adherent to her lifestyle modification program and medical therapy.

Physical examination findings, including vital signs, are normal.

Which of the following is the most appropriate next step in management?

(A) Addition of an H_2 receptor antagonist at night
(B) Ambulatory esophageal pH monitoring
(C) Fundoplication
(D) Upper endoscopy

Item 12 [Basic]

A 32-year-old man is evaluated because of a 5-week history of midepigastric abdominal pain. He also notes progressive nausea, vomiting, early satiety, and a documented weight loss of 2.7 kg (6 lb) during this time. Over the past 10 days, he has been using an over-the-counter proton pump inhibitor (PPI) once daily with only minimal improvement in his pain. Medical history is unremarkable, and he takes no prescription medications. He does not use tobacco, alcohol, or recreational drugs.

On physical examination, vital signs are normal. The abdomen is soft with mild tenderness in the epigastric area with deep palpation. The remainder of the examination is unremarkable.

Which of the following is the most appropriate next step in management?

(A) A PPI twice daily for 4 weeks
(B) Omeprazole, clarithromycin, and amoxicillin
(C) Upper gastrointestinal barium study
(D) Upper endoscopy

Item 13 [Advanced]

A 58-year-old woman is evaluated during a follow-up examination. The patient was evaluated in the emergency department 8 weeks ago because of progressively worsening epigastric pain. Upper endoscopy showed a 4-mm duodenal ulcer; biopsy specimens revealed mild gastritis with no evidence of malignancy. Histologic evaluation of the tissue showed infection with *Helicobacter pylori*.

She was treated with a 14-day course of omeprazole, clarithromycin, and amoxicillin followed by an additional 2 weeks of omeprazole alone. Her symptoms resolved at the completion of therapy. Medical history is otherwise unremarkable, and she is currently taking no medications.

On physical examination, vital signs are normal. The abdomen is soft without midepigastric tenderness. The remainder of the examination is unremarkable.

Which of the following is the most appropriate next step in management?

(A) Fecal *H. pylori* antigen testing
(B) Proton pump inhibitor therapy for at least 6 months
(C) Repeat upper endoscopy
(D) No additional testing or treatment

Item 14 [Basic]

A 66-year-old woman is evaluated for a 1-month history of abdominal discomfort. She describes a deeply painful sensation in the midepigastric region and also notes early satiety. Because of decreased appetite, she reports a 1.4-kg (3-lb) weight loss. The patient has taken an over-the-counter proton pump inhibitor for the past week that has helped relieve her symptoms. Medical history is otherwise unremarkable, and she takes no other medications.

On physical examination, vital signs are normal. The abdomen is soft with normal bowel sounds and no masses. Deep palpation in the midepigastrium produces moderate tenderness.

Upper endoscopy reveals a 9-mm ulcer in the gastric antrum proximal to the pylorus.

Which of the following is the most appropriate management for this patient's ulcer?

(A) Biopsy of the ulcer
(B) Omeprazole, amoxicillin, and clarithromycin
(C) Rapid urease test
(D) Urea breath test

Item 15 [Advanced]

A 65-year-old woman is evaluated 1 week after undergoing upper endoscopy for persistent abdominal pain. The study showed a 1-cm, clean-based ulcer in the duodenum. Biopsy specimens from the stomach showed no evidence of *Helicobacter pylori* infection, and a serum antibody test for *H. pylori* was also negative. Proton pump inhibitor therapy was started, and the patient's symptoms were alleviated. She has a history of mild osteoarthritis and osteoporosis. Medications are a nonprescription analgesic for arthritis and a calcium supplement, vitamin D, and alendronate.

On physical examination, vital signs are normal. The abdominal examination reveals no tenderness, hepatomegaly, or palpable masses.

A complete blood count is normal.

Which of the following is the most appropriate next step in this patient's management?

(A) Measure the serum gastrin level
(B) Repeat upper endoscopy with biopsy of the ulcer
(C) Review the nonprescription arthritis analgesic
(D) Stop alendronate therapy

Item 16 [Basic]

An 18-year-old man is evaluated because of slight yellowing of his eyes. He developed an upper respiratory tract infection 5 days ago with fever, sore throat, and malaise. Medical history is otherwise unremarkable. He does not smoke or use alcohol or illicit drugs and takes no prescription or over-the-counter medications.

On physical examination, temperature is 37.8°C (100.0°F). Other vital signs are normal. Significant findings include slight yellowing of the conjunctivae and mild pharyngeal erythema. Abdominal examination reveals a normal-sized liver without tenderness; there is no splenomegaly. The remainder of the examination is normal.

Laboratory studies:

Hemoglobin	14 g/dL (140 g/L)
Leukocyte count	12,000/µL (12 × 10⁹/L)
Alkaline phosphatase	75 U/L
Aspartate aminotransferase	28 U/L
Alanine aminotransferase	20 U/L
Bilirubin, total	3.6 mg/dL (62 µmol/L)
Bilirubin, direct	0.3 mg/dL (5.1 µmol/L)

Which of the following is the most likely diagnosis?

(A) Acute cholecystitis
(B) Acute hepatitis A
(C) Autoimmune hemolytic anemia
(D) Gilbert syndrome

Item 17 [Basic]

A 59-year-old woman is evaluated because of yellow discoloration of her eyes. This finding has been present for several weeks. Her only other symptom is mild fatigue. Medical history is otherwise noncontributory. She does not smoke or drink alcoholic beverages and takes no prescription or over-the-counter medications.

On physical examination, temperature is normal, blood pressure is 132/70 mm Hg, pulse rate is 85/min, and respiration rate is 12/min. There is mild scleral icterus. The liver is nontender and of normal size, and there is no splenomegaly. The remainder of the examination is normal.

Laboratory studies:

Alkaline phosphatase	375 U/L
Aspartate aminotransferase	45 U/L
Alanine aminotransferase	60 U/L
Bilirubin, total	4.1 mg/dL (70 µmol/L)
Bilirubin, direct	3.1 mg/dL (53 µmol/L)

Which of the following is the most appropriate diagnostic study to perform next?

(A) Abdominal ultrasonography
(B) Endoscopic retrograde cholangiopancreatography
(C) Liver biopsy
(D) Magnetic resonance cholangiopancreatography

Item 18 [Basic]

A 26-year-old man is evaluated for a 13-day history of fatigue, anorexia, and nausea. He also has fever, jaundice, and right upper quadrant abdominal pain that began 2 days ago. The patient has just returned from a 3-month trip to rural Mexico. He has no history of any recent sexual contacts, use of illicit drugs, blood transfusions, tattoos, or tobacco or alcohol use. He has always been in good health and takes no medications. He is unsure about his routine immunization status and did not receive any vaccines prior to travel.

On physical examination, temperature is 37.2°C (99.0°F), blood pressure is 120/86 mm Hg, pulse rate is 86/min, and respiration rate is 18/min. Body mass index is 25. Scleral icterus is present, and the liver is enlarged and tender. The remainder of the examination is unremarkable.

Laboratory studies show a serum alanine aminotransferase level of 1000 U/L, a serum aspartate aminotransferase level of 1150 U/L, and a serum total bilirubin level of 6 mg/dL (103 µmol/L).

Which of the following is the most likely diagnosis?

(A) Hepatitis A
(B) Hepatitis B
(C) Hepatitis C
(D) Hepatitis D
(E) Hepatitis E

Item 19 [Basic]

A 50-year-old man is evaluated for an insurance physical examination. The patient is well and takes no medications. He does not smoke, drink alcoholic beverages, or use illicit drugs and has been in a monogamous relationship with his wife of 25 years. He has never had a blood transfusion or a tattoo. Family history is significant for diabetes mellitus and hypertension.

On physical examination, vital signs are normal. Body mass index is 35. There is an easily palpable, nontender liver edge. The remainder of the examination is normal.

Laboratory studies:

Glucose, fasting	136 mg/dL (7.55 mmol/L)
Alanine aminotransferase	80 U/L
Aspartate aminotransferase	130 U/L
Bilirubin, total	1.5 mg/dL (26 μmol/L)
Total cholesterol	280 mg/dL (7.24 mmol/L)
Low-density lipoprotein cholesterol	160 mg/dL (4.4 mmol/L)
High-density lipoprotein cholesterol	40 mg/dL (1.03 mmol/L)
Triglycerides	400 mg/dL (4.52 mmol/L)
Hepatitis A, B, and C serology	Negative

Abdominal ultrasonography reveals fatty infiltration of the liver.

In addition to beginning statin therapy, which of the following is the most appropriate initial management?

(A) Metformin

(B) Pioglitazone

(C) Therapeutic diet and lifestyle modification

(D) Vitamin E

Item 20 [Basic]

A 32-year-old woman is evaluated for a 10-day history of malaise, right upper quadrant abdominal discomfort, and progressive jaundice. She has no recent travel history, does not drink alcoholic beverages or use illicit drugs, and takes no prescription or over-the-counter medications. She has no other medical problems.

On physical examination, the patient is awake and alert. Temperature is 37.5°C (99.5°F), blood pressure is 106/68 mm Hg, pulse rate is 90/min, and respiration rate is 18/min. Scleral icterus is noted, and the liver is enlarged and tender. The remainder of the examination is normal.

Laboratory studies:

International normalized ratio	0.9 (normal range, 0.8-1.2)
Albumin	3.8 g/dL (38 g/L)
Alkaline phosphatase	220 U/L
Alanine aminotransferase	920 U/L
Aspartate aminotransferase	850 U/L
Bilirubin, total	14.4 mg/dL (246.2 μmol/L)
Bilirubin, direct	10.6 mg/dL (181.3 μmol/L)

Abdominal ultrasonography shows hepatic enlargement. There is no bile duct dilatation, and the portal vein and spleen are normal.

Which of the following is the most likely diagnosis?

(A) Acute viral hepatitis

(B) Fulminant liver failure

(C) Hemochromatosis

(D) Primary biliary cirrhosis

Item 21 [Advanced]

A 42-year-old woman is evaluated because of a 2-week history of jaundice, low-grade fever, and fatigue. Medical history is notable for significant alcohol use, estimated at approximately 10 cans of beer daily for the past 20 years. She has no history of injection drug use, blood transfusions, or known exposure to anyone with hepatitis. Medical history is otherwise unremarkable. Her only medication is acetaminophen, 500 mg/d, for the past 3 days to treat fatigue.

On physical examination, temperature is 37.9°C (100.2°F), blood pressure is 110/70 mm Hg, and pulse rate is 100/min. Jaundice, spider angiomata, and mild muscle wasting are noted. Abdominal examination shows mild splenomegaly, a slightly enlarged and tender liver, and no ascites.

Laboratory studies:

Hemoglobin	12.8 g/dL (128 g/L)
Leukocyte count	3400/μL (3.4 × 10⁹/L)
Platelet count	99,000/μL (99 × 10⁹/L)
International normalized ratio	1.2 (normal range, 0.8-1.2)
Aspartate aminotransferase	124 U/L
Alanine aminotransferase	57 U/L
Bilirubin, total	6.2 mg/dL (106 μmol/L)
Bilirubin, direct	3.8 mg/dL (65 μmol/L)
Albumin	3.4 g/dL (34 g/L)

Which of the following is the most likely diagnosis?

(A) Acetaminophen hepatotoxicity

(B) Alcoholic hepatitis

(C) Autoimmune hepatitis

(D) Hepatitis A

Item 22 [Advanced]

A 55-year-old man is evaluated during a follow-up examination. Chronic hepatitis C virus (HCV) infection was recently diagnosed following routine screening. The patient feels well and has no symptoms. Medical history is otherwise unremarkable. He does not smoke or use alcohol or tobacco products. He takes no medications.

On physical examination, temperature is 36.8°C (98.2°F), blood pressure is 135/82 mm Hg, pulse rate is 66/min, and respiration rate is 16/min. The liver is of normal size to percussion, and there is no splenomegaly. There is no evidence of ascites and no stigmata of chronic liver disease.

Results of HCV serologic testing are positive. Abdominal ultrasonography shows a normal-appearing liver. Liver biopsy discloses mild inflammation and advanced fibrosis without evidence of cirrhosis.

Which of the following is the most appropriate management?

(A) Antiviral therapy

(B) Glucocorticoids

(C) Repeat liver biopsy in 1 year

(D) Serial aminotransferase monitoring

Item 23 [Advanced]

A 26-year-old woman is evaluated during a follow-up examination. Hepatitis B virus (HBV) was detected as part of a health examination following her recent emigration from Southeast Asia to the United States. The patient has no known history of hepatitis. Medical history is unremarkable. She does not smoke, drink alcoholic beverages, or take any medications.

On physical examination, vital signs are normal. There is no evidence of jaundice. Abdominal examination discloses a normal liver. There is no splenomegaly or stigmata of chronic liver disease.

Laboratory studies:

Aspartate aminotransferase	Normal
Alanine aminotransferase	Normal
Hepatitis B virus (HBV) serology:	
Hepatitis B surface antigen	Positive
Antibody to hepatitis B surface antigen	Negative
Hepatitis B core antibody	Positive
Hepatitis B e antigen	Positive
Antibody to hepatitis B e antigen	Negative
HBV DNA	Positive

Which of the following is the most appropriate next step in management?

(A) Antiviral therapy

(B) Hepatitis B immunization

(C) Liver biopsy

(D) Serial aminotransferase monitoring

Item 24 [Advanced]

A 45-year-old man is evaluated in the emergency department because of abdominal pain. He describes the pain as diffuse and constant. For the past month, he has had yellow discoloration of his eyes and skin, abdominal distention, and a 9.7-kg (20-lb) weight gain. There has been no fever, nausea, vomiting, or change in bowel habits. Medical history is otherwise unremarkable and he takes no medications. He drinks 6 cans of beer daily.

On physical examination, temperature is 37.7°C (99.9°F), blood pressure is 110/75 mm Hg, pulse rate is 90/min, and respiration rate is 12/min. The sclerae are icteric and the skin is jaundiced. The abdomen is distended and diffusely tender. Shifting dullness and a fluid wave are present.

A diagnostic paracentesis was performed.

Laboratory studies:

Ascitic fluid

Leukocytes	450/µL (450 × 10⁶/L), with 90% neutrophils, 5% lymphocytes, 5% macrophages
Albumin	1.0 mg/dL (10 g/L)
Serum albumin	3.2 mg/dL (32 g/L)

Which of the following is the most likely cause of this patient's abdominal pain?

(A) Malignant peritonitis

(B) Peritonitis from a perforated bowel

(C) Spontaneous bacterial peritonitis

(D) Tuberculous peritonitis

Item 25 [Basic]

A 55-year-old woman is evaluated because of new-onset yellow discoloration of her eyes and skin and brown urine. The patient also notes progressive abdominal distention for the past month associated with a 6.8-kg (15-lb) weight gain. She reports no abdominal pain, change in bowel habits, pruritus, fever, or recent travel. She has a 25-pack-year history of smoking and continues to smoke 1 pack of cigarettes each day. She has consumed 2 to 4 glasses of wine each day

for the past 12 years. Medical history is unremarkable, and she takes no medications.

On physical examination, vital signs are normal. The sclerae are icteric, and the skin appears jaundiced. Multiple spider angiomata are present over the upper chest and shoulders. The abdomen is distended and nontender with shifting dullness. There is pitting edema of both ankles.

Which of the following is the most likely cause of the patient's jaundice?

(A) Biliary tree obstruction

(B) Cirrhosis

(C) Hemolysis

(D) Hepatic vein thrombosis

Item 26 [Advanced]

A 55-year-old man is evaluated during a routine follow-up examination. The patient has compensated cirrhosis and is currently asymptomatic. Medical history is significant for chronic hepatitis B virus infection and esophageal varices. His only current medication is propranolol.

On physical examination, temperature is 37.6°C (99.7°F), blood pressure is 120/70 mm Hg, pulse rate is 68/min, and respiration rate is 16/min. Spider angiomata are present on the neck and upper chest. The spleen tip is palpable.

Screening abdominal ultrasonography discloses a nodular-appearing liver, splenomegaly, and changes consistent with portal hypertension. A 1.6-cm lesion is noted in the right hepatic lobe; the lesion was not present on an ultrasound examination done 6 months ago.

Which of the following is the most appropriate diagnostic test to perform next?

(A) Contrast-enhanced computed tomography of the abdomen

(B) Liver biopsy

(C) Repeat ultrasonography in 6 months

(D) Serum carcinoembryonic antigen measurement

Item 27 [Basic]

A 45-year-old man is evaluated in the emergency department for lethargy and disorientation. The patient has a history of alcoholic cirrhosis complicated by ascites and hepatic encephalopathy. Medications are spironolactone, propranolol, and lactulose. He has been abstinent from alcohol for 1 year.

On physical examination, the patient is somnolent but arousable. Temperature is normal, blood pressure is 100/78 mm Hg, pulse rate is 65/min, and respiration rate is 12/min. Abdominal examination discloses shifting dullness. A stool sample is negative for occult blood. There are no focal neurologic deficits.

Laboratory studies:

Electrolytes	Normal
Creatinine	1.8 mg/dL (159.1 µmol/L)
Bilirubin, total	4.0 mg/dL (68.4 µmol/L)
Ammonia	230 µg/dL (135 µmol/L)
Urinalysis	30 leukocytes/high-power field, positive leukocyte esterase

Noncontrast computed tomographic scan of the head is normal. Diagnostic paracentesis is negative for ascitic fluid findings indicative of spontaneous bacterial peritonitis.

Diuretics are discontinued, and empiric antibiotic therapy is started.

Which of the following is the most appropriate additional treatment for this patient?

(A) Glucocorticoids
(B) Hemodialysis
(C) Increased lactulose therapy
(D) Transjugular intrahepatic portosystemic shunt

Item 28 [Basic]

A 47-year-old man is admitted to the hospital because of ascites and abdominal pain. The patient has alcoholic cirrhosis. Medications are propranolol, lactulose, spironolactone, and furosemide.

On physical examination, temperature is 37.2°C (99.0°F), blood pressure is 120/60 mm Hg, pulse rate is 56/min, and respiration rate is 16/min. Tense ascites is present, and the abdomen is tender to palpation. The remainder of the examination is normal.

The admission serum creatinine level is 0.8 mg/dL (70.7 µmol/L). Ascitic fluid obtained by diagnostic paracentesis reveals 350 leukocytes/µL (350×10^6/L). Cefotaxime and albumin infusions are begun for a diagnosis of spontaneous bacterial peritonitis.

On hospital day 3, the patient is oliguric. Laboratory studies reveal a serum creatinine level of 2.0 mg/dL (176.8 µmol/L) and a random urine sodium level of 10 mEq/L (10 mmol/L). Furosemide and spironolactone are discontinued and infusions of 0.9% saline and albumin are begun, but the patient remains oliguric.

Ultrasonography shows normal kidney size and no hydronephrosis.

Which of the following is the most likely cause of this patient's clinical findings?

(A) Hepatorenal syndrome
(B) Obstructive nephropathy
(C) Prerenal azotemia
(D) Renal artery stenosis

Item 29 [Advanced]

A 50-year-old man is evaluated during a follow-up examination. Cirrhosis secondary to nonalcoholic steatohepatitis was recently diagnosed. Medical history is significant for asthma, type 2 diabetes mellitus, hyperlipidemia, and obesity. Current medications are inhaled fluticasone, montelukast, insulin glargine, insulin lispro, simvastatin, and lisinopril.

On physical examination, temperature is 37.5°C (99.5°F), blood pressure is 120/70 mm Hg, pulse rate is 80/min, and respiration rate is 16/min. Body mass index is 31. Mild diffuse wheezing is noted on lung examination. Abdominal examination reveals a palpable spleen tip.

Laboratory studies are significant for a serum total bilirubin level of 1.2 mg/dL (20.5 µmol/L), a platelet count of 100,000/µL (100×10^9/L), and a normal international normalized ratio.

Upper endoscopy shows large (>5 mm) distal esophageal varices.

Which of the following is the most appropriate treatment?

(A) Endoscopic sclerotherapy
(B) Endoscopic variceal band ligation
(C) Propranolol
(D) Transjugular intrahepatic portosystemic shunt

Item 30 [Basic]

A 47-year-old woman is evaluated following a recent emergency department visit. She was involved in a motor vehicle accident and experienced abdominal pain following the accident. Bedside ultrasonography in the emergency department showed no evidence of intra-abdominal trauma, but did show gallstones without evidence of bile duct dilatation. Prior to the motor vehicle accident she had no episodes of abdominal pain, nausea, or vomiting.

On physical examination, vital signs are normal. Body mass index is 34. Abdominal examination is normal, and the remainder of the examination is unremarkable except for obesity.

Which of the following is the most appropriate management of this patient's gallstones?

(A) Cholecystectomy
(B) Prophylactic weight loss
(C) Repeat abdominal ultrasonography in 6 months
(D) Ursodeoxycholic acid
(E) Observation

Item 31 [Advanced]

A 37-year-old man is evaluated for a 6-month history of generalized pruritus and fatigue. He has a 12-year history of ulcerative colitis treated with sulfasalazine. He does not drink alcoholic beverages or smoke cigarettes and has no other medical problems.

On physical examination, vital signs are normal. He is jaundiced, and excoriations are present on his anterior legs, forearms, and back. The remainder of the examination is normal.

Laboratory studies reveal a serum alkaline phosphatase level of 270 U/L, serum total bilirubin level of 3.5 mg/dL (60 µmol/L), and serum direct bilirubin level of 3.1 mg/dL (53 µmol/L).

Findings on endoscopic retrograde cholangiopancreatography are consistent with the diagnosis of primary sclerosing cholangitis.

Which of the following two cancers is this patient at most increased risk for developing?

(A) Cholangiocarcinoma and colorectal cancer
(B) Cholangiocarcinoma and duodenal cancer
(C) Colorectal cancer and hepatocellular carcinoma
(D) Esophageal cancer and pancreatic cancer

Item 32 [Basic]

A 35-year-old woman is evaluated because of acute abdominal pain, nausea, and vomiting of 6 hours' duration. The pain began in the midepigastrium 2 hours after eating and is now centered in the right upper abdominal quadrant. The patient has previously had similar but less intense episodes that she attributed to heartburn. She is otherwise healthy, she has two children, and her only medication is an oral contraceptive.

On physical examination, she appears uncomfortable. Temperature is 37.7°C (99.9°F), blood pressure is 130/80 mm Hg, pulse rate is 100/min, and the respiration rate is 14/min. Body mass index is 33. Abdominal examination reveals right upper quadrant tenderness, and palpation in the right upper quadrant causes inspiratory arrest when she is asked to take a deep breath. There are no peritoneal signs. Pelvic examination is normal.

Laboratory studies:

Leukocyte count	13,000/µL (13×10^9/L)
Alkaline phosphatase	300 U/L
Aspartate aminotransferase	50 U/L
Alanine aminotransferase	80 U/L
Bilirubin, total	3 mg/dL (51 µmol/L)
Amylase	Normal
Lipase	Normal

Urine pregnancy test is negative.

Which of the following is the most appropriate next step in the evaluation of this patient?

(A) Abdominal ultrasonography
(B) Computed tomographic of the abdomen and pelvis
(C) Endoscopic retrograde cholangiopancreatography
(D) Hepato-iminodiacetic acid scanning

Item 33 [Advanced]

An 80-year-old woman is evaluated in the emergency department. Her daughter, who accompanied her, reports that she has had increasing somnolence and has not "been acting normally" for several hours. The patient has hypertension and type 2 diabetes mellitus. Current medications are lisinopril, pravastatin, aspirin, and metformin.

On physical examination, the patient is lethargic and disoriented. Temperature is 38.3°C (101.0°F), blood pressure is 110/62 mm Hg, pulse rate is 100/min, and the respiration rate is 16/min. Jaundice is present. The right upper abdominal quadrant is tender to palpation without guarding. The remainder of the examination is unremarkable. Other than her altered mental status, her neurologic examination is nonfocal.

Laboratory studies:

Leukocyte count	18,600/µL (18.6×10^9/L), with 86% segmented neutrophils
Alkaline phosphatase	260 U/L
Aspartate aminotransferase	186 U/L
Alanine aminotransferase	230 U/L
Bilirubin, total	4.1 mg/dL (70 µmol/L)

Abdominal ultrasonography shows a normal liver, a common bile duct caliber of 9 mm (normal <6 mm), multiple gallstones, and no evidence of gallbladder wall thickening or pericholecystic fluid.

Broad-spectrum antibiotics are begun.

Which of the following is the most likely diagnosis?

(A) Acute hepatitis A
(B) Cholangitis
(C) Cholecystitis
(D) Pancreatitis

Item 34 [Basic]

A 34-year-old man is evaluated in the hospital. The patient was admitted because of acute pancreatitis secondary to alcohol abuse. His admission amylase was 520 units/L. He was treated with complete bowel rest, intravenous fluids, and as-needed opioid analgesics. Thirty-six hours after admission, his pain is much improved and the nausea and vomiting have resolved. He states that he is hungry.

On physical examination, vital signs are normal. Abdominal examination reveals decreased bowel sounds and no tenderness to palpation. The remainder of the physical examination is unremarkable.

Which of the following is the most appropriate next step in management?

(A) Begin nasoenteral feeding
(B) Continue bowel rest for 24 hours
(C) Obtain abdominal computed tomographic scan
(D) Repeat serum amylase measurement
(E) Resume oral intake

Item 35 [Advanced]

A 52-year-old man is evaluated in the hospital. The patient was admitted yesterday for treatment of acute pancreatitis secondary to alcohol abuse. He has remained symptomatic for 24 hours.

On physical examination, he is lying on his side with his knees drawn to his chest. Vital signs include a temperature of 38.1°C (100.6°F), blood pressure is 144/82 mm Hg, pulse rate is 102/min, and respiration rate is 14/min. Oxygen saturation on ambient air is 94%. The oral mucosa is dry. Abdominal examination discloses decreased bowel sounds and epigastric tenderness. The remainder of the examination is normal.

Laboratory studies:

Leukocyte count	11,000/µL (11×10^9/L)
Hematocrit	30%
Blood urea nitrogen	64 mg/dL (22.8 mmol/L)
Creatinine	3.1 mg/dL (53 µmol/L)
Amylase	657 U/L

Abdominal ultrasonography shows no gallstones or dilatation of the common bile duct.

Which of the following is most predictive of a poor outcome in this patient?

(A) Amylase level
(B) Anemia
(C) Blood urea nitrogen level
(D) Leukocytosis

Item 36 [Basic]

A 42-year-old woman is evaluated during a follow-up examination. The patient was hospitalized 8 weeks ago for acute pancreatitis due to gallstone disease. Imaging studies at that time showed gallstones but no evidence of a fluid collection or necrosis in the pancreas. She had an uncomplicated cholecystectomy prior to discharge. She has had no recurrent symptoms since discharge.

Two weeks ago, she was evaluated for nephrolithiasis following an episode of renal colic. A computed tomographic scan at that time showed a kidney stone in the right ureter and a 6-cm well-defined fluid collection in the pancreatic tail without other abnormalities. She has since passed the kidney stone and is asymptomatic.

On physical examination today, temperature is 37.2°C (99.0°F), blood pressure is 112/72 mm Hg, pulse rate is 66/min, and respiration rate is 18/min. No tenderness or masses are noted on abdominal examination. The remainder of the examination is normal.

Which of the following is the most appropriate next step in management?

(A) Magnetic resonance cholangiopancreatography
(B) Percutaneous drainage of the fluid collection
(C) Surgical drainage of the fluid collection
(D) No further diagnostic testing or therapy

Item 37 [Basic]

A 34-year-old woman is evaluated for a 1-day history of watery diarrhea and abdominal cramps. She has had four watery stools today but has not had fever or blood in her stool. She has been able to stay hydrated with oral intake. Several colleagues at work have had similar symptoms recently. The patient has not been recently hospitalized, has not traveled, and has not taken any antibiotics recently. She has no risk factors for HIV infection. Her medical history is otherwise unremarkable and she takes no medications. On physical examination, temperature is 36.1°C (97.0°F), blood pressure is 110/75 mm Hg, pulse rate is 86/min, and respiration rate is 12/min. Mucous membranes are moist. There is mild abdominal tenderness but no guarding or rebound; bowel sounds are normal. A urine pregnancy test is negative.

Which of the following is the most appropriate next diagnostic test?

(A) *Clostridium difficile* polymerase chain reaction
(B) Fecal leukocyte testing
(C) Flexible sigmoidoscopy with biopsies
(D) Stool culture
(E) No additional studies

Item 38 [Basic]

A 35-year-old woman is evaluated for diarrhea of 5 months' duration. Her stools are foul smelling, tan-colored, and bulky and float in the toilet bowl water. She also reports postprandial bloating and a 6.8-kg (15-lb) weight loss during this time. Iron deficiency anemia was diagnosed 6 months ago. Medical history is also significant for Hashimoto thyroiditis. Medications are levothyroxine and ferrous sulfate. There is no family history of anemia, prolonged diarrhea, inflammatory bowel disease, or colon cancer.

On physical examination, vital signs are normal. Body mass index is 20. Abdominal examination disclosed minimal midepigastric tenderness. A stool sample is negative for occult blood. The remainder of the examination is normal.

Complete blood count reveals a microcytic, hypochromic anemia. The serum ferritin level is decreased, and the serum thyroid-stimulating hormone level is slightly elevated.

Which of the following is the most appropriate diagnostic test to perform next?

(A) Colonoscopy
(B) *HLA-DQ2* or *HLA-DQ8* testing
(C) Tissue transglutaminase IgA antibody assay
(D) No additional studies

Item 39 [Basic]

A 74-year-old woman is evaluated in the emergency department for a 2-day history of abdominal pain and diarrhea. She has had 10 bowel movements daily with worsening abdominal pain and fever. Three weeks ago, the patient was hospitalized for a skin infection that was treated with antibiotics. She was discharged on oral antibiotics, which she completed taking 1 week ago. Medical history is otherwise unremarkable, and she takes no regular medications.

On physical examination, temperature is 38.6°C (101.5°F), blood pressure is 90/55 mm Hg, pulse rate is 122/min, and respiration rate is 24/min. The abdomen is distended and tender to palpation; bowel sounds are absent.

Laboratory studies indicate a leukocyte count of 32,500/µL (32.5 × 10^9/L). Stool, blood, and urine samples are obtained for culture.

Which of the following is the most likely diagnosis?

(A) *Clostridium difficile* infection
(B) Crohn disease
(C) Diverticulitis
(D) Diverticulosis
(E) Ischemic colitis

Item 40 [Advanced]

An 88-year-old woman is evaluated in the emergency department because of malaise, fever, abdominal pain, and profuse diarrhea of 3 days' duration. She has also had vomiting of 1 day's duration. The patient reports one previous episode of mild *Clostridium difficile* infection, treated successfully with oral metronidazole.

On physical examination, temperature is 39.0°C (102.2°F), blood pressure is 125/65 mm Hg, pulse rate is 105/min, and respiration rate is 16/min. Abdominal examination discloses diffuse tenderness with rebound and decreased bowel sounds but no ascites.

Laboratory studies are significant for a leukocyte count of 27,300/µL (27.3 × 10^9/L). Plain radiographs of the abdomen reveal air throughout the intestine without evidence of ileus or free intraperitoneal air. Enzyme immunoassay for *C. difficile* toxins A and B is positive.

Which of the following is the most appropriate treatment?

(A) Colectomy
(B) Intravenous metronidazole
(C) Oral vancomycin
(D) Vancomycin per rectum

Item 41 [Advanced]

A 37-year-old woman is evaluated for diarrhea. The diarrhea has been present since she developed a presumed food-borne illness 1 month ago, when she had nausea, vomiting, and watery diarrhea for 2 days. Although her symptoms improved after several days, she has continued to have episodic diarrhea with three to four watery stools each day, often following meals. She also has had excessive flatus and bloating over the past month but no nocturnal stools, weight loss, fever, or blood in her stool. She has not recently required antibiotics. Medical history is notable for a cholecystectomy performed 2 years ago.

On physical examination, vital signs are normal. Abdominal examination discloses normal bowel sounds and a nontender abdomen. Rectal examination is normal.

A complete blood count, stool cultures, stool examination for ova and parasites, and tests for *Clostridium difficile* are negative. Stool osmotic gap is 170 mOsm/kg (170 mmol/kg).

Which of the following is the most likely diagnosis?

(A) Bile-salt-induced diarrhea
(B) Irritable bowel syndrome
(C) Lactose malabsorption
(D) Microscopic colitis

Item 42 [Advanced]

A 38-year-old man is evaluated for a 3-month history of abdominal bloating and increased frequency of defecation. He has four to six loose bowel movements a day, including nocturnal bowel movements, without abdominal pain. Medical history is significant for a Roux-en-Y gastric bypass procedure 2 years ago for severe obesity; his weight loss stabilized 1 year ago, although he has lost an additional 4.5 kg (10 lb) in the past few months. Medications are daily iron and vitamin B_{12} supplements and a multivitamin.

On physical examination, vital signs are normal. Cardiopulmonary examination is normal. The abdomen is not distended or tender, and bowel sounds are normal.

Laboratory studies are normal. Stool cultures are negative. Upper endoscopy and colonoscopy are unremarkable except for the expected altered anatomy.

Which of the following is the most likely diagnosis?

(A) Bile salt malabsorption
(B) Celiac disease
(C) Irritable bowel syndrome
(D) Small intestinal bacterial overgrowth

Item 43 [Basic]

A 23-year-old woman is evaluated for abdominal pain of several years' duration. The pain is crampy in nature and occurs mostly in the lower abdomen. Her pain symptoms do not change with eating but improve somewhat with defecation. The pain is frequently associated with diarrhea, especially when she is under stress, or with intermittent constipation, although on most days she has normal bowel movements. She has not noted blood or mucus in her stools, but reports a 3.6-kg (8-lb) weight loss over the past year. Medical history is otherwise unremarkable and she takes no medications.

On physical examination, she appears thin but otherwise well. Temperature is 36.9°C (98.4°F), blood pressure is 114/53 mm Hg, pulse rate is 70/min, and respiration rate is 12/min. Body mass index is 18. The abdomen is diffusely tender. There are no abdominal masses or hepatosplenomegaly. The remainder of the examination, including pelvic and rectal examinations, is normal.

Laboratory studies are significant for a hemoglobin level of 9.5 g/dL (95 g/L), a leukocyte count of 4000/µL (4 × 10⁹/L), and a platelet count of 148,000/µL (148 × 10⁹/L).

Which of the following is the most appropriate next step in management?

(A) An antispasmodic agent
(B) A benzodiazepine
(C) Colonoscopy
(D) Computed tomography of the abdomen

Item 44 [Advanced]

A 37-year-old woman is evaluated in the emergency department for the acute onset of abdominal pain following 2 weeks of bloody diarrhea. The diarrhea has increased to 15 times per day. The patient has ulcerative colitis that was diagnosed 2 years ago and has been well controlled with daily mesalamine.

On physical examination, she appears ill. Temperature is 38.9°C (102.0°F), blood pressure is 70/40 mm Hg, pulse rate is 148/min, and respiration rate is 35/min. Abdominal examination discloses absent bowel sounds, distention, and diffuse marked tenderness with mild palpation.

Laboratory studies show a leukocyte count of 16,800/µL (16.8 × 10⁹/L).

A plain abdominal radiograph is shown.

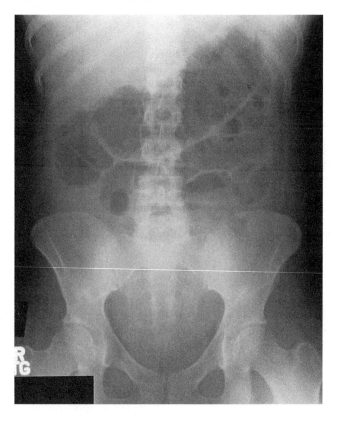

Which of the following is the most appropriate management?

(A) Schedule computed tomography of the abdomen
(B) Schedule immediate surgery
(C) Start infliximab
(D) Start intravenous methylprednisolone

Item 45 [Basic]

A 24-year-old woman is evaluated because of diarrhea, urgency, tenesmus, and abdominal pain for the past 4 to 6 weeks. She has not had fever or chills. The patient has a 5-pack-year history of smoking. Medical history is otherwise unremarkable, and she takes no medications.

On physical examination, vital signs are normal. The abdomen is soft and diffusely tender without guarding or rebound. Rectal examination is normal, and a stool sample is negative for occult blood.

Laboratory studies are significant for an erythrocyte sedimentation rate of 75 mm/h, a hemoglobin level of 11 g/dL (120 g/L), and a leukocyte count of 12,500/µL (12.5 × 10⁹/L).

Colonoscopy shows areas of inflammation scattered throughout the colon with friability, granularity, and deep ulcerations in the inflamed areas. The intervening mucosa between areas of inflammation appears normal; the rectum and ileum also appear normal.

Which of the following is the most likely diagnosis?

(A) Crohn disease
(B) Ischemic colitis
(C) Microscopic colitis
(D) Ulcerative colitis

Item 46 [Advanced]

A 38-year-old man is evaluated during a routine examination. Ulcerative colitis was diagnosed 10 years ago. He is currently asymptomatic. His last colonoscopy, performed at the time of diagnosis, showed mildly active extensive ulcerative colitis extending to the hepatic flexure. There is no family history of colon cancer or colon polyps. His only medication is mesalamine.

On physical examination, vital signs are normal. Abdominal examination is normal.

Laboratory studies, including a complete blood count, liver chemistry studies, and serum C-reactive protein level, are normal.

Which of the following is the most appropriate colonoscopy interval for this patient?

(A) Colonoscopy now and every 1 to 2 years
(B) Colonoscopy now and every 5 years
(C) Colonoscopy every 5 years starting at age 40
(D) Colonoscopy every 10 years starting at age 40

Item 47 [Basic]

A 45-year-old-man is evaluated in the emergency department for 1-day history of coffee-ground emesis and a 2-day history of melena. He last vomited 18 hours ago. The patient has been having epigastric pain for several months. He drinks 3 to 4 cans of beer weekly and takes ibuprofen daily for chronic low back pain. Medical history is otherwise unremarkable.

On physical examination, temperature is normal, blood pressure is 118/75 mm Hg, pulse rate is 100/min, and respiration rate is 18/min. There are no stigmata of chronic liver disease. The epigastrium is tender to palpation without rebound or guarding. A stool sample is positive for occult blood. The remainder of the examination is normal.

Intravenous fluids are initiated and upper endoscopy is scheduled.

Which of the following is the most appropriate treatment at this time?

(A) Erythromycin
(B) Nasogastric tube placement
(C) Octreotide
(D) Pantoprazole
(E) Ranitidine

Item 48 [Advanced]

A 72-year-old woman is evaluated during a follow-up examination. The patient has a 2-year history of chronic iron deficiency anemia associated with several episodes of melena. The source of bleeding has remained undiagnosed despite multiple upper endoscopy and colonoscopy examinations. During her last episode of melena, a technetium 99m pertechnetate red blood cell scan identified a potential source of bleeding in the small intestine. She has no other medical problems and takes no medications.

Physical examination findings, including vital signs, are normal.

Which of the following is the most likely cause of this patient's bleeding?

(A) Acute mesenteric ischemia
(B) Angiectasia
(C) Meckel diverticulum
(D) Small bowel lymphoma

Item 49 [Basic]

A 46-year-old man is evaluated for a 3-week history of occasional painless bright red rectal bleeding associated with bowel movements. He has no fatigue, lightheadedness, weight loss, or abdominal pain. His stools are frequently firm and occasionally hard, and there is no change in the frequency or consistency of his bowel movements. He has never been screened for colorectal cancer.

On physical examination, temperature is 37.2°C (98.9°F), blood pressure is 132/78 mm Hg, and pulse rate is 84/min. Digital rectal examination yields a stool sample that is positive for occult blood; the examination is otherwise normal. Anoscopy reveals a few internal hemorrhoids without active bleeding.

Laboratory studies show a hemoglobin level of 14 g/dL (140 g/L).

Which of the following is the most appropriate management of this patient?

(A) Banding of hemorrhoids
(B) Colonoscopy
(C) Fiber supplementation without further evaluation
(D) Home fecal occult blood testing

Item 50 [Basic]

A 58-year-old man is evaluated in the emergency department for painless bright red blood per rectum that began 3 hours ago. The bleeding was accompanied by a presyncopal episode. Medical history is unremarkable. He does not smoke, drink alcoholic beverages, or use illicit drugs. He is on no prescription medications but has been taking over-the-counter ibuprofen recently for a knee sprain.

On physical examination, temperature is 37.2°C (99.0°F), blood pressure is 88/58 mm Hg, pulse rate is 132/min, and respiration rate is 24/min. Abdominal examination is normal. Rectal examination discloses bright red blood in the rectal vault.

Laboratory studies reveal a hemoglobin level of 7.3 g/dL (73 g/L).

Nasogastric tube aspirate shows no evidence of blood or coffee-ground material. Intravenous fluid resuscitation is begun.

Which of the following is the most appropriate diagnostic test to perform next?

(A) Colonoscopy
(B) Tagged red blood cell scan
(C) Upper endoscopy
(D) Video capsule endoscopy

Item 51 [Advanced]

A 65-year-old man is evaluated in the emergency department for painless bright red blood per rectum that began 6 hours ago. He has no other medical problems and takes no medications.

On physical examination, temperature is 36.6°C (97.9°F), blood pressure is 130/78 mm Hg, pulse rate is 96/min, and respiration rate is 18/min. Abdominal examination is normal. Rectal examination discloses no external hemorrhoids; bright red blood is noted in the rectal vault.

Laboratory studies show a hemoglobin level of 10.4 g/dL (104 g/L), a leukocyte count of 6000/µL (6 × 10⁹/L), and a platelet count of 380,000/µL (380 × 10⁹/L).

Which of the following is the most likely cause of this patient's bleeding?

(A) Colon cancer
(B) Diverticulosis
(C) Duodenal ulcer
(D) Ischemic colitis

Item 52 [Advanced]

An 83-year-old woman is evaluated in the emergency department because of hematemesis associated with hypotension and tachycardia. Two 16-gauge intravenous catheters are placed, and intravenous fluid and erythrocyte resuscitation is initiated with bolus administration of 2 L of 0.9% saline and two units of packed erythrocytes. Intravenous omeprazole is also begun, and she is transferred to the intensive care unit (ICU). The patient has no history of gastrointestinal bleeding or liver disease. She has osteoarthritis for which she takes daily aspirin.

On physical examination in the ICU 2 hours later, blood pressure is 87/58 mm Hg, pulse rate is 112/min, and respiration rate is 12/min. The abdomen is nontender, and there is no organomegaly. There are no stigmata of chronic liver disease.

Laboratory studies show a hemoglobin level of 7 g/dL (70 g/L).

Which of the following is the most appropriate next step in management?

(A) Continue intravenous fluid and erythrocyte resuscitation
(B) Initiate octreotide
(C) Perform immediate upper endoscopy
(D) Place a diagnostic nasogastric tube

Section 3

Gastroenterology and Hepatology
Answers and Critiques

Item 1   **Answer:** **C**

Educational Objective: *Diagnose irritable bowel syndrome.*

This patient most likely has irritable bowel syndrome (IBS). The diagnosis of IBS is based solely on clinical grounds. As no biochemical, radiographic, endoscopic, or histologic markers exist, several clinical indices have been published to aid in the diagnosis of IBS, with the Rome criteria being the most widely used. Patients meeting the Rome diagnostic criteria have recurrent abdominal pain or discomfort at least 3 days each month in the past 3 months (with onset more than 6 months earlier) associated with two or more of the following: improvement with defecation; onset associated with change in frequency of stool; onset associated with change in form (appearance) of stool. In addition, this patient lacks "alarm symptoms" suggestive of an alternative diagnosis. Alarm symptoms include onset after age 50 years, brief history of symptoms, weight loss, nocturnal symptoms, family history of colon cancer, rectal bleeding, and recent antibiotic use.

Celiac disease occurs in genetically predisposed persons with haplotype *HLA-DQ2* or *HLA-DQ8* and is triggered by ingestion of gluten that is present in wheat, rye, and barley. The clinical presentation of patients with celiac disease includes diarrhea, malabsorption, and malnutrition and often iron deficiency anemia. This patient's predominant bowel pattern of constipation is not consistent with celiac disease.

The symptoms of Crohn disease, an inflammatory bowel disease, can be quite variable, depending upon the anatomic location of the inflammation. Diarrhea is associated with inflammation of both the small intestine and colon, whereas hematochezia indicates colonic disease. The absence of weight loss, nocturnal pain, and hematochezia despite symptoms for 7 months tends to preclude the diagnosis of an inflammatory bowel disease, such as Crohn disease, in this patient.

Ischemic colitis usually develops acutely in elderly patients with a history of significant cardiovascular disease that may lead to hypoperfusion of the sigmoid colon. Patients usually present with severe crampy abdominal pain with or without diarrhea followed by hematochezia. Physical examination usually reveals pain in the left lower abdominal quadrant associated with leukocytosis. Anemia may also develop. This patient does not have any findings to support a diagnosis of ischemic colitis.

Somatization disorder is characterized by multiple unexplained physical symptoms for at least 6 months, along with symptom-related social or occupational impairment. Current diagnostic criteria require at least four pain symptoms, two gastrointestinal symptoms, one pseudoneurologic symptom, and one sexual symptom. Patients attribute their symptoms to an undiagnosed disorder despite multiple negative evaluations and are often not reassured despite repeated work-ups. While patients with IBS often have associated depression, anxiety, a history of sexual abuse, phobias, and somatization, this patient has no findings to support any of these diagnoses.

KEY POINT

Patients with irritable bowel syndrome have recurrent abdominal pain or discomfort at least 3 days a month in past 3 months (with onset more than 6 months earlier) associated with two or more of the following: improvement with defecation; onset associated with change in frequency of stool; onset associated with change in form (appearance) of stool.

Bibliography
Ford AC, Talley NJ. Irritable bowel syndrome. BMJ. 2012;345:e5836. [PMID: 22951548]

Item 2   **Answer:** **A**

Educational Objective: *Diagnose acute mesenteric ischemia.*

This patient most likely has acute mesenteric ischemia based on the suggestive computed tomographic (CT) scan findings, the presence of metabolic acidosis with an elevated serum lactate level, and the presence of pain out of proportion to the examination findings (less tenderness than expected based on the patient's symptoms). A CT scan of the abdomen may show bowel wall thickening or intestinal pneumatosis (air within the wall of the bowel). The most common cause of acute mesenteric ischemia is an embolism to the superior mesenteric artery originating from the left atrium or a ventricular mural thrombus. Traditional angiography has been the diagnostic gold standard and can be used for administration of therapeutic vasodilators and stenting. CT angiography is becoming increasingly recognized as a highly sensitive and specific modality to diagnose acute mesenteric ischemia. The procedure is more readily available than traditional angiography and also permits the evaluation of the abdomen in addition to the vasculature.

Crohn disease could cause thickening of the small bowel wall on imaging, but Crohn disease is not consistent with this patient's acute onset of severe abdominal pain, hemodynamic instability, and metabolic acidosis.

An intussusception causes bowel obstruction rather than intestinal ischemia.

Acute pancreatitis is unlikely to lead to shock within 1 hour of onset. In addition, the CT scan does not support a diagnosis of acute pancreatitis, which would be characterized by pancreatic edema.

KEY POINT

Acute mesenteric ischemia should be suspected in patients with the acute onset of severe abdominal pain and an abdominal examination that discloses less tenderness than expected based on the patient's symptoms (pain out of proportion to the examination findings).

Bibliography
Sise MJ. Acute mesenteric ischemia. Surg Clin North Am. 2014;94:165-81. [PMID: 24267504]

Item 3   Answer: C

Educational Objective: *Manage acute uncomplicated diverticulitis.*

The most appropriate management for this patient with acute diverticulitis is oral antibiotic therapy with metronidazole and ciprofloxacin. Diverticulitis results from obstruction at a diverticulum neck by fecal matter, leading to mucus production and bacterial overgrowth. Left lower quadrant abdominal pain is the most common clinical manifestation, often accompanied by fever. Other symptoms may include nausea, vomiting, and anorexia. More than 50% of patients with diverticulitis have leukocytosis. Oral antibiotic therapy with agents that are effective against anaerobes and gram-negative rods is a reasonable option for initial therapy in immunocompetent patients with isolated, uncomplicated acute diverticulitis who are able to tolerate oral intake.

Colonoscopy should be avoided in the acute setting because air insufflation may increase the risk for perforation. After resolution of the acute process, however, patients who have not had a recent colonoscopy should undergo the procedure to rule out malignancy.

Hospitalization and intravenous antibiotics are generally reserved for patients with evidence of peritonitis, those with significant comorbidities, or those who cannot tolerate oral intake.

Surgical consultation can be considered for patients with acute diverticulitis that is unresponsive to antibiotic therapy, complicated diverticulitis (associated with abscess, fistula, obstruction, peritonitis, or stricture), recurrent diverticulitis, or smoldering diverticulitis, none of which is present in this patient.

KEY POINT

Oral antibiotic therapy with agents that are effective against anaerobes and gram-negative rods is a reasonable option for immunocompetent patients with isolated, uncomplicated acute diverticulitis who are able to tolerate oral intake.

Bibliography
Jacobs DO. Clinical practice. Diverticulitis. N Engl J Med. 2007;357:2057-66. [PMID: 18003962]

Item 4   Answer: A

Educational Objective: *Diagnose acute appendicitis.*

This patient has acute appendicitis. Initial symptoms usually include pain in the epigastrium or periumbilical region, which generally is mild, constant, and difficult to localize precisely. Pain eventually localizes to the right lower abdominal quadrant. Nausea and vomiting, if present, follow the onset of pain; if they precede the onset of pain, a diagnosis other than appendicitis is likely. Leukocytosis and low-grade fever are common. Urine leukocytosis, as is present in this patient, is probably due to the proximity of the inflamed appendix to the bladder and can cause a delay in diagnosis. Physical examination usually reveals localized tenderness in the right lower abdominal quadrant. Tenderness in the right lower quadrant during rectal and pelvic examinations may also be present

Ruptured ectopic pregnancy and acute pelvic inflammatory disease should always be considered in the differential diagnosis of women presenting with lower abdominal pain. A pregnancy test should always be done in a woman of reproductive age who is evaluated for abdominal or pelvic pain; the negative test in this patient makes an ectopic pregnancy unlikely. No single symptom or test is pathognomonic for pelvic inflammatory disease, but combinations of symptoms, signs, and other findings can provide a diagnosis with reasonable accuracy. The absence of a discharge and pelvic pain with cervical movement during pelvic examination makes pelvic inflammatory disease unlikely in this patient.

Acute uncomplicated pyelonephritis is suggested by the abrupt onset of fever, chills, and flank pain and the presence of costovertebral angle tenderness on physical examination. Pyuria, particularly if associated with bacteriuria or leukocyte casts, provides strong support for the presence of pyelonephritis. This patient's primarily abdominal and pelvic pain in the absence of flank pain or tenderness makes pyelonephritis less likely.

KEY POINT

Initial symptoms of acute appendicitis usually include pain in the epigastrium or periumbilical region, which eventually localizes to the right lower abdominal quadrant; nausea and vomiting follow, rather than precede, the onset of pain in patients with acute appendicitis.

Bibliography
Petroianu A. Diagnosis of acute appendicitis. Int J Surg. 2012;10:115-9. [PMID: 22349155]

Item 5   Answer: B

Educational Objective: *Diagnose chronic pancreatitis.*

A computed tomographic (CT) scan of the abdomen is most appropriate for this patient who has chronic pancreatitis secondary to alcohol abuse, which has resulted in malabsorption. The three classic findings in patients with chronic pancreatitis are abdominal pain that is usually midepigastric, postprandial diarrhea, and diabetes mellitus secondary to pancreatic endocrine insufficiency. Malabsorption causes diarrhea and steatorrhea, weight loss, and deficiencies of fat-soluble vitamins because the damaged pancreatic gland is no longer producing the pancreatic exocrine enzymes to absorb food. The presence of pancreatic calcifications on imaging studies confirms the diagnosis of chronic pancreatitis, and abdominal CT scans are able to detect calcifications in up to 90% of patients. CT scanning can also exclude other causes of pain, such as pancreatic duct dilatation, pseudocysts, or mass lesions.

Although colonoscopy is indicated as a screening study for average-risk asymptomatic persons beginning at the age of 50 years and for patients of any age with a change in bowel habits and weight loss, this patient's history suggests pancreatic malabsorption. Colonoscopy is less likely than abdominal CT scan to confirm the diagnosis.

Celiac disease is unlikely in this patient, who has a clinical picture consistent with a history of pancreatic malabsorption.

Stool studies are appropriate for determining the cause of an acute infectious diarrhea, but this patient has had diarrhea for 8 months. In addition, infectious diarrhea is not usually associated with such a degree of weight loss.

Patients with chronic pancreatitis present with abdominal pain; patients with more severe pancreatitis may also have malabsorption and endocrine insufficiency.

Bibliography

Löhr JM, Haas SL, Lindgren F, et L. Conservative treatment of chronic pancreatitis. Dig Dis. 2013;31:43-50. [PMID: 23797122]

Item 6 Answer: E

Educational Objective: *Evaluate dyspepsia with alarm features.*

The most appropriate management of this patient's symptoms is to perform upper endoscopy. Nearly 70% of patients with dyspepsia do not have a physiologic explanation for their symptoms. According to the Rome III criteria, functional dyspepsia includes one or more of the following: (1) bothersome postprandial fullness, (2) early satiety, (3) epigastric burning, and (4) epigastric pain with lack of structural disease on upper endoscopy. To establish the diagnosis, these criteria should be met for 3 months, with symptom onset at least 6 months prior to diagnosis. Guidelines recommend upper endoscopy for patients with dyspepsia and alarm features. Alarm features for dyspepsia include onset after age 50 years; anemia; dysphagia; odynophagia; vomiting; weight loss; family history of upper gastrointestinal malignancy; personal history of peptic ulcer disease, gastric surgery, or gastrointestinal malignancy; and abdominal mass or lymphadenopathy on examination. Because this patient is 52 years old and has had vomiting, upper endoscopy should be performed to evaluate for a serious underlying cause of his symptoms.

Abdominal computed tomography and abdominal ultrasonography are not as sensitive as upper endoscopy for identifying upper gastrointestinal disorders that may be confined to the mucosa, such as gastritis, peptic ulcer disease, gastric cancer, and lymphoma.

For patients younger than 50 years of age without alarm features, a test-and-treat approach for *Helicobacter pylori* infection is reasonable and cost effective when the patient is from a geographic area where the prevalence of *H. pylori* is high (such as developing countries). However, proton pump inhibitor (PPI) therapy is the most appropriate first-line strategy if the patient is from an area where the prevalence of *H. pylori* is low. However, neither empiric PPI therapy nor testing for *H. pylori* is appropriate for this patient with dyspepsia and alarm features, who requires upper endoscopy as first-line management.

Upper endoscopy is indicated for patients with dyspepsia and alarm features, including symptom onset after age 50 years; anemia; dysphagia; odynophagia; vomiting; weight loss; family history of upper gastrointestinal malignancy; personal history of peptic ulcer disease, gastric surgery, or gastrointestinal malignancy; and abdominal mass or lymphadenopathy on examination.

Bibliography

Wee EW. Evidence-based approach to dyspepsia: from Helicobacter pylori to functional disease. Postgrad Med. 2013;125:169-80. [PMID: 23933904]

Item 7 Answer: B

Educational Objective: *Diagnose dyspepsia.*

The most likely diagnosis is dyspepsia. The Rome III criteria for dyspepsia are one or more of the following predominant symptoms: (1) bothersome postprandial fullness, (2) early satiety, (3) epigastric pain, or (4) epigastric burning. The symptoms should be consistent for at least 3 months with an initial onset at least 6 months before diagnosis. This patient does not have alarm features such as unintentional weight loss, anemia, vomiting, or dysphagia that might suggest an alternative diagnosis and the need for immediate upper endoscopy.

Biliary colic is the most common clinical presentation in patients with symptomatic gallstones. The usual presentation of biliary colic is episodic severe abdominal pain typically in the epigastrium and/or right upper quadrant but occasionally in the right lower or mid abdomen. The pain rapidly intensifies over a 15-minute interval to a steady plateau that lasts as long as 3 hours and resolves slowly. The pain is often associated with nausea or vomiting and may radiate to the interscapular region or right shoulder. None of these findings are present in this patient.

Gastroesophageal reflux disease (GERD) occurs when the reflux of stomach contents causes symptoms or complications that are troublesome for the patient. GERD is diagnosed when the predominant symptom is heartburn or acid reflux. Additional signs may be belching, a sour taste in the mouth, and symptoms that are worse at night or with recumbency, none of which are present in this patient.

Peptic ulcer disease is asymptomatic in 4% to 20% of patients and is commonly diagnosed because of complications such as bleeding. Symptoms, when present, consist of discomfort typically in the epigastric region that has a burning or gnawing quality. The character of this patient's pain, the duration of symptoms, a lack of response to antacids, weight gain, and the absence of anemia make peptic ulcer disease less likely in this patient.

The Rome III criteria for the diagnosis of dyspepsia include one or more of the following predominant symptoms for at least 3 months: (1) bothersome postprandial fullness, (2) early satiety, (3) epigastric pain, or (4) epigastric burning.

Bibliography

Oustamanolakis P, Tack J. Dyspepsia: organic versus functional. J Clin Gastroenterol. 2012;46:175-90. [PMID: 22327302]

Item 8 Answer: A

Educational Objective: *Diagnose cause of gastroesophageal reflux disease.*

This patient most likely has gastroesophageal reflux disease (GERD), and the gold standard for diagnosing GERD is 24-hour esophageal pH-impedance monitoring, which establishes whether increased esophageal exposure to acid is present. This study is most helpful in patients who have GERD-like symptoms that fail to respond to an adequate trial of a proton pump inhibitor (PPI) to correlate the presence of acid in the esophagus at the time the patient is having symptoms, such as the patient described. Esophageal pH monitoring identifies the reflux of acid, and impedance monitoring detects reflux of other gastric contents in a small percentage of patients who have symptoms related to non-acid reflux.

GERD is definitively diagnosed by symptoms, upper endoscopy, or ambulatory esophageal pH/impedance monitoring. However, the presence of heartburn, regurgitation, or both is sufficient to presumptively diagnose GERD if symptoms are of sufficient severity and frequency to be troublesome for the patient. A favorable response to empiric therapy with PPIs is supportive evidence for a diagnosis of GERD and is a reasonable first step in a patient without alarm symptoms (dysphagia, anemia, vomiting, or weight loss).

When empiric therapy is not effective, upper endoscopy may be helpful to confirm GERD or identify alternative diagnoses. Endoscopy, rather than empiric therapy, is indicated as a first step in patients with alarm symptoms, which are suggestive of complications from mucosal injury. Esophagitis occurs in less than 40% of patients with GERD, and other complications develop in less than 15% of patients. The severity of reflux symptoms does not correlate well with the severity of mucosal damage seen on upper endoscopy.

Neither barium swallow radiography nor esophageal manometry is indicated because neither study is sensitive or specific for diagnosing GERD.

Although *Helicobacter pylori* testing is indicated for diagnosing peptic ulcer disease and may have a role in evaluating dyspepsia, it is generally not helpful in patients with GERD because a positive test does not confirm the diagnosis and a negative test does not exclude the presence of GERD.

KEY POINT

The gold standard for diagnosing gastroesophageal reflux disease (GERD) is 24-hour esophageal pH-impedance monitoring, which is most helpful in patients who have GERD-like symptoms that fail to respond to an adequate trial of a proton pump inhibitor.

Bibliography
Kumar AR, Katz PO. Functional esophageal disorders: a review of diagnosis and management. Expert Rev Gastroenterol Hepatol. 2013;7:453-61. [PMID: 23899284]

Item 9   Answer: E

Educational Objective: *Manage a patient with Barrett esophagus.*

The most appropriate management of this patient's Barrett esophagus (BE) is periodic upper endoscopy surveillance. BE is a complication of gastroesophageal reflux disease (GERD) in which the normal squamous epithelium of the distal esophagus is replaced by specialized columnar epithelium. The disorder is most common in white patients with long-standing and severe GERD. Patients with BE have more severe esophageal acid reflux than those with nonerosive reflux disease. BE is a premalignant condition; patients with BE have an estimated 30- to 50-fold increased risk of developing esophageal adenocarcinoma compared with those without BE and an annual incidence of esophageal adenocarcinoma of 0.5%. Approximately 10% of patients with chronic GERD symptoms have BE on upper endoscopy. Overall survival in patients with BE is comparable to that of age- and sex-matched populations. Adenocarcinoma accounts for less than 10% of the total mortality rate in patients with BE.

BE is thought to progress in a stepwise fashion from absence of dysplasia to low-grade dysplasia to high-grade dysplasia to invasive adenocarcinoma. Upper endoscopy surveillance is advisable in patients with BE to detect progression and initiate early therapy. Management of BE primarily depends on the grade of dysplasia as determined by histology, which remains the most widely accepted risk-stratification tool for BE. Progression to adenocarcinoma occurs slowly.

Proton pump inhibitors are used to control symptoms of reflux in patients with BE and can be continued in symptomatic patients.

Endoscopic ablative therapies (such as photodynamic therapy and radiofrequency ablation) and surgical resection (esophagectomy) have been shown to be effective in the management of patients with high-grade dysplasia; cohort studies show comparable outcomes with surgery and endoscopic treatment. Choice of treatment may be influenced by local expertise (endoscopic versus surgical) and patient preference. Because this patient does not have dysplasia, endoscopic ablative therapy or surgical resection is not indicated at this time.

Fundoplication, a procedure to decrease gastroesophageal reflux, is not indicated as this procedure has not been shown to reduce the risk of progression of dysplasia in patients with BE.

KEY POINT

The most appropriate management of Barrett esophagus is periodic upper endoscopy surveillance.

Bibliography
Shaheen NJ, Weinberg DS, Denberg TD, et al.; Clinical Guidelines Committee of the American College of Physicians. Upper endoscopy for gastroesophageal reflux disease: best practice advice from the clinical guidelines committee of the American College of Physicians. Ann Intern Med. 2012;157:808-16. [PMID:23208168]

Item 10   Answer: B

Educational Objective: *Manage gastroesophageal reflux disease with dyspeptic features.*

This patient is considered to have gastroesophageal reflux disease (GERD) with dyspeptic features, and the most appropriate initial management is acid suppression with a proton pump inhibitor (PPI). Studies have shown that the majority of patients with dyspepsia who undergo upper endoscopy have normal findings, and those who do have abnormalities are found to have esophagitis. Therefore, predominant heartburn or regurgitation symptoms should be categorized as GERD rather than dyspepsia. Empiric therapy with a proton pump inhibitor (PPI) is the most cost-effective management strategy. There are six PPIs available in the United States: omeprazole, esomeprazole, lansoprazole, dexlansoprazole, pantoprazole, and rabeprazole, and all have approximately similar efficacy. PPI therapy is usually given once a day before a meal, usually before breakfast. In patients who require twice-daily dosing for symptom control (for example, patients with noncardiac chest pain, extraesophageal manifestations, incomplete response to standard therapy, or Barrett esophagus), the second dose should be administered before dinner. Patients should be reassessed in 6 weeks; if symptoms respond, the drug dosage can be decreased to the lowest effective dose. Long-term PPI therapy is generally considered safe for patients who require ongoing acid suppression.

Although this patient had temporary relief with low-dose H_2 receptor antagonist therapy, PPIs are more potent and longer-acting than H_2 receptor antagonists and are considered to be superior for treatment of both dyspepsia and heartburn.

A test-and-treat strategy for *Helicobacter pylori* infection is appropriate for patients with dyspeptic symptoms without heartburn or alarm symptoms and who are from a geographic area (such as developing countries) with a high prevalence of *H. pylori* infection (>20%). Because this patient also has heartburn, this approach is not indicated. There has recently been some controversy as to whether eradication of *H. pylori* in patients with dyspepsia may increase the risk of posteradication GERD, but this has not yet been definitively established.

Upper endoscopy is not indicated because this patient does not have any dyspeptic alarm features (onset after age 50 years; anemia; dysphagia; odynophagia; vomiting; weight loss; family history of upper gastrointestinal malignancy; personal history of peptic ulcer disease, gastric surgery, or gastrointestinal malignancy; and abdominal mass or lymphadenopathy on examination). The diagnostic yield of upper endoscopy in the absence of these findings is very low.

KEY POINT

Patients with gastroesophageal reflux disease with dyspeptic features should be treated with proton pump inhibitor therapy.

Bibliography

Tack J, Talley NJ. Gastroduodenal disorders. Am J Gastroenterol. 2010;105:757-63. [PMID: 20372127]

Item 11　　　Answer:　D

Educational Objective: *Manage gastroesophageal reflux disease that does not respond to an empiric trial of proton pump inhibitor therapy.*

This patient should undergo upper endoscopy. Her symptoms suggest gastroesophageal reflux disease (GERD), but there has been no response to empiric trials of high-dose proton pump inhibitors (PPIs) for an adequate period of time (at least 8-12 weeks). Furthermore, evaluation with upper endoscopy is required for patients with symptoms of weight loss, dysphagia, odynophagia, bleeding, or anemia and in patients with long-standing symptoms (>5 years) or symptoms that are refractory to acid-suppression therapy. This patient has intermittent dysphagia for solid food, and her symptoms appear to be refractory to PPI therapy. She should therefore undergo upper endoscopy to identify possible complications or alternative diagnoses such as eosinophilic esophagitis, stricture, malignancy, or achalasia.

PPIs are much more effective in healing esophagitis (particularly severe esophagitis) than are H_2 receptor antagonists. Adding H_2 receptor antagonists to maximal PPI therapy does not result in a meaningful increase in acid blockade. Therefore, adding an H_2 receptor antagonist is unlikely to provide relief for patients who continue to have heartburn after 6 weeks of treatment with a PPI.

Ambulatory esophageal pH monitoring is most commonly used to confirm GERD in patients with persistent symptoms despite maximal medical therapy and an unrevealing upper endoscopy study (no evidence of reflux-induced esophagitis or Barrett esophagus). However, in this patient who has persistent symptoms and intermittent dysphagia, upper endoscopy is the most appropriate next diagnostic test to assess for evidence of reflux-induced complications. If this study is unrevealing, ambulatory esophageal pH monitoring should be considered.

Persistent or recurrent symptoms despite maximal medical therapy for GERD are indications for antireflux surgery such as fundoplication. However, before antireflux surgery is considered, this patient should undergo upper endoscopy (to confirm the presence of esophagitis and to eliminate the possibility of an alternative diagnosis) and possibly ambulatory esophageal pH monitoring (to document continued acid reflux while taking maximal doses of a PPI).

KEY POINT

Patients with suspected gastroesophageal reflux disease whose symptoms do not respond to an empiric trial of proton pump inhibitor therapy should undergo upper endoscopy to assess for alternative diagnoses.

Bibliography

Kahrilas PJ, Shaheen NJ, Vaezi MF, et al; American Gastroenterological Association. American Gastroenterological Association Medical Position Statement on the management of gastroesophageal reflux disease. Gastroenterology. 2008;135:1383-91. [PMID: 18789939]

Item 12　　　Answer:　D

Educational Objective: *Manage peptic ulcer disease.*

This patient should undergo upper endoscopy. His constellation of symptoms raises concern for peptic ulcer disease, particularly in the distal stomach or duodenum. Upper endoscopy is the preferred diagnostic study, as it allows direct visualization of the upper gastrointestinal tract and provides the opportunity for *Helicobacter pylori* testing of biopsy specimens as needed.

Although younger patients (≤55 years old) with mild to moderate midepigastric pain consistent with peptic ulcer disease may be treated empirically with a proton pump inhibitor (PPI) without upper endoscopy in the absence of associated symptoms, patients of any age with abdominal pain and additional symptoms such as nausea, vomiting, early satiety, or weight loss should undergo upper endoscopy. Although this patient is only 32 years old, empiric PPI therapy for peptic ulcer disease is not appropriate because of his associated symptoms.

Testing for *H. pylori* infection is indicated for patients with active peptic ulcer disease. If infection is documented, triple therapy consisting of a PPI, amoxicillin, and clarithromycin is the most commonly used initial treatment. However, treatment is not indicated in the absence of documented infection and should be withheld pending diagnostic testing in this patient.

Although an upper gastrointestinal barium study may reveal mucosal abnormalities consistent with ulceration, it does not allow direct visualization of the upper gastrointestinal tract and cannot provide biopsy specimens for *H. pylori* testing.

KEY POINT

Upper endoscopy is indicated for diagnosis in patients of any age with midepigastric abdominal pain and associated symptoms, including nausea, vomiting, early satiety, or weight loss.

Bibliography

ASGE Standards of Practice Committee, Banerjee S, Cash BD, Dominitz JA, Baron TH, et al. The role of endoscopy in the management of patients with peptic ulcer disease. Gastrointest Endosc. 2010;71:663-8. [PMID: 20363407]

Item 13　　　Answer:　A

Educational Objective: *Manage* Helicobacter pylori *infection in a patient with peptic ulcer disease.*

This patient should undergo fecal *Helicobacter pylori* antigen testing to verify eradication of the infection. The two most common causes of peptic ulcer disease are infection with *H. pylori* and the use of nonsteroidal anti-inflammatory drugs (NSAIDs). Once a diagnosis of *H. pylori* infection has been established, treatment followed by verification of eradication is essential. The initial diagnosis of *H. pylori* infection may be done by endoscopic studies (either histologic examination of biopsy tissue or rapid urease testing) or non-endoscopic studies (serum antibody tests, the urea breath test, or stool examination for *H. pylori* antigens). Because results of serum antibody studies remain positive after therapy, the urea breath test and fecal antigen testing are practical and noninvasive methods for detecting any residual *H. pylori* infection. The sensitivity of both tests is reduced when patients have recently taken a proton pump inhibitor (PPI) or antibiotic, and a period of 4 weeks without such drugs is recommended to optimize test accuracy.

Continued therapy with a PPI in a patient completing a full treatment course for peptic ulcer disease is not indicated in the absence of additional symptoms or other risk factors (such as chronic NSAID use).

Patients with uncomplicated duodenal ulcers do not require follow-up upper endoscopy to assess for healing; therefore, repeat upper endoscopy would not be indicated for this patient.

Because of the strong association of *H. pylori* infection with peptic ulcer disease, failure to confirm eradication in a patient with *H. pylori*–associated ulceration would not be appropriate.

KEY POINT

Follow-up testing using the urea breath test or fecal *Helicobacter pylori* antigen testing is indicated after treatment of *H. pylori* infection in a patient with peptic ulcer disease; testing should be performed at least 4 weeks following completion of proton pump inhibitor and antibiotic therapy.

Bibliography
Selgrad M, Malfertheiner P. Treatment of Helicobacter pylori. Curr Opin Gastroenterol. 2011;27:565-70. [PMID: 21946029]

Item 14   Answer: A

Educational Objective: *Manage a newly diagnosed gastric ulcer.*

The most appropriate management for this patient's gastric ulcer is biopsy. Biopsies of all gastric ulcers should be performed because even small, benign-appearing gastric ulcers may harbor malignancy. In benign ulcers, biopsies can also provide evidence of the presence of *Helicobacter pylori* infection and guide appropriate therapy.

Testing for *H. pylori* is indicated in patients with active peptic ulcer disease (duodenal or gastric) and in patients with a history of peptic ulcer disease who have not been previously treated for *H. pylori* infection. The most commonly used endoscopic tests are biopsy with histologic assessment and the rapid urease test. The sensitivity of the rapid urease test can be reduced by as much as 25% in patients who have taken a proton pump inhibitor (PPI), such as omeprazole, within 2 weeks or bismuth or antibiotic therapy within 4 weeks of testing. Because the rapid urease test may be influenced by her previous PPI therapy, it is not the most appropriate study for this patient.

The sensitivity of the urea breath test, like that of the rapid urease test, is also reduced by medications that affect urease production, such as a PPI, and is therefore not an appropriate test for this patient.

Treatment for peptic ulcer disease is guided by biopsy findings and the presence of *H. pylori* infection. If infection is documented, triple therapy consisting of a PPI, amoxicillin, and clarithromycin is the most commonly used initial treatment. Triple therapy is not indicated in the absence of documented infection and should therefore be withheld in this patient pending results of additional diagnostic studies.

KEY POINT

Biopsies of all gastric ulcers should be performed because even small, benign-appearing gastric ulcers may harbor malignancy.

Bibliography
McColl KE. Clinical practice. Helicobacter pylori infection. N Engl J Med. 2010 Apr 29;362(17):1597-604. [PMID: 20427808]

Item 15   Answer: C

Educational Objective: *Evaluate peptic ulcer disease.*

The type of nonprescription analgesic that this patient is taking should be identified. The two most common causes of peptic ulcer disease are nonsteroidal anti-inflammatory drugs (NSAIDs) and *Helicobacter pylori* infection, which account for more than 90% of cases. This patient has a history of arthritis for which she takes an over-the-counter analgesic. Therefore, inadvertent use of NSAIDs, which are widely available without a prescription and are often used as analgesics for arthritis, needs to be considered. Many patients who take such nonprescription medications are unaware that they are taking NSAIDs.

Measuring the serum gastrin level should be considered in a patient with a suspected acid hypersecretion state, such as a gastrinoma (Zollinger-Ellison syndrome). Clinical features include multiple peptic ulcers, ulcers in unusual locations, severe esophagitis, or fat malabsorption, none of which this patient has.

Malignancy always needs to be considered in a patient with a gastric ulcer; therefore, biopsies of the ulcer and follow-up upper endoscopy to ensure ulcer healing are recommended. However, this patient has a duodenal ulcer, which is much less likely to represent a malignancy, and biopsy of the ulcer or follow-up upper endoscopy to assess for healing is not needed.

Alendronate therapy for osteoporosis has been associated with esophagitis and rare cases of gastric or duodenal ulcers. However, stopping alendronate without considering the more common causes of peptic ulcer disease would not be appropriate at this time.

KEY POINT

In patients with peptic ulcers, nonprescription medications should be reviewed to determine whether NSAIDs are being inadvertently used.

Bibliography
Gupta S, McQuaid K. Management of nonsteroidal, anti-inflammatory, drug-associated dyspepsia. Gastroenterology. 2005;129:1711-19. [PMID: 16285968]

Item 16   Answer: D

Educational Objective: *Diagnose Gilbert syndrome.*

This patient most likely has Gilbert syndrome. His history is consistent with an upper respiratory tract viral infection. Liver chemistry studies reveal normal aminotransferase levels and indirect (unconjugated) hyperbilirubinemia. This clinical picture is consistent with Gilbert syndrome, which is a common cause of unconjugated hyperbilirubinemia that affects approximately 2% to 7% of the general population. It is caused by an inherited defect in the gene responsible for the conjugation of bilirubin with glucuronic acid. This leads to an increase in circulating unconjugated bilirubin, although the remainder of bilirubin metabolism is normal. Serum total bilirubin levels can reach 3.0 mg/dL (51.3 µmol/L) and characteristically fluctuate during concurrent illnesses. Patients are otherwise asymptomatic, although recurrent episodes leading to clinical jaundice may be bothersome.

The diagnosis is supported by the finding of an increased serum indirect bilirubin level with a normal direct (conjugated) bilirubin level, particularly after fasting. Additional diagnostic studies are generally not required for patients with normal and stable laboratory test results; expensive and invasive diagnostic studies are not indicated. Recognition of the abnormality and discussing the diagnosis with the patient are important in order to avoid additional testing or other interventions in the future. Because persons with Gilbert syndrome have a normal life expectancy, only reassurance is necessary.

The absence of right upper quadrant abdominal pain in combination with a normal serum direct bilirubin level is not consistent with acute cholecystitis.

Acute viral hepatitis most commonly presents with significant elevations of liver aminotransferase levels and increased direct hyperbilirubinemia, neither of which is present in this patient.

The patient's normal hemoglobin and direct bilirubin levels argue against the presence of hemolytic anemia.

KEY POINT

Gilbert syndrome is a common and frequently incidentally discovered cause of indirect (unconjugated) hyperbilirubinemia that usually does not require evaluation or treatment.

Bibliography

Krier M, Ahmed A. The asymptomatic outpatient with abnormal liver function tests. Clin Liver Dis. 2009;13:167-77. [PMID: 19442912]

Item 17   Answer: A

Educational Objective: *Evaluate cholestatic liver abnormalities.*

Abdominal ultrasonography is the most appropriate next diagnostic study. This patient has a cholestatic liver pattern, as evidenced by her elevated serum alkaline phosphatase and bilirubin levels but only mildly elevated serum aminotransferase levels. This type of injury can be caused by intrahepatic or extrahepatic bile duct disease (such as primary biliary cirrhosis or primary sclerosing cholangitis), infiltrative liver disease (such as metastatic disease or granulomatous disorders), and medications. Abdominal ultrasonography is the preferred initial diagnostic test to evaluate the biliary system and liver parenchyma.

If ultrasonography shows that bile duct dilatation, endoscopic retrograde cholangiopancreatography (ERCP) or magnetic resonance cholangiopancreatography would be indicated to further assess the location and cause of the obstruction. ERCP also has the advantage of possibly allowing for a tissue diagnosis (by biopsy) or a therapeutic intervention (such as biliary stone extraction, sphincterotomy, or stent placement) if indicted, although the contrast media used in this procedure increase the risk for post-procedure pancreatitis.

If imaging studies show evidence of an infiltrative hepatic process, a liver biopsy would be an appropriate next step in diagnosis.

KEY POINT

Abdominal ultrasonography to evaluate the biliary system and liver parenchyma is the initial diagnostic study of choice for diagnosing suspected cholestatic liver disease.

Bibliography

Krier M, Ahmed A. The asymptomatic outpatient with abnormal liver function tests. Clin Liver Dis. 2009;13:167-77. [PMID: 19442912]

Item 18   Answer: A

Educational Objective: *Diagnose hepatitis A infection.*

This patient most likely has hepatitis A virus (HAV) infection. HAV is a common cause of acute hepatitis. Clinical symptoms such as malaise, fatigue, nausea, and right upper quadrant abdominal discomfort develop 2 to 6 weeks after exposure. Serum aspartate aminotransferase and alanine aminotransferase elevations indicate hepatocyte inflammation or injury. Jaundice and cholestasis can develop 1 to 2 weeks after the onset of symptoms. Persons at risk for HAV infection are travelers to endemic areas, such as rural Mexico, and men who have sex with men. Vaccination of high-risk populations can prevent infection. This patient fits the epidemiologic profile for HAV infection and did not receive hepatitis A immunization prior to travel, making hepatitis A the most likely diagnosis.

Hepatitis B virus (HBV) can cause both acute and chronic hepatitis. HBV is highly transmissible by blood (including needlestick), mucocutaneous (such as sexual contact), or perinatal (infected mother to newborn) exposures. Acute HBV infection is characterized by symptoms similar to those of acute HAV infection. The incubation period of HBV infection is 4 to 16 weeks. Hepatitis D virus (HDV) is an incomplete virus that requires the presence of HBV for replication. It occurs as a coinfection with HBV or a superinfection in a patient already infected with HBV; the latter manifests as severe acute hepatitis. This patient does not have any risk factors for HBV infection, making this diagnosis and HDV infection unlikely.

As many as 4 to 5 million persons in the United States are estimated to be infected with hepatitis C virus (HCV). Infection occurs through percutaneous exposure, primarily by injection drug use or by blood transfusion prior to 1992. Most acute HCV infections are asymptomatic. Patients with chronic HCV infection often have fatigue, mild right upper quadrant abdominal discomfort, and arthralgia. This patient does not have risk factors or a clinical profile suggesting HCV infection.

KEY POINT

Hepatitis A virus infection is a common cause of acute hepatitis and results in malaise, fatigue, nausea, and right upper quadrant abdominal discomfort 2 to 6 weeks after exposure.

Bibliography

Matheny SC, Kingery JE. Hepatitis A. Am Fam Physician. 2012;86:1027-34; quiz 1010-2. [PMID: 23198670]

Item 19   Answer: C

Educational Objective: *Treat nonalcoholic fatty liver disease.*

The most appropriate management for this patient with nonalcoholic fatty liver disease (NAFLD) is therapeutic diet and lifestyle modification. Findings in patients with NAFLD can range from asymptomatic hepatic steatosis to cirrhosis. NAFLD usually results from insulin resistance and the metabolic syndrome (obesity, diabetes mellitus, dyslipidemia, and hypertension). Inflammation and fibrosis associated with NAFLD are referred to as nonalcoholic steatohepatitis (NASH). NAFLD affects as many as 30% of the adult population in the United States, and as many as 20% of these patients also have NASH. NASH progresses to cirrhosis in 10% of patients. NAFLD and NASH are diagnosed after serologic studies have excluded other causes of liver disease. Abdominal imaging with ultrasonography, computed tomography, or magnetic resonance imaging can demonstrate significant hepatic steatosis but cannot reliably identify hepatic inflammation or fibrosis. NASH may be inferred in patients who have the metabolic syndrome and elevated serum aminotransferase levels in the absence of other causes of liver disease. Liver biopsy confirms NASH and identifies the degree of hepatic inflammation and fibrosis. The mainstay of treatment of NAFLD and NASH is weight loss and management of comorbidities.

Medical therapies for NASH remain investigational. The use of statins, as indicated for the management of dyslipidemia, is not contraindicated in patients with elevated liver chemistry test results due to NASH. Antioxidants (such as vitamin E) and oral hypoglycemic medications (metformin, thiazolidinediones such as pioglitazone) have been assessed in clinical trials but have not demonstrated improved clinical outcomes.

KEY POINT

The mainstay of treatment of nonalcoholic fatty liver disease and nonalcoholic steatohepatitis is weight loss and management of comorbidities.

Bibliography

Corrado RL, Torres DM, Harrison SA. Review of treatment options for nonalcoholic fatty liver disease. Med Clin North Am. 2014;98:55-72. [PMID: 24266914]

Item 20   Answer: A

Educational Objective: *Diagnose acute viral hepatitis in a patient with new-onset jaundice.*

The most likely diagnosis is acute viral hepatitis. This patient has evidence of liver inflammation on examination and has jaundice with significant elevations of her serum aminotransferase levels (greater than 15 times the upper limit of normal). In addition, the short duration of her symptoms suggests an acute onset. The degree of elevation of the serum aminotransferase levels suggests acute viral hepatitis. Typically, the only other causes of this degree of liver chemistry test elevation are medication reactions or toxicity, autoimmune liver disease, ischemic hepatitis (sometimes referred to as "shock liver"), and acute bile duct obstruction.

Fulminant liver failure should always be considered in patients with acute hepatitis, although this typically presents with evidence of liver dysfunction in addition to the disturbance of bilirubin metabolism. Findings often include an increase in coagulation time (as measured by the international normalized ratio) due to a decrease in liver production of coagulation factors and a low serum albumin level due to decreased liver albumin production. Both of these measures are normal in this patient. Hepatic encephalopathy may also be present because of the inability of the liver to clear toxic metabolic by-products from the blood; however, this patient has normal mental status. These findings indicate that this patient's liver function remains intact despite the liver inflammation.

Hemochromatosis is a chronic metabolic cause of chronic liver disease and is associated with much lower elevations of liver inflammation markers than are present in this patient.

Primary biliary cirrhosis is an immune-mediated cause of chronic liver inflammation. However, the degree of elevation of serum aminotransferase levels in this patient vastly exceeds the levels that occur in patients with primary biliary cirrhosis, who have elevated serum alkaline phosphatase and bilirubin levels disproportionately higher than the aminotransferase elevation.

KEY POINT

Acute viral hepatitis is characterized by jaundice and significant elevations of serum aminotransferase levels (greater than 15 times the upper limit of normal).

Bibliography

Green RM, Flamm S. AGA technical review on the evaluation of liver chemistry tests. Gastroenterology. 2002;123:1367-84. [PMID: 12360498]

Item 21   Answer: B

Educational Objective: *Diagnose alcoholic hepatitis.*

The patient's clinical history is most consistent with alcoholic hepatitis. Fatigue, a history of excessive alcohol consumption, low-grade fever, jaundice, a tender enlarged liver, and examination findings consistent with chronic liver disease, along with an aspartate aminotransferase to alanine aminotransferase ratio (AST:ALT) greater than 2 are most consistent with alcoholic hepatitis. Alcoholic hepatitis refers to the development of acute liver inflammation associated with alcohol intake, although it frequently occurs in patients who have a history of heavy and prolonged alcohol use. This acute inflammation differs from cirrhosis, which is characterized by progressive hepatic fibrosis that may be a chronic condition resulting from long-term alcohol exposure. While patients with mild to moderate alcoholic hepatitis have a reasonably good prognosis with alcohol abstinence and supportive care, those with severe hepatitis have a high short-term mortality rate and may benefit from treatment, which may include glucocorticoids and pentoxifylline in addition to supportive measures.

Patients who consume excess alcohol are at greater risk for developing acetaminophen hepatotoxicity than those who drink alcohol moderately or not at all. However, acetaminophen doses of greater than 3 g/d are probably needed to cause hepatotoxicity, even for patients with alcoholism, although toxicity may occur at much lower levels of intake in certain patients. This patient has taken only 500 mg/d for 3 days, which is a very low dose. Additionally, acetaminophen toxicity typically results in serum AST and ALT values greater than 5000 U/L, which are not present in this patient.

A patient with autoimmune hepatitis would generally have serum AST and ALT values similar to those of a patient with acute viral hepatitis and the AST:ALT ratio would be less than 2.

Hepatitis A is associated with serum AST and ALT values greater than 500 U/L, often greater than 1000 U/L, with the ALT greater than the AST value, findings that are not present in this patient.

KEY POINT

Fever, a history of alcoholism, an enlarged tender liver, examination findings consistent with chronic liver disease, and an aspartate aminotransferase to alanine aminotransferase ratio greater than 2 are associated with alcoholic hepatitis.

Bibliography

O'Shea RS, Dasarathy S, McCullough AJ; Practice Guideline Committee of the American Association for the Study of Liver Diseases; Practice Parameters Committee of the American College of Gastroenterology. Alcoholic liver disease. Hepatology. 2010; 51:307-28. [PMID: 20034030]

Item 22   Answer: A

Educational Objective: *Treat chronic hepatitis C virus infection.*

Antiviral therapy is indicated for this patient with chronic hepatitis C virus (HCV) infection and advanced fibrosis. Chronic HCV infection is often progressive and may result in cirrhosis and hepatocellular carcinoma. Effective therapy for active HCV infection can delay or prevent these complications. Patients who should be considered for treatment are those who have detectable virus in their blood with some indication of liver inflammation (as indicated by elevated liver chemistry test results or inflammation on a biopsy), as well as no contraindications to therapy (decompensated liver disease [ascites, hepatic encephalopathy, jaundice], pregnancy, severe psychiatric disease, or severe preexisting cytopenia). The treatment of HCV is rapidly changing. Although previous treatments were bases on pegylated interferon and ribavirin, the introduction of protease inhibitors effective against HCV (eg, boceprevir, simeprevir, telepravir) and direct-acting antiviral agents (eg, sofosbuvir) has markedly changed HCV therapy. Therefore, multiple treatment options are increasingly available for HCV. The goal of therapy is to achieve a sustained virologic response, which is defined as undetectable HCV beyond 6 months after the end of treatment. Antiviral therapy for HCV infection is associated with significant morbidity; therefore, which patients are candidates for antiviral therapy should be carefully considered. As this patient has HCV detectable in his blood, evidence of active liver inflammation, and no contraindications to treatment, antiviral therapy is appropriate to attempt to delay or prevent progression of hepatic fibrosis associated with his chronic infection.

Extrahepatic manifestations of chronic HCV infection include hematologic conditions (mixed cryoglobulinemia, lymphoma), skin diseases, autoimmune diseases (thyroiditis), and kidney disease. Some of these conditions may benefit from glucocorticoid and antiviral therapy, but this patient has no indication for glucocorticoid therapy. Glucocorticoids result in increased viral replication and should not be given to patients with hepatitis C unless there is a defined indication for these agents.

Repeating the liver biopsy in 6 months will provide no additional information that will be helpful in this patient's management.

Serial monitoring of serum aminotransferase levels without consideration of antiviral therapy is not appropriate because this patient has advanced fibrosis. Although the overall risk of developing cirrhosis in patients with hepatitis C does not exceed 25%, one of the risk factors for progression to cirrhosis is advanced fibrosis. Therefore, the absence of established cirrhosis in this patient at this time does not mean that he will not develop cirrhosis in the future.

KEY POINT

The best available therapy for chronic hepatitis C is the combination of peginterferon and ribavirin, with the addition of an NS3/4A protease inhibitor for patients with genotype 1 hepatitis C virus.

Bibliography

Ghany MG, Strader DB, Thomas DL, Seeff LB; American Association for the Study of Liver Diseases. Diagnosis, management, and treatment of hepatitis C: an update. Hepatology. 2009;49:1335-74. [PMID: 19330875]

Item 23   Answer: D

Educational Objective: *Manage chronic hepatitis B virus infection.*

The most appropriate management for this patient is observation with serial monitoring of serum aminotransferase levels every 3 to 6 months. Based on her hepatitis B virus (HBV) serologic pattern and presence of circulating HBV DNA, the patient has chronic HBV infection (as opposed to an inactive carrier state in which there would be no evidence of active viral replication with circulating viral DNA). Patients with chronic hepatitis B may have different patterns of infection. This patient appears to be immune-tolerant, identified by the presence of a circulating viral level in the absence of markers of liver inflammation, as indicated by her normal serum aminotransferase levels. This pattern typically occurs in patients born in hepatitis B–endemic areas such as Southeast Asia or Africa in whom HBV was likely acquired perinatally. As long as patients maintain normal serum aminotransferase levels, they are at low risk for progression of liver disease. As this patient ages, she is at increased risk for active hepatitis. Other patients with chronic hepatitis B and a circulating viral level may show evidence of liver inflammation, evidenced by persistently elevated serum aminotransferase levels indicating active hepatitis. In these patients, liver biopsy should be considered and treatment should be initiated if significant inflammation or progressive liver injury is seen.

Initiation of antiviral therapy is not warranted in this patient with immune-tolerant chronic HBV infection because she is unlikely to experience progression of liver disease if her serum aminotransferase levels remain normal. In addition, antiviral therapy may potentially require life-long administration.

Immunization against HBV is not warranted because this patient has already been exposed to the virus, has significant replicating HBV, and has not developed immunity. Immunization would not result in seroconversion to the antibody to hepatitis B surface antigen–positive state.

Liver biopsy is warranted only if liver chemistry test results become elevated. The presence of significant liver inflammation or fibrosis on biopsy indicates the need for antiviral therapy.

KEY POINT

Monitoring of serum aminotransferase levels every 3 to 6 months is warranted in patients with immune-tolerant chronic hepatitis B virus infection.

Bibliography

Lok AS, McMahon BJ. Chronic hepatitis B [erratum in Hepatology. 2007;45:1347]. Hepatology. 2007;45:507-39. [PMID: 17256718]

Item 24   Answer: C

Educational Objective: *Diagnose spontaneous bacterial peritonitis.*

This patient most likely has spontaneous bacterial peritonitis. He presents with a history and physical examination findings strongly suggesting cirrhosis and ascites that are likely based on his chronic alcohol use. The ascitic fluid demonstrates a high serum ascites–albumin gradient (SAAG), calculated by subtracting the ascitic fluid albumin concentration from the serum albumin level (3.2 mg/dL – 1.0 mg/dL = 2.2 mg/dL [32 g/L –10 g/L = 22 g/L]). SAAG values ≥1.1 mg/dL (11 g/L) are consistent with ascites related to cirrhosis or portal hypertension. Additionally, the ascitic fluid leukocyte count is helpful in evaluating for the presence of infection. Neutrophil counts ≥250/µL (250 × 10^6/L) are diagnostic of spontaneous bacterial peritonitis; the ascitic fluid total neutrophil count in this patient is 405/µL (450/µL × 90%) [450 × 10^6/L × 90%], consistent with this diagnosis.

Ascites from malignancy would be expected to have a SAAG less than 1.1 mg/dL (11 g/L). Similarly, peritonitis from bowel perforation would be expected to have a SAAG less than 1.1 mg/dL and a higher leukocyte count. Tuberculous ascites would also be expected to have a SAAG less than 1.1 mg/dL and a lymphocyte predominance in the differential count.

KEY POINT

In patients with cirrhosis and ascites, an ascitic fluid neutrophil count of ≥250/µL (250 × 10^6/L) is diagnostic for spontaneous bacterial peritonitis.

Bibliography
Runyon BA, AASLD, Introduction to the revised American Association for the Study of Liver Diseases Practice Guideline management of adult patients with ascites due to cirrhosis 2012. Hepatology 2013;57:1651-3. [PMID: 23463403]

Item 25   Answer: B

Educational Objective: *Diagnose cirrhosis as a cause of jaundice.*

The patient most likely has cirrhosis as the cause of her jaundice. The physical finding of ascites (shifting dullness, abdominal distention) strongly suggests cirrhosis and portal hypertension, and the presence of spider angiomata is also associated with cirrhosis (positive likelihood ratio 4.3).

Biliary tree obstruction is a possible cause of painless jaundice, but the physical findings of cirrhosis indicate that this patient's liver disease is long-standing.

Brisk hemolysis can cause jaundice but would not produce ascites.

Hepatic vein thrombosis can cause jaundice and ascites, but is typically accompanied by abdominal pain and vomiting.

KEY POINT

Physical findings of spider angiomata and ascites strongly suggest a diagnosis of cirrhosis in a patient with jaundice.

Bibliography
Udell JA, Wang CS, Tinmouth J, et al. Does this patient with liver disease have cirrhosis? JAMA 2012;307:832-42. [PMID: 22357834]

Item 26   Answer: A

Educational Objective: *Diagnose hepatocellular carcinoma.*

The most appropriate next diagnostic test is contrast-enhanced computed tomography (CT) of the abdomen to evaluate for possible hepatocellular carcinoma (HCC). HCC often develops in patients with advanced chronic liver disease, such as hepatitis C. However, patients with hepatitis B may develop HCC in the absence of advanced liver disease. Therefore, screening for HCC every 6 to 12 months is recommended for patients with cirrhosis of any cause and for patients with chronic hepatitis B who are considered at high risk (active inflammation and age >40 years in men and >50 years in women; a family history of HCC; specific ethnic groups [Asians, African/North American blacks]).

HCC derives its blood supply by neovascularization, whereby the tumor develops a new blood supply fed through small branches of the hepatic artery. It is this characteristic vascular supply that helps identify potential cancers on contrast-enhanced imaging, such as triple-phase CT and gadolinium-enhanced magnetic resonance imaging (MRI). Although these modalities tend to be better than ultrasonography at identifying HCC, they are much more complex, inconvenient, and expensive. Therefore, current guidelines recommend the use of ultrasonography to screen for HCC, followed by CT or MRI to better define any abnormalities suggestive of HCC.

Liver biopsy is not indicated at this time. The diagnosis of HCC can be made using noninvasive radiologic criteria in patients with cirrhosis. Multiple studies have documented the high sensitivity and specificity of CT and MRI for diagnosing HCC in patients with cirrhosis who have lesions 2 cm or larger in diameter. If CT and MRI radiologic criteria are typical of HCC, a biopsy is not necessary, and the lesion should be treated as HCC.

Repeat ultrasonography at 6 months is within the recommended surveillance interval of 6 to 12 months for patients with no liver masses on previous ultrasound examinations; it is not the correct diagnostic test for a patient with a liver lesion measuring between 1 and 2 cm, such as the patient described here.

Measurement of serum carcinoembryonic antigen levels is not clinically useful in the diagnosis of HCC.

KEY POINT

In patients with chronic hepatitis B virus infection or cirrhosis and screening abdominal ultrasonography that shows findings consistent with hepatocellular carcinoma, triple-phase abdominal CT or gadolinium-enhanced MRI is the most appropriate next diagnostic test.

Bibliography
Forner A, Vilana R, Ayuso C, et al. Diagnosis of hepatic nodules 20 mm or smaller in cirrhosis: prospective validation of the noninvasive diagnostic criteria for hepatocellular carcinoma [erratum in Hepatology. 2008;47:769.]. Hepatology. 2008;47:97-104. [PMID: 18069697]

Item 27   Answer: C

Educational Objective: *Treat hepatic encephalopathy.*

The most appropriate additional treatment for this patient is to increase the lactulose therapy. This patient has severe encephalopathy manifested by worsening somnolence. If not recognized and treated, encephalopathy progresses from subtle findings, such as reversal of the sleep-wake cycle or mild mental status changes, to irritability, confusion, slurred speech, and ultimately coma. There can be multiple inciting causes of encephalopathy in patients with cirrhosis, including dehydration, infection (especially spontaneous bacterial peritonitis), dietary indiscretions, gastrointestinal bleeding, and medications. This patient likely became worse because of the development of a urinary tract infection.

The most appropriate management is to treat the infection, discontinue the diuretics, and increase the lactulose dose to reverse the encephalopathy. The dose of lactulose should be titrated to achieve two to three soft stools per day with a pH below 6.0. Approximately 70% to 80% of patients with hepatic encephalopathy improve on lactulose therapy, and treatment is usually well tolerated.

Glucocorticoids have no role in the reversal of hepatic encephalopathy.

There is also no role for hemodialysis in the treatment of hepatic encephalopathy, and this patient appears to have no other indications for dialysis (severe acidosis, hyperkalemia, kidney failure with hypervolemia).

Transjugular intrahepatic portosystemic shunt (TIPS) is not appropriate because placement of a TIPS is likely to precipitate worsening hepatic encephalopathy, as more blood is bypassed through the shunt rather than processed by the liver.

KEY POINT

First-line therapy for hepatic encephalopathy is lactulose.

Bibliography

Kalaitzakis E, Bjornsson E. Lactulose treatment for hepatic encephalopathy, gastrointestinal symptoms, and health-related quality of life. Hepatology. 2007;46:949-50. [PMID:17879365]

Item 28   **Answer: A**

Educational Objective: *Diagnose hepatorenal syndrome.*

This patient most likely has hepatorenal syndrome, which is defined as development of kidney failure in patients with portal hypertension and normal renal tubular function. Intense renal vasoconstriction leads to a syndrome of acute kidney dysfunction characterized by increased renal sodium avidity, a relatively normal urine sediment, and oliguria in some patients. This condition is diagnosed after other causes of acute kidney injury such as prerenal azotemia, renal parenchymal disease, or obstruction have been excluded. Spontaneous bacterial peritonitis, vigorous diuretic therapy, paracentesis without volume expansion, and gastrointestinal bleeding also may precipitate hepatorenal syndrome. The most effective treatment is liver transplantation.

Ultrasonography of the kidneys in most patients with obstruction reveals hydronephrosis, which was absent in this patient.

This patient has no signs of hypovolemia such as significant hypotension or tachycardia, and his kidney dysfunction did not improve after discontinuation of diuretics and administration of volume replacement with 0.9% saline and albumin. This makes prerenal azotemia an unlikely diagnosis.

The diagnosis of renal artery stenosis as the cause of this acute kidney injury is unlikely, considering this patient's end-stage cirrhosis, no evidence of hypertension, and no signs of diffuse vascular disease.

KEY POINT

The hepatorenal syndrome is defined as development of kidney dysfunction in patients with portal hypertension after exclusion of prerenal azotemia, renal parenchymal disease, and obstruction as possible causes.

Bibliography

Testino G, Ferro C. Hepatorenal syndrome: a review. Hepatogastroenterology. 2010;57:1279-84. [PMID: 21410072]

Item 29   **Answer: B**

Educational Objective: *Treat a patient with large esophageal varices and contraindication to β-blocker therapy.*

The most appropriate treatment is endoscopic variceal band ligation. The lifetime risk for a first-time variceal bleed in a patient with cirrhosis is 30%, and the mortality risk of such a bleed is 15% to 20%. Therefore, primary prophylaxis is crucial. Current guidelines recommend that all patients with cirrhosis undergo screening upper endoscopy to detect large esophageal varices. Small varices are usually less than 5 mm in diameter; large varices are larger than 5 mm. When large varices are present, as in this patient, the next step in management is use of nonselective β-blocker therapy or endoscopic variceal band ligation as primary prophylaxis to prevent variceal hemorrhage. Although no direct comparison has been performed between these treatments, each modality has a similar effect on preventing an index variceal bleed compared with placebo. However, patients with contraindications to β-blocker therapy, such as asthma or resting bradycardia, can be offered endoscopic ligation. Therefore, propranolol would not be the preferred choice in this patient.

Endoscopic sclerotherapy is also an effective therapy for prophylaxis of large varices. However, because of adverse effects such as esophageal stricturing, endoscopic sclerotherapy has been supplanted by variceal band ligation and is not recommended by major guidelines for primary prophylaxis of large varices.

In patients with active variceal hemorrhage in whom band ligation does not control primary bleeding, or if bleeding recurs or is due to gastric varices, balloon tamponade followed by portal decompression by placement of a transjugular intrahepatic portosystemic shunt (TIPS) can be performed. In the absence of recurrent or refractory variceal hemorrhage, there is no indication for TIPS in this patient.

KEY POINT

Patients with large esophageal varices and contraindications to nonselective β-blocker therapy should receive endoscopic variceal band ligation as prophylactic treatment for variceal hemorrhage.

Bibliography

Opio CK, Garcia-Tsao G. Managing varices: drugs, bands, and shunts. Gastroenterol Clin North Am. 2011;40:561-79. [PMID: 21893274]

Item 30   **Answer: E**

Educational Objective: *Manage asymptomatic gallstones.*

The most appropriate management of this patient's gallstones is observation. An estimated 60% to 80% of gallstones are asymptomatic. Over a 20-year period, 50% of patients remain asymptomatic, 30% develop biliary colic, and 20% develop more significant complications. Observation is recommended for adult patients with asymptomatic gallstones. The possible exceptions to this recommendation are groups at higher risk for gallbladder carcinoma, such as patients with a calcified (porcelain) gallbladder, certain American Indian populations, and patients with gallstones larger than 3 cm.

Once an episode of biliary colic has occurred, repeated episodes are highly likely. Ninety percent or more of significant complications, such as cholecystitis, cholangitis, or pancreatitis, are preceded by attacks of biliary colic. After 5 years without symptoms, however, the risk of repeated episodes of biliary colic and complications in patients with symptomatic gallstone disease appears to be as low as that of patients with asymptomatic gallstones. Cholecystectomy is therefore not indicated for this asymptomatic patient.

Obesity is a risk factor for gallstone disease; however, there is no evidence that weight loss prevents development of symptoms in patients with asymptomatic gallstones. Rapid weight loss is a risk factor for the development or progression of gallstones. Although this patient should be counseled to lose weight for a variety of health reasons, she should not be told that weight loss will decrease her risk of developing symptomatic gallstone disease.

Ultrasonography has high sensitivity (84%) and specificity (99%) for detecting gallstones and should be performed when features of biliary colic are present or a diagnosis of cholecystitis is suspected. However, repeat ultrasonography is not indicated unless the patient becomes symptomatic.

Ursodeoxycholic acid is indicated for patients who are at risk of developing complications of gallstones but who are unable or unwilling to undergo cholecystectomy. Even in such patients, use of ursodeoxycholic acid is limited to patients with small (<10 mm) stones who have a functioning gallbladder and unobstructed bile ducts.

KEY POINT

Prophylactic cholecystectomy is not indicated for most patients with asymptomatic gallstones.

Bibliography

Ransohoff DF, Gracie WA. Treatment of gallstones. Ann Intern Med. 1993;119(7 Pt1): 606-19. [PMID: 8363172]

Item 31   Answer: A

Educational Objective: *Predict cancer risk associated with primary sclerosing cholangitis.*

This patient is at increased risk for developing cholangiocarcinoma and colorectal cancer. Primary sclerosing cholangitis (PSC) confers an estimated annual risk for cholangiocarcinoma of 0.5% to 1.5%. In addition, 30% to 50% of patients are diagnosed with cholangiocarcinoma within 2 years of the diagnosis of PSC. When patients with PSC are found to have acute worsening of liver chemistry test results, acute worsening of symptoms, or a new dominant stricture noted on cholangiography, the possibility of cholangiocarcinoma should be considered. Ulcerative colitis is an independent risk factor for development of colorectal cancer, and patients with both ulcerative colitis and PSC may represent a distinct phenotype of disease with a particularly high rate of colorectal cancer.

Familial adenomatous polyposis (FAP) is a risk factor for colorectal cancer and duodenal cancer. FAP is characterized by hundreds to thousands of adenomatous polyps distributed throughout the colon and rectum, with a mean age at polyp diagnosis of 16 years. Without intervention, nearly all patients with FAP will develop colorectal cancer, with a mean age at cancer diagnosis of 39 years. Duodenal adenomas, particularly in the periampullary region, can be found in 50% to 90% of patients with FAP and portend a lifetime risk for duodenal cancer of 4% to 12% in such patients.

Nearly 80% of hepatocellular carcinomas occur in patients with cirrhosis. Major risk factors are male sex, chronic hepatitis B and C virus infection, hemochromatosis, and α_1-antitrypsin deficiency; however, cirrhosis from any cause can result in hepatocellular carcinoma.

Gastroesophageal reflux disease and obesity are risk factors associated with adenocarcinoma of the esophagus. Chronic pancreatitis predisposes to the development of pancreatic cancer, and tobacco use appears to increase risk. Patients with a *BRCA2* gene mutation are at increased risk for development of pancreatic cancer.

KEY POINT

Patients with ulcerative colitis and primary sclerosing cholangitis are at particularly high risk for development of cholangiocarcinoma and colorectal cancer.

Bibliography

Ehlken H, Schramm C. Primary sclerosing cholangitis and cholangiocarcinoma: pathogenesis and modes of diagnostics. Dig Dis. 2013;31:118-25. [PMID: 23797133]

Item 32   Answer: A

Educational Objective: *Diagnose acute cholecystitis.*

The patient has acute cholecystitis, and the most appropriate next diagnostic step is abdominal ultrasonography. The typical history for patients with acute cholecystitis includes prior episodes of biliary colic, midepigastric pain radiating to the right upper abdominal quadrant, fever, chills, nausea, and vomiting. Physical examination findings usually include right upper quadrant or midepigastric tenderness and pain and arrest of respiration on palpation of the right upper quadrant (Murphy sign). Leukocytosis, mild elevations in serum aminotransferase levels, and mild hyperbilirubinemia are common in patients with acute cholecystitis.

Both abdominal ultrasonography and hepato-iminodiacetic acid (HIDA) scanning are accurate for the diagnosis of acute cholecystitis. The general recommendation has been to obtain ultrasonography first, followed by a HIDA scan if necessary. Despite most organizations recommending ultrasonography as the primary diagnostic tool for acute cholecystitis, the literature shows that a HIDA scan has equal or better sensitivity and specificity; however, cost and ease of access favor the use of ultrasonography. The classic findings of acute cholecystitis on ultrasonography are pericholecystic fluid and a thickened gallbladder wall measuring 3 to 4 mm. The presence of a sonographic Murphy sign (Murphy sign elicited during palpation by the ultrasound transducer) further confirms the diagnosis. The classic finding of acute cholecystitis on a HIDA scan is nonvisualization of the gallbladder.

A contrast-enhanced computed tomographic (CT) scan can show gallstones, gallbladder wall thickening, gallbladder distention, pericholecystic fluid, and inflammation of the pericholecystic fat. An unenhanced CT scan can show gallstones and a hyperdense gallbladder wall, which can suggest the presence of gangrenous cholecystitis. However, CT scanning is expensive and is generally reserved to resolve diagnostic dilemmas and to detect possible complications of acute cholecystitis.

Endoscopic retrograde cholangiopancreatography (ERCP) is an invasive procedure used to remove common duct stones and facilitate biliary drainage and is indicated for patients with cholangitis or for those with gallstone pancreatitis complicated by cholangitis. ERCP is not indicated for the diagnosis of cholecystitis.

KEY POINT

Abdominal ultrasonography is the initial test of choice for the diagnosis of acute cholecystitis.

Bibliography

Trowbridge RL, Rutkowski NK, Shojania KG. Does this patient have acute cholecystitis? JAMA. 2003;289:80-6. [PMID: 12503981]

Item 33   Answer: B
Educational Objective: *Diagnose cholangitis.*

This elderly woman has features suggestive of severe cholangitis. Cholangitis is a syndrome of fever, jaundice, and abdominal pain that develops as a result of stasis and infection in the biliary tract with organisms that typically ascend from the small intestine; the condition is sometimes called ascending cholangitis. Results of liver chemistry tests in this patient support a diagnosis of bile duct obstruction (elevated serum alkaline phosphatase and total bilirubin concentrations), and gallstones are seen on ultrasonography. The common bile duct is also minimally dilated, which may indicate ductal obstruction caused by stones with resultant secondary cholangitis. Treatment is with broad-spectrum antibiotics directed against gram-negative bacteria, enterococci, and gut anaerobes. However, even with antibiotic therapy, the mortality rate for cholangitis is high unless ductal decompression is performed. Urgent endoscopic retrograde cholangiopancreatography is therefore warranted to document choledocholithiasis (common bile duct stones) and perform endoscopic therapy, if indicated.

Symptoms of acute hepatitis A usually include malaise, fatigue, nausea, and vomiting. Serum aminotransferase levels are generally greater than 1000 U/L. In addition, acute hepatitis A cannot explain the dilated common bile duct or the gallstones identified in this patient.

Acute cholecystitis is a syndrome of right upper quadrant abdominal pain, fever, and leukocytosis associated with gallbladder inflammation that is usually related to gallstone disease. It is not associated with infection, although antibiotic treatment is used in certain clinical situations. The diagnosis of acute cholecystitis is not supported by this patient's ultrasound findings (absence of gallbladder wall thickening and pericholecystic fluid) and cannot explain her dilated common bile duct.

Acute pancreatitis does not typically cause right upper quadrant abdominal pain and is unlikely to cause a septic state (fever, tachycardia, hypotension, and altered mental status) over just a few hours.

KEY POINT

Patients with severe cholangitis generally present with fever, jaundice, and altered mental status; abdominal pain is usually, but not invariably, present.

Bibliography

Flasar MH, Goldberg E. Acute abdominal pain. Med Clin North Am. 2006;90:481-503. [PMID: 16473101]

Item 34   Answer: E
Educational Objective: *Manage resolving acute pancreatitis.*

The most appropriate management is to resume oral intake. This patient has uncomplicated acute pancreatitis. In such patients, conservative management consisting of intravenous fluids, pain control, and bowel rest (nothing by mouth) until there is clinical improvement is appropriate. Once the patient has definite symptomatic improvement, a trial of resuming oral intake should be initiated. If the patient tolerates oral intake well, intravenous fluids may be discontinued. and the patient can be prepared for discharge. Although the time course of acute pancreatitis is variable, most patients with uncomplicated acute pancreatitis show symptomatic improvement within 72 to 96 hours.

If symptoms persist or worsen beyond 72 to 96 hours and the patient cannot resume oral intake, it is appropriate to consider nasojejunal enteral feedings. Recent evidence suggests that the use of early nasoenteral (particularly nasojejunal) feeding may reduce morbidity, particularly infectious complications, when compared with intravenous feeding. However, there is nothing to indicate that this patient cannot be fed orally, and nasoenteral feedings are not indicated at this time.

Because of this patient's clinical improvement, continued bowel rest for another 24 hours is unnecessary, and oral intake can be resumed.

Serum amylase or lipase measurements are sensitive and specific laboratory studies for evaluating acute pancreatitis. One of these tests may be used for initial diagnosis; measuring both is not routinely required in a clinical situation consistent with pancreatitis. However, the both measures may remain elevated for days to weeks after resolution of symptoms and serial measurement is therefore not useful for making management decisions in patients with uncomplicated acute pancreatitis. Repeating the test in a patient with an uncomplicated course is also not cost-effective.

In patients with severe acute pancreatitis whose condition is not improving or who continue to have fever after 3 to 5 days, contrast-enhanced computed tomographic (CT) scanning should be performed to evaluate for necrosis. This patient is obviously improving and vital signs, including temperature, are normal. He therefore does not require CT scanning prior to the initiation of oral feeding.

KEY POINT

Patients with mild acute pancreatitis should be managed conservatively with intravenous fluids, symptomatic treatment of pain and nausea, and bowel rest; oral feedings can be resumed when there is definite clinical improvement.

Bibliography

Gupta K, Wu B. In the clinic. Acute pancreatitis. Ann Intern Med. 2010;153:ITC51-5. [PMID: 21041574]

Item 35   Answer: C
Educational Objective: *Identify risk factors for poor prognosis in a patient with acute pancreatitis.*

The best predictors of higher morbidity and mortality in patients with acute pancreatitis are those associated with hemoconcentration, such as elevated blood urea nitrogen, serum creatinine, or hematocrit levels. Multiple scoring systems have been devised to prognosticate outcomes in patients with acute pancreatitis. The Ranson criteria rely on parameters that are measured at admission and at 48 hours; because of their complexity and the lag time for prognosis, these criteria are now rarely used. The Acute Physiology and Chronic Health Evaluation II score is more accurate than the Ranson criteria, but the score is cumbersome to obtain. Some studies have suggested hemoconcentration as a potential predictor of morbidity and mortality in patients with acute pancreatitis because it serves as a marker of capillary leak. Patients with severe disease tend to have elevated levels of blood urea nitrogen, serum creatinine, and occasionally hematocrit (all markers of hemoconcentration). Of these factors, the blood urea nitrogen level appears to be the most accurate for predicting severity. Other factors that predispose patients to a poor prognosis are multiple medical comorbidities, age greater than 70 years, and body mass index greater than 30.

There is no correlation between the degree of elevation of the serum amylase level and severity or prognosis of illness in patients with acute pancreatitis.

In the setting of hemoconcentration, this patient's slightly decreased hematocrit level may actually represent a more significant anemia. He should be carefully monitored for worsening anemia as he is aggressively treated with intravenous hydration. However, the anemia itself is not an indicator of a poor prognosis.

Mild leukocytosis is common in patients with acute pancreatitis and has no prognostic significance.

KEY POINT

An elevated blood urea nitrogen level indicates a poor prognosis in patients with acute pancreatitis.

Bibliography

Gupta K, Wu B. In the clinic. Acute pancreatitis. Ann Intern Med. 2010;153:ITC51-5. [PMID: 21041574]

Item 36   Answer: D

Educational Objective: *Manage an asymptomatic pancreatic pseudocyst following acute pancreatitis.*

This patient requires no further diagnostic testing or therapy. She has an asymptomatic pancreatic pseudocyst that developed as a result of her acute pancreatitis 8 weeks earlier. Pancreatic pseudocysts are the most common complication of acute pancreatitis. They are cystic collections of pancreatic juice that have a fibrous nonepithelial lining that occurs around the gland. The pseudocysts generally take at least 4 weeks to form, often resolve spontaneously, and are asymptomatic; they may, however, cause pain or obstruction by pressing against other organs. Because this patient did not have a fluid collection at the time of initial presentation, the collection is a result of the pancreatitis and not a cause. She requires no further testing or therapy because she is currently asymptomatic, and the pseudocyst will very likely resolve spontaneously.

Magnetic resonance cholangiopancreatography (MRCP) is a noninvasive technique for imaging the bile ducts and the pancreatic duct. In a patient with a pancreatic pseudocyst, MRCP might be useful to better define the extent of the cyst, particularly if the cyst may be compressing the pancreatic duct. However, in this patient, MRCP is not necessary because she is asymptomatic and without any indications for further definition of the pseudocyst.

Percutaneous or surgical drainage of the fluid collection is not indicated at this time because the patient is asymptomatic. Drainage would be advised only if she developed symptoms such as pain, fever, or anorexia.

KEY POINT

Asymptomatic pancreatic pseudocysts following acute pancreatitis typically resolve spontaneously and do not require treatment.

Bibliography

Gumaste VV, Aron J. Pseudocyst management: endoscopic drainage and other emerging techniques. J Clin Gastroenterol. 2010;44:326-31. [PMID: 20142757]

Item 37   Answer: E

Educational Objective: *Manage acute diarrhea.*

This patient needs no additional studies at this time. She has had acute diarrhea for only 1 day. For most patients, this finding represents a self-limited gastroenteritis, which is supported by the fact that this patient's work colleagues have recently had similar symptoms. Features or clinical characteristics that require additional evaluation for acute diarrhea include fever; bloody stools; diarrhea in pregnant, elderly, or immunocompromised patients; hospitalization; employment as a food handler; recent antibiotic use; volume depletion; or significant abdominal pain. This patient has none of these features. She should therefore be encouraged to stay well hydrated, use antidiarrheal agents as needed, and follow up if symptoms change or persist.

Clostridium difficile polymerase chain reaction and stool culture should be considered in patients with any features that require additional evaluation, but are not indicated for this patient unless her acute diarrhea persists.

The presence of fecal leukocytes is nonspecific and may represent infection, ischemia, or idiopathic inflammation; evaluation for fecal leukocytes rarely adds much information in the evaluation of acute diarrhea.

Flexible sigmoidoscopy with random biopsies can be used for evaluating patients with chronic watery diarrhea to assess for microscopic colitis. However, sigmoidoscopy is not indicated in the acute setting unless the patient has clinical features that suggest ischemic colitis (sudden onset of mild crampy abdominal pain and bloody diarrhea). These features are not present in this patient.

KEY POINT

Most patients with acute diarrhea have a self-limited gastroenteritis that requires no further evaluation.

Bibliography

Baldi F, Bianco MA, Nardone G, et al. Focus on acute diarrhoeal disease. World J Gastroenterol. 2009;15:3341-8. [PMID: 19610134]

Item 38   Answer: C

Educational Objective: *Diagnose celiac disease.*

The most appropriate diagnostic test to perform next in this patient is a tissue transglutaminase (tTG) IgA antibody assay to screen for celiac disease. Celiac disease is an immunologic response to dietary gliadins in patients who are genetically at risk as determined by the presence of *HLA-DQ2* or *HLA-DQ8*. The typical features of celiac disease are diarrhea, bloating, and weight loss. Iron deficiency anemia is a common finding, as are associated autoimmune diseases such as Hashimoto thyroiditis and type 1 diabetes mellitus. Patients with celiac disease may have difficulty absorbing supplemental iron and levothyroxine. The most appropriate serologic test to screen for celiac disease is the tTG IgA antibody assay. Patients with a positive tTG IgA antibody assay should undergo upper endoscopy with small bowel biopsies to establish the diagnosis of celiac disease. Characteristic histologic findings include increased intraepithelial lymphocytes and mucosal atrophy with loss of villi. The mainstay treatment of celiac disease is a gluten-free diet.

Colonoscopy is a reasonable diagnostic test if colon cancer is thought to be responsible for iron deficiency anemia, particularly in adults age 50 years or older or in patients with a family history of colon cancer. However, in addition to iron deficiency anemia, this patient has weight loss, postprandial bloating, and bulky, foul-smelling stools that float. These findings are suggestive of malabsorption, not colon cancer.

Testing of *HLA* status is in patients with suspected celiac disease is not recommended as the initial diagnostic study because 30% to 40% of the general population has *HLA-DQ2* or *HLA-DQ8* positivity. However, *HLA* testing could be considered in patients with nondiagnostic histologic findings or negative serologic markers in whom celiac disease remains a likely diagnostic possibility.

Not doing additional tests is inappropriate for a patient with unexplained iron deficiency anemia. Every effort must be made to ascertain the cause of the anemia. In addition, celiac disease is associated with a 33-fold increased risk for lymphomas of the gut as well as an increased risk for non-Hodgkin lymphoma at any site. Establishing celiac disease as the cause of this patient's iron deficiency anemia has important implications for long-term follow-up care.

KEY POINT

The most appropriate serologic test to screen for celiac disease is the tissue transglutaminase IgA antibody assay.

Bibliography

Crowe SE. In the clinic. Celiac disease. Ann Intern Med. 2011;154:ITC5-1-ITC5-15; quiz ITC5-16. [PMID: 21536935]

Item 39   Answer: A

Educational Objective: *Diagnose severe* Clostridium difficile *infection.*

This patient most likely has severe *Clostridium difficile* infection (CDI). Patients with CDI typically present with watery diarrhea, although the range of symptoms spans an asymptomatic carrier state to severe fulminant colitis with toxic megacolon. Patients with CDI and associated colitis typically have diarrhea up to 10 to 15 times daily, lower abdominal pain, cramping, fever, and leukocytosis that often exceeds 15,000/μL (15×10^9/L). CDI with colitis is most commonly associated with previous antibiotic administration. The colitis is produced by two toxins, A and B. Each has different mechanisms of action, but both toxins are highly potent and cause cytotoxicity at extremely low concentrations. The toxins can be detected by clinical laboratory testing, and the presence of either toxin confirms the diagnosis. Treatment of severe CDI with colitis consists of oral vancomycin and intravenous metronidazole.

The typical presentation of Crohn disease is abdominal pain, diarrhea, and weight loss that occur over a period of months, if not years. This patient's severe and rapidly progressive course is not consistent with Crohn disease.

Patients with uncomplicated diverticulitis present with abdominal pain and fever. Physical examination discloses left lower quadrant abdominal tenderness. Leukocytosis is present, and urinalysis may show sterile pyuria due to inflammation close to the bladder. This patient's 2-day history of severe diarrhea is not consistent with diverticulitis.

Diverticulosis refers to the presence of diverticula in the colon. Diverticulosis is common in aging Western populations and is not associated with pain or diarrhea.

Ischemic colitis symptoms include left lower quadrant abdominal pain and bloody diarrhea, which are often self-limited. Treatment is supportive and includes intravenous fluids and bowel rest. Most symptoms resolve within 48 hours. This patient's progressive symptoms are not consistent with a diagnosis of ischemic colitis.

KEY POINT

Patients with previous exposure to antibiotics may develop *Clostridium difficile* infection and associated colitis, which is characterized by diarrhea up to 10 to 15 times daily, lower abdominal pain, cramping, fever, and leukocytosis.

Bibliography

Bartlett JG, Gerding DN. Clinical recognition and diagnosis of *Clostridium difficile* infection. Clin Infect Dis. 2008;46:Suppl1:S12-8. [PMID: 18177217]

Item 40   Answer: C

Educational Objective: *Treat severe* Clostridium difficile *infection.*

The most appropriate treatment is oral vancomycin, or possibly oral vancomycin plus intravenous metronidazole. This patient presents with a first relapse of *Clostridium difficile* infection (CDI) and findings consistent with severe disease. Systemic findings, such as fever and leukocytosis, are usually absent in patients with mild disease. Colitis may develop and is associated with fever, cramps, leukocytosis, and fecal leukocytes. Colitis is documented by colonoscopy (showing pseudomembranes) or computed tomography (showing colonic wall thickening). Severe CDI may cause paralytic ileus with cessation of diarrhea and development of toxic megacolon. In accordance with current guidelines, recommended treatment of severe disease is oral vancomycin, or possibly oral vancomycin plus intravenous metronidazole for severe disease with multiorgan system failure or hypotension.

Colectomy may be considered for patients with severe CDI who do not respond to pharmacologic therapy, usually within 48 hours. Other indications for more immediate surgical intervention include the presence of toxic megacolon, perforation, or the systemic inflammatory response syndrome and multiorgan system failure.

Intravenous metronidazole alone would not be recommended as primary therapy in this patient with severe disease. Additionally, metronidazole should not be used beyond the first recurrence of CDI or for long-term chronic therapy because of the potential for cumulative neurotoxicity.

Delivery of oral therapy to the site of infection may be impaired in patients with ileus or obstruction, and, in such patients, vancomycin enemas in combination with oral vancomycin and intravenous metronidazole may facilitate more effective delivery of vancomycin to the infection site; however, in such circumstances, vancomycin enemas are used in addition to other agents.

KEY POINT

Oral vancomycin or oral vancomycin plus intravenous metronidazole is recommended for patients with severe *Clostridium difficile* infection; vancomycin per rectum combined with oral vancomycin and intravenous metronidazole is used for patients with ileus or obstruction.

Bibliography

Cohen SH, Gerding DN, Johnson S, et al. Society for Healthcare Epidemiology of America; Infectious Diseases Society of America. Clinical practice guidelines for Clostridium difficile infection in adults: 2010 update by the society for healthcare epidemiology of America (SHEA) and the infectious diseases society of America (IDSA). Infect Control Hosp Epidemiol. 2010;31:431-55. [PMID: 20307191]

Item 41   Answer: C

Educational Objective: *Diagnose lactose malabsorption.*

This patient most likely has lactose malabsorption that developed as a result of her recent food-borne illness or gastroenteritis. This is a relatively common occurrence and is usually self-limited. Evaluation for the presence of an osmotic diarrhea is performed by estimating the stool osmotic gap using stool electrolytes:

$$290 - 2 \times [\text{stool sodium} + \text{stool potassium}]$$

A gap greater than 100 mOsm/kg (100 mmol/kg) indicates an osmotic cause of diarrhea. Lactose malabsorption is the most common cause of a stool osmotic gap. Reducing this patient's lactose intake to no more than 12 g with each meal (equivalent to one glass of milk) will often result in symptom improvement. Lactose intake can slowly be increased as more time elapses after her acute illness and her lactose intolerance improves.

Bile-salt-induced diarrhea is unlikely. Even though some patients may have an increase in stool frequency after cholecystectomy, this patient's surgery was remote enough that it would not cause her current symptoms. In addition, it would not explain the stool osmotic gap, as bile-salt-induced diarrhea tends to cause a secretory diarrhea.

Features of irritable bowel syndrome (IBS) can develop after a bout of gastroenteritis. Although this patient may later develop persistent symptoms due to IBS, a stool osmotic gap is not consistent with the diagnosis of IBS.

Microscopic colitis causes a secretory diarrhea, and a stool osmotic gap does not typically occur.

KEY POINT

Lactose malabsorption is the most common cause of a stool osmotic gap and may occur transiently after an episode of self-limited gastroenteritis.

Bibliography

Shaukat A, Levitt MD, Taylor BC, et al. Systematic review: effective management strategies for lactose intolerance. Ann Intern Med. 2010;152:797-803. [PMID: 20404262]

Item 42   Answer: D

Educational Objective: *Diagnose small intestinal bacterial overgrowth as a complication of bariatric surgery.*

Patients who undergo bariatric surgery are at risk for specific early and late complications of the procedure; small intestinal bacterial overgrowth is a late complication that can manifest with bloating, diarrhea, and features of malabsorption. Having segments of small intestine excluded from the usual stream of gastric acid, bile, and proteolytic enzymes, which all act to decrease excess bacterial growth in the small intestine, is a risk factor for bacterial overgrowth. The diarrhea in bacterial overgrowth can be from deconjugation of bile salts from the intestinal bacteria, leading to fat malabsorption, as well as from decreased disaccharidase levels, leading to carbohydrate malabsorption. Culture of the normally sterile small intestine or carbohydrate (lactulose, glucose, or d-xylose) breath testing can be done to substantiate the diagnosis; alternatively, in some patients an empiric trial of antibiotic therapy can be considered.

Bile acids are normally reabsorbed in the distal small intestine, and bile salt malabsorption is associated with resection of a portion of the terminal ileum (short bowel syndrome). However, in typical Roux-en-Y procedures the bypass is significantly proximal to the distal ileum, and bile salt malabsorption is not an expected complication of a bypass procedure.

Celiac disease should be considered in any patient with diarrhea and features of malabsorption, and a tissue transglutaminase IgA antibody assay would be a reasonable study to obtain as part of this patient's evaluation. However, in a patient without a previous history of malabsorption and who has altered gastrointestinal anatomy, such as occurs with gastric bypass, bacterial overgrowth is a more likely cause of his clinical findings.

Irritable bowel syndrome should not cause nocturnal stools, weight loss, and vitamin derangements.

KEY POINT

Small intestinal bacterial overgrowth is a late complication of bariatric surgery and should be considered in patients presenting with diarrhea, bloating, and features of malabsorption after such surgery.

Bibliography

Decker GA, Swain JM, Crowell MD, Scolapio JS. Gastrointestinal and nutritional complications after bariatric surgery. Am J Gastroenterol. 2007;102:2571-80. [PMID: 17640325]

Item 43   Answer: C

Educational Objective: *Diagnose inflammatory bowel disease.*

This patient should undergo colonoscopy. Although irritable bowel syndrome (IBS) is common in this age group, and many features of this patient's presentation suggest this syndrome (including the chronicity of symptoms, their association with stress, and the pattern of alternating diarrhea and constipation), she has two alarm symptoms, weight loss and anemia. These findings are not consistent with IBS, and in a younger patient with gastrointestinal symptoms associated with weight loss and anemia, there is significant concern for inflammatory bowel disease. In patients with diarrhea in whom inflammatory bowel disease is suspected, colonoscopy is the preferred initial diagnostic study, as it allows direct visualization of the colonic mucosa and terminal ileum, which may be sufficient to diagnose both ulcerative colitis and Crohn disease. Colonoscopy also enables biopsy samples to be obtained that may help distinguish which form of inflammatory bowel disease is present.

Antispasmodic medications are helpful for symptomatic treatment of IBS. However, their use in a patient with findings incompatible with this diagnosis is inappropriate.

Benzodiazepines have only a very limited role in the treatment of IBS because of minimal effectiveness, side effects, and potential habituation. Use of benzodiazepines is therefore not indicated for this patient, even if IBS is found to be her diagnosis.

Other diagnostic studies, such as abdominal computed tomographic (CT) scanning, may have a role in establishing a diagnosis of inflammatory bowel disease, particularly in patients with abdominal pain without diarrhea. However, CT scans use ionizing radiation, which may increase the risk for future malignancy, particularly in young patients. Therefore, abdominal CT scanning should be used very judiciously in this patient population.

Patients with gastrointestinal symptoms and the presence of alarm symptoms (weight loss, anemia, fever, chronic severe diarrhea, family history of gastrointestinal disease) should undergo further evaluation; this recommendation includes evaluation for younger patients with these findings who are at increased risk for inflammatory bowel disease.

Bibliography

Halpin SJ, Ford AC. Prevalence of symptoms meeting criteria for irritable bowel syndrome in inflammatory bowel disease: systematic review and meta-analysis. Am J Gastroenterol. 2012;107:1474-82. [PMID: 22929759]

Item 44   Answer: B

Educational Objective: *Manage toxic megacolon in a patient with ulcerative colitis.*

The most appropriate management is immediate surgery for treatment of toxic megacolon. Most patients with toxic megacolon related to ulcerative colitis have at least 1 week of bloody diarrhea that is unresponsive to medical therapy. On examination, patients have tachycardia, fever, hypotension, decreased or absent bowel sounds, and lower abdominal distention and tenderness, often with peritoneal signs. On plain film radiographs, the transverse colon is most affected, with dilatation exceeding 6 cm. This patient has toxic megacolon based on the clinical history, examination findings, and imaging studies. Toxic megacolon is the most severe complication in patients with ulcerative colitis; it is associated with a 40% mortality rate in patients undergoing emergency colectomy after a perforation has occurred (compared with a 2% rate in patients without a perforation). About 50% of patients with toxic megacolon may improve with medical therapy (bowel rest, intravenous glucocorticoids, antibiotics, and fluids); however, progressive abdominal distention and tenderness with hemodynamic instability are indications for immediate surgery.

Computed tomography could further identify the extent of colonic dilatation and wall thickening as well as possible abscess formation or microperforation, but this would not change the required management of this patient and would delay the institution of definitive therapy.

Infliximab is an appropriate treatment option for some patients with severe ulcerative colitis, but it is not an effective therapy for toxic megacolon and would not be indicated in this patient.

Glucocorticoids, such as methylprednisolone, are appropriate for treatment of a flare of ulcerative colitis, and possibly less severe toxic megacolon, but are only indicated if the patient is clinically stable.

Toxic megacolon is the most severe complication associated with ulcerative colitis; progressive abdominal distention and tenderness with hemodynamic instability are indications for immediate surgery.

Bibliography

Autenrieth DM, Baumgart DC. Toxic megacolon. Inflamm Bowel Dis. 2012;18:584-91. [PMID: 22009735]

Item 45   Answer: A

Educational Objective: *Diagnose Crohn disease.*

This patient's clinical presentation is most consistent with Crohn disease. She has evidence of systemic inflammation, as indicated by her elevated erythrocyte sedimentation rate and mild anemia. The colon-oscopy shows areas of deep ulceration separated by normal mucosa (skip lesions) and rectal sparing, findings more consistent with a diagnosis of Crohn disease than with ulcerative colitis. In addition, the patient is a smoker, which increases the risk for Crohn disease.

Ischemic colitis most commonly affects older patients who have cardiovascular risk factors and a preceding hypotensive or embolic event predisposing to bowel ischemia, findings that are not present in this patient.

Microscopic colitis is typically found in middle-aged women, is often associated with other autoimmune diseases, does not cause abdominal pain, and is not associated with the changes on colonoscopy found on this patient's examination.

Although ulcerative colitis also frequently presents with evidence of systemic inflammation, the findings on colonoscopy typically show continuous inflammation, usually including the rectum, and usually do not show deep ulcers or skip lesions. Ulcerative colitis is more common in former smokers or nonsmokers than in current smokers.

Crohn disease is characterized by focal, asymmetric, transmural lesions and by skip lesions on colonoscopy, whereas ulcerative colitis is characterized by diffuse mucosal inflammation that is limited to the colon and extends proximally and continuously from the anus.

Bibliography

Baumgart DC, Sandborn WJ. Crohn's disease. Lancet. 2012;380:1590-605. [PMID: 22914295]

Item 46   Answer: A

Educational Objective: *Manage colorectal cancer screening in a patient with ulcerative colitis.*

The most appropriate management for this patient is colonoscopy now and every 1 to 2 years. Patients with ulcerative colitis with disease extending beyond the rectum are at an increased risk of developing colorectal cancer. Cancer risk has been widely reported to be between 0.5% and 1% per year after having extensive disease for 10 years or more. The exact risk for an individual patient is uncertain and is probably based on the duration and extent of disease, severity of inflammation, and other personal factors. Based on this increased cancer risk, routine surveillance colonoscopy with biopsies every 1 to 2 years is warranted beginning 8 to 10 years after diagnosis. Because cancers associated with ulcerative colitis tend to arise from the mucosa, as opposed to the usual adenoma-cancer sequence, biopsies are taken from flat mucosa throughout the colon and are evaluated for dysplastic changes. A finding of flat, high-grade dysplasia warrants recommending colectomy because of the high rate of concomitant undetected cancer. A finding of flat, low-grade dysplasia warrants either colectomy or continued surveillance colonoscopy at more frequent intervals.

Although colonoscopy now is appropriate for this patient, the interval should be every 1 to 2 years rather than every 5 years. For persons without ulcerative colitis but with a family history of colorectal cancer in a first-degree relative, screening is initiated either at age 40 years or beginning 10 years earlier than the diagnosis of the youngest affected family member. Colonoscopy every 10 years starting at age 40 is not appropriate for this patient.

Patients with ulcerative colitis with disease extending beyond the rectum should undergo routine surveillance colonoscopy with biopsies every 1 to 2 years beginning 8 to 10 years after diagnosis.

Bibliography

Kornbluth A, Sachar DB; Practice Parameters Committee of the American College of Gastroenterology. Ulcerative colitis practice guidelines in adults: American College Of Gastroenterology, Practice Parameters Committee [erratum in Am J Gastroenterol. 2010;105:500.]. Am J Gastroenterol. 2010;105:501-23. [PMID: 20068560]

Item 47   Answer: D

Educational Objective: *Treat acute upper gastrointestinal bleeding.*

This patient with acute upper gastrointestinal bleeding would benefit most from a proton pump inhibitor (PPI), such as pantoprazole. *Helicobacter pylori* infection and nonsteroidal anti-inflammatory drugs (NSAIDs) are the two most common causes of upper gastrointestinal bleeding. Ibuprofen and other NSAIDs block the enzyme cyclooxygenase and interfere with production of prostaglandins that play a central role in the defense and repair of gastric epithelium. In patients with peptic ulcer bleeding, beginning a PPI before undergoing upper endoscopy has been shown to decrease the likelihood of high-risk stigmata on subsequent upper endoscopy and to reduce the likelihood of requiring an intervention during the procedure. In patients with peptic ulcer disease, the use of intravenous PPI therapy has also been shown to reduce the risk of recurrent hemorrhage following endoscopic hemostasis.

Erythromycin and metoclopramide (motility agents) should not be used routinely prior to upper endoscopy because they have not been shown to alter the need for erythrocyte transfusion or surgery or shorten the hospital stay. However, motility agents may decrease the need for repeat upper endoscopy because of improved visibility at the initial endoscopy, particularly in patients with active bleeding. The absence of nausea and recent vomiting and stable vital signs in this patient argue against ongoing, or at least brisk, gastrointestinal bleeding being present.

Nasogastric tubes are not routinely recommended because they do not improve clinical outcomes. They may be considered in patients with persistent nausea and vomiting, particularly if associated with gastric outlet obstruction. This patient has not vomited in the last 18 hours and does not require a nasogastric tube.

Octreotide is effective in controlling variceal hemorrhage by decreasing portal venous inflow and consequently intravariceal pressure. Although the patient drinks alcohol, he has no history of liver disease or any peripheral stigmata of chronic liver disease. Variceal bleeding would therefore be unlikely.

H$_2$ receptor antagonists, such as ranitidine, are not as effective as PPIs in the treatment of upper gastrointestinal bleeding due to peptic ulcer disease.

In patients with upper gastrointestinal bleeding due to peptic ulcer disease, proton pump inhibitors can decrease the potential need for intervention during upper endoscopy and can reduce the risk of recurrent hemorrhage.

Bibliography

Prasad Kerlin M, Tokar JL. Acute gastrointestinal bleeding. Ann Intern Med. 2013;159: ITC2-1TC2-15; quiz ITC2-16. [PMID: 23922080]

Item 48   Answer: B

Educational Objective: *Diagnose obscure gastrointestinal bleeding in an elderly patient.*

The most likely cause of this patient's obscure gastrointestinal bleeding is a small bowel angiectasia. Obscure gastrointestinal bleeding is recurrent bleeding without a defined source following standard upper endoscopy and colonoscopy. Obscure bleeding in which blood is clinically apparent (such as melena) is known as overt bleeding. Occult bleeding is defined as clinically suspected bleeding without overt signs of blood loss (for example, in a patient with anemia and positive fecal occult blood testing). Many patients with obscure gastrointestinal bleeding have sources in the small intestine between the ligament of Treitz and the ileocecal valve, sometimes referred to as "mid-gastrointestinal bleeding." Angiectasia is the most common cause of small intestinal bleeding in the elderly, accounting for up to 80% of cases. While angiectasias usually causes chronic blood loss, they can also cause acute hemodynamically significant bleeding.

Acute mesenteric ischemia is caused by an inadequate blood flow to all or part of the small intestine. The most common cause is a superior mesenteric artery embolism from the left atrium or ventricular mural thrombi. The next most common cause is nonocclusive mesenteric ischemia after a cardiovascular event. Patients with acute mesenteric ischemia are typically older than 50 years and have underlying cardiac disease. The classic presentation is acute onset of severe abdominal pain; the abdomen is typically soft and less tender than expected based on the patient's symptoms (pain out of proportion to the examination findings). This patient's chronic illness and lack of abdominal pain are not consistent with the diagnosis of acute mesenteric ischemia.

Meckel diverticulum is a congenital anomaly that is located near the ileocecal valve. It often contains heterotopic gastric mucosa that can ulcerate and bleed. Technetium 99m pertechnetate has an affinity for gastric mucosa, and the Meckel scan identifies the heterotopic mucosa. Meckel diverticulum tends to cause bleeding in children and should be considered in younger patients presenting with gastrointestinal bleeding of obscure origin but is unlikely in a 72-year-old woman.

Small bowel tumors (adenocarcinomas, carcinoid, lymphoma, stromal tumors) are a cause of small intestinal gastrointestinal leading but are much less common than angiectasias.

Angiectasia is the most common cause of obscure small intestinal bleeding in elderly patients, accounting for up to 80% of cases.

Bibliography

Prasad Kerlin M, Tokar JL. Acute gastrointestinal bleeding. Ann Intern Med. 2013;159: ITC2-1TC2-15; quiz ITC2-16. [PMID: 23922080]

Item 49   Answer: B

Educational Objective: *Manage rectal bleeding.*

In this average-risk patient, the most appropriate next step is endoscopic evaluation (colonoscopy or sigmoidoscopy) to rule out colonic neoplasia as a source of bleeding. Typically, patients with hemorrhoidal bleeding report streaks of bright red blood on the toilet paper or on the outside of a firm stool. Hemorrhoids are unlikely to cause serious bleeding. Internal hemorrhoids are not painful because there is no innervation to the colonic mucosa proximal to the dentate line.

External hemorrhoids are frequently painful, particularly with bowel movements. Although hemorrhoids are a common cause of bright red blood from the rectum, rectal bleeding should not be considered hemorrhoidal without additional investigation in older patients. Most authorities agree that the type of evaluation is governed by the patient's risk for colon cancer. In young patients (age <40 years) with typical symptoms of hemorrhoid bleeding and low risk for colon cancer, additional evaluation of the colon is unnecessary. Because of the increasing incidence of colon cancer with age, patients 40 to 50 years old with typical hemorrhoidal symptoms but at low risk for colon cancer should probably at least have a sigmoidoscopy. Patients aged 50 years and older should undergo colonoscopy to evaluate the source of bleeding if routine screening has not been performed recently.

If colon cancer is excluded by colonoscopy, this patient's hemorrhoids can be treated conservatively. Banding of internal hemorrhoids and other invasive procedures for either internal or external hemorrhoids are reserved for patients who do not respond to conservative therapy.

Fiber supplementation is an appropriate treatment for this patient with hard stools but is inappropriate as the only management for his hematochezia, as this would potentially put him at risk for a missed diagnosis of colon cancer.

Home fecal occult blood testing would likely be positive, but whether positive or negative, the recommendation for this 46-year-old patient remains the same. He requires colonoscopy or sigmoidoscopy based upon the report of bright red rectal bleeding.

KEY POINT

Patients older than 40 years with hematochezia should undergo colon cancer evaluation with colonoscopy or sigmoidoscopy.

Bibliography

Schubert MC, Sridhar S, Schade RR, Wexner SD. What every gastroenterologist needs to know about common anorectal disorders. World J Gastroenterol. 2009;15:3201-9. [PMID: 19598294]

Item 50   Answer: C

Educational Objective: *Evaluate the source of suspected upper gastrointestinal bleeding.*

The most appropriate diagnostic test to perform next is upper endoscopy. In a patient with suspected upper gastrointestinal bleeding, the presenting symptoms can suggest the degree and volume of blood loss. The presence of melena (black, tarry stools) suggests an upper gastrointestinal tract source but can be associated with loss of as little as 150 to 200 mL of blood. Hematemesis of bright red blood is associated with ongoing upper gastrointestinal bleeding, whereas hematochezia secondary to an upper gastrointestinal source is suggestive of brisk ongoing bleeding of at least 1000 mL of blood. Presyncope and syncope may occur with hypovolemia secondary to bleeding. This patient has hematochezia, significant anemia, and hemodynamic instability. His use of ibuprofen for his knee injury increases the chance of an upper gastrointestinal source of bleeding. The absence of blood or coffee-ground material in the nasogastric tube aspirate does not rule out an upper gastrointestinal bleeding source; nasogastric tube placement can miss up to 15% of actively bleeding lesions, especially if no bile is noted on the aspirate. Therefore, placement of a nasogastric tube when there is a high suspicion of upper gastrointestinal bleeding is not very helpful and

should not guide a decision as to whether or not to perform upper endoscopy. A brisk upper gastrointestinal source of bleeding can cause hematochezia and can be life threatening if not acted upon early. If an upper gastrointestinal source is suspected, urgent upper endoscopy should be performed.

If the upper endoscopy is unrevealing, a rapid lavage and colonoscopy is the next study, followed by a nuclear medicine tagged red blood cell scan if no bleeding source is found.

Video capsule endoscopy is reserved for persistent occult (or overt) gastrointestinal bleeding without an identified upper or lower gastrointestinal source.

KEY POINT

If an upper gastrointestinal source of bleeding is suspected in a patient with hematochezia, upper endoscopy is the most appropriate diagnostic procedure.

Bibliography

Davila RE, Rajan E, Adler DG, et al; Standards of Practice Committee. ASGE Guideline: the role of endoscopy in the patient with lower-GI bleeding. Gastrointest Endosc. 2005;62:656-60. [PMID: 16246674]

Item 51   Answer: B

Educational Objective: *Diagnose diverticular bleeding.*

The most likely diagnosis is diverticulosis. In patients with severe hematochezia, the most common site of bleeding is the colon (75%). Within the colon, the most likely cause of bleeding is diverticula, which constitute 33% of all colonic bleeding. Bleeding is arterial, resulting from medial thinning of the vasa recta as they drape over the dome of the diverticulum. Generally, patients do not have other symptoms. Physical examination is usually unremarkable unless large blood loss results in tachycardia, hypotension, and orthostasis. Colonoscopy may identify the bleeding diverticulum and permit endoscopic treatment with epinephrine and/or electrocautery; colonoscopy may also help identify other causes of bleeding such as vascular ectasias. Vascular ectasias. or angiodysplasias (erroneously called arteriovenous malformations) account for up to 11% of episodes of lower gastrointestinal bleeding. They are painless dilated submucosal vessels that radiate from a central feeding vessel. Patients may present with iron deficiency anemia and occult gastrointestinal bleeding or with hematochezia that is indistinguishable from diverticular hemorrhage.

Colon cancer rarely, if ever, causes brisk arterial bleeding. Colon cancer typically causes chronic blood loss that is often occult; this is not compatible with this patient's findings.

The presence of melena (black, tarry stools) suggests an upper gastrointestinal tract source of bleeding (such as from a duodenal ulcer) but can be associated with loss of as little as 150 to 200 mL of blood. Hematemesis of bright red blood is associated with ongoing upper gastrointestinal bleeding, whereas hematochezia secondary to an upper gastrointestinal source is suggestive of brisk ongoing bleeding of at least 1000 mL of blood and is typically associated with hemodynamic instability, which is absent in this patient.

Ischemic colitis, which accounts for between 1% and 19% of episodes of lower gastrointestinal bleeding, results from a sudden temporary reduction in mesenteric blood flow. This hypoperfusion typically affects the "watershed" areas of the colon (that is, the splenic flexure and rectosigmoid junction). Patients may report dizziness but may not recall such episodes. They present with the sudden onset of mild crampy abdominal pain and subsequent passage of bloody stool or bloody diarrhea.

KEY POINT

The majority of patients with hematochezia have a colonic source of bleeding (75%); when bleeding is from the colon, the most frequent source is diverticula.

Bibliography

Wilkins T, Baird C, Pearson AN, Schade RR. Diverticular bleeding. Am Fam Physician. 2009;80:977-983. [PMID: 19873964]

Item 52   Answer: A

Educational Objective: *Manage upper gastrointestinal bleeding and hemodynamic instability.*

This patient should continue to receive intravenous fluid and erythrocyte resuscitation. She has experienced a large gastrointestinal hemorrhage with resultant hemodynamic instability. Her history of aspirin use suggests an upper gastrointestinal source of bleeding. Appropriate intravenous access has been obtained, and 0.9% saline fluid boluses and intravenous proton pump inhibitor infusions have been started. Despite this, she remains unstable and has a hemoglobin level of 7 g/dL (70 g/L). The most important and urgent treatment for this patient is erythrocyte transfusion and intravenous crystalloid administration to achieve hemodynamic stability, as an intensive resuscitation strategy has been shown to improve mortality in patients with severe gastrointestinal bleeding. Volume loss is estimated by pulse rate, blood pressure, and the presence of orthostatic hypotension because changes in hemoglobin and hematocrit levels may not become evident immediately. An initial hemoglobin level of less than 8 g/dL (80 g/L) is concerning because re-equilibration in the 24 to 48 hours after the initial bleeding episode may reveal an even lower hemoglobin level.

Octreotide is a somatostatin analogue that reduces portal venous pressure and has vasoconstrictive properties; it is therefore used to treat bleeding due to variceal hemorrhage, but would not be appropriately used empirically in this patient without known or suspected liver disease.

After further resuscitation with packed red blood cells and intravenous crystalloid, this patient will require upper endoscopy within 24 hours of presentation. However, upper endoscopy is not appropriate at this time in an incompletely resuscitated patient with ongoing instability. Additionally, medications administered for moderate sedation during standard upper endoscopy may result in hypotension and could cause further hemodynamic insult.

Nasogastric tube placement can be helpful in selected patients in whom the location of bleeding is in question. However, there is a high enough false-negative rate (approximately 15%) and false-positive rate (due to nasogastric tube mucosal irritation) that this is not uniformly recommended and would not be the first priority in this patient. Furthermore, this patient has hematemesis, indicating significant upper gastrointestinal hemorrhage.

KEY POINT

Patients with upper gastrointestinal bleeding should be stabilized with intravenous fluid and erythrocyte resuscitation before diagnostic upper endoscopy is performed.

Bibliography

Barkun AN, Bardou M, Kuipers EJ, et al; International Consensus Upper Gastrointestinal Bleeding Conference Group. International consensus recommendations on the management of patients with nonvariceal upper gastrointestinal bleeding. Ann Intern Med. 2010;152:101-13. [PMID: 20083829]

Section 4

General Internal Medicine

Questions

Item 1 [Basic]

A 26-year-old woman is being evaluated for a 2-day complaint of left-sided pleuritic chest pain and mild shortness of breath. Her symptoms began after she worked out at a gym and have continued since. She has no other complaints. Her medical history is unremarkable, and she takes no medications. Her family history is negative for thromboembolic disease.

Examination shows a well-appearing woman in no distress. Her blood pressure is 118/68 mm Hg, heart rate is 65 beats/min, and respiratory rate is 12 breaths/min. Oxygen saturation on ambient air is 99%. The chest is clear, and the remainder of her examination findings are unremarkable.

Using the Wells criteria, you estimate her pretest probability of pulmonary embolism (PE) as a cause of her symptoms to be 15%. A D-dimer study is obtained, and the result is negative; the sensitivity of D-dimer for PE is 96%.

Which of the following is the most appropriate next in management of this patient?

(A) Anticoagulation for likely PE
(B) Computed tomographic angiography
(C) Consider an alternative diagnosis
(D) Lower extremity Doppler ultrasonography
(E) Pulmonary angiography

Item 2 [Basic]

A blood pressure screening program is being developed. A review of data for the two communities in which the program will be implemented shows that one has a 30% prevalence of hypertension, and the other has 12% prevalence.

This difference in hypertension prevalence is most likely to affect which of the following measures associated with a specific screening intervention?

(A) Sensitivity
(B) Specificity
(C) Predictive value
(D) Likelihood ratio

Item 3 [Advanced]

A 58-year-old man is evaluated in the office for substernal chest pain. The pain is not consistently associated with exertion, nor is it always relieved by rest; it sometimes occurs when he is eating or when he is anxious. He notes no dyspnea or diaphoresis. The patient has a history of hypertension treated with lisinopril and a 25-pack-year history of cigarette smoking.

On physical examination, his blood pressure is 148/92 mm Hg and heart rate is 78 beats/min. Cardiovascular examination is unremarkable, and the remainder of the physical examination findings are normal.

The patient's pretest probability of having ischemic coronary artery disease is estimated to be 50%. Because of resting electrocardiogram (ECG) changes that would make interpreting an exercise ECG stress test difficult, a treadmill echocardiographic stress test is scheduled to further evaluate the chest pain. This test has a positive likelihood ratio (LR[+]) of 10.0 and a negative likelihood ratio (LR[-]) of 0.1. The patient's stress test result is positive.

Which of the following values best approximates the patient's posttest probability of having ischemic coronary artery disease?

(A) 5%
(B) 25%
(C) 50%
(D) 75%
(E) 95%

Item 4 [Advanced]

A series of 4 new blood tests (A, B, C, and D) are developed to diagnose a disease. The operating characteristics for a variety of different cut points for each of the four tests are shown plotted on a receiver operating characteristic (ROC) curve.

Receiver Operator Characteristic (ROC) Curve

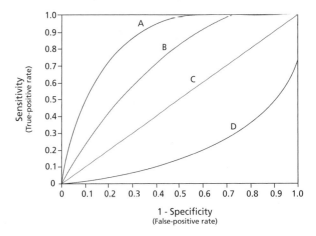

Which of the following tests has the best overall accuracy?

(A) A
(B) B
(C) C
(D) D

Item 5 [Basic]

A new medication is released (drug A) to prevent development of deep venous thrombosis (DVT). The results of a clinical trial of this medication are reviewed along with data from a trial of the most commonly used medication (drug B) for DVT prophylaxis. The following data are abstracted from these trials:

Study results:

Drug	Patients in Study (*n*)	DVT Cases (*n*)
Drug A	2500	25
Drug B	2500	50

Based on these data, how many patients need to be treated (number needed to treat [NNT]) with drug A compared with drug B to prevent one extra case of DVT?

(A) 1
(B) 2
(C) 25
(D) 100
(E) 167

Item 6 [Advanced]

A 50-year-old woman is evaluated for nonischemic cardiomyopathy. Her exercise tolerance is not limited and she is otherwise asymptomatic (New York Heart Association [NYHA] functional class I). She took a β-blocker briefly but discontinued because of fatigue. Results of the physical examination are normal.

The patient inquires whether she should receive a new medication she recently read about. You look up the primary study about the drug. The drug was studied in a randomized controlled trial (RCT) of 2000 patients ages 40 to 80 years (mean age, 63 years) with NYHA functional class III or IV heart failure. Patients received either the drug or a placebo in addition to usual medications. Eighty percent of patients in the trial also took a β-blocker. At the end of 3 years, patients taking the study drug had a significantly reduced rate of death and heart failure exacerbations. Five percent of the patients taking the study drug had serious adverse events compared with 2% in the placebo group.

Which of the following is the main reason why this patient should not be treated with the new drug?

(A) Her heart failure is too mild
(B) She is too young
(C) She should be treated with a β-blocker first
(D) The drug's adverse event rate is too high

Item 7 [Advanced]

A 75-year-old man is hospitalized with sepsis leading to multiorgan failure. The treatment team, including infectious disease and critical care consultants, concludes that the patient is deteriorating despite optimized therapy, and the prognosis is poor. A student on the team asks whether the patient should be started on a new medication for treating sepsis that she recently read about.

A review of the only trial of this medication showed that it involved treatment of 100 consecutive patients with refractory sepsis in five

intensive care units located in the same geographic region and reported that 8% of patients being treated were alive at 30 days.

Which of the following is the main reason that it is difficult to determine the effectiveness of this drug based on the published study?

(A) No comparison group
(B) Outcome assessment not blinded
(C) Patients not randomly assigned to treatment
(D) Small study size

Item 8 [Basic]

A 66-year-old man is evaluated during a routine examination. He is physically active and has no specific complaints. His medical history is significant for hypertension. He drinks three or four beers three times per week and has done so for the past 30 years. He is a former smoker, with a 15-pack-year history, but has not smoked in the past 20 years. His only medication is hydrochlorothiazide.

On physical examination, he is afebrile, his blood pressure is 124/76 mm Hg, and his pulse rate is 72 beats/min. The examination is otherwise unremarkable. A fasting lipid profile last year was within normal limits. His most recent colonoscopy was performed 5 years ago and was negative for any polyps.

Which of the following is the most appropriate screening test?

(A) Abdominal ultrasonography
(B) Chest radiography
(C) Coronary artery calcium score determination
(D) No additional testing

Item 9 [Basic]

A 30-year-old woman is evaluated during a routine examination. She received a routine tetanus, diphtheria, and acellular pertussis booster 5 years ago. She is sexually active with a single lifetime sexual partner. She has had no history of sexually transmitted infection. She reports receiving "routine shots" in childhood. She has had regular Papanicolaou smears without any abnormal results; her most recent was 3 years ago. She does not smoke cigarettes. Findings on physical examination are unremarkable.

Which of the following vaccinations should be administered?

(A) Hepatitis B vaccine series
(B) Human papillomavirus vaccine series
(C) Influenza vaccine
(D) Tetanus and diphtheria vaccine

Item 10 [Advanced]

A 65-year-old man is evaluated as a new patient. A review of his previous records shows he received a 23-valent polysaccharide pneumococcal vaccination (PPSV23) 6 years ago when he was admitted to the hospital with community-acquired pneumonia. He has never received the 13-valent pneumococcal conjugate vaccine (PCV13). He feels well with no acute symptoms. He has type 2 diabetes mellitus, hypertension, and hyperlipidemia. His medications are insulin glargine, metformin, lisinopril, and simvastatin. Results of the physical examination are unremarkable.

What additional pneumococcal vaccination should this patient receive?

(A) Both PPSV23 and PCV13 vaccinations today

(B) No further pneumococcal vaccinations are required

(C) PCV13 vaccination today and PPSV23 vaccination in 1 year

(D) PPSV23 vaccination today and PCV13 vaccination in 1 year

(E) Repeat PPSV23 vaccination only today

Item 11 [Basic]

A 52-year-old man is seen in the clinic for a new patient evaluation. He feels well and has no complaints. His medical history is negative, and he takes no medications. He does not smoke. His family history is negative for colon cancer.

On physical examination, his vital signs are normal, and his general physical examination is unremarkable. Laboratory studies are all within normal limits.

Which of the following is an appropriate screening strategy for colon cancer in this patient?

(A) Annual digital rectal examination

(B) Colonoscopy every 10 years

(C) Computed tomographic colonography every 5 years

(D) Flexible sigmoidoscopy every 10 years

Item 12 [Advanced]

A 64-year-old man is evaluated during a routine health maintenance examination. He asks about the zoster vaccine but is hesitant to receive it because it is a live vaccine and he is worried about its safety. In addition, he reports that he already had an episode of shingles when he was 45 years old. His medical history is significant for type 2 diabetes mellitus. His current medications are metformin and glipizide.

Which of the following is the most appropriate recommendation for this patient?

(A) Vaccination is contraindicated

(B) Vaccination should be offered now

(C) Vaccination should be offered at age 70 years

(D) Vaccination should be offered if varicella antibody serology is negative

Item 13 [Basic]

A 23-year-old man is evaluated during a routine examination. He is asymptomatic. He is a nonsmoker and has no history of illicit drug use. He has had two lifetime female sexual partners and is sexually active in a monogamous relationship with a woman for the past 2 years. His father is 48 years old and has hypertension; his mother is 46 years old and has hyperlipidemia. The results of the physical examination, including vital signs, are normal.

Which of the following is the most appropriate screening test to obtain?

(A) Chlamydia nucleic acid amplification test

(B) HIV antibody/p24 antigen test

(C) Resting electrocardiogram

(D) Thyroid-stimulating hormone level

Item 14 [Basic]

A 19-year-old woman is evaluated at a routine follow-up visit. She feels well and has no complaints. She states that she is not sexually active and has not engaged in prior sexual activity. She has a boyfriend whom she has dated for the past year. Her medical history is otherwise negative, and she takes no medications. She does not use alcohol or smoke. She has not received a human papillomavirus (HPV) vaccine.

On physical examination, her vital signs are normal. The rest of her physical examination findings are unremarkable.

Which of the following is the most appropriate recommendation for preventing HPV infection in this patient?

(A) HPV vaccine at age 21 years

(B) HPV vaccine at onset of sexual activity

(C) HPV vaccine at time of HPV seroconversion

(D) HPV vaccine now

Item 15 [Advanced]

A 54-year-old man is evaluated during a follow-up visit for hypertension. His office blood pressure measurements have been elevated; however, his home readings range from 118 to 140 mm Hg systolic and 82 to 88 mm Hg diastolic, averaging 124/82 mm Hg. He has no known cardiovascular disease and no family history of hypertension. He eats a relatively heart-healthy diet, exercises regularly, and does not smoke cigarettes.

Blood pressure measurements are 150/86 mm Hg and 147/83 mm Hg; comparisons with his home blood pressure cuff correlate well. Other vital signs are normal. The remainder of the examination findings are unremarkable.

Previous laboratory study results have been normal, and he had a normal electrocardiogram 2 years ago.

Which of the following is the most likely cause of this patient's blood pressure elevations?

(A) Essential hypertension

(B) Masked hypertension

(C) Primary hyperaldosteronism

(D) Renovascular hypertension

(E) White coat hypertension

Item 16 [Basic]

A 45-year-old man returns for a follow-up visit to discuss his blood pressure results. He was seen for a new patient visit 6 weeks ago. His blood pressure at that time was 138/82 mm Hg, and his evaluation was otherwise unremarkable. At a follow-up visit 2 weeks later, his blood pressure was 136/85 mm Hg. His family history is significant for his mother who has hypertension. He does not smoke cigarettes or use alcohol or drugs. He takes no medications.

On physical examination, his blood pressure is 135/84 mm Hg; his other vital signs are normal. The rest of the examination findings, including cardiac and pulmonary examinations, are normal.

Laboratory study results are significant for normal electrolytes and kidney function. An electrocardiogram is normal.

Which of the following is the most appropriate next step in the management of this patient's blood pressure?

(A) Ambulatory blood pressure monitoring
(B) Hydrochlorothiazide
(C) Recheck blood pressure in 2 weeks
(D) Recheck blood pressure in 1 year

Item 17 [Basic]

A 34-year-old man is evaluated during a follow-up visit for an elevated blood pressure measurement. On a clinic visit 3 weeks ago, his blood pressure was 150/94 mm Hg. He has no knowledge of prior blood pressure measurements. He has a family history of hypertension. He takes no medications and does not use tobacco.

On physical examination, his temperature is 37.1°C (98.8°F), blood pressure is 156/100 mm Hg, pulse rate is 82 beats/min, and respiration rate is 18 breaths/min. Funduscopic examination shows arteriolar narrowing with two arteriovenous crossing defects ("nicking"). Examination of the heart is normal as is the remainder of his physical examination.

Laboratory studies, including serum electrolytes, glucose, complete blood count, lipids, kidney function, and urinalysis, are normal.

Which of the following is the most appropriate next step in management?

(A) Echocardiography
(B) Electrocardiography
(C) Home blood pressure monitoring
(D) Plasma aldosterone–plasma renin activity ratio

Item 18 [Basic]

A 43-year-old man is evaluated during a follow-up visit for a 3-year history of type 2 diabetes mellitus and hypertension. His diabetes has been well controlled on a twice-daily dose of metformin. He takes lisinopril, 20 mg/d, for hypertension; his blood pressure measurements are typically around 125/75 mm Hg.

On physical examination, his vital signs recorded by a medical assistant show a temperature of 37.3°C (99.2°F), blood pressure of 154/78 mm Hg, and pulse rate of 82 beats/min. The rest of the examination findings are normal.

Laboratory studies reveal normal electrolytes, complete blood count, fasting lipid profile, and urine albumin–creatinine ratio as well as normal kidney function; his hemoglobin A_{1c} level is 7.1%.

Which of the following is the most appropriate next step in management?

(A) Add hydrochlorothiazide
(B) Ambulatory blood pressure monitoring
(C) Increase lisinopril
(D) Repeat blood pressure measurement

Item 19 [Basic]

An 86-year-old man is evaluated during a follow-up visit for hypertension. He has been treated for elevated blood pressure for the past 15 years and has had no hypertension-associated end-organ dam-

age. His medications are maximal daily doses of amlodipine and lisinopril, which he tolerates well.

On physical examination, his blood pressure is 146/68 mm Hg, heart rate is 72 beats/min, and the respiratory rate is 12 breaths/min. There are no significant cardiopulmonary findings, and the rest of the physical examination findings are unremarkable.

Laboratory studies reveal normal electrolytes and kidney function.

Which of the following is the most appropriate next step in managing this patient's blood pressure?

(A) Add chlorthalidone
(B) Add metoprolol
(C) Discontinue amlodipine; begin hydrochlorothiazide
(D) No change in management

Item 20 [Advanced]

A 25-year-old woman is seen in the clinic for a preconception evaluation. She has a history of hypertension that is well controlled with lisinopril. Her medical history is otherwise unremarkable.

On physical examination, her blood pressure is 134/86 mm Hg; other vital signs are normal. Cardiovascular evaluation is normal, as is the remainder of her physical examination.

Laboratory studies reveal normal electrolytes, complete blood count, thyroid-stimulating hormone level, kidney function, and urinalysis.

An electrocardiogram is normal.

In addition to starting a prenatal vitamin, which of the following medication adjustments should be made before this patient proceeds with pregnancy?

(A) Discontinue lisinopril
(B) Substitute labetalol for lisinopril
(C) Substitute losartan for lisinopril
(D) Substitute spironolactone for lisinopril

Item 21 [Basic]

A 67-year-old woman is evaluated during a follow-up appointment. She recently underwent cardiac catheterization for chest pain. A significant left anterior descending coronary artery lesion was found, and she underwent percutaneous transluminal coronary angioplasty and stenting. She reports no recurrent chest pain or other symptoms. Her medical history is significant for hypertension and hyperlipidemia. She is a nonsmoker. Her medications include metoprolol; aspirin; and atorvastatin, 10 mg, taken at bedtime.

On physical examination, her blood pressure is 128/67 mm Hg, pulse is 58/min, and respiration rate is 12/min. The cardiovascular and general medical examinations findings are normal.

Laboratory studies:

Total cholesterol	228 mg/dL
Low-density lipoprotein cholesterol	123 mg/dL
High-density lipoprotein cholesterol	93 mg/dL
Triglycerides	113 mg/dL (1.28 mmol/L)

Additional laboratory testing indicates normal kidney and liver function.

In addition to diet and exercise therapy, which of the following is the most appropriate management of this patient's lipids?

(A) Add niacin
(B) Increase the atorvastatin dose to 20 mg
(C) Increase the atorvastatin dose to 40 mg
(D) Continue the current therapy

Item 22 [Basic]

A 56-year-old woman is evaluated during a follow-up visit after presenting as a new patient 2 weeks ago. At that time, her blood pressure was 156/88 mm Hg, and follow-up laboratory tests were ordered. She has had no major illnesses. Her father had type 2 diabetes mellitus and died at age 52 years of a myocardial infarction. She is currently taking no medications.

On physical examination, her blood pressure is 160/90 mm Hg, pulse rate is 86/min, and respiration rate is 16/min. Her body mass index is 34. Results of funduscopic examination are normal. The remainder of the examination is normal.

Laboratory studies:

Creatinine	0.9 mg/dL (79.6 µmol/L)
Low-density lipoprotein cholesterol (fasting)	162 mg/dL (4.19 mmol/L)
High-density lipoprotein cholesterol (fasting)	32 mg/dL (0.83 mmol/L)
Triglycerides (fasting)	148 mg/dL (1.67 mmol/L)
Glucose (fasting)	98 mg/dL (5.4 mmol/L)
Urinalysis	Trace protein, no glucose

In addition to hypertension and obesity, which of the following is the most likely diagnosis?

(A) Hypertriglyceridemia
(B) Impaired fasting glucose
(C) Metabolic syndrome
(D) No additional diagnoses

Item 23 [Advanced]

A 19-year-old man is evaluated during a routine physical examination. He is asymptomatic, has no medical problems, and takes no medications. He is a nonsmoker and drinks two alcoholic beverages daily. His father and uncle had myocardial infarctions between the ages of 55 and 60 years.

On physical examination, vital signs are normal. His body mass index is 28. On the skin examination, he has soft, nontender, yellow plaques measuring between 0.5 and 1 cm on his upper eyelids. The remainder of the physical examination results are normal.

Which of the diagnostic studies should be done next?

(A) Aminotransferase and alkaline phosphatase
(B) Serum ferritin
(C) Serum glucose and hemoglobin A_{1c}
(D) Serum lipids
(E) Thyroid-stimulating hormone

Item 24 [Basic]

A 38-year-old white man is evaluated during a follow-up visit to discuss his lipid profile study. He was seen as a new patient several weeks ago, and a fasting lipid profile was performed. His medical history is negative for a personal or family history of heart disease; stroke; transient ischemic attack; diabetes mellitus; or renal, liver, or thyroid disease. His father has hypertension. He takes no medications and does not smoke.

On physical examination, blood pressure is 125 mm Hg; other vital signs are normal. His body mass index is 32. His cardiovascular and general medical examination findings are unremarkable.

Fasting lipid levels are as follows: total cholesterol, 234 mg/dL (6.1 mmol/L); high-density lipoprotein cholesterol, 48 mg/dL (1.2 mmol/L); low-density lipoprotein cholesterol, 158 mg/dL (4.1 mmol/L); and triglycerides: 165 mg/dL (1.9 mmol/L). All other laboratory findings are within normal limits.

In addition to dietary, weight, and exercise recommendations, which of the following is the most appropriate management option for this patient?

(A) Begin therapy with a fibrate
(B) Begin therapy with a statin
(C) Obtain lipoprotein(a) level
(D) Repeat lipid screening in 1 to 2 years

Item 25 [Advanced]

A 55-year-old woman is evaluated during a follow-up appointment for dyslipidemia. She was found to have a total cholesterol level of 325 mg/dL (8.40 mmol/L) and low-density lipoprotein (LDL) cholesterol level of 268 mg/dL (6.94 mmol/L) 2 months ago and was started on high-intensity statin therapy. She has been compliant with treatment, although she notes mild fatigue and occasional constipation. Her medical history is otherwise negative. She does not use alcohol or smoke. She is menopausal. Her only medication is atorvastatin, 80 mg, at night.

On physical examination, she is afebrile, and blood pressure is 134/82 mm Hg, pulse rate is 66/min, and respiration rate is 12/min. Her body mass index is 25. She has mildly dry skin.

Laboratory studies:

Total cholesterol	284 mg/dL (7.36 mmol/L)
LDL cholesterol	231 mg/dL (5.98 mmol/L)
HDL cholesterol	55 mg/dL (1.42 mmol/L)
Triglycerides	113 mg/dL (1.28 mmol/L)
Glucose (fasting)	100 mg/dL (5.5 mmol/L)

Additional laboratory results reveal normal kidney and liver function.

In addition to recommending diet and exercise therapy, which of the following is the most appropriate management?

(A) Add ezetimibe
(B) Switch atorvastatin to rosuvastatin
(C) Measure hemoglobin A_{1c} level
(D) Measure thyroid-stimulating hormone level

Item 26 [Basic]

A 44-year-old woman is evaluated in the office for obesity. She has been unable to lose the weight she gained during her three pregnancies. She has tried several diets but has not been successful in maintaining weight loss. She does not smoke or drink alcohol. Her other medical problems include hypertension treated with ramipril and depression treated with bupropion. The patient had a tubal ligation after her last pregnancy.

On physical examination, she is afebrile, and her blood pressure is 148/86 mm Hg, heart rate is 72 beats/min, respiratory rate is 18 breaths/min, and body mass index is 34. The rest of the physical examination findings are normal.

In addition to a low-calorie diet and increased physical activity, which of the following is the most appropriate treatment for this patient?

(A) Gastric bypass surgery
(B) Lorcaserin
(C) Orlistat
(D) Topiramate–phentermine

Item 27 [Advanced]

A 38-year-old man is evaluated in the office for treatment of depression. He also mentions that he has gained 30 lb (13.6 kg) over the past 10 years. His medical history is significant only for major depression 15 years ago treated with amitriptyline. Although the medication was effective in treating his depression, he was bothered by excessive weight gain, dry mouth, and constipation.

On physical examination, his blood pressure is 138/86, heart rate is 76 beats/min, and body mass index is 31. He had a normal fasting lipid panel and glucose 10 months ago.

In addition to a low-calorie diet and regular exercise, which of the following is the most appropriate initial drug therapy for this patient's depression and obesity?

(A) Bupropion
(B) Mirtazapine
(C) Paroxetine
(D) Venlafaxine

Item 28 [Basic]

A 48-year-old woman is evaluated during a routine examination. She is concerned about her gradual weight gain over the years and requests advice on weight reduction.

She has gained approximately 18 kg (40 lb) over the past 10 years. She has dieted many times with moderate weight loss but has always gained it back. She has a sedentary job and states she cannot fit exercise into her busy schedule. She takes no medications.

On physical examination, her vital signs are normal. Her body mass index is 32. There is no thyromegaly. The abdomen is obese and without striae. Her fasting plasma glucose level is 106 mg/dL (5.9 mmol/L), and thyroid function test results are normal.

Which of the following is the most appropriate next step to help this patient achieve long-term weight reduction?

(A) Exercise 15 to 30 minutes 5 days/week
(B) Laparoscopic adjustable band surgery
(C) Orlistat
(D) Reduce current caloric intake by 500 to 1000 kcal/d

Item 29 [Advanced]

A 42-year-old-man is evaluated for obesity. His weight has gradually increased over the past 20 years and is currently 168.2 kg (370 lb). Five years ago, he was diagnosed with type 2 diabetes mellitus, hypertension, and hyperlipidemia. He has unsuccessfully tried diet and exercise therapy for his obesity over the past 6 months. He was unable to tolerate orlistat because of gastrointestinal side effects. His medications are metformin, lisinopril, and simvastatin.

On physical examination, his temperature is normal, blood pressure is 130/80 mm Hg, pulse rate is 80 beats/min, and respiration rate is 14 breaths/min. His body mass index is 48. There is no thyromegaly. Heart sounds are normal with no murmur. There is no lower extremity edema.

Results of complete blood count, thyroid studies, and urinalysis are unremarkable.

Which of the following is the most appropriate management of this patient?

(A) Bariatric surgery evaluation
(B) Prescribe phentermine
(C) Reduce caloric intake to below 800 kcal/d
(D) Refer to an exercise program

Item 30 [Advanced]

A 47-year-old woman is evaluated for a follow-up examination. She underwent Roux-en-Y gastric bypass surgery 10 years ago and has successfully kept off the weight she lost after the surgery. Because of her stabilized weight loss and uncomplicated course, she discontinued routine medical follow-up and has not seen a physician for 5 years. Her medical history is otherwise negative. She takes no medications.

On physical examination, her vital signs are normal. Her body mass index is 24. Cardiovascular, pulmonary, and neurologic examination findings are all normal. There is no thyromegaly. Abdominal examination shows a well-healed surgical scar. The remainder of the examination is unremarkable. A stool sample is heme negative.

Laboratory studies:

Leukocyte count	4200/µL (4.2 × 10^9/L)
Hemoglobin	10.9 g/dL (109 g/L)
Mean corpuscular volume	107 fL
Platelet count	122,000/µL (122 × 10^9/L)
Reticulocyte count	1.5%

Which of the following is the most appropriate test to establish the diagnosis?

(A) Bone marrow biopsy
(B) Colonoscopy
(C) Serum thyroid-stimulating hormone level
(D) Serum vitamin B$_{12}$ level

Item 31 [Basic]

A 75-year-old woman is evaluated in the office for 3 months of back pain. She reports that the pain in her lower back began after she slipped and fell on a wet floor 3 months ago. She denies fever, weight loss, numbness or tingling in her legs, radicular pain, and bowel or bladder incontinence. She has been taking ibuprofen daily for 1 month with some improvement in her pain.

She has a 5-month history giant cell arteritis and has been on a tapering dose of prednisone since diagnosis. Her current dose of prednisone is 12 mg daily. She also takes calcium and vitamin D.

On examination, her vital signs are normal. She has point tenderness to palpation of the lumbar spine at the L4 level. Her neurologic examination findings are normal, and she has a negative straight leg raise test result.

Which of the following is the most appropriate initial imaging test?

(A) Computed tomographic myelography
(B) Lumbar spine radiography
(C) Magnetic resonance imaging of the spine
(D) Noncontrast computed tomography of the lumbar spine

Item 32 [Advanced]

A 30-year-old man is evaluated in the office for chronic low back pain. He reports the gradual onset of progressive pain and stiffness in his lower back and buttocks over 3 years. He denies any trauma at the onset of the pain. He is most stiff upon waking up in the morning and improved after he has been up and about. Acetaminophen provides no relief. He has no other medical problems and takes no additional medications.

On physical examination, his vital signs are normal. He has decreased range of motion of his back, with reduced forward flexion, and pain with palpation of the sacroiliac joints. He has a negative straight leg raise test result, and normal neurological examination findings.

Which of the following is the most appropriate initial imaging study?

(A) Anterior-posterior plain radiography of the pelvis
(B) Electromyography
(C) Magnetic resonance imaging of the spine
(D) Noncontrast computed tomography of the pelvis

Item 33 [Basic]

A 44-year-old man is evaluated for low back pain that developed acutely 5 days ago when he was playing racquetball. He felt a popping sensation in his back and a shooting pain down his leg. The pain worsened over 2 to 3 days but has improved slightly with ibuprofen. His pain is rated as 5 of 10, but he reports no numbness, weakness, or bladder or bowel incontinence.

On physical examination, his vital signs are normal. Straight leg raise test on both sides reproduces pain in the left leg. The ankle reflex is diminished on the left. There are no motor or sensory deficits observed and no saddle anesthesia. Rectal tone is normal. He is able to walk with some discomfort.

Which of the following is the most appropriate management of this patient?

(A) Analgesics and mobilization as tolerated
(B) Complete blood count and erythrocyte sedimentation rate
(C) Epidural corticosteroid injection
(D) Lumbar spine magnetic resonance imaging
(E) Lumbar spine radiography

Item 34 [Advanced]

A 24-year-old woman is seen in the office for evaluation of a cough for 2 weeks. Her symptoms began 3 weeks ago with a mild nonproductive cough, rhinorrhea, nasal congestion, and malaise. Although her other symptoms improved, the cough has persisted, is episodic, and at times is very severe with episodes of posttussive emesis. She does not have fever, shortness of breath, or chest pain. She does not have any symptoms of gastroesophageal reflux disease. Her medical history is unremarkable with no prior respiratory conditions. She works in a day care center. She does not smoke, and she takes no medications.

On examination, her temperature is 37.6°C (99.7°F), blood pressure is 118/72 mm Hg, and respiratory rate is 12 breaths/min. Oxygen saturation is 98% while she is breathing ambient air. The chest is clear, and the rest of her examination findings are normal.

Which of the following is the most likely etiology of her cough?

(A) Postinfectious
(B) Gastroesophageal reflux disease
(C) Cough-variant asthma
(D) Pertussis

Item 35 [Basic]

A 30-year-old man is evaluated in the office for a 3-month history of cough. He denies postnasal drip, rhinorrhea, acid reflux symptoms, asthma, and wheezing. He coughs during the night as well as during the day. He denies fever, sputum production, and shortness of breath. He does not smoke. He takes no medications. During the interview, he clears his throat several times.

On physical examination, his vital signs are normal. He has cobblestoning of the posterior nasal pharynx and mucoid secretions in the oropharynx. The remainder of the examination findings are unremarkable.

Which of the following should be initiated first for his cough?

(A) Diphenhydramine and pseudoephedrine
(B) Inhaled salmeterol and inhaled budesonide
(C) Loratadine
(D) Omeprazole

Item 36 [Basic]

A 58-year-old woman is evaluated for an 8-week history of persistent nonproductive cough. The cough is paroxysmal and is preceded by a tickling sensation in the back of her throat. She reports no shortness of breath, hemoptysis, fever, chills, sore throat, ear pain, wheezing, or rhinorrhea. Her medical history is significant for hyperlipidemia and hypertension that was diagnosed approximately 3 months ago. She has a 10-pack-year history of tobacco use but stopped smoking 5 years ago. Her medications include atorvastatin and lisinopril.

On physical examination, the patient is afebrile. Her blood pressure is 128/78 mm Hg, heart rate is 72 beats/min, and respiratory rate is 12 breaths/min. There is no conjunctival injection, oropharyngeal erythema, or cobblestoning. The lungs are clear, and cardiovascular examination findings are unremarkable. A chest radiograph is normal.

Which of the following is the most appropriate treatment?

(A) Albuterol inhaler
(B) Discontinue lisinopril
(C) Loratadine
(D) Omeprazole

Item 37 [Advanced]

A 45-year-old man is evaluated during a follow-up appointment for a 6-month history of nonproductive cough. The cough occurs any time he lies down and seems to also to be present after meals, but it can occur at other times as well. He experiences heartburn throughout the day. He has no shortness of breath, dyspnea on exertion, fever, chills, postnasal drip, recent upper respiratory tract infection, or wheezing. Omeprazole was prescribed 2 weeks ago, but he reports no change in his cough or heartburn symptoms. He is a nonsmoker, does not drink alcohol, and takes no other medications.

His vital signs are normal, as are the remainder of the physical examination findings. A chest radiograph is normal.

Which of the following is the most appropriate treatment?

(A) Amoxicillin–clavulanate
(B) Continue omeprazole
(C) Inhaled albuterol
(D) Loratadine with pseudoephedrine

Item 38 [Advanced]

A 50-year-old man is evaluated because of blood-tinged sputum past 2 weeks. He has smoked 1.5 packs of cigarettes daily for the past 35 years and has had a chronic morning cough ("smoker's cough") productive of clear or yellow sputum for many years. Although he has not had any change in the nature of his cough, he has noticed some streaks of blood in his usual sputum. He has no complaints of shortness of breath and reports no fever or weight loss. His medical history is otherwise unremarkable, and he takes no medications.

On physical examination, his vital signs are normal. A chest examination reveals decreased breath sounds throughout the thorax but no other symptoms. A chest radiograph is normal. The rest of the physical examination findings are unremarkable.

Which of the following is the most appropriate next step in management?

(A) Chest computed tomography
(B) Pulmonary function testing
(C) Sputum culture and cytology
(D) Reevaluation in 3 months

Item 39 [Basic]

A 42-year-old woman is evaluated for a 4-day history of a nonproductive cough, mild fever, headache, myalgia, and sore throat. She has no other medical illnesses. There is a confirmed influenza A outbreak in the local community.

On physical examination, her temperature is 38.2°C (100.8°F), blood pressure is 130/70 mm Hg, pulse rate is 88 beats/min, and respiration rate is 14 breaths/min. She does not appear ill. There is diffuse muscle tenderness to palpation. The lungs are clear. The abdomen is soft and nontender.

Which of the following is the most appropriate treatment?

(A) Amantadine
(B) Oseltamivir
(C) Rimantadine
(D) Zanamivir
(E) Symptomatic treatment

Item 40 [Advanced]

A 32-year-old man is evaluated in the office because he wishes to stop smoking. The patient has smoked 1 pack of cigarettes daily for 12 years and has made numerous unsuccessful attempts to quit on his own. His other medical problem is posttraumatic stress disorder treated with cognitive behavioral therapy and a selective serotonin reuptake inhibitor.

On physical examination, his vital signs are normal, and the rest of his physical exam findings are unremarkable.

In addition to motivational counseling, which of the following is the most appropriate drug therapy to facilitate smoking cessation?

(A) Bupropion
(B) Nicotine replacement therapy
(C) Nortriptyline
(D) Varenicline

Item 41 [Advanced]

A 57-year-old woman comes to the clinic for help in quitting smoking. She has been successful in quitting two times in the past using nicotine replacement products or varenicline, but each time she gained weight. The last attempt at smoking cessation occurred 2 years ago, and she gained 10 lb (4.5 kg) using a nicotine patch. Although she is cautiously agreeable to another trial of smoking cessation pharmacotherapy, she is concerned about additional weight gain and would prefer a therapy associated with the least amount of weight gain. She has no other medical problems and takes no medications.

On physical examination, her vital signs are normal. Her body mass index is 28. The remainder of the physical examination findings are normal.

In addition to motivational counseling, which of the following is the most appropriate drug treatment for this patient?

(A) Bupropion
(B) Clonidine
(C) Nortriptyline
(D) Varenicline

Item 42 [Basic]

A 46-year-old woman is evaluated during a routine examination. Her 72-year-old mother was just diagnosed with lung cancer, so the patient asks you for help with quitting smoking. She has a 27-pack-year smoking history. She made one previous quit attempt several years ago using over-the-counter nicotine gum, but she was unable to quit for more than a few days. Her medical history is significant for seizure disorder. Review of systems discloses mild shortness of breath with exertion and occasional wheezing. Medications are a multivitamin and phenytoin.

On physical examination, her vital signs are normal. A lung examination reveals occasional wheezing and a prolonged expiratory phase. The rest of the examination findings are normal.

In addition to counseling regarding tobacco use, which of the following is an appropriate adjunct to increase her likelihood of successful smoking cessation?

(A)　A benzodiazepine
(B)　Bupropion
(C)　Electronic cigarette use
(D)　Nicotine replacement therapy

Item 43 [Basic]

A 59-year-old man is evaluated during a follow-up examination. He has chronic obstructive pulmonary disease and hypertension. He has an 80-pack-year history of cigarette use but has recently decreased his smoking to a half pack of cigarettes daily. His medications are ipratropium and amlodipine.

On physical examination, his temperature is 37.3°C (99.2°F), blood pressure is 138/92 mm Hg, pulse rate is 96 beats/min, and respiration rate is 22 breaths/min. His body mass index is 29. He is barrel chested with diffuse wheezing on lung examination. The remainder of the physical examination findings are normal.

Which of the following is the most appropriate management regarding this patient's tobacco use?

(A)　Assess his interest in smoking cessation
(B)　Prescribe bupropion
(C)　Prescribe nicotine replacement therapy
(D)　Refer for smoking cessation counseling

Item 44 [Basic]

A 25-year-old woman is seen in the office for a 2-week history of difficulty sleeping. She reports having trouble falling asleep and staying asleep at night. On further questioning, she notes a decreased level of energy and an inability to concentrate at work. She reports a 5-lb (2.27-kg) weight gain in the past month. She comments that she is not sure that anyone would miss her if she was not here. However, she specifically denies suicidal thoughts or a plan. Her medical history is significant for irregular menses for the past 3 years but is otherwise unremarkable. She does not use tobacco, drinks 2 to 3 beers a week, and denies any drug use. Her only medication is a monthly depo-progesterone injection, which she has taken for the past 2 years.

On examination, the patient is appropriate, but her affect is flat. Her vital signs are normal, and the remainder of the physical examination is unremarkable.

Which of the following is the most appropriate next step in management?

(A)　Administer a depression screening tool
(B)　Contact her family to confirm her depressive symptoms
(C)　Discontinue depo-progesterone injections
(D)　Refer for psychiatric admission
(E)　Refer for substance abuse treatment

Item 45 [Advanced]

A 50-year-old woman is evaluated during a follow-up appointment for moderate depression. She was started on sertraline 8 weeks ago; 4 weeks ago, the dose was increased to the maximal dose. At this time, her Patient Health Questionnaire 9 score has not improved over baseline, and she confirms that her symptoms have not improved. She has no suicidal ideation and does not have hallucinations or other psychotic features. She has no previous episodes of high energy, spending sprees, lack of need of sleep, or previous psychiatric problems. She is not interested in psychotherapy at this time.

On physical examination, she has a mildly blunted affect. Her vital signs are normal, and the remainder of her physical examination findings are unremarkable.

Which of the following is the most appropriate next step in treatment?

(A)　Add venlafaxine
(B)　Continue sertraline at the current dose for an additional 8 weeks
(C)　Discontinue sertraline and begin venlafaxine
(D)　Refer for electroconvulsive therapy

Item 46 [Basic]

An 18-year-old man is evaluated in the office for follow-up of depression. He was diagnosed with major depression 2 weeks ago, and therapy with a selective serotonin reuptake inhibitor (SSRI) was begun, although he declined psychotherapy at that time. He continues with a lack of interest in all activities and relates a sense of having lost all meaning in his life. He moved to the area 6 months ago and has no family or friends in the area. He admits to having constant suicidal thoughts and has worked out plans carry this out if he does not improve soon.

On examination, the patient appears depressed but responsive. Except for his mood, his vital signs and the remainder of his physical examination findings are unremarkable.

Which of the following is the most appropriate next step in the management of this patient?

(A)　Electroconvulsive therapy
(B)　Immediate hospitalization
(C)　Refer for psychotherapy
(D)　Stop the SSRI and start a serotonin and norepinephrine uptake inhibitor

Item 47 [Advanced]

A 19-year-old man is evaluated for a complaint of depressive symptoms for 6 weeks. He started college 6 months ago and has been participating in extramural basketball, football, and soccer in addition to carrying a full academic load and having a part-time job. He began smoking cigarettes, was drinking heavily on weekends and at parties, and has had four sexual partners since beginning school. However, during the past 6 weeks, he has stopped attending classes, has seldom left his room, and his academic performance is suffering. He is having difficulty sleeping and has a poor appetite. He can identify no precipitating event related to his change in mood and recalls a prior episode of similar symptoms at age 14 years attributed to the stress of high school.

His vital signs are normal, and the remainder of his physical examination findings are unremarkable.

Which of the following is the most likely diagnosis?

(A) Bipolar disorder
(B) Dysthymia
(C) Major depressive disorder
(D) Situational adjustment reaction

Item 48 [Basic]

A 19-year-old woman is seen in the office to establish primary care. She has no medical problems, is in good health, and is not taking any medications. She does not smoke cigarettes. She is sexually active and uses condoms for birth control. Her family history is significant for hypertension and diabetes.

On physical examination, her vital signs and general examination are normal. Her body mass index is 21.

Which of the following screening tests is recommended by the U.S. Preventive Services Task Force for this patient?

(A) Alcohol use and abuse
(B) Cervical cancer
(C) Illicit drug use
(D) Ovarian cancer
(E) Skin cancer

Item 49 [Basic]

A 32-year-old man was evaluated in the emergency department for a heroin overdose. He was treated with intravenous naloxone, and after overnight monitoring, he is now alert and oriented and ready for discharge.

Physical examination shows normal vital signs and is otherwise unremarkable.

Which of the following is the best management option for this patient?

(A) Assess his interest in quitting heroin addiction
(B) Begin buprenorphine
(C) Begin methadone
(D) Enroll him in a drug rehabilitation program

Item 50 [Basic]

A 47-year-old woman is evaluated in follow-up after a recent hospitalization for acute pancreatitis secondary to alcohol abuse. She has no known medical issues but has not had any previous primary medical care. She smokes one pack of cigarettes daily, does not use illicit drugs, and takes no prescription medications. She tells you that she drinks alcohol intermittently, often once a week or less, but usually has 6 or 7 drinks when she does. She has been cited once for driving under the influence of alcohol; she has never had withdrawal symptoms.

Physical examination reveals a thin woman. Vital signs are normal. There is no evidence of jaundice or hepatomegaly. There is mild epigastric tenderness but no ascites or other stigmata of chronic liver disease.

Which of the following is the most appropriate management for this patient?

(A) Connect her drinking habits with the negative consequences
(B) Identify that she is an alcoholic and needs to abstain from drinking
(C) Initiate therapy with disulfiram
(D) Initiate therapy with naltrexone

Item 51 [Advanced]

A 36-year-old man is brought to the emergency department by his family for evaluation. He has a long history of heavy alcohol use and usually drinks around 1 bottle of whiskey daily. He decided to stop drinking several days ago after losing his job because of poor performance. His last drink was yesterday. The patient states that since then, he has felt increasingly shaky and nervous, and his family brought him in because he is having visual and auditory hallucinations. He had a seizure previously when he stopped drinking abruptly. He has no other medical problems and takes no medications.

On physical examination, his temperature is 37.2°C (99.0°F), blood pressure is 170/100 mm Hg, pulse rate is 110 beats/min, and respiration rate is 18 breaths/min. He is diaphoretic and tremulous and has difficulty focusing. The remainder of the examination findings are normal.

Which of the following medications should be administered now?

(A) Atenolol
(B) Clonidine
(C) Haloperidol
(D) Lorazepam
(E) Phenytoin

Item 52 [Advanced]

A 29-year-old man is evaluated in the emergency department for chest pain after the use of cocaine. He has no history of cardiovascular disease or other medical problems. He takes no other medications.

On physical examination, his temperature is 38.4°C (101.1°F), blood pressure is 155/95 mm Hg (identical in both arms), pulse rate is 120 beats/min, and respiration rate is 20 breaths/min. He is alert, agitated, and uncomfortable owing to ongoing chest pain. His pupils are dilated but reactive. An electrocardiogram shows a narrow complex tachycardia with T-wave inversion and ST-segment depression in the lateral leads consistent with ischemia. Urine toxicology screen is positive for cocaine.

In addition to starting aspirin and nitroglycerin, which of the following is the most appropriate treatment?

(A) Intravenous diltiazem and lorazepam
(B) Intravenous metoprolol
(C) Intravenous nitroprusside
(D) Tissue plasminogen activator

Item 53 [Advanced]

A 39-year-old woman seeks evaluation amenorrhea. Menses ceased about 8 months ago. She denies exercise or weight fluctuations. She has no other problems and takes no medications. She has never had a uterine procedure. She is currently sexually active with her husband.

General physical examination and pelvic examination are unremarkable.

Serum human choriogonadotropin, prolactin, follicle-stimulating hormone, and thyroid-stimulating hormone levels are normal.

A progesterone challenge is performed, which fails to cause endometrial bleeding. After estrogen priming followed by a progesterone challenge, bleeding fails to occur.

Which of the following is the most likely diagnosis?

(A) Hypothalamic amenorrhea
(B) Intrauterine adhesions (Asherman syndrome)
(C) Polycystic ovary syndrome
(D) Turner syndrome

Item 54 [Basic]

A 56-year-old woman is evaluated in the office for vaginal dryness and discomfort. Her symptoms have progressively worsened for the past 7 months. There is no vaginal discharge or vaginal odor. She has been menopausal since age 48 years. She has occasional hot flushing, which has diminished considerably over the past 6 years. She does not smoke cigarettes and has no history of thromboembolic disorders. Her mother, age 76 years, has osteoporosis treated with alendronate. She takes no medications. Her last Papanicolaou smear was 1 year ago, and the results were normal.

On physical examination, she has pale, dry vaginal walls with decreased rugae and petechial hemorrhages. There is no vaginal discharge. The cervix appears normal.

Which of the following is the most appropriate treatment of this patient's symptoms?

(A) Black cohosh
(B) Oral conjugated estrogen and progesterone replacement therapy
(C) Oral conjugated estrogen replacement therapy
(D) Vaginal estradiol

Item 55 [Basic]

A 23-year-old woman is evaluated after having no menses for 6 months. Menarche was at age 12 years, and her menses have always been regular and normal. She notes no recent weight gain, voice change, or facial hair growth. She is not sexually active. There is no family history of infertility or premature menopause. Her medical history is negative, and she takes no medications.

On physical examination, her vital signs are normal. Her body mass index is 22. Her thyroid is normal size and without detectable nodules. The cardiopulmonary examination findings are normal. She has no acne, hirsutism, or galactorrhea. Visual field testing results are normal.

A pregnancy test result is negative, and her thyroid-stimulating hormone level is normal.

Which of the following is the most appropriate first step in evaluation?

(A) Measurement of serum follicle-stimulating hormone and prolactin levels
(B) Measurement of total serum testosterone level
(C) Pelvic ultrasonography
(D) Pituitary magnetic resonance imaging

Item 56 [Advanced]

A 22-year-old woman is evaluated for a complaint of amenorrhea for the past 3 months. She has always had irregular periods after undergoing menarche at the age of 14 years. Her menstrual cycles have become increasingly irregular over the past 2 years, with several episodes of very heavy bleeding interspersed by several months without menstrual bleeding. She has generally felt well with no other symptoms. Her medical history is otherwise negative, and she takes no medications.

On physical examination, her vital signs are normal. Her body mass index is 29. Her cardiopulmonary examination is normal. No acne is present, although she does have several terminal hairs on her chin. Pelvic examination reveals a normal uterus on palpation and a normal speculum examination. A urine pregnancy test result is negative.

Which of the following is the most likely diagnosis?

(A) Cushing syndrome
(B) Hyperprolactinemia
(C) Hypothyroidism
(D) Polycystic ovary syndrome
(E) Uterine fibroids (leiomyomas)

Item 57 [Basic]

A 45-year-old woman is evaluated for heavy menstrual bleeding over the past 6 months. She has been menstruating steadily for the past 8 days and is using five pads or more a day with frequent clots. She is fatigued but reports no dizziness or shortness of breath. Previous evaluation for her bleeding included pelvic ultrasonography, which showed a large submucosal fibroid; a surgical procedure to treat the fibroid is scheduled in 2 weeks. Her medical history is otherwise normal, and she takes no medications.

On examination, her vital signs are normal. Her abdominal examination is benign, and the pelvic examination reveals a moderate amount of blood in the vaginal vault.

Her hemoglobin level is 10.5 g/dL (105 g/L). The pregnancy test result is negative.

Which of the following is the most appropriate next management step?

(A) Emergency surgery
(B) Intravenous estrogen
(C) Once daily oral contraceptives
(D) Oral medroxyprogesterone acetate
(E) Reevaluation in 1 week

Item 58 [Basic]

A 26-year-old woman is evaluated for amenorrhea for the past 4 months. Menarche was at age 13 years with normal periods until age 18 years when she developed heavy bleeding. She was placed on an oral contraceptive to control bleeding and for contraception. She discontinued the oral contraceptive pill 4 months ago because she and her husband want to become pregnant. However, she has had no menses since that time. There is no family history of infertility or premature menopause.

On physical examination, her vital signs are normal. Her body mass index is 24. There is no acne, hirsutism, or galactorrhea. Examination of the thyroid gland and visual field testing are normal. Pelvic examination is normal, and a pregnancy test result is negative.

Laboratory studies show normal thyroid-stimulating hormone, prolactin, and follicle-stimulating hormone levels.

Which of the following is the most appropriate next diagnostic test?

(A) Measurement of the plasma dehydroepiandrosterone sulfate level
(B) Magnetic resonance imaging of the pituitary gland
(C) Measurement of serum estradiol level
(D) Progestin withdrawal challenge

Item 59 [Advanced]

A 51-year-old woman is evaluated for vaginal bleeding for the past 3 days. She notes that around age 48 years, her periods became lighter and irregular and ceased altogether around 1 year ago. She has not had bleeding since that time. She reports no other symptoms such as pain, lightheadedness, or shortness of breath. Her medical history is negative, and she takes no medications.

On physical examination, her vital signs are normal. There is no conjunctival pallor. Cardiopulmonary examination findings are normal. Bimanual pelvic examination reveals a nontender, normal-sized, and regular uterus. Speculum examination shows a normal-appearing cervix with dark blood in the cervical os but no other abnormalities. A Papanicolaou smear is performed. A urine pregnancy test result is negative.

Which of the following is the most appropriate next management step?

(A) Begin estrogen replacement therapy
(B) Begin progestin therapy
(C) Measure follicle-stimulating hormone
(D) Perform endometrial biopsy

Item 60 [Basic]

A 73-year-old woman is evaluated in the emergency department after an episode of syncope that occurred 2 hours ago. She lost consciousness when setting the table for dinner. She denied experiencing any prodromal symptoms before the event and did not experience loss of bowel or bladder continence or tongue biting. Her husband witnessed the event and reports that she fell to the ground, had a few twitches of her extremities, and then regained consciousness in 10 to 15 seconds. There was no period of confusion after the event. She is weak but otherwise reports no symptoms. She has a past medical history of hypertension and heart failure with a left ventricular ejection fraction of 40%. She takes lisinopril, hydrochlorothiazide, and metoprolol.

On physical examination, she is afebrile, and her blood pressure is 146/87 mm Hg and heart rate is 76 beats/min sitting without orthostatic changes. Her respiratory rate is 20 breaths/min, and her oxygen saturation is 97% on ambient air. There is an S_3 on cardiac auscultation, no evidence of jugular venous distension, clear lungs, and trace peripheral edema. The neurologic examination findings are normal.

Which of the following is the most likely cause of her syncope?

(A) Arrhythmia
(B) Neurocardiogenic (vasovagal) syncope
(C) Orthostatic hypotension
(D) Seizure

Item 61 [Basic]

A 26-year-old man is evaluated in the emergency department after an episode of syncope 30 minutes ago. He works as a research assistant and was watching a subject have blood drawn for a study when he became diaphoretic and lightheaded. These symptoms persisted for about 10 seconds before he lost consciousness. He was unconscious for about 20 seconds. Upon regaining consciousness, he reported no confusion. He has no medical problems, and there is no history of cardiac disease. He takes no medications.

On physical examination, vital signs are normal, without orthostatic changes in blood pressure or pulse rate. The remainder of his physical examination findings are normal. An electrocardiogram is normal.

Which of the following is the most appropriate next step in the management of this patient?

(A) 24-Hour ambulatory electrocardiogram monitoring
(B) Echocardiogram
(C) Tilt table testing
(D) Reassurance

Item 62 [Advanced]

A 30-year-old woman is evaluated during a follow-up examination for recurrent episodes of presyncope and syncope every 3 to 4 weeks over the past few months with no discernible pattern or trigger. She reports feeling lightheaded without other associated symptoms followed by transient loss of consciousness for several seconds followed by spontaneous recovery without residual symptoms. Findings from an electrocardiogram (ECG), 24-hour continuous ambulatory ECG monitoring, and echocardiogram were normal. A cardiac event recorder showed no arrhythmia associated with her presyncopal and syncopal episodes. Her medical history is otherwise negative, and she takes no medications.

On physical examination, her temperature is normal. Her blood pressure is 122/68 mm Hg, and her pulse rate is 72 beats/min without orthostatic changes. The remainder of the examination findings are normal. Serum electrolytes, kidney function, and thyroid function study findings are normal.

Which of the following is the most appropriate next step in the evaluation of this patient?

(A) Electroencephalography
(B) Exercise cardiac stress test
(C) Implantable loop recorder
(D) Tilt-table testing

Item 63 [Advanced]

A 38-year-old woman is evaluated during a follow-up visit for two syncopal episodes experienced in the past 2 years. The first episode occurred 18 months ago at rest. The second episode occurred 5 months ago while she was walking. The patient describes an "uneasy" sensation preceding the events but reports no dyspnea, chest discomfort, palpitations, or loss of bowel or bladder control. A looping event recorder worn for 30 days did not reveal arrhythmia. She is employed as a school bus driver. She takes no medications.

On physical examination, she is afebrile, her blood pressure is 120/60 mm Hg, and her pulse rate is 60 beats/min and regular. The remaining of the examination findings are normal.

The baseline electrocardiogram findings are normal.

Which of the following is the most appropriate testing option?

(A) Continuous ambulatory electrocardiographic monitor
(B) Implantable loop recorder
(C) Postsymptom event recorder
(D) No further testing

Item 64 [Basic]

A 62-year-old man is evaluated for a syncopal event that occurred 2 nights ago. On his way to the bathroom during the night, he felt dizzy and passed out, awaking without residual symptoms. He notes that he often feels a little dizzy when he stands up. His medical history is remarkable for hypertension and benign prostatic hyperplasia. He started doxazosin 2 weeks ago for benign prostatic hyperplasia that he takes at bedtime. His other medications are lisinopril and atenolol.

On physical examination, his temperature is normal, blood pressure is 142/78 mm Hg (supine) and 106/64 mm Hg (standing), pulse rate is 74 beats/min (supine) and 80 beats/min (standing), and respiration rate is 16 breaths/min. He experiences lightheadedness when he stands up. Cardiac and neurologic examination findings are normal. Electrocardiogram findings are also normal.

Which of the following is the most appropriate management option for this patient?

(A) Admit to hospital for cardiovascular evaluation
(B) Discontinue doxazosin
(C) Perform 24-hour ambulatory electrocardiographic monitoring
(D) Perform brain magnetic resonance imaging

Item 65 [Basic]

A 48-year-old man comes to your office for evaluation of a left sided neck mass. He first noticed the mass about 2 weeks ago when he was shaving. It is not painful but has persisted without enlarging. He is without other symptoms. His medical history is unremarkable.

On examination, he appears healthy. His vital signs are normal. The mass is a left anterior cervical lymph node approximately 1.5 cm in diameter that is soft, mobile, and nontender. In addition, three smaller anterior cervical lymph nodes are noted on the right as well as a 1-cm left axillary lymph node. These nodes are also nontender, mobile, and soft. The rest of his examination findings are normal.

Which feature of this patient's clinical presentation is most suggestive of a pathologic cause of his lymphadenopathy?

(A) Age
(B) Axillary lymphadenopathy
(C) Failure to decrease in size after a week
(D) Generalized lymphadenopathy
(E) Size of 1.5 cm

Item 66 [Advanced]

A 27-year-old man is evaluated for a complaint of swollen lymph nodes associated with a 4-week history of fatigue, intermittent fever, sore throat, and left upper quadrant abdominal discomfort. He has no night sweats, weight loss, cough, dysuria, or diarrhea. His medical history is unremarkable.

On physical examination, his temperature is 38.0°C (100.4°F), blood pressure is 11/65 mm Hg, and pulse rate is 100/min. He has bilateral soft, mobile, tender cervical lymphadenopathy. The spleen is detectable 3 cm below the left costal margin and tender to palpation. There are no skin findings. The rest of the physical examination findings are unremarkable.

Laboratory studies:
Hemoglobin	11.5 g/dL (115 g/L)
Leukocyte count	9000/μL (9.0×10^9/L) with 32% neutrophils and 68% lymphocytes
Platelet count	160,000/μL (160×10^9/L)

A peripheral blood smear shows large atypical lymphocytes representing 10% of the lymphoid cells.

Which of the following is the most appropriate next step in the diagnostic evaluation?

(A) Bone marrow biopsy
(B) Epstein-Barr virus serologies
(C) Lymph node biopsy
(D) Peripheral blood flow cytometry

Item 67 [Advanced]

A 75-year-old woman is transferred to a rehabilitation facility after repair of a left intertrochanteric fracture sustained in a fall. She initially made progress in her physical rehabilitation but began to have difficulty with her stamina. Over the course of 2 weeks, she lost her appetite and was eating less than 25% of all meals. In 3 weeks, she lost 3.6 kg (8 lb). She does not have fever, nausea, cough, dyspnea, depression, or dysuria. She has soft bowel movements every 2 to 3 days with no blood. She has occasional heartburn and early satiety, which are new since her hospitalization. Her medications are acetaminophen and low-molecular weight heparin. Results of age- and sex-appropriate cancer screening tests performed 6 months ago were normal. She has never smoked cigarettes and does not consume alcohol.

On physical examination, her temperature is 37.0°C (98.6°F), blood pressure is 128/76 mm Hg, heart rate is 90 beats/min, respiratory rate is 16 breaths/min, and body mass index is 23. Her physical examination findings are normal, with a well-healing incision on the left hip.

Laboratory studies:

Hemoglobin	10.5 g/dL (105 g/L) (12.1 g/dL (121 g/L) postsurgery)
Creatinine	0.8 mg/dL (61 µmol/L)
Albumin	3.6 g/dL (36 g/L)
Calcium	10.0 mg/dL (2.50 mmol/L)
Thyroid-stimulating hormone	2.0 µU/mL (2.0 mU/L)
Aspartate aminotransferase	24 U/L
Alanine aminotransferase	27 U/L
C-reactive protein	0.1 mg/dL (1.0 mg/L)
Alkaline phosphatase	90 U/L
Lactate dehydrogenase	130 U/L

Chest radiography results are normal. Fecal occult blood test result is negative.

Which of the following is the most appropriate next step?

(A) Abdominal computed tomography
(B) Megestrol
(C) Nutritional supplements
(D) Upper endoscopy

Item 68 [Advanced]

A 55-year-old woman is evaluated in the office for weight loss. Her weight today is 4.7 kg (10.5 lb) less than it was 1 year ago, representing a 7% weight loss. Her appetite is normal, but her energy level is reduced. She denies fevers, night sweats, fatigue, dysphagia, change in bowel habits, blood in her stool, joint pain, polydipsia, skin or hair changes, depressed mood, and shortness of breath. She works as a teacher. She has never smoked or and does not drink alcohol. She takes no medications. A colonoscopy done 3 years ago was normal, and Papanicolaou smear with human papillomavirus testing was normal 2 years ago.

On physical examination, her temperature is 37.0°C (98.6°F), blood pressure is 120/74 mm Hg, heart rate is 74 beats/min, respiration rate is 16 breaths/min, and body mass index is 25. The remainder of the physical examination findings are normal.

Laboratory studies:

Hemoglobin	12.7 g/dL (127 g/L)
Creatinine	1.0 mg/dL (76.25 µmol/L)
Albumin	3.7 g/dL (37 g/L)
Thyroid-stimulating hormone	2.6 µU/mL (2.6 mU/L)
Calcium	10.5 mg/dL (2.63 mmol/L)
Aspartate aminotransferase	24 U/L
Alanine aminotransferase	27 U/L
C-reactive protein	1.3 mg/dL (13.0 mg/L)
Alkaline phosphatase	90 U/L
Urinalysis	Normal

Chest radiography results are normal. Fecal occult blood test result is negative.

Which of the following is the most appropriate next step?

(A) Abdominal and pelvis computed tomography (CT)
(B) Chest CT
(C) Colonoscopy
(D) Mammography

Item 69 [Basic]

A 70-year-old woman is evaluated in the office for fatigue and weight loss. She has noticed less energy and ability to do her normal household activities for 6 months. Her weight today is 6.8 kg (15 lb) less than it was 1 year ago. Her appetite has been increased during this time despite the weight loss. During the same time period, she has experienced worsening constipation. She denies fevers, night sweats, fatigue, dysphagia, joint pain, polyuria, polydipsia, depressed mood, and shortness of breath. She does not smoke cigarettes or drink alcohol. She has no other medical problems and takes no medications. She is current with routine health screening interventions.

On physical examination, her temperature is 37.0°C (98.6°F), blood pressure is 135/78 mm Hg, heart rate is 90 beats/min, respiratory rate is 16 breaths/min, and body mass index is 21.8. The remainder of the physical examination findings are normal.

Laboratory studies:

Hemoglobin	11.0 g/dL (110 g/L)
Creatinine	1.0 mg/dL (76.25 µmol/L)
Albumin	3.4 g/dL (34 g/L)
Thyroid-stimulating hormone	3.0 µU/L (3.0 mU/L)
Calcium	10.2 mg/dL (2.55 mmol/L)
Aspartate aminotransferase	24 U/L
Alanine aminotransferase	27 U/L
C-reactive protein	0.7 mg/dL (7.0 mg/L)
Urinalysis	Normal

One of six stool samples is positive for blood.

Which of the following is the most appropriate next diagnostic test?

(A) Abdominal computed tomography
(B) Abdominal ultrasonography
(C) Colonoscopy
(D) Mammography

Item 70 [Basic]

A 73-year-old woman is evaluated in the office for anorexia and involuntary weight loss of 6 kg (13 lb) over the past 3 months. She does not report any abdominal pain, difficulty chewing food or swallowing, nausea, vomiting, diarrhea, or change in bowel habits. She has a history of anxiety and mild depressive symptoms, and her only medication is a benzodiazepine, which she takes intermittently. She is otherwise healthy. She has never smoked and does not use alcohol. She is up to date with her routine health maintenance interventions.

On physical examination, she appears well. Her vital signs are normal. Her body mass index is 28. Her physical examination is unremarkable. Her mental status is normal, although her responses to some questions are somewhat slow.

Complete blood count, comprehensive metabolic panel, urinalysis, thyroid function tests, and a chest radiograph results are normal.

Which of the following is the most appropriate next step in this patient's management?

(A) Appetite stimulant therapy

(B) Computed tomography of the chest, abdomen, and pelvis

(C) Reassessment in 3 months

(D) Screening for depression

Item 71 [Basic]

A 79-year-old man is evaluated in the office for slowly progressive vision loss over the past year. He stopped driving at night 6 months ago because he had difficulty reading the street signs and noted increased glare from headlights. He does not have difficulty reading in his home. He has no other medical problems.

On examination, visual acuity is 20/140 on the right and 20/40 on the left. The right eye is shown (Plate 1). Left funduscopic examination findings are normal.

What is the most likely cause of this patient's vision loss?

(A) Age-related macular degeneration

(B) Cataract

(C) Glaucoma

(D) Presbyopia

Item 72 [Basic]

An 85-year-old man is urgently evaluated in the office because of difficulty urinating. His symptoms began 2 days ago with increased hesitancy and frequency and a sensation that he is not able to completely empty his bladder. He denies dysuria or hematuria. One week ago, he began taking acetaminophen and diphenhydramine at night to treat mild insomnia. He has hypertension treated with chlorthalidone and enalapril.

On physical examination, his vital signs are normal. He has suprapubic tenderness without rebound or guarding. Rectal examination reveals a mildly enlarged prostate without tenderness or nodules. Neurologic examination findings are normal, including normal sensation in the perineal area and lower extremity muscle strength.

Urinalysis is normal. Bladder catheterization reveals a postvoid residual urine volume of 75 mL (elevated).

Which of the following is the most likely cause of this patient's symptoms?

(A) Acute prostatitis

(B) Cauda equina syndrome

(C) Medication effect

(D) Prostate cancer

(E) Urinary tract infection

Item 73 [Basic]

An 80-year-old man is evaluated in the clinic after a fall at home. He has a history of three falls within the past 2 years. He denies feeling lightheaded or weak before falling, and he had no loss of consciousness. Medical issues include type 2 diabetes mellitus, peripheral neu-

ropathy, hypertension, hypothyroidism, benign prostatic hypertrophy, gastroesophageal reflux, and seasonal allergies. His medications are glipizide, gabapentin, losartan, levothyroxine, doxazosin, aspirin, omeprazole, and as-needed hydroxyzine.

On physical examination, he is afebrile, and his blood pressure is 148/76 mm Hg, heart rate is 70 beats/min, the respiratory rate is 12 breaths/min. There is no orthostasis.

Results of laboratory studies, including a complete blood count, comprehensive metabolic profile, and thyroid function studies, are normal.

Which of the following interventions would be most likely to decrease his risk of subsequent falls?

(A) Add calcium to the medication regimen

(B) Discontinue any nonessential medications

(C) Prescribe an assistive device

(D) Recommend the patient move into an assisted living facility

Item 74 [Advanced]

A 78-year-old woman living in a nursing home is evaluated for incontinence. Over the past year, she has had progressive decline in her cognitive status and now spends most of the day in bed. She requires coaxing to join the other residents in their communal meals and requires assistance for eating and bathing. When accompanied by an aide or family member, she is able to walk slowly to the bathroom without leakage and to urinate. Her medical history is significant for dementia.

On examination, she is a frail elderly woman in no acute distress. Her temperature is normal, blood pressure is 132/88 mm Hg, and pulse rate is 68 beats/min. Her body mass index is 23. Abdominal examination is without suprapubic fullness. Rectal examination reveals normal sphincter tone. Results of urinalysis are normal.

Which of the following is the most appropriate management of this patient's incontinence?

(A) Cystoscopy

(B) Indwelling urinary catheter

(C) Pelvic floor muscle training

(D) Prompted voiding

(E) Start an antimuscarinic medication

Item 75 [Advanced]

A 78-year-old-woman is evaluated in the emergency department after she fell at home last night. She has difficulty sleeping and fell when getting out of bed in the middle of the night. She had no loss of consciousness and notes left hip pain. She has hypertension and hyperlipidemia. Her current medications are lisinopril and simvastatin.

On physical examination, she appears frail with generalized weakness. She is afebrile. Her blood pressure is 138/76 mm Hg and pulse rate is 76 beats/min without orthostatic changes. She has a slow gait but no ataxia. Her lungs are clear. Her heart rhythm is regular with no murmur. There is mild tenderness in the left lateral hip and weakness of the quadriceps muscles bilaterally. There is no focal neurologic deficit. Visual acuity using glasses without bifocal lenses is normal. Radiograph of the left hip and femur reveals no fracture.

Acetaminophen is prescribed for pain. Arrangements are made for home physical therapy and for a visiting nurse to perform a home safety evaluation.

Which of the following is the most appropriate additional management of this patient?

(A) Discontinue lisinopril

(B) Prescribe vitamin D

(C) Prescribe zolpidem at bedtime

(D) Refer for prescription glasses with bifocal lenses

Item 76 [Basic]

A 78-year-old man is evaluated for routine follow-up of hypertension. He reports that he is able to perform all activities of daily living and that he only drives in the neighborhood and to nearby stores. He has used a cane while walking since he fell 3 months ago. His only medication is chlorthalidone.

On physical examination, his vital signs are normal. His corrected vision with glasses is 20/20 in both eyes. His gait is somewhat slow, but his strength is normal. The rest of the physical examination findings are unremarkable. His clinically assessed cognitive function is normal.

Which of the following is the most appropriate management of this patient?

(A) Advise the patient that he should no longer drive

(B) Advise the patient to continue to drive only locally

(C) Ask about any driving difficulties

(D) Report the patient to the state department of transportation

Item 77 [Basic]

A 42-year-old-woman is evaluated in the office for worsening of dyspnea over the past week. She has terminal breast cancer with lung metastases.

On physical examination, she appears anxious and uncomfortable. She is afebrile, and blood pressure is 130/70 mm Hg, heart rate is 98 beats/min, respiratory rate is 24 breaths/min, and oxygen saturation is 96% on ambient air. There are absent breath sounds and dullness to percussion over the right mid and lower lung fields. Cardiac examination is normal, and there is no jugular venous distention or peripheral edema.

Chest radiography shows a large, free-flowing pleural effusion that was not present 2 weeks ago.

Which of the following is the most appropriate management?

(A) Anxiolytic therapy

(B) Diuresis

(C) Morphine

(D) Oxygen via nasal cannula

(E) Therapeutic thoracentesis

Item 78 [Advanced]

An 85-year-old woman is evaluated at home for confusion. She has metastatic breast cancer to the spine, lungs, and liver and is enrolled in hospice care. Her pain has been well controlled on a fentanyl transdermal patch and immediate-release morphine as needed. Last night, the patient became confused and agitated. There is no dyspnea, fever, dysuria, chest discomfort, or abdominal discomfort. She states that she does not have any pain, and her last use of immediate-release morphine was 24 hours ago.

On physical examination, her vital signs are normal. The patient is alert but confused with inattention and poor memory. She does not seem anxious. Other than confusion and inattention, the examination reveals no abnormalities, including the cardiopulmonary, abdominal, and neurologic examinations.

Which of the following is the most appropriate management for this patient?

(A) Arterial blood gas analysis

(B) Haloperidol

(C) Immediate-release morphine

(D) Lorazepam

Item 79 [Basic]

A 76-year-old woman was evaluated 10 days ago for weight loss and occasional hemoptysis. Non–small cell lung cancer was subsequently diagnosed, as were numerous metastatic lesions. She has no significant pain. She does all of her own activities of daily living and is able to walk 1 mile before stopping because of fatigue. Her only medications are a daily multivitamin and a calcium supplement.

On physical examination, her vital signs are normal. She appears comfortable and in no distress and is interested in life-prolonging therapy.

Which of the following is the most appropriate time to begin palliative care discussions with this patient?

(A) After she develops symptoms

(B) At the current visit

(C) When admitted to hospice care

(D) When she no longer desires active treatment

Item 80 [Basic]

An 88-year-old man in hospice care is evaluated for dyspnea. He has advanced dementia and severe chronic obstructive pulmonary disease. Based on prior discussions with his family regarding the goals of care, it was decided that his treatment should consist of comfort care measures only. All of his medications except as-needed albuterol and ipratropium have been discontinued.

On physical examination, he is afebrile, and his blood pressure is 108/76 mm Hg, pulse rate is 110 beats/min, and respiration rate is 26 breaths/min. Oxygen saturation is satisfactory. He is cachectic and tachypneic and is disoriented and in moderate respiratory distress. His heart sounds are distant and tachycardic, but an S_3 is not present. Chest examination reveals decreased breath sounds but no focal findings. His extremities are warm and dry.

In addition to continuing his bronchodilator therapy, which of the following is the most appropriate next step in the treatment of this patient?

(A) Ceftriaxone and azithromycin

(B) Lorazepam

(C) Methylprednisolone

(D) Morphine

Item 81 [Advanced]

A 97-year-old woman was hospitalized 1 week ago with jaundice, abdominal pain, weight loss, and intermittent vomiting. She was found to have poorly differentiated metastatic pancreatic adenocarcinoma. Current medications are morphine, a stool softener, and a laxative. On physical examination, her vital signs are normal; she appears cachectic but comfortable.

During bedside discussions, the patient has deferred all medical decision making to her family. They have asked that "everything be done" and have declined to place the patient on do-not-resuscitate status. They have requested a surgical consultation and oncology evaluation for chemotherapy. The health care team has arranged a family meeting to address end-of-life care.

Which of the following is the best initial communication strategy for the family meeting?

(A) Ask the patient's opinion about an advanced directive
(B) Explain that curative therapy is futile
(C) Explain the diagnosis and the prognosis
(D) Explore the family's understanding about the patient's condition

Item 82 [Basic]

A 44-year-old man is evaluated during a routine examination. He is in good health, has no concerning symptoms, and takes no medications. He does not smoke, drinks alcohol socially, and exercises 30 minutes daily 5 days per week. He ingests a heart-healthy diet. All of his immunizations are up to date. The patient has no symptoms or health problems. His physical examination findings are normal.

Which of the following is the most reasonable next screening step for genetic disease in this patient?

(A) Obtain a family history of disease
(B) Obtain a three-generation pedigree
(C) Refer for genetic counseling
(D) Screen for common genetic mutations

Item 83 [Basic]

A 26-year-old man is evaluated during a routine examination. His 52-year-old mother was recently diagnosed with Huntington disease. The patient has no symptoms. He is planning on starting a family. Physical examination findings, including a complete neurologic examination, are normal.

Which of the following is the most appropriate next step in management?

(A) Obtain genetic testing for Huntington disease
(B) Order brain magnetic resonance imaging
(C) Reassure the patient that he is unlikely to develop Huntington disease
(D) Refer for genetic counseling

Item 84 [Advanced]

A 35-year-old Jewish woman of Ashkenazi descent is evaluated in the office during a routine examination. Her medical history is unremarkable. She of Ashkenazi Jewish descent, and her family history includes a paternal grandmother who had bilateral breast cancer at ages 42 and 50 years and died of metastatic breast cancer at age 53 years and a paternal great aunt who had ovarian cancer at age 45 years and breast cancer at age 51 years. Her two sisters, mother, and mother's relatives have not had breast or ovarian cancer, and her father is healthy without any cancer.

Physical examination findings, including breast and pelvic examination, are normal.

Which of the following is the most appropriate next step in management?

(A) Genetic counseling
(B) Prophylactic bilateral mastectomy
(C) Prophylactic oophorectomy
(D) Tamoxifen

Item 85 [Advanced]

A 19-year-old man is evaluated in follow-up for a diagnosis of asthma. His symptoms have not been well controlled, and he continues to have wheezing, a productive cough, and shortness of breath. Medical history is significant for multiple episodes of bronchitis since childhood but is otherwise unremarkable. His medications are a medium-dose inhaled corticosteroid and a long-acting β_2-agonist, with documented satisfactory inhaler technique.

On physical examination, his vital signs are normal except for a respiration rate of 18 breaths/min. Small nasal polyps are noted. Lung examination shows diffuse rhonchi and scattered wheezing. Cardiac examination findings are normal. Digital clubbing is noted. There is no pedal edema. Oxygen saturation breathing ambient air is 93%.

A chest radiograph shows increased bronchial markings consistent with bronchiectasis in the upper lung zones.

Which of the following is the most appropriate next step in management?

(A) Measure sweat chloride
(B) Perform bronchoscopy
(C) Perform echocardiography
(D) Record symptoms and medication use over 2 weeks

Item 86 [Advanced]

A 50-year-old woman is evaluated in the office for a rash on her legs that developed 3 days ago. The rash began as mildly itchy red spots that have expanded in number and become more prominent. She denies fever, chills, nausea, vomiting, or other systemic symptoms. She was recently treated for a urinary tract infection with a course of trimethoprim–sulfamethoxazole that was completed 2 days before her rash developed. Her medical history is otherwise unremarkable. She does not smoke or drink alcohol and is taking no medications.

On examination, her vital signs are normal. The skin shows a purpuric rash distributed across the lower extremities. The specific lesions are indurated but nontender to palpation. The rash is shown (Plate 2).

Which of the following is the most appropriate next step in management?

(A) Administer an antistaphylococcal antibiotic

(B) Perform a punch biopsy

(C) Prescribe a topical glucocorticoid

(D) Serologic testing for hepatitis A

Item 87 [Advanced]

A 57-year-old man is evaluated in the office for skin changes on his face and arms. He works as a truck driver and has noted excessive skin tanning and mild excess hair growth primarily in areas of greatest sun exposure. He also reports the development of blisters on the backs of his hands, which eventually break and leave ulcers that heal with scarring. His medical history is significant for chronic hepatitis C infection. He does not smoke, use alcohol, or take any medications.

On physical examination, his vital signs are normal. There is no jaundice, hepatosplenomegaly, or stigmata of chronic liver disease. The rash is shown (Plate 3).

Which of the following is the most likely diagnosis?

(A) Cryoglobulinemia

(B) Erythema nodosum

(C) Lichen planus

(D) Porphyria cutanea tarda

Item 88 [Advanced]

A 22-year-old man is evaluated for lip erosions and a new rash on the palms. A representative example of the skin findings is shown (Plate 4).

Which of the following infections is most commonly associated with this skin finding?

(A) Herpes simplex virus

(B) Parvovirus B19

(C) Streptococcus, group A

(D) Varicella zoster

Item 89 [Basic]

A 35-year-old man is evaluated for pain, increased warmth, erythema, and swelling on the right lower extremity of 2 days' duration. There is no pruritus. He does not recall any injury to the area. His medical history is negative, and he is currently not taking any medications.

On physical examination, his temperature is 38.4°C (100.1°F); other vital signs are normal. Skin findings are shown (Plate 5).

Which of the following is the most likely diagnosis?

(A) Cellulitis

(B) Contact dermatitis

(C) Impetigo

(D) Stasis dermatitis

Item 90 [Advanced]

A 65-year-old man is evaluated for discomfort and discoloration and occasional swelling and itching of the legs for the past 3 years. The symptoms have been gradually progressive, are worse at the end of the day and after standing for long periods of time, and are improved with elevation of his lower extremities. He has no history of trauma or deep venous thrombosis. He has no additional symptoms and no other medical problems. He takes no medication.

On physical examination, his vital signs are normal. His body mass index is 27. The cardiopulmonary examination, including peripheral pulses, is normal. Skin findings are shown (Plate 6).

The affected skin is not tender to touch.

Which of the following is the best initial management for this patient?

(A) Compression stockings

(B) Dicloxacillin

(C) Furosemide

(D) Patch testing

Item 91 [Advanced]

A 68-year-old man is evaluated for a 6-month history of a painless ulcer on the bottom of his foot. His medical history is significant for long-standing type 1 diabetes mellitus and hypertension. His medications are insulin glargine, metformin, and lisinopril.

On physical examination, his vital signs are normal. Peripheral pulses are diminished in the foot and ankle bilaterally, but the foot is appropriately warm to touch. The foot is insensate to monofilament testing over the metatarsal heads. Vibratory sensation is absent to the knee. Reflexes are diminished at the ankle but present at the knee.

Findings on examination of the foot are shown (Plate 7).

Which of the following is the most likely diagnosis?

(A) Arterial ulcer

(B) Neuropathic ulcer

(C) Vasculitic ulcer

(D) Venous stasis ulcer

Item 92 [Basic]

A 43-year-old woman is evaluated in the emergency department for widespread hives for the past 2 days. The individual lesions are extremely pruritic and seem to migrate, with each lasting 30 to 60 minutes. There is no accompanying wheezing and no lip or eyelid swelling. The patient is breathing comfortably and has no difficulty swallowing or clearing secretions. She has no known drug allergies and just finished a 3-day course of levofloxacin for a urinary tract infection.

On physical examination, her temperature is normal, blood pressure is 110/78 mm Hg, pulse rate is 90 beats/min, respiration rate is 18 breaths/min. There are scattered edematous indurated erythematous plaques consistent with wheals over the scalp, face, neck, chest, upper back, flanks, and arms. The patient has dermatographism. There is no wheezing or stridor, no mucosal lesions, and no bullae.

Which of the following is the most appropriate therapy for this patient?

(A) Cetirizine
(B) Epinephrine
(C) Indomethacin
(D) Topical high-dose prednisone

Item 93 [Basic]

A 65-year-old man is evaluated for multiple small erythematous scaly asymptomatic macules on the hands. He grew up in Florida and has a history of multiple sunburns in childhood. He rarely uses sunblock. Skin findings are shown (Plate 8).

Which of the following is the most likely diagnosis?

(A) Actinic keratoses
(B) Basal cell carcinomas
(C) Porphyria cutanea tarda
(D) Seborrheic keratoses
(E) Solar lentigines

Item 94 [Advanced]

A 31-year-old woman is evaluated in the emergency department for a 2-week history of slightly tender lesions on her anterior shins bilaterally. The lesions appeared suddenly and range from asymptomatic to slightly tender, particularly with palpation. She has no joint pain, fevers, cough, or ocular symptoms. She has no diarrhea or abdominal problems. She recently started oral contraceptives.

On physical examination, vital signs are normal. Six or seven bilateral reddish-brown subcutaneous nodules are present on the anterior shins. There is no fluctuance. Results of a chest examination are normal, ocular mucosa is normal with no conjunctivitis, joints are normal with no arthritis, crepitus, or edema. Chest radiograph is normal. Typical lesions are shown. (Plate 9)

Which of the following is the most likely diagnosis for the skin lesions?

(A) Erythema muliforme
(B) Erythema nodosum
(C) Psoriasis
(D) Pyoderma gangrenosum

Item 95 [Basic]

A 78-year-old man reports a several-year history of developing an increasing number of irregularly pigmented "moles" on the back. The lesions are mostly asymptomatic, although some itch at times, and some may be getting larger. He is concerned they could be melanoma and wonders if they can all be removed. His family history is significant for a sister with melanoma at 55 years of age.

Physical examination reveals skin lesions as shown (Plate 10).

Which of the following is the mostly likely diagnosis?

(A) Atypical nevi
(B) Melanomas
(C) Seborrheic keratoses
(D) Solar lentigines

Item 96 [Advanced]

A 75-year-old woman is evaluated in the emergency department for skin blistering. Her symptoms began 4 days ago when she developed fatigue and malaise. Yesterday she developed diffuse skin redness and blisters that break easily, leaving patches of raw skin. Ten days ago, she received trimethoprim–sulfamethoxazole for a urinary tract infection. Her medical history is otherwise unremarkable.

On physical examination, her temperature is 39.1°C (102.4°F), blood pressure is 100/75 mm Hg, pulse rate is 115 beats/min, and respiration rate is 20 breaths/min. There is generalized erythema with blistering and erosions affecting greater than 30% of her body surface area with skin sloughing of nonblistered skin. Her lips are crusted, and she has ulcers inside her mouth. Skin findings are shown (Plate 11).

The leukocyte count is 12,500/µL (12.5×10^9/L) with 15% eosinophils. The liver transaminases are elevated.

Which of the following is the most likely diagnosis?

(A) Bullous pemphigoid
(B) Erythema multiforme
(C) Staphylococcal scalded skin syndrome
(D) Toxic epidermal necrolysis

Item 97 [Advanced]

A 65-year-old woman is evaluated for a prodrome of pain on tip of the nose followed by a painful eruption involving the right periorbital tissue. On physical examination, all vital signs are normal. There are grouped vesicles on an erythematous base on the tip of her nose and about her right eye.

Which of the following is the most appropriate first step in management of this patient?

(A) Apply warm compresses
(B) Begin ophthalmic corticosteroids
(C) Begin valacyclovir and obtain an urgent ophthalmology consultation
(D) Obtain bacterial culture and start cephalexin

Item 98 [Basic]

A 22-year-old man is evaluated for recurrent outbreaks of a skin rash on the chest and back of 3 months' duration. He has not been exposed to hot tubs, whirlpool baths, or swimming pools. His health is otherwise excellent, and he takes no medication.

On physical examination, vital signs are normal. Skin findings are shown (Plate 12).

Which of the following is the most likely diagnosis?

(A) Acne
(B) Folliculitis
(C) Miliaria
(D) Rosacea

General Internal Medicine
Answers and Critiques

Item 1   Answer: C

Educational Objective: *Understand the ability of a highly sensitive diagnostic test to help exclude the presence of disease.*

The most appropriate next step in management of this patient is to consider an alternative diagnosis to pulmonary embolism (PE). The goal of diagnostic testing is to obtain additional information that helps refine the pretest probability of disease in a specific patient by using the history, physical examination, laboratory studies, or imaging. Each diagnostic intervention should help in either increasing or decreasing the likelihood that the disease of interest is present until a threshold is reached at which treatment is pursued or the diagnosis is no longer considered.

In this patient, her pretest probability of PE as the cause of her symptoms is relatively low at 15%, although PE may be potentially fatal and is usually considered a "no miss" diagnosis. Therefore, additional testing is indicated to further evaluate this diagnostic possibility. The test characteristics of a D-dimer study include a high sensitivity (96%) for detecting PE because a positive study result will detect almost all cases of PE if it is present. This high level of sensitivity allows for the application of SnOUT, in which a highly sensitive test, if the result is negative, essentially rules out the presence of the disease (or, in other words, if a highly sensitive test will detect virtually all cases of the disease is present, if the test result is negative, the disease is likely not present).

Although not applicable to this patient, a similar but opposite concept applies to tests that have a very high specificity (the ability to exclude a disease if it is truly not present). Because a highly specific test almost always has a positive result if the disease is truly present, it is useful in establishing the presence of a disease when test results are positive. The mnemonic SPIN refers to this concept (i.e., a SPecific test, when positive, rules IN disease).

KEY POINT

If a highly sensitive diagnostic test for a specific disease is negative, the presence of that disease is unlikely.

Bibliography

Jaeschke R, Guyatt GH, Sackett DL. Users' guides to the medical literature III. How to use an article about a diagnostic test. B. What are the results and will they help me in caring for my patients? The Evidence-Based Medicine Working Group. JAMA. 1994; 271:703-7. [PMID: 8309035]

Item 2   Answer: C

Educational Objective: *Understand the effect of disease prevalence on measures of a diagnostic test.*

Sensitivity and specificity describe the ability of a test, when compared with a gold standard, to detect or exclude a disease. Sensitivity is the proportion of patients with the disease who have a positive test result; specificity is the proportion of patients without the disease who have a negative test result.

Compared with the sensitivity and specificity, predictive values result from the application of a test of known sensitivity and specificity to a specific patient population. Unlike sensitivity and specificity, predictive values are highly dependent on the prevalence of the disease in the population being tested. Positive predictive value refers to the proportion of patients who have a positive test result who actually have the disease. Negative predictive value refers to the proportion of patients with a negative test result who truly do not have the disease. The positive predictive value increases with increasing disease prevalence, and the negative predictive value increases with lower disease prevalence.

A likelihood ratio (LR) is a statistical indicator of how much the result of a diagnostic test will increase or decrease the pretest probability of a disease in a specific patient. LRs may be determined from the sensitivity and specificity of a diagnostic test and therefore do not change with disease prevalence.

KEY POINT

The positive and negative predictive values of a diagnostic test are highly dependent on the prevalence of disease in the population.

Bibliography

Akobeng AK. Understanding diagnostic tests 1: sensitivity, specificity and predictive values. Acta Paediatr. 2007;96:338-41. [PMID: 17407452]

Item 3   Answer: E

Educational Objective: *Estimate posttest probability using likelihood ratios.*

The patient's posttest probability of having ischemic coronary artery disease is approximately 95%. The patient's pretest probability of having ischemic coronary artery disease is estimated to be 50% based on clinical variables (including the nature of the chest pain, age, and gender). LRs are a statistical indicator of how much the result of a diagnostic test will increase or decrease the pretest probability of a disease in a specific patient. LRs may be determined from the sensitivity and specificity of a diagnostic test, and separate LRs are calculated for use when a test result is positive (LR[+]) or when the test result is negative (LR[-]). This patient has a positive treadmill echocardiographic stress test, and the likelihood ratio for a positive result on this test is approximately 10. Although very specific posttest probabilities may be calculated or estimated using a nomogram, a clinical rule of thumb is that LR(+) values of 2, 5, and 10 correspond to an increase in disease probability by 15%, 30%, and 45%, respectively. With a pretest probability of 50%, a positive echocardiographic stress test would increase the likelihood of disease by approximately 45%, leading to a posttest probability in the range of 95%, which would be very useful clinically in making further treatment decisions.

If the stress test result had been negative, LR(-) values of 0.5, 0.2, and 0.1 correspond to a decrease in disease probability by 15%, 30%, and 45%, respectively. Tests with LRs between 0.5 and 2 do not alter the pretest probability significantly if they are either positive or negative. Evaluating the likelihood ratios of a particular test may help in selecting an appropriate study to obtain useful clinical information in the diagnostic process.

> **KEY POINT**
>
> LR(+) values of 2, 5, and 10 correspond to an increase in disease probability by 15%, 30%, and 45%, respectively; LR(-) values of 0.5, 0.2, and 0.1 correspond to a decrease in disease probability by 15%, 30%, and 45%, respectively.

Bibliography

Jaeschke R, Guyatt GH, Sackett DL. Users' guides to the medical literature. III. How to use an article about a diagnostic test. B. What are the results and will they help me in caring for my patients? The Evidence-Based Medicine Working Group. JAMA. 1994;271:703-7. [PMID: 8309035]

Item 4   Answer: A

Educational Objective: *Compare different tests using a receiver operating characteristic (ROC) curve.*

Test A has the best overall performance. Many test outcomes are continuous variables, which are arbitrarily divided at some point into normal and abnormal values by establishing a cut point. Some common examples of continuous variables are troponin, D-dimer, and prostate specific antigen (PSA) levels. It is important to realize that the process of deciding the cut point indicating the presence or absence of disease has significant implications. Decreasing the cut point to indicate an abnormal test result will help to detect more cases of the disease and decrease the number of false-negative test results (by making the test more sensitive) but at the cost of increasing the number of false-positive test results (by decreasing the specificity). Conversely, increasing the cut point to indicate an abnormal result decreases the number of false-positive test results (by decreasing the sensitivity) but at the price of increasing false-negative results (by increasing the specificity). The relationship between sensitivity and specificity may be shown graphically by the ROC curve. It demonstrates how increasing sensitivity (moving up the y axis) can decrease specificity (moving across the x axis). One way to visually compare the operating characteristics of different tests is to plot the cut points of each test on a ROC curve. A test with the best sensitivity and specificity for each of its cut points will have a curve that "crowds" the upper left margins of the ROC curve. This concept is particularly valuable when comparing different tests; the test with the greatest overall accuracy will have the largest area under the ROC curve and will be located closest to the upper left corner.

> **KEY POINT**
>
> In a comparison of two or more tests on a ROC curve, the test with the best overall accuracy for each of its cut points will have the largest area under the ROC curve.

Bibliography

Akobeng AK. Understanding diagnostic tests 3: Receiver operating characteristic curves. Acta Paediatr. 2007;96:644-7. [PMID: 17376185]

Item 5   Answer: D

Educational Objective: *Evaluate absolute risk and the number needed to treat.*

The NNT with drug A compared with drug B to prevent one additional case of DVT is 100.

Absolute risk (AR) is the risk of a specific disease based on its actual occurrence, or its event rate (ER), in a group of patients being studied, and is expressed as:

AR = Patients with event in group/Total patients in group

As seen in the table, in this study, the AR for DVT in the group treated with drug A is 25/2500, or 1%, and the AR for the group treated with drug B is 50/2500, or 2%.

Often, the event rate of a disease in an experimental group (EER) is compared with the event rate in a control group (CER). When the risk between groups is reduced, this difference is termed the absolute risk reduction (ARR), or if the outcome is of benefit, the difference is called the absolute benefit index (ABI). In this case, patients treated with drug A (EER) appear to benefit from treatment with a lower risk of DVT than patients in the group treated with drug B (CER). This is expressed as:

ABI = (EER − CER)

ABI = (1% − 2%) = 1% or 0.01

This means that treatment with drug A benefits patients compared with drug B by lowering the risk of DVT from 2% to 1%, or an absolute difference of 1%.

Assessing treatment studies using absolute measures also allows determination of "numbers needed," which are estimates of the clinical magnitude of the differences between treatments. In this case, the NNT indicates the number of patients needed to be treated with drug A compared with drug B to obtain one additional beneficial outcome. The NNT is calculated as:

NNT = 1/ABI

NNT = 1/0.01 = 100

This means that 100 patients would need to be treated with drug A compared with drug B to prevent one additional case of DVT.

Treatment study results may also be reported as relative measures; these measures compare the ratio of two outcomes without regard to the actual frequency of the outcome in a given study population. In this case, treatment with drug A leads to a 50% reduction in risk of DVT compared with treatment with drug B (25 compared with 50 events) even though the actual frequency of DVT in the study populations does not exceed 2%. Therefore, outcomes expressed in relative terms usually appear of greater magnitude than when expressed in absolute terms; they also do not allow calculations of number needed to estimate clinical impact.

> **KEY POINT**
>
> Treatment study outcomes reported in absolute terms reflect the frequency of a disease in the study population and allow estimation of "numbers needed"; outcomes reported in relative terms tend to appear to be of greater magnitude.

Bibliography

Citrome L, Ketter TA. When does a difference make a difference? Interpretation of number needed to treat, number needed to harm, and likelihood to be helped or harmed. Int J Clin Pract. 2013;67:407-11. [PMID: 23574101].

Item 6   Answer: A

Educational Objective: *Evaluate a randomized controlled trial (RCT) for generalizability.*

This patient has asymptomatic cardiomyopathy, which places her in New York Heart Association (NYHA) functional class I. Therefore, her heart failure is too mild to be appropriately considered for taking the new drug, which was tested on patients with NYHA class III and IV heart failure.

RCTs are often considered the "gold standard" for evaluating new therapies because their experimental design allows confounding variables that might obscure the benefit of a therapy to be balanced between groups. Thus, any finding in a well-designed RCT is typically considered valid. To maximize the ability of a given study to find a meaningful result, RCTs are typically restricted to relatively homogeneous individuals who meet rigidly defined inclusion and exclusion criteria. Unfortunately, the proscribed nature of patient selection and intervention in RCTs therefore makes their conclusions relatively narrow, requiring clinicians to use caution when generalizing these results to other populations. The new drug was shown to be effective for patients with NYHA class III or IV heart failure but may not be effective for a patient with more mild heart failure, such as this patient.

Although the mean age of participants in the trial was 63 years, the drug was tested on patients between the ages of 40 and 80 years. Thus, based on her age, the patient would have been eligible for the trial, and age alone is not a reason to withhold the drug from her.

Despite rigid criteria for inclusion and exclusion in an RCT, there will still likely be some variability between individual patients included in a particular study, such as concurrent medications being used. Even with these differences, however, a net benefit of treatment was found in the study population. Although most patients in the study were already taking a β-blocker, it cannot be inferred from the study whether this treatment is required to see the benefit of the new drug.

There is no arbitrary level of risk of harm that would impact a decision to use a medication; rather, each medication should be evaluated according to its risk and benefit profile. Furthermore, in this trial, drug H had net benefit despite its rate of serious adverse events.

KEY POINT

Caution should be used when generalizing the results of RCTs to populations other than those who would meet the inclusion and exclusion criteria of the study.

Bibliography

Ho PM, Peterson PN, Masoudi FA. Evaluating the evidence: is there a rigid hierarchy? Circulation. 2008;118:1675-84. [PMID: 18852378]

Item 7   Answer: A

Educational Objective: *Recognize threats to validity in a medical study.*

The main reason that it is difficult to determine the effectiveness of this drug based on the published study is that there is no comparison, or control, group. When evaluating the medical literature, it is important to consider the quality of the study design. Studies assessing treatment effectiveness should always have a control group, which can receive either an alternative treatment or a placebo. A control group is critical because it tells the investigators what would have happened if the intervention had not been done. Depending on the

study type, patients can be assigned to a control group (in an experimental study) or be part of a "natural" control (observational study). The primary threat to validity of this study is the absence of a control group; that is, there is no group with which the patients taking the new drug can be compared.

In general, it is always best for outcomes in any study to be assessed by an independent evaluator who is unaware of treatment assignment ("blinded"). In the case of unambiguous outcomes such as death, however, an unblinded outcomes assessment is permissible.

In experimental study designs, investigators often randomly assign patients to a therapy to equalize the group for measured and unmeasured confounding variables. This trial has no comparison group, so randomization would not be possible.

Increased numbers of patients in studies generally yield greater precision in measurement. In this trial, however, the key threat to validity is not trial size but absence of a control group.

KEY POINT

The primary threat to validity in a case series is the absence of a control group.

Bibliography

Ho PM, Peterson PN, Masoudi FA. Evaluating the evidence: is there a rigid hierarchy? Circulation. 2008;118:1675-84. [PMID: 18852378]

Item 8   Answer: A

Educational Objective: *Screen for abdominal aortic aneurysm.*

This patient should undergo one-time abdominal ultrasonography to screen for an abdominal aortic aneurysm (AAA) because he is a man between the ages of 65 and 75 years who has ever smoked (defined as 100 lifetime cigarettes). Screening for AAA in this patient group has been shown to decrease the risk of death from AAA by 14% over 10 years. The U.S. Preventive Services Task Force (USPSTF) therefore recommends one-time ultrasonographic screening for AAA in men ages 65 to 75 years who have ever smoked. However, there is inadequate data of benefit to recommend screening for AAA in men who have never smoked or women under any circumstances.

Coronary artery calcium (CAC) measures the amount of calcium in the walls of the coronary arteries and correlates with the degree of plaque formation. It has high sensitivity for detecting stenoses of greater than 50% but low specificity. Because of this low specificity, CAC is not recommended in asymptomatic persons. It may have a role in selected high-risk patients in whom evidence significant atherosclerotic disease may be of benefit in making treatment decisions. However, it would not be appropriate to order this screening test in this patient.

The USPSTF recommends screening for lung cancer only in patients ages 55 to 80 years who have a 30-pack-year smoking history and currently smoke or quit within the past 15 years with annual low-dose computed tomography. Although this patient is a former smoker and is in the recommended age range, his smoking history does not qualify him for screening. Additionally, plain chest radiography is not adequately sensitive for detection of small lung cancers; in patients eligible for screening, annual low-dose computed tomography scanning is the recommended modality.

One-time abdominal ultrasonography to screen for an AAA is recommended in men between the ages of 65 and 75 years who have ever smoked (defined as 100 lifetime cigarettes).

Bibliography

Thompson SG, Ashthon HA, Gao L, Scott RA; Multicentre Aneurysm Screening Study Group. Screening men for abdominal aortic aneurysm: 10 year mortality and cost effectiveness results from the randomised Multicentre Aneurysm Screening Study. BMJ. 2009;338:b2307. [PMID: 19553269]

Item 9   Answer: C

Educational Objective: *Manage influenza vaccination in a healthy woman.*

This healthy 30-year-old woman should receive a seasonal influenza vaccination. The Centers for Disease Control and Prevention currently recommends that all persons age ≥6 months be vaccinated annually against influenza regardless of risk factors. Vaccination usually takes place between September and March in the Northern Hemisphere. The trivalent or quadrivalent inactivated virus vaccine is given intramuscularly and is appropriate for all groups, including pregnant women. The intranasal live attenuated vaccine is approved for patients aged 2 to 49 years but should be avoided in pregnant women and in patients with diabetes, immunosuppression, and certain other chronic conditions.

The hepatitis B vaccine is indicated for all children and adolescents through age 18 years, persons with HIV or other recent sexually transmitted infections, persons who are sexually active but not monogamous, workers with occupational exposure to blood, clients and staff of institutions for developmentally disabled individuals, correctional facility inmates, illicit drug users, persons with diabetes mellitus who are younger than 60 years, and persons with advanced chronic kidney disease who are approaching hemodialysis. Hepatitis B vaccination is also indicated for those planning travel to an endemic area and those with an increased risk for morbidity related to the disease, as well as for persons who request vaccination. This patient has no indication for hepatitis B vaccination.

The Advisory Committee on Immunization Practices recommends routine human papillomavirus (HPV) vaccination of girls and women ages 9 to 26 years with either the bivalent or quadrivalent vaccines, and boys and men ages 11 to 21 with the quadrivalent vaccine regardless of sexual activity. HPV vaccination is also recommended for immunocompromised patients. The vaccine is not indicated for this 30-year-old woman.

Current recommendations are that a tetanus and diphtheria (Td) vaccine be routinely administered every 10 years. Owing to an increased incidence of pertussis, thought in part to be related to waning immunity from childhood vaccination, all adults are recommended to receive a single tetanus, diphtheria, and acellular pertussis (Tdap) vaccination regardless of the interval since their last Td booster (although it may be given in place of a decennial Td booster if scheduled); this is a particularly important recommendation for persons age 65 years or older because of the high burden of associated disease in this patient population. In addition, all postpartum women, health care workers, and adults who have close contact with infants younger than 12 months should receive a one-time Tdap booster if not already given. This patient is not due for a routine repeat Td booster for another 5 years and has no indications to receive either a Td or Tdap vaccination at this time.

Annual seasonal influenza vaccination is recommended for all adults regardless of risk factors.

Bibliography

National Center for Immunization and Respiratory Diseases. General recommendations on immunization–recommendations of the Advisory Committee on Immunization Practices (ACIP). MMWR Recomm Rep. 2011;60:1-64. [PMID: 21293327]

Item 10   Answer: C

Educational Objective: *Appropriately administer pneumococcal vaccination in a patient who has been previously vaccinated.*

This man should receive a dose of the PCV13 vaccine today and the PSV13 vaccination in 1 year. Two versions of pneumococcal vaccine are available: a 23-valent pneumococcal polysaccharide vaccine (PPSV23) and a 13-valent conjugate vaccine (PCV13). The PPSV23 vaccine protects against 60% of bacteremic disease and is associated with substantial reductions in morbidity and mortality among elderly and high-risk adults and is therefore recommended for all adults age ≥65 years and for adults with other risk factors (asthma, diabetes, cirrhosis, asplenia). PCV13 is more antigenic and has been used primarily in patients with significant immunocompromising conditions, such as asplenia, cerebrospinal fluid leaks, or cochlear implants. However, it has been shown that the combination of PPSV23 and PCV13 together provides the most comprehensive protection against pneumococcal disease in patients age 65 years and older. Therefore, dual immunization is recommended, although to achieve maximal immune response, the two vaccines are not administered together.

In patients 65 years or older who have never been vaccinated against pneumococcal pneumonia or who do not know their vaccination status, the vaccines should be administered sequentially with PCV13 given first, followed by the PPSV23 vaccine 6 to 12 months later. For patients who had previously received a dose of PPSV23, as in this patient, a dose of PCV13 should be given at age 65 years (at least 1 year after receiving the PPSV23 vaccine) followed by a dose of PPSV23 6 to 12 months later.

Patients receiving either vaccine before age 65 years should be vaccinated to achieve dual vaccination with PPSV23 and PCV13. Since this patient received only the PPSV23 vaccine previously, no additional immunization for pneumococcal disease would be inappropriate.

Patients aged 65 years or older should receive sequential dual immunization with both the 23-valent pneumococcal polysaccharide vaccine (PPSV23) and 13-valent pneumococcal conjugate vaccine (PCV13).

Bibliography

Centers for Disease Control and Prevention (CDC); Advisory Committee on Immunization Practices. Updated recommendations for prevention of invasive pneumococcal disease among adults using the 23-valent pneumococcal polysaccharide vaccine (PPSV23). MMWR Morb Mortal Wkly Rep. 2010;59:1102-6. [PMID: 20814406]

Item 11   Answer: B

Educational Objective: *Identify appropriate screening strategies for a patient at average risk for colon cancer.*

Colonoscopy every 10 years is the most appropriate screening recommendation for this patient among the listed options. He is at average risk for colorectal cancer, which includes persons with no personal or family history of colon adenoma or cancer and who do not have a condition that predisposes them to cancer, such as inflammatory bowel disease. Screening for colorectal cancer is cost effective and well tolerated and has been shown to decrease mortality rates. Screening for colon cancer is feasible because the 10 to 15 years needed for a polyp to develop into cancer are sufficient time to detect and remove an adenoma before it becomes malignant. Screening in the average-risk population should be started at age 50 years; there are various effective screening strategies in average-risk patients, with surveillance intervals depending on the chosen strategy.

Annual fecal occult blood testing is a screening option but requires that two samples be collected from each of three spontaneously passed stools. Digital examination to retrieve a sample is not an acceptable substitute because it is approximately five times less sensitive than the technique of obtaining two samples from each of three stools.

Flexible sigmoidoscopy is an acceptable screening option as well. However, unlike colonoscopy, sigmoidoscopy does not examine the entire colon. It must therefore be used in combination with fecal occult blood testing and should be performed in 5-year intervals.

Computed tomographic colonography is a newer method for screening. Although it does not require sedation, it does expose patients to radiation. Its effectiveness relative to existing screening modalities is under investigation, but it is not currently recommended for routine use in average risk patients.

KEY POINT

Screening for colorectal cancer in the average-risk population should be started at age 50 years.

Bibliography

Weinberg DS. In the clinic. Colorectal cancer screening. Ann Intern Med. 2008;148:ITC2-1-ITC2-16. [PMID: 18252680]

Item 12   Answer: B

Educational Objective: *Counsel a patient regarding herpes zoster vaccination.*

The herpes zoster (shingles) vaccine has been available for several years and is currently recommended for adults age 60 years and older to decrease the risk of herpes zoster and postherpetic neuralgia. The best choice in counseling this patient is to advise he have the vaccine now and explain that both efficacy and safety of the vaccine have been demonstrated. The vaccine has been shown to reduce zoster flares by half and the occurrence of postherpetic neuralgia by 67% in adults older than 60 years. In persons between the ages of 60 and 69 years, the efficacy in preventing shingles was 64%. Long-term safety studies of the vaccine have demonstrated no increase in serious adverse events compared with placebo with similar rates of serious adverse events.

The herpes zoster vaccine is a live vaccine and is contraindicated in pregnant women and in patients with primary or acquired immun-

odeficiency. This includes persons with leukemia, lymphoma, and other malignant neoplasms involving the lymphatic system or bone marrow; persons with HIV infection or AIDS; and persons on immunosuppressive therapy, including high-dose glucocorticoids. Persons with chronic medical conditions such as chronic kidney failure, diabetes mellitus, or chronic pulmonary disease can be vaccinated unless they have a contraindication. Diabetes mellitus is not a contraindication to zoster vaccine administration.

The vaccine is indicated at age 60 years regardless of the patient's history of either varicella disease (chickenpox) or shingles. Nearly all persons in the United States older than 60 years have immunity to the varicella zoster virus, and the zoster vaccine should be given even in persons who are unsure whether they ever had chickenpox. There are no recognized safety concerns in giving the vaccine to a patient who has already had shingles. Furthermore, self-reports of previous shingles may be inaccurate, and no laboratory evaluations exist to confirm a history of shingles.

KEY POINT

The herpes zoster vaccine is indicated for immunocompetent adults age 60 years and older regardless of their history of chickenpox or shingles.

Bibliography

National Center for Immunization and Respiratory Diseases. General recommendations on immunization–recommendations of the Advisory Committee on Immunization Practices (ACIP). MMWR Recomm Rep. 2011;60:1-64. [PMID: 21293327]

Item 13   Answer: B

Educational Objective: *Screen for HIV infection.*

According to guidelines published by the Centers for Disease Control and Prevention (CDC), this man should be screened for HIV infection. The guidelines recommend that all persons between the ages of 13 and 64 years be screened for HIV infection. This recommendation is based on evidence from several studies that have demonstrated that screening for HIV is effective even in low-prevalence settings. This is particularly true when screening is coupled with the availability of antiretroviral therapy. Recommended screening is with a combination assay detecting serum HIV antibody and p24 antigen. In contrast to the CDC guidelines, the U.S. Preventive Services Task Force (USPSTF) assigns a C grade to HIV screening, making no recommendation for or against routine HIV screening.

The USPSTF recommends that all sexually active women age younger than 25 years should undergo screening for chlamydial infection; this recommendation is based on evidence that screening reduces the incidence of pelvic inflammatory disease by 50%. The USPSTF also recommends that any man or woman deemed to have risk behaviors (high-risk sexual encounters, history of a sexually transmitted infection, history of sex work, inconsistent condom use) should be screened for chlamydial infection, syphilis, and gonorrhea. This patient does not fit into either category and does not require screening.

Although this patient's parents have cardiovascular risk factors, screening for coronary artery disease with a resting electrocardiogram is not recommended because abnormalities of the resting electrocardiogram are rare, are not specific for coronary artery disease, and do not predict subsequent mortality from coronary disease.

There is no agreement among major groups related to screening for hypothyroidism. The American Academy of Family Physicians and the American Association of Clinical Endocrinologists recommend screening for hypothyroidism in older women. The American Thyroid Association recommends screening adults by measuring thyroid-stimulating hormone (TSH) beginning at age 35 years, but the USPSTF does not recommend routine screening. This patient is not in a high-risk group defined by either age or sex, and screening for thyroid disease with a TSH level is not appropriate.

> **KEY POINT**
> The Centers for Disease Control and Prevention recommend that all persons between the ages of 13 and 64 years be screened for HIV infection.

Bibliography
Qaseem A, Snow V, Shekelle P, Hopkins R Jr, Owens DK; Clinical Efficacy Assessment Subcommittee, American College of Physicians. Screening for HIV in health care settings: a guidance statement from the American College of Physicians and HIV Medicine Association. Ann Intern Med. 2009;150(2):125-131. [PMID: 19047022]

Item 14   Answer: D
Educational Objective: *Immunize against human papillomavirus (HPV).*

The most appropriate option for this patient is HPV vaccination now. The Advisory Committee on Immunization Practices (ACIP) of the Centers for Disease Control and Prevention recommends HPV vaccine for cervical cancer prevention. The vaccine is recommended for all girls and women between ages 9 and 26 years regardless of sexual activity. Bivalent and quadrivalent HPV vaccines are available. Both vaccines protect against high-risk HPV subtypes (HPV-16 and HPV-18), and the quadrivalent additionally protects against subtypes that cause genital warts (HPV-6 and HPV-11). Either vaccine is recommended for use in women. Both vaccines are administered in three doses: time zero and then 1 to 2 months later, with the third dose being given 6 months after the initial dose. Pregnant women should not receive the vaccine because there is a lack of safety data in this population.

The ACIP also recommends that boys and men age 11 to 21 years receive the quadrivalent vaccine, although the vaccine may be given to boys as young as 9 years of age. Men may also be vaccinated up to age 26 years.

HPV infection is predominantly spread by sexual contact. This patient states that she is not sexually active; however, the vaccine should be recommended now because it is ideally administered before the onset of sexual activity. It is of low risk, and the vaccine efficacy lasts for at least several years. The vaccine does not protect against all types of HPV, and roughly 30% of cervical cancers will not be prevented by the vaccine, so women should continue to get regular cervical cancer screening even after completing the vaccination series.

The HPV vaccine is not effective in preventing HPV-related diseases in women who have an established infection at the time of vaccination; therefore, waiting for HPV seroconversion before vaccination is inappropriate.

> **KEY POINT**
> An HPV quadrivalent vaccination series should be offered to all girls and women ages 9 through 26 years, and women should continue to get regular Papanicolaou smears even after completing the vaccination series.

Bibliography
Advisory Committee on Immunization Practices. Recommended adult immunization schedule: United States, 2010. Ann Intern Med. 2010;152:36-9. [PMID: 20048270]

Item 15   Answer: E
Educational Objective: *Diagnose white coat hypertension.*

This patient has white coat hypertension with no evidence of target organ damage. He should therefore be advised to continue home blood pressure measurements and return for a follow-up visit in 6 months. White coat hypertension is characterized by at least three separate office blood pressure measurements above 140/90 mm Hg and at least two sets of measurements below 140/90 mm Hg obtained outside the office, accompanied by the absence of target organ damage. Ambulatory blood pressure monitoring is considered the gold standard for diagnosing this condition. Patients with white coat hypertension have a lower risk for cardiovascular events compared with those with sustained hypertension but also have a greater risk for developing sustained hypertension than those without this condition and should be carefully monitored, including with home blood pressure measurements.

This patient does not have essential hypertension because he is not hypertensive outside of the office setting. He has no family history of hypertension and no evidence of end-organ damage from untreated hypertension. Because he does not have hypertension, primary hyperaldosteronism and renovascular hypertension, which are causes of secondary hypertension, are unlikely.

Masked hypertension is elevated blood pressure in the ambulatory setting that is missed in the office setting. If this patient had masked hypertension, ambulatory blood pressure readings would be elevated, and office readings would be low. In addition, this patient might have evidence of end-organ damage from chronic untreated hypertension.

> **KEY POINT**
> Patients with white coat hypertension are at higher risk for developing sustained hypertension and should be carefully monitored.

Bibliography
Franklin SS, Thijs L, Hansen TW, O'Brien E, Staessen JA. White-coat hypertension: new insights from recent studies. Hypertension. 2013;62:982-7. [PMID: 24041952]

Item 16   Answer: D
Educational Objective: *Manage prehypertension.*

This patient has prehypertension, and rechecking his blood pressure in 1 year is indicated. The prehypertension category established by the Seventh Report of the Joint National Committee on Prevention, Detection, Evaluation, and Treatment of High Blood Pressure (JNC 7) designates a group at high risk for progression to hypertension in whom lifestyle modifications may be preemptive. Although this is not considered a mild form of hypertension, it is a category used to define persons considered at increased risk for the development of true hypertension. Increasing age and family history are also associated with an increased risk of eventually developing hypertension requiring treatment. The patient should be advised to make appropriate lifestyle changes if indicated, such as weight loss (if overweight), increase his exercise level, and control his dietary intake of cholesterol and saturated fats. His blood pressure should then be rechecked in 1 year.

Repeat blood pressure measurement in 2 weeks, given his stable but borderline blood pressures on his previous determinations and before implementation of lifestyle changes, would not be indicated.

Ambulatory blood pressure monitoring is indicated for patients with suspected white coat hypertension, to monitor patients with difficult-to-control blood pressure or those with significant symptoms such as hypotension on therapy, or if autonomic dysfunction is suspected. None of these situations is present in this patient.

This patient has not met the diagnostic criteria for sustained hypertension; therefore, initiation of long-term medical treatment is not appropriate.

KEY POINT

Lifestyle modifications and a repeat blood pressure measurement in 1 year are indicated for patients with prehypertension.

Bibliography

Chobanian AV, Bakris GL, Black HR, et al; National Heart, Lung, and Blood Institute; Joint National Committee on Prevention, Detection, Evaluation, and Treatment of High Blood Pressure; National High Blood Pressure Education Program Coordinating Committee. The Seventh Report of the Joint National Committee on Prevention, Detection, Evaluation, and Treatment of High Blood Pressure: the JNC 7 report [erratum in JAMA. 2003;290:197]. JAMA. 2003;289:2560-72. [PMID: 12748199]

Item 17   Answer: B

Educational Objective: *Evaluate a patient with high blood pressure.*

Electrocardiography (ECG) is the most appropriate next step for this patient with high blood pressure. The evaluation of a patient with high blood pressure is directed toward determining if the blood pressure is elevated as a primary phenomenon or is secondary to another cause, if there are other cardiovascular risk factors present, and if there is evidence of target organ damage. ECG is a means of assessing for the presence of cardiac effects of sustained blood pressure elevation. On ECG, cardiac damage from hypertension is manifested by the presence of left ventricular hypertrophy and possibly Q waves. These findings also indicate an increased risk for cardiovascular events. Measures of kidney function and the urinalysis are also used to evaluate for possible end-organ damage caused by sustained hypertension. Measurement of lipids is useful in assessing for other cardiovascular risks.

Echocardiography is not indicated in this patient. It is a relatively expensive and unnecessary test in this asymptomatic patient with elevated blood pressure and normal cardiac examination findings. An echocardiogram may be indicated if there are abnormal findings on his ECG but should not be an initial test in this patient. Home blood pressure monitoring is reasonable if white coat hypertension is suspected; however, it is more important to complete the initial evaluation of this patient, which lacks an ECG. This patient's retinal arteriolar changes support target organ effect of blood pressure, particularly in this patient who is young, making white coat hypertension less likely.

Secondary hypertension should be considered in patients with hypertension who have atypical clinical features (onset at a young age, absent family history, severe hypertension) and are resistant to antihypertensive therapy. Although secondary hypertension makes up only a very small percentage of patients with elevated blood pressure, a clinical clue suggestive of primary hyperaldosteronism is spontaneous hypokalemia. If present a plasma aldosterone–plasma renin activity ratio (ARR) is an appropriate screening test. However, this patient has no features suggestive of a secondary cause of hypertension, including hypokalemia, and screening with an ARR is not needed.

KEY POINT

Evaluation of a patient with high blood pressure includes determining if the blood pressure is elevated as a secondary phenomenon, if there are other cardiovascular risk factors present, and if there is evidence of target organ damage.

Bibliography

American College of Physicians. In the clinic. Hypertension. Ann Intern Med. 2008;149:ITC6(1-15). [PMID: 19047024]

Item 18   Answer: D

Educational Objective: *Identify the cause of a patient's change in blood pressure.*

A repeat blood pressure measurement is indicated for this patient to ensure proper technique. Poor technique in measuring blood pressure is a common cause of apparent fluctuations in blood pressure. The American Heart Association recommendations require 5 minutes of rest, the bladder empty, the back supported with the feet on the floor (not in the supine position on an examination table), and proper cuff size with the cuff bladder encircling at least 80% of the arm. Errors in positioning the patient, incorrect cuff size relative to arm circumference, measuring through clothing and coats, intercurrent conversation, and interferences such as recent caffeine intake or cigarette smoking contribute to variability in blood pressure measurement. The increasing use of devices that allow patients to have repeated blood pressure measurements without a health care worker (physician or nurse) in the room may obviate some of this controversy, although these may also be associated with different forms of technical error. Similar issues may arise in inpatient settings in which variable assessment techniques and use of automated blood pressure devices may yield significant fluctuations in measured blood pressure. Such changes warrant clinician confirmation before making changes in therapy.

It is important to make adjustments to a patient's antihypertensive regimen, regardless of setting, only if the blood pressure measurements on which those adjustments are being made are accurate and reflect evidence of sustained, inadequate control.

Ambulatory blood pressure monitoring is used to diagnose white coat hypertension and masked hypertension and to determine whether treatment of hypertension is adequate outside the office or hospital setting. However, it is not indicated in this patient with generally well-controlled blood pressure and a single abnormal determination.

KEY POINT

Errors in positioning the patient, incorrect cuff size relative to arm circumference, intercurrent conversation, and interferences such as recent caffeine intake or cigarette smoking contribute to variability in blood pressure measurement.

Bibliography

Chobanian AV, Bakris GL, Black HR, et al; National Heart, Lung, and Blood Institute Joint National Committee on Prevention, Detection, Evaluation, and Treatment of High Blood Pressure; National High Blood Pressure Education Program Coordinating Committee. The Seventh Report of the Joint National Committee on Prevention, Detection, Evaluation, and Treatment of High Blood Pressure: the JNC 7 report. JAMA. 2003;289:2560-72. [PMID: 12748199]

Item 19   Answer: D

Educational Objective: *Manage hypertension in a patient who is older than the age of 80 years.*

No change in management is required at this time. This 86-year-old man has hypertension and currently takes a calcium channel blocker (amlodipine) and an angiotensin-converting enzyme (ACE) inhibitor (lisinopril); his blood pressure measurements have been less than 150 mm Hg systolic. The pattern of blood pressure elevation in older patients is typically characterized by a prominent systolic blood pressure. This relates in large part to the significant role of vascular stiffness in the blood pressure increases of older patients, which, in addition to raising systolic pressure, also leads to a decline in the diastolic pressure. Treatment of elevated systolic blood pressure in older patients has been shown to improve cardiovascular outcomes. Although a target blood pressure of <140/90 mm Hg is generally accepted for most patients with hypertension younger than age 60 years, evidence supports that a blood pressure goal of <150/90 mm Hg is of benefit in those 60 years of age or older. This older patient with near-target blood pressure measurements does not require additional treatment.

Adding an additional antihypertensive agent such as diuretics or a β-blocker (metoprolol) to this patient's regimen is not appropriate because no change is indicated in his current level of treatment. Furthermore, an additional agent with a different mechanism of action may cause adverse effects in older patients who may not be able to compensate effectively for the physiologic changes induced by multiple medications.

This patient's current regimen of the calcium channel blocker amlodipine and an ACE inhibitor appears to be reasonably effective; therefore, a diuretic substitution is unnecessary.

KEY POINT

The blood pressure target for treatment of hypertension in patients 60 years of age or older is <150/90 mm Hg.

Bibliography

James PA, Oparil S, Carter BL, et al. 2014 Evidence-Based Guideline for the Management of High Blood Pressure in Adults: Report From the Panel Members Appointed to the Eighth Joint National Committee (JNC 8). JAMA. 2014;311:507-20. [Epub ahead of print] [PMID: 24352797]

Item 20   Answer: B

Educational Objective: *Manage hypertension in a woman of childbearing age.*

This patient has essential hypertension and should be switched from lisinopril to labetalol before pregnancy. Exposure to angiotensin-converting enzyme (ACE) inhibitors such as lisinopril during the first trimester has been associated with fetal cardiac abnormalities, and exposure during the second and third trimesters has been associated with neonatal kidney failure and death. Angiotensin receptor antagonists such as losartan have been associated with similar fetal toxicity as ACE inhibitors, most likely because of the dependence of the fetal kidney on the renin–angiotensin system. Therefore, both of these agents are pregnancy category X drugs and are contraindicated throughout pregnancy and in women planning to conceive.

Labetalol is a pregnancy risk category C drug and is commonly used during pregnancy owing to its combined α- and β-blocking properties and because it does not compromise uteroplacental blood flow. Methyldopa also is used extensively in pregnancy and is one of the

only agents in which long-term follow-up of infants exposed in utero has proved to be safe. Furthermore, methyldopa is the only agent classified as a pregnancy category B drug. However, controlling blood pressure with single-agent methyldopa is often difficult, and many women are bothered by its sedating properties.

Cessation of antihypertensive therapy in a patient with hypertension is not recommended before pregnancy.

Aldosterone antagonists such as spironolactone have an antiandrogenic effect on the fetus when exposure occurs during the first trimester and should be avoided in women planning to conceive.

KEY POINT

ACE inhibitors, angiotensin receptor blockers, and aldosterone antagonists should be avoided during pregnancy and in women planning to conceive.

Bibliography

Cooper WO, Hernandez-Diaz S, Arbogast PG, et al. Major congenital malformations after first-trimester exposure to ACE inhibitors. N Engl J Med. 2006;354:2443-51. [PMID: 16760444]

Item 21   Answer: C

Educational Objective: *Prescribe appropriate antilipidemic therapy for a high-risk patient.*

The most appropriate lipid management is to recommend high-intensity statin therapy in this patient with atherosclerotic cardiovascular disease (ASCVD). Her newly diagnosed ASCVD places her into one of the four statin benefit groups described in the 2013 American College of Cardiology/American Heart Association lipid management guidelines. Other statin benefit groups include patients with a low-density lipoprotein (LDL) cholesterol level >190 mg/dL, patients with diabetes, and patients with a 10-year risk of developing ASCVD of >7.5%. The guidelines recommend high-intensity statin for patients with ASCVD who are younger than age 75 years, as in this patient. High-intensity statin therapy is defined as atorvastatin, 40 mg to 80 mg/day, or rosuvastatin, 20 mg to 40 mg/day. These two agents are recommended because they have documented efficacy in improving outcomes in multiple randomized controlled trials. The 80-mg dose is best tolerated in younger patients and those without multiple medications or multiple comorbidities and could be considered for use in this patient. The goal of high-intensity statin therapy is to lower the LDL cholesterol level by ≥50%, although routine follow-up of LDL cholesterol levels to guide therapy is not recommended, which differs from previous guidelines.

Moderate-intensity statin therapy includes atorvastatin, 10 to 20 mg/day. Therefore, maintaining her current dose of atorvastatin at 10 mg/day or increasing it to 20 mg/day would not provide high-intensity therapy.

Niacin and other non-statin drugs are no longer recommended as first-line treatments for hyperlipidemia. Although niacin may effectively lower non–high-density lipoprotein cholesterol, it has not been shown to reduce ASCVD outcomes. However, despite the limited evidence for the effectiveness of non-statin drugs, they are sometimes prescribed when patients are intolerant of statins.

KEY POINT

High-intensity statin therapy is indicated in high-risk patients who are younger than age 75 years.

Bibliography

Goff DC Jr, Lloyd-Jones DM, Bennett G, et al. 2013 ACC/AHA Guideline on the assessment of cardiovascular risk: a report of the American College of Cardiology/American Heart Association Task Force on Practice Guidelines. J Am Coll Cardiol.2014;63(25 Pt B):2935-59. [PMID: 24239921]

Item 22   Answer: C

Educational Objective: *Diagnose metabolic syndrome.*

Given this patient's hypertension, lipid profile, and abdominal obesity, she meets the criteria for metabolic syndrome. The diagnosis of metabolic syndrome is made by the presence of three or more of the following five criteria: (1) waist circumference >40 in (102 cm) in men and >35 in (88 cm) in women, (2) systolic blood pressure ≥130 mm Hg or diastolic blood pressure ≥85 mm Hg, (3) high-density lipoprotein (HDL) cholesterol level <40 mg/dL (1.04 mmol/L) in men and <50 mg/dL (1.30 mmol/L) in women, (4) triglyceride level ≥150 mg/dL (1.70 mmol/L), and (5) fasting plasma glucose level ≥110 mg/dL (6.1 mmol/L).

The clinical importance of identifying the metabolic syndrome is the increased risk for cardiovascular disease and type 2 diabetes mellitus in those with this diagnosis. Persons with the metabolic syndrome should receive aggressive intervention focused on lifestyle modification to decrease weight, increase physical activity, and implement a nonatherogenic diet in addition to undergoing treatment for the significant metabolic abnormalities that define the syndrome. The metabolic syndrome is frequently identified in patients with polycystic ovary syndrome and has also been associated with the development of other disorders, including fatty liver disease, obstructive sleep apnea, hyperuricemia, and gout.

The patient does not meet the criteria for hypertriglyceridemia, although American Heart Association guidelines recommend an optimal triglyceride level of below 100 mg/dL (1.13 mmol/L), and this would be an appropriate goal for this patient for lifestyle modifications.

Impaired fasting glucose (prediabetes) is defined as a fasting plasma glucose level of 100 to 125 mg/dL (5.6–6.9 mmol/L). She does not have this diagnosis, and the diagnosis of the metabolic syndrome does not strictly require abnormalities in glucose metabolism.

KEY POINT

Metabolic syndrome is diagnosed by the presence of three or more of five abnormalities: increased waist circumference, elevated systolic or diastolic blood pressure, decreased HDL cholesterol level, elevated triglyceride level, and elevated fasting plasma glucose level.

Bibliography

Tota-Maharaj R, Defilippis AP, Blumenthal RS, Blaha MJ. A practical approach to the metabolic syndrome: review of current concepts and management. Curr Opin Cardiol. 2010;25:502-12. [PMID: 20644468]

Item 23   Answer: D

Educational Objective: *Diagnose xanthelasma.*

The patient's skin lesions are xanthelasmas, which are the most common type of xanthomas. Xanthomas are the characteristic skin conditions associated with primary (due to genetic defects) or secondary hyperlipidemias. Xanthomas are yellow, orange, reddish, or yellow-brown papules, plaques, or nodules. If the infiltration is deep, the xanthoma may be nodular and have normal-appearing overly-

ing skin. The type of xanthoma closely correlates with the type of lipoprotein that is elevated. Xanthelasma is a type of xanthoma characterized by soft, nontender, nonpruritic plaques localized to the eyelids. Xanthelasma can occur without hyperlipidemia, particularly in older individuals, but is often associated with familial dyslipidemias when seen in a younger person.

Other types of xanthomas include eruptive xanthomas, which present as clusters of erythematous papules typically on the extensor surfaces. They are most often associated with extremely high (>3000 mg/dL [33.9 mmol/L]) serum triglyceride levels. Eruptive xanthomas regress with treatment of hypertriglyceridemia. Plane xanthomas are yellow-to-red plaques found in skin folds of the neck and trunk. They can be associated with familial dyslipidemias and a variety of hematologic malignancies. Tendon xanthomas are subcutaneous nodules occurring on the extensor tendons. They are associated with familial hypercholesterolemia.

Hypothyroidism is associated with elevated lipid levels and can be a cause of secondary hyperlipidemias. However, hypothyroidism is not directly associated with the formation of xanthomas and usually does not result in lipid levels high enough to cause xanthomas. An elevated serum ferritin level suggests the diagnosis of hemochromatosis, but hemochromatosis is not associated with xanthomas. Although liver chemistry test results may be abnormal in patients with extremely elevated lipid levels and are important to monitor during lipid therapy with statins, they are not associated with xanthoma formation. Type 2 diabetes is often seen in association with dyslipidemias, but abnormal glucose levels are not directly related to xanthoma formation.

KEY POINT

Xanthelasma is characterized by soft, nontender, nonpruritic plaques localized to the eyelids and may be associated with familial dyslipidemias.

Bibliography

Pitambe HV, Schulz EJ. Life-threatening dermatoses due to metabolic and endocrine disorders. Clin Dermatol. 2005;23:258-66. [PMID: 15896541]

Item 24   Answer: D

Educational Objective: *Manage hyperlipidemia in a low-risk patient.*

The most appropriate management for this patient is to repeat a fasting lipid level in the future. Traditionally, hyperlipidemia has been as a total cholesterol level >200 mg/dL (5.2 mmol/L) or a low-density lipoprotein (LDL) cholesterol level of >130 mg/dL (3.36 mmol/L). Other lipid abnormalities include a high-density lipoprotein (HDL) cholesterol level of <40 mg/dL (1.04 mmol/L) and fasting triglycerides ≥150 mg/dL (1.69 mmol/L). Although this patient has several lipid abnormalities, the most recent American College of Cardiology/American Heart Association (ACC/AHA) cholesterol treatment guidelines discuss four high-risk groups that warrant treatment for hyperlipidemia. These include patients with established atherosclerotic cardiovascular disease (ASCVD), patients with LDL cholesterol levels >190 mg/dL (4.92 mmol/L), patients with diabetes, and patients with a 10-year risk of developing ASCVD of >7.5% as estimated using the Pooled Cohort Equations calculator. This patient's estimated 10-year ASCVD risk is approximately 5%. He therefore does not meet treatment criteria, and the focus should be on dietary intervention, weight control, and exercise. Follow-up lipid testing in this patient is appropriate, although the optimal interval for doing so is unclear. The U.S. Preventive Services Task Force recommends screening at 5-year intervals in otherwise average risk patients unless their risk profile has changed, and the ACC/AHA guidelines recommend repeat testing based on an individual patient's risk factor profile. A follow-up fasting lipid profile in 1 to 2 years would be reasonable in this patient.

In patients eligible for therapy, statins are first-line therapy, with the intensity of treatment based on individual patient risk factors. Because there is no indication for treatment in this patient, initiating a statin would not be appropriate.

Fibrates are most effective in lowering triglycerides , although triglycerides are no longer considered as separate targets for therapy unless levels are very high, generally considered to be >500 mg/ dL (5.7 mmol/L), which is not present in this patient. Fibrates are also not recommended as first-line therapy for elevated total or LDL cholesterol or low HDL cholesterol.

Lipoprotein(a) (Lp[a]) level determination is not recommended for routine practice. Lp(a) is associated with increased risk for coronary artery disease (CAD) but does not appear to be an independent predictor of risk of CAD.

KEY POINT

Management of lipid abnormalities includes dietary, weight, and exercise recommendations, with statin therapy indicated for those most likely to benefit from treatment (patients with atherosclerotic cardiovascular disease, patients with LDL cholesterol level >190 mg/dL [4.92 mmol/L], patients with diabetes, and patients with a 10-year ASCVD risk of >7.5%).

Bibliography

Stone NJ, Robinson JG, Lichtenstein AH, et al; for the 2013 ACC/AHA Cholesterol Guideline Panel. Treatment of blood cholesterol to reduce atherosclerotic cardiovascular disease risk in adults: Synopsis of the 2013 ACC/AHA Cholesterol Guideline. Ann Intern Med. 2014;160:339-43. [Epub ahead of print]. [PMID: 24474185]

Item 25   Answer: D
Educational Objective: *Diagnose secondary causes of dyslipidemia.*

This patient's serum thyroid-stimulating hormone level should be measured. Her total cholesterol and low-density lipoprotein (LDL) cholesterol levels are markedly elevated despite adherence to treatment with high-intensity atorvastatin. High-intensity statin therapy seeks to decrease the LDL cholesterol level by ≥50%, and her response to treatment has been significantly less than what would be expected. This failure to respond should raise concern for possible secondary causes of dyslipidemia. Even high-intensity statin therapy may be ineffective in the setting of untreated hypothyroidism, diabetes mellitus, obstructive liver disease, or nephrotic syndrome. There are several clinical clues that suggest the diagnosis of hypothyroidism in this patient, including symptoms of fatigue and constipation and dry skin noted on physical examination. Undiagnosed thyroid disease may be contributing to this patient's apparent treatment-refractory dyslipidemia and should be evaluated.

Ezetimibe inhibits cholesterol absorption from the intestine and is effective in lowering serum cholesterol levels. However, it has not been shown to improve cardiovascular outcomes relative to the effect of statin therapy alone. It is therefore used primarily in patients unable to tolerate statins or possibly as add-on treatment for patients inadequately controlled with a statin medication. Use as a single agent in this patient would not be appropriate.

Rosuvastatin is the second drug recommended for high-intensity statin therapy in high-risk patients. However, evaluation of this patient's failure to respond to high-intensity atorvastatin would be indicated before switching to an alternative agent.

Undiagnosed diabetes mellitus should be considered in patients with unresponsive hyperlipidemia and may be diagnosed by a hemoglobin A_{1c} level of 6.5% or greater. In this patient, her fasting glucose and triglyceride levels are normal, making a diagnosis of diabetes less likely; therefore, obtaining a hemoglobin A_{1c} level would not be an appropriate next step in management.

KEY POINT

In patients with hyperlipidemia that is refractory to medical therapy, secondary causes, including hypothyroidism, diabetes mellitus, nephrotic syndrome, and obstructive liver disease, should be considered.

Bibliography

Alwaili K, Alrasadi K, Awan Z, Genest J. Approach to the diagnosis and management of lipoprotein disorders. Curr Opin Endocrinol Diabetes Obes. 2009;16:132-40. [PMID: 19306526]

Item 26   Answer: C
Educational Objective: *Treat obesity with orlistat.*

The most appropriate drug for this patient is orlistat. Current Food and Drug Administration (FDA)–approved options for drug therapy in the United States include sympathomimetic drugs that suppress appetite (phentermine, diethylpropion) and drugs that alter fat absorption (orlistat). Orlistat, now available over the counter, is a lipase inhibitor that leads to fat malabsorption. In a recent meta-analysis on the pharmacologic treatment of obesity, the mean weight loss in patients treated with orlistat was 2.9 kg (6.4 lb) at 12 months. Secondary benefits included reductions in low-density lipoprotein cholesterol level and blood pressure and, in patients with diabetes, improvement in glycemic control. Approximately 15% to 30% of patients experience gastrointestinal side effects (flatus, abdominal cramps, fecal incontinence, oily spottage), especially while consuming high-fat diets. Orlistat has not been associated with serious cardiovascular side effects. However, a recently completed review by the Food and Drug Administration (FDA) noted rare reports of severe liver injury with orlistat. Malabsorption of fat-soluble vitamins A, D, and E has been reported, and vitamin supplementation is advisable while taking the medication.

Bariatric surgery is recommended as a treatment option for patients who have been unable to maintain weight loss with diet and exercise with or without drug therapy with class III obesity, defined as patients who have a body mass index (BMI) ≥40, or those with BMIs of 35 to 39.9 (class II) who have obesity-related comorbid conditions, such as hypertension, impaired glucose tolerance, diabetes mellitus, hyperlipidemia, and obstructive sleep apnea. This patient does not meet these criteria.

In 2012, lorcaserin, a brain serotonin 2C receptor agonist, was approved by the for adults with BMIs greater than 30 or greater than 27 with obesity-related complications. In conjunction with a reduced-calorie diet and exercise counseling, lorcaserin was associated with an average weight loss of 3% at 1 year. Lorcaserin is as effective as orlistat but with fewer side effects, but long-term safety data are limited. Lorcaserin should be used with caution in patients who are on medications that increase serotonin levels such as selective serotonin reuptake inhibitors and bupropion because of the risk of precipitating the serotonin syndrome.

In a study of low-dose, controlled-release phentermine plus topiramate combined with office-based lifestyle intervention, modest weight loss was achieved (8.1 kg [17.8 lb] at 56 weeks compared with 1.4 kg [3.1 lb] in the placebo group). Significant improvement was noted in waist circumference, blood pressure, and lipid levels in the treatment group. Combination phentermine–topiramate has been approved by the FDA for the treatment of obesity. However, significant increases in blood pressure and arrhythmias can occur with phentermine; caution is indicated in patients with hypertension and cardiovascular disease. Clinicians who prescribe combination phentermine–topiramate are asked to enroll in a Risk Evaluation and Mitigation Strategy (REMS) formal training module detailing safety information. Because this patient's blood pressure is not adequately controlled, combination phentermine–topiramate is not the best medication choice.

KEY POINT

Orlistat, available over the counter, is a lipase inhibitor that leads to fat malabsorption and weight loss.

Bibliography

Tsai AG, Wadden TA. In the clinic: obesity. Ann Intern Med. 2013;159:ITC3-1-ITC3-15; quiz ITC3-16. [PMID: 24026335]

Item 27   Answer: A

Educational Objective: *Treat depression and overweight with bupropion.*

The most appropriate initial drug therapy for this patient is bupropion. Many classes of medications can cause weight gain. In patients with diabetes, thiazolidinediones, oral hypoglycemic medications, and insulin can all cause modest weight gain. Certain psychiatric medications, including tricyclic antidepressants, selective serotonin reuptake inhibitors (SSRIs), lithium, and many antipsychotic agents (thioridazine, clozapine, olanzapine) are also associated with weight gain. Finally, several anticonvulsants such as valproic acid and carbamazepine can cause weight gain.

Because different classes of antidepressants appear to be equally effective, the selection of a particular agent should be driven by its side effect profile, other comorbid disorders, and cost, matching the medication to the individual patient. Bupropion is a good alternative for patients who wish to avoid gaining weight. In a randomized, placebo-controlled trial, bupropion was associated with significantly more weight loss than placebo. Bupropion has also been shown to reduce the amount of weight gain associated with smoking cessation compared with placebo.

Mirtazapine is often a good choice for underweight depressed patients because it is more likely to stimulate appetite and cause weight gain and somnolence. In general, SSRI (eg, paroxetine) are well tolerated with low toxicity; however, weight gain can be a problem. The serotonin-norepinephrine reuptake inhibitor venlafaxine appears to be weight neutral in most patients but is unlikely to help this patient lose weight.

KEY POINT

Bupropion is an antidepressant medication that is associated with weight loss and may be an effective choice for overweight patients.

Bibliography

Fancher TL, Kravitz RL. In the clinic. Depression. Ann Intern Med. 2010;152:ITC51-15; quiz ITC5-16. [PMID: 20439571]

Item 28   Answer: D

Educational Objective: *Counsel an obese patient regarding weight reduction.*

This patient should reduce her current caloric intake by 500 to 1000 kcal/d. A consistent reduction in daily dietary caloric intake is the most successful long-term and safest weight loss strategy in obese and overweight patients. Patients who follow a diet that reduces their caloric intake by 500 to 1000 kcal/d compared with their intake that is currently maintaining weight will lose an average of 0.45 to 0.91 kg (1–2 lb) per week. The initial goal should be a loss of 10% of total body weight. If this patient adheres to this recommendation, she should lose 9.1 kg (20 lb) in 4 to 5 months. This degree of weight loss has been shown to decrease the health-related consequences of obesity, including diabetes mellitus. Because she already has prediabetes, weight loss is important to her long-term health.

Exercise is an important part of a comprehensive weight loss program that focuses on lifestyle modification. However, without attention to eating habits and caloric restriction, exercise alone is not adequate for weight loss.

Current guidelines recommend consideration of bariatric interventions, such as laparoscopic band surgery, in patients with body mass index (BMI) greater than 40 or patients with BMI of 35 to 40 with obesity-related comorbidities, such as diabetes mellitus, obstructive sleep apnea, or severe joint disease. This patient does not meet these recommendations.

Orlistat is a lipase inhibitor that leads to fat malabsorption that should be used in conjunction with a reduced calorie diet. It is moderately effective in weight loss (2.9 kg [6.4 lb] at 12 months), but gastrointestinal side effects are common. More serious adverse effects, such as severe liver injury and malabsorption of fat-soluble vitamins, have been reported. Lifestyle management with diet and exercise should be the first step in any weight loss program. Medications can be used in conjunction with, but not as a substitute for, diet and exercise.

KEY POINT

Consistent reduction in daily dietary caloric intake is the most successful long-term and safest weight loss strategy in obese and overweight patients.

Bibliography

Moyer VA; U.S. Preventive Services Task Force. Screening for and management of obesity in adults: U.S. Preventive Services Task Force recommendation statement. Ann Intern Med. 2012;157:373-8. [PMID: 22733087]

Item 29   Answer: A

Educational Objective: *Manage obesity with bariatric surgery.*

This patient should be referred for bariatric surgery. For patients with extreme obesity (body mass index [BMI] ≥40) or severe obesity (BMI of 35.0–39.9) with related complications, the National Institutes of Health recommends consideration of bariatric surgery if diet, exercise, and medication are ineffective. Patients should be motivated and well informed about this option and undergo multidisciplinary evaluation by a medical, surgical, psychiatric, and nutritionist team. The most common procedure is gastric bypass surgery, but laparoscopic banding is becoming common as well. Bariatric surgery results in more dramatic and sustained weight loss than nonsurgical interventions and leads to improvement in obesity-related complications (diabetes mellitus, obstructive sleep apnea, hypertension, and hyperlipidemia). This patient has not successfully lost weight after a 6-month trial of diet and medication and has obesity-related complications that likely will improve with weight loss.

Phentermine is a sympathomimetic drug that is approved by the Food and Drug Administration for short-term use (up to 12 weeks) as an adjunctive treatment of obesity. However, this patient's severe obesity would require treatment for much longer than 12 weeks. In addition, most persons regain any weight that is lost with this medication upon its discontinuation.

Restricting caloric intake to below 800 kcal/d (a very-low-calorie diet) is no more effective for long-term weight loss than a moderate strategy of restricting intake to 500 to 1000 kcal/d below what is estimated to maintain current body weight. In addition, long-term compliance with a very-low-calorie diet is nearly impossible.

Exercise is an important part of a comprehensive weight loss program that focuses on lifestyle modification. However, the patient has already not benefited from an exercise program. It is unlikely that exercise alone will meet his weight loss goals.

KEY POINT

Bariatric surgery should be considered for patients with BMIs of 40 or greater or BMIs of 35.0 to 39.9 with obesity-related complications in whom diet, exercise, and medication are ineffective.

Bibliography

Karmali S, Johnson Stoklossa C, Sharma A, et al. Bariatric surgery: a primer. Can Fam Physician. 2010;56:873-9. [PMID: 20841586]

Item 30   Answer: D

Educational Objective: *Diagnose vitamin B$_{12}$ deficiency in a patient who has undergone gastric bypass surgery.*

This patient's serum vitamin B$_{12}$ level should be measured. Macrocytic anemia, thrombocytopenia, mild neutropenia, and an inappropriately low reticulocyte count are the hallmark hematologic findings in vitamin B$_{12}$ deficiency. Vitamin B$_{12}$ deficiency is one the most common nonoperative complications of Roux-en-Y gastric bypass surgery. It results from decreased absorption of vitamin B$_{12}$, mainly through lack of intrinsic factor production from the bypassed gastric mucosa. It is essential for patients who undergo a roux-en-Y gastric bypass procedure to participate in postoperative monitoring of vitamin B$_{12}$ levels and to maintain lifelong adequate vitamin B$_{12}$ supplementation (500–1000 micrograms/d orally or 1000 micrograms intramuscularly monthly). Recent guidelines recommend that serum vitamin B$_{12}$ levels, along with ferritin, folate, vitamin D, and calcium, be monitored twice yearly for the first 2 years after Roux-en-Y gastric bypass surgery and yearly thereafter.

A bone marrow biopsy, a relatively invasive and costly test, is premature at this point. Bone marrow biopsy is indicated for unexplained anemia, leukopenia, thrombocytopenia, or pancytopenia. The patient has a high likelihood of vitamin B$_{12}$ deficiency that can explain her hematologic findings, and performing a bone marrow biopsy before measuring the serum vitamin B$_{12}$ level would be inappropriate.

With no gastrointestinal (GI) symptoms, no family history of colorectal cancer, a benign abdominal examination, heme-negative stool, and a macrocytic (not microcytic) anemia with neutropenia and thrombocytopenia, the suspicion for GI malignancy or other lower GI tract disease leading to bleeding and iron deficiency is very low. Therefore, a colonoscopy is not indicated at present.

Based on history and physical examination, there is no strong clinical suspicion for thyroid disease. Although hypothyroidism can be associated with mild macrocytosis, the presence of neutropenia and thrombocytopenia is inconsistent with this diagnosis. Therefore, measuring the serum thyroid-stimulating hormone level is not indicated.

KEY POINT

Vitamin B$_{12}$ deficiency is common after Roux-en-Y gastric bypass surgery.

Bibliography

Buchwald H, Ikramuddin S, Dorman RB, Schone JL, Dixon JB. Management of the metabolic/bariatric surgery patient. Am J Med. 2011;124:1099-105. [PMID: 22014789]

Item 31   Answer: B

Educational Objective: *Diagnose a vertebral compression fracture.*

The most appropriate initial imaging test is lumbar spine radiography. This patient most likely has a vertebral compression fracture. Vertebral compression fractures should be suspected in patients at risk for osteoporosis (glucocorticoid use, advanced age) and trauma. Point tenderness to palpation suggests either vertebral fracture or infection. This patient's chronic daily prednisone use increases her risk for osteoporosis, despite her use of calcium and vitamin D, and her age older than 65 years also adds to her risk. Patients with osteoporosis are susceptible to vertebral compression fractures with low-impact trauma, such as a fall from standing, as in this patient. Plain radiography of the spine is the imaging test of choice to diagnose a compression fracture.

In patients with rapidly progressive neurologic symptoms (but not stable mild neurologic symptoms), cauda equina syndrome, or suspicion for epidural abscess or osteomyelitis, magnetic resonance imaging (MRI) is the preferred modality because of better visualization of soft tissues and the spinal canal. If MRI is not feasible, computed tomography (CT) myelography is a viable alternative. Noncontrast CT is useful for detecting sacroiliitis and is a reasonable diagnostic study in patients in whom an inflammatory spondyloarthropathy is suspected.

KEY POINT

Plain radiography is the diagnostic test of choice for suspected vertebral fracture.

Bibliography

Chou R, Qaseem A, Owens DK, Shekelle P; Clinical Guidelines Committee of the American College of Physicians. Diagnostic imaging for low back pain: advice for high-value health care from the American College of Physicians. Ann Intern Med. 2011;154:181-9. Erratum in: Ann Intern Med. 2012;156(1 Pt 1):71. [PMID: 21282698]

Item 32   Answer: A

Educational Objective: *Diagnose ankylosing spondylitis.*

The most appropriate initial imaging study is single anteroposterior (AP) radiography of the pelvis. This patient most likely has ankylosing spondylitis. This disorder has a male predominance, and the peak age of onset is between 20 and 30 years. Patients classically present with progressive inflammatory back pain and stiffness, usually with elevation of systemic inflammatory markers such as erythrocyte sedimentation rate or C-reactive protein. Initially, pain can be localized to the low back, buttocks, or posterior thighs. With time, inflammation and bony changes usually ascend the spine, producing a stooped posture with limited mobility of the spine and chest. Disease activity typically fluctuates, with slow progression of bony changes, including ankylosis. A single AP radiograph of the pelvis provides a view of the sacroiliac joints and the hips and is indicated for patients with suspected spondyloarthritis. The earliest changes typically occur at the iliac portion of the sacroiliac joint where the subchondral bone becomes less distinct. Erosive changes can subsequently produce irregularity of the cortex. In late disease, the joint space may be obliterated. Sacroiliitis may be evident on plain radiographs in only 40% of patients with ankylosing spondylitis even after 10 years of disease. If the diagnosis remains in question, magnetic resonance imaging (MRI) of the sacroiliac joints should be considered to evaluate for local bone marrow edema, which occurs in acute sacroiliitis. Computed tomography (CT) can detect erosive or sclerotic changes when plain radiographs are insufficient; however, MRI is preferred for the detection of active inflammation and does not expose patients to the radiation of CT.

KEY POINT

The initial imaging study for suspected spondylarthritis is single anteroposterior radiography of the pelvis providing a view of the sacroiliac joints and the hips.

Bibliography
Wilson JF. In the clinic. Low back pain. Ann Intern Med. 2008;148:ITC5-1-ITC5-16. [PMID: 18458275]

Item 33   Answer: A
Educational Objective: *Manage acute low back pain.*

In this patient presenting with uncomplicated low back pain and examination findings suggesting radiculopathy, initial treatment with nonopioid analgesics and mobilization as tolerated is most appropriate. The overall prognosis for acute musculoskeletal low back pain is excellent; most patients without sciatica show substantial improvement within 2 weeks, and three quarters of those with sciatica are substantially better after 3 months; therefore, therapeutic interventions should focus on mitigating symptoms and maintaining function while the patient recovers.

Complete blood count and erythrocyte sedimentation rate are helpful in assessing for infection, inflammatory spondylitis, and malignancy. This patient has no signs or symptoms suggestive of systemic illness, and specific laboratory testing is therefore not indicated at this time.

Epidural corticosteroid injection is sometimes considered in patients with chronic radiculopathy, although the literature is mixed regarding its value. This patient has an excellent prognosis without intervention, so invasive treatments would be inappropriate as initial therapy.

Lumbar spine imaging is not indicated for most patients with acute lumbosacral back pain with radiculopathy because it does not add clinically significant information. Situations in which imaging is necessary include patients with rapidly progressing neurologic symptoms, evidence of cord compression, or cauda equina syndrome or if infection or malignancy is a possible cause of the patient's symptoms and examination findings.

Lumbar spine radiography is helpful to assess for possible malignancy or compression fracture. In this younger patient without evidence of systemic illness, radiography is not indicated. Magnetic res-onance imaging would likely demonstrate the disk herniation and nerve root compression that are already evident on physical examination, but the management plan would still be analgesics and gentle mobilization.

KEY POINT

Therapeutic interventions for most patients with acute low back pain should focus on mitigating symptoms and maintaining function while the patient recovers.

Bibliography
Chou R, Qaseem A, Snow V, et al; Clinical Efficacy Assessment Subcommittee of the American College of Physicians; American College of Physicians; American Pain Society Low Back Pain Guidelines Panel. Diagnosis and treatment of low back pain: a joint clinical practice guideline from the American College of Physicians and the American Pain Society. Ann Intern Med. 2007;147:478-91. [PMID: 17909209]

Item 34   Answer: D
Educational Objective: *Recognize the presentation of pertussis in adults.*

The patient's presentation is most consistent with pertussis. Pertussis is caused by *Bordetella pertussis* and has traditionally been associated with infection in children. However, with vaccination, more than half of cases now occur in adolescents and adults. Symptoms in adults may be less severe than the "whooping cough" usually associated with infection in children, and a severe, persistent cough may be the primary clinical manifestation in adults. The incubation period is 7 to 10 days, which is then followed by the catarrhal phase that lasts for 1 to 2 weeks and is characterized by malaise, rhinorrhea, and mild cough. The paroxysmal phase follows in which the other symptoms improve but the cough becomes severe, often being triggered by specific activities (eg, yawning or stretching) or exposure to environmental respiratory irritants. Vigorous inspiration during paroxysms of cough causes the characteristic "whooping" sound, and the episodes of coughing may be severe enough to trigger emesis. This phase may last weeks to months if untreated followed by the convalescent phase that lasts 1 to 3 months during which the cough slowly resolves. Pertussis is highly communicable, and treatment with a macrolide antibiotic in the first 2 weeks of infection decreases the severity of symptoms and decreases transmission of disease.

Postinfectious cough is common after viral respiratory tract infections, although the cough tends to be mild, generally improves progressively from the time of initial infection, and is not usually as severe and paroxysmal as with pertussis as seen in this patient. Gastroesophageal reflux disease is a common cause of persistent, mild cough, although the onset of her cough with an acute infectious process, its severity, and the lack gastrointestinal symptoms make this a less likely diagnosis. Cough-variant asthma is a manifestation of asthma in which cough is the predominant presenting symptom. This patient has no other history or respiratory symptoms suggestive of asthma, and her clinical presentation is more consistent with a diagnosis of pertussis.

KEY POINT

Pertussis should be considered in cough ≥2 weeks associated without other apparent cause when associated with one of the following: paroxysms of coughing, inspiratory whoop, or posttussive emesis.

Bibliography
Braman SS. Postinfectious cough: ACCP Evidence-based clinical practice guidelines. Chest 2006;129:138S-46S.

Item 35   Answer: A

Educational Objective: *Treat upper airway cough syndrome*

The patient should be started on diphenhydramine and pseudoephedrine. This patient has upper airway cough syndrome (UACS), which is the most common cause of chronic cough. In several case series, UACS, asthma, and gastrointestinal reflux disease (GERD) accounted for 90% of patients with chronic cough (excluding those with cough related to smoking or angiotensin-converting enzyme inhibitors). Symptoms of UACS include cough, nasal discharge, sensation of postnasal drip, and frequent throat clearing. Physical examination findings of UACS are cobblestoning of the posterior pharyngeal mucosa and mucoid or mucopurulent secretions at the nasopharynx or oropharynx. Treatment of UACS includes a first-generation antihistamine and a decongestant. Because of their stronger anticholinergic effect, first-generation agents are preferred relative to second-generation antihistamines, such as loratadine. However, their sedating effect may limit their use. An adequate trial of therapy for UACS is 2 to 3 weeks.

Cough-variant asthma is present in patients who have cough as their main symptom. The cough is typically dry and is sometimes the only symptom of asthma. Patients with cough-variant asthma may demonstrate reversible airflow obstruction or airway hyperreactivity with bronchoprovocation testing. However, because bronchoprovocation testing may yield false-positive results, asthma should be diagnosed as a cause of chronic cough only if symptoms abate after 2 to 4 weeks of standard asthma therapy with an inhaled bronchodilator and inhaled glucocorticosteroid.

GERD is common in patients with symptoms of UACS, and treatment of GERD should be considered if cough persists despite a trial of antihistamines and decongestants. Because chronic cough often has more than one etiology, treatment of GERD should be added to treatment of UACS.

KEY POINT

Upper airway cough syndrome is the most common cause of chronic cough and is treated with a first-generation antihistamine and decongestant.

Bibliography

Dudha M, Lehrman SG, Aronow WS, Butt A. Evaluation and management of cough. Compr Ther. 2009;35:9-17. [PMID: 19351100]

Item 36   Answer: B

Educational Objective: *Treat cough in a patient taking an angiotensin-converting enzyme (ACE) inhibitor.*

In this patient with a nonproductive cough, the best option is to discontinue lisinopril. Clinical evaluation of chronic cough (>8 weeks in duration) includes a careful history and physical examination focusing on the common causes of chronic cough. All patients should undergo chest radiography. Smoking cessation and discontinuation of ACE inhibitors should be recommended for 4 weeks before additional evaluation. Cough is a common side effect of ACE inhibitors. Approximately 15% of patients who are prescribed these medications will develop a nonproductive cough. Reported causative factors include bradykinin and substance P, which are metabolized by ACE and prostaglandins. The onset may be delayed, as in this patient, and may take up to 4 weeks to resolve upon discontinuation of the drug (rarely, up to 3 months). Although the cough is frequently mild, in some patients it is significant enough to interfere with quality of life,

and alternate therapy needs to be considered. Substitution of an angiotensin receptor blocker, such as losartan, is a good alternative in this patient; these medications generally do not cause cough (incidence is similar to that of placebo), and evidence supports their renal protective benefits in patients with diabetes mellitus.

Because this patient's cough has been present for 8 weeks, other causes of chronic cough should be considered. Because the clinical picture is most consistent with ACE inhibitor–induced cough and there is no symptom predominance to support bronchospasm (history of asthma, wheezing and cough with exertion, exposure to allergens or cold air), upper airway cough syndrome (postnasal drip with frequent nasal discharge, a sensation of liquid dripping into the back of the throat, and frequent throat clearing), or gastroesophageal reflux disease (heartburn or regurgitation), initial empiric treatment with albuterol, an antihistamine, intranasal corticosteroids, or omeprazole is not indicated at this time. ACE inhibitor–induced cough generally abates within 4 weeks after the drug is discontinued. If this patient's cough persists beyond this time, a systemic approach to treatment of chronic cough should ensue.

KEY POINT

In patients with chronic cough and a normal chest radiograph, smoking cessation and discontinuation of ACE inhibitors should be recommended for 4 weeks before additional evaluation for the cough.

Bibliography

Dicpinigaitis PV. Angiotensin-converting enzyme inhibitor-induced cough: ACCP evidence-based clinical practice guidelines. Chest. 2006;129(1 suppl):169S-73S. [PMID: 16428706]

Item 37   Answer: B

Educational Objective: *Treat chronic cough caused by gastroesophageal reflux disease (GERD).*

Omeprazole should be continued in this patient. He presents with chronic cough (>8 weeks) most likely caused by GERD. Although typical heartburn symptoms are absent in more than one-third of patients with GERD-related cough, this patient's clinical profile and symptoms of heartburn and cough exacerbated by the recumbent position are classic for GERD. The treatment of chronic cough caused by GERD is challenging. If lifestyle modification (weight loss, elevation of the head of the bed, avoidance of tobacco and alcohol) is unsuccessful, targeted and prolonged treatment with histamine blockers or proton pump inhibitors is recommended. Improvement in the cough may require therapy for 2 to 3 months. Because this patient has been on therapy for only 2 weeks and his clinical picture is without any interim change, continuation for 8 to 12 weeks would be recommended.

The American College of Chest Physicians recommends a symptom-guided, systematic, algorithmic approach to chronic cough. There is no evidence of infection; therefore, antibiotics are not indicated. The patient does not present with symptoms or signs of upper airway cough syndrome (postnasal drainage, frequent throat clearing, nasal discharge, cobblestone appearance of the oropharyngeal mucosa, or mucus dripping down the oropharynx). The use of antihistamines and decongestants, such as loratadine with pseudoephedrine, should be reserved until the empiric trial of treatment for GERD is completed and found to be ineffective.

Cough-variant asthma (in which cough is the predominant symptom) occurs in up to 57% of patients with asthma. Cough-variant asthma is suggested by the presence of airway hyperresponsiveness and confirmed when cough resolves with asthma medications. The treatment for cough-variant asthma is the same as for asthma in general, but the maximum symptomatic benefit may not occur for 6 to 8 weeks in cough-variant asthma. This patient does not have asthma and has a reasonable alternative explanation for his chronic cough; therefore, treatment with an inhaled bronchodilator such as albuterol is not indicated at this time.

KEY POINT

The duration of empiric proton pump inhibitor therapy for a patient with gastro-esophageal reflux disease-related cough is 8 to 12 weeks.

Bibliography

Chang AB, Lasserson TJ, Gaffney J, Connor FL, Garske LA. Gastro-oesophageal reflux treatment for prolonged non-specific cough in children and adults. Cochrane Database Syst Rev. 2011;(1):CD004823. [PMID: 21249664]

Item 38   Answer: A

Educational Objective: *Use chest computed tomography (CT) to evaluate a patient with hemoptysis for lung cancer.*

The most appropriate next step in the management of this patient is chest CT. The most commonly encountered causes of hemoptysis in ambulatory patients are infection (bronchitis or pneumonia) and malignancy. All patients with hemoptysis should have a chest radiograph. Risk factors that increase the risk of malignancy include male sex, age older than 40 years, a smoking history of more than 40 pack-years, and symptoms lasting for more than 1 week. These patients should be referred for chest CT and fiberoptic bronchoscopy even if the chest radiograph is normal.

Sputum cytology examination is of low sensitivity for detection of lung cancer. It is therefore not an appropriate stand-alone test for evaluating for this possibility in a high-risk patient.

Pulmonary function testing is useful for diagnosing the presence of obstructive lung disease, which might be present in this patient who is a long-term smoker. However, it has no role in the diagnosis of possible lung cancer and would not be an appropriate diagnostic study in this patient.

Because this patient is considered at high risk for lung cancer, clinical follow-up in 3 months is not appropriate because a delayed diagnosis may result in a suboptimal outcome.

KEY POINT

All patients with hemoptysis should have a chest radiograph; patients at high risk for lung cancer should be referred for chest CT and fiberoptic bronchoscopy even if the chest radiograph is normal.

Bibliography

Dudha M, Lehrman S, Aronow WS, Rosa J. Hemoptysis: diagnosis and treatment. Compr Ther. 2009;35:139-49. PMID: 20043609]

Item 39   Answer: E

Educational Objective: *Manage influenza virus infection during an outbreak in the community.*

This patient has classic symptoms of influenza occurring during a confirmed outbreak of influenza A (H1N1) virus infection in the community. She has mild illness and is otherwise healthy; therefore, she does not need treatment with an antiviral medication.

The Advisory Committee on Immunization Practices (ACIP) recommends early antiviral treatment of suspected or confirmed influenza for hospitalized patients; those with severe, complicated, or progressive illness; and those at high risk for influenza complications. Other high-risk medical conditions include cardiovascular disease (except isolated hypertension), active cancer, chronic kidney disease, chronic liver disease, hemoglobinopathies, immunocompromise (including HIV disease), and neurologic diseases that impair handling of respiratory secretions.

When treatment is indicated, it should be started within the first 2 days of symptom onset to reduce the duration of illness and decrease the risk for serious complications. Oseltamivir or zanamivir is indicated for those with influenza A or influenza B virus infection and for those in whom the influenza virus type is unknown. Oseltamivir and zanamivir differ in their pharmacokinetics, safety profiles, routes of administration, approved age groups, and recommended dosages. Zanamivir is administered by an inhaler device and is not recommended for persons with underlying airways disease such as asthma or chronic obstructive pulmonary disease.

Amantadine and rimantadine are related antiviral medications in the adamantane class that are active against influenza A viruses but not influenza B viruses. In recent years, widespread adamantane resistance among influenza A strains has been noted. These agents are not recommended for antiviral treatment or chemoprophylaxis for circulating influenza A strains.

KEY POINT

Antiviral therapy is not indicated for mild influenza in healthy persons.

Bibliography

Fiore AE, Fry A, Shay D, Gubareva L, et al; Centers for Disease Control and Prevention (CDC). Antiviral agents for the treatment and chemoprophylaxis of influenza – recommendations of the Advisory Committee on Immunization Practices (ACIP). MMWR Recomm Rep. 2011;60:1-24. [PMID: 21248682]

Item 40   Answer: B

Educational Objective: *Treat tobacco addiction with nicotine replacement therapy in a patient with psychiatric disease.*

The most appropriate drug therapy for this patient is nicotine replacement therapy. Combining motivational counseling with pharmacotherapy use is more effective than either intervention alone. The use of pharmacotherapy (nicotine replacement, bupropion, or varenicline) doubles the odds of smoking cessation. Nicotine replacement therapy is considered safe in most patients. Three nicotine replacement products are available over the counter (nicotine gum, lozenge, and patch), and two are available by prescription (inhaler and nasal spray). Combinations of nicotine replacement therapy with bupropion have been shown to be more effective than either alone and combinations of nicotine replacement therapy (e.g., patch and gum) have been shown to be more effective than nicotine replacement monotherapy. Varenicline has been demonstrated to be more effective than bupropion, and combinations of varenicline with various nicotine replacement therapies have showed cessation rates higher than nicotine replacement or bupropion alone.

Bupropion is contraindicated in patients taking monoamine oxidase inhibitors or with seizure or eating disorders. Varenicline must be used with caution in patients with kidney impairment or on dialysis and in patients with cardiovascular disorders. Both bupropion and varenicline must be used with caution in patients with serious psychiatric illness because they may cause neuropsychiatric symptoms such as personality changes, vivid dreams, or suicidal ideation. The risk of serious neuropsychiatric events is highlighted in the Boxed Warning and Warnings and Precautions section of the physician label. Nortriptyline has demonstrated only modest effectiveness in smoking cessation trials and is considered a second-line agent by the U.S. Preventive Services Task Force. Finally, combining either nortriptyline or bupropion with a selective serotonin reuptake inhibitor is relatively contraindicated.

KEY POINT

Nicotine replacement therapy is considered safe in most patients.

Bibliography

Cahill K, Stevens S, Perera R, Lancaster T. Pharmacological interventions for smoking cessation: an overview and network meta-analysis. Cochrane Database Syst Rev. 2013;5:CD009329. [PMID: 23728690]

Item 41   Answer: A
Educational Objective: *Prevent smoking cessation-related weight gain.*

The most appropriate drug therapy for this overweight patient who wishes to avoid further weight gain during smoking cessation therapy is bupropion. The average weight gain associated with smoking cessation is 10 lb (4.5 kg) and is higher in women than it is in men. In both men and women, the benefits of smoking cessation outweigh any risks associated with weight gain. Nevertheless, fear of weight gain can be an impediment to successful smoking cessation efforts, particularly in women. Bupropion is a drug that has been shown to be effective in preventing weight gain in nonsmokers. Bupropion has also been shown to reduce the amount of weight gain associated with smoking cessation compared with placebo. In one reported trial of sustained-release bupropion therapy release versus placebo, bupropion was associated with less weight gain (2.7 lb [1.3 kg]) than placebo. Nicotine gum has also been shown to delay but not prevent the weight gain associated with smoking cessation.

Clonidine and nortriptyline are both second-line choices for smoking cessation, and this patient does not have any contraindications to first-line therapies. In head-to-head comparisons, varenicline was found to be more effective than bupropion in achieving smoking cessation. However, for this patient, the slower rate of rate of weight gain associated with bupropion may make it preferable to varenicline as a smoking cessation agent.

KEY POINT

Bupropion and nicotine gum delay but do not prevent weight gain associated with smoking cessation.

Bibliography

Wilson JF. In the clinic. Smoking cessation. Ann Intern Med. 2007;146:ITC2-1-ICT2-16. [PMID: 17283345]

Item 42   Answer: D
Educational Objective: *Counsel a patient regarding methods for smoking cessation.*

Although both counseling and pharmacotherapy are effective strategies for smoking cessation, the combination of counseling with medication use is more effective than either intervention alone. Nicotine replacement is effective for smoking cessation; its availability in multiple formulations (gum, lozenge, patch, aerosol) allows for alternative options in patients who have not benefited from one type of therapy, as in this patient. Although centrally acting agents (bupropion, varenicline) are also effective treatment options, bupropion would be contraindicated in this patient with an underlying seizure disorder. The choice of cessation method is less important than that an effective method is used correctly by the patient; the array of treatment options allows for individualization based on patient preference, previous experience, cost, and potential side effects. Counseling may be brief or intensive; the two most effective counseling components include practical problem-solving skills and social support.

Many smokers indicate that stress reduction is a primary reason for their tobacco use. Although selected individuals with true anxiety disorders may benefit from anxiolytic therapy, the use of benzodiazepines as a smoking cessation medication has not been documented.

Electronic cigarettes deliver a warmed aerosol through a cigarette-like device that bears the appearance, physical sensation, and possibly the taste of tobacco smoke, with the intention of helping smokers maintain the activities associated with smoking but without the harmful effects. However, their use in smoking cessation has not been established.

KEY POINT

Smoking cessation is achieved more effectively with a combination of counseling and anti-smoking medication use than with either intervention alone.

Bibliography

Rennard SI, Daughton DM. Smoking cessation. Clin Chest Med. 2014;35:165-76. [PMID: 24507844]

Item 43   Answer: A
Educational Objective: *Counsel a patient regarding smoking cessation.*

Current recommendations are that all clinicians assess tobacco use at every visit, encourage every patient to make a quit attempt, and counsel patients appropriately. Patients who exhibit medical illnesses related to smoking present an opportunity for clinicians to increase the patient's awareness of the connection between the unhealthy behavior and its negative consequences. Even if time does not allow for an in-depth counseling session, all patients should be asked about their smoking at every visit, and a brief, clear message about quitting should be provided to all patients. A recommended strategy for counseling is to follow the "five As": ask every patient at every visit about their smoking, advise all smokers to quit, assess their current interest in quitting, assist by offering resources or medications, and arrange for follow-up.

It is not clear yet whether this patient is truly interested in quitting. Thus, it would be inappropriate to prescribe either smoking cessation aids or counseling until the physician has determined that the patient is indeed ready to quit.

> **KEY POINT**
>
> **Tobacco use should be assessed at every visit, and patients who smoke should be encouraged to make a quit attempt and counseled appropriately.**

Bibliography

Rennard SI, Daughton DM. Smoking cessation. Clin Chest Med. 2014;35:165-76. [PMID: 24507844]

Item 44   Answer: A
Educational Objective: Diagnose depression.

A depression screening tool should be administered to this patient. When initially evaluating a patient with a history suggestive of depression, using a validated screening tool improves diagnostic accuracy and is helpful in guiding further intervention. Validated tools, such as the Patient Health Questionnaire 9, have robust sensitivity and specificity for detecting or excluding depression and assessing the severity of depression if it is present. This patient presents with sleep changes, decreased energy and interest, and reported decreased concentration, all symptoms of depression that should be further evaluated.

Although input from family members may be helpful in specific situations to assess the details and severity of a patient's depressive symptoms, doing so in this situation without establishing a definitive diagnosis and without patient consent would be inappropriate. A validated screening tool should give provide adequate information to pursue further evaluation and treatment at this time.

Discontinuation of the patient's depo-progesterone would not be indicated because she has been on this medication without prior interceding symptoms, suggesting that her symptoms are not clearly associated with this treatment. Additionally, discontinuation of a previously stable medication regimen can be stressful for patients and further complicate management of possible depression.

Inpatient psychiatric evaluation is indicated in patients who have an active plan for committing suicide or have psychotic features, neither of which is present in this patient.

Referral for substance abuse treatment is indicated if there is evidence that it is contributing to or complicating the patient's symptoms. Although self-reporting of substance use is not always reliable, it is not clear that substance use is associated with this patient's depressive symptoms, and evaluation of her presenting symptoms would be the most appropriate initial step in management.

> **KEY POINT**
>
> **When depression is considered, a validated tool should be used to establish its presence and degree of severity.**

Bibliography

Fancher TL, Kravitz RL. In the clinic. Depression. Ann Intern Med. 2010;152:ITC51-15; quiz ITC5-16. [PMID: 20439571]

Item 45   Answer: C
Educational Objective: *Treat depression.*

The most appropriate next treatment step for this patient is to discontinue sertraline and begin a different antidepressant, such as venlafaxine. She has moderate depression that is refractory to initial single-agent treatment. The goal of treatment is to achieve complete remission within 6 to 12 weeks and continue treatment for 4 to 9 months thereafter. Patients should be assessed 2 and 4 weeks after starting therapy for adherence, adverse drug reactions, and suicide risk and again at 6 to 8 weeks for response to therapy. Using a formal tool for severity assessment (e.g., the Patient Health Questionnaire 9 [PHQ-9]) helps quantify the nature of the response; patients are considered to have at least a partial response if a 50% or greater decrease in symptom score has occurred. Using the PHQ-9, patients can be classified as complete responders, partial responders, or nonresponders. Complete responders should continue the same therapy modality for an additional 4 to 9 months. Treatment options for partial responders and nonresponders include using a higher dose of the same agent (ineffective in this patient), adding a second agent, switching to a new drug, or adding psychotherapy (patient not interested). Any change in therapy requires periodic follow-up as outlined above.

Although some patients with resistant depression require more than one antidepressant medication, a patient's depression is usually not considered resistant until after the failure of two trials of medication monotherapy. Therefore, adding a second antidepressant would not be an appropriate next step.

This patient remains unresponsive to treatment with sertraline after a dose escalated to the maximal dose. Waiting an additional 8 weeks is unlikely to change management and will slow this patient's recovery. Switching to a new drug, either of the same class or different class (e.g., venlafaxine), is indicated.

Electroconvulsive therapy (ECT) is indicated in severely depressed patients, such as those with profound suicidal ideation or psychotic features in whom a rapid response to therapy is particularly desirable. This patient has no indication for ECT.

> **KEY POINT**
>
> **Patients refractory to a single antidepressant may respond to a change in therapy, which may include replacement with another antidepressant, either from the same or a different class; addition of a second antidepressant; or a psychotherapeutic intervention.**

Bibliography

Fancher TL, Kravitz RL. In the clinic. Depression. Ann Intern Med. 2010;152:ITC51-15; quiz ITC5-16. [PMID: 20439571]

Item 46   Answer: B
Educational Objective: *Treat a suicidal patient.*

This patient should be hospitalized for further care. Depressed patients who have an intent or plan for suicide are at the highest risk for actually committing suicide and should be hospitalized if they have poor social support (as in this patient), are intoxicated, are actively delusional, or are likely to be noncompliant with medication. If these features are absent and the patient is deemed able to make a contract for safety, outpatient therapy can proceed with psychiatry consultation and close follow-up.

Electroconvulsive therapy (ECT) can be considered for depressed patients who have psychotic features, suicidal thoughts, or no response to antidepressants or who cannot tolerate antidepressants. ECT should be managed by a psychiatrist, most often as part of comprehensive inpatient treatment.

Major depression is ideally treated with a combination of medication and psychotherapy, which this patient declined. He has also not had a sufficient trial of antidepressant pharmacotherapy to warrant switching medications. Therefore, making either of these changes in his treatment regimen would not be an appropriate next step in management given his active suicidal ideation.

KEY POINT

Patients who have identified a suicidal plan or intent are at the highest risk for committing suicide and should be hospitalized if they have poor social support, are intoxicated, are actively delusional, or are likely to be noncompliant with medication.

Bibliography
Fancher TL, Kravitz RL. In the clinic. Depression. Ann Intern Med. 2010;152:ITC51-15; quiz ITC5-16. [PMID: 20439571]

Item 47   Answer: A
Educational Objective: *Diagnose bipolar disorder.*

This patient most likely has bipolar disorder. Among young depressed adults, the presence of prior hypomanic symptoms in a patient with depression is suggestive of the possibility of the presence of bipolar disorder. Diagnostic criteria for mania include a distinct period of abnormally and persistently elevated, expansive, or irritable mood lasting at least 1 week. Typical symptoms include inflated self-esteem or grandiosity, a decreased need for sleep, distractibility, increased goal-directed behavior, and excessive involvement in pleasurable activities that have a high potential for consequences (unrestrained buying sprees, sexual indiscretions). It is important to diagnose bipolar disorder because this condition is frequently overlooked, and the treatment may differ significantly from the treatment of depression.

The characteristics of a major depressive disorder include depressed mood most of the day nearly every day for at least 2 weeks; loss of all interest and pleasure; disturbances of appetite, weight, sleep, or activity; fatigue or loss of energy; self-reproach or inappropriate guilt; poor concentration or indecisiveness; morbid thoughts of death (not just fear of dying) or suicide; or all of these. Although this patient meets many of these clinical criteria, his episodes of hypomania and current episode of depression are more compatible with bipolar disorder than major depressive disorder.

Dysthymia is a chronic mood disorder characterized by depressed mood or anhedonia at least half the time for at least 2 years accompanied by two or more vegetative or psychological symptoms and functional impairment. The patient's 6-week course of depressed mood is not compatible with dysthymia, which also cannot account for his hypomanic episodes or substance abuse.

Situational adjustment reaction with depressed mood is a subsyndromal depression with a clear precipitant; it usually resolves with resolution of the acute stressor without medication. The patient cannot identify a precipitating event for his altered mood, making this diagnosis unlikely.

KEY POINT

Among young depressed adults, the presence of prior hypomanic symptoms is indicative of a bipolar disorder.

Bibliography
Muzina DJ, Colangelo E, Manning JS, et al. Differentiating bipolar disorder from depression in primary care. Cleve Clin J Med. 2007;74:89-105. [PMID: 17333635]

Item 48   Answer: A
Educational Objective: *Screen for substance abuse.*

The U.S. Preventive Services Task Force (USPSTF) recommends screening and counseling for all adults for alcohol use and abuse, identifying the quantity and frequency of drinking, adverse consequences, and patterns of use. The Alcohol Use Disorders Identification Test (AUDIT) is the most studied screening tool for detecting alcohol-related problems in primary care settings. It consists of 10 questions and is easy to administer; a three-question version (the AUDIT-C) is more sensitive but less specific than the 10-question AUDIT. The four-item CAGE questionnaire may also be used. (Have you ever felt you should cut down on your drinking? Have people annoyed you by criticizing your drinking? Have you ever felt bad or guilty about your drinking? Have you ever had a drink first thing in the morning to steady your nerves or get rid of a hangover [eye opener]?) With a cut-off of two positive answers, the CAGE questionnaire is 77% to 95% sensitive and 79% to 97% specific for detecting alcohol abuse or dependence in primary care settings and indicates that further assessment is warranted. The AUDIT is more sensitive than the CAGE questionnaire in identifying hazardous drinking and alcohol dependence, but the CAGE is easier to deliver in a primary care setting. The TWEAK test, designed specifically for pregnant women, identifies a lower level of alcohol use because any amount of alcohol may be considered hazardous to fetuses. Clinicians should choose a screening test appropriate to their practice and provide counseling and intervention when patients screen positive.

Screening with conventional cervical cytology (Papanicolaou smear) results in a 95% decrease in mortality rate from cervical cancer. The USPSTF recommends initiating cervical cancer screening at age 21 years regardless of the age initiation of sexual activity.

The prevalence of drug use (illicit and prescription) is much lower than for alcohol and depends on the clinical setting. Several screening instruments have been validated for drug use in the primary care setting. Currently, no practice guidelines exist for screening patients for unhealthy drug use.

The USPSTF recommends against routine screening for bladder, ovarian, and pancreatic cancers. The USPSTF concludes that the evidence is insufficient to recommend for or against screening for skin and oral cancer. The USPSTF recommends that fair-skinned persons age 10 to 24 years be counseled about reducing their exposure to ultraviolet radiation to reduce the risk of skin cancer.

Additional age-appropriate screening interventions recommended by the USPSTF for this patient include screening for chlamydia in sexually active women, HIV testing, and checking the blood pressure; testing for syphilis is indicated in patients with risk factors.

KEY POINT

The USPSTF recommends screening and counseling for all adults for alcohol use and abuse, identifying quantity and frequency of drinking, adverse consequences, and patterns of use.

Bibliography
Moyer VA; Preventive Services Task Force. Screening and behavioral counseling interventions in primary care to reduce alcohol misuse: U.S. preventive services task force recommendation statement. Ann Intern Med. 2013;159:210-8. [PMID: 23698791]

Item 49   Answer: A

Educational Objective: *Assess a patient with a substance abuse disorder.*

Assess his interest in quitting opioid addiction will be the next best step in his management. After patients have been identified as using drugs, interventional techniques used for alcohol abuse (brief interventions, motivational interviewing) may be used for counseling, although data are limited regarding outcomes of these interventions for drug abuse. One simple approach for use in the clinical setting is the 5 As (ask, advise, assess, assist, and arrange), wherein the clinician *asks* patients about their illicit drug use at every visit, *advises* them to quit, *assesses* their willingness or readiness to quit at this time, *assists* them with a quit plan, and *arranges* for follow-up. For patients not ready to quit, motivational interviewing, with emphasis on nonconfrontational strategies and discussion of patient choices, is recommended. Challenges unique to this population include the high likelihood of drug dependence and polysubstance use; the legal ramifications of illicit drug use; and in the case of prescription drug use, the distinction between appropriate and inappropriate use. Behavioral counseling intervention starts with assessing patient's perception of risk of the consequences of a particular behavior and willingness to modify behavior to avoid such negative consequences.

Pharmacologic treatment of withdrawal often involves substituting a long-acting agent for the abused drug and then gradually tapering its dosage. The desirable qualities for outpatient medications include administration by mouth, low potential for abuse and overdose, and low incidence of side effects. Methadone is used to treat acute withdrawal symptoms and may be used as maintenance therapy for weeks to years. Methadone dosage is titrated to balance sedation and patient discomfort. Buprenorphine may be preferred over methadone because it is a partial opioid agonist that has superior ability in reducing withdrawal symptoms, and its combination with naloxone allows for less abuse potential and respiratory depression in overdose. Buprenorphine is restricted to qualified physicians who have received training and a waiver to practice medication-assisted opioid addiction therapy.

Drug rehabilitation programs address motivation, teach coping skills, provide reinforcement, improve interpersonal functioning, and foster compliance with pharmacotherapy. For both drug rehabilitation program and pharmacotherapy to be successful, first we need to connect the negative consequences with specific behavior(s) and assess patient's perception about it and their willingness to modify such behavior.

KEY POINT

One simple approach for use in counseling patients who abuse illicit drugs is the 5 As (ask, advise, assess, assist, and arrange), wherein the clinician *asks* patients about their illicit drug use at every visit, *advises* them to quit, *assesses* their willingness or readiness to quit at this time, *assists* them with a quit plan, and *arranges* for follow-up.

Bibliography
Polen MR, Whitlock EP, Wisdom JP, Nygren P, Bougatsos C. Screening in primary care settings for illicit drug use: staged systematic review for the United States Preventive Services Task Force [Internet]. Rockville (MD): Agency for Healthcare Research and Quality (US); 2008 Jan. Available from www.ncbi.nlm.nih.gov/books/NBK33960/ [PMID: 20722153]

Item 50   Answer: A

Educational Objective: *Manage a patient with harmful alcohol use.*

This patient is exhibiting harmful use of alcohol and should be counseled appropriately, including connecting her drinking habits with the negative consequences that she has recently experienced. Harmful drinking is drinking that causes physical or psychological harm. This patient's drinking has resulted in serious illness as well as legal action for driving under the influence of alcohol. Optimal management would include a discussion of appropriate amounts of alcohol, negative consequences, and agreement of goals for reducing alcohol intake. This should be performed in the setting of frequent follow-up and reassessment and should incorporate the patient's ideas about her drinking behaviors and ways to change them, barriers she may face in reducing her alcohol consumption, and previous experiences with attempting to stop or reduce her drinking.

Labeling a patient an alcoholic is neither productive nor a medically useful term. Goals of managing this patient may not require complete abstinence, and abstinence may be difficult for the patient to accomplish immediately.

Adjunct management strategies may include medications (e.g., disulfiram or naltrexone) or referral to Alcoholics Anonymous or a psychiatrist, but these measures are more effective when done in combination with primary counseling.

The National Institute on Alcohol Abuse and Alcoholism defines at-risk drinking as more than 14 drinks per week or 4 drinks per occasion in men and more than 7 drinks per week or 3 drinks per occasion in women. However, harmful drinking is defined by consequences and not by the quantity consumed.

KEY POINT

Management of harmful drinking patterns includes counseling to help patients connect the negative consequences to their drinking, discussion of appropriate amounts of alcohol, and agreement of goals for reducing alcohol intake, performed in a patient-centered manner in a setting of frequent follow-up and reassessment.

Bibliography
Friedmann PD. Clinical practice. Alcohol use in adults. N Engl J Med. 2013. 24;368:365-73. [PMID: 23343065]

Item 51   Answer: D

Educational Objective: *Prevent seizures in acute alcohol withdrawal syndrome.*

Lorazepam should be administered now. This patient with heavy, chronic alcohol use is showing evidence of acute alcohol withdrawal syndrome as seen by his hypertension, tachycardia, sweating, agitation, tremulousness, and cognitive changes. His history of a prior alcohol withdrawal seizure is another indication for aggressive treatment for alcohol withdrawal. Benzodiazepines, such as lorazepam, are first-line therapy for patients who require pharmacologic prophylaxis or treatment for alcohol withdrawal. Patients with the alcohol withdrawal syndrome who are treated with benzodiazepines have fewer complications, including alcohol withdrawal seizures and delirium tremens. Although shorter acting agents such as lorazepam are more commonly used, longer acting agents (chlordiazepoxide or diazepam) may be more effective in preventing seizures but can pose a risk for excess sedation in older adults and in patients with liver disease. Patients with a history of seizures should receive a prophylactic benzodiazepine on a fixed schedule even if they are asymptomatic during the acute alcohol withdrawal period.

β-Blockers, such as atenolol, and clonidine can be used to control tachycardia and hypertension when needed but are adjunctive, not primary, treatments for alcohol withdrawal. Antipsychotic agents such as haloperidol can be used to treat agitation and hallucinosis in patients exhibiting these signs. However, β-blockers are associated with a greater incidence of delirium, and neuroleptics such as haloperidol are associated with a greater incidence of seizures during withdrawal. The use of antiepileptics, such as phenytoin, is ineffective compared with benzodiazepines in preventing alcohol-related seizures.

KEY POINT

Benzodiazepines are the drug class of choice for prophylaxis of alcohol withdrawal seizures.

Bibliography

Manasco A, Chang S, Larriviere J, et al. Alcohol withdrawal. South Med J. 2012;105:607-12. [PMID: 23128805]

Item 52   Answer: A

Educational Objective: *Treat cocaine-induced chest pain.*

The most appropriate treatment is intravenous diltiazem and lorazepam. This patient is having acute chest pain and electrocardiographic changes associated with cocaine use. Cocaine raises blood pressure, heart rate, and myocardial oxygen requirements. It can also induce spasm of the coronary circulation even if there is no preexisting coronary artery stenosis. Patients with chest pain in the setting of cocaine use should be evaluated and managed as any other patient with chest pain except for the use of β-blockers. Instead, calcium channel blockers and benzodiazepines are safe in this setting and are effective in lowering the heart rate, blood pressure, and myocardial oxygen demand that occur primarily because of the sympathetic stimulation due to cocaine.

The use of β-blockers in patients with cocaine-induced chest pain is controversial because of the pharmacologic concern that they may leave the patient with unopposed α-mediated vasoconstriction, leading to increased blood pressure and myocardial ischemia. Although β-blockade is considered beneficial in most patients with possible ischemic cardiac disease, in this situation, it is generally recommended to use a calcium channel blocker to decrease the blood pressure and heart rate and lower myocardial oxygen demand.

Thrombolytic therapy with an agent such as tissue plasminogen activator is not appropriate because the patient does not meet the criteria for thrombolytic therapy, which is usually used only in cases of ST-elevation myocardial infarction, particularly if a percutaneous coronary intervention cannot be provided. Because there is no ST-segment elevation on this patient's ECG, thrombolysis would not be appropriate.

Intravenous nitroprusside is not indicated because this patient's clinical presentation is not consistent with a hypertensive urgency, aortic dissection, or other acute need to lower the blood pressure primarily. The blood pressure is elevated, but it is in a range consistent with the patient's cocaine ingestion and agitation.

KEY POINT

Calcium channel blockers and benzodiazepines are safe in patients with cocaine-associated chest pain and are effective in lowering the heart rate, blood pressure, and myocardial oxygen demand.

Bibliography

McCord J, Jneid H, Hollander JE, et al; American Heart Association Acute Cardiac Care Committee of the Council on Clinical Cardiology. Management of cocaine-associated chest pain and myocardial infarction: a scientific statement from the American Heart Association Acute Cardiac Care Committee of the Council on Clinical Cardiology. Circulation. 2008;117:1897-907. [PMID: 18347214]

Item 53   Answer: A

Educational Objective: *Diagnose secondary ovarian failure.*

The most likely diagnosis is hypothalamic amenorrhea. Secondary amenorrhea is defined as the absence of a menstrual cycle for three cycles or 6 months in previously menstruating women. Pregnancy is the most common cause of secondary amenorrhea. The initial evaluation of amenorrhea includes a thorough history and physical examination and measurement of serum human chorionic gonadotropin, prolactin, follicle-stimulating hormone, and thyroid-stimulating hormone levels to assess for pregnancy, hyperprolactinemia, primary ovarian insufficiency, and thyroid disease, respectively.

If the results of the laboratory tests are normal, the next step is to assess estrogen sufficiency with a progesterone challenge test. Estradiol levels can be variable in amenorrhea of differing causes, but results of a progesterone challenge test will clearly delineate between an estrogen-deficient state (no bleeding) and an estrogen-sufficient state (withdrawal bleeding). If the patient is producing estrogen, she will have withdrawal bleeding within 1 week of completing a course of progesterone. This will mean that the patient is not estrogen deficient, and polycystic ovary syndrome (or a similar diagnosis) should be considered. If no withdrawal bleeding occurs after the progesterone challenge, then the patient has a low-estrogen state, and hypothalamic amenorrhea is the diagnosis. If no clear cause of the hypothalamic amenorrhea is present, then pituitary magnetic resonance imaging should be ordered to rule out a pituitary adenoma. This patient's absence of bleeding to a progesterone challenge supports the diagnosis of hypothalamic amenorrhea.

Uterine or outflow tract disorders secondary to intrauterine adhesions (Asherman syndrome), although rare, also must always be considered as a possible cause of secondary amenorrhea. Asherman syndrome is caused by endometrial scarring after a uterine procedure (usually repeated dilation and curettage) and should be considered in any woman with amenorrhea and past exposure to uterine instrumentation. This patient has no history of uterine procedures.

This patient does not have Turner syndrome. The physical findings of Turner syndrome include short stature, a shield-shaped chest, and a webbed neck. Primary amenorrhea is common in Turner syndrome. Turner syndrome is caused by the absence of one of the X chromosomes and is generally diagnosed early in life because of characteristic physical findings.

KEY POINT

Hypothalamic amenorrhea is associated with normal follicle-stimulating hormone, thyroid-stimulating hormone, and prolactin levels and absence of bleeding with a progesterone challenge test.

Bibliography
Klein DA, Poth MA. Amenorrhea: an approach to diagnosis and management. Am Fam Physician. 2013;87:781-8. [PMID: 23939500]

Item 54   Answer: D

Educational Objective: *Treat menopausal symptoms with topical estrogen.*

The most appropriate management of this patient is vaginal estradiol. The clinical history and physical examination are most helpful for making the diagnosis of vaginal atrophy; pale vaginal walls, decreased rugae, and petechiae are characteristic findings. Symptoms related to vaginal atrophy include vulvar itching, vaginal dryness, and dyspareunia. Vaginal atrophy is frequently progressive and often requires treatment. Mild to moderate symptoms can be treated with vaginal moisturizers and lubricants, but more severe symptoms are best treated with vaginal estrogen.

Systemic hormone therapy is the most effective treatment for moderate to severe vasomotor symptoms and has Food and Drug Administration approval for this indication. It may be considered as a treatment option for women who have a thorough understanding of the risks and benefits associated with therapy. All women with an intact uterus who are treated with hormone therapy must receive progesterone to avoid estrogen-induced endometrial hyperplasia and cancer. Although oral estrogen therapy is effective for relieving vaginal atrophy symptoms, it has been associated with several adverse outcomes, including increased rates of coronary heart disease, stroke, venous thromboembolism, and invasive breast cancer. For that reason, current guidelines recommend the use of low-dose topical, rather than systemic, estrogen therapy for the treatment of patients who only have vaginal symptoms. Because this patient has primarily vaginal symptoms, systemic estrogen therapy, with or without progesterone, is not indicated.

Several nonhormonal therapies have been proposed for women who have contraindications to hormone therapy or want to avoid its attendant risks. Red clover extract and black cohosh are ineffective for treating hot flushes and have no demonstrated effectiveness in treating vaginal atrophy.

KEY POINT

Mild to moderate symptoms of vaginal atrophy can be treated with vaginal moisturizers and lubricants, but more severe symptoms are best treated with vaginal estrogen.

Bibliography
Col NF, Fairfield KM, Ewan-Whyte C, Miller H. In the clinic. Menopause. Ann Intern Med. 2009;150:ITC4-1-15; quiz ITC4-16. [PMID: 19349628]

Item 55   Answer: A

Educational Objective: *Evaluate secondary amenorrhea with measurement of serum follicle-stimulating hormone (FSH) and prolactin levels.*

This patient has secondary amenorrhea, and the initial diagnostic studies should include thyroid-stimulating hormone (TSH), FSH, and prolactin levels. Secondary amenorrhea is defined by the absence of menses for 3 or more consecutive months in a woman who has menstruated previously. Menstrual failure can be complete amenorrhea or varying degrees of oligomenorrhea, the latter being much more common. Pregnancy should be excluded in all patients before other evaluations. Polycystic ovary syndrome is the most common cause of secondary amenorrhea, and hypogonadotropic hypogonadism (low FSH and low estrogen levels) is most commonly caused by hyperprolactinemia (elevated serum prolactin level). In young women, secondary amenorrhea may be associated with hypergonatrophic hypogonadism. This group includes primary ovarian failure (often caused by Turner syndrome mosaicism and autoimmune disorders) and in cancer survivors can be traced to chemotherapy or radiation treatments.

Laboratory evaluation is first directed toward ovarian failure, hyperprolactinemia, and thyroid disease. Therefore, FSH, prolactin, TSH, and free thyroxine levels are generally measured. An FSH level greater than 20 mU/mL (20 U/L) suggests ovarian failure.

If serum FSH and prolactin levels are normal on laboratory studies, the next step in the evaluation is a progestin withdrawal challenge. If the progestin challenge does not result in withdrawal bleeding, then assessment of the pelvic anatomy with ultrasonography would be appropriate.

A high serum prolactin level requires additional pituitary evaluation, including magnetic resonance imaging (MRI). Obtaining an MRI before this patient's serum prolactin level has been determined, however, is premature.

This patient has no symptoms of hyperandrogenemia. Therefore, measurement of her total serum testosterone level is of little value.

KEY POINT

After pregnancy is excluded, the initial evaluation of secondary amenorrhea includes measurement of FSH, TSH, and prolactin levels.

Bibliography
Klein DA, Poth MA. Amenorrhea: an approach to diagnosis and management. Am Fam Physician. 2013;87:781-8. [PMID: 23939500]

Item 56   Answer: D

Educational Objective: *Diagnose polycystic ovary syndrome.*

The patient's irregular menstrual bleeding interspersed with amenorrhea, obesity, and signs of hyperandrogenism are consistent with a diagnosis of polycystic ovary syndrome (PCOS). PCOS is the most common cause of irregular menstrual bleeding in premenopausal patients. The early onset of symptoms is the most important part of the history for differentiating PCOS from other causes of anovulatory menstrual irregularities. Most girls develop regular menses within 1 year of menarche, and failure to do so suggests the diagnosis of PCOS. If symptoms begin years after puberty or have relatively sudden onset, other causes should be considered. Diagnosis requires two of following three criteria: ovulatory dysfunction, laboratory or clinical evidence of hyperandrogenism, and ultrasound evidence of polycystic ovaries. Signs of ovulatory dysfunction include amenorrhea, oligomenorrhea, and infertility. Typical signs of androgen excess include hirsutism, acne, and occasionally alopecia. Laboratory abnormalities in PCOS may include a ratio of luteinizing hormone to follicle-stimulating hormone >2 and mild elevations in serum testosterone and dehydroepiandrosterone sulfate levels; these findings, however, are not diagnostic. Insulin resistance is an important feature, as is obesity, although only 50% of affected women are obese.

Hypothyroidism can cause irregular menstrual cycles and often periods of heavy bleeding. Cold intolerance is common, as is coarsening of hair and nails. Physical examination may reveal an enlarged thyroid gland and often delayed reflexes. Signs of hyperandrogenism are not present.

Cushing syndrome is often associated with both hyperandrogenism and amenorrhea but may also be associated with hypertension, wide purple abdominal striae, and easy bruising. Affected patients frequently have central obesity, and physical examination may reveal a prominent dorsal cervical fat pad. It is important to exclude Cushing syndrome when a diagnosis of PCOS is being considered, but onset of Cushing syndrome during adolescence is rare.

Hyperprolactinemia is a frequent cause of amenorrhea and may be associated with certain medications (tricyclic antidepressants, phenothiazines, metoclopramide). Pituitary tumors may also lead to hyperprolactinemia, often with associated visual changes and headache. Obesity and signs of androgen excess are typically absent.

Uterine fibroids are a common cause of irregular and often heavy menstrual bleeding. Depending on size and location, they can often be palpated on physical examination. They are not associated with oligomenorrhea, amenorrhea, or signs of androgen excess.

KEY POINTS

Polycystic ovary syndrome should be considered in the differential diagnosis of patients with oligomenorrhea, amenorrhea, and abnormal uterine bleeding.

Diagnostic criteria for polycystic ovary syndrome include ovulatory dysfunction, laboratory or clinical evidence of androgen excess, and polycystic ovaries on ultrasonography.

Bibliography
Wilson JF. In the clinic. The polycystic ovary syndrome. Ann Intern Med. 2011;154: ITC2-2-ITC2-15 [PMID: 21282692]

Item 57   Answer: D
Educational Objective: *Treat heavy menstrual bleeding with oral medroxyprogesterone.*

The most appropriate next management step is oral medroxyprogesterone acetate. In patients who present with menorrhagia (heavy menstrual bleeding) with a known etiology, several therapeutic agents can decrease bleeding. For moderate bleeding that can be managed on an outpatient basis, a progestational agent such as medroxyprogesterone acetate can be given for 10 to 21 days. The progesterone will typically act to stabilize the endometrium and stop uterine blood flow. Alternatively, a monophasic oral contraceptive may be dosed four times a day for 5 to 7 days and subsequently reduced to daily dosing for 3 weeks followed by withdrawal bleeding.

Nonsteroidal antiinflammatory drugs act by inhibiting prostaglandin synthesis and may decrease mild bleeding by approximately 30%. Once-daily oral contraceptives are effective in decreasing menstrual blood loss by 50%; however, in bleeding that is as heavy as this case, neither of these medications would be as effective as medroxyprogesterone.

If the patient were heavily symptomatic from her bleeding, intravenous estrogen might be appropriate. Parenteral conjugated estrogens are approximately 70% effective in stopping the bleeding entirely. However, pulmonary embolism and venous thrombosis are associated with intravenous estrogen therapy, making its use appropriate only under specific clinical circumstance.

Surgical options are reserved for cases in which medical treatment fails, but it is likely in this case that medical treatment can provide a

bridge until her scheduled surgical procedure. Monitoring her for a week will not be helpful because it is likely she will sustain a great deal of additional blood loss during this time.

KEY POINT

Medroxyprogesterone acetate for 10 to 21 days is effective treatment for moderate menstrual bleeding.

Bibliography
Fazio SB, Ship AN. Abnormal uterine bleeding. South Med J. 2007;100:376-82; quiz 383, 402. [PMID: 17458397]

Item 58   Answer: D
Educational Objective: *Evaluate secondary amenorrhea with a progestin withdrawal challenge.*

The next step in the evaluation of this patient with secondary amenorrhea after stopping her oral contraceptive pill is a progestin withdrawal challenge. This patient has an unremarkable personal and family medical history and no evidence of androgen excess. Results of her initial laboratory studies are negative for thyroid disorders, ovarian dysfunction, and hyperprolactinemia. Given these data, the differential diagnosis of this patient's secondary amenorrhea includes anatomic defects and chronic anovulation, with or without estrogen. The differential diagnosis can be narrowed most effectively with a progestin withdrawal challenge. Menses after challenge excludes anatomic defects and chronic anovulation without estrogen. Therefore, a progestin withdrawal challenge is the most appropriate next step.

Polycystic ovary syndrome (PCOS) affects 6% of women of childbearing age and typically presents with oligomenorrhea and signs of androgen excess (hirsutism, acne, and occasionally alopecia). Insulin resistance is a major feature of the disorder, as is overweight and obesity (although only 50% of women with PCOS are obese). Typically, testosterone and dehydroepiandrosterone sulfate levels are mildly elevated, and the luteinizing hormone to FSH ratio is greater than 2:1. However, measurement of dehydroepiandrosterone sulfate is rarely clinically useful in establishing or excluding this diagnosis.

Positive withdrawal bleeding after the progestin withdrawal challenge suggests an estradiol level of greater than 40 pg/mL (146.8 pmol/L) and thus obviates the need for measurement of serum estradiol levels.

Magnetic resonance imaging of the pituitary gland is unnecessary at this point because her follicle-stimulating hormone, prolactin, and thyroid-stimulating hormone levels are all normal, and there is no suggestion of a central process leading to her amenorrhea.

KEY POINT

Menstrual flow on progestin withdrawal indicates relatively normal estrogen production and a patent outflow tract, which limits the differential diagnosis of secondary amenorrhea to chronic anovulation with estrogen present.

Bibliography
Klein DA, Poth MA. Amenorrhea: an approach to diagnosis and management. Am Fam Physician. 2013;87:781-8. [PMID: 23939500]

Item 59   Answer: D
Educational Objective: *Diagnose abnormal uterine bleeding with an endometrial biopsy.*

The most appropriate next step in the management of this patient with abnormal uterine bleeding is to perform an endometrial biopsy. Abnormal uterine bleeding can take many forms, including infrequent menses, excessive flow, prolonged duration of menses, intermenstrual bleeding, and postmenopausal bleeding. Patients at perimenopause frequently experience irregular bleeding secondary to anovulation and fluctuating hormone levels. Shortened intermenstrual cycles (more frequent bleeding), a longer duration of bleeding, episodes of heavy bleeding, or menstruation after ≥6 months of amenorrhea warrants further evaluation. For women with prolonged or excessively heavy perimenopausal bleeding, pelvic ultrasonography should be performed. If the endometrial lining is <4 mm in thickness, an endometrial biopsy may occasionally be deferred. However, any uterine bleeding in a postmenopausal woman (usually considered the absence of menses for ≥1 year) is abnormal and warrants evaluation by endometrial biopsy, particularly for the possible presence of endometrial cancer.

Estrogen is the most effective treatment for the relief of perimenopausal symptoms such as hot flushes in selected patients in whom the benefits outweigh the risks of therapy. However, estrogen replacement is not indicated in the management of abnormal uterine bleeding and would be harmful if the bleeding is caused by an endometrial cancer.

Progestins may be useful in managing patients with heavy vaginal bleeding (menorrhagia) with a known cause such as leiomyoma and in patients with anovulatory bleeding to help maintain regular cycles. However, this intervention would be inappropriate without first eliminating the possibility of endometrial cancer as the cause of the abnormal uterine bleeding in this patient.

A follicle-stimulating hormone level would affirm menopause if significantly elevated but cannot exclude the possibility of endometrial carcinoma.

KEY POINT

An assessment of the endometrial lining with an endometrial biopsy is appropriate to rule out endometrial cancer or hyperplasia in postmenopausal women with uterine bleeding.

Bibliography
Col NF, Fairfield KM, Ewan-Whyte C, Miller H. In the clinic. Menopause. Ann Intern Med. 2009;150:ITC4-1-15; quiz ITC4-16. [PMID: 19349628]

Item 60   Answer: A
Educational Objective: *Diagnose arrhythmia as the cause of syncope.*

The most likely cause of this patient's syncope is an arrhythmia, probably ventricular tachycardia. Cardiac diseases predominate as cause of syncope in elderly adults and include bradycardias (sinus and atrioventricular node dysfunction) as well as tachyarrhythmias (supraventricular and ventricular). Patients with an arrhythmogenic cause of syncope usually have less than 5 seconds of warning symptoms before each episode. Patients often have underlying structural heart disease as a contributing cause. This patient's history of heart failure and low ejection fraction make ventricular tachycardia the most likely cause of her syncopal episode.

Neurocardiogenic or vasovagal syncope, the most common type, is predominantly a clinical diagnosis. Vasovagal neurocardiogenic syncope (the common "faint") results from a reflex withdrawal of sympathetic tone accompanied by an increase in vagal tone, precipitating a drop in blood pressure and heart rate. Patients with neurocardiogenic syncope often experience a prodromal phase, usually longer than 10 seconds, characterized by palpitations, nausea, blurred vision, warmth, diaphoresis, or lightheadedness, although these symptoms are less common in elderly adults. Provoking factors include prolonged standing, postural change, hot environments, emotional distress, dehydration, and use of diuretics or vasodilators. The first episode usually occurs at a young age, and recurrences are common.

Orthostatic hypotension is characterized by an abnormal drop in blood pressure with standing (>20 mm Hg systolic or 10 mm Hg diastolic). Orthostatic syncope is more common in elderly adults; in those taking vasoactive drugs, diuretics, or alcohol; and in the setting of volume depletion or autonomic failure, such as primary or idiopathic autonomic neuropathy. Patients commonly have symptoms of dizziness, weakness, and fatigue, both before and after the event.

Seizure can cause a transient loss of consciousness but is often associated with tongue biting and incontinence and is typically associated with a prolonged episode of post-event confusion. Twitching of the extremities can accompany syncope from any cause and does not establish the diagnosis of seizure.

KEY POINT

Cardiac diseases predominate as cause of syncope in elderly adults and include bradycardias (sinus and atrioventricular node dysfunction) as well as tachyarrhythmias (supraventricular and ventricular).

Bibliography
Saklani P, Krahn A, Klein G. Syncope. Circulation. 2013;127:1330-9. [PMID: 23529534]

Item 61   Answer: D
Educational Objective: *Evaluate neurocardiogenic syncope.*

The most appropriate next step in the management of this patient is reassurance. Neurocardiogenic syncope, the most common type, is predominantly a clinical diagnosis. Patients with neurocardiogenic syncope often experience a prodromal phase, usually longer than 10 seconds, characterized by palpitations, nausea, blurred vision, warmth, diaphoresis, or lightheadedness.

The diagnostic evaluation of syncope begins with a thorough history and physical examination. The history and physical examination reveal a cause in one-third to two-thirds of patients. Any witnesses should be interviewed because patients may not remember important aspects of the event. Important aspects of the history include age, position, prodrome, triggers, associated symptoms, duration of symptoms, previous episodes and duration between episodes, medications, family history (especially in young patients), and underlying medical conditions. Vital signs, including orthostatic vital signs, often contribute to the diagnosis.

Despite its low diagnostic yield, 12-lead electrocardiography remains the first and most widely recommended test to perform in patients being evaluated for syncope, partly owing to its noninvasive nature, availability, and low cost. Although this test is relatively insensitive for finding a specific cause of syncope, its specificity is high, and an abnormal ECG result is used to identify and stratify patients for additional testing. The remainder of the evaluation should be directed by the unique circumstances of the patient's event. Echocardiography is recommended in patients suspected of having structural heart disease. If an arrhythmia is suspected, documentation of the arrhythmia is indicated either by inpatient telemetry or ambulatory monitoring. Tilt-table testing should be reserved for patients with recurrent episodes of syncope in the absence of known heart disease or in patients with documented heart disease in whom a cardiac cause has been excluded. Tilt-table testing may also have a role in evaluating patients in whom documenting neurocardiogenic syncope is important (such as in high-risk occupational settings) and differentiating the cause of syncope from neurologic (such as seizure) or psychiatric etiologies. This patient has no indication for arrhythmia monitoring, echocardiography, or tilt-table testing.

KEY POINT

ECG is the first and most widely recommended test to perform in patients being evaluated for syncope; the remainder of the evaluation should be directed by the unique circumstances of the patient's event.

Bibliography

Saklani P, Krahn A, Klein G. Syncope. Circulation. 2013;127:1330-9. [PMID: 23529534]

Item 62   Answer: D

Educational Objective: *Evaluate a patient with recurrent syncope.*

The most appropriate next step in the evaluation of this patient is tilt-table testing. Tilt-table testing is useful in evaluating recurrent syncope in the absence of heart disease to discriminate neurocardiogenic from orthostatic syncope and to evaluate frequent syncope in patients with psychiatric disease. This patient continues to have recurrent syncopal episodes despite normal cardiac and metabolic evaluations without definitive evidence of orthostasis or other explanation for her symptoms.

Electroencephalography may be useful in patients in whom a seizure is suspected as a cause of syncope. However, this patient has no risk factors for seizure, and her episodes are without a prodromal aura, evidence of seizure activity, or postictal symptoms suggestive of seizure activity.

Exercise cardiac stress testing has a low yield for syncope in patients at low risk for ischemic heart disease. In this patient with normal ECG and echocardiogram findings, cardiac stress testing would not be expected to contribute significant diagnostic information.

An implantable loop recorder is a device that is placed subcutaneously that has a looping memory capable of storing ECG rhythm events over a period of months to years. It is used primarily in patients with unexplained symptoms in whom an arrhythmia is suspected but an episode has not been captured with shorter periods of monitoring. However, this patient has had presyncopal and syncopal events while under active ECG monitoring that have not shown evidence of an associated arrhythmia. Therefore, more prolonged monitoring would likely not be helpful.

KEY POINT

Tilt-table testing is useful in evaluating recurrent syncope in the absence of heart disease, to discriminate neurocardiogenic from orthostatic syncope, and to evaluate frequent syncope in patients with psychiatric disease.

Bibliography

Moya A, Sutton R, Ammirati F, et al; Task Force for the Diagnosis and Management of Syncope; European Society of Cardiology (ESC); European Heart Rhythm Association (EHRA); Heart Failure Association (HFA); Heart Rhythm Society (HRS). Guidelines for the diagnosis and management of syncope (version 2009). Eur Heart J. 2009;30:2631-71. [PMID: 19713422]

Item 63   Answer: B

Educational Objective: *Determine the optimal cardiac monitoring device in a patient with infrequent syncopal episodes.*

An implantable loop recorder (ILR) should be placed in this patient. Her physical examination and baseline electrocardiographic (ECG) findings do not suggest cardiovascular abnormalities. The concern for arrhythmia is significant given her previous syncopal events and her occupation, which requires driving. An ILR is placed subcutaneously under local anesthesia and has a solid-state looping memory capable of storing ECG rhythm events, with a total capacity of up to 42 minutes. Battery life is approximately 3 years, a duration likely long enough to capture an event in this patient. ILRs are often useful in identifying an arrhythmia when previous, shorter duration monitoring is not diagnostic.

A continuous ambulatory ECG monitor may detect asymptomatic arrhythmias but is typically worn for only 24 to 48 hours. External event recorders (looping event recorders and postsymptom event recorders) are used for more infrequent symptoms and record ECG tracings only when triggered by the patient. In this patient, a looping event recorder worn for 30 days did not reveal any arrhythmias. Because of the fleeting and infrequent nature of this patient's symptoms, it is unlikely that 24- or 48-hour ambulatory monitoring or an event recorder would capture an event. For arrhythmia evaluation, recent studies have shown improved diagnostic yield of mobile cardiac outpatient telemetry systems, another noninvasive monitoring tool, compared with looping event recorders. However, these systems are not yet widely available.

Further testing would be appropriate in this patient who has a high-risk occupation and has experienced syncope at rest.

KEY POINT

An implantable loop recorder is useful in identifying an infrequent arrhythmia when previous, shorter-duration monitoring is not diagnostic.

Bibliography

Parry SW, Matthews IG. Implantable loop recorders in the investigation of unexplained syncope: a state of the art review. Heart. 2010;96:1611-6. [PMID: 20937748]

Item 64   Answer: B

Educational Objective: *Diagnose orthostatic hypotension as a cause of syncope.*

The patient's history and examination findings are consistent with orthostatic hypotension. A drop in systolic blood pressure of 20 mm Hg or more or diastolic blood pressure of 10 mm Hg or more after standing for 3 minutes is diagnostic of orthostatic hypotension. Medications are a common cause of orthostatic hypotension, and α-adrenergic blockers, such as doxazosin, are a class of medications that may precipitate this condition. Because the episode of syncope was temporally related to initiation of the doxazosin, a prudent strategy would be to discontinue the medication.

Structural heart disease is common in this patient's age group, but nothing in his clinical history or physical examination suggests a cardiac abnormality. In the presence of a likely explanation for his syncope, there is no indication for admitting him for inpatient cardiovascular evaluation.

Cerebrovascular causes of syncope are invariably associated with neurologic signs and symptoms, such as ataxia, vertigo, and diplopia. Because the patient has no neurologic signs, a cerebrovascular cause is unlikely and a brain magnetic resonance image would be of limited use.

24-Hour ambulatory electrocardiographic monitoring has poor yield in the evaluation of syncope unless the patient has frequent episodes of syncope or lightheadedness that could be captured during testing. For patients with infrequent symptoms, continuous-loop recorders are recommended. However, in a patient with historical and clinical findings strongly suggesting orthostatic hypotension, additional diagnostic evaluation for arrhythmia is not indicated.

KEY POINT

Doxazosin should be discontinued in this patient. Orthostatic hypotension is usually diagnosed by a suggestive history or a systolic blood pressure decrease of at least 20 mm Hg or a diastolic blood pressure decrease of at least 10 mm Hg within 3 minutes of standing.

Bibliography

Pretorius RW, Gataric G, Swedlund SK, Miller JR. Reducing the risk of adverse drug events in older adults. Am Fam Physician. 2013;87:331-6. [PMID: 23547549]

Item 65   Answer: A

Educational Objective: *Diagnose benign versus pathologic lymphadenopathy.*

Age is the most suggestive clinical feature of pathologic lymphadenopathy. People older than 40 years of age are 20 times more likely to have a pathologic cause of lymphadenopathy than those who are younger given the prevalence of benign causes of lymph node enlargement in that age range.

Classifying lymphadenopathy as localized or generalized is not a useful predictor of its likelihood of being pathologic.

The location of the lymphadenopathy can be a helpful predictor of the likelihood of a pathologic versus benign cause. Specifically, whereas mediastinal, supraclavicular, and abdominal lymphadenopathy have a greater likelihood of a pathologic cause, cervical, axillary, and inguinal lymphadenopathy have a greater likelihood of a benign cause, as is present in this patient.

Size can be a helpful predictor of whether lymphadenopathy is benign or pathological, lymph nodes <2 cm frequently are from benign causes, and those ≥2 cm are more likely to be associated with a pathological cause.

Most infectious and immunologic causes of lymphadenopathy resolve within 2 weeks, and persistence for less than 2 weeks is reassuring for a benign cause of lymphadenopathy. If a benign cause of lymphadenopathy is suspected, an observation period of at least 4 weeks is considered appropriate before pursuing additional diagnostic studies.

KEY POINT

Clinical features of lymphadenopathy as assessed by history and physical examination can help predict the likelihood that the underlying cause is either benign or pathologic.

Bibliography

Pangalis GA, Vassilakopoulos TP, Boussiotis VA, Fessas P. Clinical approach to lymphadenopathy. Semin Oncol. 1993;20:570-82. [PMID: 8296196]

Item 66   Answer: B

Educational Objective: *Evaluate a patient with benign lymphadenopathy.*

The most appropriate next step in the diagnostic evaluation is anti–Epstein-Barr virus (EBV) antibody assay. The history and physical examination are critical in determining which patients need further evaluation for lymphadenopathy. The patient's age is one of the most helpful pieces of information; age older than 40 years is associated with a 20-fold higher risk for malignancy or granulomatous disease compared with younger patients. The setting in which the lymphadenopathy occurs is also important; whereas acute onset after an infection suggests an infectious or reactive lymphadenopathy, subacute onset in a cigarette smoker suggests malignancy. Timing is another helpful clue because most benign immunologic reactions resolve in 2 to 4 weeks, but more serious conditions are associated with persistent or progressive lymphadenopathy. Systemic symptoms (specifically fever, night sweats, and weight loss) in this clinical context are often referred to as "B symptoms" based on the Ann Arbor staging system for lymphoma in which the designation "B" is added to the stage if constitutional symptoms are present. Systemic symptoms may suggest a more serious underlying illness. However, a 1-month history of fatigue and intermittent fever with tender but soft and freely movable lymphadenopathy and splenomegaly associated with atypical lymphocytosis in a young male patient are most consistent with infectious mononucleosis caused by EBV infection.

A bone marrow biopsy to diagnose leukemia or malignancy would be unnecessary before the presence of mononucleosis is confirmed. Similarly, a lymph node biopsy would not be necessary until mononucleosis is confirmed or excluded.

Peripheral blood flow cytometry would not add useful information because this patient's illness would result in a polyclonal increase in lymphocytes. Flow cytometry is best used to help establish a diagnosis when evaluating for a malignancy that would reveal a monoclonal population of cells with a specific phenotype.

KEY POINT

Cervical lymphadenopathy that is soft, tender to the touch, and freely movable in association with fever is usually not of malignant origin.

Bibliography

Pangalis GA, Vassilakopoulos TP, Boussiotis VA, Fessas P. Clinical approach to lymphadenopathy. Semin Oncol. 1993;20:570-82. [PMID: 8296196]

Item 67   Answer: D

Educational Objective: *Diagnose an upper gastrointestinal (GI) cause of involuntary weight loss in an elderly patient.*

Upper endoscopy is the most appropriate next step. Of all patients with involuntary weight loss, approximately 50% will have a physical cause for the weight loss. Although malignancy is the most common physical cause of weight loss, a significant proportion of those with a physical cause have a nonmalignant GI disease. This patient's loss of appetite, heartburn, and anemia should prompt further investigation for upper GI causes of weight loss and investigation for ulcer or gastritis with an upper endoscopy is reasonable.

In a patient with a recent onset of heartburn, early satiety, and anemia, direct visualization of the upper GI system is more likely to yield a diagnosis than is abdominal computed tomography scan. Megestrol is an appetite stimulate that has marginal ability to induce weight gain and is associated with an increased risk of edema, heart failure, and deep venous thrombosis. Nutritional supplements may improve mortality rates in hospitalized, older, malnourished patients but are unlikely to be helpful for this patient. In addition, appetite and nutritional supplements do not address the potential cause of this patient's involuntary weight loss and anemia.

KEY POINT

In patients with symptoms or signs suggestive of a physical cause of weight loss, nonmalignant GI causes are common.

Bibliography

Huffman GB. Evaluating and treating unintentional weight loss in the elderly. Am Fam Physician. 2002:15;65:640-50. [PMID: 11871682]

Item 68   Answer: D

Educational Objective: *Perform age- and sex-appropriate cancer screening for involuntary weight loss.*

Mammography would be a reasonable next step in the evaluation of this patient's involuntary weight loss. Of all community-dwelling patients with involuntary weight loss, approximately 16% to 38% will have a malignancy as the cause. Malignancy is the most common physical cause of involuntary weight loss. Given her loss of energy and elevated C-reactive protein level, the possibility of a physical cause of weight loss is higher. Having a normal appetite suggests gastrointestinal (GI) causes are less likely. Age-appropriate cancer screening should be part of the initial workup for people with involuntary weight loss. For this woman, that includes mammography, cervical cytology, and colonoscopy. She had a normal colonoscopy 3 years ago and a Papanicolaou smear with human papillomavirus testing 2 years ago, which makes repeating these studies much less useful. Without a smoking history, screening for lung cancer with chest computed tomography (CT) is also low yield.

In cases when the cause of involuntary weight loss is not clear, it is reasonable to consider the following studies: complete blood count; erythrocyte sedimentation rate or C-reactive protein; serum chemistry tests, including calcium and liver chemistry tests; HIV test; thyroid-stimulating hormone level; urinalysis; chest radiography; and stool for occult blood. In patients with GI symptoms, also consider upper endoscopy, abdominal CT, or abdominal ultrasonography. However, screening mammography would be a logical next step to complete her age-and sex-appropriate cancer screening.

KEY POINT

Malignancy is the most common cause of involuntary weight loss among adults with signs of a physical cause for weight loss.

Bibliography

Vanderschueren S, Geens E, Knockaert D, Bobbaers H. The diagnostic spectrum of unintentional weight loss. Eur J Intern Med. 2005;16:160-4. [PMID: 15967329]

Item 69   Answer: C

Educational Objective: *Diagnose colon cancer as the cause of unintentional weight loss.*

The most appropriate next diagnostic test is colonoscopy. Although the differential diagnosis of involuntary weight loss is often broad, a patient's presenting symptoms and findings frequently allow a tailored approach to the evaluation. This patient has fatigue, increased appetite, worsening constipation and anemia, and a positive stool for occult blood suggesting that evaluation for a gastrointestinal (GI)-related disorder, such as colonoscopy, should be the initial focus of evaluation.

The most common causes of involuntary weight loss belong to four major categories: malignancy; chronic infections or inflammation, especially GI; metabolic, such as hyperthyroidism; and psychiatric. Other causes are drugs, social factors, and age related. In some patients, more than one of these causes is responsible. A small prospective study of patients with unintentional weight loss found that the following factors were associated with a physical cause of involuntary weight loss: fatigue, smoking (>20 pack-year history), nausea or vomiting, change in cough, and increased appetite. Cancer is the most common physical cause of unintentional weight loss, and GI causes are the second most common physical cause.

Although mammography may ultimately be needed to evaluate this patient's weight loss, the patient's findings most strongly suggest a GI cause of her findings. Direct visualization of the colonic mucosa with colonoscopy is more likely to establish a diagnosis accounting for her constipation and anemia than is mammography, abdominal computed tomography, or abdominal ultrasonography.

KEY POINT

The patient's presenting symptoms will often appropriately direct the initial evaluation for unintentional weight loss and eliminate unnecessary testing.

Bibliography

Vanderschueren S, Geens E, Knockaert D, Bobbaers H. The diagnostic spectrum of unintentional weight loss. Eur J Intern Med. 2005;16:160-4. [PMID: 15967329]

Item 70   Answer: D

Educational Objective: *Diagnose a psychiatric cause of involuntary weight loss.*

This patient should be screened for depression as a cause of her weight loss. Her history of anxiety and depression with current weight loss without another explanation raises the possibility that depression might be a cause of her clinical findings. Depression accounts for 9% to 15% of all cases of involuntary weight loss and is the most common psychiatric cause. Depression is also the second most common chronic disorder in primary care medicine. Screening for depression is the first step in the diagnosis of mood disorders in all adults and should be considered in the differential diagnosis of patients with involuntary weight loss. There is little evidence to recommend one screening method over another, so physicians can choose the method that best suits their patient population and practice setting. After screening verifies the clinical impression of depression, treatment should be prescribed.

Initial diagnostic testing for the evaluation of involuntary weight loss is limited to basic studies unless the history and physical examination suggest a specific cause.

Occult malignancy is uncommon, and imaging of the thorax and abdomen for cancer in the absence of specific historical information or physical examination findings has not been shown to help determine the cause of involuntary weight loss.

Beginning an appetite stimulant does not address the cause of the weight loss and is not indicated.

Observation and reevaluation of the patient is not appropriate without further evaluation for the cause of her unexplained weight loss.

KEY POINTS

Depression accounts for 9% to 15% of all cases of involuntary weight loss and is the most common psychiatric cause of involuntary weight loss.

Imaging with computed tomography or magnetic resonance imaging in the absence of historical information or physical examination findings suggesting disorders of the thorax or abdomen has not been shown to help determine the cause of involuntary weight loss.

Bibliography

Huffman GB. Evaluating and treating unintentional weight loss in the elderly. Am Fam Physician. 2002;65:640-50. PMID: 11871682.

Item 71   Answer: B
Educational Objective: *Diagnose a cataract.*

The most likely cause of this patient's vision loss is a cataract. Cataracts are a common cause of progressive painless vision loss in elderly adults. Risk factors include older age, ultraviolet B radiation exposure, smoking, diabetes mellitus, a family history of cataracts, and systemic corticosteroid use. A common symptom is difficulty with night vision. Nondilated examination of the eye may reveal an opacified lens and a decreased red reflex. Surgery is indicated if symptoms from the cataract interfere with the patient's ability to meet his or her needs of daily living; there are no criteria based on the level of visual acuity.

Age-related macular degeneration (AMD) is the most common cause of blindness in developed countries. There are two types of AMD, dry (atrophic) and wet (neovascular). In dry AMD, soft drusen (deposits of extracellular material) form in the area of the macula. It may be asymptomatic in the early stages and subsequently progress, with the gradual loss of central vision. Wet AMD is caused by neovascularization of the macula with subsequent bleeding or scar formation. Visual loss may be more sudden (over a period of weeks) and is often more severe. This patient has no findings to support the diagnosis of AMD.

Primary open-angle glaucoma (POAG) is a progressive optic neuropathy associated with increased intraocular pressure without an identifiable blockage of the normal drainage pathways of the aqueous humor. It is the most common form of glaucoma and is the leading cause of irreversible blindness in the world. POAG is characterized by painless, gradual loss of peripheral vision in both eyes, which may be unnoticed by the patient. It is often asymmetric. In later

stages, it may progress to involve central visual acuity. Clinical findings include an increased optic cup to disc ratio (>0.5), disc hemorrhages, and vertical extension of the central cup.

Presbyopia describes an age-related change partly caused by reduced elasticity of the lens that results in difficulty seeing at a close range because of the diminished ability of the lens to accommodate. Other than decreased visual acuity, the physical examination of the eye is normal.

KEY POINT

Cataract can be diagnosed when a nondilated examination of the eye reveals an opacified lens and a decreased red reflex.

Bibliography

Rosenberg EA, Sperazza LC. The visually impaired patient. Am Fam Physician. 2008; 77:1431-6. [PMID: 18533377]

Item 72   Answer: C
Educational Objective: *Diagnose drug-induced urinary retention.*

This patient's urinary retention is most likely a result of anticholinergic side effects of diphenhydramine in the setting of preexisting prostate enlargement. Using a modified Delphi method, a consensus panel from the American Geriatrics Society identified medications or classes of medications that should be avoided in older patients; the list of medications known as Beers criteria was most recently updated in 2012. Two types of recommendations were made: (1) medications or medication classes that should generally be avoided in persons age 65 years or older because they are either ineffective or pose unnecessarily high risk for older persons and a safer alternative is available and (2) medications that should not be used in older persons known to have specific medical contraindication. Diphenhydramine is listed as a drug that poses an unnecessary risk for older patients because it is highly anticholinergic and increases the risk of confusion, dry mouth, constipation, and urinary retention. Diphenhydramine may be appropriate in selected clinical situations such as severe allergic reactions.

Urinary tract infection, including acute prostatitis, is an uncommon cause of urinary retention, accounting for only 2% of cases in most studies. The normal urinalysis makes urinary tract infection unlikely. Acute prostatitis typically presents with fever, pelvic pain, and urinary symptoms. The absence of these symptoms and nontender prostate examination make the diagnosis of acute prostatitis an unlikely cause of urinary retention.

Prostate cancer is responsible for approximately 7% of urinary retention cases. However, the timing of his symptoms in relation to diphenhydramine use makes a medication side effect in the setting of prostatic enlargement a much more likely explanation of his symptoms.

Cauda equina syndrome and other neurologic disorders account for 2% of urinary retention cases. Symptoms of cauda equina syndrome may include saddle anesthesia, urinary retention and sometimes overflow incontinence, and lower extremity weakness. Cauda equina syndrome has many potential etiologies, including myelopathy, and cord compression caused by cancer, infection, and disk herniation. This patient does not have any additional findings to suggest this disorder.

Diphenhydramine is a drug that poses an unnecessary risk for older patients because it is highly anticholinergic and increases the risk of confusion, dry mouth, constipation, and urinary retention.

Bibliography

American Geriatrics Society 2012 Beers Criteria Update Expert Panel. American Geriatrics Society updated Beers Criteria for potentially inappropriate medication use in older adults. J Am Geriatr Soc. 2012;60:616-31. [PMID: 22376048]

Item 73   Answer: B

Educational Objective: *Understand interventions to decrease fall risk in geriatric patients.*

Reviewing and discontinuing any nonessential medications would be the most likely intervention to decrease falls in this patient. A geriatric patient's risk of falling increases with the number of medications he or she takes. Polypharmacy, typically defined as taking more than medications, is associated with an increased risk of falls. In addition to the absolute number of medications, many classes of medications are particularly high risk; these include psychoactive medications such as sedatives, antipsychotics, antidepressants, anticonvulsants, and antihypertensive medications. Although there may be multiple factors contributing to this patient's falls, his medication list is concerning not only for the number of medications but also for the types of medications it includes. Specifically, he is taking an antihistamine (hydroxyzine), which may be sedating; an α-blocker (doxazosin) and an antihypertensive (Losartan), which may cause orthostatic changes; and an anticonvulsant (gabapentin) that acts on the central nervous system and can promote falls. Although not all of these medications can be appropriately discontinued, minimizing the number of high-risk types of medicine is the most important first step in addressing fall risk.

Vitamin D supplementation with 800 IU/day has been shown to decrease falls in high-risk patients, although the addition of calcium is not associated with a reduction in falls.

Although an assistive device may be useful for preventing falls in selected patients, they should be prescribed only to individuals with specific indications based on gait and balance assessment coupled with strength training and education regarding appropriate use of the device.

Assisted living provides help to patients who may have difficulty in carrying out routine activities of daily living. However, an assisted living setting does not necessarily reduce the risk of falls in susceptible patients.

Polypharmacy is a major contributing factor to falls in elderly adults; a review of the number and types of medications prescribed to a patient with falls should be an initial step in evaluation.

Bibliography

Pretorius RW, Gataric G, Swedlund SK, Miller JR. Reducing the risk of adverse drug events in older adults. Am Fam Physician. 2013;87:331-6. [PMID: 23547549]

Item 74   Answer: D

Educational Objective: *Treat functional urinary incontinence.*

This patient would be best managed by establishing a prompted voiding protocol. Urinary incontinence affects more than 50% of nursing home patients and is associated with significant morbidity and cost. Most of these patients have limited mobility or significant cognitive impairment, leading to a high prevalence of functional incontinence, defined as simply not getting to the toilet quickly enough. Systematic reviews have shown that the use of prompted (or timed) voiding (periodically asking the patient about incontinence, often at specified time intervals, reminding the patient to go to the toilet, and providing praise for maintaining continence and using the toilet) was associated with modest short-term improvement in urinary incontinence.

History, focused examination, and urinalysis are often adequate to classify urinary incontinence. Postvoid residual urine volume determination is most useful if overflow incontinence caused by outlet obstruction or a flaccid neurogenic bladder is suspected. Detailed urologic evaluations, such as cystoscopy and urodynamic testing, are unnecessary in uncomplicated urinary incontinence.

An indwelling urinary catheter is not advised as a first-line measure to manage urinary incontinence owing to an increased risk of urinary tract infections, resultant antibiotic treatment, and the development of antibiotic complications and resistance.

Pelvic floor muscle training is effective for stress incontinence, which may be coexistent in this patient, but successful implementation requires a cooperative and cognitively intact patient who can understand and participate in the exercise program, which this patient is unlikely to do.

Antimuscarinic medications are indicated primarily for urge incontinence and are not of benefit in functional incontinence. In addition, anticholinergic adverse side effects, such as dry mouth and worsening cognitive function, render its use in this patient ill advised.

Prompted voiding is an effective management strategy for patients with functional urinary incontinence.

Bibliography

Fink HA, Taylor BC, Tacklind JW, et al. Treatment interventions in nursing home residents with urinary incontinence: a systematic review of randomized trials. Mayo Clin Proc. 2008;83:1332-43. [PMID: 19046552]

Item 75   Answer: B

Educational Objective: *Manage a fall in an elderly patient.*

In this patient with generalized weakness as well as leg muscle weakness, a slow gait, and a recent fall, it is appropriate to prescribe vitamin D. Vitamin D deficiency increases the risk for falls in elderly adults, and vitamin D supplementation reduces this risk. According to U.S. Preventive Services Task Force recommendations, vitamin D supplementation can be prescribed without first obtaining a serum vitamin D level for patients with an increased risk of falling. The proposed mechanism of action of vitamin D is its beneficial effect on muscle strength and function and on gait. Although calcium supplementation may have a beneficial effect on bone loss, there is no clear benefit to adding calcium in reducing falls.

Discontinuing lisinopril is not appropriate because the patient does not demonstrate orthostatic blood pressure changes that would account for her fall, and her blood pressure is reasonably well controlled on this medication.

Zolpidem is a nonbenzodiazepine sedative hypnotic with a short half-life that can be prescribed for a limited time period for insomnia. Caution must be exercised, however, because of adverse effects, including an increased risk for falls, especially among older adults. Reviewing sleep hygiene would be a better first step in managing her insomnia.

Bifocal lenses are associated with an increased risk for falling. If needed, reading glasses could be obtained to improve her near vision.

KEY POINT

Vitamin D supplementation reduces the risk for falls in elderly patients and can be prescribed without obtaining a serum vitamin D level in patients with an increased risk of falling.

Bibliography

Kalyani RR, Stein B, Valiyil R, et al. Vitamin D treatment for the prevention of falls in older adults: systematic review and meta-analysis. J Am Geriatr Soc. 2010;58:1299-310. [PMID: 20579169]

Item 76   Answer: C

Educational Objective: *Manage risk for motor vehicle accidents in an older adult driver.*

This patient has a number of factors that increase his risk of being involved in a motor vehicle accident, and his physician has a responsibility to reduce this risk. This patient's risk factors for a motor vehicle accident include his age, visual deficits (corrected with glasses), and decreased motor function (including a history of falling). The first step in assessing driving ability in older adults is to ask the patient and family members about driving difficulties. This assessment should include questions about whether friends and family members are worried about their driving, getting lost while driving, near misses, and recent accidents. A more complete set of questions to assess driving risk can be found in the "Am I a Safe Driver?" self-assessment tool (www.ama-assn.org/ama1/pub/upload/mm/433/am_i_a_safe_driver.pdf). A positive response to any of the questions suggests unsafe driving.

It would be premature to advise this patient to stop driving before assessing driving-related skills, providing the patient with information on safe driving, and suggesting that the patient enroll in a driving course designed to improve skills. Referral to a driver rehabilitation specialist can also assist in assessment and skill improvement.

Advising the patient to drive only locally is not advised because so-called "low-mileage" drivers may be at the greatest risk. Older drivers who are having driving difficulties often self-restrict their driving, but local roads often have more hazards, including more signs and signals and confusing and congested intersections.

Guidelines for reporting patients to the department of transportation vary by state and include immediate threats to driving safety such as new seizures. Even in states that require reporting of immediate threats to driving safety, there is no indication to report this patient before a more complete evaluation is performed.

KEY POINT

The first step in assessing driving ability in older adults is to ask the patient and family members about driving difficulties, including whether friends and family members are worried about their driving, getting lost while driving, near misses, and recent accidents.

Bibliography

Carr DB, Schwartzberg JG, Manning L, Sempek J. Physician's Guide to Assessing and Counseling Older Drivers. 2nd edition. Washington, DC. NHTSA. 2010. Available at www.ama-assn.org/ama/pub/physician-resources/public-health/promoting-healthy-lifestyles/geriatric-health/older-driver-safety/assessing-counseling-older-drivers.page.

Item 77   Answer: E

Educational Objective: *Manage terminal dyspnea.*

The most appropriate management for this patient to perform a therapeutic thoracentesis. This patient presents with dyspnea that is most likely related to a malignant pleural effusion. The most common symptoms associated with pleural effusions are dyspnea, pleuritic chest pain, and nonproductive cough. Dyspnea related to pleural effusions may be related to abnormal activation of stretch and flow receptors within the lung parenchyma and chest wall, with resultant mismatch between efferent central nervous system signaling and afferent input. Even in patients with terminal illness, the initial goals of symptom management should focus on therapies that alleviate the cause of symptoms, in this case drainage of the pleural effusion. The effusion may recur after drainage, but if the patient experiences symptom relief with thoracentesis, a tunneled catheter for intermittent drainage can be placed.

Diuresis is an effective therapy for patients with dyspnea secondary to heart failure and hypervolemia but will not alleviate dyspnea caused by a malignant pleural effusion when volume status is normal. This patient has normal cardiovascular examination findings and no evidence of jugular venous distension or peripheral edema that would warrant diuretic therapy. Opioids are frequently used in cancer-related dyspnea, but this patient has a potential remediable cause of dyspnea, and thoracentesis is the best initial management. Benzodiazepines may alleviate the anxiety associated with her dyspnea but will not address the underlying cause nor will oxygen administration via nasal cannula. Furthermore, the data behind oxygen therapy for management of dyspnea in malignancy is inconclusive, particularly in the absence of hypoxia, as in this case.

KEY POINT

In patients with terminal illness, the initial goals of symptom management should focus on therapies that alleviate the cause of symptoms even if these interventions may be invasive.

Bibliography

Pinna MÁ. Dyspnea review for the palliative care professional: treatment goals and therapeutic options. J Palliat Med. 2012;15:730. [PMID: 22780112]

Item 78   Answer: B

Educational Objective: *Treat delirium associated with terminal disease.*

The most appropriate management for this patient is haloperidol. This patient demonstrates confusion, agitation, and a deficit in attention, pointing to a likely diagnosis of delirium. Delirium is common at the end of life and can be caused by advanced medical conditions, the medications being used to palliate symptoms, or a combination of both. Family members frequently need to be reassured that delirium is common. There are no U.S. Food and Drug Administration–approved therapies for delirium. However, evidence demonstrates that low-dose antipsychotic agents are effective in the treatment of delirium.

The patient does not complain of dyspnea, her vital signs are normal, and her pulmonary examination findings are normal. There is no indication for arterial blood gas analysis at this time. Although this patient is confused, she is able to convey that she is not experiencing pain; therefore, the administration of short-acting morphine is not appropriate. Opioid analgesia can be reduced provided pain remains controlled, and this may help control or lessen delirium. Because benzodiazepines, including lorazepam, can cause or worsen delirium, they should only be used if there is a strong component of patient anxiety, which is not present in this case.

KEY POINT

Low-dose antipsychotic agents are effective in the treatment of delirium associated with terminal disease.

Bibliography

Lorenz KA, Lynn J, Dy SM, et al. Evidence for improving palliative care at the end of life: a systematic review. Ann Intern Med. 2008;148:147-59. [PMID: 18195339]

Item 79   Answer: B

Educational Objective: *Manage palliative care discussion.*

Palliative care discussions with this patient should begin now. It is important to stress to patients that a palliative care discussion is not a discussion of withholding or withdrawal of treatment or patient abandonment. Palliative care is a multidisciplinary, boarded specialty that focuses on preventing and relieving suffering and establishing goals of treatment that are consistent with the patient's wishes. This often involves efforts at pain and symptom control and encouraging and enabling patients to be actively involved in the decisions regarding their care. Nonhospice palliative care does not exclude testing, treatment, or hospitalization but seeks to ensure that these interventions are consistent with what the patient wants and the expected goals and outcomes of care. Whereas care in a hospice setting may be palliative in nature, not all palliative care takes place in patients with terminal illness. Palliative care input may be particularly valuable in assisting this patient, who has a new diagnosis of severe disease, with understanding her illness and making key decisions regarding her care. Although studies are limited, palliative care has been shown to improve overall quality of life in the setting of various diseases relative to usual care for severely ill individuals.

Waiting until the patient develops symptoms, refuses active treatment, or is admitted to hospice care does not take full advantage of the benefits of early and appropriately administered palliative care.

KEY POINT

Early referral for palliative care in addition to oncologic care improves quality of life and decreases depressive symptoms compared with standard oncologic care only.

Bibliography

Temel JS, Greer JA, Muzikansky A, et al. Early palliative care for patients with metastatic non-small-cell lung cancer. N Engl J Med. 2010;363:733-42. [PMID: 20818875]

Item 80   Answer: D

Educational Objective: *Treat dyspnea at the end of life.*

This patient on comfort care should be given morphine. Dyspnea is one of the most common symptoms encountered in palliative care. It is most often the result of direct cardiothoracic pathology, such as pleural effusion, heart failure, chronic obstructive pulmonary disease (COPD), pulmonary embolism, pneumonia, or lung metastases. Dyspnea can also be caused by systemic conditions, such as anemia, muscle weakness, or conditions causing abdominal distention. Patients with underlying lung disease on bronchodilator therapy should have this therapy continued to maintain comfort. Opioids are effective in reducing dyspnea in patients with underlying cardiopulmonary disease and malignancy. In patients already receiving opioids, using the breakthrough pain dose for dyspnea and increasing this dose by 25% if not fully effective may be helpful. A 5-mg dose of oral morphine given four times daily has been shown to help relieve dyspnea in patients with end-stage heart failure. Low-dose (20 mg) extended-release morphine given daily has been used to relieve dyspnea in patients with advanced COPD.

Antibiotics and corticosteroids are appropriately used in patients with exacerbations of severe COPD. However, neither would be expected to provide immediate relief of the patient's respiratory distress and would also be inconsistent with care focusing primarily on comfort measures at the end of life.

In contrast to opioids, benzodiazepines have not demonstrated consistent benefit in treating dyspnea. However, they may be useful in specific patients who have significant anxiety associated with their dyspnea.

KEY POINT

Opioids are effective in reducing dyspnea in patients with underlying cardiopulmonary disease and malignancy.

Bibliography

Swetz KM, Kamal AH. Palliative care. Ann Intern Med. 2012;156:ITC21. [PMID: 22312158]

Item 81   Answer: D

Educational Objective: *Initiate a discussion about palliative care with the family of a cancer patient.*

The cornerstone of establishing goals of care in the end-of-life setting is to communicate in a patient-centered, open-ended format. This is true regardless of whether a patient or patient's family is angry or is requesting inappropriately aggressive care. The first step in this process in this case is to ask the family to tell you what they understand about the patient's condition. Active, empathic listening allows the caregiver to establish what the patient and family understand about the diagnosis and prognosis. It also shows respect for the myriad ways in which loved ones process information about medical conditions and helps to establish trust. The family should be allowed to vent their frustration and to articulate what they believe the patient's condition and chance of meaningful recovery to be. Given the feelings of distress about the patient's condition, it is entirely possible that one meeting may not be enough to establish clearly defined goals of care. Asking open-ended questions and being comfortable with silences are important in building a trusting relationship with the patient and family.

The upcoming dialogue with the family is likely to be emotionally charged, and a series of visits may be needed to cover all appropriate areas. It would not be appropriate to initiate the discussion with the patient and family about advanced directives until it is learned what the family knows about the diagnosis and prognosis.

It would not be helpful to begin a meeting with a distraught family or patient by stating that curative therapy would be futile. This approach is likely to further alienate a family struggling with a distressing diagnosis.

Although explaining the diagnosis and prognosis may be an important goal for a family meeting, it is usually more effective to begin the meeting with an open-ended question that allows the physician to better understand the family's perspective. Explanations can then be better tailored to what the family knows and understands about the patient's condition.

KEY POINT

The cornerstone of establishing goals of care in the end-of-life setting is to communicate in a patient-centered, open-ended format.

Bibliography

Swetz KM, Kamal AH. Palliative care. Ann Intern Med. 2012;156:ITC21. [PMID: 22312158]

Item 82   Answer: A

Educational Objective: *Understand the most appropriate screening strategy for possible genetic disease in an average risk patient.*

The most appropriate screening step for genetic diseases in this patient is to inquire about any diseases that "run in the family" and, specifically, to inquire about a family history of the more common and important inherited diseases, including breast, ovarian, prostate, and colon cancer, as well as early cardiovascular disease. A detailed family history should follow for the conditions identified through this preliminary questioning.

Genetic counseling with the option for testing should be offered when the patient has a personal or family history suggestive of a genetic susceptibility condition for which testing is available and in which the test results will aid in diagnosis or influence the management of the patient or family at hereditary risk. It is premature to refer for genetic counseling without first determining if there is concern for a genetic disorder.

The process of taking a family history typically used by medical genetics professionals is both labor and time intensive, typically involves a three-generation pedigree, and may require hours to complete. Gathering this degree of detail on individuals of average risk is not feasible or indicated.

Although it is standard of care to perform genetic testing for certain mutations in unselected preconception, prenatal, and newborn populations and direct-to-consumer genomic kits are commercially available, the clinical validity of such testing may be lacking, there may be a high likelihood of false-positive test results, and the potential harms and costs of performing genetic testing may outweigh any benefits.

KEY POINT

The most appropriate first screening step for genetic diseases is to inquire about any diseases that "run in the family" and to inquire specifically about a family

history of the more common and important inherited diseases, including breast, ovarian, prostate, and colon cancer, as well as early cardiovascular disease.

Bibliography

Berg AO, Baird MA, Botkin JR, et al. National Institute of Health State-of-the-Science Conference Statement: Family History and Improving Health. Ann Intern Med. 2009;151:872-7. [PMID: 19884615]

Item 83   Answer: D

Educational Objective: *Understand the indications for referral for genetic counseling.*

This patient should be referred for genetic counseling. Huntington disease is an autosomal dominant disorder caused by a CAG repeat within a gene on chromosome 4 that leads to a progressive neurodegenerative disorder characterized by choreiform movements, psychiatric problems, and dementia. It is currently untreatable. Because of the potential harms from genetic test information and the need for patients and their families to receive appropriate information for decision making, patients with possible inherited diseases should undergo genetic testing only in the context of genetic counseling. Genetic counseling should include discussion of possible risks and benefits of early detection and prevention modalities. Genetic counseling with the option for testing should be offered when (1) the patient has a personal or family history suggestive of a genetic susceptibility condition, (2) the genetic test can be adequately interpreted, and (3) the test results will aid in diagnosis or influence the medical or surgical management of the patient or family at hereditary risk.

Brain magnetic resonance imaging in patients with well-defined findings of Huntington disease demonstrates caudate atrophy. Such imaging is unlikely to be helpful in an asymptomatic patient and is not preferred to genetic counseling in estimating the likelihood of disease.

Symptoms of Huntington disease typically begin in the fourth and fifth decades of life, but 10% of patients have symptoms in the second decade. It is premature to reassure the patient, considering his young age and absence of genetic test data.

KEY POINT

Patients with possible inherited diseases should be referred for genetic testing only in the context of genetic counseling.

Bibliography

Berg AO, Baird MA, Botkin JR, et al. National Institute of Health State-of-the-Science Conference Statement: Family History and Improving Health. Ann Intern Med. 2009; 151:872-7. [PMID: 19884615]

Item 84   Answer: A

Educational Objective: *Understand the appropriate management of patients at high risk for germline-susceptibility cancers.*

This patient should be referred for genetic counseling and evaluation for *BRCA1/BRCA2* testing. Certain family backgrounds and patterns of disease are associated with deleterious *BRCA1/BRCA2* mutations that confer a significantly higher risk for breast and ovarian cancer compared with persons without these mutations. Compared with the general population, women who are of Ashkenazi Jewish descent are five times more likely to harbor *BRCA1* or *BRCA2* mutations, and an increased-risk family history includes any first-degree relative (or two second-degree relatives on the same side of the family) with breast or ovarian cancer, as in this patient. Therefore, referral to a genetic counselor is appropriate for this patient and will enable her to become informed about her options for reducing cancer risk. Although women with *BRCA1/BRCA2*-positive breast or ovarian cancer do not necessarily have a worse prognosis than those without these genetic mutations, they do have a substantially higher risk for death from cancer simply because of the enormously increased frequency with which breast and ovarian cancers occur in these higher risk populations. For patients not in this risk group, the family history pattern of breast or ovarian cancer is used to assess the degree of risk; an unremarkable family history pattern suggests a very low probability of having a *BRCA1/BRCA2* mutation.

Studies have suggested that prophylactic bilateral mastectomy in high-risk patients decreases the risks for breast cancer incidence and mortality by 90% or more. Likewise, prophylactic oophorectomy should be considered in women who have tested positive for a *BRCA1/BRCA2* mutation and who have completed childbearing. However, these are drastic approaches and not a consideration for this patient until she learns more about her degree of cancer risk by genetic counseling.

Tamoxifen has shown some effectiveness in preventing breast cancer regardless of *BRCA1* or *BRCA2* status and appears to lower risk in patients with the *BRCA2* mutation. However, initiating therapy would be premature in this patient before she is determined to be at high risk for breast or ovarian cancer.

KEY POINT

Patients with a family history suggestive of germline-susceptibility cancer should be referred for genetic counseling.

Bibliography

U.S. Preventive Services Task Force. Genetic risk assessment and BRCA mutation testing for breast and ovarian cancer susceptibility: recommendation statement. Ann Intern Med. 2005;143:355-61. [PMID: 16144894]

Item 85   Answer: A

Educational Objective: *Evaluate for cystic fibrosis in a patient whose disease mimics asthma.*

The most appropriate management is measurement of sweat chloride. This young man has been diagnosed with asthma, but he is more likely to have cystic fibrosis based on his symptoms and the presence of clubbing and upper lobe bronchiectasis. Most cases of cystic fibrosis are diagnosed during childhood; however, a delayed diagnosis can occur in patients with a mild form of cystic fibrosis, who are often misdiagnosed as having asthma when the symptoms are limited to the respiratory tract. The atypical features of his clinical presentation should raise suspicion for a possible underlying genetic disorder; a high level of suspicion should be maintained so that a heritable condition is not overlooked. In this patient, the diagnosis should be confirmed with measurement of sweat chloride, which is elevated (>60 meq/L [60 mmol/L]) in patients with cystic fibrosis. Genetic testing for cystic fibrosis is recommended for patients who have positive sweat chloride test results and helps support the diagnosis.

Diagnostic bronchoscopy can be helpful in patients with regional bronchiectasis to exclude proximal airway obstruction. However, in this patient, bronchoscopy is unlikely to lead to additional information, and it is a more invasive test than the measurement of sweat chloride.

Echocardiography is helpful in evaluating patients with clubbing suspected of having congenital heart disease; however, this patient has no other stigmata to suggest congenital heart disease, such as a loud pathologic murmur, asymmetric pulses, evidence of heart failure, or cyanosis.

Keeping a home diary of asthma symptoms or peak expiratory flow rate can be helpful to assess asthma control; however, in this patient with good inhaler technique, the persistence of symptoms is not likely to be related to asthma. In addition, uncontrolled asthma cannot explain the presence of bronchiectasis and clubbing in this patient.

KEY POINT

Delayed diagnosis can occur in patients with a mild form of cystic fibrosis; these patients are often misdiagnosed as having asthma when symptoms are limited to the respiratory tract.

Bibliography

National Asthma Education and Prevention Program. Expert Panel Report 3. Guidelines for the Diagnosis and Management of Asthma. Available at www.nhlbi.nih.gov/guidelines/asthma/asthsumm.pdf.

Item 86   Answer: B

Educational Objective: *Diagnose cutaneous small-vessel vasculitis.*

A punch biopsy should be performed on one of the patient's skin lesions. She has a purpuric rash indicating bleeding under the skin. Her purpuric lesions are also palpable; palpable purpura is a characteristic associated with vasculitis. A biopsy is indicated to confirm the presence of vasculitis and to guide therapy. This patient likely has cutaneous small-vessel vasculitis. This is a general description of infiltration of neutrophils in the dermis causing inflammation of the blood vessels as seen with the presence of a characteristic histologic pattern termed leukocytoclastic vasculitis. Vessel injury is immune complex mediated and is nonspecific; it may be triggered by medications, infections, connective tissue diseases, or malignancy, although a cause is not identifiable in 60% of cases. Although a leukocytoclastic vasculitis may be a part of a more system-wide vasculitic process, it is termed cutaneous small-vessel vasculitis when limited to the skin without other organ involvement.

When the diagnosis of vasculitis in the skin is made and there is no evidence of systemic vasculitis or specific organ involvement, treatment involves identifying a potential cause and removing it, which may be adequate therapy. This patient's recent exposure to antibiotics before development of her rash is a suggestive etiology. Elevation and external compression may be helpful for those with swelling, and antihistamine and anti-inflammatory agents can be provided for patients with significant pruritus. In severe cases, a short course of systemic glucocorticoid (e.g., prednisone) may be helpful. Topical glucocorticoids are not an effective therapy.

Staphylococcal skin infections more typically appear as pustules or furuncles as opposed to palpable purpura as in this patient. Therefore, antistaphylococcal antibiotic treatment would not be appropriate.

A leukocytoclastic vasculitis may be present with active hepatitis B and C infections. However, hepatitis A is self-limited, does not have a chronic form, and is not associated with a cutaneous vasculitis.

KEY POINT

Cutaneous small-vessel vasculitis, often presenting as palpable purpura on dependent areas, has an unknown cause in upward of 60% of patients. Treatment is often supportive.

Bibliography

Chen KR, Carlson JA. Clinical approach to cutaneous vasculitis. Am J Clin Dermatol. 2008;9:71-92. [PMID: 18284262]

Item 87   Answer: D
Educational Objective: *Diagnose porphyria cutanea tarda*

This patient most likely has porphyria cutanea tarda (PCT). Dermatologic findings are commonly seen in systemic disease, and a number of skin conditions may be associated with chronic hepatitis C infection. There is a very strong association of PCT with chronic hepatitis C infection, although why this relationship occurs is not known. PCT is the most common of the porphyrias worldwide. PCT is caused by a deficiency in uroporphyrinogen decarboxylase, an enzyme in the heme biosynthesis pathway. PCT may be acquired (type 1) and familial (type 2); 80% are of the acquired type, and the enzymatic defect is limited to the liver. Whereas this type develops most often in mid-adult life, type 2 develops in younger patients and represents a decrease in enzymatic activity in all tissues. Both types of PCT often require susceptibility factors such as alcohol, hepatitis C or HIV infection, iron overload (e.g., hemochromatosis), or estrogen use for clinical evidence of PCT to occur. Sunlight activates the large amounts of uroporphyrinogen that are deposited in the skin, leading to photosensitization and tissue damage. The result is a variety of cutaneous findings, which include blisters, erosions, hyperpigmentation, hypertrichosis, and sclerodermoid plaques. Involvement of the liver usually is seen with modest elevations of the hepatic transaminases. The diagnosis should be suspected in at-risk patients with consistent skin findings and with reddish-to-brown urine in natural light (and pink to red with fluorescence). Measurement of urinary porphyrins confirms the diagnosis. Treatment is by sunlight avoidance, phlebotomy, or hydroxychloroquine (which mobilizes accumulated porphyrins), and treatment of hepatitis C.

Lichen planus is a mucocutaneous disorder of unclear etiology that also appears to have an association with hepatitis C, although it may also be found as an isolated disorder or in association with autoimmune disorders and some medications. The skin findings are a generalized rash that is characteristically polygonal, pruritic, papular, planar, purple, and with plaques (the six Ps). This patient's skin findings are not consistent with this diagnosis.

Cryoglobulinemia, in which temperature-dependent circulating immune complexes are deposited in small- to medium-sized blood vessels, is also associated with hepatitis C infection. The most common clinical manifestations include cutaneous palpable purpura, which often involves the lower legs, may come in "crops," and can leave areas of hyperpigmentation after resolution. Cryoglobulins may also involve the kidney (causing glomerulonephritis) and other organ systems (e.g., the central nervous system). This patient's clinical presentation is not consistent with cryoglobulinemia.

Erythema nodosum causes tender, reddish, palpable inflammatory nodules that typically occur on the anterior lower legs. It is a hypersensitivity immune reaction to infection or systemic inflammation and may be seen with hepatitis C. However, it is a nonspecific finding that may occur in a wide range of systemic diseases or with different medications. This patient's rash is not consistent with this diagnosis.

KEY POINT
PCT is the most common porphyria. Skin manifestations are varied and include blisters, erosions, hyperpigmentation, and hypertrichosis.

Bibliography
Kapoor R, Johnson RA. Images in clinical medicine. Porphyria cutanea tarda and hypertrichosis. N Engl J Med. 2013;369:1356. [PMID: 24088095]

Item 88   Answer: A
Educational Objective: *Recognize the association of herpes simplex virus infection and erythema multiforme.*

This patient has erythema multiforme (EM), which is an acute, often recurrent mucocutaneous eruption that usually follows an acute infection, most frequently recurrent herpes simplex virus (HSV) infection. It may also be idiopathic or drug related. Most patients are between 20 and 40 years of age. Lesions range in size from several millimeters to several centimeters and consist of erythematous plaques with concentric rings of color. The dusky center may become necrotic and can form a discrete blister or eschar. Few to hundreds of lesions develop within several days and are most commonly located on the extensor surfaces of the extremities, particularly the hands and feet. Lesions occur less frequently on the face, trunk, and thighs. Mucosal lesions are present in up to 70% of patients and involve the cutaneous and mucosal lips, gingival sulcus, and the sides of the tongue. Mucosal lesions consist of painful erosions or, less commonly, intact bullae. The conjunctival, nasal, and genital mucosal surfaces can also be affected. Patients may have low-grade fever during an EM outbreak. Lesions usually last 1 to 2 weeks before healing; however, hyperpigmentation may persist. Recurrences are common, particularly in HSV-associated infection. Treatment of EM is primarily symptomatic. Systemic corticosteroids may provide symptomatic improvement but may be associated with complications. Antiviral therapy does not shorten the EM outbreak in HSV-associated infection, but continuous prophylactic antiviral therapy may help prevent further episodes. Treatment for bacterial infection-associated EM is appropriate for management of the specific active infection; however, there are no studies that demonstrate that treatment impacts the duration of the EM lesions. Antibiotic therapy is based on identification of an infectious cause. If EM is thought to be due to a new drug, the drug should be discontinued.

EM is not caused by streptococcal infection but may be triggered by the antibiotics used to treat this or other bacterial infections. Parvovirus B19 and varicella zoster virus are rarely associated with EM.

KEY POINT
Erythema multiforme is an acute dermatosis of the skin and mucosae that can be triggered by infections, most commonly herpes simplex virus.

Bibliography
Usatine RP, Sandy N. Dermatologic emergencies. Am Fam Physician. 2010;82:773-80. [PMID: 20879700]

Item 89   Answer: A
Educational Objective: *Diagnose cellulitis.*

This patient has cellulitis. Cellulitis is a rapidly spreading, deep, bacterial skin infection involving the dermis and subcutaneous tissues characterized by a well-demarcated area of warmth, swelling, tenderness, and erythema that may be accompanied by lymphatic streaking. Fever, although common, is not uniformly present. Patients with severe disease may have associated systemic toxicity. The diagnosis is usually clinical because superficial skin cultures are typically nondiagnostic, and blood culture results are not commonly positive except in severe cases.

Cellulitis may occur at the site of any break in the skin, although it is frequently associated with existing dermatologic conditions, such as eczema, tinea pedis, or chronic skin ulcers, and conditions leading to chronic lymphedema, such as mastectomy and lymph node dissections or saphenous vein grafts used in bypass surgery. The most common pathogens are *Staphylococcus aureus* and the β-hemolytic streptococci, especially group A β-hemolytic streptococci (GABHS). Whereas GABHS is most often associated with nonpurulent cellulitis, *S. aureus* may cause concomitant abscesses, furuncles, carbuncles, and bullous impetigo.

This patient has nonpurulent cellulitis, or cellulitis without purulent drainage or exudate, most likely caused by β-hemolytic streptococci; empiric outpatient treatment with a β-lactam agent such as cephalexin or dicloxacillin is recommended. Because purulent cellulitis is more likely to be caused by *S. aureus*, and possibly methicillin-resistant *S. aureus*, empiric outpatient treatment with agents potentially effective against many community-acquired strains, which may include trimethoprim–sulfamethoxazole, a tetracycline (e.g., doxycycline), clindamycin, and linezolid.

Impetigo is a superficial skin infection characterized by a yellowish, crusted surface that may be caused by staphylococci or streptococci. If *S. aureus* is the cause, secretion of exfoliative toxin may result in superficial blister formation, and systemic spread of the same toxins causes staphylococcal scalded skin syndrome. This patient's skin infection is not superficial and his systemic features are not consistent with a diagnosis of impetigo.

Contact dermatitis can also present with swelling, erythema, and warmth, but it is almost always accompanied by pruritus, which helps distinguish this condition from cellulitis, as in this patient; however, areas of contact and other types of dermatitis can become secondarily infected.

Stasis dermatitis can also look similar to cellulitis when it is inflammatory and is often confused with an infectious process. However, stasis dermatitis is almost always bilateral and usually not tender.

KEY POINT

Cellulitis is a rapidly spreading, deep, subcutaneous-based infection characterized by a well-demarcated area of warmth, swelling, tenderness, and erythema that may be accompanied by lymphatic streaking and fever and chills.

Bibliography
Gunderson CG. Cellulitis: definition, etiology, and clinical features. Am J Med. 2011;124:1113-22. [PMID: 22014791]

Item 90   Answer: A
Educational Objective: *Treat chronic venous insufficiency.*

This patient has chronic venous insufficiency, and the best initial management is knee-high compression stockings that provide pressure of 20 to 40 mm Hg of external compression. Chronic venous insufficiency results from persistent venous hypertension caused by venous incompetence or occlusion, commonly seen in older or overweight people or those with previous conditions (thrombophlebitis, trauma) in which the lower extremity venous system may have been damaged. Manifestations of chronic venous insufficiency include edema, skin hyperpigmentation, stasis dermatitis, varicose veins, cellulitis, and ulceration. The diagnosis is usually made based on history and examination; biopsy is usually avoided because it may result in a nonhealing ulcer. Medications should be reviewed because certain drugs (e.g., dihydropyridine calcium channel blockers) can exacerbate dependent edema. The goal of therapy is to reduce venous

hypertension, which is accomplished with leg elevation and compression therapy.

Antibiotics, topical or oral, are used when there is evidence of secondary infection. Because venous insufficiency causes lower extremity erythema, it is frequently confused with infection. However, cellulitis tends to be unilateral and associated with pain and possibly systemic symptoms. This patient's normal vital signs, absence of fever and pain, and absence of acute change associated with cutaneous erythema and warmth do not support the presence of an infection.

Because venous insufficiency impedes drainage of fluid to drain from dependent areas, diuretics are typically not effective in significantly reducing edema because they are unable to selectively remove fluid from the extremities. They may be helpful in patients with volume overload, although this is absent in this patient.

Patch testing is done to evaluate for allergic contact dermatitis, which is a potential complication from a disrupted skin barrier and use of multiple topical medications. Contact dermatitis may be difficult to distinguish from cellulitis because symptoms typically include redness, pruritus, and vesicles or bullae.

KEY POINT

The best initial management for chronic venous insufficiency is leg elevation and compression stockings.

Bibliography
Wolinsky CD, Waldorf H. Chronic venous disease. Med Clin North Am. 2009;93: 1333-46. [PMID: 19932334]

Item 91   Answer: B
Educational Objective: *Diagnose neuropathic ulcers.*

This patient has a neuropathic ulcer. Neuropathic ulcers develop in skin with decreased or absent sensation and are most commonly found in areas of trauma or friction, particularly on the feet under the metatarsal heads. Neuropathic ulcers are painless. They are often surrounded by a thick, macerated rim of hyperkeratosis. The ulcer may extend under the rim, so debridement to determine the full extent of the ulcer is necessary early in the management of the ulcer. Treatment of neuropathic ulcers is challenging and, in addition to debridement, requires offloading of any contributory pressure through use of footwear or casting. Infections should be treated aggressively, watching for any evidence of associated osteomyelitis.

Arterial ulcers arise in the setting of severe peripheral vascular disease. They are usually painful, well-demarcated ulcers, which may arise on any part of the limb but frequently overlie bony prominences. There may be other evidence of arterial insufficiency, including absent peripheral pulses, cool skin, and pallor.

Palpable purpura is the clinical hallmark of small vessel vasculitis. Skin ulcers more commonly result from vasculitis involving larger arteries. They are often painful, irregularly shaped, punched-out appearing ulcers. There may be surrounding erythema or purpura, but they lack the hyperkeratosis found in neuropathic ulcers.

Venous stasis ulcers, which may be associated with varicose veins, more commonly arise on the medial legs around the malleolus. The surrounding skin may be hyperpigmented and sclerotic, a condition known as lipodermatosclerosis.

Neuropathic ulcers are most commonly found in areas of trauma or friction, particularly on the feet under the metatarsal heads, and are commonly surrounded by a thick, macerated rim of hyperkeratosis.

Bibliography

Boulton AJ. What you can't feel can hurt you. J Vasc Surg. 2010;52(3 suppl):28S-30S. [PMID: 20804930]

Item 92   Answer: A

Educational Objective: *Manage a patient with acute urticaria.*

This patient is presenting with acute urticaria, most likely as a result of her levofloxacin exposure, and should be treated initially with an H_1-blocking nonsedating antihistamine (e.g., cetirizine), which will stop the likely allergic cause of her urticaria. A short course of systemic glucocorticoids may also be helpful for patients with widespread or highly symptomatic involvement. In persistent cases, an H_2-blocking antihistamine is sometimes added, although the effectiveness of doing so has not been established.

Although she has widespread cutaneous involvement with multiple hives, the patient lacks concerning features such as wheezing; stridor; and lip, tongue, or eyelid swelling, and she is breathing comfortably and able to clear secretions. If she did exhibit dyspnea, difficulty clearing her secretions, had lip or tongue swelling, or had hemodynamic instability, administration of epinephrine would be indicated.

Indomethacin is a nonsteroidal antiinflammatory drug and can cause mast cell degranulation and worsen urticaria. It has no role in the management of this condition.

Topical corticosteroids can occasionally provide additional relief for symptomatic urticarial lesions, but given this patient's widespread urticarial eruption, it would be impractical and inappropriate to treat with topical therapy alone.

Combination H_1 antihistamines are the first-line therapy for patients with acute urticaria.

Bibliography

Limsuwan T, Demoly P. Acute symptoms of drug hypersensitivity (urticaria, angioedema, anaphylaxis, anaphylactic shock). Med Clin North Am. 2010;94:691-710. [PMID: 20609858]

Item 93   Answer: A

Educational Objective: *Diagnose actinic keratoses.*

This patient has actinic keratoses (AKs), which are common erythematous scaly macules that typically occur on sun-exposed areas of older persons with fair skin. They are premalignant lesions, and approximately 1% to 5% will develop into squamous cell carcinomas over time. Multiple treatment options are available, including cryotherapy, topical imiquimod, topical 5-fluorouracil, and photodynamic therapy.

AKs are often easier to palpate than to identify visually because of the predominance of the scale. Biopsy is indicated for lesions that are particularly scaly and substantive or those that do not respond readily to treatment.

In contrast, basal cell carcinomas (BCCs) most commonly appear as pearly telangiectatic papules. because the most important risk factors for the development of BCCs are fair skin and sun exposure (the same risk factors as for AKs), the two often occur in the same area.

Porphyria cutanea tarda is a blistering disorder caused by a deficiency of the enzyme uroporphyrinogen decarboxylase; both familial and acquired forms exist. Patients with porphyria cutanea tarda develop bullae on the dorsal hands after sun exposure; these eventually rupture, forming erosions, dyspigmentation, and scarring. The involved areas are often tender.

Seborrheic keratoses are brown, scaly, waxy papules and plaques with a "stuck-on" appearance that occur in older persons. They lack the erythema typically seen with actinic keratoses. They are harmless but may occasionally resemble more worrisome lesions and thus warrant biopsy.

Solar lentigines are brown macules and patches that occur in elderly fair-skinned persons in areas of substantial sun damage. They are benign but are indicative of a region that is at risk for developing skin cancer because they are a marker for sun exposure.

AKs are premalignant, erythematous, scaly macules that occur on sun-exposed areas of older persons with fair skin and that may develop into squamous cell carcinomas over time.

Bibliography

Kim RH, Armstrong AW. Nonmelanoma skin cancer. Dermatol Clin. 2012;30:125-39. [PMID: 22117874]

Item 94   Answer: B

Educational Objective: *Diagnose erythema nodosum.*

This patient's skin lesions are characteristic of erythema nodosum, consisting of painful, erythematous nodules on the anterior surfaces of both legs that evolve into bruise-like lesions that resolve in several weeks. The nodules are more easily palpated than visualized. Erythema nodosum is the result of a hypersensitivity immune reaction that may be secondary to drugs (possibly the oral contraceptive that was recently started in this patient), infection (such as fungal or streptococcal), or systemic inflammation due to sarcoidosis, tuberculosis, lymphoma, or inflammatory bowel disease. At least 50% of cases are idiopathic. The condition usually is acute and self-limited, and treatment is supportive following treatment of any associated cause.

Erythema multiforme (EM) is an acute, often recurrent mucocutaneous eruption characterized by circular erythematous plaques with a raised, darker central circle ("target lesions"). EM usually follows an acute infection, most often recurrent herpes simplex virus or mycoplasma pneumoniae infection. It may also be drug related or idiopathic. Lesions generally are located on the extremities, palms, and soles, and painful oral mucosal erosions and bullae are common. However, this patient's skin lesions are not consistent with EM.

Psoriasis consists of well-demarcated, symmetrically distributed, erythematous plaques affecting extensor surfaces with an overlying silvery scale that are usually nontender. This patient's skin findings are painful, erythematous, nodular, and without plaque formation or scaling, which do not support this diagnosis.

Pyoderma gangrenosum is an ulcerative skin condition typically associated with an underlying systemic condition, such as inflammatory bowel disease, rheumatoid arthritis, spondyloarthritis, or a hematologic disease or malignancy (most commonly acute myelogenous leukemia). Lesions often are multiple and tend to appear on the lower extremities. They begin as tender papules, pustules, or vesicles that spontaneously ulcerate and progress to painful ulcers with a purulent base and undermined, ragged, violaceous borders. However, this patient's skin lesions are not ulcerative and she has no evidence of an underlying inflammatory condition, making this diagnosis unlikely.

KEY POINT

The skin lesions of erythema nodosum consist of painful, erythematous nodules on the anterior surfaces of both legs.

Bibliography

Gilchrist H, Patterson JW. Erythema nodosum and erythema induratum (nodular vasculitis): diagnosis and management. Dermatol Ther. 2010;23:320-7. PMID: 20666819

Item 95   Answer: C

Educational Objective: *Diagnose benign seborrheic keratoses.*

This patient has multiple seborrheic keratoses. Seborrheic keratoses range in color from flesh colored to yellow or tan, and they may be irregularly pigmented. These growths are extremely common, developing around age 30 years, and increase with age; they can number from a few to hundreds on a given person. They can be smooth but are often waxy or verrucous in texture, and on the extremities, they may be thin and flaky. They are most frequently located on the torso, particularly on the back, between the breasts, and on the face and scalp. They are benign and do not have a premalignant potential, but they must be distinguished from atypical nevi and from malignant melanoma. Their treatment is usually considered cosmetic unless they become inflamed, itch, or are otherwise irritated. They are not usually associated with any other medical conditions, although rarely the rapid development of multiple seborrheic keratoses, the sign of Leser-Trélat, has been associated with malignancy. However, this sign is very nonspecific and it is rarely diagnosed.

Atypical nevi appear to benign nevi but have atypical features. They are also frequently located on the torso, but they are usually macular (flat) and lack the verrucous texture of most seborrheic keratoses.

Melanomas may sometimes be difficult to distinguish clinically from seborrheic keratoses. They are usually darkly pigmented and have irregular borders; the borders of seborrheic keratoses are usually well demarcated. Any darkly pigmented or black lesion with equivocal characteristics should be evaluated for melanoma; a diagnostic biopsy may be indicated in some cases.

Solar lentigines ("age" or "liver" spots) are uniform, brown, scaly, regularly shaped macules and patches that occur in sun-exposed areas that lack the features characteristic of melanoma; although benign, they are indicative of areas of high cumulative sun exposure and thus at risk for the development of cancers and precancers.

This patient has seborrheic keratoses, which are brown, scaly, waxy papules and plaques that commonly occur in older persons. They frequently have a "stuck-on" appearance and often have verrucous (warty) features as well. Seborrheic keratoses typically exhibit horn cysts (epidermal cysts filled with keratin) on the surface that can best be visualized with a magnifying lens. Although benign, they may occasionally resemble melanoma because of the presence of asym-

metry, an irregular border, irregular pigmentation, large size, and progressive enlargement; thus, the "ABCDE" warning signs that apply to melanocytic lesions do not apply to them. Atypical lesions are often biopsied to rule out malignancy. There appears to be a hereditary component to the development of seborrheic keratoses because patients with large numbers of them often have family members with similar findings. No treatment is required; irritated lesions may be removed with cryotherapy or electrodessication and curettage. The appearance of new lesions is common, particularly with advancing age.

Melanomas are malignant melanocytic lesions that typically have asymmetry, irregular borders, color variation, a large diameter, and evolution over time (ABCDEs); they tend to lack the scale and verrucous features often seen in seborrheic keratoses. Pigmented basal cell carcinomas may sometimes resemble waxy seborrheic keratoses, but the presence of telangiectasias and pearliness is a good diagnostic clue for the presence of basal cell carcinoma.

KEY POINT

Seborrheic keratoses are benign waxy to verrucous papules ranging in color from flesh colored to yellow or tan, and they may be irregularly pigmented.

Bibliography

Luba MC, Bangs SA, Mohler AM, Stulberg DL. Common benign skin tumors. Am Fam Physician. 2003;67:729-38. [PMID: 12613727]

Item 96   Answer: D

Educational Objective: *Diagnose toxic epidermal necrolysis (TEN).*

This patient has TEN. Stevens-Johnson syndrome (SJS) and TEN are severe, idiosyncratic reactions that lead to sloughing of the epidermis. The two syndromes are differentiated by the degree of epidermal detachment, with SJS defined as involvement of ≤10% of body surface area and TEN involving at least 30% of body surface area; intermediate degrees of body surface area involvement are considered to be overlap syndromes (SJS/TEN). Both typically begins with a prodrome that may include fatigue, malaise, fever, sore throat, or a burning sensation in the eyes 1 to 3 days before skin lesions appear. Skin findings may be characterized by flat, purpuric, targetoid lesions that coalesce into patches, or there may be diffuse, tender erythema without identifiable individual lesions. The involved epidermis blisters and sloughs, leaving behind denuded dermis, and a positive Nikolsky sign (lateral pressure on nonblistered skin leads to denudation) is usually present. Skin pain is prominent. Two or more mucosal surfaces, such as the eyes, nasopharynx, mouth, and genitals, are involved in more than 80% of cases. SJS/TEN is most commonly caused by medications; antiepileptic agents, nonsteroidal anti-inflammatory drugs, antibiotics, pantoprazole, sertraline, tramadol, and allopurinol are the most frequently implicated drugs. The reaction most commonly occurs within 4 and 28 days of exposure. The diagnosis is often made clinically, but a biopsy can be confirmatory. Treatment requires discontinuation of the suspected causative medication and is otherwise supportive.

Erythema multiforme (EM) is an acute, often recurrent mucocutaneous eruption that usually follows an acute infection, most frequently recurrent herpes simplex virus infection, but it may also be drug related or idiopathic. Lesions range in size from several millimeters to several centimeters and consist of erythematous plaques with concentric rings of color. On biopsy, EM lesions appear similar to those found in SJS/TEN, suggesting that it may be may be on a continuum with these more severe conditions. However, EM does not cause skin sloughing, eosinophilia, or aminotransferase levels as seen in this patient.

Bullous pemphigoid is a chronic, vesiculobullous eruption that predominantly involves nonmucosal surfaces. It has been associated with several autoimmune diseases and is characterized by antibodies directed to the epidermal basement membrane that lead to development of subepidermal vesicles and blisters that are tense and do not rupture easily unlike the easily ruptured blisters and skin sloughing seen in this patient.

Staphylococcal scalded skin syndrome (SSSS) is most common in children, but adults with underlying immunosuppression or acute kidney injury may be affected. Clinical features that are characteristic of SSSS include perioral crusting and fissuring and early involvement of the intertriginous areas. Skin detachment and mucosal involvement do not occur.

KEY POINT

TEN is a potentially lethal drug eruption with acute onset of widespread skin and mucosal necrosis.

Bibliography

Bruno TF, Grewal P. Erythroderma: a dermatologic emergency. CJEM. 2009;11:244-6. [PMID: 19523275]

Item 97   Answer: C
Educational Objective: *Manage ophthalmic herpes zoster infection.*

This patient has herpes zoster ophthalmicus (shingles), and referral to an ophthalmologist and empiric treatment with an antiviral agent (acyclovir, valacyclovir, or famciclovir) are imperative. Ophthalmic zoster, if not treated promptly, can lead to blindness. Shingles, which is reactivation of varicella-zoster virus, can occur any time after the primary varicella infection. It often begins with a prodrome of intense pain, and in more than 90% of patients, it is associated with pruritus, tingling, tenderness, or hyperesthesia. The cutaneous eruption typically involves a single dermatome and rarely crosses the midline. In a recent, prospective multicenter study, eye redness and rash in the supratrochlear nerve distribution had a statistically significant association with clinically relevant eye disease. One hundred percent of patients who developed moderate to severe eye disease presented with a red eye. Hutchinson sign (zoster eruption on the tip of the nose) was not predictive of clinically relevant eye disease. Clinical diagnosis is based on both history and physical examination. Testing by direct fluorescent-antibody testing or by polymerase chain reaction can confirm the diagnosis; however, decisions regarding antiviral therapy are often based on the history and physical examination rather than reliance on laboratory testing.

Applying warm compresses or obtaining bacterial culture and starting antibiotics would not be appropriate treatment for a viral infection, and delaying treatment could result in blindness. Ophthalmic corticosteroids are frequently administered as an adjunctive agent to antiviral therapy in the treatment of ophthalmic zoster but are never used as a single agent and should be administered by a specialist.

KEY POINT

Ophthalmic herpes zoster infection should be considered a medical emergency that requires prompt referral to an ophthalmologist and initiation of an antiviral agent.

Bibliography

Adam RS, Vale N, Bona MD, et al. Triaging herpes zoster ophthalmicus patients in the emergency department: do all patients require referral? Acad Emerg Med. 2010;17:1183-8. [PMID: 21175516]

Item 98   Answer: B
Educational Objective: *Diagnose folliculitis.*

The patient has folliculitis, which is most commonly caused by bacteria and tends to center around hair follicles. Culture of a pustule can confirm the diagnosis but is often not necessary. Clinical diagnosis is sufficient, and further testing should be pursued if empiric treatment does not cause improvement. The most common cause is *Staphylococcus aureus*. Treatment is usually with topical antibiotics such as clindamycin or topical agents such as benzoyl peroxide. Systemic oral antibiotics such as doxycycline can be used in recalcitrant or recurrent cases.

Although bacterial folliculitis is the most common type, other types include *Malassezia* folliculitis, *Candida* folliculitis, eosinophilic folliculitis, and *Pseudomonas* folliculitis.

Although acne could present as erythematous papules and pustules in this location, close clinical examination can help distinguish it from folliculitis by looking for the primary lesion of acne, a comedone. Culturing a pustule can also help to distinguish these two entities. A pustule of acne is usually sterile.

Miliaria is often referred to as "prickly heat" or "heat rash" and appears as erythematous papules that occur after occlusion of sweat ducts. Pustules are not present.

Rosacea appears as papules and pustules but usually only affects the central face.

KEY POINT

Bacterial folliculitis is an eruption of papules and pustules most commonly caused by *S. aureus* that centers around hair follicles.

Bibliography

Stevens DL, Eron LL. Cellulitis and soft-tissue infections. Ann Intern Med. 2009;150:ITC11. [PMID: 19124814].

Section 5

Hematology

Questions

Item 1 [Advanced]

A 53-year-old woman is evaluated for anemia. She has taken low-dose methotrexate for 5 months for treatment of rheumatoid arthritis. Her only source of obvious bleeding is menstrual blood loss. She continues to have menses every 28 days, with flow lasting 5 days and requiring three to four pad changes daily.

Laboratory studies:

	Before Methotrexate Therapy	Current Values
Hemoglobin	10.8 g/dL (108 g/L)	9.7 g/dL (97 g/L)
Leukocyte count	6200/µL (6.2×10⁹/L)	6750/µL (6.75×10⁹/L)
Platelet count	372,000/µL (372×10⁹/L)	382,000/µL (382×10⁹/L)
Reticulocyte count	0.7% of erythrocytes	0.8% of erythrocytes
Mean corpuscular volume	92 fL	93 fL
Iron	49 µg/dL (8.8 µmol/L)	15 µg/dL (2.7 µmol/L)
Iron-binding capacity, total	394 µg/dL (70.6 µmol/L)	317 µg/dL (56.8 µmol/L)
Ferritin	36 ng/mL (36 µg/L)	29 ng/mL (29 µg/L)

Which of the following is the most likely cause of this patient's anemia?

(A) Anemia of inflammation alone
(B) Anemia of inflammation plus iron deficiency
(C) Iron deficiency alone
(D) Methotrexate-induced anemia

Item 2 [Basic]

A 64-year-old man is evaluated for decreased exercise tolerance and dyspnea on exertion for 3 weeks. He underwent gastric bypass surgery 6 months ago and has lost 27 kg (60 lb).

On physical examination, temperature is 36.7°C (98.0°F), blood pressure is 137/78 mm Hg, pulse rate is 104/min, and respiration rate is 17/min. Body mass index is 32. The patient has pale conjunctivae. Cardiopulmonary and neurologic examination findings are normal.

Results of initial laboratory studies show a hemoglobin level of 7.4 g/dL (74 g/L), a mean corpuscular volume of 104 fL, a serum cobalamin (vitamin B$_{12}$) level in the low-normal range, and a normal red blood cell folate level. An electrocardiogram is normal.

Which of the following is the most appropriate next diagnostic test?

(A) Bone marrow aspiration and biopsy
(B) Hemoglobin electrophoresis
(C) Serum homocysteine and methylmalonic acid measurement
(D) Serum iron studies

Item 3 [Advanced]

A 19-year-old man undergoes follow-up evaluation for anemia. The anemia was identified when he attempted to donate blood. He is otherwise healthy and is asymptomatic. Medical and family histories are noncontributory. He takes no medications

On physical examination, temperature is normal, blood pressure is 117/78 mm Hg, pulse rate is 88/min, and respiration rate is 17/min. Body mass index is 19. The patient has pale conjunctivae. The remainder of the examination is unremarkable.

Laboratory studies:

Hemoglobin	11.6 g/dL (116 g/L)
Mean corpuscular volume	60 fL
Leukocyte count	5400/µL (5.4×10⁹/L)
Platelet count	179,000/µL (179×10⁹/L)
Red blood cell distribution width	Normal
Reticulocyte count	2.3% of erythrocytes
Ferritin	58 ng/mL (58 µg/L)

Hemoglobin electrophoresis is normal. The peripheral blood smear shows target cells.

Which of the following is the most likely diagnosis?

(A) Hereditary spherocytosis
(B) Iron deficiency
(C) Sideroblastic anemia
(D) α-Thalassemia trait

Item 4 [Basic]

A 22-year-old woman is evaluated for a 6-month history of decreased exercise tolerance, particularly with activities such as running. She is otherwise healthy and eats a normal diet. Medical history is unremarkable. She notes no menstrual abnormalities and takes no medications.

On physical examination, temperature is 36.7°C (98.0°F), blood pressure is 110/72 mm Hg, pulse rate is 88/min, and respiration rate is 16/min. Body mass index is 22. The patient has pale conjunctivae. Examination of the heart and lungs is normal. There is no splenomegaly. The neurologic examination is normal.

Laboratory studies:

Hemoglobin	7.9 g/dL (79 g/L)
Leukocyte count	5600/µL (5.6 × 10⁹/L)
Mean corpuscular volume	62 fL
Platelet count	625,000/µL (625 × 10⁹/L)
Red blood cell distribution width	22% (normal range: 14.6-16.5%)

A peripheral blood smear is notable for microcytic, hypochromic erythrocytes with marked anisopoikilocytosis.

Which of the following is the most appropriate treatment for this patient?

(A) Erythropoietin

(B) Erythrocyte transfusion

(C) Oral ferrous sulfate

(D) Parenteral (intramuscular or intravenous) iron

Item 5 [Advanced]

A 57-year-old woman with chronic lymphocytic leukemia (CLL) is evaluated in the emergency department because of a 2-week history of increasing malaise, decreased exercise tolerance, and darkened urine. Her CLL was last treated 2 months ago with fludarabine, cyclophosphamide, and rituximab.

On physical examination, the patient has scleral icterus. Temperature is 37.3°C (99.2°F), blood pressure is 142/82 mm Hg, pulse rate is 117/min, and respiration rate is 18/min. Mild lymphadenopathy is palpated in the cervical area. Cardiopulmonary examination discloses a regular tachycardia and crackles at the bases of both lungs. Splenomegaly is found on abdominal examination.

Laboratory studies:

Hemoglobin	6.9 g/dL (69 g/L)
Leukocyte count	6500/µL (6.5 × 10⁹/L)
Platelet count	250,000/µL (250 × 10⁹/L)
Reticulocyte count	10% of erythrocytes
Total bilirubin	6.3 mg/dL (107.7 µmol/L)
Direct bilirubin	0.5 mg/dL (8.6 µmol/L)
Lactate dehydrogenase	357 U/L
Direct antiglobulin (Coombs) test	Positive for IgG

A peripheral blood smear reveals spherocytosis but is otherwise unremarkable.

Which of the following is the most likely diagnosis?

(A) α-Thalassemia

(B) Autoimmune hemolytic anemia

(C) Hereditary spherocytosis

(D) Microangiopathic hemolytic anemia

Item 6 [Basic]

A 77-year-old woman is evaluated for anemia that has developed over the past year. She is asymptomatic and is active and able to engage in her usual activities without shortness of breath or excessive fatigue. Medical history is significant for hypertension and hyperlipidemia for which she takes lisinopril and atorvastatin.

On physical examination, temperature is 36.7°C (98.0°F), blood pressure is 137/78 mm Hg, pulse rate is 88/min, and respiration rate is 17/min. Body mass index is 19. Cardiac examination reveals an S₄. The remainder of the examination is normal.

Laboratory studies:

Hemoglobin	11.4 g/dL (114 g/L)
Leukocyte count	6200/µL (6.2 × 10⁹/L) with a normal differential
Platelet count	225,000/µL (225 × 10⁹/L)
Mean corpuscular volume	90 fL
Reticulocyte count	0.8% of erythrocytes
Ferritin	187 ng/mL (187 µg/L)
Iron	78 µg/dL (14 µmol/L)
Iron-binding capacity, total	356 µg/dL (64 µmol/L)
Creatinine	1.5 mg/dL (132 µmol/L)

The peripheral blood smear is compatible with a normochromic, normocytic anemia.

Which of the following is the most likely cause of this patient's anemia?

(A) Advanced age

(B) Anemia of inflammation

(C) Iron deficiency

(D) Kidney disease

Item 7 [Advanced]

A 32-year-old man is hospitalized because of a 2-day history of acute pain in his back, chest, and extremities, along with nausea and vomiting. The pain has not responded to oral hydromorphone therapy. The patient has sickle cell disease and has been hospitalized twice in the past year for similar problems.

On physical examination, temperature is 38.7°C (101.7°F), blood pressure is 130/80 mm Hg, pulse rate is 104/min, and respiration rate is 20/min. Oxygen saturation (ambient air) is 92%. Cardiac examination reveals an S₄. Wheezes are heard on auscultation of the lungs. The abdomen is nontender.

Laboratory studies are significant for normal kidney function and no evidence of proteinuria. A chest radiograph shows an infiltrate in the right upper lobe of the lung.

Treatment is started with intravenous 0.9% (normal) saline, patient-controlled morphine, ceftriaxone, azithromycin, and an inhaled β-agonist. Erythrocyte transfusion is also begun. Over the next 3 days, the patient's symptoms resolve.

Which of the following is the most appropriate long-term management of this patient's sickle cell disease?

(A) Captopril

(B) Hydroxyurea

(C) Prophylactic penicillin

(D) Recombinant erythropoietin

Item 8 [Basic]

A 17-year-old girl is evaluated in the emergency department for progressive fatigue, shortness of breath, and lethargy over the past week. The patient had mild flu-like symptoms several weeks ago with fever and joint pains, but these symptoms have improved. Medical history is significant for sickle cell disease (Hb SS). She has had several pain crises but no acute chest syndrome or stroke. Her only medication is folic acid daily.

On physical examination, temperature is 35.7°C (96.4°F), blood pressure is 96/55 mm Hg, pulse rate is 114/min, and respiration rate is 22/min. Other than tachycardia, the cardiopulmonary examination is normal. There is no lymphadenopathy or splenomegaly and no rash.

Results of laboratory studies show a hemoglobin level of 5.2 g/dL (52 g/L) (compared with 8.2 g/dL [82 g/L] 3 months ago) and a reticulocyte count of 0.1% of erythrocytes.

A chest radiograph is normal.

Which of the following is the most likely diagnosis?

(A) Aplastic crisis
(B) Hyperhemolytic crisis
(C) Megaloblastic crisis
(D) Splenic sequestration crisis

Item 9 [Basic]

A 19-year-old man is admitted to the hospital because of a sickle cell pain crisis. Over the next 48 hours, he develops worsening dyspnea, chest pain, and fever.

On physical examination, temperature is 38.0°C (100.4°F), blood pressure is 123/65 mm Hg, pulse rate is 118/min, and respiration rate is 22/min and labored. Oxygen saturation is 86% with the patient breathing oxygen, 6 L/min by nasal cannula. There is no jugular venous distention. Cardiopulmonary examination discloses decreased bilateral breath sounds at the lung bases, but no crackles or S_3. There is no peripheral edema.

Results of laboratory studies show a hemoglobin level of 4.9 g/dL (49 g/L), a reticulocyte count of 4.4% of erythrocytes, and a leukocyte count of 6900/µL (6.9 × 10⁹/L) with a normal differential.

Chest radiograph shows multilobar infiltrates that were not present on the admission chest radiograph.

Broad-spectrum antibiotics are begun, and incentive spirometry is initiated.

Which of the following is the most appropriate additional treatment?

(A) Erythrocyte transfusion
(B) Fluid bolus
(C) Furosemide
(D) Hydroxyurea

Item 10 [Advanced]

A 38-year-old woman is evaluated in the emergency department because of severe diffuse pain. The patient has sickle cell disease. She is treated with hydration and opioid medication for an acute pain crisis. Her pain is significantly relieved, and she is subsequently admitted to the hospital.

Three days after admission, she continues to have significant pain in her right hip that is only moderately relieved with pain medication. On physical examination, temperature is 37.1°C (98.8°F), blood pressure is 128/75 mm Hg, pulse rate is 85/min and respiration rate is 12/min. Cardiopulmonary and abdominal examinations are unre-

markable. There is tenderness to palpation over the right hip and marked pain on passive or active range of motion of the hip. She is unable to bear weight on her right side.

Results of laboratory studies are significant for a hemoglobin level of 9.7 g/dL (97 g/L) and a leukocyte count of 5500/µL (5.5 × 10⁹/L) with a normal differential.

Which of the following is the most likely cause of this patient's persistent hip pain?

(A) Avascular necrosis
(B) Osteoarthritis
(C) Osteomyelitis
(D) Rheumatoid arthritis

Item 11 [Basic]

A 30-year-old woman is evaluated for a 2-week history of easy bruising and epistaxis. She had previously been well and takes no medications or supplements.

On physical examination, vital signs are normal. There are numerous petechiae, particularly on the lower extremities, and several ecchymoses on her arms and legs. Crusted blood is visible in both nares. There is no lymphadenopathy or liver or spleen enlargement. The remainder of the examination is normal.

Laboratory studies:

Hemoglobin	12.5 g/dL (125 g/L)
Leukocyte count	5700/µL (5.7 ×10⁹/L)
Platelet count	10,000/µL (10 ×10⁹/L)
Comprehensive metabolic panel	Normal

The peripheral blood smear shows a paucity of platelets and several large platelets.

Which of the following is the most likely diagnosis?

(A) Henoch-Schönlein purpura
(B) Immune thrombocytopenic purpura
(C) Thrombotic thrombocytopenic purpura
(D) Von Willebrand disease

Item 12 [Basic]

A 65-year-old man with is evaluated in the emergency department after developing a swollen and painful left leg. Left iliofemoral deep venous thrombosis is diagnosed, and the patient is hospitalized. Unfractionated heparin and warfarin are begun. He has no other medical problems and was taking no medications prior to admission.

The platelet count on the first hospital day is 175,000/µL (175 × 10⁹/L) but drops to 80,000/µL (80 × 10⁹/L) on hospital day 5.

On physical examination on hospital day 5, vital signs are normal. The left leg is swollen and painful but improved since the day of admission. The remainder of the examination is normal.

Other than thrombocytopenia, the complete blood count and comprehensive metabolic panel are normal. The activated partial thromboplastin time is in the therapeutic range, and the international normalized ratio is 1.5. With the exception of decreased platelet numbers, the peripheral blood smear is normal.

This patient is at greatest risk for which of the following events?

(A) Anaphylaxis
(B) Arterial thrombosis
(C) Bleeding
(D) Additional venous thrombosis

Item 13 [Advanced]

A 24-year-old woman is evaluated in the emergency department for the recent onset of headache and fever. Symptoms began 48 hours ago and have been steadily progressive. Nausea, vomiting, and epigastric pain developed 6 hours ago. The patient was previously well and takes no medications.

On physical examination, she appears restless and confused with dysarthric speech. Temperature is 38.1°C (100.5°F), blood pressure is 150/92 mm Hg, pulse rate is 110/min, and respiration rate is 22/min. Oxygen saturation is 95% (ambient air). There is no nuchal rigidity. Cardiopulmonary examination is normal. Abdominal examination discloses tenderness without guarding to palpation; bowel sounds are present.

Laboratory studies:

Hemoglobin	9.7 g/dL (97 g/L)
Mean corpuscular volume	102 fL
Reticulocyte count	6.6% of erythrocytes
Leukocyte count	6600/µL (6.6 × 10⁹/L)
Platelet count	5000/µL (5.0 × 10⁹/L)
Prothrombin time	12.1 s
Activated partial thromboplastin time	24.3 s
Haptoglobin	10 mg/dL (100 mg/L)
Lactate dehydrogenase	546 U/L
Bilirubin, total	1.1 mg/dL (19 µmol/L)
Creatinine	1.7 mg/dL (150 µmol/L)

A peripheral blood smear is shown (Plate 13).

Which of the following is the most likely diagnosis?

(A) Aplastic anemia
(B) Disseminated intravascular coagulation
(C) Thrombotic thrombocytopenic purpura
(D) Warm autoimmune hemolytic anemia with immune thrombocytopenic purpura

Item 14 [Advanced]

A 35-year-old woman is evaluated for thrombocytopenia. This finding was identified on a complete blood count obtained as part of an insurance application. The patient feels well and has no history of bleeding symptoms. Her medical history is unremarkable, and she takes no medications.

On physical examination, vital signs are normal. Examination of the skin discloses no petechiae or ecchymoses. The remainder of the examination is normal.

Hemoglobin is 13.5 g/dL (135 g/L), the leukocyte count is 8000/µL (8.0 × 10⁹/L) with a normal differential, and the platelet count is 12,000/µL (12×10⁹/L). A peripheral blood smear is shown (Plate 14).

Which of the following is the most appropriate management?

(A) Intravenous immune globulin
(B) Platelet transfusion
(C) Prednisone
(D) Repeat platelet count

Item 15 [Basic]

A 35-year-old woman undergoes evaluation following the incidental detection of thrombocytopenia. The patient has no evidence or history of bruising, nosebleeds, menorrhagia, or upper gastrointestinal or genitourinary bleeding and no family history of bleeding disorders. Medications are an oral contraceptive pill and occasional ibuprofen for menstrual discomfort.

On physical examination, vital signs are normal. Examination of the skin discloses no bruising or hematomas. Abdominal examination is normal, with no splenomegaly.

Laboratory studies:

Hematocrit	35%
Hemoglobin	12.9 g/dL (129 g/L)
Leukocyte count	6500/µL (6.5 × 10⁹/L)
Mean corpuscular volume	85 fL
Platelet count	55,000/µL (55 × 10⁹/L)

The peripheral blood smear shows large platelets, slightly decreased in number.

Which of the following is the most appropriate management?

(A) Initiate glucocorticoid therapy
(B) Perform antiplatelet antibody assay
(C) Perform bone marrow biopsy
(D) Repeat complete blood count in 1 week

Item 16 [Advanced]

A 58-year-old woman is evaluated for an elevated hemoglobin level detected during a routine health screening examination. She is asymptomatic except for the onset of daily headaches and fatigue beginning 3 months ago. Medical history is unremarkable, and she takes no medications.

On physical examination, temperature is normal, blood pressure is 140/85 mm Hg, pulse rate is 80/min, and respiration rate is 18/min. Oxygen saturation is 98% (ambient air). She has a ruddy complexion. There is no lymphadenopathy. Cardiopulmonary examination is normal. A spleen tip is palpable, and the liver is enlarged.

Laboratory studies:

Hemoglobin	16.8 g/dL (168 g/L)
Leukocyte count	15,800/µL (15.8 × 10⁹/L) with 70% polymorphonuclear cells, 10% bands, 3% metamyelocytes, 5% basophils, and 12% lymphocytes
Platelet count	800,000/µL (800 × 10⁹/L)
Comprehensive metabolic panel	Normal

Analysis for the *JAK2 V617F* mutation is positive.

Which of the following is the most appropriate initial treatment?

(A) Aspirin and phlebotomy
(B) Busulfan
(C) Chlorambucil
(D) Hydroxyurea
(E) Radioisotope phosphorus 32 (^{32}P)

Item 17 [Advanced]

A 40-year-old man is evaluated for progressive abdominal pain, early satiety, and a 6.8-kg (15-lb) weight loss over the past 4 months. Medical history is unremarkable, and he takes no medications.

On physical examination, vital signs are normal. The spleen is markedly enlarged, with the inferior border extending into the pelvic rim. The liver is also enlarged and measures 16 cm in total span. The remainder of the examination is unremarkable.

Laboratory studies:

Hemoglobin	8.3 mg/dL (83 g/L)
Leukocyte count	85,000/µL (85 × 10^9/L) with 60% polymorphonuclear cells, 15% bands, 5% metamyelocytes, 3% myelocytes, 1% promyelocytes, 5% basophils, and 11% lymphocytes
Platelet count	900,000/µL (900 × 10^9/L)

Fluorescence in situ hybridization (FISH) assay for (9;22) translocation is positive. The peripheral blood smear shows neutrophilia and left-shifted granulopoiesis without evidence of dysplasia.

Which of the following is the most likely diagnosis?

(A) Acute myeloid leukemia
(B) Chronic myeloid leukemia
(C) Myelodysplastic syndrome
(D) Leukemoid reaction

Item 18 [Basic]

A 19-year-old man is admitted to the hospital because of a 3-week history of nosebleeds, malaise, and fever. He recently had a viral syndrome, which resolved about 6 weeks ago. Medical history is otherwise unremarkable. He takes no medications and has no known allergies.

On physical examination, temperature is 38.6°C (101.6°F), blood pressure is 102/54 mm Hg, pulse rate is 114/min, and respiration rate is 12/min. Examination of the skin discloses petechiae and bruising of the lower extremities. There is no lymphadenopathy or splenomegaly.

Laboratory studies:

Hemoglobin	7.8 g/dL (78 g/L)
Leukocyte count	1000/µL (1 × 10^9/L) with 20% neutrophils and 80% lymphocytes
Platelet count	28,000/µL (28 × 10^9/L)
Reticulocyte count	0.2% of erythrocytes

Findings from a bone marrow biopsy are shown (Plate 15).

Which of the following is the most likely diagnosis?

(A) Acute myeloid leukemia
(B) Aplastic anemia
(C) Chronic lymphocytic leukemia
(D) Myelodysplasia

Item 19 [Basic]

A 70-year-old man is evaluated for a 1-year history of progressive fatigue and easy bruising. Medical history is significant for Hodgkin lymphoma, which was diagnosed 20 years ago and treated with combination chemotherapy plus radiation therapy. He has no other symptoms and takes no medications.

On physical examination, temperature is normal, blood pressure is 110/60 mm Hg, and pulse rate is 75/min. Conjunctival pallor is present. There are scattered petechiae on the mucus membranes but no other skin findings. The remainder of the examination is unremarkable.

Laboratory studies:

Hemoglobin	7 g/dL (70 g/L)
Leukocyte count	1100/µL (1.1 × 10^9/L) with 28% neutrophils, 69% lymphocytes, and 3% myeloid blasts
Platelet count	40,000/µL (40 × 10^9/L)

A bone marrow biopsy reveals enlarged and atypical erythroid precursors with ringed sideroblasts, reduced mononuclear megakaryocytes, and 6% myeloblasts. Bone marrow cytogenetic studies demonstrate multiple chromosomal translocations and deletions.

Which of the following is the most likely cause of this patient's findings?

(A) Acute lymphoblastic leukemia
(B) Myelodysplastic syndrome
(C) Parvovirus B19 infection
(D) Recurrent Hodgkin lymphoma

Item 20 [Advanced]

A 57-year-old woman is evaluated in the emergency department for fever and shaking chills. Her symptoms began earlier in the day and have progressed over the past 8 hours. Medical history is significant for myelodysplastic syndrome diagnosed 1 year ago. Her only medication is azacitidine.

On physical examination, temperature is 39.2°C (102.6°F), blood pressure is 100/70 mm Hg, pulse rate is 110/min, and respiration rate is 20/min. Physical examination findings are otherwise unremarkable. There is no rash, lymphadenopathy, costovertebral angle tenderness, abdominal tenderness, or splenomegaly.

Laboratory studies:

Hemoglobin	10.6 g/dL (106 g/L)
Leukocyte count	33,600/µL (33.6 × 10^9/L)
Platelet count	88,000/µL (88 × 10^9/L)
Urinalysis	Normal

A chest radiograph is normal. A peripheral blood smear is shown (Plate 16).

Which of the following is the most likely diagnosis?

(A) Acute lymphoblastic leukemia
(B) Acute myeloid leukemia
(C) Acute promyelocytic leukemia
(D) Chronic myeloid leukemia

Item 21 [Basic]

A 75-year-old woman is evaluated after an elevated total serum protein level is noted as an incidental laboratory finding. The abnormality was identified during an evaluation for osteoporosis. She is asymptomatic, and her only medications are calcium, vitamin D, and alendronate.

Physical examination findings, including vital signs, are normal.

Laboratory studies:

Hemoglobin	13 g/dL (130 g/L)
Leukocyte count	6200/µL (6.2 × 10⁹/L)
Platelet count	240,000/µL (240 × 10⁹/L)
Protein, total	8.6 g/dL (86 g/L)
Albumin	4.0 g/dL (40 g/L)
Calcium	10 mg/dL (2.5 mmol/L)
Creatinine	1.2 mg/dL (106 µmol/L)
Urinalysis	Normal

Serum protein electrophoresis shows a monoclonal spike. Immunofixation reveals a serum monoclonal IgG λ level of 1.5 g/dL (15 g/L); serum IgM and IgA levels are normal. A radiographic bone survey shows no abnormalities.

Which of the following is the most likely diagnosis?

(A) AL amyloidosis
(B) Asymptomatic multiple myeloma
(C) Monoclonal gammopathy of unknown significance
(D) Waldenström macroglobulinemia

Item 22 [Basic]

A 60-year-old man is evaluated for unexplained low back pain, fatigue, nausea, anorexia, and an unexplained 6.8-kg (15-lb) weight loss. These symptoms have been gradually progressive over the past 9 weeks. The patient was previously healthy and takes no medications.

On physical examination, temperature is normal, blood pressure is 148/92 mm Hg, pulse rate is 90/min, and respiration rate is 20/min. Body mass index is 24. Mucous membranes are dry, and there is no jugular venous distention. Cardiopulmonary examination is normal. There is no hepatosplenomegaly. The remainder of the examination is unremarkable.

Laboratory studies:

Hemoglobin	9 g/dL (90 g/L)
Leukocyte count	3200/µL (3.2 × 10⁹/L)
Platelet count	100,000/µL (100 × 10⁹/L)
Calcium	12 mg/dL (3.0 mmol/L)
Creatinine	2.2 mg/dL (194 µmol/L)
Dipstick urinalysis	Negative for protein

Serum protein electrophoresis shows hypogammaglobulinemia, and urine protein electrophoresis is positive for a monoclonal protein.

Which of the following tests will be most helpful in establishing the diagnosis?

(A) Fat pad aspirate
(B) Peripheral blood smear
(C) Serum immunofixation
(D) Urine immunofixation

Item 23 [Advanced]

A 70-year-old woman is evaluated for a 1 week history of progressive fatigue and anorexia. Medical history is significant for hypertension. Her only medication is hydrochlorothiazide.

On physical examination, temperature is normal, supine blood pressure is 150/95 mm Hg and pulse rate is 80/min with orthostatic changes noted on standing, and respiration rate is 20/min. The remainder of the examination is unremarkable.

Laboratory studies:

Hematocrit	29%
Blood urea nitrogen	62 mg/dL (22.1 mmol/L)
Creatinine	4.6 mg/dL (407 µmol/L)
Electrolytes	
Sodium	134 mEq/L (134 mmol/L)
Potassium	5 mEq/L (5 mmol/L)
Chloride	114 mEq/L (114 mmol/L)
Bicarbonate	15 mEq/L (15 mmol/L)
Calcium	12.5 mg/dL (3.1 mmol/L)
Phosphorus	8.5 mg/dL (2.7 mmol/L)
Urinalysis	Specific gravity 1.010; trace protein; no glucose or ketones

Which of the following is the most likely diagnosis?

(A) Hypercalcemia secondary to thiazide therapy
(B) Milk-alkali syndrome
(C) Multiple myeloma
(D) Primary hyperparathyroidism

Item 24 [Advanced]

A 16-year-old girl is evaluated because of fatigue for the past 3 to 4 months. She reports a history of heavy menstrual bleeding since onset of menarche at 13 years, requiring several pads each day during her menstrual cycle. Her mother and sister also have a history of heavy menstrual bleeding. She has no known medical problems, but recalls continued bleeding for 2 to 3 days following an uncomplicated tooth extraction 1 year earlier. She takes no prescription or over-the-counter medications.

On physical examination, temperature is normal, blood pressure is 108/68 mm Hg, pulse rate is 90/min, and respiration rate is 10/min. There is mild conjunctival pallor. The remainder of the examination is normal.

Laboratory studies:

Hemoglobin	8.5 g/dL (85 g/L)
Leukocyte count	6800/µL (6.8 × 10⁹/L) with a normal differential
Platelet count	260,000/µL (260 × 10⁹/L)
Mean corpuscular volume	68 fL

Examination of a peripheral blood smear shows microcytosis and hypochromia but is otherwise normal.

Which of the following is the most appropriate diagnostic test to perform next?

(A) Plasma fibrinogen measurement

(B) Platelet function testing

(C) Prothrombin time and activated partial thromboplastin time

(D) Von Willebrand factor antigen determination

Item 25 [Basic]

A 60-year-old woman is evaluated for a nosebleed that had persisted for several hours and is unaccompanied by trauma. She has lost 9 kg (20 lb) over the last 4 months and has had new-onset low back pain for the last several weeks that has not responded to acetaminophen. The patient has hypertension. Her only medication is lisinopril. An extensive review of her history does not reveal any previous bleeding problems.

On physical examination, temperature is normal, blood pressure is 128/73 mm Hg, pulse rate is 88/min, and respiration rate is 12/min. There is no orthostasis. Oozing from the nares is evident. The lumbosacral spine is tender to palpation, and petechiae are noted on both lower extremities.

Results of laboratory studies are significant for a hemoglobin level of 9 g/dL (90 g/L), a leukocyte count of 1200/µL (1.2 × 10⁹/L), and a platelet count of 15,000/uL (15 × 10⁹/L).

Which of the following is the most appropriate next diagnostic step?

(A) Antiplatelet antibody determination

(B) Peripheral blood smear examination

(C) Platelet function testing

(D) Prothrombin time and activated partial thromboplastin time

Item 26 [Basic]

A 50-year-old man undergoes preoperative evaluation. He is scheduled to have elective arthroscopic knee surgery. Medical history is unremarkable, he takes no medications, and he has had no previous surgical procedures.

Physical examination findings are normal.

Which of the following is the most appropriate screening approach to detect any bleeding disorders in this patient?

(A) Clinical history

(B) Complete blood count with platelet count and differential

(C) Platelet function testing

(D) Prothrombin time and activated partial thromboplastin time

Item 27 [Advanced]

A 66-year-old woman is evaluated in the hospital for abnormal bleeding. She was admitted yesterday with a urinary tract infection and bacteremia. The patient has no other medical problems and was on no medications before admission.

On physical examination, temperature is 39.2°C (102.6°F), blood pressure is 85/60 mm Hg, pulse rate is 115/min, and respiration rate is 18/min. Bleeding is noted on mucous membranes around intravenous access sites. Multiple ecchymoses are present on her arms and legs.

Laboratory studies:

Hemoglobin	8.5 g/dL (85 g/L)
Platelet count	35,000/µL (35 × 10⁹/L)
Prothrombin time	15 s
Activated partial thromboplastin time	30 s
D-dimer	Elevated
Fibrinogen	Decreased

Examination of a peripheral blood smear shows many fragmented erythrocytes and diminished platelets.

Which of the following is the most likely cause of this patient's bleeding?

(A) Disseminated intravascular coagulation

(B) Hemolytic uremic syndrome

(C) Immune thrombocytopenic purpura

(D) Thrombotic thrombocytopenic purpura

Item 28 [Basic]

A 24-year-old man is evaluated for severe bleeding following arthroscopic surgery of the right knee 24 hours ago. The patient sustained a sports-related injury 1 year ago and since that time has had repeated swelling of the knee requiring aspiration of bloody fluid. Medical history is significant for compartment syndrome in the left forearm after sustaining an injury. He is an only child. His only medication is acetaminophen.

On physical examination, temperature is normal, blood pressure is 100/55 mm Hg, pulse rate is 120/min, and respiration rate is 22/min. The wound dressing shows fresh bleeding from the arthroscopy sites.

Laboratory studies:

Platelet count	Normal
Prothrombin time	11 s
Activated partial thromboplastin time (aPTT)	60 s
aPTT mixing study	Corrects

Which of the following is the most appropriate next diagnostic study?

(A) Factor VIII inhibitor testing

(B) Factor VIII and factor IX measurement

(C) Platelet function testing

(D) Von Willebrand factor antigen measurement

Item 29 [Basic]

A 65-year-old man is evaluated during a follow-up examination. The patient has a first-time diagnosis of left popliteal venous thrombosis made 10 days ago in the emergency department. He reports no recent travel, surgery, trauma, or period of immobilization. There is no family history of venous thromboembolism. He has a 30 pack-year history of smoking and quit 5 years ago.

On physical examination, vital signs and general examination findings are normal.

Which of the following is the most appropriate evaluation?

(A) Age- and sex-specific cancer screening

(B) Factor V Leiden, prothrombin gene (PT G20210A), protein C, protein S, and antithrombin deficiency testing

(C) Lupus anticoagulant and anticardiolipin antibody titers

(D) Plasma homocysteine measurement

(E) No additional diagnostic testing is indicated

Item 30 [Basic]

A 42-year-old man is diagnosed with idiopathic deep venous thrombosis of the right common femoral vein. He will be started on heparin followed by warfarin for a minimum of 3 months' duration. He has a strong family history of idiopathic deep venous thrombosis, and an evaluation for thrombophilia will be undertaken. Protein C deficiency is most strongly suspected.

Which of the following is the most appropriate time to initiate the evaluation for thrombophilia in this patient?

(A) Before beginning anticoagulation therapy

(B) During anticoagulation with heparin

(C) During anticoagulation with warfarin

(D) Two weeks following the completion of warfarin therapy

Item 31 [Advanced]

A 35-year-old woman is evaluated in the emergency department for the acute onset of right leg swelling and pain and associated dyspnea. Symptoms were present upon arising this morning. She reports no recent travel, periods of immobilization, trauma, or surgery. Medical history is significant for two pregnancies ending in miscarriages. She does not smoke or drink alcoholic beverages. Her mother was diagnosed with systemic lupus erythematosus at age 32 years.

On physical examination, temperature is normal, blood pressure is 138/78 mm Hg, pulse rate is 96/min, and respiration rate is 24/min. Oxygen saturation is 86% (ambient air). Cardiopulmonary examination reveals a right sternal lift and increased intensity of P_2. The right calf is swollen and tender to palpation.

Lower extremity Doppler ultrasound reveals a right popliteal and common femoral deep venous thrombosis.

Prior to initiating anticoagulation therapy, the activated partial thromboplastin time is obtained and is prolonged.

Which of the following is the most likely diagnosis?

(A) Antiphospholipid syndrome

(B) Factor V Leiden mutation

(C) Homozygous antithrombin deficiency

(D) Prothrombin gene mutation (PT^{G20210A})

Item 32 [Advanced]

A 42-year-woman is evaluated in the emergency department for swelling of the right leg after an 8-hour plane ride. She does not have shortness of breath, chest pain, or previous episodes of venous thromboembolic disease. The patient does have an 8-year history of systemic lupus erythematosus treated with hydroxychloroquine. She also reports two miscarriages, 7 and 5 years ago.

On physical examination, vital signs are normal. The right leg is obviously swollen. The remainder of the examination is normal.

Doppler ultrasound shows a deep venous thrombosis of the right femoral vein. Laboratory testing reveals a prolonged activated partial thromboplastin time and positive β_2-glycoprotein 1 IgG antibody assay.

The patient is started on heparin followed by warfarin. Twelve weeks later, the β_2-glycoprotein 1 IgG antibody assay is repeated and is again positive.

Which of the following is the most appropriate anticoagulation management?

(A) Continue warfarin for an additional 3 months

(B) Continue warfarin indefinitely

(C) Discontinue warfarin

(D) Discontinue warfarin and begin aspirin

Item 33 [Advanced]

A 35-year-old woman is evaluated preoperatively before undergoing a complex orthopedic procedure. Her medical history is significant for IgA deficiency and a severe anaphylactic reaction during an erythrocyte transfusion that she received for postpartum hemorrhage at age 25 years.

On physical examination, temperature is 37.4°C (99.3°F), blood pressure is 128/78 mm Hg, pulse rate is 82/min, and respiration rate is 16/min. The remainder of the examination is unremarkable.

Results of laboratory studies indicate a hemoglobin level of 13.6 g/dL (136 g/L), a platelet count of 186,000/µL (186 × 10^9/L), and normal prothrombin and activated partial thromboplastin times. Previous laboratory study results showed an undetectable serum IgA level but otherwise normal immunoglobulin levels and no other abnormalities on serum protein electrophoresis.

Which of the following is the most appropriate erythrocyte product for this patient if transfusion is needed?

(A) Cytomegalovirus negative

(B) γ-Irradiated

(C) Leukoreduced

(D) Phenotypically matched

(E) Washed

Item 34 [Basic]

A 22-year-old man is evaluated in the emergency department for injuries sustained in a motorcycle accident. There is no head trauma, but he reports severe left-sided abdominal pain.

On physical examination, temperature is 37.3°C (99.1°F), blood pressure is 85/44 mm Hg, pulse rate is 118/min, and respiration rate is 16/min. Abdominal examination discloses guarding and rebound tenderness in the left upper quadrant. The patient's mental status and neurologic examination findings are normal.

Results of laboratory studies are significant for a hemoglobin level of 8.7 g/dL (87 g/L), a normal platelet count, and normal prothrombin and activated partial thromboplastin times.

The patient's blood type is A, Rh negative.

Computed tomography of the abdomen confirms splenic laceration. The blood bank indicates that type A-negative blood is not available.

Which of the following is the most appropriate erythrocyte product for emergency transfusion in this patient?

(A) A positive
(B) AB negative
(C) B positive
(D) O negative

Item 35 [Basic]

A 34-year-old woman is evaluated for increasing bone pain, dyspnea, and fatigue for the past 2 days. The patient has sickle cell anemia. She was hospitalized 7 days ago for an elective cholecystectomy for which she received 2 units of matched erythrocytes. The operation was uneventful, and she was discharged home in 24 hours. Current medications are hydroxyurea and folic acid.

On physical examination, the patient is in pain and has jaundice. Temperature is 37.4°C (99.4°F), blood pressure is 146/85 mm Hg, pulse rate is 116/min, and respiration rate is 12/min. The cardiopulmonary and neurologic examinations are normal.

Laboratory studies:

	Current value	Values at hospital discharge
Hemoglobin	7.4 g/dL (74 g/L)	9.9 g/dL (99 g/L)
Leukocyte count	12,000/µL (12 × 10⁹/L)	8000/µL (8 × 10⁹/L)
Platelet count	187,000/µL (187 × 10⁹/L)	207,000/µL (207 × 10⁹/L)
Reticulocyte count	2.3% of erythrocytes	5.3% of erythrocytes
Bilirubin, total	4.8 mg/dL (82 µmol/L)	Not applicable
Bilirubin, direct	0.6 mg/dL (10.2 µmol/L)	Not applicable

Which of the following laboratory findings would best explain this patient's current clinical presentation?

(A) Antineutrophil antibodies
(B) HLA antibodies
(C) IgA deficiency
(D) New alloantibodies

Item 36 [Advanced]

A 48-year-old woman is evaluated in the hospital for shortness of breath, chills, and fever. These findings developed during transfusion of a single unit of packed erythrocytes that she received following an uncomplicated left total hip arthroplasty.

On physical examination, temperature is 38.9°C (102.0°F), blood pressure is 116/68 mm Hg, pulse rate is 111/min, and respiration rate is 22/min. Oxygen saturation is 86% (breathing oxygen, 2 liters/min by nasal cannula). There is no jugular venous distention or peripheral edema. Cardiopulmonary examination discloses tachycardia but is otherwise normal.

Results of laboratory studies indicate a hemoglobin level of 9.3 g/dL (93 g/L), a leukocyte count of 9600/µL (9.6 × 10⁹/L), and a platelet count of 198,000/µL (198 × 10⁹/L).

Diffuse bilateral infiltrates are seen on a chest radiograph. An electrocardiogram shows sinus tachycardia but no ST changes.

Which of the following is the most likely diagnosis?

(A) Acute hemolytic transfusion reaction
(B) Febrile nonhemolytic transfusion reaction
(C) Transfusion-associated circulatory overload
(D) Transfusion-related acute lung injury

Section 5

Hematology

Answers and Critiques

Item 1   **Answer: B**

Educational Objective: *Diagnose iron deficiency in the setting of anemia of inflammation.*

The most likely cause of this patient's anemia is iron deficiency and anemia of inflammation. This patient has rheumatoid arthritis, a cause of anemia of inflammation. Inflammatory cytokines block iron utilization and decrease transferrin saturation and calculated serum total iron-binding capacity (TIBC) levels. Because ferritin is an acute phase reactant, serum ferritin levels tend to increase in patients with anemia of inflammation. In contrast, iron deficiency is associated with increased transferrin saturation and calculated serum TIBC levels and decreased serum ferritin levels. When inflammation accompanies iron deficiency, inflammatory cytokines always confound the expected pattern of serum iron studies.

Virtually all patients with serum ferritin levels less than 10 to 15 ng/mL (10-15 µg/L) are iron deficient. However, 25% of menstruating women with absent stainable bone marrow iron have serum ferritin levels greater than 15 ng/mL (15 µg/L). Assuming absence of inflammation, higher serum ferritin cutoff limits of 30 to 41 ng/mL (30-41 µg/L) improve the accuracy of diagnosing iron deficiency in women during their reproductive years. In patients with rheumatoid arthritis, serum ferritin levels are expected to rise by as much as threefold as a result of the effects of inflammatory cytokines. Therefore, this patient's serum ferritin levels of 29 and 36 ng/mL (29 and 36 µg/L) support a diagnosis of iron deficiency in the setting of her inflammatory illness. Generally, serum ferritin levels less than 100 to 120 ng/mL (100-120 µg/L) reflect iron deficiency in patients with inflammatory conditions.

While monthly menstrual blood loss is the most likely cause of iron deficiency in this patient, she should undergo colon cancer screening to exclude gastrointestinal causes of occult blood loss.

Methotrexate is an antimetabolite that inhibits dihydrofolate reductase and causes megaloblastic maturation. However, low-dose methotrexate is unlikely to cause significant megaloblastic anemia, whereas higher doses may do so with a significant rise in mean corpuscular volume (MCV). This patient's normal and unchanging MCV values exclude a diagnosis of methotrexate-induced anemia.

KEY POINT

Serum ferritin levels less than 100 to 120 ng/mL (100-120 µg/L) may reflect coexisting iron deficiency in patients with inflammatory states.

Bibliography

Weiss G, Goodnough LT. Anemia of chronic disease. N Engl J Med. 2005;352:1011-23. [PMID: 15758012]

Item 2   **Answer: C**

Educational Objective: *Diagnose cobalamin (vitamin B_{12}) deficiency.*

The most appropriate next step in diagnosis is to obtain serum homocysteine and methylmalonic acid levels. This patient has a history of gastric bypass surgery that puts him at risk for cobalamin (vitamin B_{12}) deficiency. His serum vitamin B_{12} level is in the low-normal range and requires further assessment. An elevated methylmalonic acid level is more sensitive and specific for diagnosing cobalamin deficiency than a low serum vitamin B_{12} level because serum vitamin B_{12} levels do not adequately assess tissue vitamin B_{12} stores, especially in patients with serum vitamin B_{12} levels in the low-normal range. In patients with cobalamin deficiency, both methylmalonic acid and homocysteine levels are increased. Therefore, determining the serum homocysteine level is also indicated.

Bone marrow aspiration and biopsy are helpful in evaluating causes of megaloblastic anemia, but are not typically done until cobalamin and folate deficiencies have been excluded.

Hemoglobin electrophoresis is a method for identifying hemoglobin subcomponents by separating out individual hemoglobin species in an electric field. This test may be helpful in diagnosing sickle cell anemia, sickle cell trait, and some thalassemias. Hemoglobinopathies tend to be characterized by abnormal erythrocyte morphology and microcytosis, neither of which is present in this patient.

This patient has a macrocytic anemia and is unlikely to have iron deficiency, which causes a microcytic anemia. Serum iron studies are therefore not indicated.

KEY POINT

An elevated serum methylmalonic acid level is more sensitive and specific for diagnosing cobalamin (vitamin B_{12}) deficiency than a low serum vitamin B_{12} level.

Bibliography

Galloway M, Hamilton M. Macrocytosis: pitfalls in testing and summary of guidance. BMJ. 2007;335:884-6. [PMID: 17962289]

Item 3   **Answer: D**

Educational Objective: *Diagnose α-thalassemia trait.*

The most likely diagnosis is α-thalassemia trait. Decreased or absent synthesis of normal α or β chains resulting from genetic defects is the hallmark of the thalassemic syndromes. The result is ineffective erythropoiesis, intravascular hemolysis caused by precipitation of the excess insoluble globin chain, and decreased hemoglobin production. α-Thalassemia trait (-α/-α or –/αα) is associated with mild anemia, microcytosis, hypochromia, target cells on the peripheral blood smear, and, in adults, normal hemoglobin electrophoresis results. The (-α/-α) variant is found in 2% to 3% of black persons and is often mistaken for iron deficiency. This patient's peripheral blood smear demonstrating target cells makes a thalassemic syndrome the most likely diagnosis, and the normal hemoglobin electrophoresis results are suggestive of α-thalassemia trait. α-Thalassemia trait can be more definitively diagnosed by globin gene synthesis studies but is more often suggested by chronic microcytic anemia, target cells, normal serum iron studies, and normal hemoglobin electrophoresis results. No treatment is necessary for α-thalassemia trait.

Hereditary spherocytosis is characterized by a normal to increased mean corpuscular volume (MCV), depending on the degree of erythrocytosis, and by erythrocytes on a peripheral blood smear that lack the normal central pallor. Patients with iron deficiency may note fatigue, malaise, irritability, decreased exercise tolerance, and headaches, which may appear before symptoms of overt anemia occur. These findings are not consistent with those identified in this patient.

Sideroblastic anemia is characterized by a decreased erythrocyte count caused by ineffective erythropoiesis and hypochromic normocytic or macrocytic erythrocytes with basophilic stippling that stain positive for iron. These findings are not consistent with this patient's laboratory study results.

KEY POINT

α-Thalassemia trait is associated with mild anemia, microcytosis, hypochromia, target cells on the peripheral blood smear, and, in adults, normal hemoglobin electrophoresis.

Bibliography

Cunningham MJ. Update on thalassemia: clinical care and complications. Hematol Oncol Clin North Am. 2010;(1):215-27. [PMID: 20113904]

Item 4   Answer: C

Educational Objective: *Treat iron deficiency in a menstruating woman.*

The most appropriate treatment is oral ferrous sulfate. Iron deficiency can result from blood loss or malabsorption in addition to increased iron use. Women of reproductive age may lose enough iron through normal menstrual blood loss to become iron deficient in the absence of uterine or gastrointestinal disease. Patients with mild iron deficiency may note fatigue, malaise, irritability, decreased exercise tolerance, and headaches before symptoms of overt anemia occur. This patient has signs and symptoms of iron deficiency, likely secondary to menstrual blood loss. The variation in the size of erythrocytes is quantified in the red blood cell distribution width (RDW) measurement. An increased RDW is most often associated with a nutrient deficiency such as iron, folate, or vitamin B_{12}. Patients with iron deficiency anemia caused by blood loss can have mild thrombocytosis, which resolves with treatment of iron deficiency. For simple iron deficiency, oral ferrous sulfate, which is relatively inexpensive and available without a prescription, would be effective and is therefore the most appropriate treatment option.

Initiation of erythropoiesis-stimulating agents should only be considered after patients have been evaluated for other causes of anemia and iron stores are adequate (serum ferritin level >100 ng/mL [100 μg/L] and transferrin saturation >20%).

Erythrocyte transfusions are reserved for patients with severe symptomatic anemia in whom rapid correction is necessary to prevent cardiovascular complications, including heart failure and infarction.

Parenteral iron, either intramuscular iron dextran or intravenous iron sucrose, is reserved for patients receiving dialysis or for patients who cannot absorb or tolerate oral iron replacement.

KEY POINT

For patients with simple iron deficiency, oral ferrous sulfate is the least expensive and simplest treatment option.

Bibliography

Killip S, Bennett JM, Chambers MD. Iron deficiency anemia. Am Fam Physician. 2007; 75:671-8. [PMID: 17375513]

Item 5   Answer: B

Educational Objective: *Diagnose warm agglutinin-mediated hemolytic anemia.*

This patient most likely has autoimmune hemolytic anemia. The hemolytic anemias are characterized by increased destruction of erythrocytes associated with a marrow response (reticulocytosis). Elevated levels of unconjugated bilirubin, lactate dehydrogenase, and uric acid, and depressed levels of haptoglobin are characteristic of hemolysis. Autoimmune hemolytic anemia may be idiopathic or result from drugs, lymphoproliferative disorders (as in this patient), collagen vascular diseases, or malignancies. The disorder occurs when IgG, IgM, or, rarely IgA, autoantibodies bind to erythrocyte antigens. The most common type of autoimmune hemolytic anemia is warm antibody–mediated. In this condition, IgG antibodies bind to Rh-type antigens on the erythrocyte surface at 37.0°C (98.6°F) . Although these antibodies may fix complement, they more commonly bind to the cell surface and facilitate Fc-receptor–mediated erythrocyte destruction by splenic macrophages. Warm antibodies are diagnosed by the direct antiglobulin (Coombs) test, which detects IgG or complement on the cell surface. Spherocytes are seen on the peripheral blood smear. Glucocorticoids are usual first-line therapy to interrupt antibody production.

α-Thalassemia is a congenital hemolytic anemia. Patients with a two-α-gene defect have target cells and an absence of spherocytes on the peripheral blood smear, and will not have a positive direct antiglobulin test.

Hereditary spherocytosis is a membrane defect resulting in a spherocytic shape, reduced deformability, and trapping with subsequent destruction in the spleen. Spherocytes are present on the peripheral blood smear and the direct Coombs test is negative. Diagnosis is with the osmotic fragility test demonstrating increased erythrocyte fragility in hypotonic saline compared with normal erythrocytes.

Microangiopathic hemolytic anemia is a nonimmune hemolytic anemia. Like other hemolytic anemias, it is characterized by reticulocytosis, elevated levels of unconjugated bilirubin, lactate dehydrogenase, and depressed levels of haptoglobin. Microangiopathic hemolysis may be associated with thrombocytopenia. Another distinguishing characteristic of microangiopathic hemolytic anemia is the presence of schistocytes on the peripheral blood smear.

KEY POINT

Warm antibody-mediated hemolytic anemia is characterized by spherocytes on the peripheral blood smear and a positive direct antiglobulin (Coombs) test.

Bibliography

Bass GF, Tuscano ET, Tuscano JM. Diagnosis and classification of autoimmune hemolytic anemia. Autoimmun Rev. 2014 Apr-May;13(4-5):560-4. [PMID: 24418298]

Item 6   Answer: D

Educational Objective: *Diagnose anemia secondary to kidney disease in an older patient.*

This patient most likely has anemia secondary to kidney disease. Because erythropoietin is produced in the kidney, kidney disease is associated with an underproduction anemia caused by renal cortical loss. The anemia of kidney disease is usually normochromic and normocytic with an inappropriately low reticulocyte count for the level of anemia present. Patients with minor increases in serum creatinine levels may have reduced erythropoietin levels. Before attributing anemia to chronic kidney disease, other potential causes of anemia should be eliminated. The typical evaluation includes a complete blood count with erythrocyte indices, absolute reticulocyte count, serum iron and total iron-binding capacity (TIBC), percent transferrin saturation, serum ferritin, and exclusion of gastrointestinal bleeding with appropriate testing.

Although the prevalence of anemia does increase with age, most patients have an associated disease process, such as chronic kidney disease, iron deficiency, or an inflammatory state. Ascribing anemia to advanced age, per se, would be inappropriate in the presence of a known cause of anemia.

Anemia of inflammation is associated with normal or low serum iron levels, low TIBC, and an elevated serum ferritin level. Iron deficiency is associated with an elevated TIBC and a reduced serum ferritin level. This patient has a normal serum iron level, TIBC, and serum ferritin level.

KEY POINT

Anemia due to kidney disease is caused by underproduction of erythropoietin, is usually normochromic and normocytic, and associated with an inappropriately low reticulocyte count for the level of anemia present.

Bibliography
Fishbane S, Nissenson AR. Anemia management in chronic kidney disease. Kidney Int Suppl. 2010;(117):S3-S9. [PMID: 20671741]

Item 7   Answer: B

Educational Objective: *Prevent acute chest syndrome in patients with sickle cell disease.*

This patient has the acute chest syndrome and will likely benefit from long-term hydroxyurea therapy. Acute chest syndrome is the most common form of pulmonary disease in patients with sickle cell disease and is a major cause of morbidity and mortality. Therapy with hydroxyurea augments levels of hemoglobin F, which inhibits intracellular polymerization of hemoglobin S, reduces the number of acute pain episodes in patients with sickle cell disease by 50%, and decreases the frequency of the acute chest syndrome by 40%. Nine-year follow-up data from a 2-year multicenter double-blind, randomized, placebo-controlled trial showed that hydroxyurea use was associated with a 40% reduction in mortality rates in such patients. Daily oral hydroxyurea therapy is indicated for patients who have three or more acute pain episodes yearly that require inpatient parenteral opioid therapy.

The diagnosis of the acute chest syndrome is established by identifying an infiltrate on chest radiographs that involves at least one lung segment and that is not thought to be due to atelectasis; associated findings include one or more of the following: chest pain; temperature greater than 38.5°C (101.3°F); tachypnea, wheezing, cough, or the development of increased work of breathing (such as retractions); and hypoxemia relative to baseline oxygen saturation values.

Patients with sickle cell disease are at risk for proteinuria and chronic kidney failure. Angiotensin-converting enzyme (ACE) inhibitors such as captopril may help to prevent kidney disease in patients who show signs of developing kidney dysfunction. However, this patient has a normal serum creatinine level and normal levels of microalbumin; therefore, ACE inhibitor therapy is not indicated at this time.

In children up to the age of 5 years, prophylactic penicillin (or a macrolide antibiotic in patients with penicillin allergy) decreases the risk of infections known to trigger the acute chest syndrome, but antibiotic therapy is not useful in older patients.

Recombinant erythropoietin is used primarily to manage anemia due to underproduction of erythropoietin in patients with sickle cell disease who develop chronic kidney failure, which has not occurred in this patient.

KEY POINT

In patients with sickle cell disease, hydroxyurea therapy reduces the number of acute pain episodes by 50% and decreases the frequency of the acute chest syndrome by 40%.

Bibliography
Steinberg MH, Barton F, Castro O, et al. Effect of hydroxyurea on mortality and morbidity in adult sickle cell anemia: risks and benefits up to 9 years of treatment. JAMA. 2003;289:1645-51. Erratum in: JAMA. 2003;290:756. [PMID: 12672732]

Item 8   Answer: A

Educational Objective: *Diagnose aplastic crisis in a patient with sickle cell disease.*

The most likely diagnosis is aplastic crisis. This patient with sickle cell disease has acute worsening of her chronic anemia. Her recent viral syndrome, which presented with fever and arthralgia, is consistent with parvovirus B19 infection. Aplastic crisis can occur when patients with chronic hemolytic anemia and shortened erythrocyte survival are infected with parvovirus B19, which leads to suppression of erythrocyte production (red blood cell aplasia) and the inability to maintain erythrocyte production needed to replace the hemolyzed cells, as reflected in her very low reticulocyte count. Confirmation may be obtained by demonstrating IgM antibodies against parvovirus B19 or polymerase chain reaction studies detecting parvovirus B19 DNA.

Hyperhemolytic crisis is characterized by sudden worsening of sickle cell disease with reticulocytosis. This complication is rare, and its cause is unknown.

Megaloblastic crisis refers to an acquired anemia occurring in patients with increased folate demands, such as those with chronic hemolysis, and, rarely, pregnant women, children with accelerated growth, or the elderly. Although a low reticulocyte count may be consistent with a megaloblastic crisis, this condition would be unlikely to occur so acutely after a viral illness and would be very unlikely in a patient who takes chronic folic acid replacement.

Splenic sequestration crisis is the result of splenic vaso-occlusion and splenic pooling of erythrocytes, causing a rapid drop in hemoglobin concentration, reticulocytosis, and a rapidly enlarging spleen. Splenic sequestration is also often accompanied by left upper quadrant abdominal pain and splenomegaly and would not be characterized by a very low reticulocyte count.

Aplastic crisis can occur when patients with chronic hemolytic anemia and shortened erythrocyte survival are infected with parvovirus B19, which leads to suppression of erythrocyte production.

Bibliography

Servey JT, Reamy BV, Hodge J. Clinical presentations of parvovirus B19 infection. Am Fam Physician. 2007;75:373-6. [PMID: 17304869]

Item 9 Answer: A

Educational Objective: *Treat acute chest syndrome in a patient with sickle cell disease.*

The most appropriate treatment is erythrocyte transfusion. This patient meets the criteria for the acute chest syndrome, which include identification of a new infiltrate on a chest radiograph that involves at least one lung segment and one or more of the following: chest pain; temperature less than 38.5°C (101.3°F); tachypnea, wheezing, or cough or labored breathing; and hypoxia relative to baseline oxygen saturation values. Management includes empiric broad-spectrum antibiotics, supplemental oxygen, pain medication to diminish chest splinting, bronchodilators if reactive airways disease is present, and avoidance of overhydration. Erythrocyte transfusion is indicated if hypoxia persists despite supplemental oxygen, as has occurred in this patient. Erythrocyte exchange transfusion may be preferred if the hypoxia continues to progress.

A fluid bolus is not indicated in this patient because he does not have hypovolemia or hypotension, although maintenance intravenous fluid should be continued to maintain euvolemia.

Furosemide may be helpful in patients who have hypovolemia, but there is no clinical evidence to support this diagnosis in this patient. Furosemide-induced hypovolemia should be avoided because it can lead to increased sickling.

Hydroxyurea is effective for decreasing the incidence of acute chest syndrome but is not indicated for treatment in the acute setting.

Management of the acute chest syndrome in patients with sickle cell disease includes empiric broad-spectrum antibiotics, supplemental oxygen, pain medication, avoidance of overhydration, bronchodilators as needed, and erythrocyte transfusion for persistent hypoxia despite supplemental oxygen.

Bibliography

Gladwin MT, Vichinsky E. Pulmonary complications of sickle cell disease. N Engl J Med. 2008;359:2254-65. [PMID: 19020327]

Item 10 Answer: A

Educational Objective: *Diagnose avascular necrosis in a patient with sickle cell disease.*

This patient has avascular necrosis (AVN), which is a very common complication in adults with sickle cell disease in whom repeated vaso-occlusive crises lead to infarcts and degeneration in marrow-containing bone. AVN most commonly affects the femoral and humoral heads and may be asymptomatic and identified only radiographically. Symptomatic AVN of the hip can be extremely painful in patients with sickle cell disease; treatment is typically similar to treatment of pain crises and includes hydration and appropriate analgesia. Symptomatic AVN has a high likelihood of progressing to femoral head collapse, necessitating surgical intervention with

decompression or possibly joint replacement. However, joint replacement is usually delayed as long as possible because of the high failure rate in patients with sickle cell disease.

Although osteoarthritis in multiple joints occurs in patients with long-standing sickle cell disease, development of osteoarthritis would be unusual in a young adult.

Patients with sickle cell disease and AVN are at increased risk of osteomyelitis because of areas of necrotic bone and splenic dysfunction. The clinical presentation of AVN and osteomyelitis may be similar, although this patient's persistent pain following an acute pain crisis and lack of evidence of active infection suggest AVN as the most likely diagnosis.

Rheumatoid arthritis is unlikely because involvement of only one hip would be an unusual presentation for this disorder.

Avascular necrosis results from repeated vaso-occlusive crises causing infarcts and degeneration in marrow-containing bone and most commonly affects the femoral and humoral heads.

Bibliography

Al-Mousawi FR, Malki AA. Managing femoral head osteonecrosis in patients with sickle cell disease. Surgeon. 2007;(5):282-9. [PMID: 17958228]

Item 11 Answer: B

Educational Objective: *Diagnose immune thrombocytopenic purpura.*

The most likely diagnosis is immune thrombocytopenic purpura (ITP), an acquired autoimmune condition in which autoantibodies are directed against platelet surface proteins, leading to platelet destruction. Clinical findings may include signs or symptoms of mild to severe bleeding. Although ITP is a diagnosis of exclusion, supportive clinical findings include an otherwise normal blood count or concomitant anemia from bleeding and the absence of additional organ dysfunction. Variants of ITP may be drug induced or part of a broader illness of abnormal immune regulation, such as systemic lupus erythematosus, HIV infection, or lymphoproliferative malignancies. Platelets, when present, may be large because they typically have recently been released from the bone marrow. Because of the enhanced hemostatic function of these young platelets, patients may experience less severe bleeding than that associated with other diseases with a similar platelet count.

Henoch-Schönlein purpura is a small-vessel vasculitis that most commonly occurs in children; the syndrome may affect adults with greater severity. Presenting features include a purpuric rash predominantly affecting the distal lower extremities, arthritis, abdominal pain, and hematuria. Attacks are usually self-limited and resolve in several weeks, although a subset of patients experience persistent progressive kidney disease.

Thrombotic thrombocytopenic purpura (TTP) is a process characterized by abnormal activation of platelets and endothelial cells, deposition of fibrin in the microvasculature, and peripheral destruction of erythrocytes and platelets. TTP should be suspected in patients who have microangiopathic hemolytic anemia and thrombocytopenia. A peripheral blood smear is essential to determine whether the anemia is caused by a microangiopathic hemolytic process, as indicated by the presence of schistocytes.

Von Willebrand disease (vWD) is the most common inherited bleeding disorder. It is an autosomal dominant disorder. Von Willebrand factor protects factor VIII from degradation. Factor VIII levels can be low enough in patients with vWD to cause slight prolongation of the activated partial thromboplastin time, although the hemorrhagic manifestations are characterized by mucocutaneous bleeding rather than by hemarthroses, as occurs in patients with hemophilia. Patients with vWD have normal platelet counts.

KEY POINT

The diagnosis of immune thrombocytopenic purpura is suggested by isolated thrombocytopenia or thrombocytopenia and anemia from bleeding, an otherwise normal peripheral blood smear, and absence of additional organ dysfunction.

Bibliography

Provan D, Stasi R, Newland AC, et al. International consensus report on the investigation and management of primary immune thrombocytopenia. Blood. 2010;115:168-86. [PMID: 19846889]

Item 12   Answer: D

Educational Objective: *Predict the most common complication of heparin-induced thrombocytopenia.*

The patient is at greatest risk for venous thrombosis. Heparin-induced thrombocytopenia (HIT), the most common drug-induced immune thrombocytopenia, is caused by antibodies directed against a complex of heparin and platelet factor 4, a protein released from platelets. HIT occurs in approximately 5% of patients treated with unfractionated heparin for 5 or more days but develops in only about 1% of patients treated with low-molecular-weight heparin. The criteria for diagnosing HIT include: (1) thrombocytopenia (defined as a platelet count <150,000/µL [150 × 10⁹/L] or a 50% decrease in the platelet count from baseline) in the presence of current heparin administration or its use over the past 3 months; (2) exclusion of other causes of thrombocytopenia; (3) reversal of thrombocytopenia on cessation of heparin. Although several HIT-related assays can confirm the diagnosis, the results take several days to be completed, and decisions related to treatment are typically based on clinical findings. The most serious complication of HIT is a thrombotic event, triggered by a number of mechanisms including release of procoagulant agents from platelets and endothelial activation. Venous thromboses are most common (about two thirds of events), but arterial thromboses also occur and can be life-threatening. Once HIT is detected or even suspected, heparin must be stopped immediately and an alternative rapidly acting anticoagulant begun, even if thrombosis has not occurred. A new thrombotic event develops in 20% to 50% of patients who do not receive subsequent antithrombotic prophylaxis.

Rarely, patients may develop a systemic allergic reaction to heparin manifested by fever, hives, dyspnea, and hypotension. HIT is an antibody-mediated phenomenon that can also rarely be associated with systemic allergic symptoms. However, anaphylaxis associated with heparin is uncommon.

Thrombocytopenia associated with HIT tends to be relatively mild, with mean platelet counts being approximately 60,000/µL (60 × 10⁹/L). Additionally, the coagulation pathways are unaffected directly by HIT. Therefore, these patients typically do not bleed excessively.

KEY POINT

Venous thromboses are the most common complication of heparin-induced thrombocytopenia, but arterial thromboses also occur and can be life-threatening.

Bibliography

Dasararaju R, Singh N, Mehta A. Heparin induced thrombocytopenia: review. Expert Rev Hematol. 2013;6:419-28. [PMID: 23991928]

Item 13   Answer: C

Educational Objective: *Diagnose thrombotic thrombocytopenic purpura.*

The most likely diagnosis is thrombotic thrombocytopenic purpura (TTP). TTP is a pathologic process characterized by abnormal activation of platelets and endothelial cells, deposition of fibrin in the microvasculature, and peripheral destruction of erythrocytes and platelets. TTP should be suspected in patients who have: (1) microangiopathic hemolytic anemia, characterized by schistocytes on the peripheral blood smear and increased serum lactate dehydrogenase (LDH) levels; and (2) thrombocytopenia. A peripheral blood smear is essential to determine whether the anemia is caused by a microangiopathic hemolytic process, as indicated by the presence of schistocytes. Patients may also have fever; kidney manifestations, such as hematuria, elevated serum creatinine levels, and proteinuria; and fluctuating neurologic manifestations, such as headache, confusion, sleepiness, coma, seizures, and stroke, but the absence of these symptoms does not exclude the diagnosis. Other clinical features may include nausea, vomiting, and abdominal pain with or without elevations of serum amylase and lipase levels. This patient has fever in association with neurologic symptoms, anemia, and thrombocytopenia with normal coagulation parameters (prothrombin time and activated partial thromboplastin time) and a peripheral blood smear showing fragmented erythrocytes (schistocytes), the hallmark of a microangiopathic process. Plasma exchange should be instituted emergently at diagnosis because 10% of patients die of this disease despite therapy.

Although aplastic anemia also causes thrombocytopenia, it is not associated with reticulocytosis or schistocytes on the peripheral blood smear.

Schistocytes, a sign of fragmentation hemolysis, are associated with both TTP and disseminated intravascular coagulation (DIC), but DIC results in abnormal coagulation parameters due to fibrinogen consumption, whereas coagulation parameters remain normal with TTP. Other features that favor TTP rather than DIC in this patient are the very high LDH level (attributed to tissue necrosis in addition to hemolysis) and the very high schistocyte density on the peripheral blood smear; schistocyte density is generally low in patients with DIC.

Spherocytes, not schistocytes, are the expected erythrocyte finding in patients with warm autoimmune hemolytic anemia. Immune thrombocytopenia is caused by accelerated platelet destruction caused by antibodies directed toward platelet antigens. The combination of these two disorders would not account for the clinical findings in this patient.

KEY POINT

High-density schistocytes on a peripheral blood smear with very high serum lactate dehydrogenase levels and normal coagulation parameters are features that distinguish the microangiopathic hemolytic anemia–associated thrombotic thrombocytopenic purpura from that of disseminated intravascular coagulation.

Bibliography

George JN, Charania RS. Evaluation of patients with microangiopathic hemolytic anemia and thrombocytopenia. Semin Thromb Hemost. 2013;39:153-60. [PMID: 23390027]

Item 14   Answer: D

Educational Objective: *Manage a patient with pseudothrombocytopenia.*

The patient's peripheral blood smear shows platelet clumping, which suggests pseudothrombocytopenia. Pseudothrombocytopenia is a laboratory artifact in which platelets drawn into an ethylenediaminetetraacetic acid (EDTA)–anticoagulated test tube clump and fail to be counted accurately by the automated counter, resulting in a spuriously low platelet count. This patient's thrombocytopenia is therefore a laboratory artifact and requires no therapy. Pseudothrombocytopenia can be confirmed when the platelet count normalizes after the count is repeated in a tube containing citrate or heparin as the anticoagulant.

Immune thrombocytopenic purpura (ITP) is a relatively common cause of thrombocytopenia. The diagnosis is based on excluding other causes of thrombocytopenia, other systemic illnesses, and medications. The complete blood count is generally normal except for thrombocytopenia. Pseudothrombocytopenia must be excluded as the cause for a decreased platelet count. For patients with established ITP, initial treatment includes high-dose glucocorticoids. Intravenous immune globulin (IVIG) may increase very low platelet counts in patients with ITP; however, the effect is transient (days to weeks). Because this patient has another explanation for her thrombocytopenia, ITP is not confirmed, and treatment with prednisone or IVIG is not indicated.

As the low platelet counts in pseudothrombocytopenia are artifactual, platelet transfusions are not indicated.

KEY POINT

Pseudothrombocytopenia is a laboratory artifact with no clinical sequelae, characterized by platelet clumping on the peripheral blood smear and a spuriously low platelet count.

Bibliography
Froom P, Barak M. Prevalence and course of pseudothrombocytopenia in outpatients. Clin Chem Lab Med. 2011;49:111-4. [PMID: 20961195]

Item 15   Answer: D

Educational Objective: *Manage a patient with immune thrombocytopenic purpura.*

This patient should have a repeat complete blood count in 1 week. She has new-onset thrombocytopenia with an otherwise normal complete blood count. The lack of clinical manifestations or systemic symptoms; normal physical examination findings, including absence of splenomegaly; and the normal peripheral blood smear provide no clues to an underlying disorder. She is not taking any medications known to cause thrombocytopenia. She therefore most likely has immune thrombocytopenic purpura (ITP). ITP is a diagnosis of exclusion and is often discovered incidentally, but patients may have clinical signs or symptoms of mild to severe bleeding or hemorrhage in the setting of an otherwise normal blood count and the absence of organ dysfunction. ITP can be drug induced or part of a broader illness associated with abnormal immune regulation. Asymptomatic patients without evidence of bleeding and with platelet counts greater than 30,000 to 40,000/µL (30-40 × 10⁹/L) have less than a 15% chance of developing more severe thrombocytopenia requiring treatment. The most appropriate course of action is to counsel this patient about potential bleeding symptoms and repeat the complete blood count at a designated interval such as 1 week.

In adult patients with ITP, therapy may be required for those with platelet counts lower than 30,000 to 40,000/µL (30-40 × 10⁹/L) or if bleeding is present. Given this patient's lack of bleeding symptoms and a platelet count greater than 50,000/µL (50 × 10⁹/L), she does not require glucocorticoid therapy or other treatment.

Antibody testing in patients with suspected ITP commonly results in both false-negative and false-positive results. Consequently, antiplatelet antibody testing is found to have little predictive value in the diagnosis of ITP and is not recommended.

The patient's complete blood count is normal except for thrombocytopenia, which makes bone marrow dysfunction less likely; therefore, bone marrow biopsy is not indicated.

KEY POINT

Asymptomatic patients with immune thrombocytopenic purpura without evidence of bleeding and with platelet counts greater than 30,000 to 40,000/µL (30-40 × 10⁹/L) have a very low incidence of developing more severe thrombocytopenia requiring treatment.

Bibliography
Provan D, Stasi R, Newland AC, et al. International consensus report on the investigation and management of primary immune thrombocytopenia. Blood. 2010;115:168-86. [PMID: 19846889]

Item 16   Answer: A

Educational Objective: *Treat polycythemia vera.*

This patient most likely has polycythemia vera (PV), and the most appropriate treatment is aspirin and phlebotomy. PV is a neoplastic disorder that originates from pluripotent hematopoietic progenitor cells. The symptoms of PV are the same as those of erythrocytosis from any cause and include confusion, transient ischemic attack–like symptoms, tinnitus, blurred vision, and headache, the last of which occurs in 50% of patients. Symptoms that are more specific for PV and other myeloproliferative disorders include generalized pruritus that often worsens after bathing, erythromelalgia (a burning sensation in the palms and soles possibly caused by platelet activation), and hypermetabolic symptoms such as fever, weight loss, and sweating. On physical examination, patients may have plethora and hepatosplenomegaly. Findings of a hemoglobin level greater than 18.5 g/dL (185 g/L) in men or greater than 16.5 g/dL (16.5 g/L) in women invariably indicate an elevated red blood cell mass. Concomitant leukocytosis (often with basophilia) and thrombocytosis (suggesting trilineage myeloproliferation) as well as hepatosplenomegaly further support the diagnosis. In addition, more than 97% of patients with PV have an activating mutation in the signaling protein JAK2 (*JAK2 V617F* mutation). Serum erythropoietin levels are usually suppressed; measurement of the red blood cell mass, previously a diagnostic study for PV, is no longer done. Low-dose aspirin has been shown to decrease the risk of thrombosis and should be given to all patients in the absence of contraindications. Phlebotomy results in the highest overall survival rates and should be performed once or twice weekly until a target hematocrit value of less than 45% is achieved, followed by intermittent phlebotomy to maintain the hematocrit value between 40% and 45%.

The addition of the myelosuppressive agent hydroxyurea to phlebotomy decreases thrombotic events. Patients with PV and an increased risk for thrombosis, defined as age older than 60 years or having a history of a previous thrombotic event, should be treated with hydroxyurea. However, this patient does not require hydroxyurea because of her younger age and no history of thrombosis. Other myelosuppressive agents, such as chlorambucil or busulfan, are leukemogenic and should not be used.

A single dose of the radioisotope phosphorus 32 (^{32}P) may control the hemoglobin level and platelet count for 1 year or more in patients with PV. Although it confers an increased risk for leukemia (up to 11%), ^{32}P may be beneficial for patients who are intolerant of hydroxyurea or who have a limited expected survival. However, it is not first-line therapy and should not be given to this patient at this time.

KEY POINT

Phlebotomy and aspirin are the initial treatments for patients with polycythemia vera.

Bibliography

Hensley B, Geyer H, Mesa R. Polycythemia vera: current pharmacotherapy and future directions. Expert Opin Pharmacother. 2013;14:609-17. [PMID: 23480062]

Item 17   Answer: B

Educational Objective: *Diagnose chronic myeloid leukemia.*

The most likely diagnosis is chronic myeloid leukemia (CML). CML is a clonal hematopoietic progenitor cell disorder characterized by myeloid proliferation. CML consists of a chronic, accelerated, and blast phase. The diagnosis may be established incidentally, or patients may present with symptoms including fatigue, night sweats, weight loss, abdominal discomfort, early satiety, and bleeding. On physical examination, splenomegaly is the most common finding. In chronic-phase CML, the leukocyte count is high, the hemoglobin level is low or normal, and the platelet count is normal or high. The peripheral blood smear shows neutrophilia and left-shifted granulopoiesis. Basophilia is common. An increasing proportion of blasts are seen as the disease progresses to more advanced phases.

Acute myeloid leukemia (AML) is a malignancy of myeloid progenitor cells. Clinical manifestations of marrow failure develop over days to months and include fatigue, dyspnea, and easy bleeding. Fever is commonly caused by infection. The leukocyte count can be low, normal, or high, but circulating myeloblasts are present in most patients. Auer rods, which are clumps of azurophilic granular material that form elongated needles seen in the cytoplasm of leukemic blasts are sometimes seen on the peripheral smear and suggest a diagnosis of AML rather than acute lymphoblastic leukemia.

The myelodysplastic syndromes are clonal hematopoietic progenitor cell disorders characterized by ineffective hematopoiesis and a variable rate of transformation to acute myeloid leukemia. Symptoms include fatigue and easy bleeding. Infections due to neutropenia are a common cause of death. Laboratory studies reveal normocytic or macrocytic anemia. Dysplastic changes on the peripheral blood smear may include nucleated erythrocytes and hypolobated, hypogranular neutrophils, which were not present in this patient.

CML must be distinguished from leukemoid reactions and other myeloproliferative disorders. Detection of the (9;22) translocation by routine cytogenetic studies or fluorescence in situ hybridization assay or of the *BCR-ABL* fusion transcript by reverse transcriptase-polymerase chain reaction is diagnostic of CML and excludes a leukemoid reaction and other diagnoses. A leukemoid reaction is usually defined as a non-leukemic leukocytosis exceeding 50,000/µL (50 × 10^9/L) and is characterized by an increase in early neutrophil precursors in the peripheral blood.

KEY POINT

Detection of the (9;22) translocation by routine cytogenetic studies or fluorescence in situ hybridization (FISH) assay or of the *BCR-ABL* fusion transcript by reverse transcriptase-polymerase chain reaction is diagnostic of chronic myeloid leukemia.

Bibliography

Jabbour E, Kantarjian H. Chronic myeloid leukemia: 2012 update on diagnosis, monitoring, and management. Am J Hematol. 2012;87:1037-45. [PMID: 23090888]

Item 18   Answer: B

Educational Objective: *Diagnose aplastic anemia.*

The most likely diagnosis is aplastic anemia. Aplastic anemia refers to a condition in which the bone marrow fails to produce blood cells, resulting in a hypocellular bone marrow and pancytopenia. This patient's nosebleeds (thrombocytopenia), malaise and fatigue (anemia), and fever (neutropenia) are the classic symptoms associated with pancytopenia. He also had a viral syndrome approximately 6 weeks ago, which may be significant because certain viral illnesses, such as Epstein-Barr virus and cytomegalovirus infection, can cause aplastic anemia. This patient has a very low reticulocyte count and a bone marrow biopsy that is essentially devoid of cellular elements, findings that are consistent with aplastic anemia.

Acute myeloid leukemia (AML) is a malignancy of myeloid progenitor cells characterized by a median age at diagnosis of 67 years. The presentation of AML is similar to that of aplastic anemia. However, the bone marrow biopsy in patients with AML would show an abundance of myeloid blasts, which are not present in this patient's bone marrow findings.

Chronic lymphocytic leukemia (CLL) is the most common form of lymphoid malignancy, with a median age at diagnosis of 70 years. Symptoms vary greatly, and many patients are asymptomatic at diagnosis. Development of CLL would be quite unusual in a younger patient, such as the patient described here. In addition, the leukocyte count in patients with CLL is typically elevated, not depressed, at presentation, and the bone marrow biopsy would show a preponderance of lymphocytes.

The myelodysplastic syndromes (MDS) are a group of clonal hematopoietic progenitor cell disorders characterized by ineffective hematopoiesis and a variable rate of transformation to AML. The incidence of MDS increases with age. In this patient, myelodysplasia is unlikely because of the acute onset of his symptoms and his young age. In addition, the bone marrow findings in myelodysplasia are typically hypercellular, although, less commonly, hypocellular variants occur.

KEY POINT

Aplastic anemia is characterized by hypocellular bone marrow and symptoms associated with pancytopenia, such as bleeding, fever, and fatigue.

Bibliography

Marsh JC, Ball SE, Cavaenagh J, et al. Guidelines for the diagnosis and management of aplastic anaemia. Br J Haematol. 2009;147:43-70. [PMID: 19673883]

Item 19   Answer: B

Educational Objective: *Diagnose myelodysplastic syndrome related to combination chemotherapy and radiation therapy.*

The most likely cause of this patient's findings is a myelodysplastic syndrome related to combination chemotherapy and radiation therapy. The adverse consequences of multiagent chemotherapy and radiation can occur many years after completion of therapy. The myelodysplastic syndromes are progenitor cell clonal disorders characterized by ineffective hematopoiesis and various peripheral cytopenias. Patients have signs and symptoms referable to a specific cytopenia (most often, megaloblastic anemia) and bone marrow findings showing a hypercellular marrow with dyserythropoiesis. Many chromosomal abnormalities are associated with myelodysplastic syndromes, including abnormal numbers of chromosomes, translocations, and structural abnormalities. This patient's absence of lymphadenopathy and hepatosplenomegaly and presence of multiple chromosomal abnormalities on cytogenetic examination of the bone marrow make this diagnosis likely; the multiple chromosomal translocations and deletions present in the bone marrow confirm the diagnosis.

Acute lymphoblastic leukemia (ALL) is a disorder of committed progenitor cells characterized by a proliferation of immature lymphoblasts. ALL constitutes less than 20% of acute leukemias in adult patients, with the highest incidence occurring in the seventh decade of life. Patients present with lymphocytosis, neutropenia, anemia, and thrombocytopenia, as well as lymphadenopathy and hepatosplenomegaly.

Parvovirus B19 infection can lead to abnormal-appearing erythroid precursors but would not be associated with the multiple abnormal cytogenetic changes or excess blasts demonstrated in this patient.

Disease in almost all patients with recurrent Hodgkin lymphoma is detected within 12 years of initial therapy, most often within 2 years. Relapsed Hodgkin lymphoma is characterized by the finding of a palpable mass on physical examination or the presence of lymphoma symptoms, such as fever, anorexia, weight loss, and pruritus. Finally, recurrent Hodgkin lymphoma would not account for this patient's peripheral blood findings or bone marrow chromosomal abnormalities.

KEY POINT

Myelodysplastic syndrome can be a late adverse consequence of combination chemotherapy and radiation therapy.

Bibliography

Borthakur G, Estey AE. Therapy-related acute myelogenous leukemia and myelodysplastic syndrome. Curr Oncol Rep. 2007;9:373-7. [PMID: 17706165]

Item 20   Answer: B

Educational Objective: *Diagnose acute myeloid leukemia.*

The most likely diagnosis is acute myeloid leukemia (AML). Myelodysplastic syndromes are clonal disorders of the hematopoietic progenitor cells that usually occur in patients older than 50 years of age and are characterized by ineffective hematopoiesis and peripheral cytopenia. Although the natural history of distinct subtypes of myelodysplasia ranges from indolent chronic anemia to rapid death from progression to acute leukemia, most patients eventually progress to leukemic syndromes or die of complications of bone marrow failure. Patients with myelodysplastic syndrome treated with azacitidine have significantly delayed transformation to leukemia and improved quality of life. Despite treatment with azacitidine, this patient has AML, as indicated by the peripheral blood smear showing a myeloblast with Auer rods. Auer rods are clumps of azurophilic, needle-shaped crystals made from primary cytoplasmic granules. They occur most often in patients with AML and rarely in patients with myelodysplasia. Fever in patients with AML is almost always related to infection; therefore, this patient must be quickly and thoroughly evaluated for a source of infection and treated empirically with broad-spectrum antibiotics.

Acute lymphoblastic leukemia (ALL) is an extremely aggressive disease of precursor T or B cells, usually of explosive onset. Rapidly increasing blast cells in the blood and bone marrow, bulky lymphadenopathy (especially in the mediastinum), and cytopenia secondary to bone marrow involvement are the usual presenting clinical features. Auer rods do not occur in patients with ALL.

Acute promyelocytic leukemia (APL) is a subtype of AML that occurs in 10% of patients with AML. Patients with APL may have circulating blasts, but the predominant cell is a large immature granulocyte with multiple granules overlying the cytoplasm and nucleus. The disorder is exquisitely sensitive to anthracycline cytotoxic therapy. The addition of all-*trans*-retinoic acid and arsenic trioxide to the therapy has resulted in high cure and salvage rates in patients with APL.

Typically, chronic myeloid leukemia (CML) is diagnosed as a result of a routine blood count that shows leukocytosis with circulating myeloid precursors in all stages of development. Patients with CML may have circulating blasts but also will have more mature granulocytes and will not have Auer rods.

KEY POINT

A peripheral blood smear showing myeloblasts that contain Auer rods is diagnostic of acute myeloid leukemia.

Bibliography

O'Donnell MR, Appelbaum FR, Coutre SE, et al. Acute myeloid leukemia. J Natl Compr Canc Netw. 2008;6:962-93. [PMID: 19176196]

Item 21   Answer: C

Educational Objective: *Diagnose monoclonal gammopathy of unknown significance.*

The most likely diagnosis is monoclonal gammopathy of unknown significance (MGUS). MGUS is defined as the presence of a serum monoclonal (M) protein level of less than 3 g/dL (30 g/L), fewer than 10% plasma cells on bone marrow examination, and no evidence of anemia, kidney failure, bone disease, or other myeloma-related end-organ damage. MGUS is always asymptomatic and is usually discovered by means of incidental laboratory findings, most often, hyperproteinemia. Although MGUS precedes most cases of multiple myeloma, most patients with MGUS do not develop a plasma cell dyscrasia requiring therapy. Therefore, screening for monoclonal gammopathies should not be done, but testing should be considered for patients with incidentally discovered hyperproteinemia, unexplained anemia or kidney dysfunction, hypercalcemia, peripheral neuropathy, or lytic bone lesions. The initial evaluation of most patients with an established M protein abnormality includes a complete blood count; serum calcium, albumin, and creatinine measurement; urinalysis; serum protein and urine electrophoresis and immunofixation; quantitative immunoglobulin measurement (IgG, IgM, IgA); serum free light-chain testing; and a skeletal survey.

AL amyloidosis is the most common amyloidosis and is caused by the deposition of monoclonal light chains. Clinical manifestations include nephrotic-range proteinuria with worsening kidney function, restrictive cardiomyopathy, and hepatomegaly. Neurologic findings include a symmetric distal sensorimotor neuropathy, carpal tunnel syndrome, and autonomic neuropathy with orthostatic hypotension. Periorbital purpura and macroglossia are characteristic of AL amyloidosis. A diagnosis of AL amyloidosis requires characteristic findings on tissue biopsy, the presence of a monoclonal plasma cell disorder, and evidence that the amyloid deposits are composed of clonal light chains.

Asymptomatic (smoldering) multiple myeloma is characterized by a serum M protein level of 3 g/dL (30 g/L) or more, regardless of isotype, or 10% or more of clonal plasma cells on bone marrow examination and the absence of myeloma-related end-organ damage. The risk of asymptomatic multiple myeloma progressing to symptomatic multiple myeloma or AL amyloidosis is 73% at 15 years, with a median time to progression of 4.8 years.

Waldenström macroglobulinemia is a lymphoplasmacytic lymphoma characterized by production of monoclonal IgM antibodies. Constitutional symptoms, lymphadenopathy, and hepatosplenomegaly may be present. Diagnosis requires demonstration of lymphoplasmacytic lymphoma comprising 10% or more of the bone marrow cellularity and the presence of an IgM M protein.

KEY POINT

Monoclonal gammopathy of unknown significance is defined as the presence of a serum monoclonal protein level of less than 3 g/dL (30 g/L) fewer than 10% plasma cells on bone marrow examination, and no evidence of anemia, kidney failure, bone disease, or other myeloma-related end-organ damage.

Bibliography
Anguille S, Bryant C. Monoclonal gammopathy of undetermined significance. CMAJ. 2013;185:1345. [PMID: 23695605]

Item 22   Answer: D
Educational Objective: *Diagnose multiple myeloma.*

The test that will be most helpful in establishing the diagnosis is urine immunofixation. This patient has many features of multiple myeloma, including bone pain, pancytopenia, kidney disease, and hypercalcemia. Multiple myeloma is a malignancy of plasma cells. Most myelomas produce a monoclonal (M) protein consisting of an intact immunoglobulin composed of a heavy chain (IgG, IgA, or IgD) and a κ or λ light chain, but they may secrete free light chains alone (16% of cases), or, rarely, no immunoglobulin. Symptomatic myeloma is diagnosed by the presence of 10% or more clonal plasma cells on bone marrow biopsy, the presence of an M protein, and evidence of myeloma-related end-organ damage. The M protein is produced and secreted by the malignant plasma cells and is detected by serum protein electrophoresis and/or of urine protein electrophoresis combined with immunofixation of the serum and urine. Immunofixation confirms the presence of an M protein and determines its type. The absence of an M protein in the serum and the finding of hypogammaglobulinemia suggest that the M protein is a light chain, which is filtered by the glomerulus and is readily found by urine immunofixation but not found in the serum. Although fil-

tered light chains are proteins, most routine urinalysis dipsticks test primarily for albumin and may not detect the presence of the myeloma protein in the urine, as in this patient.

An abdominal fat pad aspirate revealing amorphous eosinophilic material that demonstrates apple-green birefringence when stained with Congo red and viewed under polarized light will establish the diagnosis of AL amyloidosis. However, this patient lacks the characteristic clinical findings of AL amyloidosis, such as proteinuria, restrictive cardiomyopathy, and hepatomegaly, which makes this diagnosis unlikely.

The most common finding in the peripheral blood smear of patients with multiple myeloma is rouleaux formation followed by leukopenia and thrombocytopenia. Monoclonal plasma cells are rarely detected in the peripheral blood. The peripheral blood smear findings will support a diagnosis of multiple myeloma but will not help establish the diagnosis.

KEY POINT

Monoclonal protein is produced and secreted by the malignant plasma cells and is detected by serum protein electrophoresis and/or urine protein electrophoresis combined with immunofixation.

Bibliography
Smith D, Yong K. Multiple myeloma. BMJ. 2013;346:f3863. [PMID: 23803862]

Item 23   Answer: C
Educational Objective: *Diagnose multiple myeloma.*

Multiple myeloma is the most likely explanation for this patient's clinical findings. Multiple myeloma may cause acute kidney injury, anemia, hypercalcemia, and a decreased anion gap (as is seen in this patient), although not all of these findings may be present in every patient.

Acute kidney injury is the initial presentation in as many as 50% of patients with multiple myeloma and may be the result of direct toxicity of myeloma proteins on the renal tubule or myeloma-associated hypercalcemia. Hypercalcemia in multiple myeloma results from osteoclast activation. Hypercalcemia in the presence of kidney failure should raise suspicion for multiple myeloma, as kidney injury is usually associated with hypocalcemia due to hyperphosphatemia and a decrease in kidney 1-α hydroxylation of 25-hydroxycholecalciferol (25-hydroxy vitamin D_3). Hypercalcemia may contribute to kidney failure by several mechanisms, including hemodynamic effects of vasoconstriction that mediate kidney sodium and water retention and direct effects on renal tubular sodium and water handling, resulting in prerenal azotemia secondary to volume depletion. Anemia results from the uncontrolled clonal proliferation of plasma cells and typically causes a normocytic anemia but may progress to other cytopenias. The anion gap, normally approximately 12 plus or minus 2 mEq/L (12 ± 2 mmol/L), may be decreased in patients with multiple myeloma because of the presence of an unmeasured cationic light chain that causes an increase in negative ions to maintain electroneutrality, thereby decreasing the calculated gap between measured positive and negative serum ions.

Although patients with hydrochlorothiazide toxicity may have volume depletion and prerenal azotemia, the presence of this patient's hematologic and metabolic abnormalities makes hydrochlorothiazide toxicity less likely as a unifying diagnosis.

The hypercalcemia that characterizes the milk-alkali syndrome is not associated with anemia and is usually associated with metabolic alkalosis.

Primary hyperparathyroidism is generally associated with hypophosphatemia and not anemia or proteinuria.

KEY POINT

A decreased anion gap in the presence of anemia, proteinuria, hypercalcemia, and kidney failure suggests the diagnosis of multiple myeloma.

Bibliography

Smith D, Yong K. Multiple myeloma. BMJ. 2013;346:f3863. [PMID: 23803862]

Item 24   Answer: D

Educational Objective: *Diagnose von Willebrand disease.*

A von Willebrand factor (vWF) antigen determination should be performed next. The most likely diagnosis is von Willebrand disease (vWD) given the patient's history of bleeding, her quantitatively normal platelet count, and her suggestive family history. vWD is the most common inherited bleeding disorder, affecting 1% of the population. Because vWF plays an important role in platelet adherence to injured epithelium, patients with symptomatic disease have easy bruising or mild to moderate nasal or gingival bleeding or heavy menstrual flow and excessive bleeding following surgical procedures, as in this patient. Although vWF antigen can be falsely elevated during periods of acute inflammation, pregnancy, or use of estrogen products, this study will most likely reveal decreased levels of vWF reflecting the presence of type 1 vWD in this otherwise healthy patient. Desmopressin, which releases stored vWF and factor VIII from endothelial cells, is first-line therapy for most subtypes of vWD and can be administered intravenously or intranasally.

Plasma fibrinogen measurement is not indicated. The plasma fibrinogen level would likely be normal, as this patient has a disorder of primary hemostasis given her history suggesting mucocutaneous bleeding and her family history.

Platelet function testing measures qualitative platelet defects and may be abnormal in patients with vWD, but is not considered adequately sensitive to establish the diagnosis, particularly for mild forms of the disease that tend to predominate in the general population.

The prothrombin time (PT) and activated partial thromboplastin time (aPTT) or other studies assessing the coagulation pathways are more appropriate in the evaluation of suggested secondary hemostasis bleeding disorders. The aPTT may be abnormal if factor VIII activity is decreased in patients with moderate or severe disease.

KEY POINT

Von Willebrand disease should be suspected in a patient presenting with easy bruising or mucocutaneous bleeding, or heavy menstrual blood flow, or excessive postoperative bleeding, and a strong family history of a bleeding disorder.

Bibliography

Sadler JE, Mannucci PM, Berntorp E, et al.: Impact, diagnosis and treatment of von Willebrand disease. Thromb Haemost 2000;84:160-74. [PMID: 10959685]

Item 25   Answer: B

Educational Objective: *Diagnose an acquired bleeding disorder.*

Examination of a peripheral blood smear is the most appropriate next diagnostic step. This patient's low hemoglobin level, leukocyte count, and platelet count (pancytopenia) suggest a primary bone marrow disorder as a cause of her bleeding. Examination of a peripheral blood smear provides an assessment of bone marrow function and in this patient with pancytopenia, weight loss, and new-onset low back pain may provide indirect evidence of malignancy involving the bone marrow if immature granulocytes or erythroid precursors are present (termed a leukoerythroblastic smear).

The presence of antiplatelet antibodies is a nonspecific finding and is not diagnostic of immune thrombocytopenia, as antiplatelet antibodies may also be present in patients with a history of taking medication associated with development of antibodies toward platelets that may not be responsible for the thrombocytopenia. Additionally, immune thrombocytopenia would not explain this patient's other hematologic abnormalities and is unlikely in this patient.

Platelet function testing would not be helpful, as this patient has a quantitative platelet abnormality in addition to other abnormalities suggesting a bone marrow process that requires further evaluation. Additionally, automated platelet function testing may be abnormal in a patient with a low platelet count but would not be diagnostic of a primary platelet abnormality.

Prothrombin time and activated partial thromboplastin time test coagulation factors. However, this patient has mucocutaneous bleeding, which is suggestive of a disorder of primary hemostasis. This is also supported by the presence of petechiae on physical examination.

KEY POINT

In patients with a bleeding disorder with evidence of a primary bone marrow abnormality as a possible cause, examination of the peripheral blood smear should be the initial diagnostic step.

Bibliography

Hayward CP, Diagnosis and management of mild bleeding disorders. Am Soc Hematol Edu Program. 2005;423-8 [PMID: 16304414]

Item 26   Answer: A

Educational Objective: *Screen for bleeding disorders in a patient prior to surgery.*

The most appropriate screening approach to detect bleeding disorders is obtaining a thorough clinical history. The clinical history should focus on whether the patient has had any abnormal bleeding in the past (particularly following any previous surgical procedures) or any systemic illnesses that might increase bleeding risk (such as liver disease). If bleeding is reported, its severity should be determined. Also determine whether the bleeding is spontaneous or is an excessive response to normal bleeding after injury, surgery, or dental procedures; whether the bleeding pattern is lifelong or recently acquired; and whether the bleeding suggests a platelet or a coagulation defect.

Disorders of primary hemostasis, such as platelet-related bleeding, tend to occur immediately after injury and often affect the mucous membranes or the skin in the form of petechiae. Disorders of secondary hemostasis, such as coagulation-related bleeding, may be delayed in onset and manifested more by deep tissue bruises (ecchy-moses) and may produce hemarthroses in patients with congenital factor deficiencies. Women should be asked about the pattern of menstrual bleeding or, if postmenopausal, about whether any abnormal bleeding has occurred. Obtaining a detailed medication history, including use of medications that may increase the risk of bleeding (such as nonsteroidal anti-inflammatory drugs), and a family history of any bleeding disorders is an essential part of the evaluation process.

In the absence of a personal or family history of abnormal bleeding, liver disease, significant alcohol use, malabsorption, or anticoagulation therapy, the likelihood of a bleeding disorder is low, and no further preoperative testing is required. Patients with any of these risk factors should be evaluated further by obtaining a prothrombin time, an activated partial thromboplastin time, and a platelet count. Additional testing, including evaluation for conditions such as von Willebrand disease, may be indicated in patients with a history of bleeding problems.

Although preoperative evaluation has traditionally involved obtaining complete blood counts and coagulation studies, the yield of these tests in low-risk patients undergoing low-risk procedures is extremely low; individual assessment of bleeding risk and the potential risks and benefits of preoperative testing are key elements of practicing high value care.

KEY POINT

In the absence of a personal or family history of abnormal bleeding, liver disease, significant alcohol use, malabsorption, or anticoagulation therapy, the likelihood of a bleeding disorder is low in a patient being evaluated prior to surgery, and no further preoperative testing for bleeding disorders is required.

Bibliography
Smetana GW, Macpherson DS. The case against routine preoperative laboratory testing. Med Clin North Am. 2003;87:7-40. [PMID: 12575882]

Item 27   Answer: A
Educational Objective: *Diagnose disseminated intravascular coagulation.*

The most likely diagnosis is disseminated intravascular coagulation (DIC). DIC results from the widespread activation of coagulation that causes formation of fibrin clots that may lead to a thrombotic disorder. However, in most patients, secondary fibrinolysis dissolves the fibrin clots, and consumption of platelets and coagulation factors causes thrombocytopenia, clotting factor deficiencies, bleeding, and vascular injury. Erythrocyte consumption causes a microangiopathic hemolytic anemia with characteristic fragmented erythrocytes seen on a peripheral blood smear. DIC most commonly occurs in patients with infections (with gram-negative organisms being the most common), cancer, and obstetrical complications.

The diagnosis of DIC is based on prolonged coagulation times (prothrombin time and activated partial thromboplastin time), an elevated D-dimer titer, a decreased serum fibrinogen level and platelet count, and the presence of microangiopathic hemolytic anemia. The degree of these abnormalities depends on the extent of consumption of platelets and coagulation factors and the ability of the patient to compensate for these findings.

The differential diagnosis of DIC includes two thrombotic microangiopathies: thrombotic thrombocytopenic purpura (TTP) and hemolytic uremic syndrome (HUS). These two syndromes overlap,

and it is often difficult to distinguish between them. The pentad of TTP includes thrombocytopenia, microangiopathic hemolytic anemia, neurologic deficits, kidney impairment, and fever; however, all five findings do not need to be present for the diagnosis to be established. HUS is a condition primarily of children and mainly affects the kidneys as a result of intrarenal platelet-fibrin thrombi. Neither TTP nor HUS is associated with a prolonged prothrombin time or activated partial thromboplastin time, elevated D-dimer titer, or decreased serum fibrinogen level.

Immune thrombocytopenic purpura (ITP) may be autoimmune mediated or drug induced. The diagnosis is based on excluding other causes of thrombocytopenia, other systemic illnesses, and medications. The only laboratory disorder associated with ITP is thrombocytopenia, which would not explain the other clinical and laboratory findings in this patient.

KEY POINT

The diagnosis of disseminated intravascular coagulation is based on a prolonged prothrombin time and activated partial thromboplastin time, an elevated D-dimer titer, a decreased serum fibrinogen level and platelet count, and the presence of microangiopathic hemolytic anemia.

Bibliography
Levi M, Toh CH, Thachil J, Watson HG. Guidelines for the diagnosis and management of disseminated intravascular coagulation. British Committee for Standards in Haematology. Br J Haematol. 2009 Apr;145(1):24-33. [PMID: 19222477]

Item 28   Answer: B
Educational Objective: *Diagnose factor VIII or factor IX deficiency (hemophilia).*

This patient most likely has hemophilia, and the most appropriate next diagnostic study is measurement of factor VIII and factor IX levels for hemophilia A and B, respectively. Although usually diagnosed in childhood, mild hemophilia may not become apparent until an older age, particularly in the absence of a clear family history of X-linked bleeding disorders. This patient's bleeding is suggestive of a disorder of secondary hemostasis with bleeding into the joints and soft tissues. Results of laboratory studies are consistent with this diagnosis based on a normal prothrombin time (PT) and prolonged activated partial thromboplastin time (aPTT) that fully corrects on mixing with a 1:1 ratio of normal plasma (as opposed to the presence of an inhibitor, such as to factor VIII, which does not correct on a mixing study). Laboratory findings in hemophilia A and B are indistinguishable. Replacement of the deficient factor is the treatment of choice. Aspirin and nonsteroidal anti-inflammatory drugs are contraindicated in patients with hemophilia.

Primary hemostatic disorders, including von Willebrand disease, usually present with diffuse mucocutaneous bleeding, which is inconsistent with the clinical findings in this patient. Therefore, platelet function studies or testing for von Willebrand factor antigen would not be indicated.

KEY POINT

Factor deficiencies, such as hemophilia, are characterized by a normal prothrombin time and prolonged activated partial thromboplastin time that fully corrects with a mixing study.

Bibliography
Stine KC, Becton DL. Bleeding disorders: when is normal bleeding not normal? J Ark Med Soc. 2009;106:40-2. [PMID: 19715248]

Item 29   Answer: A

Educational Objective: *Perform age- and sex-specific cancer screening for a patient with idiopathic venous thromboembolism.*

The most appropriate evaluation is to ensure that this patient's age- and sex-specific cancer screening is up to date. Acquired thrombophilia is much more common than inherited thrombophilia and is often associated with greater thrombotic risks. Venous thromboembolic (VTE) disease incidence increases with age, perhaps because of the increased prevalence of acquired VTE risk factors such as surgery and cancer in the aging population. Cancer increases the risk of VTE by 4- to 20-fold. Cancers express tissue factor on their surface and induce tissue factor expression by endothelial cells and monocytes, contributing to a prothrombotic state. Thrombotic risk varies by cancer type and stage; risk is highest with pancreatic and brain tumors, intermediate with lung cancer and lymphoma, and lower with breast and prostate cancer. Metastatic disease increases thrombotic risk twofold. While aggressive screening for cancer in patients with idiopathic VTE makes intuitive sense, there is no evidence from prospective studies that aggressive cancer screening either is cost effective or improves survival. A rationale approach is to perform a careful history and physical examination, follow up on potential cancer symptoms and signs, and ensure that the patient's age- and sex-specific cancer screening is up to date.

Testing for inherited thrombophilias is probably not indicated in this patient at this time. Generally, the clinical setting of a thrombotic event (unprovoked versus provoked) provides greater prognostic information as to recurrence risk than the results of thrombophilia testing. Common thrombophilic defects such as factor V Leiden heterozygosity modestly increase recurrence risks (1.5 fold). In contrast, more potent thrombophilic states such as antithrombin deficiency that are associated with significant recurrence risks are rarely identified. Therefore, in most instances, the results of thrombophilia testing will not influence treatment duration and such testing is not generally recommended.

KEY POINT

The most appropriate evaluation for idiopathic venous thromboembolism is to ensure that the patient's age- and sex-appropriate cancer screening is up to date.

Bibliography

Van Doormaal FF, Terpstra W, Van Der Griend R, et al. Is extensive screening for cancer in idiopathic venous thromboembolism warranted? J Thromb Haemost. 2011;9: 79-84. [[PMID: 20946181]

Item 30   Answer: D

Educational Objective: *Diagnose inherited thrombophilia.*

Evaluation for thrombophilia should be initiated 2 weeks after the patient completes warfarin therapy. Screening for factor V Leiden and the prothrombin gene mutation (PT^{G2021A}) can be done at any time, but antithrombin, protein C, protein S, and dysfibrinogenemia testing may be altered during acute thrombotic events and their treatment. Therefore, these levels are most accurately assessed after the acute thrombotic event has resolved and anticoagulants have been discontinued for at least 2 to 4 weeks. In particular, warfarin reduces vitamin K-dependent protein C and protein S levels. Heparin lowers antithrombin III levels. Acute venous thromboembolic disease (VTE) may cause transient lowering of protein C, protein S, and antithrombin III levels as well as elevated antiphospholipid titers. Testing for these inherited hypercoagulable states is best done after the treatment of the acute VTE has been completed for approximately 2 weeks.

KEY POINT

Avoid testing for inherited thrombophilias during the acute phase of a venous thromboembolic disease, especially if anticoagulant therapy has already been initiated, since many false-positive test results may occur during this period.

Bibliography

Chong LY, Fenu E, Stansby G, Hodgkinson S; Guideline Development Group. Management of venous thromboembolic diseases and the role of thrombophilia testing: summary of NICE guidance. BMJ. 2012;344:e3979. [PMID: 22740565]

Item 31   Answer: A

Educational Objective: *Diagnose antiphospholipid syndrome.*

The most likely diagnosis is antiphospholipid syndrome (APS). APS is an acquired autoimmune disorder associated with venous or arterial thromboembolism, pregnancy loss, thrombocytopenia, kidney impairment, vasculitis, and cardiac valvular abnormalities. APS can occur in a primary form or in association with other autoimmune diseases such as systemic lupus erythematosus. APS is characterized by the presence of antibodies against phospholipids (for example, cardiolipin) or phospholipid-binding proteins (for example, β_2-glycoprotein 1) that can be detected with enzyme immunoassays or phospholipid-dependent coagulation tests such as the (prolonged) activated partial thromboplastin time (aPTT) and the dilute Russell viper venom time. APS can cause thrombosis by inducing tissue factor expression, disrupting protein C and antithrombin function, or activating platelets and the complement cascade. APS is associated with a high risk of thromboembolism.

Of the inherited thrombophilic conditions, factor V Leiden mutation is the most common. This mutation can be detected by gene analysis or by a coagulation assay (the activated protein C resistance assay). This mutation is found in approximately 20% of all individuals with deep venous thrombosis (DVT) and occurs much more frequently in those with idiopathic DVT; it is also associated with DVT in women who take oral contraceptive pills.

Antithrombin deficiency is an autosomal dominant disorder. The prevalence of the heterozygous condition is 0.02% in the general population. Homozygous antithrombin deficiency is generally not compatible with life. Heterozygous antithrombin deficiency is associated with a risk for venous thromboembolism of approximately 1% per year.

Another common genetic thrombophilia is a guanine to adenine mutation in the prothrombin gene at position 20210 ($PT^{G20210A}$), resulting in higher prothrombin levels in affected individuals. This confers a three- to fourfold increased risk of venous thromboembolism. Neither factor V Leiden mutation nor prothrombin gene mutation is associated with fetal loss or a prolonged aPTT.

KEY POINT

The antiphospholipid syndrome is an acquired autoimmune disorder associated with venous or arterial thromboembolism, pregnancy loss, thrombocytopenia, kidney impairment, vasculitis, cardiac valvular abnormalities and a prolonged activated partial thromboplastin time.

Bibliography

Miyakis S, Lockshin MD, Atsumi T, et al. International consensus statement on an update of the classification criteria for definite antiphospholipid syndrome (APS). J Thromb Haemost. 2006 Feb;4(2):295-306. [PMID: 16420554]

Item 32   Answer: B

Educational Objective: *Treat antiphospholipid syndrome with warfarin.*

In this patient with antiphospholipid syndrome (APS), warfarin should be continued indefinitely. APS is defined by the presence of antiphospholipid antibodies and typical clinical manifestations. Clinical criteria for the diagnosis of APS are arterial or venous thrombosis and pregnancy loss or complications; other manifestations include livedo reticularis (a lattice-like skin rash), thrombocytopenia, valvular heart disease, unexplained prolongation of the activated partial thromboplastin time, and microangiopathic kidney impairment.

This disorder may occur as an independent syndrome (primary APS) or secondary to underlying systemic lupus erythematosus (SLE). Antiphospholipid antibodies include anticardiolipin antibodies, anti-β_2-glycoprotein 1 antibodies, and the lupus anticoagulant and are found in 30% to 40% of patients with SLE. Positive results for anticardiolipin antibody or lupus inhibitor assay should be confirmed over time to ensure that these are not transient changes, which can occur after viral infections. Ideally, at least two positive laboratory tests (anticardiolipin antibody or lupus inhibitor assay) at least 12 weeks apart should be documented to confirm the presence of APS before a patient is committed to lifelong anticoagulation therapy.

A systematic review reported that the absolute risk of new venous thromboembolic (VTE) disease in patients with antiphospholipid antibodies is low (less than 1% per year). However, this risk may be increased to up to 10% per year in women with antiphospholipid antibodies or APS and recurrent fetal loss and more than 10% per year in patients with antiphospholipid antibodies and previous VTE who have discontinued anticoagulants within 6 months. Current recommendations are to treat these latter high-risk patients with anticoagulants indefinitely. The benefit of VTE prevention with long-term anticoagulation in these high-risk patients may outweigh the risk for bleeding complications.

KEY POINT

The risk of venous thromboembolic disease is increased to up to 10% per year in women with antiphospholipid antibodies or antiphospholipid syndrome and recurrent fetal loss; current recommendations are to treat these patients with anticoagulation therapy indefinitely.

Bibliography

Kwak-Kim J, Agcaoili MS, Aleta L, et al. Management of women with recurrent pregnancy losses and antiphospholipid antibody syndrome. Am J Reprod Immunol. 2013;69:596-607. [PMID: 23521391]

Item 33   Answer: E

Educational Objective: *Manage a patient with a history of transfusion-associated anaphylaxis.*

The most appropriate erythrocyte product to minimize the risk of an anaphylactic transfusion reaction in this patient is washed erythrocytes. The diagnosis of severe IgA deficiency should be considered in any patient with a history of anaphylaxis during a blood transfusion. Most patients with IgA deficiency are asymptomatic, although they are also prone to gastrointestinal infections (particularly *Giardia lamblia*) and have an increased risk for autoimmune disorders, including rheumatoid arthritis and systemic lupus erythematosus. Some patients with severe IgA deficiency develop anti-IgA antibodies, which may lead to an anaphylactic reaction when blood products containing IgA are used in transfusion. Erythrocyte and platelet products may contain small amounts of plasma (with IgA present); consequently, anaphylaxis may occur with fresh frozen plasma (FFP), platelets, and erythrocytes if given in these patients. Washing erythrocytes and platelets can remove plasma proteins and greatly decrease the incidence of anaphylaxis. Transfusion of blood products from an IgA-deficient donor would be another option to minimize the transfusion-associated risk of anaphylaxis.

Cytomegalovirus (CMV)-negative blood would not be indicated for this patient who has normal T-cell function and is not at risk for CMV infection.

γ-Irradiation of erythrocytes is used to minimize the incidence of graft-versus-host disease by eradicating any lymphocytes present in the transfusion when given to an immunocompromised recipient, but would not decrease the risk for anaphylaxis and would not be indicated for this immunocompetent patient.

Leukoreduction of erythrocytes decreases the incidence of febrile nonhemolytic transfusion reactions, CMV transmission, and alloimmunization but does not decrease the risk for anaphylaxis.

Phenotypically matched erythrocytes are indicated for patients who have a high risk for alloimmunization and subsequent delayed hemolytic transfusion reaction, such as patients with sickle cell disease; however, phenotypically matched (matched for ABO, Rh, and Kell antigens) erythrocytes would not decrease the risk for anaphylaxis.

KEY POINT

Using washed erythrocytes and platelets minimizes the risk for transfusion-associated anaphylaxis.

Bibliography

Sandler SG. How I manage patients suspected of having had an IgA anaphylactic transfusion reaction. Transfusion. 2006;46:10-13. [PMID: 16398725]

Item 34   Answer: D

Educational Objective: *Manage ABO and Rh compatibility issues in a patient who requires emergent erythrocyte transfusion.*

This patient should undergo transfusion with O-negative erythrocyte products. Whenever possible, erythrocytes should be ABO and Rh compatible between the recipient and the donor. When an exact ABO and Rh match is not available or when there is not time for blood typing and screening to be done for patients who require emergent transfusion, the least incompatible blood products should be transfused. Humans develop antibodies against ABO and Rh antigens not present on their erythrocytes. Therefore, this patient will have developed antibodies against blood group B but not blood group A. He will also have developed antibodies against Rh(D) because his blood type is Rh negative. Consequently, the most compatible blood type of the choices listed is O negative. Because type O-negative blood lacks both A and B antigens, as well as the Rh(D) antigen, it is considered the universal erythrocyte donor product and should be given when emergent transfusion is indicated and the recipient's blood type is unknown or when an exact ABO and Rh match is not available.

The use of A-positive erythrocytes is not the best option because of Rh incompatibility, which could lead to an acute or delayed hemolytic transfusion reaction. However, this approach could be considered in emergency situations if A-negative and O-negative blood is not available.

AB-negative erythrocytes would be incompatible because of anti-B antibodies present in the patient's plasma, which would react against donor erythrocytes and could lead to an acute hemolytic transfusion reaction.

B-positive erythrocytes would also be both ABO and Rh incompatible and are therefore not an appropriate transfusion product for this patient.

KEY POINT

Type O-negative is the universal erythrocyte donor product because it lacks both A and B antigens as well as the Rh(D) antigen and can be given when emergent transfusion is indicated and the recipient's blood type is unknown or when an exact ABO and Rh match is not available to avoid a hemolytic transfusion reaction.

Bibliography
Goodell PP, Uhl L, Mohammed M, Powers AA. Risk of hemolytic transfusion reactions following emergency-release RBC transfusion. Am J Clin Pathol. 2010;134:202-6. [PMID: 20660321]

Item 35   Answer: D

Educational Objective: *Evaluate a patient with a delayed hemolytic transfusion reaction.*

The presence of new alloantibodies leading to a delayed hemolytic transfusion reaction (DHTR) would best explain this patient's current clinical presentation. She has sickle cell anemia and has received a blood transfusion in the past week. This patient's severe pain crisis occurring 5 to 10 days after a receiving a transfusion is classic for a DHTR. Her clinical course, including jaundice, an elevated serum indirect bilirubin level, and a current hemoglobin level lower than a recent value, is most characteristic of a DHTR. Delayed transfusion reactions are caused by an amnestic minor, non-ABO erythrocyte antibody. Following a transfusion, there is a 1% to 1.6% chance of developing these minor non-ABO alloantibodies, and DHTR occurs when the patient is re-exposed to the same antigen with a subsequent transfusion. Alloantibodies tend to occur in patients who receive multiple blood transfusions over time, such as those with sickle cell anemia.

The presence of antibodies against recipient neutrophils present in donor plasma is known to cause transfusion-related acute lung injury (TRALI), which may mimic noncardiogenic pulmonary edema, including radiographic evidence of pulmonary edema and pulmonary infiltrates. Patients may also have fever and hypotension. This constellation of symptoms and findings is not consistent with this patient's presentation, which is most characteristic of a pain crisis. In addition, TRALI occurs during or soon after a transfusion, and this patient's findings were delayed several days after the transfusion.

Platelet refractoriness is an inappropriately low increment in the platelet count following a transfusion, generally defined as an increment of less than 10,000/µL $(10 \times 10^9/L)$. HLA alloimmunization can cause platelet refractoriness, but this patient did not receive platelets, and HLA alloimmunization would not explain her current findings.

Anaphylaxis during blood transfusion can rarely occur in patients with a severe IgA deficiency, but this patient did not experience anaphylaxis.

KEY POINT

Clinical findings of delayed hemolytic transfusion reaction typically develop approximately 5 to 10 days after erythrocyte transfusion and include anemia, jaundice, and fever and a worsening pain crisis in patients with sickle cell anemia.

Bibliography
Scheunemann LP, Ataga KI. Delayed hemolytic transfusion reaction in sickle cell disease. Am J Med Sci. 2010;339:266-9. [PMID: 20051821]

Item 36   Answer: D

Educational Objective: *Diagnose transfusion-related acute lung injury.*

The most likely diagnosis is transfusion-related acute lung injury (TRALI). This patient developed a fever, dyspnea, diffuse pulmonary infiltrates, and hypoxia during a blood transfusion. This presentation is consistent with TRALI, a reaction caused by antileukocyte antibodies in the donor blood product directed against recipient leukocytes, which then sequester in the lungs, usually during or within 6 hours of a transfusion. TRALI can occur with any blood product, even erythrocytes and platelets, which may have small amounts of plasma. Because of the diffuse pulmonary infiltrates, dyspnea, and hypoxia, differentiating TRALI from noncardiac pulmonary edema may be difficult. Treatment of TRALI is primarily supportive, and most patients fully recover within several days to 1 week.

An acute hemolytic transfusion reaction (AHTR) is most commonly caused by a clerical error leading to ABO incompatibility. Very early in the transfusion, patients develop hypotension and disseminated intravascular coagulation, but this patient presented primarily with hypoxia and is therefore unlikely to be experiencing an AHTR.

Febrile nonhemolytic transfusion reactions occur commonly during transfusion and are also characterized by fever. However, a febrile nonhemolytic transfusion reaction would not lead to hypoxia and pulmonary infiltrates.

TRALI can be difficult to distinguish from transfusion-associated circulatory overload. However, transfusion-associated circulatory overload is less likely than TRALI in this patient because she had only received a single unit of packed erythrocytes and had no underlying cardiac disease, jugular venous distention, S_3, or peripheral edema.

KEY POINT

Transfusion-related acute lung injury is characterized by fever, dyspnea, diffuse pulmonary infiltrates, and hypoxia occurring during or within hours of a transfusion and resembles noncardiac pulmonary edema.

Bibliography
Silliman CC, Fung YL, Ball JB, Khan SY. Transfusion-related acute lung injury (TRALI): current concepts and misconceptions. Blood Rev. 2009;23:245-55. [PMID: 19699017]

Section 6

Infectious Disease Medicine

Questions

Item 1 [Advanced]

A 54-year-old woman is evaluated in the emergency department because of fever, muscle stiffness, and altered mental status. The patient was well until 2 days ago, when she had fever and myalgia. Today, she also had muscle stiffness, restlessness, and difficulty remembering things. She reports no respiratory infection, headache, gastrointestinal symptoms, or rash. She has hypertension treated with lisinopril and depression treated with sertraline. The dose of sertraline was increased to 200 mg daily last week.

On physical examination, temperature is 38.9°C (102.1°F), blood pressure is 144/74 mm Hg, pulse rate is 112/min, respiratory rate is 18/min, and oxygen saturation is 96% on ambient air. She is agitated, diaphoretic, and shivering. Her gait is ataxic, muscle tone is increased, and deep tendon reflexes are increased. Myoclonus is present.

Which of the following is the most likely diagnosis?

(A) Heat stroke
(B) Malignant hyperthermia
(C) Neuroleptic malignant syndrome
(D) Serotonin syndrome

Item 2 [Advanced]

A 32-year-old man is evaluated in the emergency department for a 12-hour history of severe agitation and tremors. The patient has a history of developmental delay and chronic schizoaffective disorder and resides in a group home. Medications are lithium, valproic acid, and fluphenazine.

Physical examination shows an agitated overweight man in three-point restraints. Temperature is 39.4°C (103.0°F), blood pressure is 110/65 mm Hg, and pulse rate is 110/min. Generalized tremors, rigidity, agitation, and diaphoresis are noted.

Results of laboratory studies show a serum creatine kinase level of 1480 units/L.

Which of the following is the most likely diagnosis?

(A) Lithium intoxication
(B) Malignant hyperthermia
(C) Neuroleptic malignant syndrome
(D) Serotonin syndrome

Item 3 [Basic]

A 45-year-old woman is evaluated in the clinic because of a 1-week history of fever. One week ago, she was diagnosed with pyelonephritis and prescribed a 10-day course of trimethoprim-sulfamethoxa-

zole based on culture results. The urinary tract symptoms resolved over 3 days, but she continued to feel feverish. She took her temperature at that time, and it was 38.5°C (101.3° F). The fever has persisted. She reports feeling well otherwise and has returned to normal activities. Medical history is unremarkable. The only medication is trimethoprim-sulfamethoxazole.

On physical examination, temperature is 38.3°C (101.1°F). Vital signs are otherwise normal. There is no rash, and the other findings on physical examination are normal.

Findings of complete blood count are normal. Repeat urinalysis shows 3 leukocytes/hpf, and findings are otherwise normal.

Which of the following is the most likely cause of the patient's fever?

(A) Antibiotic-resistant urinary tract infection
(B) Drug fever
(C) Factitious fever
(D) Normal resolving urinary tract infection

Item 4 [Basic]

A 52-year-old man is evaluated because of nasal congestion, frontal headache, and rhinorrhea. He was well until 4 days ago, when rhinorrhea developed. Two days ago, the nasal discharge increased and has become dark green. He has a frontal headache that worsens when he bends over and right upper maxillary tooth pain. He has no other medical problems and takes no medications.

On physical examination, vital signs are normal. Nasal examination shows red, swollen mucosa and a green discharge. He has no lymphadenopathy. He has no pain with palpation over the maxillary sinuses.

What is the best management plan?

(A) Begin treatment with amoxicillin
(B) Begin treatment with imipenem
(C) Obtain sinus computed tomography
(D) Order sinus radiography
(E) Provide symptomatic therapy

Item 5 [Basic]

A 19-year-old man is evaluated because of a 2-day history of sore throat, cough, fever, and chills. On physical examination, temperature is 38.9°C (102.0°F), blood pressure is 122/82 mm Hg, pulse rate is 88/min, and respiration rate is 14/min. The pharynx is erythematous, with tonsillar enlargement and exudates bilaterally. There is no cervical lymphadenopathy.

Which of the following is the most appropriate management?

(A) Obtain throat culture and start penicillin therapy

(B) Perform rapid antigen detection testing

(C) Start penicillin therapy

(D) No further testing or treatment

Item 6 [Advanced]

A 19-year-old woman is evaluated for a 1-week history of left ear canal pruritus, redness, and pain. She swims 1 mile each day and has recently started wearing plastic earplugs to keep water out of her ears while swimming. Her hearing is normal.

On physical examination, she is afebrile, blood pressure is 98/66 mm Hg, pulse rate is 62/min, and respiration rate is 16/min. She appears healthy and is in no distress. There is pain with tugging on the pinna and compression or movement of the tragus. The left ear canal is shown (Plate 17). With irrigation, the left tympanic membrane appears normal. There is no preauricular or cervical lymphadenopathy.

Which of the following is the most likely diagnosis?

(A) Acute otitis externa

(B) Delayed-type hypersensitivity reaction to ear plugs

(C) Malignant otitis externa

(D) Otitis media

Item 7 [Basic]

An 84-year-old man is evaluated because of a 5-day history of rhinitis, nasal congestion, sneezing, and nonproductive cough. The symptoms began with a sore throat, which resolved after 24 hours. He has mild ear pain when blowing his nose or coughing. He has a history of coronary artery disease and hypertension. Medications are aspirin, metoprolol, and hydrochlorothiazide.

On physical examination, temperature is 36.5°C (97.7°F), blood pressure is 130/72 mm Hg, pulse rate is 82/min, and respiration rate is 16/min. He has nasal congestion and occasional cough. There is mild clear nasal discharge with no sinus tenderness. The oropharynx has no injection or exudate. There is no lymphadenopathy. External auditory canals are normal. The tympanic membranes are dull bilaterally without injection. A small left middle ear effusion is noted.

Which of the following is the most appropriate management?

(A) Amoxicillin

(B) Azithromycin

(C) Referral to an otorhinolaryngologist

(D) Reassurance and observation

Item 8 [Advanced]

A 26-year-old woman is evaluated in the emergency department for an 8-day history of sore throat, fever, and neck pain. She has severe pain on the left side of her neck with swallowing. She has had fevers for the last week, with rigors starting today. Over the last 3 to 4 days, she has had increasing cough. She is otherwise healthy and takes no medications.

On physical examination, temperature is 39.1°C (102.3°F), blood pressure is 108/68 mm Hg, pulse rate is 116/min, and respiration rate

is 20/min. Body mass index is 19. She appears ill. The neck is tender to palpation along the left side, without lymphadenopathy. The pharynx is erythematous, with tonsillar enlargement and no exudates. The chest is clear to auscultation. The remainder of the examination is normal.

Chest radiograph is shown. Leukocyte count is 18,400/µL (18.4 × 10^9/L) with 17% band forms. Serum creatinine level is 0.8 mg/dL (70.7 µmol/L).

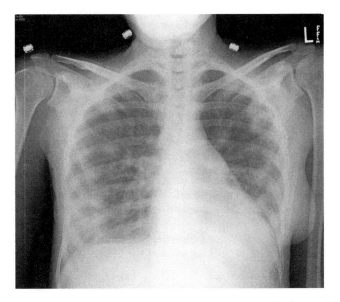

Which of the following tests is most likely to establish the diagnosis?

(A) Computed tomography (CT) of the chest with contrast

(B) CT of the neck with contrast

(C) Radiography of the pharyngeal soft tissues

(D) Transthoracic echocardiography

Item 9 [Advanced]

A 68-year-old man is evaluated in the emergency department because of fever, shortness of breath, and productive cough. He felt ill a week ago, and his symptoms have progressively worsened. A month ago, he was hospitalized in the intensive care unit because of respiratory failure. He has a history of chronic obstructive pulmonary disease and uses an ipratropium and albuterol inhaler. He has a 45-pack-year history of smoking and continues to smoke.

On physical examination, temperature is 38.4°C (101.1°F), blood pressure is 110/68 mm Hg, pulse rate is 114/min, respiration rate is 24/min, and oxygen saturation is 90% on ambient air. Body mass index is 19. Pulmonary examination shows crackles at the right base.

Leukocyte count is 19,000/µL (19 × 10^9/L) with 70% segmented neutrophils and 10% band forms. Chest radiograph shows a right lower lobe consolidation. Blood cultures are obtained, and treatment with intravenous fluids is initiated.

Which of the following is the most appropriate empiric antibiotic treatment?

(A) Cefazolin

(B) Ceftriaxone and azithromycin

(C) Ceftriaxone and ciprofloxacin

(D) Piperacillin-tazobactam and amikacin

Item 10 [Basic]

A 70-year-old man is evaluated in the emergency department because of shortness of breath, cough, and purulent sputum. His symptoms began a week ago and have progressively worsened. He has never smoked.

On physical examination, the patient is alert and oriented and appears dyspneic. Temperature is 40.2°C (104.4°F), blood pressure is 112/60 mm Hg, pulse rate is 100/min, respiration rate is 30/min, and oxygen saturation is 89% on ambient air. Pulmonary examination shows right-sided crackles and dullness to percussion.

Chest radiograph shows a right-sided consolidation. Blood cultures are obtained, and treatment with empiric antibiotics is initiated.

Which of the following is the most appropriate disposition for this patient?

(A) Admit for overnight observation
(B) Admit to the intensive care unit
(C) Admit to the medical ward
(D) Discharge home on oral antibiotics

Item 11 [Basic]

A 26-year-old man is evaluated because of a 3-day history of fever, myalgia, dry cough, and malaise. He has no known drug allergies. The remainder of the medical history is noncontributory.

On physical examination, temperature is 38.3°C (100.9°F), blood pressure is 125/75 mm Hg, pulse rate is 95/min, and respiration rate is 16/min. Oxygen saturation is 100% on ambient air. Crackles are heard in the left lung base.

Chest radiograph shows left lower lobe airspace disease.

Which of the following oral agents is the most appropriate treatment?

(A) Amoxicillin
(B) Azithromycin
(C) Cefuroxime
(D) Ciprofloxacin

Item 12 [Advanced]

A 56-year-old man is evaluated in the emergency department because of a 1-week history of fever, headache, diarrhea, and cough productive of yellow sputum. He also has a 2-day history of progressive dyspnea.

On physical examination, temperature is 38.8°C (101.8°F), blood pressure is 110/60 mm Hg, pulse rate is 110/min, and respiration rate is 28/min. Oxygen saturation is 85% while breathing 100% oxygen by nonrebreather mask. Bronchial breath sounds are heard over the left and right lower lung fields.

Laboratory studies show a leukocyte count of 4000/µL (4.0×10^9/L), platelet count of 97,000/µL (97×10^9/L), and serum sodium level of 131 meq/L (131 mmol/L).

Chest radiograph shows findings consistent with consolidation in the left and right middle and lower lobes.

The patient is intubated, and mechanical ventilation is initiated. Blood cultures are obtained, empiric antibiotic therapy is begun, and the patient is admitted to the intensive care unit.

In addition to an endotracheal aspirate for Gram stain and culture, which of the following is the most appropriate next step in the evaluation?

(A) Bronchoscopy with quantitative cultures
(B) *Legionella* and *Streptococcus pneumoniae* urine antigen assays
(C) *Legionella* serologic testing
(D) No further testing

Item 13 [Basic]

A 47-year-old man was admitted to the hospital 3 days ago with community-acquired pneumonia. Oxygen saturation was 89% on ambient air. Pulmonary examination showed bronchial breath sounds localized to the right lower lung field. Chest radiograph confirmed a right lower lobe consolidation. He was treated with intravenous ceftriaxone and azithromycin.

On the second hospital day, blood cultures obtained on admission are positive for *Streptococcus pneumoniae* susceptible to penicillin. Treatment with ceftriaxone was continued, and azithromycin was discontinued.

On the morning of hospital day 3, the patient is feeling better, has been afebrile for the last 12 hours, and is eating and drinking well. Temperature is 37.0°C (98.6°F), blood pressure is 140/80 mm Hg, pulse rate is 88/min, and respiration rate is 16/min. Oxygen saturation is 97% on ambient air.

Which of the following is the most appropriate management?

(A) Discharge on oral levofloxacin to complete 7 days of therapy
(B) Discharge on oral amoxicillin to complete 14 days of therapy
(C) Discharge on oral amoxicillin to complete 7 days of therapy
(D) Switch to oral amoxicillin and discharge tomorrow, if stable

Item 14 [Basic]

A 35-year-old man is evaluated in the office for a preemployment physical examination. He emigrated to the United States from Vietnam last year and has been employed by the public school system. He is asymptomatic and takes no medications. He does not drink alcohol, smoke cigarettes, or use illicit drugs. At 12 years of age, he received the bacillus Calmette-Guérin vaccine.

On physical examination, vital signs are normal. The remainder of the physical examination is normal.

Which of the following is indicated to screen for tuberculosis?

(A) Chest radiograph
(B) Interferon-γ-releasing assay
(C) Sputum stain and culture
(D) Tuberculin skin test
(E) No additional testing

Item 15 [Basic]

A 70-year-old man is evaluated for placement in an extended care facility. Other than dementia, the patient has no medical problems, including fever, cough, or recent weight loss. He is a retired army officer who served in logistics and supply. He has no history of previous tuberculosis infection or exposure to persons with tuberculosis. He does not smoke cigarettes, drink alcohol, or use illicit drugs. His only medication is donepezil.

On examination, vital signs are normal. His score on the Mini–Mental State Examination is 23.

A tuberculin skin test is applied and shows 8 mm of induration 48 hours later.

Which of the following is the most appropriate management?

(A) Chest radiograph

(B) Isolation

(C) Treatment with isoniazid for 9 months

(D) No further evaluation or therapy

Item 16 [Advanced]

A 35-year-old woman is evaluated before the initiation of infliximab treatment for rheumatoid arthritis. She was diagnosed with rheumatoid arthritis 5 years ago, and her disease is inadequately controlled on methotrexate and naproxen. She has no other symptoms or medical problems. She has no history of known exposure to tuberculosis or other risk factors for tuberculosis.

Findings on physical examination are unremarkable except for changes compatible with active rheumatoid arthritis involving the hands and feet.

Which of the following studies should be performed before the initiation of therapy?

(A) Chest computed tomography

(B) Induced sputum examination and culture

(C) Serologic studies for tuberculosis antibodies

(D) Tuberculin skin test or interferon-γ-releasing assay

Item 17 [Advanced]

A 35-year-old man is evaluated in the emergency department because of a 1-month history of chronic cough that produces blood-tinged sputum. He has no significant medical history. He works as a merchant mariner and travels frequently to Russia, India, and Southeast Asia.

On physical examination, the patient appears thin and ill. Temperature is 38.8°C (100.9°F), blood pressure is 125/75 mm Hg, pulse rate is 95/min, and respiration rate is 30/min. Crackles are heard over the upper lung fields. The remainder of the findings on examination are unremarkable.

Chest radiograph shows bilateral upper lobe cavitary lesions. Acid-fast bacillus is found on direct sputum smear.

Which of the following is the most appropriate therapy for this patient?

(A) Ciprofloxacin, pyrazinamide, and ethambutol

(B) Isoniazid

(C) Isoniazid and rifampin

(D) Isoniazid, rifampin, pyrazinamide, and ethambutol

Item 18 [Basic]

A 55-year-old man is screened for tuberculosis with a tuberculin skin test during a preemployment physical examination. Forty-eight hours later, he has 16 mm of induration at the site of the injection. He has never had a reactive tuberculin skin test and has no known exposure to tuberculosis. History shows no risk factors for tuberculosis. He has no other medical problems and takes no medications. Findings on physical examination and review of systems are normal.

Results of blood tests, including HIV and aminotransferase levels, are normal, as are the results of chest radiography.

Which of the following is the most appropriate management for this patient?

(A) Administration of bacillus Calmette-Guérin vaccination

(B) Testing with interferon-γ-releasing assay

(C) Treatment with isoniazid for 9 months

(D) Treatment with isoniazid, rifampin, pyrazinamide, and ethambutol for 9 months

(E) Observation

Item 19 [Basic]

A 35-year-old man is seen for a follow-up evaluation. He is scheduled to have dental work, including several extractions and placement of implants. Medical history is significant for a heart murmur, but is otherwise unremarkable. He takes no medications and has no known allergies.

On physical examination, vital signs are normal. Heart examination shows a normal S1 and physiologically split S2. There is a grade 2/6 midsystolic murmur heard best at the second right intercostal space that radiates to the right carotid artery. The remainder of the examination is normal.

A previous transthoracic echocardiogram demonstrated a bicuspid aortic valve with normal left ventricular function.

Which of the following is the most appropriate antibiotic prophylaxis for this patient before his dental procedure?

(A) Amoxicillin, orally

(B) Trimethoprim-sulfamethoxazole, orally

(C) Vancomycin, intravenously

(D) No antibiotic prophylaxis

Item 20 [Basic]

A 50-year-old woman is evaluated in the emergency department because of a 1-week history of fever and weakness. She has not been hospitalized recently. The remainder of her history is noncontributory.

On physical examination, temperature is 101.0°F (38.3°C), blood pressure is 130/80 mm Hg, pulse rate is 80/min, and respiration rate is 19/min. A grade 3/6 holosystolic murmur is heard over the apex of the heart, with radiation to the midaxillary region. The remainder of the findings on physical examination are normal.

Echocardiogram shows mitral valve regurgitation with an oscillating vegetation on the mitral valve. Multiple blood cultures are obtained, and empiric vancomycin plus gentamicin is initiated for native value endocarditis. Twenty-four hours later, blood cultures grow methicillin-resistant *Staphylococcus aureus*.

The current antibiotic regimen should be changed to which of the following intravenous antibiotics?

(A) Imipenem
(B) Nafcillin
(C) Oxacillin
(D) Piperacillin-tazobactam
(E) Vancomycin monotherapy

Item 21 [Basic]

A 47-year-old woman is evaluated before undergoing a dental procedure involving placement of several implants with bone grafting. Her medical history is significant for mitral valve prolapse with an episode of methicillin-resistant *Staphylococcus aureus* endocarditis 10 years ago that was treated successfully with antibiotics. The remainder of the history is noncontributory. She notes no drug allergies.

On physical examination, vital signs are normal. Cardiopulmonary examination shows a late systolic click. The remainder of the examination is normal.

Which of the following is the most appropriate prophylactic regimen for this patient before her dental procedure?

(A) Amoxicillin, orally
(B) Trimethoprim-sulfamethoxazole, orally
(C) Vancomycin, intravenously
(D) No antibiotic prophylaxis

Item 22 [Advanced]

A 58-year-old man is admitted to the hospital with a 3-week history of intermittent fevers and shortness of breath. He has a mechanical aortic valve. He takes warfarin and no other medications.

On physical examination, temperature is 40.0°C (104.0°F), blood pressure is 148/50 mm Hg, pulse rate is 93/min, and respiration rate is 22/min. A grade 2/6 early systolic murmur and early diastolic murmur are noted at the cardiac base.

Electrocardiogram shows sinus tachycardia with a new first-degree atrioventricular block (prolonged P-R interval). Blood cultures obtained on admission show gram-positive cocci in clusters. Serum creatinine level is 2.3 mg/dL (203 µmol/L).

Which of the following is the most appropriate initial study to obtain?

(A) Cardiac computed tomographic angiography
(B) Cardiovascular magnetic resonance imaging
(C) Transesophageal echocardiography
(D) Transthoracic echocardiography

Item 23 [Advanced]

A 38-year-old man is admitted to the hospital for a 4-week history of fever, shortness of breath, myalgia, and decreased appetite.

On physical examination, temperature is 39.0°C (102.2°F), blood pressure is 138/60 mm Hg, and pulse rate is 112/min. Jugular venous distention is increased. A grade 3/6 crescendo-decrescendo systolic ejection murmur is noted at the right upper sternal border, and a grade 3/6 decrescendo diastolic murmur is noted at the left lower

sternal border. Bibasilar crackles are heard on examination of the lungs.

Laboratory findings include a hemoglobin level of 9.0 g/dL (90 g/L) and a leukocyte count of 17,500/µL (17.5×10^9/L) with a left shift. The patient is treated empirically with vancomycin and gentamicin intravenously.

Blood cultures are positive for viridans group streptococci, which are susceptible to penicillin.

Transesophageal echocardiogram shows normal left ventricular size and systolic function, a bicuspid aortic valve with mild aortic stenosis, and severe aortic valve regurgitation. A 0.5-cm vegetation is seen on the aortic valve with echolucency (fluid) around the posterior aortic annulus.

Which of the following is the most appropriate next step in management?

(A) Aortic valve replacement
(B) Cardiac catheterization
(C) Intravenous heparin
(D) Intravenous penicillin for 4 to 6 weeks

Item 24 [Basic]

A 62-year-old woman is evaluated in the emergency department for a 3-day history of fever, vomiting, confusion, and left-sided abdominal pain. Medical history includes hypertension and type 2 diabetes mellitus. Current medications are lisinopril and metformin. The patient's medical record confirms a previous hospitalization for penicillin-rated anaphylaxis.

On physical examination, temperature is 39.4°C (102.9°F), blood pressure is 86/52 mm Hg, pulse rate is 128/min, respiration rate is 24/min, and oxygen saturation is 94% on ambient air. Left-sided costovertebral angle tenderness is present.

Leukocyte count is 24,000/µL (24.0×10^9/L) and creatinine is 2.8 mg/dL (247.5 µmol/L). Urinalysis shows 220 leukocytes/high-power field and many bacteria. Urine and blood cultures are obtained. Volume resuscitation is begun.

Which of the following is the most appropriate empiric antibiotic treatment?

(A) Ampicillin and gentamicin
(B) Ciprofloxacin
(C) Imipenem
(D) Vancomycin

Item 25 [Basic]

A 73-year-old man is evaluated during a routine office visit. He has a 35-year history of type 2 diabetes mellitus that is treated with metformin. He has an indwelling urinary catheter that was placed 9 months ago for bladder dysfunction related to diabetic autonomic neuropathy. A visiting home nurse has left a message that the patient's urine has turned cloudy. She has ordered a urinalysis and has sent along the report to the office. The patient currently feels well and has no symptoms.

On physical examination, the patient's mental status and vital signs, including temperature, are normal. There is no suprapubic or costovertebral angle tenderness. An indwelling urinary catheter with a collection bag is present. The urine appears cloudy.

Urinalysis shows 40 leukocytes/high-power field and bacteria.

Which of the following is the most appropriate next step in management?

(A) Ciprofloxacin
(B) Repeat urinalysis
(C) Trimethoprim-sulfamethoxazole administration
(D) Urine culture
(E) No additional testing or treatment

Item 26 [Basic]

A 22-year-old woman is evaluated for a 1-day history of dysuria and urinary urgency and frequency. She had an episode of cystitis 2 years ago. She has a sulfa allergy.

On physical examination, temperature is normal, blood pressure is 110/60 mm Hg, pulse rate is 60/min, and respiration rate is 14/min. There is mild suprapubic tenderness, but no flank tenderness. The remainder of the findings on examination are normal.

Urine dipstick analysis shows 3+ leukocyte esterase. A pregnancy test is negative.

Treatment with which of the following antibiotics is most appropriate in this patient?

(A) Amoxicillin
(B) Fosfomycin
(C) Ciprofloxacin
(D) Nitrofurantoin

Item 27 [Advanced]

A 26-year-old woman undergoes follow-up evaluation after completing an appropriate antibiotic course for a urinary tract infection that was diagnosed 3 days ago. She is currently asymptomatic. She has had five similar episodes in the last year. In all cases, the symptoms began after sexual intercourse and responded well to antibiotic treatment. She has increased her fluid intake and routinely voids after sexual intercourse. She is otherwise healthy, with no medical problems and no history of sexually transmitted infections. She currently takes no medications and does not use spermicides.

Physical examination, including vital signs, is normal.

Which of the following is the most appropriate next step to reduce this patient's risk of urinary tract infection?

(A) Long-term daily suppressive antibiotic therapy
(B) Postcoital antimicrobial prophylaxis
(C) Recommendation to drink cranberry juice
(D) Use of a spermicide before intercourse

Item 28 [Advanced]

A 62-year-old man is evaluated in the emergency department for a 2-day history of fever, vomiting, dysuria, and lower abdominal and perineal pain.

On physical examination, temperature is 39.2°C (102.6°F), blood pressure is 95/65 mm Hg, and pulse rate is 122/min. The mucous membranes are dry. Suprapubic tenderness is present. Rectal examination shows an enlarged and extremely tender prostate.

Laboratory studies show a leukocyte count of 18,000/μL (18×10^9/L) with 70% segmented neutrophils. Urinalysis shows more than 50 leukocytes/high-power field and many bacteria. The serum creatinine level is normal.

Treatment with intravenous fluids and parenteral ciprofloxacin is started. Urine culture grows *Escherichia coli* sensitive to fluoroquinolones. Three days after admission, the patient continues to have fever and abdominal and perineal pain. A repeat leukocyte count shows a result of 16,000/μL (16×10^9/L).

Which of the following is the most appropriate management for this patient?

(A) Discontinue ciprofloxacin and start gentamicin
(B) Insert a catheter for bladder drainage
(C) Obtain a transrectal ultrasound
(D) Perform prostate massage

Item 29 [Basic]

A 20-year-old woman is evaluated because of a 4-day history of abdominal pain. She is sexually active and reports that her last menstrual period began 5 days ago. Symptoms include nausea but no vomiting.

Physical examination shows temperature of 38.4°C (101.1°F), blood pressure of 130/82 mm Hg, pulse rate of 100/min, and respiratory rate of 18/min. There is moderate tenderness in the lower quadrants bilaterally, with no rebound or guarding. Pelvic examination shows cervical motion tenderness and bilateral adnexal tenderness.

Which of the following organisms most commonly cause this condition?

(A) *Bacteroides* species
(B) *Chlamydia trachomatis* and *Neisseria gonorrhoeae*
(C) *Gardnerella vaginalis* and herpes simplex virus
(D) *Trichomonas vaginalis* and *Mycoplasma genitalium*

Item 30 [Basic]

A 30-year-old man is evaluated in an urgent care clinic because of a 2-day history of pain that is localized to the right testicle. He reports no recent trauma. He had unprotected intercourse with a new female partner within the last week.

On physical examination, temperature is 37.7°C (99.9°F). The remainder of the vital signs are normal. No testicular masses are noted, but the posterior aspect of the right testicle is tender to palpation, as is the right spermatic cord.

A urine sample is obtained for nucleic acid amplification testing.

Which of the following is the most appropriate treatment?

(A) Ceftriaxone and doxycycline
(B) Ceftriaxone and levofloxacin
(C) Levofloxacin and azithromycin
(D) Levofloxacin and doxycycline

Item 31 [Advanced]

A 19-year-old man is admitted to the hospital with a 4-day history of fever, fatigue, and pain in the elbows, wrists, and knees. He has also had progressive pain and swelling of the right knee and a rash on the right arm.

On physical examination, temperature is 38.2°C (100.8°F), blood pressure is 110/60 mm Hg, pulse rate is 95/min, and respiration rate is 12/min. There is pain to palpation over the left wrist. The right knee is swollen and warm, with significant effusion. The rash on the arm is shown (Plate 18).

Blood cultures are obtained, and arthrocentesis of the right knee is performed. The synovial fluid leukocyte count is 60,000/µL (60 × 10⁹/L) with 90% polymorphonuclear neutrophils. The results of Gram stain are negative.

Which of the following is the most appropriate diagnostic test to perform next?

(A) Antinuclear antibody and rheumatoid factor assays
(B) Biopsy and culture of a skin lesion
(C) HLA B27 testing
(D) Nucleic acid amplification urine test for *Neisseria gonorrhoeae*

Item 32 [Basic]

A 24-year-old man is evaluated because of a 3-day history of painful penile lesions accompanied by dysuria, generalized myalgia, malaise, and fever. The patient is sexually active.

On physical examination, temperature is 37.8°C (100.0°F) and the remaining vital signs are normal. Examination of the genital area shows painful vesicular lesions on an erythematous base.

Which of the following is the most appropriate treatment?

(A) Acyclovir
(B) Benzathine penicillin G
(C) Ceftriaxone and azithromycin
(D) Fluconazole

Item 33 [Basic]

A 26-year-old man is evaluated because of a painless penile lesion that he first noted 3 days ago. He has no fever or other symptoms. He has had three male sexual partners in the last 6 months and uses condoms inconsistently. He undergoes HIV testing every year, and his most recent results 7 months ago were negative.

On physical examination, vital signs are normal. Skin findings on the shaft of the penis are shown (Plate 19).

There is no evidence of penile discharge or other genital lesions. He has no other skin or oral lesions. Shotty, nontender inguinal lymphadenopathy is noted.

Which of the following is the most likely diagnosis?

(A) Chancroid
(B) Herpes simplex virus infection
(C) Human papillomavirus infection
(D) Syphilis

Item 34 [Advanced]

A 27-year-old man is evaluated in the clinic 6 months after initiation of antiretroviral therapy for newly diagnosed HIV infection. He is asymptomatic. At the time of diagnosis, his HIV-RNA (viral load) was 500,000 copies/mL and CD4 cell count was 298/µL. Medications are emtricitabine, tenofovir, and efavirenz, and omeprazole, which he takes on occasion for heartburn.

On physical examination, temperature is 37°C (98.6°F). The remainder of the vital signs and physical examination are normal.

Today's laboratory results show a viral load of 200,000 copies/mL and CD4 cell count of 225/µL (0.23 × 10⁹/L).

Which of the following is the most appropriate management?

(A) Add a protease inhibitor
(B) Add trimethoprim-sulfamethoxazole
(C) Monitor and repeat viral load testing and CD4 cell count in 6 months
(D) Obtain viral resistance testing

Item 35 [Advanced]

A 39-year-old woman is evaluated because of a 1-week history of painless blurred vision in the right eye. Her only other visual symptom has been an increased number of floaters in the right eye for the last 3 months. She reports no discomfort, photophobia, pain with reading, trauma, or recent illness. She has a history of intravenous drug use 9 years ago. She has no other medical problems and takes no medications.

On physical examination, temperature is 36.8°C (98.2°F). The rest of the vital signs are normal. There is no conjunctival injection. Pupils react to light and accommodation. Visual acuity in the right eye is 20/30 and in the left eye is 20/20. Funduscopic evaluation shows fluffy yellow retinal lesions with some associated hemorrhage, consistent with cytomegalovirus retinitis.

Which of the following is the most likely underlying disease?

(A) Endocarditis
(B) Hepatitis C
(C) HIV infection
(D) Multiple sclerosis

Item 36 [Basic]

A 33-year-old woman is seen for a routine evaluation. She and her husband are thinking about starting a family, and she asks whether she should be screened for HIV. She has had several sexual partners, but always within monogamous relationships and always using condoms. None of her partners had known HIV infection, used injection drugs, or had sex with men. She has no history of sexually transmitted infections, has never been pregnant, and is sexually active only with her husband of 8 years. Her husband is healthy but has never been tested for HIV infection. She takes no medications.

Findings on physical examination are normal.

Which of the following is the most appropriate next step in the management of this patient?

(A) HIV antibody/p24 antigen test

(B) HIV Western blot assay

(C) HIV nucleic acid amplification test

(D) No testing indicated

Item 37 [Advanced]

A 23-year-old woman is evaluated in the emergency department because of a 10-day history of fever, cervical lymphadenopathy, malaise and fatigue, sore throat, headache, and nausea. She reports no vomiting, diarrhea, abdominal pain, nasal congestion, or cough. She had a rash a few days ago that has resolved. She is sexually active with multiple male partners and does not use condoms.

On physical examination, temperature is 38.1°C (100.6°F), blood pressure is 110/88 mm Hg, pulse rate is 96/min, and respiration rate is 16/min. Significant lymphadenopathy is noted in the cervical, axillary, and inguinal regions. The oropharynx is erythematous, with mildly enlarged tonsils but no exudate. There is no skin rash. The remainder of the physical examination is unremarkable.

Results of heterophile antibody test, rapid streptococcal antigen test, HIV antibody/p24 antigen test, pregnancy test, and rapid plasma reagin test are negative.

Which of the following is the most appropriate diagnostic test to perform next?

(A) CD4 cell count

(B) HIV nucleic acid amplification test

(C) HIV Western blot assay

(D) Repeat HIV antibody/p24 antigen test

Item 38 [Basic]

A 32-year-old man is admitted to the hospital for a 3-week history of increasing dyspnea on exertion, dry cough, pleuritic chest pain, and fever. The patient has had multiple sexual partners of both genders.

On physical examination, temperature is 38.6°C (101.5°F), blood pressure is 110/66 mm Hg, pulse rate is 112/min, and respiration rate is 24/min. Oxygen saturation is 89% on ambient air. The oropharynx shows scattered white plaques. Lung auscultation shows diffuse crackles bilaterally. The remainder of the examination is normal.

The result of a rapid HIV test is positive. Sputum Gram stain shows few neutrophils, pseudohyphae, and mixed bacteria. Chest radiograph shows bilateral diffuse reticular infiltrates.

Which of the following is the most likely diagnosis?

(A) Cytomegalovirus pneumonia

(B) *Mycobacterium avium* complex infection

(C) *Pneumocystis jirovecii* pneumonia

(D) Pulmonary candidiasis

Item 39 [Basic]

A 46-year-old man underwent a total right hip replacement 5 months ago after a motorcycle accident. He presents now with a 3-week history of progressively increasing pain in the right hip, initially with ambulation and now at rest. He has no other symptoms. Medical history is unremarkable, and he takes no medications.

On physical examination, temperature is 37.9°C (100.2°F). Vital signs are otherwise normal. The right hip shows a well-healed surgical scar without drainage. The remainder of the examination is unremarkable.

Plain radiograph of the right hip shows soft tissue swelling and lucency along the bone-prosthesis interface. Aspiration of the joint shows many polymorphonuclear leukocytes and gram-positive cocci in clusters. Culture of the aspirated fluid grows coagulase-negative staphylococci.

Which of the following is the most appropriate next step in management?

(A) Hyperbaric oxygen and intravenous antibiotics

(B) Intravenous antibiotics

(C) Removal of the hip prosthesis and intravenous antibiotics

(D) Surgical irrigation of the prosthetic joint and intravenous antibiotics

Item 40 [Advanced]

A 68-year-old woman is admitted to the hospital because of fever and back pain that has worsened over the last several weeks. Medical history is significant for kidney failure secondary to hypertension. She has been treated with hemodialysis for the last 4 months.

On physical examination, temperature is 38.2°C (100.8°F), blood pressure is 138/82 mm Hg, pulse rate is 92/min, and respiration rate is 12/min. There is a tunneled dialysis catheter in the left upper chest without evidence of inflammation. There is tenderness to palpation over the lumbar spine. The remainder of the physical examination is normal, with no focal neurologic findings.

Laboratory studies include leukocyte count of 13,000/µL (13.0×10⁹/L) with 72% neutrophils. Magnetic resonance imaging shows destructive changes to the T12 and L1 vertebral bodies, with no paraspinal collections or spinal cord impingement. Blood culture findings are positive for methicillin-resistant *Staphylococcus aureus*.

In addition to removal of the dialysis catheter, which of the following is the most appropriate next step in management?

(A) Antibiotic therapy alone

(B) Antibiotic therapy with debridement of the involved vertebral bodies

(C) Percutaneous biopsy and culture of paraspinal tissue before antibiotic administration

(D) Technetium 99m bone scan of the spine before antibiotic administration

Item 41 [Basic]

A 25-year-old man is evaluated because of a 2-week history of purulent drainage from a small opening in a previously healed right lower extremity wound. Six months ago, the patient had an open comminuted fracture of the proximal tibia that was treated with internal fixation with a metal plate. He recovered well after surgery, with complete healing of his surgical incisions. He has otherwise felt well.

On physical examination, temperature is 37.2°C (98.9°F), blood pressure is 120/75 mm Hg, and respiration rate is 12/min. There is a well-healed surgical incision overlying the right tibia except for a 2-mm opening at the distal margin, with minimal surrounding erythema and slight purulent drainage. The remainder of the examination is normal.

Swab samples from the wound grow an *Enterococcus* species that is susceptible to all antibiotics tested.

Which of the following is the most appropriate next step in management?

(A) Bone biopsy culture

(B) Intravenous vancomycin

(C) Nuclear medicine bone scan

(D) Oral ampicillin

Item 42 [Basic]

A 59-year-old woman is evaluated because of a 1-week history of increasing pain in the right foot. She recalls stepping on a nail about 1 month before the symptoms began. She reports no drainage from the previous puncture wound site, which has healed completely. Medical history is otherwise unremarkable. She takes no medications.

On physical examination, vital signs are normal. Examination of the foot shows tenderness and warmth directly below the proximal fifth metatarsal bone.

Plain radiograph of the right foot is normal.

Which of the following is the most appropriate next step to establish the diagnosis?

(A) Computed tomography

(B) Gallium scan

(C) Magnetic resonance imaging

(D) Three-phase bone scan

Item 43 [Basic]

A 75-year-old man is evaluated in the emergency department because of a 2-day history of confusion, falls, and urinary incontinence. History includes diabetes mellitus, hypertension, and chronic kidney disease, with a baseline serum creatinine level of 2.2 mg/dL (167.8 μmol/L). Medications are glargine insulin, metoprolol, and lisinopril.

On physical examination, temperature is 38.5°C (101.3°F), blood pressure is 89/55 mm Hg, pulse rate is 112/min, respiration rate is 24/min, and oxygen saturation is 93% on ambient air. The patient is disoriented and has moderate word finding difficulty. Findings of cardiovascular and respiratory examinations are normal. There is suprapubic tenderness. The remainder of the physical examination is normal.

Laboratory:

Leukocyte count	18,000/μL (18.0 × 10⁹/L)
Serum creatinine level	3.0 mg/dL (228.8 μmol/L)
Plasma glucose level	160 mg/dL (8.9 mmol/L)
Blood urea nitrogen level	48 mg/dL (17.1 mmol/L)
Lactic acid level	40.5 mg/dL (4.5 mmol/L)
Urinalysis findings	Dipstick results are positive for leukocyte esterase and nitrates. Microscopic analysis shows too many leukocytes to count.

Blood and urine cultures are obtained.

Which of the following is the most appropriate next step in the management of this patient?

(A) Intravenous crystalloid solution and broad-spectrum antibiotics

(B) Intravenous crystalloid solution and vasopressor therapy

(C) Intravenous glucocorticoid and broad-spectrum antibiotics

(D) Intravenous insulin and broad-spectrum antibiotics

Item 44 [Basic]

A 47-year-old man is evaluated in the hospital because of right knee pain, fever, and rigors 3 days after repair of a right tibial plateau fracture. He has no other symptoms. Current medications include enoxaparin and oxycodone.

On examination, temperature is 39.0°C (102.2°F), blood pressure is 100/60 mm Hg, pulse rate is 110/min, respiration rate is 22/min, and oxygen saturation is 95% on ambient air. The right knee is swollen, tender, and erythematous, with reduced mobility.

Arthrocentesis of the right knee shows purulent synovial fluid.

Synovial fluid and blood cultures are obtained.

Which of the following is the best antibiotic management of this infection?

(A) Begin treatment with empiric antibiotics after adequate fluid resuscitation

(B) Begin treatment with empiric antibiotics within 1 hour

(C) Withhold antibiotics pending arthroscopic joint drainage

(D) Withhold antibiotics until culture results are available

Item 45 [Basic]

A 64-year-old woman is evaluated in the emergency department because of a 3-day history of weakness, fever, chills, dyspnea, and cough. She has no other medical problems and takes no medications.

On physical examination, she appears ill and the extremities are warm. Temperature is 38.9°C (102.0°F), blood pressure is 105/50 mm Hg, pulse rate is 125/min, and respiration rate is 28/min. Oxygen saturation is 92% while breathing 100% oxygen via a nonrebreather mask. Pulmonary examination shows right lower posterior chest egophony and dullness to percussion.

Laboratory studies show hemoglobin level of 9 g/dL (90 g/L), leukocyte count of 18,000/μL (18 × 10⁹/L) with 80% segmented neutrophils, and serum creatinine level of 1.8 mg/dL (159 μmol/L). Electrolyte levels are normal. Chest radiograph shows right lower lobe consolidation.

Treatment with intravenous ceftriaxone and levofloxacin is initiated.

Which of the following is the most appropriate additional initial treatment?

(A) Erythrocyte transfusion

(B) Hydrocortisone

(C) Norepinephrine

(D) Normal saline

Item 46 [Advanced]

A 41-year-old woman is admitted to the intensive care unit because of a 1-day history of progressively worsening mental status and jaundice. Medical history is significant for advanced autoimmune hepatitis.

On physical examination, temperature is 33.0°C (91.4°F), blood pressure is 105/55 mm Hg, pulse rate is 110/min, and respiration rate is 27/min. Body mass index is 18. She is unresponsive and jaundiced. The lungs are clear, and findings on cardiac examination are normal. Abdominal examination shows a distended abdomen with a detectable fluid wave.

Laboratory studies show a leukocyte count of 9800/µL (9.8 × 10⁹/L), serum creatinine level of 1.6 mg/dL (141 µmol/L), and lactic acid level of 6 mg/dL (0.7 mmol/L).

Chest radiograph is normal, and findings of urinalysis are unremarkable. Blood and urine culture results are pending. Treatment is initiated with intravenous fluids and empiric broad-spectrum antibiotics.

Which of the following is the most appropriate next step in management?

(A) Abdominal computed tomography
(B) Diagnostic paracentesis
(C) Hydrocortisone
(D) Norepinephrine

Item 47 [Advanced]

A 78-year-old woman is treated in the intensive care unit (ICU) for a 24-hour history of altered mental status that has been progressively worsening.

On arrival to the emergency department, she was disoriented. Temperature was 38.7°C (101.7°F). Blood pressure was 82/40 mm Hg and the heart rate was 115/min.

Laboratory studies showed a leukocyte count of 33,000/µL (33 × 10⁹/L) and a hemoglobin level of 11 g/dL (110 g/L). Urine dipstick was positive for nitrites and leukocyte esterase. Chest radiograph was normal.

Results of blood and urine culture are pending. Central venous access was obtained, and treatment with broad-spectrum antibiotics was initiated. A 1000-mL normal saline fluid challenge was administered over 30 minutes.

Current examination in the ICU shows blood pressure of 85/45 mm Hg and pulse rate of 100/min. Findings on physical examination are unchanged.

Which of the following is the most appropriate immediate next step in management?

(A) Erythrocyte transfusion
(B) Hydrocortisone
(C) Norepinephrine
(D) Normal saline at 200 mL/h

Item 48 [Basic]

A 69-year-old man is admitted to the intensive care unit with respiratory failure as the result of an exacerbation of heart failure. He is intubated and mechanically ventilated. Treatment with an intravenous diuretic and an angiotensin-converting enzyme inhibitor is initiated. A urinary catheter is placed.

In addition to meticulous hand hygiene, which of the following is most effective in preventing catheter-associated urinary tract infection?

(A) Changing the urinary catheter every 72 hours
(B) Providing antibiotic prophylaxis
(C) Removing the urinary catheter immediately
(D) Screening for and treating asymptomatic bacteriuria
(E) Using silver-impregnated urinary catheters

Item 49 [Basic]

A 52-year-old woman is admitted to the intensive care unit with acute respiratory distress secondary to left lower lobe pneumonia. She has chronic obstructive pulmonary disease. She is intubated, mechanically ventilated, and treated appropriately with intravenous antibiotics. Her hospital stay is prolonged and requires placement of a central venous line. By hospital day 10, her fever resolved and oxygenation improved. Mechanical ventilation was discontinued. On hospital day 12, her temperature spiked to 38.7°C (101.6°F). The patient has no localizing symptoms.

On physical examination, the patient is alert and in no distress. Blood pressure is 130/78 mm Hg, pulse rate is 90/min, and respiration rate is 14/min. Oxygen saturation is 90% on 2 L/min oxygen delivered by nasal cannula. This value is unchanged from 24 hours ago. Other than decreased breath sounds and persistent crackles in the left lower lobe, which are unchanged since hospital day 10, the patient's findings on physical examination are unremarkable.

Leukocyte count increased from 6700/µL (6.70 × 10⁹/L) on hospital day 10 to 12,400/µL today (12.4 × 10⁹/L). Chest radiograph shows an infiltrate in the left lower lobe that is improved from hospital day 10. Echocardiogram is normal. Three sets of blood cultures are obtained peripherally and through the central venous catheter.

Which of the following is the most appropriate next step?

(A) Begin empiric ciprofloxacin and gentamicin treatment
(B) Remove the central venous line
(C) Repeat the echocardiogram in 24 hours
(D) Order urinalysis with culture

Item 50 [Advanced]

A 58-year-old man is evaluated in the emergency department because of a 3-week history of cough and dyspnea. He now has hemoptysis. He has also had fevers, night sweats, and a 13.6-kg (30-lb) weight loss over the last 3 months. He has no significant medical history and does not smoke, use alcohol, or take drugs. He takes no medications. He recently immigrated to the United States from Africa.

On physical examination, he appears thin and coughs frequently. Temperature is 38.3°C (101.0°F), blood pressure is 100/60 mm Hg, pulse rate is 101/min, and respiration rate is 30/min. Pulmonary examination shows crackles over the right upper lung field.

Which of the following are the most appropriate infectious precautions to order for this patient?

(A) Airborne
(B) Contact
(C) Droplet
(D) Standard

Item 51 [Advanced]

A 58-year-old woman undergoes preoperative evaluation before coronary artery bypass surgery that is scheduled for tomorrow. She has been hospitalized in the cardiac intensive care unit (ICU) for 4 days after collapsing and experiencing cardiogenic shock. She was intubated in the field and given mechanical ventilation in the ICU. She is being treated with both paralytic and sedating medications in addition to a proton pump inhibitor and intravenous nitroglycerin.

On physical examination, the patient's condition has stabilized and she is afebrile. No attempts are made to wean her from the ventilator because of her impending surgery and her heart condition.

Which of the following is the most appropriate measure to prevent ventilator-associated pneumonia in this patient?

(A) Bathe the patient daily in chlorhexidine
(B) Begin preoperative antimicrobial prophylaxis immediately and continue until extubation
(C) Maintain the head of bed at an angle of greater than 30 degrees
(D) Perform tracheotomy and remove the endotracheal tube

Item 52 [Basic]

A 21-year-old man is being treated in the hospital for multiple gunshot wounds. He was admitted 2 weeks ago, has undergone multiple abdominal surgical procedures, and has been treated with broad-spectrum antibiotics. Fever developed 3 days ago, and a strain of Enterobacteraiceae that is resistant to multiple antibiotics was isolated from blood cultures drawn from a central line catheter and an abdominal drain. The patient shares a room with another patient.

Which of the following is most likely to reduce spread of this patient's resistant organism to his roommate?

(A) Cleaning the room with bleach
(B) Following strict staff hand hygiene practices
(C) Providing prophylactic antimicrobial treatment to the roommate
(D) Replacing the patient's central line catheter and abdominal drain with new devices

Section 6

Infectious Disease Medicine

Answers and Critiques

Item 1   **Answer: D**

Educational Objective: *Diagnose serotonin syndrome.*

The most likely diagnosis is serotonin syndrome. Serotonin syndrome can develop in patients taking any selective serotonin reuptake inhibitor or serotonin-norepinephrine reuptake inhibitor, alone or in combination with other medications, such as opiates, triptans, or over-the-counter medications, such as dextromethorphan. Symptoms can develop in as little as 24 hours or several weeks after initiation of therapy or a change in therapy. Serotonin syndrome may be mild, with symptoms of anxiety, tremor, restlessness, or diarrhea, or may present with high fever, muscle rigidity, and cognitive changes. Findings unique to serotonin syndrome are shivering, hyperreflexia, myoclonus, and ataxia. This patient recently had an increase in the dose of her selective serotonin reuptake inhibitor and has the symptoms and signs of serotonin syndrome.

Heat stroke results from failure of the body's thermoregulatory system; the system may be impaired or overwhelmed. Thermoregulation may be impaired in the elderly and in patients who have or are being treated for conditions that can lead to dehydration or anhidrosis. Diuretics and anticholinergic medications are commonly implicated. Heat stroke is not associated with muscle rigidity, hyperreflexia, myoclonus, or ataxia.

Malignant hyperthermia is a reaction to certain classes of drugs, including inhaled anesthetics (halothane and others) and depolarizing neuromuscular blockers (succinylcholine and decamethonium). It causes markedly increased intracellular calcium, increased cellular metabolism, and sustained muscle tetany. Severe muscle rigidity, masseter spasm, hyperthermia with core temperature of up to 45.0°C (113.0°F), cardiac tachyarrhythmias, and rhabdomyolysis usually manifest quickly when susceptible patients are exposed to a triggering agent. This patient has not been exposed to the implicated drugs.

Neuroleptic malignant syndrome is an idiosyncratic reaction to neuroleptic antipsychotic agents. It is characterized by muscle rigidity, hyperthermia, and autonomic dysregulation. Temperature is only modestly elevated in some patients, and delirium is common. All neuroleptic agents have been associated with the syndrome. It often occurs when drug treatment is started or after rapid dose escalation. The patient was not exposed to the implicated drugs, and neuroleptic malignant syndrome is not associated with hyperreflexia or myoclonus.

KEY POINT

Serotonin syndrome presents with high fever, muscle rigidity, and cognitive changes. Findings unique to serotonin syndrome are shivering, hyperreflexia, myoclonus, and ataxia.

Bibliography

Boyer EW, Shannon M. The serotonin syndrome. N Engl J Med. 2005;352:1112-20. [PMID: 15784664]

Item 2   **Answer: C**

Educational Objective: *Diagnose neuroleptic malignant syndrome.*

This patient, who has fever, tremors, agitation, and parkinsonism on examination, is most likely to have neuroleptic malignant syndrome (NMS). This potentially life-threatening disorder is characterized by hyperthermia that is usually accompanied by autonomic dysfunction, such as tachycardia, diaphoresis, or labile blood pressure; extrapyramidal signs, typically muscle rigidity or dystonia and elevated muscle enzyme levels; and altered mental status. The syndrome is an idiosyncratic reaction to exposure to antipsychotic neuroleptic medications. The most common agents that cause NMS are haloperidol and fluphenazine. NMS usually develops over 24 hours and peaks within 72 hours. The syndrome can occur with all drugs that cause central dopamine type 2 receptor blockade and usually occurs soon after the start of treatment with a new drug or with dose escalation. NMS also has been reported in patients with Parkinson disease who abruptly discontinue the use of dopamine drugs. Most patients with NMS have muscle rigidity, hyperthermia, cognitive changes, autonomic instability, diaphoresis, sialorrhea, seizures, cardiac arrhythmias, and rhabdomyolysis within 2 weeks after initiation of drug treatment. Symptoms can occur at any time during drug therapy and may persist for up to 1 month. Symptoms may persist longer if parenteral medications were given.

Acute lithium toxicity can produce neurologic findings, including ataxia, agitation, tremors, fasciculations, or myoclonic jerks. Lithium toxicity does not produce hyperthermia.

Malignant hyperthermia is an inherited skeletal muscle disorder characterized by a hypermetabolic state that is precipitated by exposure to volatile inhalational anesthetics (halothane, isoflurane, enflurane, desflurane, and sevoflurane) and the depolarizing muscle relaxants succinylcholine and decamethonium. Increased intracellular calcium leads to sustained muscle contractions, with skeletal muscle rigidity, tachycardia, hypercarbia, hypertension, hyperthermia, tachypnea, and cardiac arrhythmias. Rhabdomyolysis and acute kidney injury can develop. The patient has not been exposed to the drugs that account for this diagnosis.

Like NMS, serotonin syndrome presents with high fever, muscle rigidity, and cognitive changes. Findings unique to serotonin syndrome are shivering, hyperreflexia, myoclonus, and ataxia. Serotonin syndrome is caused by the use of serotonin reuptake inhibitors, and this patient does not take these medications.

KEY POINT

Neuroleptic malignant syndrome is a potentially lethal condition that develops after exposure to dopamine receptor antagonists. It is characterized by muscle rigidity, hyperthermia, cognitive changes, autonomic instability, diaphoresis, sialorrhea, seizures, cardiac arrhythmias, and rhabdomyolysis.

Bibliography

Gillman PK. Neuroleptic malignant syndrome: mechanisms, interactions, and causality. Mov Disord. 2010;25:1780-90. [PMID: 20623765]

Item 3   Answer: B

Educational Objective: *Diagnose drug fever.*

This patient most likely has drug fever. Antibiotics can cause or prolong fever, creating confusion for the clinician. A common cause of drug fever is sulfonamide and β-lactam antibiotics and nitrofurantoin. This patient was treated for pyelonephritis and responded well to treatment. She is otherwise asymptomatic and feels well. Findings on physical examination are normal despite documented fever. Eosinophilia and rash accompany drug fever in only 25% of cases; their absence does not exclude drug fever. The diagnosis of drug fever is made by discontinuing use of the suspected drug. In some cases, drug challenge is attempted to document the source of fever. In most patients, the fever abates within 72 hours after discontinuation of the drug. Substitution of the suspected drug with a drug from the same class may cause fever to persist or recur. In this patient, the appropriate management is to stop treatment with trimethoprim-sulfamethoxazole. Whether another antibiotic needs to be prescribed depends on the underlying infection, the response to therapy, and the duration of treatment before the antibiotic is stopped. Because drug fever tends to be a diagnosis of exclusion, all patients with suspected drug fever should be carefully observed for the possible presence of an alternative diagnosis.

Although antimicrobial resistance is possible, the patient's symptoms responded quickly to antibiotic therapy, with complete resolution of symptoms. Repeat urinalysis does not suggest persistent infection.

Factitious fever, although uncommon, does occur. Patients with factitious fever often have an underlying psychiatric disease and cause elevation of their temperature in a number of ways. There is no suggestion in this patient of a possible factitious cause of fever.

In most patients with uncomplicated pyelonephritis, fever resolves with appropriate antibiotic therapy in approximately 3 to 4 days. Fever persisting after that time frame raises the issue of a potential complication of the infection (e.g., abscess) or drug fever. This patient has no other symptoms associated with a complicated infection (e.g., evidence of ongoing infection, fatigue, pain, or leukocytosis), making the possibility of drug fever more likely.

KEY POINT

Drug fever should be suspected in patients who recently started treatment with a new drug, particularly an antibiotic, and who have fever without other obvious signs of infection or inflammation.

Bibliography

Johnson DH, Cunha BA. Drug fever. Infect Dis Clin North Am. 1996;10:85-91. [PMID: 8698996]

Item 4   Answer: E

Educational Objective: *Treat acute sinusitis*

The most appropriate management for this patient is symptomatic relief. Common symptoms associated with sinusitis (such as headache, facial pain and pressure that increases when bending forward, fever, and toothache) have not been well assessed in comparison with gold standard tests, such as sinus aspiration or radiography.

Physical examination findings that have been shown to add diagnostic value include purulent rhinorrhea with unilateral predominance, local pain with unilateral predominance, bilateral purulent rhinorrhea, and pus in the nasal cavity. The presence of three or more of these symptoms has a positive likelihood ratio of 6.75 for the presence of bacterial sinusitis. Imaging, such as with sinus computed tomography, is rarely necessary in a patient who is at average risk for infection with resistant organisms, but should be considered in immunocompromised patients who are at risk for infection with unusual organisms, such as fungus or *Pseudomonas* species.

Initial treatment of patients with symptoms that suggest acute sinusitis is largely symptomatic. Systemic antihistamines, intranasal glucocorticoids, and topical decongestants have all been shown to be helpful. Topical decongestants should be limited to a few days of use to avoid rebound rhinitis (rhinitis medicamentosa). Evidence suggests a small increase in the number of patients with acute sinusitis whose symptoms resolve if antibiotics are used when symptoms have been present for at least 7 days. However, the cure rate is high in placebo-treated patients (80%). Therefore, the number needed to treat is also high. Eight to 15 patients would need to be treated with antibiotics to produce one additional cure. For this reason, some guidelines recommend initial symptomatic treatment, with initiation of antibiotics only in patients with 3 to 4 days of severe symptoms (e.g., temperature ≥39.0°C [102.2°F], purulent drainage, and facial pain), worsening of symptoms that were initially improving after a typical upper respiratory tract infection, or symptoms that do not improve after 10 days. If antibiotics are used, there is no evidence that any particular agent is superior in patients who are not at risk for infection with resistant organisms. Amoxicillin-clavulanate and doxycycline are both appropriate first-line agents; an extremely broad-coverage antibiotic such as imipenem would not be appropriate for treatment of bacterial sinusitis unless required by culture and sensitivity data.

KEY POINT

Guidelines recommend initiation of antibiotic treatment only in patients with 3 to 4 days of severe symptoms (e.g., temperature ≥39.0°C [102.2°F], purulent drainage, and facial pain), worsening of symptoms that were initially improving after a typical upper respiratory tract infection, or symptoms that do not improve after 10 days.

Bibliography

Wilson JF. In the clinic. Acute sinusitis. Ann Intern Med. 2010;153:ITC3-1-15; quiz ITC-3-16. Erratum in: Ann Intern Med. 2010;153:851. Ann Intern Med. 2010;153:620. [PMID: 20820036]

Item 5   Answer: B

Educational Objective: *Manage acute pharyngitis.*

This patient should be given a rapid streptococcal antigen test before initiation of antibiotic therapy. The patient's primary symptoms (fever, cough, and sore throat) are compatible with either a viral upper respiratory tract infection or streptococcal pharyngitis. The Centor criteria (temperature >38.1°C [100.5°F], tonsillar exudates, and tender cervical lymphadenopathy; absence of cough) predict the likelihood of streptococcal pharyngitis. The use of these criteria is a reasonable way to triage patients with pharyngitis to empiric treatment with antibiotics, symptomatic treatment only, or testing with treatment if the test result is positive. Patients with all four criteria have a 40% or greater chance of having group A β-hemolytic streptococcal (GABHS) pharyngitis; patients with zero or one criterion have a low (<3%) probability of having GABHS pharyngitis. This patient has two criteria. Patients with two or three criteria have an intermediate probability of having GABHS pharyngitis. For these patients, some guidelines recommend throat culture and others recommend rapid antigen detection test (RADT) with confirmation of negative results. The advantage of RADT is the immediate availability of the results. RADT has sensitivity and specificity similar to those of throat culture. The throat swab for either culture or RADT should be obtained from both tonsils or tonsillar fossae and the posterior pharyngeal wall. In high-risk patients, a negative antigen test result should be confirmed by throat culture.

No guidelines recommend antibiotic treatment without further testing. Some recommend treating patients with three or four Centor criteria while the test results are pending, although guidelines differ on this point.

KEY POINT

Use of the four-point Centor criteria is a reasonable way to triage patients with pharyngitis to empiric treatment with antibiotics, symptomatic treatment only, or testing with treatment if the test result is positive.

Bibliography
Wessels MR. Clinical practice. Streptococcal pharyngitis. N Engl J Med. 2011;364:648-55. [PMID: 21323542]

Item 6   Answer: A
Educational Objective: *Diagnose acute otitis externa.*

This patient most likely has uncomplicated acute otitis externa. Her swimming puts her at risk for otitis externa because of the moist conditions created by daily water immersion. Symptoms include otalgia, itching or fullness with or without hearing loss, and pain intensified by jaw motion. Signs include internal tenderness when the tragus or pinna is pushed or pulled and diffuse ear canal edema, purulent debris, and erythema, with or without otorrhea. Otitis externa can cause erythema of the tympanic membrane and mimic otitis media. In otitis externa, however, pneumatic otoscopy shows good tympanic membrane mobility. Management consists of clearing the canal of debris to optimize penetration of ototopical agents and allow visualization of the tympanic membrane to ensure that it is intact before initiating treatment. Topical agents have been the mainstay of therapy for uncomplicated otitis, although there is little information on the effectiveness of one topical treatment compared with another. An ototopical agent containing neomycin, polymyxin B, and hydrocortisone is frequently used and is effective when given for 7 to 10 days. Mild otitis externa can be treated with a dilute acetic acid solution.

Although an allergic reaction to the plastic earplugs should be considered, a delayed-type (type IV) hypersensitivity reaction is unlikely because of the purulent discharge and the much higher likelihood that the patient has bacterial acute otitis externa. Delayed-type hypersensitivity reactions (contact dermatitis) are typically characterized by erythema and edema with vesicles or bullae that often rupture, leaving a crust. Allergic reactions to plastic in hearing aids, metal in earrings, or even otic suspension drops used to treat otitis externa should always be considered in the differential diagnosis of an inflamed external auditory canal.

Malignant otitis externa is a much more serious condition in which infection in the ear canal spreads to the cartilage and bones nearby. It is frequently accompanied by fever, significant pain, and otorrhea.

Patients usually appear much more ill than this healthy-appearing woman with localized ear discomfort. On physical examination, granulation tissue is often visible along the inferior margin of the external canal.

Pain with tugging on the pinna and movement of the tragus and an inflamed external auditory canal make otitis media highly unlikely as a diagnostic possibility. In addition, acute otitis media is associated with signs of middle ear effusion and inflammation (erythema of the tympanic membrane), which are not present in this patient.

KEY POINT

Symptoms of otitis externa include otalgia, itching or fullness, and pain intensified by jaw motion. Signs include internal tenderness when the tragus or pinna is pushed or pulled and diffuse ear canal edema, purulent debris, and erythema.

Bibliography
Osguthorpe JD, Nielsen DR. Otitis externa: review and clinical update. Am Fam Physician. 2006;74:1510-6. [PMID: 17111889]

Item 7   Answer: D
Educational Objective: *Manage upper respiratory tract infection with ear pain.*

This patient has signs and symptoms of a viral upper respiratory tract infection (URI). The recent development of ear pain and the findings of a dull tympanic membrane and a small middle ear effusion are compatible with either otitis media or a viral URI without otitis media. Treatment of otitis media in adults has not been well studied. There are no guidelines for antibiotic use in adults separate from those for children. In children older than 2 years without severe illness, outcomes appear to be similar for observation without antibiotics compared with antibiotic treatment. This strategy to reduce the use of antimicrobials has not been evaluated in adults, and it is not known whether antibiotics are associated with improved short- or long-term outcomes. However, antibiotic use is associated with adverse effects and higher levels of antibiotic resistance that should be considered in conjunction with the lack of evidence regarding benefit. Considering the patient's equivocal diagnosis of otitis media and mild symptoms, it would be reasonable to withhold antibiotic therapy.

When an antibiotic is prescribed, amoxicillin is recommended as first-line therapy in adults. Azithromycin can be used in a patient who is allergic to penicillin, but there is no evidence that it is more effective than penicillin.

Consultation with an otorhinolaryngologist is not indicated because the patient only has a URI.

KEY POINT

Do not routinely prescribe antibiotic therapy for adults with otitis media.

Bibliography
Harmes KM, Blackwood RA, Burrows HL, et al. Otitis media: diagnosis and treatment. Am Fam Physician. 2013;88:435-40. [PMID: 24134083]

Item 8   Answer: B
Educational Objective: *Diagnose Lemierre syndrome.*

The patient should undergo computed tomography (CT) of the neck with contrast. She has fever, leukocytosis, sore throat, unilateral neck tenderness, and multiple densities on chest radiograph, suggestive of septic emboli. The combination of these factors points strongly toward

Lemierre syndrome, which is septic thrombosis of the internal jugular vein. The diagnosis should be suspected in anyone with pharyngitis, persistent fever, neck pain, and septic pulmonary emboli. CT of the affected vessel with contrast would confirm the diagnosis. Treatment includes intravenous antibiotics that cover streptococci, anaerobes, and β-lactamase-producing organisms. Penicillin with a β-lactamase inhibitor and carbapenem are both reasonable choices (e.g., ampicillin-sulbactam, piperacillin-tazobactam, ticarcillin-clavulanate).

Chest CT would better characterize the pulmonary infiltrates, but this information would not provide specific diagnostic information that would guide therapy.

Soft tissue radiography of the neck cannot detect jugular vein filling defects or thromboses, which are diagnostic of septic thrombophlebitis.

Echocardiography would be helpful to exclude right-sided endocarditis as a cause of septic emboli. However, there is nothing in the history or on cardiac examination to suggest a cardiac source of septic emboli.

KEY POINT

The diagnosis of septic thrombosis of the jugular vein (Lemierre syndrome) should be suspected in patients with pharyngitis, persistent fever, neck pain, and septic pulmonary emboli.

Bibliography

Centor RM, Samlowski R. Avoiding sore throat morbidity and mortality: when is it not "just a sore throat?" Am Fam Physician. 2011;83:26, 28. [PMID: 21888123]

Item 9   Answer: D

Educational Objective: *Treat* Pseudomonas aeruginosa *pneumonia.*

The most appropriate empiric antibiotic therapy for this patient is piperacillin-tazobactam and amikacin. *Pseudomonas aeruginosa* pneumonia should be suspected in patients with a history of smoking and chronic lung disease. Other risk factors for *Pseudomonas* pneumonia include broad-spectrum antibiotic use in the previous month, recent hospitalization, malnutrition, neutropenia, and glucocorticoid use. *P. aeruginosa* pneumonia can be severe and life-threatening, and appropriate initial antibiotic selection is crucial. Treatment with a combination of two antimicrobial agents to which *P. aeruginosa* shows in vitro susceptibility, typically a β-lactam and an aminoglycoside, should be started empirically. Although it remains controversial whether combination therapy is more efficacious than monotherapy, traditionally, combination therapy has been recommended to broaden the empiric coverage and prevent the emergence of antibiotic resistance during therapy.

Empiric treatment with cefazolin, ceftriaxone and azithromycin, or ceftriaxone and ciprofloxacin is not appropriate for a patient with suspected *P. aeruginosa* pneumonia because these antibiotics are ineffective in the treatment of *Pseudomonas* infections.

KEY POINT

Initial empiric therapy with two antipseudomonal agents should be initiated in patients with risk factors for *Pseudomonas* pneumonia.

Bibliography

Tamma PD, Cosgrove SE, Maragakis LL. Combination therapy for treatment of infections with gram-negative bacteria. Clin Microbiol Rev. 2012;25:450-70. [PMID: 22763634]

Item 10   Answer: C

Educational Objective: *Determine the setting for treatment of community-acquired pneumonia.*

The most appropriate disposition for the patient is admission to the medical ward. The decision regarding admission is often complex. Prognostic models, such as CURB-65 (Confusion, blood Urea nitrogen >19.6 mg/dL, Respiration rate ≥30/min, systolic Blood pressure <90 mm Hg or diastolic <60 mm Hg, and age ≥65 years) and the Pneumonia Severity Index (PSI), have been developed to identify patients who require hospitalization and avoid unnecessary admissions. CURB-65 is used to identify patients who are at risk for complications. Patients who meet zero criteria have a 0% mortality rate. The mortality rate increases to 8.3% when patients meet two criteria and 20% when they meet three criteria. those with a score of two had an 8.3% mortality rate, and those with a score of three or higher had a mortality rate of >20%. Patients who meet two criteria usually are admitted to the hospital, and those who meet three criteria are considered for intensive care unit (ICU) admission. The patient is at moderate risk, considering his age and tachypnea, and needs to be admitted to the hospital. He is hemodynamically stable, and ICU admission is not indicated.

The PSI predicts the mortality risk based on 20 clinical factors, including patient age, comorbidities, physical examination findings, and laboratory data, and stratifies patients into five mortality risk classes. Patients who are at medium or high risk (>70 points) should be admitted to the hospital. Based on this model, the patient is at medium risk because of his age, fever, tachypnea, and hypoxia. Therefore, he requires hospital admission. One study that compared the PSI with the CURB-65 criteria found that both approaches identified low-risk patients but the CURB-65 was more discriminating in predicting individual mortality risk in high-risk patients.

Overnight observation or discharge on oral antibiotics would not be appropriate because of the severity of the patient's illness.

KEY POINT

Prognostic models, such as CURB-65 and the Pneumonia Severity Index, may help to identify patients with community-acquired pneumonia who are at risk for complications and require admission to the hospital.

Bibliography

Mandell LA, Wunderink RG, Anzueto A, et al. Infectious Diseases Society of America/American Thoracic Society consensus guidelines on the management of community-acquired pneumonia in adults. Clin Infect Dis. 2007;44(suppl 2):S27-72. [PMID: 17278083]

Item 11   Answer: B

Educational Objective: *Treat community-acquired pneumonia in an outpatient.*

The patient should be treated with azithromycin. His clinical presentation and radiographic findings are consistent with community-acquired pneumonia (CAP). In outpatients, risk factors for drug-resistant *Streptococcus pneumoniae* infection influence the selection of empiric therapy. These risk factors include age older than 65 years, recent (within the last 3 months) β-lactam therapy, medical comorbidities, immunocompromising conditions and immunosuppressive therapy, alcoholism, and exposure to a child in day care. This patient is a young, healthy man with no risk factors for drug-resistant *S. pneumoniae* infection. Therefore, treatment with a macrolide agent, such as azithromycin, will provide adequate coverage for the likely pathogens, including drug-susceptible *S. pneumoniae*, *Haemophilus influenzae*, *Mycoplasma* species, and *Chlamydophila* species.

Amoxicillin would not provide coverage for atypical pathogens, such as *Mycoplasma* or *Chlamydophila,* and would not cover all *H. influenzae* strains because an increasing number of strains produce β-lactamase. Although few studies have examined the microbiology of CAP in outpatients, *Mycoplasma* and *Chlamydophila* are more likely to cause pneumonia in ambulatory patients. High-dose amoxicillin combined with a macrolide is an alternative for patients with risk factors for drug-resistant *S. pneumoniae* infection.

Cefuroxime provides coverage for drug-susceptible *S. pneumoniae* and *H. influenzae* but not for atypical pathogens. A respiratory fluoroquinolone, such as moxifloxacin or levofloxacin, provides appropriate coverage for the likely pathogens associated with CAP but is unnecessarily broad for this indication. A respiratory fluoroquinolone would be appropriate if this patient had risk factors for infection with drug-resistant *S. pneumoniae*.

Ciprofloxacin has very poor activity against *S. pneumoniae* and should not be used as empiric therapy for CAP.

KEY POINT

In previously healthy patients with pneumonia but no risk factors for drug-resistant S*treptococcus pneumoniae* infection, treatment with a macrolide agent, such as azithromycin, provides adequate coverage for the likely pathogens.

Bibliography

Mandell LA, Wunderink RG, Anzueto A, et al. Infectious Diseases Society of America/American Thoracic Society consensus guidelines on the management of community-acquired pneumonia in adults. Clin Infect Dis. 2007;44(suppl 2):S27-72. [PMID: 17278083]

Item 12   Answer: B

Educational Objective: *Diagnose severe community-acquired pneumonia.*

This patient requires *Legionella* and *Streptococcus pneumoniae* urine antigen assays. The role of routine diagnostic testing to determine the microbial cause of community-acquired pneumonia (CAP) is controversial. The Infectious Diseases Society of America/American Thoracic Society consensus guidelines suggest that diagnostic testing in outpatients, except for pulse oximetry, is optional. However, this hospitalized patient has severe CAP, defined as CAP in a patient who requires admission to an intensive care unit or transfer to an intensive care unit within 24 hours of admission. Blood cultures, *Legionella* and *Streptococcus pneumoniae* urine antigen assays, and endotracheal aspirate for Gram stain and culture are recommended for hospitalized patients with severe CAP. *Legionella* should be suspected in this patient, who is older than 50 years of age and presents with severe pneumonia with extrapulmonary symptoms (headache, diarrhea, hyponatremia).

Bronchoscopy with quantitative culture can be used as a diagnostic tool in the evaluation of patients with pneumonia. Bronchoscopy was compared with evaluation using clinical features suggesting pneumonia and endotracheal aspirate for Gram stain and qualitative culture in patients with ventilator-associated pneumonia. Clinical outcomes for the two approaches were equivalent. However, bronchoscopy with quantitative culture has not been prospectively studied for the management of patients with severe CAP.

Serologic testing for atypical pathogens such as *Legionella* species is not recommended because convalescent titers would need to be obtained 6 to 8 weeks after initial testing to establish a diagnosis.

This hospitalized patient has severe CAP. Therefore, providing no further evaluation would not be appropriate.

KEY POINT

Blood cultures, *Legionella* and *Streptococcus pneumoniae* urine antigen assays, and endotracheal aspirate for Gram stain and culture are recommended for hospitalized patients with severe community-acquired pneumonia.

Bibliography

Niederman N. In the clinic. Community-acquired pneumonia. Ann Intern Med. 2009;151(7):ITC-4-2-ITC-4-14; quiz ITC-4-16. [PMID: 19805767]

Item 13   Answer: C

Educational Objective: *Manage a hospitalized patient with bacteremic pneumococcal pneumonia.*

This patient with bacteremic pneumococcal pneumonia should be discharged on oral amoxicillin to complete 7 days of therapy. Physical examination findings on hospital day 3 (afebrile, systolic blood pressure ≥90 mm Hg, pulse rate ≤100/min, and respiration rate ≤24/min) plus normal oxygen saturation on ambient air indicate that the patient is clinically stable and should be considered for discharge. In addition, patients who are considered stable for discharge should have a normal (or baseline) mental status and should be able to tolerate oral therapy. Pneumococcal bacteremia does not warrant a more prolonged course of intravenous therapy. Once patients are clinically stable, they are at very low risk for subsequent clinical deterioration and can be safely discharged from the hospital.

Levofloxacin would provide unnecessarily broad-spectrum coverage for this patient's penicillin-susceptible pneumonia, and levofloxacin would be a more expensive treatment option.

In most patients, especially those who have a prompt clinical response to treatment, 7 to 10 days of therapy is sufficient for treatment of community-acquired pneumonia, even in the setting of bacteremic infection. A 14-day treatment regimen would be unnecessarily long for this patient.

Studies have shown that continued observation after switching from intravenous to oral therapy is not necessary.

KEY POINT

Hospitalized patients with bacteremic community-acquired pneumonia who respond promptly to therapy do not require a more prolonged course of intravenous therapy. They can be discharged home on oral medication when they are clinically stable.

Bibliography

Weinstein MP, Klugman KP, Jones RN. Rationale for revised penicillin susceptibility breakpoints versus *Streptococcus pneumoniae:* coping with antimicrobial susceptibility in an era of resistance. Clin Infect Dis. 2009;48:1596-600. [PMID: 19400744]

Item 14   Answer: B

Educational Objective: *Screen for latent tuberculosis.*

The most appropriate next test for this patient is an interferon-γ-releasing assay (IGRA). This patient recently emigrated from an area with high rates of tuberculosis, so screening for tuberculosis is recommended. The Centers for Disease Control and Prevention endorses the use of IGRAs in all clinical settings in which the tuberculin skin test (TST) is recommended. Two types of IGRAs are increasingly being used. Both indicate sensitization to *Mycobacterium tuberculosis* by measuring the release of interferon-γ in the blood by T cells as a response to *M. tuberculosis*–associated antigens. IGRAs are generally believed to be as sensitive as the TST but more specific in diagnosing tuberculosis. As with the TST, a more vigorous IGRA response is needed for a low-risk person to be considered infected. Similar to the TST, IGRAs are not recommended for testing persons who are at low risk for latent tuberculosis infection. IGRAs are preferred to the TST in those have received bacillus Calmette-Guérin vaccine either as treatment for cancer or as a vaccine. IGRAs are also preferred when testing persons who often do not return for a follow-up reading of the TST (e.g., injection drug users or homeless persons). Generally, IGRAs are done in place of the TST and not in addition to this test. IGRA testing is significantly more expensive than the TST and may not be readily available in some areas. These factors should be considered when deciding which testing strategy to pursue.

Neither the TST nor IGRAs can distinguish between latent and active infection. Therefore, any person who has a positive test result should be carefully evaluated for the possibility of active infection with a chest radiograph. Sputum staining and culture are done if changes are seen on the chest radiograph that are consistent with pulmonary tuberculosis or when the patient's presentation suggests the presence of active tuberculosis.

KEY POINT

Interferon-γ-releasing assay is preferred to the tuberculin skin test in those who have received bacillus Calmette-Guérin vaccine either as treatment for cancer or as a vaccine. Interferon-γ-releasing assay is also preferred when testing persons who often do not return for a follow-up reading of the tuberculin skin test.

Bibliography
Escalante P. In the clinic. Tuberculosis. Ann Intern Med. 2009;150:ITC-6-1-14; quiz ITV-6-16. [PMID: 19487708]

Item 15   Answer: D
Educational Objective: *Interpret results of the tuberculin skin test.*

No further evaluation or therapy is needed. The Mantoux tuberculin skin test (TST) involves injecting purified protein derivative intradermally (usually into the volar aspect of the forearm) and assessing the skin response. Induration (not erythema) is measured 48 to 72 hours later. A positive response indicates a delayed-type hypersensitivity response. To increase the specificity of the test, criteria for positivity are based on the patient's risk factors for infection with *Mycobacterium tuberculosis*. A TST response of 5 mm or greater is considered positive for HIV-positive persons; recent contacts of persons with active tuberculosis; those with fibrotic changes on chest radiograph that are consistent with previous tuberculosis infection; and patients with organ transplants and other immunosuppressive conditions (receiving the equivalent of ≥15 mg/d prednisone for >4 weeks). A TST response of 10 mm or greater is considered positive for recent (<5 years) arrivals from high-prevalence countries; injection drug users; residents or employees of high-risk congregate settings, including prisons and jails, nursing homes and other long-term facilities for the elderly, hospitals and other health care facilities, residential facilities for patients with AIDS, and homeless shelters; mycobacteriology laboratory personnel; persons with clinical conditions that put them at high risk for active disease; and children who are younger than 4 years of age or are exposed to adults in high-risk categories. A response of 15 mm or greater is considered positive for all other persons.

A chest radiograph is indicated for patients with symptoms that are compatible with tuberculosis or persons with a positive screening test for tuberculosis, such as a positive result on the TST or interferon γ-releasing assay. Treatment with isoniazid for 9 months would be appropriate for a person diagnosed with latent tuberculosis. Airborne precautions are recommended for patients infected with microorganisms such as rubella virus and *M. tuberculosis*, which are transmitted by airborne droplet nuclei smaller than 5 μm. This patient has no indications for chest radiography, isoniazid treatment, or isolation.

KEY POINT

To increase the specificity of the tuberculin skin test, criteria for positivity are based on the patient's risk factors for infection with *Mycobacterium tuberculosis*.

Bibliography
Escalante P. In the clinic. Tuberculosis. Ann Intern Med. 2009;150:ITC-6-1-14; quiz ITV-6-16. [PMID: 19487708]

Item 16   Answer: D
Educational Objective: *Evaluate for latent tuberculosis before the administration of a biologic agent for immunosuppression.*

The most appropriate study to be performed before the initiation of therapy with a biologic immunosuppressant is evaluation for the presence of latent tuberculosis (TB). This evaluation is done with a tuberculin skin test or interferon-γ-releasing assay (IGRA). Because of their potent suppression of cell-mediated immunity, biologic agents used to treat rheumatic and other diseases carry an increased risk for serious infection, in particular, reactivation TB and extrapulmonary TB. Therefore, all patients who are considered for such therapy should undergo screening for latent TB infection. Screening includes a full medical history, physical examination, and tuberculin skin testing with purified protein derivative or IGRA. If the results of screening are negative, treatment with a biologic agent is appropriate. However, clinical monitoring for TB should be continued throughout the course of treatment. If the results of screening are positive, further evaluation is indicated to confirm latent TB or the possibility of active disease. Treatment for either latent TB or active disease is required before initiation of biologic therapy, based on the diagnosis. It is considered reasonable to start treatment with a biologic agent after at least 1 month of therapy for latent TB or after completion of a full course of therapy for active disease.

Although chest radiography is a component of diagnosing latent or active TB, skin or IGRA testing is indicated as the first test in screening.

Induced sputum for microscopic analysis, nucleic amplification testing, and culture may be helpful in patients with suspected active TB. However, this testing would not be appropriate for screening in this patient.

Serologic studies for TB have not been shown to be effective and currently have no role in screening for or diagnosing TB infection.

KEY POINT

Testing for tuberculosis with a tuberculin skin test or interferon-γ-releasing assay is indicated before the initiation of immunosuppressive biologic agents.

Bibliography

Singh JA, Furst DE, Bharat A, et al. 2012 update of the 2008 American College of Rheumatology recommendations for the use of disease-modifying antirheumatic drugs and biologic agents in the treatment of rheumatoid arthritis. Arthritis Care Res. 2012;64:625–39. [PMID:22473917]

Item 17   Answer: D

Educational Objective: *Manage initial therapy for active tuberculosis.*

The patient should be given a four-drug regimen as initial therapy for newly diagnosed, previously untreated tuberculosis (TB). A diagnosis of pulmonary TB should be considered in any patient who has cough for longer than 3 weeks accompanied by loss of appetite, unexplained weight loss, night sweats, bloody sputum or hemoptysis, hoarseness, fever, fatigue, or chest pain. The index of suspicion should be substantially higher for patients who have increased risk of exposure to TB.

Four-drug therapy is used in patients with suspected, previously untreated TB in whom resistance patterns are unknown to allow coverage for possible multidrug resistance, followed by de-escalation of antimicrobial therapy once drug susceptibility is known. Isoniazid, rifampin, pyrazinamide, and ethambutol are the most commonly used first-line drugs. All four drugs are used during the first 2 months of treatment, and depending on the results of susceptibility testing, treatment continues with isoniazid and rifampin for the remaining 7 months, for a total of 9 months of treatment.

Drug-resistant TB is resistant to at least one first-line antituberculosis drug. Multidrug-resistant TB is defined as an organism that is resistant to more than one antituberculosis drug and at least isoniazid and rifampin.

Treatment with fluoroquinolones or other drugs, such as ethionamide or cycloserine, would be appropriate only after a diagnosis of multidrug-resistant TB is confirmed. They are considered second-line therapies because they tend to be less effective than those typically used for initial treatment and should be used only if resistance has been documented.

Treatment with isoniazid alone is not acceptable because isoniazid monotherapy is typically used to treat latent TB when multidrug-resistant TB is not suspected.

Dual therapy with isoniazid and rifampin is typically used to complete a full course of therapy in patients with susceptible TB but not to initiate therapy in patients with active disease.

KEY POINT

The initial therapeutic regimen for all adults with previously untreated tuberculosis consists of a 2-month initial phase of treatment with isoniazid, rifampin, pyrazinamide, and ethambutol pending the results of drug susceptibility tests.

Bibliography

American Thoracic Society; CDC; Infectious Diseases Society of America. Treatment of tuberculosis. MMWR Recomm Rep. 2003;52:1-77. Erratum in MMWR Recomm Rep. 2005;53:1203. [PMID: 12836625]

Item 18   Answer: C

Educational Objective: *Treat latent tuberculosis infection.*

This patient meets the clinical criteria for latent tuberculosis infection and should receive treatment with isoniazid for 9 months to pre-

vent reactivation tuberculosis. He has a greater than 15-mm induration on tuberculin skin testing. Therefore, he is at high risk (5%-10%) for the development of reactivation tuberculosis. Because the patient has no signs or symptoms of active tuberculosis or HIV infection and has normal results on chest radiography, he has latent infection. Treatment with isoniazid for 9 months is the appropriate therapy. In patients who are at high risk for active tuberculosis, treatment with isoniazid may reduce the risk of active disease by up to 90%.

Although the incidence of isoniazid-related hepatotoxicity is slightly increased in older patients, age is not a limitation to treatment of latent tuberculosis. The U.S. Centers for Disease Control and Prevention, the American Thoracic Society, and the Infectious Diseases Society of America guidelines call for treatment for all high-risk persons with latent tuberculosis unless previous treatment can be documented or such treatment is medically contraindicated.

Bacillus Calmette-Guérin (BCG) vaccination has no role in the prevention or treatment of tuberculosis in the United States. Although BCG vaccine has been used extensively in other countries, its efficacy for the prevention of tuberculosis has varied in controlled trials conducted with different populations around the world. In addition, it appears to be less effect than isoniazid in treating latent tuberculosis.

Results of testing with an interferon-γ-releasing assay (IGRA) would be expected to be positive in this patient and would not provide additional clinical information. Neither tuberculin skin testing nor IGRA can distinguish between latent and active tuberculosis.

Four-drug treatment with isoniazid, rifampin, pyrazinamide, and ethambutol is not indicated in the absence of active disease.

Observation alone is insufficient protection for this patient because he is at risk for reactivation tuberculosis.

KEY POINT

In patients who are at high risk for active tuberculosis, treatment may reduce the risk of active disease by up to 90%.

Bibliography

American Thoracic Society; Centers for Disease Control and Prevention; Infectious Diseases Society of America. American Thoracic Society/Centers for Disease Control and Prevention/Infectious Diseases Society of America: controlling tuberculosis in the United States. Am J Respir Crit Care Med. 2005;172:1169-227. [PMID: 16249321]

Item 19   Answer: D

Educational Objective: *Appropriately withhold infective endocarditis prophylaxis in a patient with a heart murmur associated with a native valve abnormality.*

No antibiotic prophylaxis is required prior to this patient's dental procedure. Although prophylaxis for dental procedures had been widely provided to individuals with most cardiac issues, it has been found that the bacteremia associated with dental procedures is much less likely to cause endocarditis than the bacteremia resulting from normal, daily activities, and that only an extremely small number of cases of infective endocarditis are prevented by prophylaxis. Therefore, antibiotic prophylaxis is now recommended only for patients with underlying cardiac conditions associated with the highest risk of adverse outcome from infective endocarditis, and only when those patients undergoing specific procedures in which significant bacteremia is most likely. High risk cardiac conditions include patients with prosthetic cardiac valves, a history of prior infective endocarditis, unrepaired cyanotic congenital heart disease or completely repaired congenital heart disease for 6 months following repair, repaired congenital heart disease with residual defects or abnormalities, and cardiac transplantation recipients with cardiac valvulopathy. Prophylaxis is not indicated in patients with heart murmurs associated with native valve abnormalities such as mitral valve prolapse or a congenital bicuspid aortic valve as in this patient.

In patients with an indication for treatment, antibiotics directed toward viridans streptococci are recommended, which is usually amoxicillin or clindamycin in penicillin-allergic patients.

KEY POINT

Antibiotic prophylaxis to prevent infective endocarditis is recommended only for patients with underlying conditions associated with the highest risk of adverse outcome from infective endocarditis; this does not include heart murmurs associated with native valve abnormalities.

Bibliography
Duval X, Leport C. Prophylaxis of infective endocarditis: current tendencies, continuing controversies. Lancet Infect Dis. 2008;8(4):225-32. [PMID: 18353264]

Item 20   Answer: E

Educational Objective: *Treat native valve infective endocarditis.*

This patient should be switched to intravenous vancomycin monotherapy. When clinical suspicion for endocarditis is intermediate or high, initiation of empiric antibiotic therapy is appropriate after multiple blood cultures have been drawn. Tailored antibiotic therapy is guided by the causative organism and its microbiologic susceptibilities. Recommended empiric treatment of community-acquired endocarditis includes a combination of vancomycin plus gentamicin or ampicillin-sulbactam plus gentamicin. The Infectious Diseases Society of America Clinical has practice guidelines that recommend intravenous vancomycin (or daptomycin) for the treatment of methicillin-resistant *Staphylococcus aureus* (MRSA) infective endocarditis. The recommended duration of treatment for *S. aureus*-associated native valve infective endocarditis is 6 weeks.

β-Lactam antibiotics (e.g., imipenem) and β-lactam plus β-lactamase inhibitor combinations (e.g., piperacillin-tazobactam) are not effective in the management of MRSA infections.

Penicillinase-resistant penicillins, such as nafcillin and oxacillin, are effective against methicillin-susceptible *S. aureus* but are not active against MRSA.

KEY POINT

Endocarditis caused by methicillin-resistant *Staphylococcus aureus* is treated with either intravenous vancomycin or daptomycin. Empiric antibiotic therapy for infective endocarditis should be narrowed in spectrum based on culture results and antibiotic susceptibility when available.

Bibliography
Liu C, Bayer A, Cosgrove SE, et al. Clinical practice guidelines by the Infectious Diseases Society of America for the treatment of methicillin-resistant *Staphylococcus aureus* infections in adults and children: executive summary. Clin Infect Dis. 2011;52:285-92. [PMID: 21217178]

Item 21   Answer: A

Educational Objective: *Manage a patient with a history of infective endocarditis before a dental procedure.*

This patient with a history of infective endocarditis and requires antimicrobial prophylaxis with amoxicillin before her dental procedure. The American Heart Association (AHA) infective endocarditis guidelines were revised in 2007. These guidelines recommend antibiotic prophylaxis to prevent endocarditis only in patients who have cardiac conditions associated with the highest risk of adverse outcome from endocarditis when undergoing procedures associated with a high risk of bacteremia. High-risk cardiac conditions include the presence of a prosthetic cardiac valve, unrepaired cyanotic congenital heart disease, congenital heart disease repair with prosthetic material or device within the last 6 months, presence of palliative shunts and conduits, cardiac valvulopathy in cardiac transplant recipients, and a history of infective endocarditis, as in this patient. High-risk surgical procedures include dental procedures involving manipulation of gingival tissue or the periapical region of teeth or perforation of the oral mucosa as well as respiratory tract procedures that involve perforation of the respiratory mucosa (tonsillectomy, adenoidectomy). In patients with an indication for prophylaxis, the suggested antibiotic regimen before dental procedures is an agent directed against viridans group streptococci, administered as a single dose 30 to 60 minutes before the procedure. Amoxicillin and cephalosporins, such as cephalexin, are frequently prescribed. Clindamycin, azithromycin, or clarithromycin are appropriate alternatives in patients with penicillin allergy.

Vancomycin is not required because, despite this patient's history of methicillin-resistant *Staphylococcus aureus* endocarditis, the previous infection does not influence the antibiotic choice for prophylactic endocarditis treatment.

Trimethoprim-sulfamethoxazole does not have activity against viridans streptococci and would not be an appropriate choice of antibiotic prophylaxis in this patient.

According to the AHA guidelines, a history of infective endocarditis is one of the indications for infective endocarditis prophylaxis before a dental procedure involving gingival manipulation. Therefore, providing no prophylaxis to this patient would not be appropriate.

KEY POINT

There are specific indications for infective endocarditis prophylaxis for patients before certain dental or surgical procedures that involve manipulation of gingival tissue or the periapical region of teeth or perforation of the oral mucosa. Prophylaxis is needed in patients with a prosthetic cardiac valve, a history of infective endocarditis, unrepaired cyanotic congenital heart disease, congenital heart disease repair with prosthetic material or device within the last 6 months, palliative shunts and conduits, or cardiac valvulopathy in cardiac transplant recipients.

Bibliography
Wilson W, Taubert KA, Gewitz M, et al. Prevention of infective endocarditis. Guidelines from the American Heart Association. A guideline from the American Heart Association Rheumatic Cardiovascular Disease in the Young, and the Council on Clinical Cardiology, Council on Cardiovascular Surgery and Anesthesia, and the Quality of Care and Outcomes Research Interdisciplinary Working Group. Circulation. 2007;116:1736-54. [PMID: 17446442]

Item 22   Answer: C

Educational Objective: *Evaluate a patient with a high pretest probability of endocarditis.*

This patient likely has prosthetic valve endocarditis, and transesophageal echocardiography (TEE) is the initial test of choice when there is a moderate or high pretest probability of endocarditis (e.g., in patients with staphylococcal bacteremia or fungemia, a prosthetic heart valve, or an intracardiac device). There is concern about multiple associated complications in this patient, including aortic regurgitation (widened pulse pressure and diastolic murmur) as well as aortic root abscess (prolonged P-R interval). TEE is the initial imaging test in some clinical situations, such as detection of left atrial thrombus, evaluation of prosthetic mitral valve dysfunction, and evaluation of suspected aortic dissection, as well as in patients with a moderate to high pretest probability of endocarditis. Some studies have shown that TEE has greater than 95% sensitivity in the diagnosis of endocarditis compared with only 50% to 80% for transthoracic echocardiography (TTE). Patients who are at high risk for endocarditis and its complications should undergo early TEE rather than TTE.

Cardiac computed tomographic angiography and cardiovascular magnetic resonance imaging may be of help in identifying an aortic root abscess. However, TEE is more likely to identify cardiac vegetations and is as likely to identify aortic abscess. In addition, this patient has an elevated serum creatinine level, and these two imaging modalities should be avoided in this setting because of the increased risk of complications associated with contrast required for both studies.

KEY POINT

Transesophageal echocardiography is the initial test of choice in patients who have a moderate or high pretest probability of endocarditis.

Bibliography

Douglas PS, Garcia MJ, Haines DE, et al. ACCF/ASE/AHA/ASNC/HFSA/HRS/SCAI/SCCM/SCCT/SCMR 2011 appropriate use criteria for echocardiography. A Report of the American College of Cardiology Foundation Appropriate Use Criteria Task Force, American Society of Echocardiography, American Heart Association, American Society of Nuclear Cardiology, Heart Failure Society of America, Heart Rhythm Society, Society for Cardiovascular Angiography and Interventions, Society of Critical Care Medicine, Society of Cardiovascular Computed Tomography, and Society for Cardiovascular Magnetic Resonance endorsed by the American College of Chest Physicians. J Am Coll Cardiol. 2011;57:1126-66. [PMID: 21349406]

Item 23   Answer: A

Educational Objective: *Manage complicated infective endocarditis.*

This patient should undergo replacement of the aortic valve. He has aortic valve endocarditis complicated by perivalvular extension, resulting in an abscess and severe aortic regurgitation. Urgent surgical intervention is indicated for patients with heart failure; abscess or fistula formation; severe left-sided valvular regurgitation; refractory infection despite appropriate antibiotic therapy; or recurrent embolic events, especially with residual vegetation larger than 1.0 cm. There should be no delay in surgical intervention for observation of the patient's response to antibiotic therapy once the surgical indications are met. In this patient, the complications of endocarditis would not likely improve or resolve without surgical therapy. Continuing antibiotic therapy alone without immediate surgical intervention may result in further decompensation of the patient's clinical status and an increased operative risk for intervention at a later time.

Although antibiotic therapy with coverage narrowed to an identified susceptible organism is appropriate treatment for uncomplicated infective endocarditis, because of this patient's associated valve dysfunction and likely perivalvular abscess, surgical treatment is needed in addition to antibiotic therapy.

Cardiac catheterization is not indicated in this patient and may increase the risk of embolization of the vegetation or worsening of the patient's hemodynamic status. Cardiac catheterization before planned cardiac surgery is indicated in patients with risk factors for coronary artery disease. These risk factors are not present in this patient.

Although the vegetative lesion in endocarditis is a product of both bacterial and platelet adhesion, no studies have shown a reduction in embolic events in patients treated with heparin.

KEY POINT

In patients with endocarditis complicated by heart failure, abscess, severe regurgitation, or hemodynamic derangements, valve replacement should be performed urgently, without delay to determine the response to antibiotic therapy.

Bibliography

Stout KK, Verrier ED. Acute valvular regurgitation. Circulation. 2009;119:3232-41. [PMID: 19564568]

Item 24   Answer: B

Educational Objective: *Treat pyelonephritis.*

The most appropriate treatment for this patient is intravenous ciprofloxacin. This patient has sepsis as a result of acute pyelonephritis. Pyelonephritis is associated with abrupt onset of fever, chills, sweats, nausea, vomiting, diarrhea, myalgia, and flank or abdominal pain. Hypotension and septic shock may occur in severe cases. Urinary frequency and dysuria may precede pyelonephritis. Consider outpatient management for patients with pyelonephritis who are medically stable and able to take oral medication. Fluoroquinolones are used as first-line empiric oral therapy (except in pregnancy) because of the higher urine drug concentrations achieved compared with trimethoprim–sulfamethoxazole (TMP-SMX). Ampicillin, TMP-SMX, and first-generation cephalosporins are no longer used for empiric therapy because of unacceptably high rates of resistance. Patients with pyelonephritis who are acutely ill, hypotensive, nauseated, or vomiting are admitted to the hospital for intravenous fluids and parenteral antibiotics. Empiric therapy is begun with a fluoroquinolone, an extended-spectrum cephalosporin or penicillin, or an aminoglycoside, and treatment is continued for 7 to 14 days. Cephalosporins or aminoglycosides alone are insufficient for treating infections caused by enterococci. Persistent fever and unilateral flank pain despite adequate treatment suggest perinephric or intrarenal abscess and the need for kidney computed tomography.

Ampicillin and imipenem should be avoided, considering the patient's severe allergy to penicillin. Aminoglycoside should be avoided in patients with kidney disease. Vancomycin does not provide coverage for gram-negative organisms.

KEY POINT

Empiric therapy for hospitalized patients with pyelonephritis includes a fluoroquinolone, an extended-spectrum cephalosporin or penicillin, or an aminoglycoside. Treatment is continued for 7 to 14 days.

Bibliography

Gupta K, Hooton TM, Naber KG, et al. International clinical practice guidelines for the treatment of acute uncomplicated cystitis and pyelonephritis in women: a 2010 update by the Infectious Diseases Society of America and the European Society for Microbiology and Infectious Diseases. Clin Infect Dis. 2011;52:e103-20. [PMID: 21292654]

Item 25   Answer: E
Educational Objective: *Manage asymptomatic bacteriuria.*

No additional testing or treatment is indicated. The prevalence of asymptomatic bacteriuria is higher in women than in men. Asymptomatic bacteriuria occurs more commonly in pregnancy, patients with diabetes, and older patients, particularly men who are 65 years of age or older. Asymptomatic bacteriuria is also often seen in patients with indwelling urinary catheters. However, treatment of asymptomatic bacteriuria in adult nonpregnant patients (including patients with diabetes and the elderly) generally is not indicated. However, screening for and treatment of bacteriuria in pregnancy have been shown to be effective in preventing pyelonephritis.

Symptoms and signs compatible with a catheter-associated urinary tract infection include fever, rigors, altered mental status, malaise or lethargy, flank pain, costovertebral angle tenderness, and hematuria. In asymptomatic patients with indwelling urethral or suprapubic catheters, screening for bacteriuria is not recommended, except in pregnant women. The finding of pyuria in a patient with a chronic indwelling urinary catheter and asymptomatic bacteriuria should not be interpreted as an indication for antimicrobial treatment. Urinary collection systems concentrate normal urinary components and are frequently colonized with bacteria, making interpretation of urinalysis findings difficult. Thus, treatment with trimethoprim-sulfamethoxazole or ciprofloxacin is not indicated in this patient. Repeat urinalysis or urine culture is unnecessary in a patient without urinary symptoms.

KEY POINT

In patients with indwelling urinary catheters, screening for and treating asymptomatic bacteriuria is not recommended, except in pregnant women.

Bibliography

Hooton TM, Bradley SF, Cardenas DD, et al. Diagnosis, prevention, and treatment of catheter-associated urinary tract infection in adults: 2009 International Clinical Practice Guidelines from the Infectious Diseases Society of America. Clin Infect Dis. 2010;50:625-63. [PMID: 20175247]

Item 26   Answer: D
Educational Objective: *Manage acute, uncomplicated cystitis in a woman.*

This patient has acute, uncomplicated cystitis and is therefore a candidate for a short course of antibiotics. Although a number of antimicrobial agents are appropriate, the preferred initial therapy is a 3-day course of trimethoprim-sulfamethoxazole if local resistance rates of urinary tract pathogens do not exceed 20% or if the infecting organism is known to be susceptible. However, this patient has a reported sulfa allergy. Therefore, she should be treated with nitrofurantoin for 5 days. Nitrofurantoin has excellent coverage for common organisms responsible for cystitis and has minimal propensity to select for drug-resistant organisms. However, a 3-day regimen of nitrofurantoin is not as effective as a 3-day regimen of trimethoprim-sulfamethoxazole or fluoroquinolone agents. Therefore, treatment of uncomplicated cystitis with nitrofurantoin is recommended for 5 days. Nitrofurantoin should not be used if early pyelonephritis is suspected.

Amoxicillin or ampicillin should not be used unless the infecting organism is known to be susceptible because of the relatively high frequency of *Escherichia coli* species resistant to these agents among patients with community-acquired urinary tract infections.

Fluoroquinolone agents, such as ciprofloxacin, are alternatives for patients who are allergic to or intolerant of first-line agents or who live in areas where resistance to trimethoprim-sulfamethoxazole is higher than 20%. Fluoroquinolones are highly effective agents, and 3-day regimens are equivalent in efficacy to longer treatment courses. They should be reserved for more serious infections than acute cystitis.

Fosfomycin is another alternative first-line agent for uncomplicated cystitis if it is available, but its efficacy is inferior compared with other short-course, first-line agents. However, it is extremely expensive relative to most other agents used to treat uncomplicated cystitis and it should not be used if early pyelonephritis is suspected.

KEY POINT

Trimethoprim-sulfamethoxazole or nitrofurantoin is the preferred management strategy for acute, uncomplicated cystitis in nonpregnant young women.

Bibliography

Gupta K, Hooton TM, Naber KG, et al. International clinical practice guidelines for the treatment of acute uncomplicated cystitis and pyelonephritis in women: a 2010 update by the Infectious Diseases Society of America and the European Society for Microbiology and Infectious Diseases. Clin Infect Dis. 2011;52:e103-20. [PMID: 21292654]

Item 27   Answer: B
Educational Objective: *Manage postcoital urinary tract infection.*

The most appropriate next step in preventing recurrent urinary tract infections (UTIs) in this patient is postcoital ciprofloxacin. Recurrent UTIs in young, sexually active women are more commonly a reinfection rather than relapse and are often associated with sexual intercourse. Consequently, a detailed sexual history should be obtained from female patients with a presentation such as that in this patient. Symptoms of UTI are often related to the use of spermicidal agents because spermicides decrease the number of healthy vaginal lactobacilli and predispose women to UTIs. However, this patient does not use spermicidal agents. The recommended prophylaxis against recurrent UTIs is liberal fluid intake and postcoital voiding. Although these are not evidenced-based recommendations, they are unlikely to be harmful. If UTIs continue to occur despite these measures, as they have in this patient, prophylaxis with a postcoital antibiotic, such as ciprofloxacin, is appropriate.

Long-term suppressive antibiotic therapy can be an effective method for preventing postcoital UTIs, but patients may have difficulty adhering to this regimen. In addition, it is associated with increased costs, antimicrobial resistance, and candidal superinfections.

Randomized clinical trials have not shown that drinking cranberry juice reduces the incidence of recurrent UTIs, including postcoital UTIs.

Adding a spermicide is likely to increase, not decrease, this patient's incidence of UTI.

Antibiotic prophylaxis after intercourse is appropriate for preventing recurrent postcoital urinary tract infections in women.

Bibliography

Dielubanza EJ, Schaeffer AJ. Urinary tract infections in women. Med Clin North Am. 2011;95:27-41. [PMID: 21095409]

Item 28   Answer: C

Educational Objective: *Diagnose prostatic abscess.*

The most appropriate management for this patient is transrectal ultrasound to evaluate for a prostatic abscess. The patient presents with a clinical picture that is consistent with acute prostatitis, and treatment with an appropriate intravenous antibiotic is initiated. If there is no clinical improvement after 36 to 72 hours of treatment, with continued fever, pain, and leukocytosis, the most likely cause is a complication, such as a prostatic abscess. Further evaluation with a transrectal ultrasound or abdominal/pelvic computed tomography is indicated. If a prostatic abscess is identified, ultrasound-guided or surgical drainage may be indicated.

Parenteral administration of empiric antibiotics is appropriate for a patient who presents with acute prostatitis and systemic signs of illness and requires hospital admission. Causative organisms of acute prostatitis in older men are usually gram-negative bacteria, with *Escherichia coli* being the most common. Fluoroquinolones and trimethoprim-sulfamethoxazole have a broad spectrum of antibacterial activity against gram-negative pathogens, have excellent prostate penetration, and are usually well tolerated. Intravenous antibiotic therapy may be changed to oral treatment when the patient shows clinical improvement and can tolerate oral intake.

Although aminoglycosides have excellent coverage for gram-negative organisms and would be reasonable to use as dual therapy with another antibiotic in an acutely ill patient, it would not be appropriate to switch to an aminoglycoside as monotherapy in a patient who has not benefited from treatment with a sensitive antibiotic without excluding a potential complication, such as abscess.

Transurethral catheterization should be avoided in acute prostatitis. If bladder drainage is necessary, it should be suprapubic to reduce the risk of prostatic abscess and septicemia. Furthermore, there is no indication for placement of a bladder catheter, such as outflow obstruction.

Prostate massage, or application of pressure to the prostate during a digital rectal examination, is used to express secretions from the prostate. At one time, this method was believed to be therapeutically useful as a treatment for acute prostatitis. However, vigorous massage of the prostate should be avoided in acute prostatitis. It is not helpful diagnostically, is uncomfortable for the patient, and potentially increases the risk of bacteremia.

Patients with acute prostatitis who do not respond to appropriate antibiotic therapy within 36 to 72 hours may have a complication, such as a prostatic abscess.

Bibliography

Ramakrishnan K, Salinas RC. Prostatitis: acute and chronic. Prim Care. 2010;37:547-63, viii-ix. [PMID: 20705198]

Item 29   Answer: B

Educational Objective: *Diagnose the bacterial cause of pelvic inflammatory disease.*

This patient has findings consistent with pelvic inflammatory disease (PID). The organisms most likely responsible for this condition are *Chlamydia trachomatis* and *Neisseria gonorrhoeae*. PID is an ascending infection of the genital tract. Patients may present with endometritis, salpingitis, or both, and PID can be complicated by the development of a tubo-ovarian abscess. PID is considered a polymicrobial infection. *C. trachomatis* and *N. gonorrhoeae* cause most infections, and other possible pathogens include enteric gram-negative organisms, organisms that originate from the normal vaginal flora (especially anaerobes), and streptococci. The risk of PID is particularly high in sexually active young women (especially adolescents). All women with suspected PID should be tested for gonorrhea and chlamydia. They should also have a pregnancy test to exclude normal or ectopic implantation. The clinical diagnosis of PID is imprecise. PID should be considered in sexually active women who present with lower abdominal or pelvic pain and one or more of the following findings: cervical motion tenderness, uterine tenderness, or adnexal tenderness. The presence of mucopurulent cervical discharge or numerous leukocytes in a wet mount of vaginal secretions increases the specificity of the diagnosis. Other findings that increase diagnostic specificity include fever (temperature >38.3°C [100.9°F]), increased erythrocyte sedimentation rate or C-reactive protein concentration, and confirmation of infection with either *N. gonorrhoeae* or *C. trachomatis*. If the diagnosis is suspected, the patient should be tested for these two pathogens, although recommended antimicrobial regimens for PID target all possible causative organisms.

In women, herpes simplex virus (HSV) may also cause cervicitis. In men, urethritis may be caused by HSV, *Trichomonas vaginalis*, or *Mycoplasma genitalium*. *N. gonorrhoeae* and *C. trachomatis* may cause proctitis in both men and women who have receptive anal intercourse. However, these organisms are not the most likely causes of PID.

Chlamydia trachomatis and *Neisseria gonorrhoeae* are the primary causes of pelvic inflammatory disease.

Bibliography

Markle W, Conti T, Kad M. Sexually transmitted diseases. Prim Care. 2013;40:557-87. [PubMed PMID: 23958358]

Item 30   Answer: A

Educational Objective: *Treat epididymitis in a young man.*

A combination of ceftriaxone and doxycycline is the most appropriate treatment for this patient. Acute epididymitis in sexually active men younger than 35 years of age is most frequently caused by *Chlamydia trachomatis*. *Neisseria gonorrhoeae* also causes epididymitis in this age group. In older men, most infections occur in conjunction with urinary tract infection caused by enteric gram-negative organisms. Infection caused by Enterobacteriaceae should also be considered in men who have sex with men and who are the insertive partner in anal intercourse.

Patients with epididymitis present with unilateral pain and tenderness in the epididymis and testis (epididymitis-orchitis). The spermatic cord is enlarged and tender on palpation. Some patients may find relief with elevation of the testicle, whereas elevation usually exacerbates the pain of testicular torsion. The finding of leukocytes on urine microscopic examination or positive leukocyte esterase on urine dipstick is supportive of the diagnosis. When *N. gonorrhoeae* or *C. trachomatis* infection is suspected, a urethral swab or urine sample should be obtained for nucleic acid amplification testing. Urine culture and susceptibility testing should also be done.

In 2010, the Centers for Disease Control and Prevention recommended administration of ceftriaxone, 250 mg intramuscularly as a single dose, for the treatment of all infections caused by *N. gonorrhoeae* because of reports of decreased susceptibility of *N. gonorrhoeae* isolates to cephalosporins and increasing reports of clinical failure with lower doses of ceftriaxone (125 mg). In addition, all patients treated for *N. gonorrhoeae* should receive azithromycin or doxycycline because of the high rate of coinfection with *C. trachomatis* and the additional activity of these agents against isolates with decreased susceptibility to cephalosporins. For men who have sex with men and are at risk for both sexually transmitted infection and infection with enteric organisms (e.g., insertive anal intercourse), treatment with ceftriaxone and a fluoroquinolone (e.g., levofloxacin) is recommended.

KEY POINT

Empiric treatment for acute epididymitis in sexually active men younger than than 35 years of age consists of ceftriaxone and doxycycline (or azithromycin).

Bibliography

Sexually Transmitted Diseases Treatment Guidelines, 2010. Centers for Disease Control and Prevention. www.cdc.gov/std/treatment/2010/epididymitis.htm. Accessed October 27, 2013.

Item 31   Answer: D

Educational Objective: *Diagnose disseminated gonococcal infection.*

The most appropriate next step in diagnosis is a nucleic acid amplification urine test for *Neisseria gonorrhoeae*. The patient has evidence of an arthritis-dermatitis syndrome and should be evaluated for disseminated gonococcal infection (DGI). In contrast to nongonococcal septic arthritis, patients with DGI present with migratory joint symptoms and often have involvement of several joints with tenosynovitis rather than involvement of a single joint. Asymmetric joint involvement helps to distinguish DGI from autoimmune disease–associated polyarthritis, which is typically symmetric. Skin lesions are found in more than 75% of patients with DGI but may be few in number; consequently, a careful examination of the skin must be performed. Lesions are most likely to be found on the extremities. The classic lesion is characterized by a small number of necrotic vesicopustules on an erythematous base. Organisms are rarely cultured from the skin lesions of DGI, although they may be shown through nucleic acid amplification techniques.

The nucleic acid amplification urine test for *Neisseria gonorrhoeae* is a noninvasive, sensitive test for diagnosing gonorrhea in men. This test provides rapid results (within hours) and can help to guide therapy pending return of blood and synovial fluid culture results. Mucosal cultures, including of the throat, anus, urethra, or cervix (in women), may also be helpful in establishing the diagnosis. These cultures tend to have a higher diagnostic yield than blood and synovial fluid cultures in patients with DGI.

Although this young patient may have autoimmune inflammatory arthritis, such as systemic lupus erythematosus or rheumatoid arthritis, the prevalence of HLA B27 in patients with reactive arthritis is only 50%. Consequently, HLA B27 testing is not very useful in establishing a diagnosis. In addition, reactive arthritis tends to present as a symmetric oligoarthritis, and this patient's arthritis is asymmetric. The associated rash, keratoderma blennorrhagica, consists of hyperkeratotic lesions on the palms and soles, which are not present in this patient. Patients with reactive arthritis may also have conjunctivitis, urethritis, oral ulcers, and circinate balanitis.

KEY POINT

Mucosal specimens from the throat, anus, and urethra, or cervix (in women) tested for nucleic acid amplification or culture have a higher diagnostic yield than blood and synovial fluid cultures in patients with disseminated gonococcal infection.

Bibliography

García-De La Torre I, Nava-Zavala A. Gonococcal and nongonococcal arthritis. Rheum Dis Clin North Am. 2009;35:63-73. [PMID: 19480997]

Item 32   Answer: A

Educational Objective: *Treat primary genital herpes simplex virus infection.*

The most appropriate treatment is acyclovir. The patient's findings on clinical examination are consistent with herpes simplex virus (HSV) infection. Because he has several lesions accompanied by systemic symptoms (malaise, fever), he most likely has a primary infection. Both HSV-1 and HSV-2 can cause primary genital infection, and the incidence of primary infection from HSV-1 has increased in recent years. HSV-1 genital infections are less likely to be associated with recurrences and subclinical viral shedding. Although the clinical presentation is consistent with HSV infection, the diagnosis should be confirmed by viral culture or polymerase chain reaction testing. Direct fluorescence antibody testing is a much less sensitive diagnostic modality. Pending the results of diagnostic testing, the patient should begin antiviral therapy to reduce the severity and duration of symptoms. Acyclovir, valacyclovir, and famciclovir are appropriate agents for the treatment of HSV infection. In primary infection, treatment is ideally started within 72 hours of onset and continued for 7 to 10 days. In recurrent HSV outbreaks, antiviral therapy is ideally started within 24 hours of onset and continued for 5 days. Although antiviral therapy does not eradicate the infection, it has been shown to decrease the duration of symptoms and lesions.

Benzathine penicillin G is the appropriate treatment choice for primary syphilis. Syphilis is characterized by chancres, which are usually single painless lesions with a clean base (unless secondarily infected). However, multiple lesions can also occur.

Ceftriaxone plus azithromycin would be appropriate for treatment of a sexually transmitted infection with *Neisseria gonorrhoeae* and *Chlamydia trachomatis*. However, neither of these infections typically presents with the clinical findings seen in this patient. Although this patient may be at risk for these infections, treatment without a specific diagnosis would not be indicated.

Fluconazole is an antifungal and would be appropriate for a candidal infection. However, vesicular lesions are not a common presentation of cutaneous infection with candida; therefore, treatment with fluconazole would not be appropriate.

Pending the results of diagnostic testing, patients with suspected primary herpes simplex virus infection should begin receiving empiric antiviral therapy with acyclovir, valacyclovir, or famciclovir to reduce the severity and duration of symptoms.

Bibliography

Workowski KA, Berman S; Centers for Disease Control and Prevention (CDC). Sexually Transmitted Diseases Treatment Guidelines, 2010. MMWR Recomm Rep. 2010;59:1-110. [PMID: 21160459]

Item 33   Answer: D

Educational Objective: *Diagnose primary syphilis.*

This patient's clinical presentation and examination findings are most consistent with a syphilitic chancre. Chancres are most frequently single lesions, but multiple lesions can occur. The lesions are generally painless. The border of the ulcer is raised and has a firm, cartilaginous consistency. The incidence of primary and secondary syphilis in the United States has increased among certain populations, especially young men who have sex with men and patients with HIV infection. Because the method needed to demonstrate *Treponema pallidum* organisms in clinical specimens is not available in most settings, the clinical diagnosis can be confirmed by serologic testing. However, findings on serum rapid plasma reagin titer are frequently negative in primary syphilis. This patient should be offered HIV testing, screening for gonorrhea and chlamydia infection, and counseling on risk reduction. In addition to syphilis, the differential diagnosis of genital ulcer disease includes chancroid and herpes simplex virus infection. Bacterial secondary infection of traumatic genital lesions can also have the appearance of an ulcer.

Chancroid causes single or multiple painful ulcers with a ragged border. The base of the ulcer has a granulomatous appearance, frequently with a purulent exudate. This patient does not have symptoms of chancroid.

Herpes simplex virus infection generally presents with multiple painful ulcers that were initially vesicular on an erythematous base.

Human papillomavirus infection causes genital warts, not ulcerative lesions.

Syphilitic chancres are most frequently single, painless lesions, with a raised border and a firm cartilaginous consistency. Multiple lesions can also occur.

Bibliography

Su JR, Beltrami JF, Zaidi AA, Weinstock HS. Primary and secondary syphilis among black and Hispanic men who have sex with men: case report data from 27 States. Ann Intern Med. 2011;155:145-51. [PMID: 21810707]

Item 34   Answer: D

Educational Objective: *Manage an unsuccessful antiretroviral regimen in a patient with HIV.*

The most appropriate management for this patient is to obtain a viral resistance test (genotype ± phenotype) and to consult an infectious disease specialist. Suppression of HIV viral load to less than 50 copies/mL should occur by 24 weeks of effective therapy. Virologic failure is suspected when suppression of viral replication to less than 200 copies/mL cannot be achieved or maintained. Potential causes for virologic failure include poor adherence to the regimen, medica-

tion intolerance, pharmacokinetic issues (such as individual variation in drug metabolism), and suspected drug resistance. Resistance testing should be performed while the patient is taking the unsuccessful regimen or within 4 weeks of discontinuation. Distinguishing among the reasons for virologic failure can be challenging, and assistance from an infectious disease specialist is warranted.

Although protease inhibitors are one of the preferred classes of drugs for HIV treatment, changes in the antiretroviral regimen should be made after evaluation for factors leading to failure, including viral resistance. In this patient, drug interactions must also be considered because proton pump inhibitors such as omeprazole can have a significant effect on the concentration of protease inhibitors.

Routine monitoring of HIV-RNA and CD4 cell counts can be performed every 3 to 6 months in clinically stable patients with suppressed viral load. The poor response as shown by this patient's viral load should trigger prompt evaluation.

Trimethoprim-sulfamethoxazole is used for *Pneumocystis jirovecii* prophylaxis when the CD4 cell count is less than 200/µL or when it is less than 100/µL in patients with positive serologic findings for toxoplasmosis. This patient does not have an indication for antibiotic prophylaxis for either *Pneumocystis* or toxoplasmosis.

In patients who do not achieve viral suppression, evaluating for factors that lead to failure should be undertaken, including viral resistance testing and assistance from an infectious disease specialist.

Bibliography

Thompson MA, Aberg JA, Hoy JF, et al. Antiretroviral treatment of adult HIV infection: 2012 recommendations of the International Antiviral Society-USA panel. JAMA. 2012;308:387-402. [PMID: 22820792]

Item 35   Answer: C

Educational Objective: *Diagnose cytomegalovirus retinitis associated with HIV infection.*

The most likely underlying disease in this patient is advanced HIV infection. End-organ disease caused by cytomegalovirus (CMV) infection usually occurs in patients with significant immunosuppression, generally in patients who have HIV infection with CD4 count of less than 50/µL. Cytomegalovirus infection in those infected with HIV usually involves the eye or the gastrointestinal tract. Although the incidence of CMV retinitis has significantly declined since the introduction of highly active antiretroviral therapy, its occurrence persists as a result of poor antiretroviral adherence, antiretroviral resistance, and late presentation to clinical attention. Patients may be asymptomatic or present with floaters, scotomata, or peripheral visual field defects. If the macula or optic nerve is involved, patients present with decreased visual acuity. Characteristic funduscopic appearance is fluffy yellow-white retinal lesions, with or without intraretinal hemorrhage. Treatment includes ganciclovir, foscarnet, or valganciclovir, depending on the location and severity of disease. Concomitant treatment of HIV with antiretroviral therapy is reported to lead to a better outcome.

Although endocarditis is a potential sequela of intravenous drug use, this patient's drug use is too remote to consider this diagnosis. In addition, bacterial endocarditis is associated with exudative, hemorrhagic retinal lesions (Roth spots). The patient's retinal findings are not consistent with endocarditis.

Hepatitis C is a common complication of intravenous drug use, and clinical manifestations can occur years after inoculation. However, hepatitis C is not associated with ophthalmologic findings.

Optic neuritis, which causes acute loss of vision and pain with eye movement, is a common presenting syndrome. Funduscopic examination sometimes shows inflammation of the optic nerve in the affected eye and an afferent pupillary defect, such as dilation of the affected pupil when light is moved from the unaffected eye. The patient's symptoms and findings are not consistent with optic neuritis.

KEY POINT

Cytomegalovirus retinitis is a well-established complication of HIV infection.

Bibliography

Barrett L, Walmsley S. CMV retinopathy in the antiretroviral therapy era: prevention, diagnosis, and management. Curr Infect Dis Rep. 2012;14:435-44. [PMID: 22688820]

Item 36   Answer: A

Educational Objective: *Screen for HIV infection.*

The first step in the management of this patient is screening by HIV antibody/p24 antigen testing. Although this patient has no symptoms or significant risk factors for HIV infection, the Centers for Disease Control and Prevention recommends that all persons between 13 and 64 years of age undergo HIV screening at least once and that those with risk factors undergo annual testing. In addition, the American College of Physicians has issued a guidance statement recommending that this age range be expanded to include patients through 75 years of age because of increased rates of infection in this population. Recommended screening testing is with a combination immunoassay that detects both HIV antibody and p24 antigen, a viral capsid protein that is elevated early in infection. This combination testing reduces the "window period" when false-negative results may occur and may diagnose HIV as early as 2 weeks after infection occurs.

Western blot testing had previously been used as a more specific confirmatory test for HIV if an initial highly sensitive enzyme-linked immunosorbent assay (ELISA) for antibodies directed toward HIV or a rapid HIV test were positive. However, Western blot testing is no longer recommended due to the improved sensitivity and specificity of the combined HIV antibody/p24 antigen assay as an initial test and removal of the need for sequential testing to document HIV infection.

Nucleic acid amplification testing is not used for screening for HIV infection in asymptomatic, low-risk patients. It may be helpful in diagnosis of patients who may be in the "window period" following acute HIV infection before seroconversion occurs, which may lead to false-negative antibody testing. However, the currently recommended initial combination HIV antibody/p2 antigen test reduces the window period to as little as 2 weeks.

Because this patient has never had HIV screening and is eligible, initiating no testing would not be the most appropriate management.

KEY POINT

All persons between 13 and 75 years of age should be tested for HIV infection at least once, and those with risk factors should undergo annual testing.

Bibliography

Qaseem A, Snow V, Shekelle P. Screening for HIV in health care settings: a guidance statement from the American College of Physicians and HIV Medicine Association. Ann Intern Med. 2009;150:125-31. [PMID: 19047022]

Item 37   Answer: B

Educational Objective: *Diagnose acute retroviral syndrome.*

The most appropriate next diagnostic test is an HIV nucleic acid amplification test. The patient's medical history and timing of symptoms are typical of acute HIV infection. Although her symptoms could also represent infectious mononucleosis or syphilis, preliminary results for those conditions are negative. In most cases, when HIV infection develops, an acute symptomatic illness occurs within 2 to 4 weeks of infection. Symptoms typically last for a few weeks and range from a simple febrile illness to a full-blown mononucleosis-like syndrome. Because patients have no immune response during this period, virus levels tend to be very high, resulting in high levels of infectivity. Symptoms of acute HIV infection resolve with or without treatment, and most acute infections are undiagnosed. Patients who present with symptomatic acute HIV infection (acute retroviral syndrome) are usually in the "window period," which may extend for 3 to 6 weeks. During this time, seroconversion of the disease has not yet occurred and results of HIV antibody testing are negative. The currently recommended, newer generation HIV assays combine HIV antibody testing with detection of the HIV p24 antigen, which may shorten the length of the window period to as little as 2 weeks, although this assay was negative in this patient with a high suspicion for acute HIV infection. Repeating this test would not be expected to be definitive in this patient with a previously negative result. However, results of viral-specific tests, such as those for nucleic acid, are usually positive at quite high levels during this time frame and can be used to definitively establish the diagnosis.

Measurement of CD4 cell count is neither sensitive nor specific for HIV infection and should be performed only after the diagnosis of HIV is already established. CD4 cell count can be normal in a patient with HIV infection. Conversely, it can be depressed as a result of many other conditions that can present similarly to acute HIV infection.

During the window period of acute HIV infection, results of antibody testing are unreliable. Therefore, antibody-based testing, such as Western blot, would not be useful.

KEY POINT

Most patients with acute HIV infection have nonspecific symptoms that range from a simple febrile illness to a mononucleosis-like syndrome within 2 to 4 weeks of infection.

Bibliography

Cohen MS, Gay CL, Busch MP, Hecht FM. The detection of acute HIV infection. J Infect Dis. 2010;202(suppl 2):S270-7. [PMID: 20846033]

Item 38   Answer: C

Educational Objective: *Diagnose* Pneumocystis *pneumonia in a patient with AIDS.*

The most likely diagnosis is *Pneumocystis jirovecii* pneumonia (PCP). This patient has known risk factors for HIV infection and a reactive rapid HIV test. He very likely has HIV infection, although confirmation with Western blot testing still must be performed. His subacute presentation with dry cough and dyspnea and chest radiograph findings of diffuse interstitial disease is the typical presentation of PCP in patients with AIDS. PCP is also the most common opportunistic infection in patients who are not taking *Pneumocystis* prophylaxis. Bronchoscopy with lavage can be done with special stains to confirm the diagnosis.

Although it can cause pneumonia in transplant recipients, cytomegalovirus (CMV) is an unusual cause of pneumonia in patients with AIDS. In such patients, CMV is more likely to present as retinitis or gastrointestinal disease, with a CD4 cell count of less than 50/µL.

Mycobacterium avium complex usually causes disseminated disease in patients with AIDS and a CD4 cell count of less than 50/µL who present with systemic symptoms, such as fevers, sweats, weight loss, and involvement of the liver, spleen, and lymph nodes, not as pulmonary disease.

Candida is generally a very rare cause of pulmonary infection, even in immunocompromised hosts. The presence of pseudohyphae in this patient's sputum is most likely a result of his oral candidiasis, as seen on examination findings, and is not evidence of pulmonary involvement.

KEY POINT

Pneumocystis jirovecii pneumonia is characterized by a subacute presentation with dry cough and dyspnea, hypoxia, and findings of diffuse interstitial disease on chest radiograph.

Bibliography

Carmona EM, Limper AH. Update on the diagnosis and treatment of *Pneumocystis* pneumonia. Ther Adv Respir Dis. 2011;5:41-59. [PMID: 20736243]

Item 39   Answer: C
Educational Objective: *Manage prosthetic joint infection.*

The patient's prosthetic joint should be removed, and he should be treated with appropriate intravenous antibiotics for 4 to 6 weeks. Effective treatment of prosthetic joint infection generally requires removal of all foreign material (joint and cement). In the presence of a foreign body, bacteria produce a biofilm (glycocalyx) that allow the organism to persist protected from the host defenses and blocks penetration of many antibiotics. Hence, eradication of the infection requires removal of the hardware, 4 to 6 weeks of appropriate antibiotic therapy, and in many cases reimplantation arthroplasty (two-stage strategy). Antibiotic–impregnated polymethylmethacrylate is commonly used in cement spacers to maintain normal anatomic alignment once the prosthetic joint has been removed for the duration of antibiotic therapy. The antibiotic agent achieves high concentrations in the surrounding tissues as it elutes from the polymethylmethacrylate. The spacer is removed at the time of reimplantation.

Antibiotic treatment with retention of the infected prosthetic joint is associated with very high failure rates. This includes treatment with either intravenous antibiotics alone or antibiotics used in conjunction with surgical debridement and irrigation of the prosthesis.

Hyperbaric oxygen therapy may have an adjunctive role in the setting of decreased tissue oxygen levels, such as osteomyelitis in the setting of diabetes mellitus and peripheral vascular disease, but not in prosthetic joint infection.

KEY POINT

Infection of an orthopedic implant requires removal of the prosthesis followed by an extended course of antibiotics.

Bibliography

Osmon DR, Berbari EF, Berendt AR, et al. Diagnosis and Management of Prosthetic Joint Infection: Clinical Practice Guidelines by the Infectious Diseases Society of America. Clin Infect Dis. 2013;56:e1-25. doi:10.1093/cid/cis803. [PMID: 3223583]

Item 40   Answer: A
Educational Objective: *Manage hematogenous vertebral osteomyelitis.*

This patient should be treated with antibiotic therapy for 4 to 6 weeks. Hematogenous vertebral osteomyelitis can often be successfully treated with antibiotics alone, with relapse rates of less than 10% at 6 to 12 months of follow-up.

Blood cultures are very important in the diagnostic assessment of osteomyelitis. Findings are positive in approximately 58% of cases of vertebral osteomyelitis. A positive blood culture finding precludes the need for more invasive diagnostic procedures, such as percutaneous interventions for biopsy or culture.

Bone scans in vertebral osteomyelitis often become positive early in the course of infection but have lower specificity than MRI. A bone scan would be unlikely to provide additional information in this case and therefore is not indicated.

Indications for surgical intervention include the need for abscess drainage, removal of an orthopedic implant, and need for stabilization of the spine. None of these features is present in this case. Therefore, surgical treatment is not indicated pending a course of antibiotic therapy.

KEY POINT

Blood culture findings that are positive for pathogenic bacteria in the setting of hematogenous vertebral osteomyelitis have a high level of diagnostic accuracy and preclude the need for more invasive diagnostic testing.

Bibliography

Zimmerli W. Vertebral osteomyelitis. N Engl J Med 2010;362:1022-9. [PMID: 20237348]

Item 41   Answer: A
Educational Objective: *Manage a patient with possible osteomyelitis.*

The most appropriate next step in management is deep bone biopsy culture before antimicrobial therapy is begun. The development of a draining sinus tract from the wound above a bone that underwent surgical instrumentation is highly suspicious for underlying contiguous osteomyelitis. The patient's current condition is presumably related to his initial open trauma and the associated surgery 6 months ago. Microbiologic isolates from cultures obtained from a wound or draining sinus tract generally do not reliably correlate with the pathogen in the infected bone, with the occasional exception of *Staphylococcus aureus*. Because of limited utility and the possibility of providing misinformation, the use of microbiologic isolates from culture of a wound or a draining sinus tract to guide antibiotic therapy is discouraged. Instead, identification of the causative pathogens is best attempted by bone biopsy performed surgically or percutaneously with radiographic guidance. Once the causative organism is recovered, treatment (usually consisting of at least 6 weeks of parenteral antimicrobial therapy) can be initiated. Debridement of necrotic material is often necessary, and if feasible, removal of the metallic hardware is performed to promote microbiologic eradication and clinical success.

Although many isolates of *Enterococcus* are susceptible to either ampicillin or vancomycin, initiation of prolonged antibiotic therapy would not be indicated without further confirmation of osteomyelitis and identification of this organism as its cause. Additionally, antibiotic therapy for osteomyelitis is usually given parenterally to ensure adequate penetration into bone. Therefore, treatment with an oral antibiotic likely would not be effective.

A nuclear medicine study, such as a three-phase technetium 99m-labeled bone scan, is a very sensitive imaging modality for detecting osteomyelitis. However, this study lacks specificity and findings would be expected to be abnormal because of the patient's recent surgery. Therefore, this test could not reliably confirm a diagnosis of bone infection or identify its causative agent.

KEY POINT

In patients with suspected osteomyelitis, the microbiologic isolates from cultures obtained from a wound or a draining sinus tract generally do not reliably correlate with the pathogen in the infected bone, with the occasional exception of *Staphylococcus aureus*.

Bibliography
Sanders J, Mauffrey C. Long bone osteomyelitis in adults: fundamental concepts and current techniques. Orthopedics. 2013;36:368-75. [PMID: 23672894]

Item 42   Answer: C
Educational Objective: *Evaluate a patient with osteomyelitis.*

The next study that should be performed is magnetic resonance imaging (MRI) of the foot. The clinical hallmarks of acute osteomyelitis are local pain and fever, particularly in patients with acute hematogenous osteomyelitis. However, these symptoms may be absent in patients with chronic and contiguous osteomyelitis.

Given the limitations of physical examination findings in the diagnosis of osteomyelitis, radiologic studies are frequently used. In patients who have normal findings on plain radiographs in the presence of high clinical suspicion for osteomyelitis, more advanced imaging techniques are indicated. MRI is the preferred imaging study for the evaluation of possible osteomyelitis. MRI can show changes of acute osteomyelitis within days of infection and are superior to and more sensitive (90%) and specific (80%) than plain films and computed tomography. They can also detect soft tissue abscesses and epidural, paravertebral, or psoas abscesses that may require surgical drainage. They can also be used to delineate anatomy before surgery. Nonetheless, false-positive MRI results may occur in patients with noninfectious conditions, such as fractures, tumors, and healed osteomyelitis.

In patients with a pacemaker or metal hardware precluding MRI or in those in whom MRI results are inconclusive, CT or (if metal hardware is likely to impair CT imaging) nuclear studies may be used instead. CT show excellent anatomic detail, and CT is the imaging study of choice for patients with osteomyelitis when MRI cannot be obtained.

Nuclear imaging studies can reliably detect inflammation as a result of acute infection. However, such visualized abnormalities, which may be caused by bone turnover or inflammation, can also have other noninfectious causes, including trauma, neoplasm, and degenerative joint disease. Gallium scanning, once the gold standard for cancer diagnosis, may still be used to visualize inflammation and chronic infection, partly because gallium binds to the membranes of neutrophils that are recruited to a site of infection. However, leukocyte-labeled nuclear scans have almost entirely replaced this imaging technique. Except in the setting of diminished blood flow to the affected area, a negative finding on three-phase bone scan confers a high negative predictive value for osteomyelitis.

KEY POINT

Magnetic resonance imaging is the imaging study of choice for suspected osteomyelitis.

Bibliography
Chihara S, Segreti J. Osteomyelitis. Dis Mon. 2010;56:5-31. [PMID: 19995624]

Item 43   Answer: A
Educational Objective: *Treat severe sepsis.*

This patient should receive intravenous crystalloid solution and broad-spectrum antibiotics. Systemic inflammatory response syndrome (SIRS) is a term that was introduced to describe findings of altered temperature, tachycardia, hyperventilation, and abnormal leukocyte count, regardless of cause (inflammatory or infectious). Sepsis is defined as SIRS plus suspected infection. Severe sepsis is associated with systemic effects, including hypotension, confusion, decreased urine output, and metabolic acidosis. This patient has severe sepsis.

The source of the patient's infection should be identified and controlled. Blood and source cultures should be collected before administration of antibiotics when possible. Treatment with broad-spectrum empiric antibiotics, chosen based on the site of infection (lung, gastrointestinal, or unknown), should be implemented within 1 hour after recognition of sepsis. Crystalloid solution (e.g., normal saline or lactated Ringer solution) should be given to achieve central venous pressure of 8 to 12 mm Hg. Repetitive fluid challenges are performed by giving 500- to 1000-mL boluses of crystalloid solution over short intervals while assessing the response to target central venous pressure. If mean arterial pressure is less than 65 mm Hg despite fluid challenge and adequate preload, treatment with vasoactive agents should be started and titrated as needed.

High-dose glucocorticoids are of no benefit in sepsis and were shown to harm patients in earlier studies. The Surviving Sepsis Campaign suggests that replacement-dose intravenous hydrocortisone be given only to adult patients with septic shock after blood pressure is found to be poorly responsive to fluid resuscitation and vasopressor therapy. The American College of Physicians Clinical Practice Guideline for Use of Intensive Insulin Therapy for the Management of Glycemic Control in Hospitalized Patients recommends that, after initial stabilization, patients with severe sepsis and hyperglycemia who are admitted to the intensive care unit should receive insulin therapy to achieve a plasma glucose level of 140 to 200 mg/dL. This patient has no indication for intravenous insulin therapy at this time.

KEY POINT

The goals of sepsis management are to treat infection and optimize tissue perfusion.

Bibliography

Dellinger RP, Levy MM, Rhodes A, et al. Surviving Sepsis Campaign: international guidelines for management of severe sepsis and septic shock. Intensive Care Med. 2013;39:2165-228. [PMID: 24067755]

Item 44   Answer: B

Educational Objective: *Treat sepsis with early antibiotic therapy.*

The best antibiotic management of this infection is to begin treatment with empiric antibiotics within 1 hour. The source of infection should be identified and controlled. Removal of infected devices and drainage of abscesses may be life-saving interventions. Blood and source cultures should be collected before administration of antibiotics when possible. Broad-spectrum empiric antibiotics, chosen based on the site of infection (lung, gastrointestinal, or unknown) should be implemented within 1 hour after recognition of sepsis. Even with early implementation, use of inappropriate antibiotics (i.e., antibiotics to which bacteria are resistant) is associated with a mortality rate of 42%, whereas the mortality rate is 17% if appropriate antibiotics are used. Delay in initiation of antibiotic treatment to await culture results, or the choice of an inappropriate antibiotic agent is associated with an increased mortality rate.

Adequate fluid resuscitation is essential in the management of sepsis. Most patients need 4 to 6 L of fluid in the first 6 hours. Use of crystalloid or colloid solution is likely equivalent; however, colloid solution is far more expensive. Therefore, most practitioners use crystalloid solution, such as lactated Ringer solution, or normal saline. Antibiotic therapy should not be delayed pending adequate fluid resuscitation.

Thorough drainage of infected joints is essential to promote successful resolution and prevent joint damage. Joints that are readily accessible (such as knees) can be managed with either needle aspiration or arthroscopic drainage. Needle aspiration should be performed repeatedly, usually daily, with complete removal of synovial fluid until reaccumulation ceases. Arthroscopic drainage or open surgical debridement is mandatory when the joint space is irregular, the fluid is loculated, or it is otherwise difficult or impractical to thoroughly and regularly evacuate the joint space using needle drainage. Although arthroscopic joint drainage may be necessary, antibiotic therapy should be initiated immediately, not pending drainage.

KEY POINT

Broad-spectrum empiric antibiotics, chosen based on the site of infection (lung, gastrointestinal, or unknown) should be implemented within 1 hour after recognition of sepsis.

Bibliography

Dellinger RP, Levy MM, Rhodes A, et al. Surviving Sepsis Campaign: international guidelines for management of severe sepsis and septic shock. Intensive Care Med. 2013;39:2165-228. [PMID: 24067755]

Item 45   Answer: D

Educational Objective: *Treat sepsis.*

The most appropriate initial treatment is administration of normal saline. The diagnosis of sepsis requires at least two of the following criteria for systemic inflammatory response syndrome (SIRS): temperature greater than 38.0°C (100.4°F) or less than 36.0°C (96.8°F), leukocyte count greater than 12,000/µL (12 × 10⁹/L) or less than 4000/µL (4.0 × 10⁹/L), respiration rate greater than 20/min, and pulse rate greater than 90/min in the setting of a known or suspected infection (documented positive cultures are not required). This patient meets the criteria for SIRS, with clinical and radiographic evidence of pneumonia, consistent with a diagnosis of sepsis.

Initial resuscitation of a patient with severe sepsis and septic shock should begin early, with a goal of maintaining adequate tissue perfusion. Most patients need at least 4 to 6 L of intravascular volume replacement within the first 6 hours. One of the biggest pitfalls of management is underestimating the intravascular volume deficit. Early aggressive fluid resuscitation with intravenous crystalloid solution has been shown to improve the mortality rate in these patients.

Except in select cases, such as elderly patients with myocardial infarction, target hemoglobin concentrations of greater than 7 g/dL (70 g/L) should be considered adequate in the setting of sepsis. Although this patient is anemic, there is no evidence of active bleeding. Therefore, at this time, erythrocyte transfusion would not be appropriate.

The Surviving Sepsis guidelines recommend avoiding the use of glucocorticoids in patients with sepsis in the absence of shock unless the patient's endocrine or glucocorticoid history warrants this treatment. Intravenous hydrocortisone may also be considered for adults with septic shock when hypotension responds poorly to adequate fluid resuscitation and vasopressors.

The patient's blood pressure is stable, and she has no signs of hypoperfusion. Therefore, there is no indication for vasopressor therapy at this time. In patients with known or suspected infection, persistent hypotension despite adequate fluid resuscitation mandates the use of vasopressors.

KEY POINT

Initial resuscitation of a patient with severe sepsis and septic shock should begin early, with a goal of maintaining adequate tissue perfusion with intravascular volume replacement.

Bibliography

Dellinger RP, Levy MM, Rhodes A, et al. Surviving Sepsis Campaign: international guidelines for management of severe sepsis and septic shock. Intensive Care Med. 2013;39:2165-228. [PMID: 24067755]

Item 46   Answer: B

Educational Objective: *Manage septic shock.*

The most appropriate next step in management is diagnostic paracentesis to identify a potential source of infection. The findings on physical examination are characteristic of shock. Although advanced liver failure and sepsis can both present in this manner, septic shock should be assumed first and excluded as a cause. The patient meets the criteria for systemic inflammatory response syndrome (SIRS) (altered temperature, tachycardia, hyperventilation, and abnormal leukocyte count). The combination of organ dysfunction and SIRS is diagnostic of severe sepsis. In addition to aggressive intravenous fluid therapy and treatment with empiric broad-spectrum antibiotics, identifying the source of potential infection is the next step in management. The ascites associated with this patient's chronic liver disease represents a potential source of infection that should be evaluated. Identification of a source of infection is important in guiding the choice of appropriate empiric antibiotic coverage and focusing longer-term antibiotic therapy once an organism has been identified. This patient's worsening liver failure and new-onset encephalopathy can be precipitated by infection.

Abdominal computed tomography is not helpful in the diagnosis of bacterial peritonitis, and direct examination of the ascitic fluid is necessary to assess this as a potential source of infection. Imaging for other potential abdominal sources of infection may be indicated if no other cause is found once peritonitis is excluded.

Vasopressors such as norepinephrine are recommended for patients with septic shock and mean arterial blood pressure of less than 65 mm Hg after an adequate trial of intravenous fluids. This patient's current blood pressure is adequate, and so a vasopressor is not indicated.

Glucocorticoid therapy is not recommended in the setting of septic shock unless the patient's endocrine or glucocorticoid history warrants treatment or if undetected adrenal insufficiency is suspected. This patient has no clear history of chronic or intermittent glucocorticoid use and has not had an adequate trial of volume expansion.

KEY POINT

The primary goals of sepsis management are to control the source of infection and to initiate antibiotic treatment promptly.

Bibliography
Dellinger RP, Levy MM, Rhodes A, et al. Surviving Sepsis Campaign: International Guidelines for Management of Severe Sepsis and Septic Shock. Intensive Care Med. 2013;39:2165-228. [PMID: 24067755]

Item 47   Answer: C
Educational Objective: *Manage septic shock.*

The most appropriate next step in management is to start vasopressor therapy with norepinephrine. This patient's clinical picture is consistent with sepsis, likely as the result of a urinary tract infection. The goals of sepsis management are to treat infection and optimize tissue perfusion. This is accomplished by starting early and appropriate antibiotic therapy and using crystalloids to maintain an adequate preload. If an initial fluid challenge of 1000 mL crystalloid solution does not achieve an adequate blood pressure, defined as mean arterial pressure of 65 mm Hg or greater or central venous pressure of 8 to 12 mm Hg, initiation of a vasoactive agent is indicated to ensure that tissue perfusion is maintained. Mean arterial pressure is calculated as follows:

([2 × diastolic blood pressure] + systolic blood pressure)/3

Despite an initial 1000-mL normal saline bolus, the patient's mean arterial pressure remains less than 65 mm Hg. The recommended vasopressor for initial treatment is norepinephrine, administered centrally.

Although erythrocyte transfusions act as colloidal substances and may be useful in resuscitation when oxygen-carrying capacity is impaired (such as with acute blood loss), the patient's measured hemoglobin level appears adequate to maintain tissue oxygenation without the need for erythrocyte transfusion. Transfusion for volume expansion in the absence of another clear indication is not appropriate.

Intravenous hydrocortisone in stress doses is indicated only when hypotension remains unresponsive to adequate fluid resuscitation

and vasopressor therapy, or if there is concern about possible underlying adrenal insufficiency.

Although patients with sepsis often have significant fluid requirements because of hemodynamic instability, increasing the infusion rate is not an effective means to acutely restore intravascular volume and by itself would not be adequate to optimize tissue perfusion.

KEY POINT

Vasopressor therapy is indicated to maintain mean arterial pressure of 65 mm Hg or greater or central venous pressure of 8 to 12 mm Hg in patients with sepsis who have not benefited from an initial fluid challenge with crystalloid solution.

Bibliography
Dellinger RP, Levy MM, Rhodes, A, et al. Surviving Sepsis Campaign: International Guidelines for Management of Severe Sepsis and Septic Shock. Intensive Care Med. 2013;39:2165-228. [PMID: 24067755]

Item 48   Answer: C
Educational Objective: *Prevent catheter-associated urinary tract infection.*

The most effective way to prevent catheter-associated urinary tract infections (CAUTIs) is to decrease catheter use. CAUTI is defined as a urinary tract infection occurring in a catheterized patient. These infections account for more than 97% of hospital-acquired urinary tract infections. CAUTI is the most common type of hospital-acquired infection, with an average of 16.8 cases per 1000 catheter days. Urinary catheters should be used for specific indications, not for convenience, and should be removed as soon as possible. If a urinary catheter is needed, measures should be taken to decrease the risk of urinary colonization and infection. These include hand washing, using an aseptic technique for catheter placement and sterile equipment for catheter insertion and care, securing the catheter properly, and maintaining unobstructed urine flow with closed sterile drainage.

Factors that have no role in the prevention of CAUTIs include screening for asymptomatic bacteriuria in catheterized patients; treating asymptomatic bacteriuria, except in pregnant women and before invasive urologic procedures; irrigating the catheter; performing routine catheter changes; cleaning the meatal area with antiseptics before or during catheterization; and administering prophylactic antibiotics. The effect of using catheters coated with antiseptics (silver alloy or antibiotic) on the incidence of CAUTIs is unclear. Studies have shown that antiseptic-coated catheters decrease the incidence of asymptomatic bacteriuria but do not significantly reduce the risk of symptomatic urinary tract infections. Antiseptic-coated catheters cost more than standard urinary catheters. However, in the absence of new evidence showing their efficacy, they should not be used as a primary modality for preventing CAUTIs.

KEY POINT

The most effective way to prevent catheter-associated urinary tract infections is to decrease catheter use.

Bibliography
Lo E, Nicolle L, Classen D, et al. Strategies to prevent catheter-associated urinary tract infections in acute care hospitals. Infect Control Hosp Epidemiol. 2008;29(suppl 1):S41-50. [PMID: 18840088]

Item 49   Answer: B

Educational Objective: *Treat a central line-associated bloodstream infection.*

The most appropriate next step is to remove the central venous line. Central line-associated bloodstream infection (CLABSI) should be suspected in patients who have no obvious source of infection from a site other than the central line. This is likely when the same pathogen is isolated from a peripheral blood culture specimen and from a specimen obtained either by aspirating blood through the central line or culture of the catheter tip. Removal of the central line is the most important intervention in treating CLABSI. It is especially important when the central venous line is no longer needed. Empiric antibiotic therapy is initiated with broad-spectrum agents. Coagulase-negative staphylococci, enterococci, and *Staphylococcus aureus*, and gram-negative rods (*Escherichia coli, Klebsiella, Pseudomonas*) are common pathogens. Vancomycin is used for empiric coverage because of its activity against coagulase-negative staphylococci and *S. aureus*. In severely ill or immunocompromised patients, additional empiric coverage with a third-generation cephalosporin (ceftriaxone, ceftazidime) or fourth-generation cephalosporin (cefepime) may be needed for enteric gram-negative bacilli and *Pseudomonas aeruginosa*.

Empiric treatment with ciprofloxacin and gentamicin would not provide adequate coverage for methicillin-resistant *S. aureus* infection. Even appropriately selected antibiotics may be inadequate to treat CLABSI if the central venous catheter is not removed. Routine repetition of echocardiography to diagnose endocarditis in the absence of supporting clinical findings, such as a new or changing heart murmur, is not likely to be helpful. An asymptomatic urinary tract infection is an unlikely source of spiking fever and leukocytosis, and urinalysis is not indicated.

KEY POINT

Removal of the central venous line is generally the most important intervention in treating central line-associated bloodstream infection.

Bibliography

Liang SY, Khair H, Durkin MJ, Marschall J. Prevention and management of central line-associated bloodstream infections in hospital practice. Hosp Pract 2012;40:106-18. [PMID:22406886]

Item 50   Answer: A

Educational Objective: *Institute effective infection control measures in the setting of possible tuberculosis.*

Airborne respiratory precautions should be used because of this patient's high risk of active tuberculosis (TB) and compatible clinical picture. He is from a location in which TB is endemic, and his current clinical presentation is consistent with a reactivation of pulmonary TB. A diagnosis of pulmonary TB should be considered in any patient with cough for greater than 3 weeks, loss of appetite, unexplained weight loss, night sweats, hoarseness, fever, fatigue, or chest pain. The index of suspicion should be substantially higher for patients who have spent time in developing countries, in certain urban areas in the United States with a high prevalence of TB, or in a correctional facility.

Airborne precautions are recommended for patients infected with microorganisms such as *Mycobacterium tuberculosis* or rubella virus that are transmitted by airborne droplet nuclei smaller than 5 μm. Organisms that cause avian influenza, varicella, disseminated zoster, severe acute respiratory syndrome, or smallpox and the agents of viral hemorrhagic fever also require airborne precautions. Airborne precautions include placing the patient in an isolation room with high-efficiency particulate air filtration and negative pressure. Anyone entering the room should wear a fit-tested N-95 or higher disposable respirator, as should the patient during transport out of the room. Goggles, gowns, and gloves should be worn if substantial spraying of respiratory secretions is anticipated.

Contact precautions are indicated for patients with known or suspected infections that are transmitted by direct contact, such as vancomycin-resistant enterococci and methicillin-resistant *Staphylococcus aureus*. The patient is isolated in a private room or with patients who have the same active infection. Nonsterile gloves and gowns are required for direct contact with the patient or with any infective material. Gowns and gloves are removed before exiting isolation rooms. Because this patient potentially has a disease that is transmitted through airborne droplets, contact precautions would not be appropriate.

Droplet precautions are used for protection against microorganisms transmitted by respiratory droplets larger than 5 μm. These droplets can usually be transmitted to susceptible recipient mucosal surfaces over distances of less than 3 to 10 feet. Examples of pathogens and diseases that require the institution of droplet isolation precautions include *Neisseria meningitidis*, pneumonic plague, diphtheria, *Haemophilus influenzae* type b, *Bordetella pertussis*, influenza, mumps, rubella, and parvovirus B19. Droplet precautions include placing the patient in an isolation room, wearing a face or surgical mask when in the room, and wearing goggles, gowns, and gloves if substantial spraying of respiratory secretions is anticipated. Droplet precautions alone would not be considered adequate for protection against communication of TB.

Standard precautions are used with all patients and include protecting breaks in the skin or mucous membranes from possible pathogenic exposures, washing the hands before and after patient contact, wearing gloves when contacting blood or bodily fluids, washing the hands after glove removal, and wearing a mask and eye protection when needed to decrease the risk of splash- or aerosol-associated exposure. However, using only standard precautions in this patient with suspected TB would provide inadequate protection.

KEY POINT

Airborne precautions should be initiated immediately for any patient who has suspected tuberculosis to reduce the risk of transmission to health care workers and other patients.

Bibliography

Siegel JD, Rhinehart E, Jackson M, et al. 2007 Guideline for Isolation Precautions: Preventing Transmission of Infectious Agents in Health Care Settings. Am J Infect Control. 2007;35(10 suppl 2):S65-164. [PMID: 18068815]

Item 51   Answer: C

Educational Objective: *Prevent ventilator-associated pneumonia.*

The head of this patient's bed should be maintained at an angle of greater than 30 degrees. Ventilator-associated pneumonia (VAP) is a subset of hospital-acquired pneumonia that develops more than 48 to 72 hours after initiation of mechanical ventilation. To reduce the rate of VAP, a prevention "bundle" should be implemented. Components include maintaining the head of the patient's bed at an angle of greater than 30 degrees; performing daily assessment of the patient's readiness to wean from the ventilator; and using chlorhexidine mouthwash.

Use of chlorhexidine-based antiseptic to bathe hospitalized patients in intensive care units is a common practice that has been studied as a means of preventing CLABSI and the spread of multidrug-resistant organisms. However, there are no controlled data on the specific role of chlorhexidine-based bathing in preventing VAP.

Prolonged duration of the use of perioperative surgical prophylactic antimicrobial agents has not been shown to reduce the risk of VAP.

Performing early tracheotomy has not been clearly identified as a method for reducing VAP.

KEY POINT

In patients who are receiving mechanical ventilation, maintaining the head of the bed at an angle of greater than 30 degrees helps to reduce the risk of ventilator-associated pneumonia.

Bibliography

American Thoracic Society; Infectious Diseases Society of America. Guidelines for the management of adults with hospital-acquired, ventilator-associated, and health-care-associated pneumonia. Am J Respir Crit Care Med. 2005;171:388-416. [PMID: 15699079]

Item 52   Answer: B

Educational Objective: *Prevent transmission of hospital-acquired infection.*

Hand hygiene is the single most important measure to prevent transmission of infectious agents, including multidrug-resistant organisms. Hand hygiene before and after patient contact consists of hand washing with soap and water for at least 15 to 30 seconds. Alcohol-based hand disinfectants are acceptable alternatives to soap and water. The only exception to the use of alcohol-based disinfectants is with possible *Clostridium difficile* infection. The spores produced by this organism are not susceptible to these agents. Therefore, hand washing should be used in that setting. In addition to hand hygiene, standard precautions include the use of barrier protection, including wearing gloves and personal protective equipment for the mouth, nose, and eyes; appropriate handling of patient care equipment and instruments/devices (avoiding exposure to skin and using appropriate cleaning techniques); and proper handling, transporting, and processing of used or contaminated linen.

Room cleaning, disinfection, and sterilization are important components of infection control. Although many agents are used for this purpose, bleach has a potential role in cleaning the rooms of patients with *C. difficile* infection because of its ability to kill the spores produced by that organism. However, the role of bleach in controlling patient-to-patient transmission of other infectious agents has not been established.

Prophylactically treating the roommate for a resistant infection is not nearly as effective or safe as the use of proper hand hygiene. Furthermore, improper use of antibiotics in this fashion can quickly lead to additional antibiotic resistance.

Removing the contaminated catheters and drains from a source patient has not been found to reduce the risk of spread of pathogens to other patients.

KEY POINT

Hand hygiene is the single most important measure to prevent spread of hospital-acquired infections.

Bibliography

Boyce JM. Update on hand hygiene. Am J Infect Control. 2013;41(5 Suppl):S94-6. [PMID: 23622758]

Section 7

Nephrology

Questions

Item 1 [Basic]

A 67-year-old woman is admitted to the hospital after falling and fracturing her left hip. The patient resides in a nursing home. A review of her medical records reveals a serum creatinine level of 1.3 mg/dL (115 µmol/L) 12 months ago and 1.4 mg/dL (124 µmol/L) 3 months ago. Her serum creatinine level today is 1.4 mg/dL (124 µmol/L).

Which of the following will best estimate her glomerular filtration rate?

(A) Blood urea nitrogen clearance
(B) Chronic Kidney Disease Epidemiology Collaboration (CKD-EPI) equation
(C) Creatinine clearance
(D) Serum creatinine measurement

Item 2 [Advanced]

A 34-year-old man is evaluated in the emergency department for a 1-month history of worsening dyspnea and "cola-colored urine." For the past week, he has had decreased urine output and a cough productive of blood-tinged sputum. Until 1 month ago, he felt well. He has no significant medical history and takes no medications.

On physical examination, temperature is normal, blood pressure is 155/102 mm Hg, pulse rate is 104/min, and respiration rate is 22/min. Oxygen saturation is 88% (ambient air). Body mass index is 27. There is no jugular venous distention. Other than tachycardia, the cardiac examination is normal. Inspiratory crackles are heard over both lower lung lobes. There is no peripheral edema.

Laboratory studies:

Hemoglobin	10.4 g/dL (104 g/L)
Blood urea nitrogen	22 mg/dL (7.7 mmol/L)
Serum creatinine	3.8 mg/dL (336 µmol/L)
Albumin	3.4 g/dL (34 g/L)
Urinalysis	2+ blood; 2+ protein; 10 leukocytes/high-power field; 15-20 dysmorphic erythrocytes/high-power field with hyaline casts
Urine protein–creatinine ratio	5 mg/mg

A chest radiograph shows bilateral lower lobe patchy infiltrates. A kidney biopsy is performed.

Which of the following glomerular lesions is most likely to be seen?

(A) Crescentic glomerulonephritis
(B) Focal segmental glomerulosclerosis
(C) Membranous glomerulopathy
(D) Minimal change disease

Item 3 [Advanced]

A 34-year-old woman is evaluated for urinary frequency. She has no dysuria, fever, chills, or excessive sweating. She is otherwise healthy, and her only medication is a daily multivitamin.

On physical examination, temperature is 37.1°C (98.7°F), blood pressure is 149/95 mm Hg, pulse rate is 72/min, and respiration rate is 18/min. The remainder of the examination is normal.

Dipstick urinalysis shows a pH of 5.5, 1+ blood, 1+ protein, and negative leukocyte esterase. Urine microscopy findings are shown.

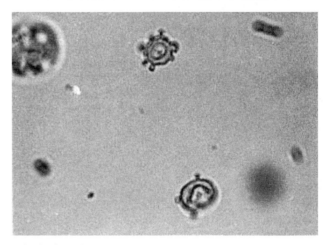

Which of the following diagnostic tests is most appropriate to perform next?

(A) Kidney biopsy
(B) Kidney ultrasonography
(C) Urine culture
(D) Urine protein–creatinine ratio and serum creatinine measurement

Item 4 [Basic]

A 28-year-old man is evaluated for hematuria. Blood in the urine was found on testing related to an insurance physical examination. Medical history is unremarkable, and the patient takes no medications. His father died of metastatic bladder cancer at the age of 55 years.

On physical examination, temperature is 36.9°C (98.4°F), blood pressure is 138/85 mm Hg, pulse rate is 72/min, and respiration rate is 12/min. The remainder of the examination is normal.

Urinalysis reveals no protein, 5-10 erythrocytes/high-power field (all of which are isomorphic), and 0-2 leukocytes/high-power field.

Which of the following is the most appropriate diagnostic test to perform next?

(A) Computed tomographic urography
(B) Cystoscopy
(C) Repeat urinalysis
(D) Urine culture
(E) Urine cytology

Item 5 [Basic]

A 28-year-old woman is evaluated during a follow-up visit. A recent life insurance examination revealed proteinuria on dipstick urinalysis. She is otherwise healthy and has no pertinent personal or family medical history.

On physical examination, temperature is 36.1°C (97.0°F), blood pressure is 110/64 mm Hg, pulse rate is 72/min, and respiration rate is 12/min. Body mass index is 23. The remainder of the examination is normal.

Laboratory studies:

Serum creatinine	0.8 mg/dL (70.7 μmol/L)
Estimated glomerular filtration rate	>60 mL/min/1.73 m²
Urinalysis	1+ protein; 0-2 erythrocytes/high-power field; 0 leukocytes/high-power field
24-Hour urine collection for protein	200 mg/24 h (normal, <150 mg/24 h)

Which of the following is the most appropriate next step in management?

(A) Kidney biopsy
(B) Repeat 24-hour urine collection for protein
(C) Split urine collection
(D) Spot urine protein–creatinine ratio
(E) Reassurance

Item 6 [Advanced]

A 26-year-old man is evaluated in the emergency department after being found on the floor in his apartment by friends.

On physical examination, the patient is minimally responsive. Temperature is normal, blood pressure is 92/54 mm Hg, pulse rate is 118/min, and respiration rate is 14/min. Oxygen saturation is 97% (ambient air). Skin is mottled on the posterior buttocks and back. Neurologic examination findings are nonfocal.

Laboratory studies:

Serum creatinine	6.3 mg/dL (734 μmol/L)
Electrolytes	
Sodium	151 mEq/L (151 mmol/L)
Potassium	5.8 mEq/L (5.8 mmol/L)
Chloride	121 mEq/L (121 mmol/L)
Bicarbonate	19 mEq/L (19 mmol/L)
Creatine kinase	85,000 U/L
Urinalysis	Specific gravity 1.012; 3+ blood; 0-5 erythrocytes/high-power field; dark granular casts

Electrocardiogram shows sinus tachycardia but is otherwise normal. Results of a toxicology screen are pending.

Which of the following is the most appropriate treatment for this patient?

(A) Hemodialysis
(B) Intravenous mannitol
(C) Rapid infusion of intravenous 0.9% saline
(D) Rapid infusion of 5% dextrose in water

Item 7 [Basic]

A 72-year-old woman is evaluated in the emergency department for increasing dyspnea on exertion, orthopnea, and bilateral lower extremity swelling over the last week. She has a history of systolic heart failure for which she takes lisinopril, metoprolol, and furosemide.

On physical examination, temperature is normal, blood pressure is 100/50 mm Hg, pulse rate is 104/min, and respiration rate is 26/min. Oxygen saturation is 92% (on 100% oxygen by non-rebreather mask). She has marked jugular venous distention while sitting upright. Cardiopulmonary examination shows a summation gallop and bibasilar crackles. There is 3+ pitting edema of the lower extremities.

Laboratory studies:

Serum creatinine	1.2 mg/dL (106 μmol/L)
Blood urea nitrogen	25 mg/dL (8.9 mmol/L)
Electrolytes	
Sodium	122 mEq/L (122 mmol/L)
Potassium	4.4 mEq/L (4.4 mmol/L)
Chloride	95 mEq/L (95 mmol/L)
Bicarbonate	22 mEq/L (22 mmol/L)
Glucose, random plasma	110 mg/dL (6.4 mmol/L)
Spot urine sodium	10 mEq/L (10 mmol/L)
Urine osmolality	475 mOsm/kg H₂O

Which of the following best characterizes this patient's hyponatremia?

(A) Hyperosmolal hyponatremia with decreased effective arterial blood volume
(B) Hypo-osmolol hyponatremia with decreased effective arterial blood volume
(C) Hypo-osmolol hyponatremia with normal effective arterial blood volume
(D) Isosmotic hyponatremia with adequate effective arterial blood volume

Item 8 [Basic]

A 34-year-old fireman is evaluated in the emergency department after falling from a second story balcony. He is unconscious and on a back board. Vital signs were stable in the field and on transport to the hospital.

On physical examination, blood pressure is 120/60 mm Hg, pulse rate is 100/min, and respiration rate is 18/min. Oxygen saturation is 98% (on 100% oxygen by non-rebreather mask). There is bruising over the left chest, flank, and hip area and a large laceration over the left occipital skull. Cardiopulmonary and abdominal examinations are normal. He responds to painful stimuli. The neurologic examination is nonfocal.

Imaging studies show fractures of the left 8th and 9th ribs, a fractured pelvis, and a large left retroperitoneal hematoma. Computed tomography scan of the head shows no evidence of subdural hematoma or intracerebral bleeding.

Urinalysis is dipstick positive for blood. Microscopic urine examination shows no erythrocytes.

Laboratory studies one hour after the fall:

Electrolytes

Sodium	139 mEq/L (139 mmol/L)
Potassium	6.6 mEq/L (6.6 mmol/L)
Chloride	100 mEq/L (100 mmol/L)
Bicarbonate	20 mEq/L (20 mmol/L)
Glucose, random plasma	114 mg/dL (6.3 mmol/L)
Serum creatinine	1.6 mg/dL (141 µmol/L)
Creatine kinase	6554 U/L

Which of the following mechanisms is responsible for this patient's hyperkalemia?

(A) Decreased distal tubule urine flow

(B) Decreased glomerular filtration rate

(C) Disrupted cell membranes

(D) Increased aldosterone effect

Item 9 [Advanced]

A 66-year-old woman is evaluated in the emergency department for a 1-day history of nausea, vomiting, weakness, and confusion. Today, she has difficulty walking and has fallen several times. Medical history is significant for a recent diagnosis of depression for which fluoxetine was started 3 weeks ago. She takes no other medications.

On physical examination, the patient appears chronically ill. She is unable to stand without assistance because of generalized weakness. Temperature is normal, blood pressure is 130/78 mm Hg and pulse rate is 68/min without orthostatic changes; respiration rate is 18/min. Cardiopulmonary examination is normal. There is no peripheral edema. The neurologic examination is nonfocal.

Laboratory studies:

Serum creatinine	0.9 mg/dL (79.6 µmol/L)
Serum sodium	115 mEq/L (115 mmol/L)
Glucose, random plasma	105 mg/dL (5.8 mmol/L)
Serum osmolality	245 mOsm/kg H$_2$O
Urine osmolality	408 mOsm/kg H$_2$O
Urine sodium	90 mEq/L (90 mmol/L)

Which of the following is the most appropriate treatment?

(A) 0.9% Saline infusion

(B) 3% Saline infusion

(C) Furosemide

(D) Tolvaptan

Item 10 [Advanced]

A 68-year-old man is evaluated in the hospital. The patient was hospitalized 3 days ago for acute kidney injury secondary to a bladder outlet obstruction due to benign prostatic hyperplasia. Medical history is otherwise unremarkable, and he took no medications prior to admission.

On admission, a bladder catheter was placed and resulted in immediate drainage of 800 mL of urine. Urine volume increased to 130 mL/h over the initial 48 hours of hospitalization.

On physical examination today (hospital day 3), temperature is normal, blood pressure is 135/60 mm Hg, pulse rate is 68/min, and respiration rate is 14/min. Cardiopulmonary examination is normal. There is 1+ bilateral lower extremity edema.

Laboratory studies (hospital day 3):

Serum creatinine	3.4 mg/dL (301 µmol/L); value was 6.2 mg/dL (548 µmol/L) on admission
Serum sodium	151 mEq/L (151 mmol/L)
Urine osmolality	326 mOsm/kg H$_2$O (normal, 300-900 mOsm/kg H$_2$O)
Urinalysis	Specific gravity 1.012; pH 5.0; no blood; trace protein; no glucose

Kidney ultrasound reveals bilateral hydronephrosis.

Which of the following is the most appropriate next step in treatment?

(A) 0.45% Saline

(B) 0.9% Saline

(C) 5% Dextrose in water

(D) Desmopressin

Item 11 [Advanced]

A 44-year-old man is evaluated in the emergency department because of polyuria and polydipsia. Over the past week he has noted increased urination and almost constant thirst. Medical history is significant for bipolar disorder. His only medication is lithium, and he does not take any over-the-counter preparations.

On physical examination, temperature is normal, blood pressure is 135/80 mm Hg, pulse rate is 78/min, and respiration rate is 12/min. The remainder of the examination is normal.

Results of laboratory studies show a serum sodium level of 152 mEq/L (152 mmol/L), random plasma glucose level of 125 mg/dL (6.9 mmol/L), and urine osmolality of 117 mOsm/kg. Injection of arginine vasopressin results in no significant increase in urine osmolality within 1 to 2 hours.

Which of the following is the most likely cause of this patient's hypernatremia?

(A) Central diabetes insipidus

(B) Nephrogenic diabetes insipidus

(C) Osmotic diuresis

(D) Primary polydipsia

Item 12 [Basic]

A 65-year-old man is evaluated in the hospital after undergoing emergent sigmoid colectomy for a perforated diverticulum. Medical history is significant for stage 4 chronic kidney disease due to autosomal dominant polycystic kidney disease. He also has hypertension treated with amlodipine.

On physical examination, temperature is normal, blood pressure is 150/95 mm Hg, pulse rate is 102/min, and respiration rate is 18/min. Abdominal examination reveals a clean and dry surgical incision.

Postoperative urine output decreases to 50 mL over 8 hours and does not improve following a fluid challenge.

Laboratory studies:

	Current	On admission
Serum creatinine	6.4 mg/dL (566 µmol/L)	5.4 mg/dL (477 µmol/L)
Serum potassium	6.9 mEq/L (6.9 mmol/L)	4.8 mEq/L (4.8 mmol/L)

Electrocardiogram shows tall, symmetric, peaked T waves and a shortened QT interval.

Intravenous calcium, insulin, and dextrose are given.

Which of the following is the most appropriate next step in treatment?

(A) Furosemide
(B) Hemodialysis
(C) Sodium bicarbonate
(D) Sodium polystyrene sulfonate

Item 13 [Basic]

A 36-year-old man is evaluated in the emergency department because of a 3-hour history of colicky right flank pain. His medical history is unremarkable and he takes no medications.

On physical examination, vital signs are normal. The patient is in moderate discomfort with pain localized to the costovertebral region of the right flank. The remainder of the physical examination is unremarkable.

Laboratory studies:

Electrolytes	Normal
Albumin	4.1 g/dL (41 g/L)
Calcium	11.4 mg/dL (2.9 mmol/L)
Phosphorus	2.4 mg/dL (0.77 mmol/L)
Parathyroid hormone	85 pg/mL (65 ng/L)

A urinalysis shows microscopic hematuria without evidence of infection. A noncontrast computed tomographic scan of the kidneys shows a 1.5-mm stone at the right ureteropelvic junction with mild hydronephrosis.

Which of the following best describes the mechanism of hypercalcemia in this patient?

(A) Calcium mobilized from bone, with increased gastrointestinal (GI) absorption and increased kidney absorption
(B) Calcium mobilized from bone, with increased GI absorption but no increased kidney absorption
(C) Calcium not mobilized from bone, with increased GI absorption and increased kidney absorption
(D) Calcium not mobilized from bone, with increased GI absorption but no increased kidney absorption

Item 14 [Advanced]

A 62-year-old woman is evaluated for weakness of 1 week's duration. The patient has a 35-year history of Crohn disease. Two months

ago, she underwent resection of the distal ileum and right colon because of entero-enteric fistula formation. After the resection, she developed profuse diarrhea while on enteral feedings and also had significant weight loss amounting to 15% of her body weight. Home intravenous total parenteral nutrition was started 1 week ago. Since the initiation of intravenous nutrition, her diarrhea has resolved completely, but she has developed new muscle weakness and mild dyspnea on exertion.

On physical examination, temperature is normal, blood pressure is 106/68 mm Hg, pulse rate is 78 min, and respiration rate is 18/min. Body mass index is 17. Cardiopulmonary examination is normal. The abdomen is soft with well-healed surgical scars. There is generalized muscular weakness and symmetrically diminished reflexes throughout.

Laboratory studies:
Electrolytes:

Sodium	136 mEq/L (136 mmol/L)
Potassium	3.3 mEq/L (3.3 mmol/L)
Chloride	96 mEq/L (96 mmol/L)
Bicarbonate	18 mEq/L (19 mmol/L)
Random glucose	122 mg/dL (6.8 mmol/L)
Calcium	8.3 mg/dL (2.1 mmol/L)
Phosphorus	1.1 mg/dL (0.36 mmol/L)
Magnesium	1.2 mg/dL (0.50 mmol/L)
Albumin	2.7 g/dL (27 g/L)

Which of the following is the most immediate cause of this patient's recent symptoms?

(A) Gastrointestinal losses of phosphorus
(B) Poor oral intake of phosphorus-containing foods
(C) Renal losses of phosphorus
(D) Shift of phosphorus into the intracellular space

Item 15 [Basic]

A 43-year-old man is evaluated in the hospital for perioral paresthesias and severe cramping of both hands. He underwent total thyroidectomy yesterday because of papillary thyroid cancer. The surgery was uncomplicated, and no involved lymph nodes were found.

On physical examination, vital signs are normal. Cardiopulmonary and abdominal examinations are unremarkable. Results of muscle strength testing are normal. Although the patient reports cramps, no tetany is detected.

Results of laboratory studies show a serum calcium level of 4.1 mg/dL (1.0 mmol/L), a serum magnesium level of 1.7 mg/dL (0.70 mmol/L), and a serum phosphorus level of 4.7 mg/dL (1.52 mmol/L); kidney function studies are normal.

An electrocardiogram is normal.

Which of the following is the most appropriate immediate treatment for this patient?

(A) Calcitriol
(B) Calcium
(C) Magnesium
(D) Recombinant parathyroid hormone

Item 16 [Basic]

A 62-year-old woman is evaluated for a 1-week history of fatigue, lethargy, constipation, and nocturnal polyuria and polydipsia. The patient has advanced breast cancer, which has metastasized to her liver. Conventional therapy is no longer helpful, and she is scheduled to see her oncologist to discuss the next steps in management.

On physical examination, she is pale and somnolent. Blood pressure is 98/65 mm Hg and resting pulse rate is 103/min. The mucous membranes are dry. Cardiopulmonary examination is normal.

Laboratory studies:

Blood urea nitrogen	37 mg/dL (13.2 mmol/L)
Calcium	15.7 mg/dL (3.9 mmol/L)
Serum creatinine	1.6 mg/dL (141 µmol/L)
Sodium	151 mEq/L (151 mmol/L)

Which of the following is the most appropriate immediate next step in treating this patient?

(A) An intravenous bisphosphonate
(B) Intravenous furosemide
(C) Intravenous glucocorticoids
(D) Intravenous 0.9% saline

Item 17 [Advanced]

A 23-year-old woman is evaluated in the emergency department because she has been unable to walk for 1 day. The patient has a 2-month history of progressive weakness of both lower extremities. She reports no diarrhea or weight loss. Medical history is remarkable for Sjögren syndrome. She takes no medications.

On physical examination, vital signs are normal. Diffuse grade 3/5 weakness is noted most prominently in the lower extremities. There is no muscle atrophy or tenderness.

Laboratory studies:

Electrolytes	
Sodium	141 mEq/L (141 mmol/L)
Potassium	1.9 mEq/L (1.9 mmol/L)
Chloride	117 mEq/L (117 mmol/L)
Bicarbonate	14 mEq/L (14 mmol/L)
Urine anion gap	Positive
Urinalysis	Specific gravity 1.014; pH 7.0; otherwise normal

Kidney ultrasound shows bilateral nephrocalcinosis.

Which of the following is the most likely diagnosis?

(A) Gitelman syndrome
(B) Laxative abuse
(C) Type 1 (distal) renal tubular acidosis
(D) Type 2 (proximal) renal tubular acidosis

Item 18 [Basic]

A 25-year-old woman is evaluated in the emergency department because of the sudden onset of dyspnea. Symptoms started while she was in a meeting at her workplace. Medical history is unremarkable, and she has no known cardiovascular or pulmonary disorders. She takes no medications.

On physical examination, she appears in moderate respiratory distress. Temperature is 36.7°C (98.0°F), blood pressure is 155/85 mm Hg, pulse rate is 105/min, and respiration rate is 32/min. Cardiovascular and pulmonary examinations are normal.

Laboratory studies:

Electrolytes:	
Sodium	140 mEq/L (140 mmol/L)
Potassium	4.7 mEq/L (4.7 mmol/L)
Chloride	108 mEq/L (108 mmol/L)
Bicarbonate	22 mEq/L (22 mmol/L)
Arterial blood gas studies (ambient air):	
pH	7.49
Pco_2	30 mm Hg (4.0 kPa)
Po_2	99 mm Hg (13.2 kPa)

Which of the following best characterizes this patient's acid–base disorder?

(A) Mixed anion gap metabolic acidosis and respiratory alkalosis
(B) Mixed metabolic alkalosis and respiratory alkalosis
(C) Respiratory acidosis
(D) Respiratory alkalosis

Item 19 [Basic]

A 66-year-old man is evaluated in the emergency department for a 3-day history of productive cough and worsening dyspnea. Medical history is significant for chronic obstructive pulmonary disease (COPD). Medications are tiotropium, salmeterol, and as-needed albuterol.

On physical examination he is using the accessory muscles of respiration and has pursed-lipped breathing. Temperature is normal, blood pressure is 148/82 mm Hg, pulse rate is 95/min and respiration rate is 20/min. There is a prolonged expiratory-to-inspiratory phase, and scattered wheezes are auscultated throughout both lung fields.

Laboratory studies:

Electrolytes	
Sodium	140 mEq/L (140 mmol/L)
Potassium	3.5 mEq/L (3.5 mmol/L)
Chloride	98 mEq/L (98 mmol/L)
Bicarbonate	32 mEq/L (32 mmol/L)
Arterial blood gas studies (ambient air)	
pH	7.32
Pco_2	64 mm Hg (8.5 kPa)
Po_2	59 mm Hg (7.8 kPa)

Chest radiograph shows findings consistent with COPD but is otherwise unchanged from baseline.

Which of the following acid-base disorders is most likely present?

(A) Metabolic acidosis
(B) Respiratory acidosis
(C) Respiratory acidosis and metabolic acidosis
(D) Respiratory alkalosis

Item 20 [Advanced]

A 26-year-old man is evaluated for a 6-month history of fatigue. He is subsequently diagnosed with hypokalemic metabolic alkalosis. Medical history is unremarkable, and he takes no medications.

On physical examination, temperature is 36.6°C (97.9°F), blood pressure is 110/64 mm Hg and pulse rate is 78/min without orthostatic changes; respiration rate is 14/min. Cardiopulmonary examination is normal. There is no edema. The remainder of the examination is unremarkable.

Laboratory studies:

Serum creatinine	0.8 mg/dL (70.7 µmol/L)
Electrolytes:	
Sodium	142 mEq/L (142 mmol/L)
Potassium	2.9 mEq/L (2.9 mmol/L)
Chloride	100 mEq/L (100 mmol/L)
Bicarbonate	32 mEq/L (32 mmol/L)

Which of the following is the most appropriate diagnostic test to perform next?

(A) Plasma aldosterone and renin measurement

(B) Serum magnesium measurement

(C) Urine chloride measurement

(D) Urine osmolal gap

Item 21 [Advanced]

A 45-year-old man is brought to the emergency department after being found unresponsive in an alleyway. Medical history is unknown, although his breath smells of alcohol.

On physical examination, he is obtunded and responds only to noxious stimuli. Temperature is normal, blood pressure is 95/70 mm Hg, pulse rate is 115/min, and respiration rate is 12/min. General physical examination is unremarkable. Except for his altered mental status, the neurologic evaluation is nonfocal.

Laboratory studies:

Electrolytes:	
Sodium	135 mEq/L (135 mmol/L)
Potassium	3.8 mEq/L (3.8 mmol/L)
Chloride	92 mEq/L (92 mmol/L)
Bicarbonate	12 mEq/L (12 mmol/L)
Arterial blood gas studies (ambient air):	
pH	7.08
Pco$_2$	42 mm Hg (5.6 kPa)

Which of the following acid-base disorders is most likely present?

(A) Metabolic acidosis, metabolic alkalosis, and respiratory acidosis

(B) Metabolic acidosis and respiratory alkalosis

(C) Metabolic alkalosis and respiratory acidosis

(D) Respiratory acidosis and metabolic acidosis

(E) Simple metabolic acidosis

Item 22 [Basic]

A 39-year-old man is evaluated in the emergency department because of the acute onset of severe right flank pain. The pain is described as sharp and radiates to the groin. He vomited six times

prior to presentation. Medical history is unremarkable, and he takes no medications.

On physical examination, the patient is in distress because of the pain. Temperature is normal, blood pressure is 148/88 mm Hg, pulse rate is 110/min, and respiration rate is 30/min. There is tenderness to palpation over the right flank. The remainder of the examination is unremarkable.

Laboratory studies:

Electrolytes:	
Sodium	141 mEq/L (141 mmol/L)
Potassium	4.0 mEq/L (4.0 mmol/L)
Chloride	100 mEq/L (100 mmol/L)
Bicarbonate	34 mEq/L (34 mmol/L)
Arterial blood gas studies (ambient air):	
pH	7.60
Pco$_2$	36 mm Hg (4.8 kPa)
Po$_2$	59 mm Hg (7.8 kPa)

A computed tomographic scan of the kidneys demonstrates a nonobstructing kidney stone at the ureteropelvic junction on the right.

Which of the following best describes this patient's acid-base disorder?

(A) Metabolic alkalosis

(B) Metabolic alkalosis and respiratory acidosis

(C) Metabolic alkalosis and respiratory alkalosis

(D) Respiratory alkalosis

Item 23 [Basic]

A 48-year-old woman is evaluated in the emergency department for fatigue, diffuse weakness, and lightheadedness. Her symptoms developed after attending an outdoor music festival, where she was exposed to the sun most of the day. Medical history is significant for hypertension, which is treated with hydrochlorothiazide. She took a single dose of ibuprofen 3 hours ago.

On physical examination, temperature is normal, supine blood pressure is 97/52 mm Hg, supine pulse rate is 98/min, and respiration rate is 12/min. When standing, blood pressure is 90/45 mm Hg, and the pulse rate is 108/min. The remainder of the examination is normal.

Laboratory studies:

Serum creatinine	1.1 mg/dL (97.2 µmol/L) (baseline: 0.7 mg/dL [61.9 µmol/L])
Electrolytes	Normal
Fractional excretion of sodium	1.2%
Fractional excretion of urea	27.4%
Urinalysis	Specific gravity 1.035; pH 6.5; trace protein; no cells; 3-5 hyaline casts

Which of the following is the most likely diagnosis?

(A) Acute interstitial nephritis

(B) Acute tubular necrosis

(C) Nonsteroidal anti-inflammatory drug nephrotoxicity

(D) Prerenal azotemia

Item 24 [Basic]

A 67-year-old man is evaluated in the hospital for an increasing serum creatinine level. The patient was hospitalized for pneumonia 2 days ago and is improving on antibiotic therapy. He has experienced no episodes of hypotension during the hospitalization. His only other medication is tamsulosin for benign prostatic hyperplasia.

On physical examination, the patient is afebrile. Blood pressure is 144/75 mm Hg, and pulse rate is 64/min. Cardiopulmonary examination is normal. The abdomen is nontender, with normal bowel sounds and some suprapubic fullness. Urine output was 1200 mL in the past 24 hours.

The serum creatinine level is 1.9 mg/dL (168 µmol/L). Urinalysis shows a specific gravity of 1.011; pH 6.0; trace leukocyte esterase; 0-3 erythrocytes/high-power field; and 0-5 leukocytes/high-power field.

Which of the following is the most appropriate diagnostic test to perform next?

(A) Fractional excretion of sodium
(B) Kidney biopsy
(C) Kidney ultrasonography
(D) Serum creatine kinase measurement

Item 25 [Basic]

A 64-year-old man is evaluated in the emergency department for a 7-day history of fever and cough. His wife reports that he has had progressively decreasing oral intake and lethargy for the past 2 days.

On physical examination, the patient is confused but responsive. Temperature is 40.2°C (104.3°F), blood pressure is 70/48 mm Hg, pulse rate is 120/min, and respiration rate is 18/min. Oxygen saturation is 86% (ambient air). Pulmonary examination reveals decreased breath sounds at both bases. The remainder of the examination is normal.

Bladder catheterization produces 350 mL of dark urine.

Laboratory studies:
Serum creatinine	5 mg/dL (442 µmol/L)
Urine sodium	70 mEq/L (70 mmol/L)
Fractional excretion of sodium	1.3%
Urinalysis	Specific gravity 1.023; 1+ protein; many casts

A photomicrograph of the urine sediment is shown (Plate 20). Chest radiograph shows bilateral lower lobe pulmonary infiltrates.

Supplemental oxygen and antibiotics are started.

Which of the following is the most likely cause of this patient's acute kidney failure?

(A) Acute interstitial nephritis
(B) Acute tubular necrosis
(C) Bladder outlet obstruction
(D) Prerenal acute kidney failure

Item 26 [Advanced]

A 71-year-old woman is hospitalized for chest pain. She has type 2 diabetes mellitus, hypertension, hyperlipidemia, and chronic kidney disease. Medications are lisinopril, rosuvastatin, furosemide, carvedilol, insulin, and aspirin.

On physical examination, temperature is normal, blood pressure is 118/50 mm Hg, pulse rate is 70/min, and respiration rate is 14/min. Cardiopulmonary and abdominal examinations are normal. There is trace edema of the lower extremities, which is a baseline finding in this patient.

Laboratory studies:
Serum creatinine	2.1 mg/dL (186 µmol/L)
Electrolytes	Normal
Estimated glomerular filtration rate	19 mL/min/1.73 m^2

Adenosine thallium scan reveals an area of reversible ischemia in the left anterior descending coronary artery distribution. Cardiac catheterization is scheduled. Lisinopril is stopped prior to the procedure.

Which of the following interventions will decrease this patient's risk for contrast-induced nephropathy?

(A) Hydration with intravenous isotonic saline
(B) Hydration with intravenous isotonic saline and furosemide diuresis
(C) Oral hydration
(D) Prophylactic hemodialysis

Item 27 [Advanced]

A 68-year-old man is hospitalized for a 3-month history of dark brown urine, malaise, and an unintentional 6.8-kg (15-lb) weight loss. He has felt febrile but reports no urinary hesitancy or frequency, dysuria, nausea, vomiting, or diarrhea. Medical history is otherwise unremarkable, and he takes no medications.

On physical examination, the patient appears fatigued. Temperature is 37.6°C (99.6°F), blood pressure is 162/93 mm Hg, pulse rate is 88/min, and respiration rate is 16/min. Periorbital edema is present. Cardiopulmonary examination is normal. The abdomen is nontender and nondistended. There is 1+ bilateral pitting lower extremity edema.

Results of laboratory studies are significant for a serum creatinine level of 3.2 mg/dL (283 µmol/L) (6 months ago: 1.1 mg/dL [97.2 µmol/L]) and a urinalysis showing 1+ blood. 1+ protein, 5-10 erythrocytes/high-power field, 50% acanthocytes, and erythrocyte casts.

Which of the following is the most likely diagnosis?

(A) Acute interstitial nephritis
(B) Acute tubular necrosis
(C) Polyarteritis nodosa
(D) Rapidly progressive glomerulonephritis

Item 28 [Advanced]

A 19-year-old woman is hospitalized for acute kidney injury associated with bloody diarrhea. She also has nausea, vomiting, abdominal pain, fever, chills, and decreased urine output. Medical history is otherwise unremarkable, and she takes no medications.

On physical examination, temperature is 37.8°C (100.0°F), blood pressure is 135/90 mm Hg, and pulse rate is 110/min. The oral mucosa is dry. There is diffuse abdominal pain with guarding. The remainder of the examination is normal.

Laboratory studies:

Haptoglobin	8 mg/dL (80 mg/L)
Hemoglobin	5.2 g/dL (52 g/L)
Platelet count	36,000/µL (36 × 10⁹/L)
Reticulocyte count	7.8% of erythrocytes
Serum creatinine	5.7 mg/dL (504 µmol/L)
Lactate dehydrogenase	2396 U/L
Urinalysis	Many erythrocytes and erythrocyte casts

The peripheral blood smear shows many schistocytes.

Which of the following is the most likely cause of this patient's acute kidney injury?

(A) Acute tubular necrosis
(B) Hemolytic uremic syndrome
(C) Postinfectious glomerulonephritis
(D) Scleroderma renal crisis

Item 29 [Basic]

A 67-year-old man is evaluated during a routine examination. He has a history of hypertension and type 2 diabetes mellitus treated with losartan, chlorthalidone, amlodipine, atorvastatin, aspirin, and insulin glargine.

On physical examination, temperature is normal, blood pressure is 155/92 mm Hg, pulse rate is 88/min, and respiration rate is 20/min. Body mass index is 28. The remainder of the examination is normal.

Laboratory studies:

Hemoglobin	13 g/dL (130 g/L)
Hemoglobin A₁c	6.8%
Serum creatinine	1.7 mg/dL (150 µmol/L)
Estimated glomerular filtration rate	41 mL/min/1.73 m²
Spot urine albumin-creatinine ratio	2.5 mg/g

Which of the following interventions is most likely to slow the progression of this patient's chronic kidney disease?

(A) Decrease blood pressure to less than 140/90 mm Hg
(B) Decrease the hemoglobin A₁c value to less than 6.5%
(C) Decrease the urine albumin-creatinine ratio to less than 30 mg/g
(D) Increase the hemoglobin level to 14 g/dL (140 g/L)

Item 30 [Basic]

A 32-year-old woman is evaluated during a new patient visit. She is healthy, exercises regularly without symptoms, and takes no medications. Medical history is unremarkable. Family history is notable for her father and paternal aunt who both have hypertension and chronic kidney disease. There is no family history of polycystic kidney disease. Her father began dialysis when he was 50 years old and now has a kidney transplant.

Physical examination findings, including vital signs, are normal.

Which of the following should be done to screen for chronic kidney disease in this patient?

(A) 24-Hour urine collection for creatinine clearance
(B) Kidney ultrasonography
(C) Radionuclide kidney clearance scanning
(D) Serum creatinine measurement, estimated glomerular filtration rate, and urinalysis

Item 31 [Basic]

A 59-year-old woman is evaluated during a routine follow-up visit. Type 2 diabetes mellitus and hyperlipidemia were recently diagnosed. She feels well. Medications are metformin, atorvastatin, and aspirin.

Physical examination findings, including vital signs, are normal.

Results of laboratory studies show a serum creatinine level of 0.9 mg/dL (79.6 µmol/L), an estimated glomerular filtration rate of greater than 60 mL/min/1.73 m², and a normal urinalysis.

Which of the following is the most appropriate diagnostic test to perform next?

(A) 24-Hour urine collection for protein
(B) Kidney ultrasonography
(C) Spot urine albumin-creatinine ratio
(D) No additional testing

Item 32 [Basic]

A 69-year-old man is evaluated during a new patient visit. Medical history includes hypertension and several episodes of kidney stones. Family history is significant for chronic kidney disease in his mother, who required dialysis. His only medication is lisinopril.

On physical examination, temperature is 36.9°C (98.4°F), blood pressure is 134/72 mm Hg, pulse rate is 72/min, and respiration rate is 14/min. The remainder of the examination is normal.

Laboratory studies:

Hemoglobin	12 g/dL (120 g/L)
Serum creatinine	1.9 mg/dL (168 µmol/L); 5 years ago: 1.4 mg/dL (124 µmol/L)
Estimated glomerular filtration rate	37 mL/min/1.73 m²
Urinalysis	2+ protein; 0-2 erythrocytes/high-power field; 0-1 leukocytes/high-power field

Which of the following is the most appropriate diagnostic test to perform next?

(A) Abdominal computed tomography with contrast
(B) Kidney biopsy
(C) Kidney ultrasonography
(D) Radionuclide kidney clearance scanning

Item 33 [Advanced]

A 55-year-old woman is evaluated during a routine examination. Chronic kidney disease was diagnosed 3 years ago. For the past year, she has had increasing fatigue. She reports no shortness of breath or chest pain. Medications are lisinopril, calcium acetate, ferrous sulfate, and a multivitamin.

On physical examination, temperature is normal, blood pressure is 110/70 mm Hg, pulse rate is 76/min, and respiration rate is 14/min. The remainder of the examination is normal. A stool specimen is negative for occult blood.

Laboratory studies:

Hemoglobin	8.9 g/dL (89 g/L); 1 year ago, 11 g/dL (110 g/L)
Mean corpuscular volume	91 fL
Reticulocyte count	1% of erythrocytes
Serum creatinine	2 mg/dL (177 µmol/L)
Ferritin	250 ng/mL (250 µg/L)
Transferrin saturation	33%
Vitamin B_{12} and folate	Normal

Which of the following is the most appropriate intervention for this patient's management?

(A) Add ascorbic acid
(B) Add an erythropoiesis-stimulating agent
(C) Schedule a blood transfusion
(D) Switch from oral to intravenous iron therapy

Item 34 [Basic]

A 51-year-old man is evaluated for left-sided flank pain and a low-grade fever of several days' duration. He reports no nausea or vomiting. He has not experienced urinary changes such as hesitancy or frequency. Medical history is unremarkable, and he takes no medications.

On physical examination, temperature is 37.8°C (100.0°F), blood pressure is 159/93 mm Hg, pulse rate is 92/min, and respiration rate is 12/min. Abdominal examination is significant for mild discomfort to palpation across the left flank but is otherwise normal. The remainder of the examination is unremarkable.

Results of laboratory studies are significant for a leukocyte count of 11,500/µL (11.5 × 10⁹/L) and a urinalysis showing a pH of 5.5; 2+ blood; trace protein; 1+ leukocyte esterase; 5-10 erythrocytes/high-power field; 2-5 leukocytes/high-power field; and no nitrites.

Which of the following is the most appropriate test to perform next?

(A) Abdominal magnetic resonance imaging
(B) Abdominal radiography of the kidneys, ureters, and bladder
(C) Intravenous pyelography
(D) Noncontrast abdominal helical computed tomography

Item 35 [Basic]

A 50-year-old man undergoes follow-up examination. He was evaluated in the emergency department 2 days ago for right flank pain and was found to have a 4-mm stone in the distal right ureter on non-contrast computed tomography (CT). Results of laboratory studies at the time, including kidney function tests, were normal. He was treated with low-dose opioid medication and was discharged home with follow-up scheduled today. The patient continues to report mild pain that is controlled with the medication.

On physical examination, vital signs are normal. There is mild tenderness to palpation over the right costovertebral angle, and the remainder of the examination is normal.

Which of the following is the most appropriate next step in management?

(A) α-Blocker therapy
(B) Extracorporeal shock wave lithotripsy
(C) 24-Hour urine collection for calcium, oxalate, and uric acid
(D) Repeat noncontrast CT
(E) Ureteroscopy and intracorporeal lithotripsy

Item 36 [Advanced]

A 35-year-old man is seen in the clinic for follow-up evaluation for recurrent symptomatic calcium oxalate kidney stones. His episodes of nephrolithiasis are associated with significant pain and are disabling. His last attack was 1 month ago. He first developed kidney stones 5 years ago and typically has one to two episodes each year. He has been adherent to recommendations to increase his fluid intake and maintain a low-sodium diet.

On physical examination, vital signs are normal. The remainder of the examination is unremarkable.

Laboratory studies:

Urinalysis	pH 5.0; 1+ blood; no protein; 0-3 erythrocytes/high-power field; no bacteria; no glucose

24 hour urine collection:

Calcium	Normal
Uric acid	Normal
Citric acid	Normal
Oxalate	High

Radiograph of the kidneys, ureters, and bladder reveals a 3-mm calculus in the right upper pole.

In addition to avoiding foods high in oxalate and adhering to a low-protein diet, which of the following is the most appropriate next step in this patient's management?

(A) Begin allopurinol
(B) Begin hydrochlorothiazide
(C) Begin sodium citrate
(D) Increase dietary calcium intake

Section 7

Nephrology

Answers and Critiques

Item 1   **Answer: B**

Educational Objective: *Estimate glomerular filtration rate.*

The Chronic Kidney Disease Epidemiology Collaboration (CKD-EPI) equation will best estimate this patient's glomerular filtration rate (GFR). The National Kidney Foundation Kidney Disease Outcomes Quality Initiative (NKF KDOQI) recommends the use of mathematical equations to estimate GFR. These equations should only be used when the serum creatinine level has been stable for at least 24 to 48 hours. The CKD-EPI equation is a validated measurement derived from a large population of patients with both normal and abnormal kidney function. The CKD-EPI equation performs better at higher (normal) values of GFR and in patients with mild chronic kidney disease, such as this patient. Although the Modification of Diet in Renal Disease (MDRD) study equation has been validated in multiple populations with chronic kidney disease (CKD), this equation frequently underestimates GFR when it is greater than 60 mL/min/1.73 m^2.

Blood urea nitrogen (BUN) is derived from the metabolism of proteins. Although widely used, BUN concentration is a poor marker of kidney function for several reasons: it is not produced at a constant rate; it is reabsorbed along the tubules; and alterations in kidney blood flow markedly influence tubular reabsorption and excretion. Serum BUN measurement should not be used in isolation to predict kidney function. Measurement of urea clearance significantly underestimates GFR but may be useful in estimating GFR when it is less than 15 mL/min/1.73 m^2.

Because creatinine is secreted by renal tubules, creatinine clearance overestimates GFR. Additional inaccuracies arise because of over- or undercollection of urine. Observed creatinine excretion can be compared with expected excretion to assess the accuracy of the sample. When kidney function is normal, urine creatinine excretion occurs principally via glomerular filtration, with an additional smaller quantity excreted via tubular secretion; thus, an accurately measured creatinine clearance will approximate the true GFR. However, in patients with CKD, as the GFR declines, an increasing percentage of total urine creatinine excretion occurs via tubular secretion; thus, both the estimated and the measured creatinine clearances will progressively overestimate the true GFR in patients with worsening CKD.

Although the serum creatinine concentration is one of the most commonly used markers of GFR, it is an imperfect measure of kidney function. Reduction of muscle mass, as occurs in amputees and patients with malnutrition or muscle wasting, can result in a lower serum creatinine level without a corresponding change in GFR. Younger persons, men, and black persons often have higher muscle mass and higher serum creatinine levels at a given level of GFR compared with older persons with decreased muscle mass. Patients with advanced liver disease produce lower concentrations of precursors of serum creatinine and often have muscle wasting, with a corre-spondingly lower serum creatinine level at a particular level of GFR. Finally, serum creatinine concentration overestimates kidney function in elderly persons, especially women.

> **KEY POINT**
>
> The National Kidney Foundation Kidney Disease Outcomes Quality Initiative (NKF KDOQI) recommends the use of mathematical equations to estimate glomerular filtration rate.

Bibliography

Delanaye P, Mariat C. The applicability of eGFR equations to different populations. Nat Rev Nephrol. 2013;9:513-22. [PMID: 23856996]

Item 2   **Answer: A**

Educational Objective: *Diagnose crescentic glomerulonephritis.*

The most likely glomerular lesion seen on kidney biopsy is crescentic glomerulonephritis. This patient has pulmonary-renal syndrome characterized by hemoptysis and rapidly progressive kidney failure associated with the nephritic syndrome. The nephritic syndrome is a glomerular inflammatory condition (glomerulonephritis) characterized by hematuria, oliguria, hypertension, and acute kidney failure. Urinalysis usually reveals pyuria, hematuria, and cellular and granular casts; nephrotic-range proteinuria may also be present. The most likely histologic correlate of a rapidly progressive glomerulonephritis is crescentic glomerulonephritis. The crescent formation results from necrosis and rupture of the basement membrane, allowing coagulation proteins, macrophages, epithelial cells, and fibroblasts to enter and replace Bowman space. The two most common conditions causing adult-onset pulmonary-renal syndrome are antineutrophil cytoplasmic antibody (ANCA)–positive vasculitis (either granulomatosis with polyangiitis [formerly known as Wegener granulomatosis] or microscopic polyangiitis) and anti–glomerular basement membrane antibody disease (Goodpasture syndrome).

Minimal change disease, focal segmental glomerulosclerosis, and membranous glomerulopathy are not inflammatory glomerular lesions and are not associated with the nephritic syndrome. These glomerular diseases are more likely to be associated with the nephrotic syndrome characterized by edema, hypoalbuminemia, heavy proteinuria, and bland urine sediment (absent leukocytes, erythrocytes, and erythrocyte casts).

> **KEY POINT**
>
> The most likely histologic correlate of a rapidly progressive glomerulonephritis is crescentic glomerulonephritis.

Bibliography

West SC, Arulkumaran N, Ind PW, et al. Pulmonary-renal syndrome: a life threatening but treatable condition. Postgrad Med J. 2013 May;89:274-83. [PMID: 23349383]

Item 3   Answer: D
Educational Objective: *Diagnose glomerular hematuria.*

The most appropriate diagnostic tests to perform next are a urine protein–creatinine ratio and a serum creatinine measurement to determine the degree of proteinuria and level of kidney function. This patient has microscopic hematuria that appears glomerular in origin. Glomerular hematuria on urine microscopy is characterized by the presence of dysmorphic erythrocytes or acanthocytes, which are erythrocytes that retain a ring shape but have "blebs" protruding from their membrane, giving them a characteristic shape (compared with acanthocytes in the blood, in which the membrane protrusions appear to have a "spiked" shape). Significant hematuria may also be associated with the presence of erythrocyte casts. These findings are highly associated with a glomerular cause of bleeding and are specifically suggestive of glomerulonephritis. Urine microscopy in patients with glomerular disease also may detect intact erythrocytes; however, these are less specific for a diagnosis of glomerular disease.

After determining this patient's degree of proteinuria and level of kidney function, further evaluation for glomerular disease may include measurement of serum complement levels, a hepatitis panel, and blood cultures as well as testing for antinuclear antibodies, antineutrophil cytoplasmic antibodies (ANCA), anti–glomerular basement membrane antibodies, and antistreptolysin O antibodies.

Depending on the serologic test results, this patient may undergo a kidney biopsy to determine the cause of the glomerulonephritis, but biopsy is not indicated at this time.

If this patient's asymptomatic microscopic hematuria were nonglomerular in origin, ultrasonography would be appropriate to assess for a possible cause of urinary tract bleeding. However, imaging of the upper urinary tract would not be helpful in further evaluating her abnormal urinalysis results that suggest a glomerular process.

There is no indication that this patient has a urinary tract infection (negative leukocyte esterase and absent leukocytes on microscopic urinalysis); therefore, a urine culture is not indicated.

> **KEY POINT**
>
> **Glomerular hematuria on urine microscopy is characterized by the presence of dysmorphic erythrocytes or acanthocytes, and significant hematuria may also be associated with the presence of erythrocyte casts; these findings are specifically suggestive of glomerulonephritis.**

Bibliography
Sharp VJ, Barnes KT, Erickson BA. Assessment of asymptomatic microscopic hematuria in adults. Am Fam Physician. 2013;88:747-54. [PMID: 24364522]

Item 4   Answer: C
Educational Objective: *Diagnose hematuria.*

A repeat urinalysis is appropriate for this low-risk patient with possible hematuria. Evaluation should ensure that a patient does not have any of the known risk factors for microscopic hematuria, including a smoking history, occupational exposure to chemicals or dyes, age older than 40 years, a history of gross hematuria, a urologic disorder, irritative voiding symptoms, urinary tract infection, analgesic abuse, or pelvic irradiation. In a patient age younger than age 40 years, greater than 3 erythrocytes/high-power field on two or more occasions constitutes hematuria and is a common finding on urinalysis. A single episode in older patients or in those at risk should initiate a full evaluation of the upper and lower urinary tract. This patient has had hematuria documented on one occasion; thus, urinalysis should be repeated before further evaluation, despite his family history. A family history of bladder cancer does not increase the patient's risk of developing a malignancy unless both family members have been exposed to similar toxins.

If hematuria is established after the repeat urinalysis, this patient should then be evaluated for its cause. Bleeding in patients with persistent hematuria may originate anywhere along the genitourinary tract, and the location of the bleeding must be identified in order to determine the next steps in evaluation. Therefore, differentiating between glomerular and nonglomerular hematuria by urine microscopy is important. Glomerular hematuria is characterized by the presence of dysmorphic erythrocytes or acanthocytes (erythrocytes that retain a ring shape but have "blebs" protruding from their membrane, giving them a characteristic shape) on urine microscopy, and hematuria associated with the presence of erythrocyte casts is specifically indicative of glomerulonephritis. Nonglomerular hematuria refers to blood in the urine that originates outside of the glomerulus. This condition is associated with isomorphic erythrocytes that usually appear normal on urine microscopy. The most common causes of asymptomatic nonglomerular hematuria are urinary tract infections and kidney stones. Kidney or bladder cancer may also cause nonglomerular hematuria.

An appropriate evaluation for persistent nonglomerular hematuria in this patient may begin with upper urinary tract imaging. The American Urological Association recommends computed tomography (CT), ultrasonography, or intravenous urography and notes that CT urography is the best choice, if available. This should be followed by cystoscopy and possibly by urine cytology. Urine culture is unlikely to be helpful in this patient in the absence of dysuria or voiding symptoms and no evidence of infection on urinalysis.

> **KEY POINT**
>
> **In patients younger than age 40 years, the finding of greater than 3 erythrocytes/high-power field on urinalysis should be confirmed on two or more occasions to establish the diagnosis of hematuria.**

Bibliography
Margulis V, Sagalowsky AI. Assessment of hematuria. Med Clin North Am. 2011;95: 153-9. [PMID: 21095418]

Item 5   Answer: C
Educational Objective: *Diagnose orthostatic proteinuria.*

A split urine collection is an appropriate initial evaluation for sustained, isolated proteinuria. Protein excretion may vary based on time of collection and, in a small percentage of children and young adults, may also vary with changes in posture. Orthostatic (postural) proteinuria refers to protein excretion that increases during the day but decreases at night during recumbency. The diagnosis of orthostatic proteinuria is established by comparing the urine protein excretion during the day with findings from a separate urine collection obtained during the night. An 8-hour nighttime urine collection containing ≤50 mg of protein is required for diagnosis. Typically, urine protein excretion in patients with orthostatic proteinuria is less than 1 g/24 h but can rarely be greater than 3 g/24 h. Orthostatic proteinuria is benign and has not been associated with long-term kidney disease. Other benign causes of transient or isolated proteinuria include febrile illnesses and rigorous exercise.

Because transient or isolated proteinuria is typically benign, further evaluation is not warranted.

Kidney biopsy is recommended when histologic confirmation is needed to help diagnose kidney disease, implement medical therapy, or change medical treatment. Kidney biopsy is used predominantly in patients with glomerular disease, and the most common indications for kidney biopsy include the nephrotic syndrome, acute glomerulonephritis, or kidney transplant dysfunction. It is inappropriate to consider a kidney biopsy before excluding benign causes of proteinuria, such as orthostatic proteinuria.

A repeat 24-hour urine collection for protein is unnecessary for this patient who already has a urine dipstick test that is positive for albuminuria and a previous 24-hour urine collection (gold standard test) that is positive for proteinuria.

Although a spot urine protein–creatinine ratio correlates well with a 24-hour urine collection (which is considered the gold standard for quantifying urine protein if accurately collected) and is more convenient for patients than an extended collection, this patient has already had a 24-hour urine study and a spot collection would not add additional information.

More than 95% of adults will excrete less than 130 mg/24 h of protein in the urine, and the normal value is defined as less than 150 mg/24 h. Reassurance is incorrect for this patient because if orthostatic proteinuria is not established as the cause of her proteinuria, this finding may be an indication of early kidney dysfunction.

KEY POINT

A split urine collection is an appropriate initial evaluation for sustained, isolated proteinuria.

Bibliography

Naderi AS, Reilly RF. Primary care approach to proteinuria. J Am Board Fam Med. 2008;21:569-74. [PMID: 18988725]

Item 6   Answer: C
Educational Objective: *Manage rhabdomyolysis.*

Treatment using rapid infusion of intravenous 0.9% saline is indicated for this patient with rhabdomyolysis, which develops when muscle injury leads to the release of myoglobin and other intracellular muscle contents into the circulation. Rhabdomyolysis most commonly develops after exposure to myotoxic drugs, infection, excessive exertion, or prolonged immobilization. Diagnosis should be considered in patients with a serum creatine kinase level above 5000 U/L who demonstrate blood on urine dipstick testing in the absence of significant hematuria. Complications of rhabdomyolysis include hypocalcemia, hyperphosphatemia, hyperuricemia, metabolic acidosis, acute muscle compartment syndrome, and limb ischemia. Treatment consists of aggressive fluid resuscitation; fluids should be adjusted to maintain an hourly urine output of at least 300 mL until the urine is negative for myoglobin. Acute kidney injury resulting from acute tubular necrosis occurs in approximately one third of patients.

Although dialysis may ultimately be necessary if this patient does not respond to intravenous saline, there are no acute hemodialysis needs at this time. Although he has hyperkalemia, he has no abnormal electrocardiogram findings, and increasing sodium delivery with intravenous fluids through the renal tubules should help renal potassium excretion. If the potassium concentration does not

improve after a trial of intravenous fluids or the patient develops volume overload, dialysis may need to be initiated.

Mannitol is an osmotic agent that increases renal tubular flow; however, in this patient mannitol may also lead to further hypovolemia and has not been shown to be superior to hydration in the treatment of rhabdomyolysis.

This patient's hypernatremia indicates a free water deficit, and his history and examination findings suggest a hypovolemic hypernatremia. Rapid infusion of 5% glucose in water will help correct this patient's water deficit but will not expand his volume and promote urine flow as effectively as sodium-containing intravenous fluid.

KEY POINT

Infusion of intravenous saline is the treatment of choice for rhabdomyolysis.

Bibliography

Better OS, Abassi ZA. Early fluid resuscitation in patients with rhabdomyolysis. Nat Rev Nephrol. 2011;7:416-22. [PMID: 21587227]

Item 7   Answer: B
Educational Objective: *Diagnose hypo-osmolol hyponatremia with decreased effective arterial blood volume.*

This patient's hyponatremia can be characterized as hypo-osmolol hyponatremia with decreased effective arterial blood volume. Hyponatremia is most commonly a marker of hypo-osmolality. Hypo-osmolol hyponatremia is diagnosed by either directly measuring or calculating the serum osmolality: Serum osmolality = $2[Na+] + [blood urea nitrogen]/2.8 + [glucose]/18$. In this patient, the serum osmolality is calculated as 259 mOsm/kg H_2O, indicating hypo-osmolol hyponatremia.

Hypo-osmolol hyponatremia is the most common form of hyponatremia. It may occur in patients with normal, increased, or decreased extracellular fluid (ECF) volumes. The cause of hypo-osmolal hyponatremia can be established by patient history, volume status, urine osmolality, and urine sodium level. This patient's clinical findings of heart failure, high urine osmolality in relation to her serum osmolality, and spot urine sodium level less than 20 mEq/L (20 mmol/L) are consistent with a prerenal state due to decreased effective arterial blood volume. The decreased effective arterial blood volume is the consequence of poor cardiac output in the setting of decompensated heart failure.

Hyperosmolal hyponatremia is caused by marked hyperglycemia or exogenously administered solutes such as mannitol or sucrose. Hyperglycemia causes the translocation of water from the intracellular to the ECF compartment, which results in a decrease in the serum sodium level by approximately 1.6 mEq/L (1.6 mmol/L) for every 100 mg/dL (5.55 mmol/L) increase in the plasma glucose level above 100 mg/dL (5.55 mmol/L). Patients with hypertonic hyponatremia may have decreased effective arterial blood volume as the result of osmotic diuresis.

Absorption of isosmotic irrigating solutions such as glycine or sorbitol can cause isosmotic hyponatremia with a normal effective arterial blood volume. Isosmotic hyponatremia may also occur as a result of pseudohyponatremia. Pseudohyponatremia is a laboratory artifact that may be observed in patients with hyperglobulinemia or severe hyperlipidemia; an increase in the solid phase of a specimen displaces and decreases the effective volume analyzed for sodium content, leading to reporting of an artificially low serum sodium level. Measured serum osmolality is normal in patients with pseudohyponatremia, as is the effective arterial blood volume.

KEY POINT

The cause of hypo-osmolal hyponatremia can be established by patient history, volume status, urine osmolality, and urine sodium level; in a patient with heart failure, increased urine concentration and low urine sodium suggests decreased effective arterial blood volume and hyponatremia due to poor cardiac output and kidney hypoperfusion.

Bibliography
Lien, YH, Shapiro, JI. Hyponatremia: Clinical diagnosis and management. Am J Med. 2007;120:653-8. [PMID:17679119]

Item 8   Answer: C
Educational Objective: *Diagnose rhabdomyolysis-induced hyperkalemia.*

The mechanism of this patient's hyperkalemia is disrupted cell membranes. Hyperkalemia is defined as a serum potassium concentration greater than 5 mEq/L (5 mmol/L). Risk factors include extensive tissue injury, underlying acute or chronic kidney disease, and decreased renin-angiotensin-aldosterone activity. This patient has crush-related rhabdomyolysis as evidenced by the serum creatine kinase elevation and a urinalysis that is dipstick positive for blood in the absence of erythrocytes on urine microscopic examination. Skeletal muscle has higher intracellular potassium content than most other tissues, and large muscle injuries may cause hyperkalemia as the result of cell membrane disruption.

This patient's blood pressure has been stable and adequate to ensure kidney perfusion. Generally, a mean arterial blood pressure (MAP) less than 60 mm Hg is associated with a decreased glomerular filtration rate. This patient's MAP is 80 mm Hg (MAP = diastolic blood pressure + [systolic blood pressure - diastolic blood pressure]/3). This suggests that his glomerular filtration rate is preserved and distal tubule urine flow is maintained.

The presence of hypotension is a stimulus for activation of the renin-angiotensin-aldosterone system. Increased levels of aldosterone result in increased sodium absorption distally in exchange for potassium excretion. Such an exchange may be associated with the development of hypokalemia, not hyperkalemia.

KEY POINT

Skeletal muscle has higher intracellular potassium content than most other tissues, and large muscle injuries may cause hyperkalemia as the result of cell membrane disruption.

Bibliography
Wingo CS. Introduction: potassium homeostasis in humans: our current understanding. Semin Nephrol. 2013;33:205-6. [PMID: 23953796]

Item 9   Answer: B
Educational Objective: *Treat a patient who has symptomatic hyponatremia.*

This patient has symptomatic hypo-omolar hyponatremia, and a rapid increase in the serum sodium level using 3% saline infusion is indicated. The patient's presentation is consistent with the syndrome of inappropriate antidiuretic hormone secretion (SIADH) as the cause of her hyponatremia, likely from her recently started antide-

pressant medication. This diagnosis is based on her low serum osmolality associated with a urine sodium level exceeding 40 mEq/L (40 mmol/L) and urine osmolality that is inappropriately concentrated relative to her serum osmolality (above 100 mOsm/ kg H_2O and usually greater than 300 mOsm/kg H_2O) without evidence of hypovolemia. Although free water restriction is the recommended therapy for asymptomatic patients with SIADH, hypertonic saline (such as 3% saline) is used to treat patients who are symptomatic. Because of its hypertonicity, 3% saline rapidly increases the serum sodium level; a typical goal for treating symptomatic hyponatremia is to increase the serum sodium level to approximately 120 mEq/L (120 mmol/L). However, hypertonic saline must be used with extreme caution to avoid overcorrection and the risk of central nervous system damage resulting from changes in serum osmolality. Recent evidence suggests than an increase in the serum sodium level by approximately 4 to 6 mEq/L (4-6 mmol/L) over the first 24 hours is sufficient in symptomatic patients. If the extracellular fluid osmolality rapidly normalizes in a patient with chronic hyponatremia, cell shrinkage may occur and can precipitate osmotic demyelination syndrome.

Use of 0.9% (normal) saline in patients with SIADH can result in excretion of most of the infused sodium and retention of a significant portion of the infused water, leading to positive water balance and worsening hyponatremia.

Furosemide can be used as adjunctive management of hyponatremia caused by SIADH because this agent interferes with urine concentration and causes excretion of a more dilute urine, thus increasing total water excretion. However, the rapidity of correction expected with furosemide alone is insufficient to increase the serum sodium concentration to an appropriate level in a symptomatic patient.

Tolvaptan, an oral V_2 receptor vasopressin antagonist, is approved to treat patients with asymptomatic euvolemic and hypervolemic hyponatremia. However, the safety of this agent in the management of patients with symptomatic hyponatremia has yet to be established, and too rapid correction and overcorrection of the serum sodium level have been reported.

KEY POINT

Patients with symptomatic hyponatremia due to the syndrome of inappropriate antidiuretic hormone secretion (SIADH) require a rapid increase in the serum sodium level using 3% (hypertonic) saline infusion.

Bibliography
Sterns RH, Hix JK, Silver S. Treating profound hyponatremia: a strategy for controlled correction. Am J Kidney Dis. 2010;56:774-9. [PMID: 20709440]

Item 10   Answer: C
Educational Objective: *Treat hypernatremia.*

The presence of significant hypernatremia indicates a relative deficit of water to sodium, and correction of the water deficit with 5% dextrose in water is indicated for this patient. He is experiencing a postobstructive diuresis and electrolyte imbalance that may occur when chronic urine obstruction causes retention of solute and acute tubular injury. The resulting diuresis is osmotic owing to the retained solute (consistent with the urine osmolality greater than 300 mOsm/kg H_2O) with hypernatremia being caused by a tubular concentrating defect that leads to difficulty in maintaining normal water balance. Administration of free water is indicated to correct the hypernatremia until the osmotic diuresis and tubular injury resolve.

There is little evidence to guide the optimal rate of correction of hypernatremia, but a correction rate of 6 to 10 mEq/L (6-10 mmol/L) per day is reasonable.

The presence of edema and hypernatremia in this patient is indicative of excess total body sodium; therefore, volume expansion with either 0.9% or 0.45% saline is not indicated.

Desmopressin is indicated to treat patients with central diabetes insipidus and can also be used as an adjunct in the management of nephrogenic diabetes insipidus, but this patient's relatively high urine osmolality and high urine volume are most consistent with a solute diuresis.

KEY POINT

Correction of the water deficit using 5% dextrose in water is appropriate in patients with significant hypernatremia without evidence of hypovolemia or sodium depletion.

Bibliography

Pokaharel M, Block CA. Dysnatremia in the ICU. Curr Opin Crit Care. 2011;17: 581-93. [PMID: 22027406]

Item 11   Answer: B

Educational Objective: *Diagnose nephrogenic diabetes insipidus.*

The most likely cause of this patient's hypernatremia is nephrogenic diabetes insipidus (DI). This patient has serum hyperosmolality, as estimated by multiplying the serum sodium level by 2 (304 mOsm/kg [304 μmol/kg]; normal, 275-295 mOsm/kg [275-295 μmol/kg]). The appropriate kidney response to hyperosmolality is to retain free water, which results in concentration of the urine above serum osmolality, up to a potential maximally concentration of greater than 800 mOsm/kg [800 μmol/kg] in younger, healthy patients. This response is not seen in this patient. Therefore, he has either DI or an osmotic diuresis.

Patients with hyperosmolality who have submaximally concentrated urine without evidence of an osmotic diuresis have DI by definition. The diagnosis may be confirmed by a water deprivation test, which should normally demonstrate an increase in urine osmolality with decreased water intake and the resulting increase in serum osmolality; patients with DI fail to show an appropriate increase in urine osmolality as the serum osmolality rises. Distinguishing between central and nephrogenic DI in a patient who already demonstrates hyperosmolality can be done by measuring antidiuretic hormone (ADH) levels (patients with central DI have an inappropriately low level, whereas patients with nephrogenic DI have a normal to elevated level) or by evaluating the response to administering the vasopressor analogue desmopressin (arginine vasopressin). A significant increase in urine osmolality (greater than 50%) within 1 to 2 hours after administration indicates insufficient endogenous ADH secretion, and, therefore, central DI, whereas a lack of response indicates kidney resistance to the effects of arginine vasopressin and, therefore, nephrogenic ID. Nephrogenic DI is an insensitivity of the cortical collecting duct to circulating ADH and can be caused by medications (for example, lithium), hypokalemia, hypercalcemia, sickle cell disease and trait, and amyloidosis. Treatment requires adequate water intake, salt restriction, and, in some patients, a thiazide diuretic. Thiazide diuretics effectively block sodium reabsorption in the distal renal tubule, thereby causing natriuresis.

An osmotic diuresis is most often caused by hyperglycemia and may be occur with ingestion of osmotically active substances such as mannitol. This patient's plasma glucose level does not exceed the kidney threshold for glucose reabsorption (which in most persons is 200 to 225 mg/dL [11.1-12.5 mmol/L]), and he does not report intake of any other potentially causative agents. Furthermore, solute diuresis is usually characterized by isotonicity of the urine, whereas this patient has a markedly hypotonic urine. Consequently, an osmotic diuresis is an unlikely cause of his hypernatremia.

Patients with primary polydipsia also manifest polyuria and polydipsia but do not develop hypernatremia and hyperosmolality. These patients may develop hyponatremia and typically have a clearly identifiable psychiatric illness.

KEY POINT

Patients with hyperosmolality without glucosuria who have submaximally concentrated urine have diabetes insipidus by definition.

Bibliography

Khanna A. Acquired nephrogenic diabetes insipidus. Semin Nephrol. 2006;26:244-8. [PMID: 16713497]

Item 12   Answer: B

Educational Objective: *Treat hyperkalemia in a patient with acute kidney injury.*

In addition to intravenous calcium , insulin, and dextrose, hemodialysis is appropriate for this patient who has significant hyperkalemia with evidence of cardiac conduction abnormalities. These findings warrant emergency treatment. Hyperkalemia is defined as a serum potassium concentration greater than 5 mEq/L (5 mmol/L). Risk factors include underlying acute or chronic kidney disease and decreased renin-angiotensin-aldosterone activity. Clinical manifestations include ascending muscle weakness, electrocardiographic changes, and life-threatening cardiac arrhythmias and paralysis when the hyperkalemia is severe. Intravenous calcium and insulin-dextrose are temporizing measures to decrease the arrhythmogenic effect of excessive potassium on the myocardium, and definitive therapy ultimately requires potassium removal. The presence of concurrent acute kidney injury (AKI) and recent surgery in this patient favor use of hemodialysis.

The efficacy of furosemide in promoting a kaliuresis would likely be impaired in this patient with AKI and low urine output and is not considered a reliable way to treat this degree of life-threatening hyperkalemia.

Sodium bicarbonate has limited efficacy in the management of hyperkalemia in patients with end-stage kidney disease or severe AKI. In these patients, the hypokalemic response is often minimal and is delayed by several hours, which is insufficient to bring about a clinically meaningful decrease in the serum potassium level. Conversely, patients with hyperkalemia, hypovolemia, and metabolic acidosis usually respond well to hydration with sodium bicarbonate.

The cation exchange resin sodium polystyrene sulfonate removes potassium from the body and is useful in long-term control of hyperkalemia in some patients. However, the decrease in the serum potassium concentration with this therapy is not immediate, making this an inadequate treatment for hyperkalemia in patients with acute electrocardiographic changes. Additionally, sodium polystyrene sulfonate is contraindicated in patients who have had recent bowel surgery because these patients are at risk for intestinal necrosis.

Sodium polystyrene sulfonate is contraindicated in the treatment of hyperkalemia in patients who have had recent bowel surgery.

Bibliography

Elliott MJ, Ronksley PE, Clase CM, et al. Management of patients with acute hyperkalemia. CMAJ. 2010;182:1631-5. [PMID: 20855477]

Item 13   Answer: A

Educational Objective: *Understand the mechanism of hypercalcemia in hyperparathyroidism.*

This patient has primary hyperparathyroidism, and the mechanisms responsible for hypercalcemia in this patient include calcium mobilized from bone with increased gastrointestinal (GI) absorption and increased kidney absorption. Primary hyperparathyroidism is the most common cause of hypercalcemia diagnosed in the outpatient setting. The hypercalcemia of primary hyperparathyroidism often is diagnosed incidentally by routine blood testing before the development of symptoms. This disorder also may be found during the evaluation of osteoporosis or nephrolithiasis. Effects of excess parathyroid hormone (PTH) include increased 1,25-dihydroxy vitamin D levels, increased osteoclast-mediated bone resorption, enhanced distal tubular reabsorption of calcium, decreased proximal tubular reabsorption of phosphorus, hypercalcemia, hypophosphatemia, and increased urine phosphate and calcium levels. PTH also up-regulates 1α-hydroxylase expression in the kidney, leading to increased production of 1,25-dihydroxy vitamin D, which further increases GI calcium absorption.

Excessive ingestion of calcium carbonate to treat osteoporosis or dyspepsia can result in hypercalcemia, metabolic alkalosis, and kidney insufficiency. Metabolic alkalosis stimulates the distal tubule to reabsorb calcium, contributing to hypercalcemia. This is commonly termed the "milk-alkali syndrome" and is an example of hypercalcemia due to increased GI and kidney absorption of calcium.

Patients with chronic kidney disease who are receiving calcium carbonate or calcium acetate to bind dietary calcium may develop hypercalcemia because of increased GI absorption of calcium.

Hypercalcemia can result from excessive ingestion or production of either 25-hydroxy vitamin D (calcidiol) or 1,25-dihydroxy vitamin D (calcitriol). The mechanism of hypercalcemia is the result of increasing GI calcium absorption and bone resorption. Two examples of conditions that can lead to endogenous hypervitaminosis D are lymphoma and granulomatous diseases such as sarcoidosis.

Effects of excess parathyroid hormone include increased 1,25-dihydroxy vitamin D levels, increased osteoclast-mediated bone resorption, enhanced distal tubular reabsorption of calcium, decreased proximal tubular reabsorption of phosphorus, hypercalcemia, hypophosphatemia, and increased urine phosphate and calcium levels.

Bibliography

Marcocci C, Cetani F. Clinical practice. Primary hyperparathyroidism. N Engl J Med. 2011;365:2389-97. [PMID: 22187986]

Item 14   Answer: D

Educational Objective: *Evaluate a patient with refeeding syndrome.*

The most likely cause of this patient's hypophosphatemia and associated symptoms is a shift of extracellular phosphorus into the intracellular space resulting in the refeeding syndrome. Hypophosphatemia is defined as a serum phosphorus concentration less than 2.5 mg/dL (0.81 mmol/L) and is most common in patients with a history of chronic alcohol use, critical illness, or malnutrition. Most patients with hypophosphatemia are asymptomatic, but symptoms of weakness may manifest at serum phosphorus levels less than 2.0 mg/dL (0.65 mmol/L). Levels less than 1.0 mg/dL (0.32 mmol/L) may result in respiratory muscle weakness, hemolysis, and rhabdomyolysis. If the refeeding syndrome occurs, the level of nutritional support should be reduced, and the hypophosphatemia, hypokalemia, and hypomagnesemia should be corrected. Moderately to severely ill patients with marked edema or a serum phosphorus level less than 2.0 mg/dL (0.65 mmol/L) should be hospitalized for intravenous therapy to correct electrolyte deficiencies. Continuous telemetry may also be needed to monitor cardiopulmonary physiology.

Hypophosphatemia may result from impaired gastrointestinal absorption, increased renal excretion, or intracellular shift of phosphorus. Refeeding syndrome is caused by an intracellular shift of phosphorus; calories provided to a patient after a prolonged period of starvation serve as a stimulus for cellular growth, which consumes phosphorus in the form of phosphorylated intermediates such as adenosine triphosphate. Persons who chronically abuse alcohol frequently may develop refeeding syndrome, largely because of underlying poor nutrition. The syndrome may also be the result of intravenous infusion of glucose in malnourished patients, as occurred with this patient.

Other causes of hypophosphatemia include renal phosphate wasting, as occurs with proximal (type 2) renal tubular acidosis, hyperparathyroidism, and vitamin D deficiency or resistance. Chronic diarrhea and poor oral intake of phosphorus may cause hypophosphatemia and could be a consideration in this patient. However, her diarrhea resolved and her weakness and other symptoms developed with the onset of intravenous feeding, suggesting the refeeding syndrome as the acute precipitant of her hypophosphatemia.

Refeeding syndrome is caused by an intracellular shift of phosphorus; calories provided to a patient after a prolonged period of starvation serve as a stimulus for cellular growth, which consumes phosphorus in the form of phosphorylated intermediates such as adenosine triphosphate.

Bibliography

Mehanna HM, Moledina J, Travis J. Clinical Review: Refeeding syndrome: what it is, and how to prevent and treat it. BMJ 2008;336:1495-8. [PMID: 18583681]

Item 15   Answer: B

Educational Objective: *Treat hypoparathyroidism occurring after thyroidectomy.*

Calcium is most likely to diminish the acute symptoms in this patient who recently underwent thyroidectomy. Complications of thyroidectomy include the inadvertent removal of or injury to the parathyroid glands. If a substantial amount of parathyroid tissue is not left in vivo, hypoparathyroidism accompanied by hypocalcemia will result postoperatively. Symptoms are primarily neuromuscular, such as paresthesias and muscle cramps, and tend to be prominent in patients who experience a rapid drop in the serum calcium level after surgery. This patient requires an emergent rapid increase in his serum calcium concentration, which is best accomplished by oral calcium (carbonate or citrate) supplementation. Intravenous calcium more rapidly increases the serum calcium level and may be indicated in patients with very low (<7.5 mg/dL [1.9 mmol/L]) calcium levels or more significant clinical findings associated with the hypocalcemia, such as severe musculoskeletal weakness, tetany, or electrocardiographic conduction abnormalities. Ultimately, this patient most likely will require more prolonged calcium therapy, depending on the degree of hypoparathyroidism after surgery.

Although this patient also may require chronic vitamin D supplementation to maintain his serum calcium concentration, this would not be an initial intervention in a symptomatic patient with hypocalcemia. If chronic supplementation is needed, calcitriol (1,25-dihydroxyvitamin D) should be used because the lack of parathyroid hormone will diminish the endogenous conversion of 25-hydroxyvitamin D to the more potent 1,25-dihydroxyvitamin D. However, calcitriol by itself will not effectively increase serum calcium levels until several days have elapsed.

Patients with hypomagnesemia may have hypocalcemia that is refractory to correction until the low magnesium concentrations are repleted. This patient has no evidence of significant hypomagnesemia.

A recombinant form of parathyroid hormone (teriparatide) is available, although its primary use is in the treatment of advanced osteoporosis in selected patients. Although teriparatide holds promise as a potential therapy for chronic hypoparathyroidism, its safety and long-term effectiveness for this indication have not been established, and it does not have Food and Drug Administration approval for treatment of acute hypoparathyroidism.

KEY POINT

In most patients with hypoparathyroidism and hypocalcemia, oral calcium is appropriate emergent therapy because it is rapidly absorbed and will increase the serum calcium level within minutes.

Bibliography

Khan MI, Waguespack SG, Hu MI. Medical management of postsurgical hypoparathyroidism [erratum in: Endocr Pract. 2011;17:967]. Endocr Pract. 2011;17(Suppl 1):18-25. [PMID: 21134871]

Item 16   Answer: D

Educational Objective: *Treat hypercalcemia.*

This patient should be hydrated with 0.9% saline as the next step in treatment. She has severe symptomatic hypercalcemia in the setting of advanced metastatic breast cancer. The history of polyuria and polydipsia and the physical examination findings of tachycardia and dry mucous membranes suggest significant dehydration, which is confirmed by the elevated blood urea nitrogen and serum creatinine levels. High calcium levels impair the ability of the nephron to concentrate urine, which results in inappropriate water loss from the kidney. Therefore, the most appropriate next step in this patient's treatment is to restore euvolemia and begin to lower the serum calcium level by saline diuresis. Normalization of intravascular volume with saline will improve delivery of calcium to the renal tubule and aid in excretion of calcium. As the kidneys excrete excess sodium from the saline, excretion of calcium will follow.

Hypercalcemia of malignancy may be due to local osteolytic hypercalcemia or to humoral hypercalcemia of malignancy, in which a tumor that does not involve the skeleton secretes a circulating factor that activates bone resorption. In this patient, the liver metastases are likely secreting parathyroid hormone–related protein. Control of the tumor with chemotherapy may help with longer-term control of this patient's hypercalcemia.

Bisphosphonate therapy may be needed if this patient's hypercalcemia continues after rehydration, and intravenous furosemide may be appropriate after she is adequately hydrated in order to maintain euvolemia. Glucocorticoid therapy could be considered if bisphosphonate treatment does not adequately lower the serum calcium level. However, none of these treatments should be attempted before the patient is rehydrated with 0.9% saline.

KEY POINT

In patients with acute hypercalcemia, normalization of intravascular volume with saline will improve delivery of calcium to the renal tubule and aid in excretion of calcium.

Bibliography

Stewart, AF. Clinical practice. Hypercalcemia associated with cancer. N Engl J Med. 2005;352:373-9. [PMID: 15673803]

Item 17   Answer: C

Educational Objective: *Diagnose hypokalemic type 1 (distal) renal tubular acidosis.*

This patient most likely has type 1 (distal) renal tubular acidosis (RTA), a disorder characterized by normal anion gap metabolic acidosis and hypokalemia. Causes of type 1 RTA include autoimmune disorders such as Sjögren syndrome, systemic lupus erythematosus, or rheumatoid arthritis; drugs such as lithium or amphotericin B; hypercalciuria; and hyperglobulinemia. The kidney's ability to excrete hydrogen ions in response to acidemia is impaired in patients with type 1 RTA, resulting in an inappropriately alkali pH of the urine in the presence of a systemic acidosis. The persistently increased pH encourages the development of kidney stones. Therefore, the pH above 6.0 in the setting of acidemia and the presence of nephrocalcinosis in this patient support the diagnosis of hypokalemic type 1 RTA.

Gitelman syndrome is an autosomal recessive syndrome characterized by hypokalemic metabolic alkalosis, not acidosis as noted in this patient. The defect is due to inactivating mutations in the gene for the thiazide-sensitive sodium chloride cotransporter in the distal convoluted tubule, and the electrolyte profile is analogous to that induced by thiazide diuretics.

Laxative abuse may also present with a hypokalemic normal anion gap metabolic acidosis. Patients with increased gastrointestinal losses of bicarbonate and potassium have intact renal tubular function that results in a compensatory increase in urine ammonium production, indicating increased acid secretion by the kidney. Urine ammonium may be estimated by calculating the urine anion gap using the formula:

Urine anion gap (UAG) = ([urine sodium] + [urine potassium]) – [urine chloride]

The UAG is normally between 30 and 50 mEq/L (30-50 mmol/L). Metabolic acidosis originating outside the kidney is suggested by a large negative UAG caused by significantly increased urine ammonium excretion. Conversely, metabolic acidosis of kidney origin is suggested by a positive UAG related to minimal urine ammonium excretion. This patient's urine anion gap is positive and is therefore not consistent with laxative abuse.

Type 2 (proximal) RTA, a defect in regenerating bicarbonate in the proximal tubule, is characterized by a normal anion gap metabolic acidosis, hypokalemia, glycosuria (in the setting of a normal plasma glucose level), low-molecular-weight proteinuria, and kidney phosphate wasting. However, distal urine acidification mechanisms are intact, and the urine pH is less than 5.5 in the absence of alkali therapy. Type 2 RTA is not associated with nephrocalcinosis or nephrolithiasis. This patient's normal urinalysis, high urine pH, and nephrocalcinosis are inconsistent with Type 2 RTA.

KEY POINT

Hypokalemic distal (type 1) renal tubular acidosis is characterized by normal anion gap metabolic acidosis, hypokalemia, a urine pH greater than 6.0, and nephrocalcinosis.

Bibliography

Comer DM, Droogan AG, Young IS, et al. Hypokalaemic paralysis precipitated by distal renal tubular acidosis secondary to Sjögren's syndrome. Ann Clin Biochem. 2008;45(Pt 2):221-5. [PMID: 18325192]

Item 18   Answer: D

Educational Objective: *Diagnose respiratory alkalosis.*

This patient has a respiratory alkalosis. The presence of an alkaline arterial pH with a low Pco_2 is compatible with respiratory alkalosis. There is complete, appropriate compensation for the primary process, which is often described as being a "pure" acid-base disorder. In acute respiratory alkalosis, for each 10 mm Hg (1.3 kPa) decline in Pco_2 the expected decline in the serum bicarbonate level is 2 mEq/L (2 mmol/L). Since this patient's Pco_2 declined by 10 mm Hg (1.3 kPa) to 30 mm Hg (4.0 kPa), the expected decline in the serum bicarbonate level is 2 mEq/L (2 mmol/L); this matches the measured serum bicarbonate concentration exactly.

Because the decline in the serum bicarbonate level is appropriate for the degree of respiratory alkalosis, this patient cannot have an accompanying metabolic acidosis or metabolic alkalosis. Furthermore, because her anion gap is normal, there is no possibility that an anion-gap metabolic acidosis is present in addition to the respiratory alkalosis. The anion gap is 10, calculated as $[Na^+] - ([Cl^-] + [HCO_3^-])$. The normal anion gap is 12 ± 2.

Because the Pco_2 is depressed rather than elevated, the diagnosis cannot be respiratory acidosis.

There are many potential causes of respiratory alkalosis, and the physical examination is often helpful in identifying the correct diagnosis. Common causes of respiratory alkalosis include psychogenic causes (for example, hyperventilation associated with anxiety), pulmonary vascular disease (for example, pulmonary hypertension or pulmonary embolism), pulmonary parenchymal disease (for example, pneumonia or pulmonary fibrosis), heart failure, sepsis, cirrhosis, and normal pregnancy.

KEY POINT

In acute respiratory alkalosis, for each 10 mm Hg (1.3 kPa) decline in Pco_2, the expected decline in the serum bicarbonate level is 2 mEq/L (2 mmol/L).

Bibliography

Palmer BF. Approach to fluid and electrolyte disorders and acid-base problems. Prim Care. 2008;35:195-213. [PMID: 18486713]

Item 19   Answer: B

Educational Objective: *Diagnose respiratory acidosis due to COPD.*

This patient's acid-base disorder is a respiratory acidosis. Respiratory acidosis is caused by any process associated with primary retention of carbon dioxide. In this patient, the arterial pH is less than 7.38 and the Pco_2 is greater than 40 mm Hg (5.3 kPa), indicating the presence of a respiratory acidosis. Kidney compensation for persistent hypercapnia results from stimulation of secretion of protons at the level of the distal nephron. The urine pH decreases, and excretion of urine ammonium, titratable acid, and chloride is enhanced. Consequently, the reabsorption of bicarbonate throughout the nephron is enhanced. The predicted increase in the serum bicarbonate level is calculated as 1 mEq/L (1 mmol/L) for each 10 mm Hg (1.3 kPa) increase in Pco_2 (acute) or 4 mEq/L (4 mmol/L) for each 10 mm Hg (1.3 kPa) increase in Pco_2 (chronic). Because this patient with COPD probably has chronic retention of carbon dioxide, an increase in the serum bicarbonate level by at least 8 mEq/L (8 mmol/L) is expected. This is consistent with the measured serum bicarbonate level. Therefore, there is appropriate compensation for the respiratory acidosis.

There is no evidence for a coexisting metabolic acidosis with an elevated serum bicarbonate level. Respiratory alkalosis is not consistent with the observed decrease in the arterial pH.

KEY POINT

In respiratory acidosis, the predicted increase in the serum bicarbonate level is calculated as 1 mEq/L (1 mmol/L) for each 10 mm Hg (1.3 kPa) increase in Pco_2 (acute) or 4 mEq/L (4 mmol/L) for each 10 mm Hg (1.3 kPa) increase in Pco_2 (chronic).

Bibliography

Palmer BF. Approach to fluid and electrolyte disorders and acid-base problems. Prim Care. 2008;35:195-213. [PMID: 18486713]

Item 20   Answer: C

Educational Objective: *Evaluate a patient who has hypokalemic metabolic alkalosis.*

Measurement of the urine chloride level is the most appropriate test to determine the cause of this patient's hypokalemic metabolic alkalosis. Metabolic alkalosis is caused by the net loss of acid or the retention of bicarbonate. The diagnostic evaluation of metabolic alkalosis begins with the clinical assessment of volume status and blood pressure. Metabolic alkalosis that is associated with hypovolemia will correct with the administration of isotonic saline and volume expansion and is thus considered saline-responsive. Metabolic alkalosis that is associated with increased extracellular fluid volume and hypertension will not respond to isotonic saline and is termed saline-resistant. In this patient who does not have hypertension and has a normal or slightly decreased effective arterial blood volume, the urine chloride level can help distinguish the various causes of metabolic alkalosis. Patients with low urine chloride levels (<15 mEq/L [15 mmol/L]; normal for men, 25-371 mEq/L [25-371 mmol/L]) are usually either vomiting or have a decreased effective arterial blood volume from various causes, including prior use of diuretics or low cardiac output. Patients with high urine chloride levels (>15 mEq/L [15 mmol/L]) most commonly are currently receiving therapy with diuretics or, more rarely, may have a genetically based tubular disorder such as Bartter syndrome or Gitelman syndrome.

Measurement of plasma aldosterone and renin levels is most helpful in the diagnostic evaluation of metabolic alkalosis with associated hypertension. A plasma aldosterone-plasma renin activity ratio of 20 to 30 when the plasma aldosterone level is greater than 15 ng/dL (414 pmol/L) is highly suggestive of primary hyperaldosteronism, whereas suppression of both renin and aldosterone is consistent with syndromes of apparent mineralocorticoid excess. Plasma aldosterone and renin levels are elevated in patients with malignant hypertension, renin-secreting tumors, and renovascular hypertension.

Hypomagnesemia can lead to urine magnesium wasting and metabolic alkalosis and can be observed in patients with Bartter syndrome or Gitelman syndrome. However, the serum magnesium level is not as helpful as the urine chloride value in distinguishing between the various causes of hypokalemic metabolic alkalosis.

The urine osmolal gap is a method of estimating urine ammonium excretion and is useful in the evaluation of normal anion gap metabolic acidosis. Ammonium excretion is variable in metabolic alkalosis and depends on numerous factors, including the magnitude of potassium depletion, protein intake, and volume status.

KEY POINT

The diagnostic evaluation of metabolic alkalosis begins with the clinical assessment of volume status and blood pressure; measurement of urine sodium and chloride levels can help distinguish the various causes.

Bibliography
Khanna A, Kurtzman NA. Metabolic alkalosis. J Nephrol. 2006;19 Suppl 9:S86-96. [PMID: 16736446]

Item 21   Answer: A

Educational Objective: *Diagnose a mixed acid-base disorder.*

The most likely acid-base disorder is metabolic acidosis, metabolic alkalosis, and respiratory acidosis. The low arterial pH defines acidosis; the finding of a low serum bicarbonate level further defines the acidosis as metabolic acidosis. The increased anion gap categorizes the metabolic acidosis as an increased anion-gap acidosis. The Pco_2 measurement determines if respiratory compensation is appropriate for the degree of metabolic acidosis. The adequacy of respiratory compensation can be checked using the Winter formula:

$$\text{Expected } Pco_2 = (1.5 \times [HCO_3] + 8) \pm 2 = 26 \pm 2$$

This formula confirms that the measured Pco_2 is inappropriately elevated for the degree of expected compensation for metabolic acidosis, establishing the diagnosis of concurrent respiratory acidosis. Finally, the corrected serum bicarbonate level is calculated to determine if a complicating metabolic disturbance is present:

$$\text{Corrected } [HCO_3] = \text{measured } [HCO_3] + (\text{measured anion gap} - 12)$$

Using this formula, the corrected serum bicarbonate level (the expected bicarbonate concentration if no other acid-base disturbances are present) is 31 mEq/L (31 mmol/L); this level suggests the presence of a complicating metabolic alkalosis.

Mixed acid-base disturbances are common in patients with multiple medical issues affecting the metabolic and respiratory systems; therefore, careful evaluation is required to understand the underlying processes involved.

KEY POINT

To diagnose a mixed acid-base disorder, it is necessary to evaluate the arterial pH, expected Pco_2, anion gap, and serum bicarbonate and corrected serum bicarbonate levels.

Bibliography
Palmer BF. Approach to fluid and electrolyte disorders and acid-base problems. Prim Care. 2008;35:195-213. [PMID: 18486713]

Item 22   Answer: C

Educational Objective: *Diagnose a mixed metabolic alkalosis and respiratory alkalosis disorder.*

The patient has metabolic alkalosis and respiratory alkalosis. Metabolic alkalosis is indicated by the high serum bicarbonate level and an arterial pH greater than 7.40. Respiratory compensation for the metabolic alkalosis is not appropriate; the Pco_2 would be expected to increase by 0.7 mm Hg (0.09 kPa) for each 1 mEq/L (1 mmol/L) increase in the serum bicarbonate level (to approximately 47 mm Hg (6.3 kPa) in this patient). However, his Pco_2 has decreased to 36 mm Hg (4.8 kPa), indicating the presence of a concurrent respiratory alkalosis. The metabolic alkalosis is probably a result of vomiting, and the respiratory alkalosis is most likely due to pain-induced hyperventilation, both of which are effects of the patient's kidney stone.

KEY POINT

A mixed metabolic alkalosis and respiratory alkalosis is suggested by an elevated arterial pH and serum bicarbonate concentration and a Pco_2 concentration that is lower than expected for the degree of alkalosis.

Bibliography
Palmer BF. Approach to fluid and electrolyte disorders and acid-base problems. Prim Care. 2008;35:195-213. [PMID: 18486713]

Item 23   Answer: D

Educational Objective: *Diagnose prerenal azotemia.*

This patient most likely has prerenal azotemia. Prerenal azotemia generally occurs in patients with a mean arterial pressure below 60 mm Hg but may occur at higher pressures in patients with chronic kidney disease or in those who take medications, such as nonsteroidal anti-inflammatory drugs (NSAIDs), that can alter glomerular hemodynamics. Patients with prerenal azotemia may have a history of decreased fluid intake accompanied by examination findings consistent with volume depletion. This patient was exposed to the sun for a prolonged period and took ibuprofen before going to the emergency department. She also takes hydrochlorothiazide daily for hypertension. Although her fractional excretion of sodium (FE_{Na}) is greater than 1%, she is on a diuretic, which can increase the FE_{Na} even in patients with prerenal azotemia. Because the fractional excretion of urea is less influenced by diuretics, it can be helpful in evaluating patients on diuretic therapy. It is calculated similarly to the FE_{Na} using the serum and urine urea levels. In euvolemic patients, the fractional excretion of urea is usually ≥35%, and in those with prerenal azotemia, the fractional excretion of urea is typically below 35%, as in this patient. Finally, her urine is concentrated, with hyaline casts and a high urine specific gravity.

Acute interstitial nephritis is most commonly caused by a hypersensitivity reaction to a medication. Urinalysis findings include leukocyte casts and eosinophils, neither of which is present in this patient.

Acute tubular necrosis (ATN) is characterized by damage to the renal tubule due to a physiologic insult to the kidney, such as hypoxia, toxins, or prolonged hypoperfusion. Kidney failure tends to be rapid, and the urine traditionally contains muddy brown casts. Although ATN may result from prolonged prerenal azotemia, this patient's clinical presentation and urinalysis are not consistent with this diagnosis.

NSAIDs can induce acute kidney injury (AKI) by several mechanisms and may also exacerbate other causes of AKI. Although ibuprofen taken prior to presentation may have worsened the effect of volume contraction on this patient's kidney function, a single dose would likely not be the primary cause of her AKI.

KEY POINT

Patients with prerenal azotemia may have a history of decreased fluid intake accompanied by examination findings consistent with volume depletion.

Bibliography

Gotfried J, Wiesen J, Raina R, et al. Finding the cause of acute kidney injury: which index of fractional excretion is better? Cleve Clin J Med. 2012;79:121-6. [PMID: 22301562]

Item 24   Answer: C

Educational Objective: *Diagnose obstructive acute kidney injury.*

Kidney ultrasonography is indicated for this patient with acute kidney injury (AKI) most likely caused by urinary obstruction. Because relief of obstruction can reverse kidney injury and prevent chronic damage, timely diagnosis is essential. Urinary obstruction can be asymptomatic and can be associated with no noted change in urine output. Because of the lack of definitive symptoms on presentation, kidney imaging, typically ultrasonography, should be considered for all patients with AKI, particularly when risk factors for obstruction are present. Medical history findings (including pelvic tumors or irradiation, congenital urinary tract abnormalities, kidney stones, genitourinary infections, various procedures or surgeries, and prostatic enlargement) should increase suspicion for obstruction. Bladder ultrasonography, rather than kidney imaging, can be done as a quick bedside procedure and may also diagnose bladder obstruction; however, it will not reveal hydronephrosis or kidney anatomy.

In obstruction, the urine sediment is bland (no leukocytes, erythrocytes, or erythrocyte casts). Urine electrolytes are variable; in early obstruction, the urine sodium concentration and fractional excretion of sodium (FE_{Na}) may be low, but in late obstruction, the urine sodium concentration and FE_{Na} may be high, indicative of tubular damage. Therefore, the FE_{Na} is not helpful in evaluating for possible obstruction. Because of impaired kidney excretion of potassium, acid, and water, hyperkalemic metabolic acidosis and hyponatremia may also be present.

Kidney biopsy is performed to evaluate for kidney injury of unknown cause. In this patient with a history suggestive of obstruction, imaging to exclude obstruction should be done first.

Rhabdomyolysis is associated with an increased serum creatine kinase level and can cause elevated serum creatinine and potassium levels; however, this patient has no risk factors for rhabdomyolysis (crush injury, muscle pain, or medications known to cause rhabdomyolysis), and serum creatine kinase measurement is not indicated.

KEY POINT

Kidney imaging, typically ultrasonography, should be considered in all patients with acute kidney injury, particularly when risk factors for obstruction are present.

Bibliography

Licurse A, Kim MC, Dziura J, et al. Renal ultrasonography in the evaluation of acute kidney injury: developing a risk stratification framework. Arch Intern Med. 2010;170:1900-7. [PMID: 21098348]

Item 25   Answer: B

Educational Objective: *Diagnose ischemic acute tubular necrosis.*

This patient's urine sediment findings and clinical presentation support a diagnosis of acute tubular necrosis (ATN). In this patient, ATN was likely precipitated by pneumonia with associated hypotension and hypoxemia. Aside from prerenal acute kidney failure, ATN is the most common cause of acute kidney failure in the hospital setting. The urine findings of muddy brown casts, tubular epithelial cell casts, high urine sodium concentration (>20 mEq/L [20 mmol/L]) in a patient with oliguria and a fractional excretion of sodium (FE_{Na}) greater than 1% are characteristic of ATN.

Acute interstitial nephritis is characterized by pyuria, leukocyte casts, and urine eosinophils; often there is a history of medication use (especially β-lactam agents or nonsteroidal anti-inflammatory drugs, although almost any drug can be causative) and rash.

Bladder outlet obstruction, a form of postrenal acute kidney failure, may occur in older men with prostate enlargement. Chronic urinary retention due to bladder outlet obstruction may cause tubular damage due to increased pressure within the urinary tract. Although there is no specific bladder volume of urine samples obtained by catheterization that is diagnostic of chronic urinary retention, volumes less than 400 mL are less likely to be associated with significant obstruction.

Prerenal acute kidney failure also occurs in the setting of volume depletion, cirrhosis (including hepatorenal syndrome), heart failure, sepsis, and impaired kidney autoregulation. However, prerenal azotemia is associated with sodium retention, as evidenced by a urine sodium concentration less than 10 mEq/L (10 mmol/L), FE_{Na} less than 1%, and a bland urine sediment (no leukocytes, erythrocytes, or erythrocyte casts).

KEY POINT

Acute tubular necrosis is associated with muddy brown casts and tubular epithelial cell casts in the urine sediment, and, in a patient with oliguria, a high urine sodium concentration and a fractional excretion of sodium greater than 1%.

Bibliography

Gill N, Nally JV Jr, Fatica RA. Renal failure secondary to acute tubular necrosis: epidemiology, diagnosis, and management. Chest. 2005;128:2847-63. [PMID: 16236963]

Item 26   Answer: A

Educational Objective: *Assess the risk of contrast-induced nephropathy in a patient with chronic kidney disease.*

Hydration with intravenous isotonic saline is indicated to decrease this patient's risk for contrast-induced nephropathy (CIN) associated with her scheduled cardiac catheterization. Patients with underlying kidney injury are particularly susceptible to additional kidney injury caused by exposure of the renal tubule to nephrotoxic contrast media. Thus, avoidance of exposure to contrast in high-risk patients is preferable. However, in patients who require contrast studies, use of low osmolar contrast agents and hydration to promote urine flow and avoid volume contraction has been shown to decrease the risk for CIN. There is some evidence that isotonic saline is preferable to hypotonic solutions for periprocedural hydration. Multiple studies have evaluated use of intravenous 0.9% saline or intravenous fluids containing isotonic sodium bicarbonate as the prophylactic fluid. At this time, neither formulation appears significantly more effective than the other.

Although given to increasing urine flow, diuresis with a loop diuretic (such as furosemide) or mannitol has not been shown to decrease the risk for CIN and may even increase the risk.

Oral hydration, with or without sodium loading, has not been shown to be more effective, and may even be less effective, than intravenous hydration with isotonic saline.

Prophylactic hemodialysis has been evaluated as a method for removing nephrotoxic contrast agents in patients with existing kidney failure. No benefit has been shown, and outcomes may possibly be poorer than outcomes following medical therapy.

KEY POINT

Hydration with intravenous isotonic saline is indicated to decrease the risk of contrast-induced nephropathy in patients with underlying kidney injury.

Bibliography

Solomon R, Dauerman HL. Contrast-induced acute kidney injury. Circulation. 2010;122:2451-5. [PMID: 21135373]

Item 27   Answer: D

Educational Objective: *Diagnose rapidly progressive glomerulonephritis.*

This patient most likely has rapidly progressive glomerulonephritis (RPGN), a clinical syndrome characterized by urine findings consistent with glomerular disease and rapid loss of kidney function over a period of days, weeks, or months. RPGN is most typically due to either anti–glomerular basement membrane antibody disease, immune complex deposition (for example, lupus nephritis), or an antineutrophil cytoplasmic antibody-positive vasculitis. Glomerulonephritis is characterized by hematuria, oliguria, hypertension, and kidney insufficiency caused by glomerular inflammation. Urinalysis usually reveals hematuria as well as cellular and granular casts, and proteinuria is typically present. This patient has a subacute illness with generalized symptoms of decline, poorly controlled hypertension, and periorbital and lower extremity edema. These findings, along with the presence of erythrocyte casts on urinalysis, make the diagnosis of RPGN most likely.

Acute interstitial nephritis may present with hematuria but more often with pyuria and leukocyte casts. Furthermore, poorly con-

trolled hypertension and periorbital edema are not in the typical constellation of symptoms associated with this disorder.

Acute tubular necrosis (ATN) is a common form of intrarenal disease that usually occurs after a sustained period of ischemia or exposure to nephrotoxic agents. More than 70% of patients with ATN have muddy brown casts in the urine. This patient's rapid clinical course, absence of risk factors for ATN, and presence of erythrocyte casts in the urine are inconsistent with ATN.

Polyarteritis nodosa is a vasculitis of medium-sized vessels. Clinical features include hypertension, variable kidney insufficiency, and, occasionally, bleeding due to kidney infarction caused by rupture of a renal artery microaneurysm. Urinalysis may show hematuria and subnephrotic-range proteinuria; however, because there is no inflammation or necrosis of glomeruli, erythrocyte casts are not seen.

KEY POINT

Rapidly progressive glomerulonephritis is characterized by hematuria, oliguria, hypertension, and kidney injury caused by glomerular inflammation.

Bibliography

Mukhtyar C, Guillevin L, Cid MC, et al; European Vasculitis Study Group. EULAR recommendations for the management of primary small and medium vessel vasculitis. Ann Rheum Dis. 2009;68:310-7. [PMID: 18413444]

Item 28   Answer: B

Educational Objective: *Diagnose hemolytic uremic syndrome.*

The most likely cause of this patient's acute kidney injury (AKI) is hemolytic uremic syndrome (HUS), which is caused by some strains of *Escherichia coli*, including the O157:H7 strain that produces Shiga-like toxin. Shiga-like toxin is destructive against small blood vessels such as those found in the digestive tract and the kidneys; one specific target for the toxin is the vascular endothelium of the glomerulus, causing cell death, breakdown of the endothelium, hemorrhage, and activation of platelets and inflammatory pathways resulting in intravascular thrombosis and hemolysis. This patient manifests the classic triad for HUS, including microangiopathic hemolytic anemia (anemia, elevated reticulocyte count and lactate dehydrogenase level, low haptoglobin level, and schistocytes on the peripheral blood smear), thrombocytopenia, and AKI in the setting of dysentery caused by an enteric pathogen.

Acute tubular necrosis is an unlikely diagnosis in a patient with microangiopathic hemolytic anemia, thrombocytopenia, and evidence of glomerular damage (erythrocyte casts in the urine). Patients with acute tubular necrosis are more likely to present with muddy brown casts.

Postinfectious glomerulonephritis more commonly occurs after streptococcal and staphylococcal infections and characteristically has a latency period of 7 to 120 days before the onset of AKI. Postinfectious glomerulonephritis is not associated with microangiopathic hemolytic anemia.

Scleroderma renal crisis (SRC) occurs almost exclusively in patients with early diffuse cutaneous systemic sclerosis. This condition is characterized by the acute onset of severe hypertension, kidney failure, and microangiopathic hemolytic anemia. SRC is not associated with bloody diarrhea, and the absence of skin findings in this patient makes this diagnosis unlikely.

Patients with hemolytic uremic syndrome typically present with the classic triad of microangiopathic hemolytic anemia, thrombocytopenia, and acute kidney injury.

Bibliography

Zipfel PF, Heinen S, Skerka C. Thrombotic microangiopathies: new insights and new challenges. Curr Opin Nephrol Hypertens. 2010;19:372-8. [PMID: 20539230]

Item 29   Answer: A

Educational Objective: *Prevent progression of chronic kidney disease.*

The intervention most likely to slow the progression of this patient's chronic kidney disease (CKD) is to decrease the blood pressure to at least less than 140/90 mm Hg, and possibly to less than 130/80 mm Hg. Blood pressure control has been shown to delay CKD progression. The Eighth Report of the Joint National Committee on Prevention, Detection, Evaluation, and Treatment of High Blood Pressure recommends a target blood pressure of less than 140/90 mm Hg for patients with kidney disease, preferably with agents that block angiotensin (angiotensin-converting enzyme [ACE] inhibitors or angiotensin receptor blockers [ARBs]) to treat patients with hypertension and CKD because of evidence showing that these agents improve kidney outcomes, regardless of whether or not proteinuria is present. This recommendation applies to patients with hypertension and CKD regardless of diabetic status or race. Other guidelines suggest a lower blood pressure goal of 130/80 mm Hg in patients with chronic kidney disease and significant proteinuria (eg, 500 mg/d) or with diabetes. Because this patient's blood pressure is above either goal level, more aggressive control of his blood pressure would be the most effective intervention in slowing the progression of his kidney disease.

In patients with type 1 or type 2 diabetes mellitus and microalbuminuria, findings from randomized controlled trials indicate that achieving a hemoglobin A_{1c} value of approximately 7% significantly decreases the risk of developing overt proteinuria. This patient's hemoglobin A_{1c} value is already below 7%, and interventions should now target blood pressure control.

Proteinuria may be one of the earliest indicators of diabetic kidney disease, and severe proteinuria, such as in this patient, indicates an increased risk of progression to advanced kidney disease. A primary goal of treatment in patients with diabetes and proteinuria is aggressive blood pressure control with an ACE inhibitor or ARB that decrease the risk of cardiovascular risks and progression of diabetic kidney disease. Although some treatment guidelines recommend a reduction of the daily protein loss in diabetics to 500-1000 mg/d, there is no evidence that lowering urinary protein into the normal range of <300 mg/d (or a urine albumin-creatinine ration of <30 mg/g) is of additional benefit. Overly aggressive therapy with antihypertensive medications or the combination of an ACE inhibitor and ARB are not recommended due to the risks of reducing glomerular capillary perfusion pressure or electrolyte abnormalities, such as hyperkalemia.

Erythropoietin stimulating agents (ESAs) should be considered for patients with symptomatic anemia attributable to erythropoietin deficiency when the hemoglobin level is less than 10 g/dL (100 g/L), adjusting the dose to a target hemoglobin level of 10 to 11 g/dL (100-110 g/L). Use of ESAs, however, is not associated with decreasing the progression of kidney disease. Additionally, using ESAs to increase the hemoglobin level above 11 to 12 g/dL (110-120 g/L) is associated with increased mortality for patients on kidney dialysis.

The Eighth Report of the Joint National Committee on Prevention, Detection, Evaluation, and Treatment of High Blood Pressure recommends a target blood pressure of less than 140/90 mm Hg for patients with kidney disease.

Bibliography

James PA, Oparil S, Carter BL, et al. 2014 Evidence-Based Guideline for the Management of High Blood Pressure in Adults. Report from the Panel Members Appointed to the Eighth Joint National Committee (JNC8). JAMA. 2014;311:507-20. [PMID: 24352797]

Item 30   Answer: D

Educational Objective: *Screen for chronic kidney disease.*

This patient should be screened for chronic kidney disease (CKD) with a serum creatinine measurement, estimated glomerular filtration rate (GFR), and urinalysis. Although there is no clear benefit to screening average-risk adults for kidney disease (including serum creatinine testing or urinalysis as part of routine health surveillance), recognizing patients at risk for CKD is imperative because this disease can be asymptomatic. Certain findings on the medical history, including diabetes mellitus and hypertension, and predisposing risk factors should prompt screening for CKD. In particular, evaluation for diseases that can damage the kidneys directly (such as scleroderma) or can cause damage because of the treatment required (such as cisplatin) is indicated. A family history of CKD is a risk factor, as more evidence points to an inherited predisposition to CKD. A history of acute kidney injury (AKI) is recognized as a risk for future AKI and CKD. Various genitourinary abnormalities also can cause CKD. Screening for CKD includes measurement of the serum creatinine level and estimation of GFR as well as urinalysis to evaluate for blood, protein, and casts. Although evidence is lacking that targeted screening improves clinical outcomes, the National Kidney Foundation guidelines recommend targeted screening for CKD. Guidelines, however, do not support screening of the general population for kidney disease.

A 24-hour urine collection for creatinine clearance is generally used to obtain a precise estimation of kidney function, which is needed in circumstances such as the evaluation of living-donor kidney transplant candidates. It is not a screening test for CKD because of the difficulty and inconvenience in obtaining the specimen.

Kidney imaging (usually ultrasonography) should be considered if results of the serum creatinine measurement or urinalysis are abnormal. Except for patients with a family history of polycystic kidney disease, imaging is not an initial screening study for CKD.

Radionuclide kidney clearance scanning is considered the gold standard for estimating GFR in healthy persons and in patients with AKI. However, use of these studies is limited because of cost, lack of widespread availability, and operator technical difficulties.

Patients with a family history of chronic kidney disease should be screened for the disease with a serum creatinine measurement, estimated glomerular filtration rate, and urinalysis.

Bibliography

Drawz P, Rahman M. In the clinic. Chronic kidney disease. Ann Intern Med. 2009;150: ITC2-1-15. [PMID: 19189903]

Item 31   Answer: C

Educational Objective: *Screen for chronic kidney disease in a patient with diabetes mellitus.*

A spot urine albumin–creatinine ratio is indicated to evaluate this patient for chronic kidney disease (CKD). She has type 2 diabetes mellitus, a disease associated with increased risk for CKD, and testing for moderately increased albuminuria (microalbuminuria) is appropriate. The National Kidney Foundation and the American Diabetes Association recommend annual testing to assess urine albumin excretion in patients with type 1 diabetes of 5 years' duration and in all patients with type 2 diabetes starting at the time of diagnosis by measuring the urine albumin–creatinine ratio. Moderately increased albuminuria (microalbuminuria) is defined as an albumin–creatinine ratio of 30 to 300 mg/g; diagnosis requires an elevated albumin–creatinine ratio on two of three random samples obtained over 6 months. Patients with diabetes and moderately increased albuminuria (microalbuminuria) are at increased risk for progression of CKD and cardiovascular disease. Use of angiotensin-converting enzyme inhibitors or angiotensin receptor blockers delays progression of CKD in patients with proteinuric kidney disease or in patients with diabetes and microalbuminuria, underscoring the importance of early detection.

The gold standard for measuring urine protein excretion is a 24-hour urine collection. However, this test is cumbersome and unreliable if not collected correctly. Patients have a difficult time accurately collecting and storing urine for 24 hours. Therefore, obtaining urine ratios on random urine samples is recommended as an alternative method of estimating proteinuria in the clinical assessment of kidney disease. Furthermore, a 24-hour urine collection may not diagnose low-grade microalbuminuria.

Kidney ultrasonography can be performed once a diagnosis of CKD is made but should not be used to screen for CKD.

Although this patient has an estimated glomerular filtration rate of greater than 60 mL/min/1.73 m^2 and normal urinalysis results, she has diabetes and should therefore be evaluated for CKD.

KEY POINT

Annual testing is recommended to assess urine albumin excretion in patients with type 1 diabetes mellitus of 5 years' duration and in all patients with type 2 diabetes starting at the time of diagnosis by measuring the urine albumin–creatinine ratio.

Bibliography

KDOQI. KDOQI clinical practice guidelines and clinical practice recommendations for diabetes and chronic kidney disease. Am J Kidney Dis. 2007;49(2 Suppl 2):S12-S154. [PMID: 17276798]

Item 32   Answer: C

Educational Objective: *Evaluate a patient with chronic kidney disease.*

Kidney ultrasonography is indicated for this patient with stage 3 chronic kidney disease (CKD), based on an estimated glomerular filtration rate (GFR) of 37 mL/min/1.73 m^2. He has not yet been evaluated for the cause of his CKD, which may have implications for therapy, including future kidney transplantation. The patient's mother had known CKD, raising the possibility that there is a genetic component to this patient's CKD. Kidney ultrasonography is often the first imaging choice to assess kidney disease because it is safe, not dependent upon kidney function, noninvasive, and relatively inexpensive. Because it does not require contrast dye, ultrasonography does not place patients at risk for contrast-induced nephropathy. Kidney ultrasonography can show small echogenic kidneys, elements of obstruction, or other chronic entities such as autosomal dominant polycystic kidney disease.

Abdominal computed tomography (CT) can reveal information regarding causes of CKD and may be used for patients who are not suitable for ultrasonography (for example, unable to undergo imaging because of obesity or large amounts of intestinal gas). However, CT is more costly than ultrasonography, exposes patients to additional radiation, and may involve use of intravenous iodinated contrast agents, which are associated with a risk for contrast-induced nephropathy in patients with an estimated GFR of less than 60 mL/min/1.73 m^2. Experts therefore recommend against the use of these agents in this population group.

Kidney biopsy is predominantly used in patients with glomerular disease. The most common indications for kidney biopsy include the nephrotic syndrome, acute glomerulonephritis, and kidney transplant dysfunction. None of these indications is present in this patient.

Radionuclide kidney clearance scanning can calculate GFR and renal plasma flow very accurately. However, its use is limited because of cost, lack of widespread availability, and operator technical difficulties. Estimating equations for GFR are reasonably accurate in patients with stage 3 CKD, such as the patient described here; these equations can be calculated without the need for invasive studies and are generally preferred to radionuclide kidney clearance scanning.

KEY POINT

Kidney ultrasonography is often the first choice for imaging studies to assess kidney disease because it is safe, not dependent upon kidney function, noninvasive, and relatively inexpensive.

Bibliography

Drawz P, Rahman M. In the clinic. Chronic kidney disease. Ann Intern Med. 2009; 150(3):ITC2-1-15. [PMID: 19189903]

Item 33   Answer: B

Educational Objective: *Manage anemia associated with chronic kidney disease.*

This patient has anemia associated with chronic kidney disease (CKD), and the most appropriate intervention is initiation of an erythropoiesis-stimulating agent (ESA). Anemia may develop in patients with stages 3 and 4 CKD and is primarily caused by reduced production of erythropoietin. Anemia is associated with decreased quality of life, left ventricular hypertrophy, and cardiovascular complications in patients with CKD. ESAs are indicated for patients with CKD who have hemoglobin levels less than 10 g/dL (100 g/L), but other causes of anemia, including iron deficiency, hemoglobinopathies, vitamin B$_{12}$ deficiency, and gastrointestinal blood loss, should be considered before beginning this therapy. Because use of ESAs to correct hemoglobin levels to the normal range may be associated with an increased risk for cardiovascular events, ESAs should not be initiated in patients with hemoglobin levels greater than 12 g/dL (120 g/L). It is therefore recommended that patients with CKD who have not yet started dialysis have a hemoglobin level less than 10 g/dL (100 g/L) before initiating an ESA with a target hemoglobin level of 10 to 11 g/dL (100-110 g/L) during maintenance therapy.

Although ascorbic acid has been shown to augment oral iron absorption, there are no convincing data suggesting that the addition of this agent is worth the cost or increase in gastrointestinal side effects.

Blood transfusion is generally avoided in patients with chronic anemia in the absence of critical tissue ischemia (for example, chest pain and neurologic symptoms). This intervention can sensitize persons to HLA antigens, which may complicate the potential for kidney transplantation.

Because this patient's serum iron levels are adequate, switching from oral to intravenous iron therapy would not help to improve her anemia and is associated with an increased risk of anaphylaxis.

KEY POINT

Initiation of an erythropoiesis-stimulating agent is indicated for patients with anemia associated with chronic kidney disease who have hemoglobin levels less than 10 g/dL (100 g/L); however, other causes of anemia, including iron deficiency, hemoglobinopathies, vitamin B_{12} deficiency, and gastrointestinal blood loss, should be considered before beginning this therapy.

Bibliography

Biggar P, Ketteler M. ESA therapy - the quest continues: anemia treatment following recent national and international recommendations 2011 and 2012. Clin Nephrol. 2013;79:335-50. [PMID: 23391317]

Item 34   Answer: D
Educational Objective: *Evaluate a patient with probable kidney stones.*

The most appropriate test to perform next in this patient is noncontrast abdominal helical computed tomography (CT). This patient has new-onset gradual abdominal and flank pain and a urinalysis revealing hematuria with low-grade pyuria, all of which are associated with kidney stones. Noncontrast abdominal helical CT is the most frequently used method for diagnosing kidney stones. This study identifies urinary tract obstruction with hydronephrosis, detects stones as small as 1 mm in diameter, and helps evaluate other potential causes of abdominal pain and hematuria. However, noncontrast abdominal helical CT is expensive relative to plain radiography. It also has a higher radiation exposure than other imaging studies, and therefore its use is contraindicated in pregnant women and should be minimized in younger patients. Ultrasonography is the study of choice in these patients. Ultrasonography is also an increasingly acceptable alternative method to CT for evaluating for nephrolithiasis in other patients who do not have a contraindication to CT. Although it is less sensitive or specific for kidney stones than CT, particularly for small stones or those in the distal ureter, it is a reasonable initial study for evaluating for kidney stones due to convenience, minimal radiation exposure, and lower cost, with CT reserved for those in whom nephrolithiasis is highly suspected but who have a nondiagnostic ultrasound study.

Magnetic resonance imaging does not typically visualize stones; therefore, a negative study cannot exclude the diagnosis of nephrolithiasis.

Most kidney stones are radiopaque and are easily visualized on abdominal radiography of the kidneys, ureters, and bladder (KUB), which is inexpensive, noninvasive, and widely available. However, false-negative results may occur in patients with small stones, radiolucent stones (such as those composed of uric acid), and interference of the overlying bowel. Therefore, KUB radiography can be used to follow stone burden but should not be used diagnostically because of possible false-negative results.

Intravenous pyelography also has lower sensitivity and specificity relative to CT and also requires administration of intravenous contrast. Because of this it is not a preferred method for diagnosing nephrolithiasis.

KEY POINT

Noncontrast abdominal helical CT is the gold standard for diagnosing kidney stones.

Bibliography

Goldfarb DS. In the clinic. Nephrolithiasis. Ann Intern Med. 2009;151:ITC2. [PMID: 19652185]

Item 35   Answer: A
Educational Objective: *Treat a patient who has a kidney stone.*

Treatment with an α-blocker is indicated for this patient who has a kidney stone that became symptomatic several days ago. The stone is of moderate size at 4 mm. Ninety percent of stones less than 5 mm pass spontaneously. In contrast, stones that are more than 10 mm are unlikely to pass without intervention. Although several days have passed, there is still a significant chance that he will pass the stone without surgical intervention. To increase the chance of stone passage, medical expulsive therapy using agents such as an α-blocker (such as tamsulosin) or a calcium channel blocker (such as nifedipine) should be employed. Using these agents for the facilitation of kidney stone passage is "off label" but is common practice for patients with stones less than 10 mm and well-controlled symptoms and is recommended by the American Urological Association and the European Association of Urology.

Patients who do not have an urgent indication for urologic intervention may still require intervention if the stone does not pass after a period of observation. The choice of intervention may depend on the characteristics of the stone and the practice of the particular center. Extracorporeal shock wave lithotripsy is a widely used, noninvasive method to treat symptomatic calculi located in the proximal ureter or within the kidney.

24-Hour urine collections are essential to identify specific abnormalities in urine composition and to tailor therapy for patients with a propensity to nephrolithiasis. If indicated because of multiple episodes of nephrolithiasis, collections should be performed several weeks after stone passage when the patient is consuming a regular diet.

Repeat imaging by noncontrast computed tomography would expose this patient to more radiation without providing additional important diagnostic or prognostic information and is not indicated at this time.

Stones located in the distal ureter are usually accessible by directed therapy guided by ureteroscopy. During ureteroscopy, "intracorporeal" lithotripsy can be performed using lasers, ultrasonography, or other techniques. However, this intervention is premature at this time.

KEY POINT

Medical expulsive therapy using the α-blocker tamsulosin or a calcium channel blocker such as nifedipine is appropriate to increase the chance of passage of kidney stones less than 10 mm in patients with well-controlled symptoms.

Bibliography

Parsons JK, Hergan LA, Sakamoto K, et al. Efficacy of alpha-blockers for the treatment of ureteral stones. J Urol. 2007;177:983-7. [PMID: 17296392]

Item 36 Answer: D

Educational Objective: *Manage a patient with recurrent calcium oxalate stone formation.*

An increase in dietary calcium intake and initiation of a low-protein diet are indicated for this patient. This patient most likely has recurrent calcium oxalate stones due to secondary hyperoxaluria. Hyperoxaluria is caused by increased gastrointestinal absorption of oxalate, whereas secondary hyperoxaluria is usually caused by increased intake of oxalate-rich foods such as rhubarb, peanuts, spinach, beets, and chocolate. Therefore, dietary restriction of oxalate-rich foods would decrease this patient's risk of recurrent calcium oxalate stones. Furthermore, oxalate binds to urine calcium as it is eliminated by the kidneys, which results in calcium oxalate stone formation. With a high-calcium diet, the calcium binds to oxalate in the gut and prevents its absorption and ultimate filtration at the level of the kidneys.

Allopurinol decreases the production of uric acid available for stone formation and is indicated to treat recurrent uric acid stones. This agent would not affect this patient's calcium oxalate stone formation.

In patients with calcium-containing stones and hypercalciuria, hydrochlorothiazide is recommended to treat hypercalciuria, increase calcium reabsorption in the kidney, and therefore reduce the amount of calcium available in the urine to form stones. However, this patient's 24-hour urine collection findings suggest that hyperoxaluria is the causative factor for stone formation, not hypercalciuria.

Alkalinization of the urine with citrate decreases the solubility of calcium oxalate and may help to prevent recurrent kidney stones, but potassium citrate would be more appropriate than sodium citrate in this patient. Sodium increases calcium excretion in the urine and may exacerbate hypercalciuria and calcium-containing stone formation. The use of citrate to alkalinize the urine also may cause calcium phosphate stone formation.

KEY POINT

In patients with recurrent calcium oxalate stones and hyperoxaluria, increased dietary calcium intake and avoidance of oxalate-rich foods such as rhubarb, peanuts, spinach, beets, and chocolate are recommended to decrease the risk of stone formation.

Bibliography

Goldfarb DS. In the clinic. Nephrolithiasis. Ann Intern Med. 2009;151:ITC2. [PMID: 19652185]

Section 8

Neurology

Questions

Item 1 [Basic]

A 56-year-old man is evaluated because of headaches. He has had sporadic headaches over the past 20 years that occur once or twice monthly. The headaches frequently develop in the afternoon, worsen in the evening, and typically resolve during sleep. Discomfort is described as tightness in the occipital and temporal regions and is moderate in intensity but is not disabling. The patient also reports neck stiffness but no nausea, phonophobia, or photophobia. He usually takes as-needed acetaminophen, although this only partially improves his symptoms. Medical history is otherwise negative and he takes no other medications.

On physical examination, vital signs are normal. Tenderness is noted in the paraspinal cervical muscles with normal cervical range of motion. Neurologic examination findings are normal.

Which of the following is the most appropriate next step in management?

(A) Amitriptyline, daily
(B) Cyclobenzaprine
(C) Ibuprofen
(D) Magnetic resonance imaging of the cervical spine
(E) Physical therapy

Item 2 [Basic]

A 44-year-old woman is evaluated for a 30-year history of severe headache that occurs once or twice each month and lasts 1 to 2 days. The pain affects the left side of her head, is pulsating in nature, and is associated with nausea and photophobia. Once or twice each year, the attacks are preceded by 30 minutes of unilateral flashing lights followed by partial visual loss. Several different nonsteroidal anti-inflammatory drugs have been ineffective; she currently takes ibuprofen as needed.

Physical examination findings, including vital signs and neurologic examination, are normal.

Which of the following is the most appropriate treatment?

(A) Butalbital with acetaminophen and caffeine
(B) Dihydroergotamine
(C) Propranolol
(D) Sumatriptan

Item 3 [Basic]

A 27-year-old man is evaluated for a 16-year history of gradually worsening headache. He describes attacks of severe periorbital throbbing pain that occurs exclusively on the left, lasts 6 to 8 hours, and is accompanied by slight nausea, bilateral tearing, and moderate photophobia and phonophobia. He does not experience aura

associated with his headaches. The frequency of these attacks has increased to approximately 15 days per month. High-dose ibuprofen and naproxen have become less effective in relieving the pain over the past year. The patient also has asthma treated with albuterol and salmeterol-fluticasone. He has no symptoms of depression.

Findings on physical examination, including vital signs and neurologic examination, are normal.

Results of laboratory studies also are normal.

Which of the following is the most appropriate treatment?

(A) Fluoxetine
(B) Propranolol
(C) Verapamil
(D) Vitamin D

Item 4 [Advanced]

A 42-year-old woman is evaluated because of worsening headaches. The patient has had a diagnosis of migraine for 10 years. The headaches typically occur once or twice monthly with unilateral severe throbbing pain, nausea with vomiting, and photophobia. She sometimes experiences a visual aura preceding the headache pain by 45 minutes, and the headache lasts for 36 to 48 hours. Over the past 3 months, her headaches have increased in frequency and intensity, and she now reports daily bilateral frontotemporal discomfort with associated visual blurring. Although previously helpful, oral triptan and nonsteroidal anti-inflammatory drug (NSAID) therapy has not provided any relief for the past 3 months. In addition to oral sumatriptan and an NSAID, her only other medication is an oral contraceptive.

Physical examination findings, including vital signs and neurologic examination, are normal.

Which of the following is the most appropriate next step in management?

(A) Analgesic discontinuation
(B) Change to another triptan
(C) Lumbar puncture
(D) Magnetic resonance imaging of the brain

Item 5 [Advanced]

A 75-year-old woman is evaluated in the emergency department for a 3-day history of headache and fever. Over the past 24 hours she has also become confused. Medical history is significant for hypertension treated with chlorthalidone.

On physical examination, the patient is disoriented to time and place. Temperature is 38.9°C (102.2°F), blood pressure is 110/70 mm

Hg, pulse rate is 105/min, and respiration rate is 19/min. Oxygen saturation is 94% (ambient air). There are no focal neurologic abnormalities, but neck stiffness is noted.

Empiric treatment is initiated with ampicillin, ceftriaxone, and vancomycin.

Complete blood count reveals a leukocyte count of 20,000/µL (20 × 10^9/L). Noncontrast computed tomographic scan of the head is normal. Blood cultures are obtained.

A lumbar puncture is performed, and the cerebrospinal fluid (CSF) examination reveals an opening pressure of 220 mm H_2O; the leukocyte count is 1000/µL (1.0 × 10^9/L) with 80% neutrophils and 20% lymphocytes; the protein level is 100 mg/dL (1000 mg/L); and the glucose level is 15 mg/dL (0.83 mmol/L). Gram stain of the CSF is shown (Plate 21).

This patient's antibiotic regimen should be narrowed to intravenous administration of which of the following?

(A) Ampicillin
(B) Ceftriaxone
(C) Vancomycin
(D) No change of antibiotic regimen

Item 6 [Advanced]

A 21-year-old man is evaluated in the emergency department for headache, confusion, and a seizure. A generalized and persistent headache began 48 hours ago. The patient is a college student, and earlier today he was unable to recognize the other students in his dormitory. Just before being transported to the emergency department, he had a generalized seizure. He has no history of other medical problems, including seizure disorders, and takes no medications.

On physical examination, temperature is 38.6°C (101.5°F), blood pressure is 130/80 mm Hg, pulse rate is 96/min, and respiration rate is 20/min. Oxygen saturation is 95% (ambient air). He is obtunded but has no other abnormalities on physical examination.

Results of a complete blood count and routine blood chemistry tests are normal. Computed tomographic scan of the head reveals focal low-density lesions in the left temporoparietal region.

A lumbar puncture is performed. Cerebrospinal fluid (CSF) analysis reveals a leukocyte count of 75/µL (0.075 × 10^9/L) with 95% lymphocytes; an erythrocyte count of 60/µL (60 × 10^{12}/L); a glucose concentration of 70 mg/dL (3.89 mmol/L); and a protein level of 80 mg/dL (800 mg/L). Gram stain of the CSF is negative for microorganisms.

Intravenous ampicillin, ceftriaxone, and vancomycin are initiated.

Which of the following should be done next?

(A) Brain biopsy
(B) CSF polymerase chain reaction assay for herpes simplex virus
(C) Electroencephalography
(D) Magnetic resonance imaging of the brain

Item 7 [Basic]

A 55-year-old woman is evaluated for a 2-day history of fever, headache, and confusion. Medical history is unremarkable, and she takes no medications. The patient has no known drug allergies.

On physical examination, temperature is 39.2°C (102.6°F), blood pressure is 100/60 mm Hg, pulse rate is 118/min, and respiration rate is 24/min. She is confused but responds to vigorous stimulation. There are no rashes. Neurologic examination findings are nonfocal.

Laboratory studies show a leukocyte count of 22,000/µL (22 × 10^9/L) with 40% band forms.

A computed tomographic scan of the head without contrast is normal.

Lumbar puncture is performed. Cerebrospinal fluid (CSF) leukocyte count is 1500/µL (1.5 × 10^9/L) with 95% neutrophils, the glucose level is 26 mg/dL (1.4 mmol/L), and the protein level is 200 mg/dL (2000 mg/L). A CSF Gram stain shows gram-positive diplococci.

Which of the following antimicrobial regimens should be initiated at this time?

(A) Ceftriaxone and acyclovir
(B) Ceftriaxone and ampicillin
(C) Ceftriaxone and levofloxacin
(D) Ceftriaxone and vancomycin

Item 8 [Basic]

An 18-year-old woman is evaluated in the emergency department for a 2-day history of fever, headache, vomiting, and photosensitivity. She noted painful ulcers on the vulva 10 days ago, but otherwise has felt well and has no other symptoms. Medical history is otherwise unremarkable.

On physical examination, temperature is 38.5°C (101.3°F), blood pressure is 100/60 mm Hg, pulse rate is 110/min, and respiration rate is 14/min. Nuchal rigidity is noted. Ophthalmoscopic examination is unremarkable with no evidence of papilledema. She has no oral or skin lesions. A few shallow ulcers are present on the vulva. There are no changes in sensorium. Neurologic examination findings are nonfocal.

Lumbar puncture is performed.

Cerebrospinal fluid (CSF) analysis:

Leukocyte count	200/µL (0.20 × 10^9/L) with 90% lymphocytes
Erythrocyte count	10/µL (10 × 10^{12}/L)
Glucose	60 mg/dL (3.3 mmol/L)

Plasma glucose level is 100 mg/dL (5.6 mmol/L).

A Gram stain of the CSF is negative.

Which of the following is the most likely diagnosis?

(A) Acute bacterial meningitis
(B) Acute HIV infection
(C) Aseptic meningitis
(D) Behçet disease

Item 9 [Basic]

A 56-year-old woman is evaluated in the emergency department for difficulty speaking and clumsiness of the right hand. The symptoms began approximately 2 hours ago. Medical history is significant for type 2 diabetes mellitus treated with metformin and hypertension treated with ramipril.

On physical examination, the patient is alert. Temperature is normal, blood pressure is 170/100 mm Hg, pulse rate is 90/min, and respiration rate is 22/min. Oxygen saturation is 96% (ambient air). Cardiopulmonary examination is normal. Neurologic examination discloses right-sided extremity weakness, arm greater than leg, right-sided facial paralysis, and word-finding difficulty.

Results of complete blood count, plasma glucose level, metabolic panel, serum troponin level, and coagulation panel are normal. An electrocardiogram is normal.

Which of the following is the most appropriate next step in management?

(A) Labetalol, intravenously
(B) Magnetic resonance imaging of the brain
(C) Noncontrast computed tomography of the head
(D) Recombinant tissue plasminogen activator, intravenously

Item 10 [Basic]

A 48-year-old woman is evaluated in the emergency department for impaired speech and right arm weakness. Symptoms began 5 hours ago and are rapidly resolving. The patient has a history of type 2 diabetes mellitus treated with metformin.

On physical examination, temperature is normal, blood pressure is 178/104 mm Hg, pulse rate is 100/min, and respiration rate is 22/min. Oxygen saturation is 96% (ambient air). BMI is 28. Cardiopulmonary examination is normal. There is minimal right arm and right facial weakness and mild word-finding difficulty.

Complete blood count, metabolic and coagulation panels, and serum troponin level are normal. Random plasma glucose level is 126 mg/dL (6.99 mmol/L).

An electrocardiogram reveals sinus rhythm and no evidence of myocardial infarction or ischemia. Noncontrast CT of the head is normal.

Which of the following is the most appropriate treatment?

(A) Aspirin
(B) Enoxaparin
(C) Low-molecular-weight heparin
(D) Recombinant tissue plasminogen activator
(E) Warfarin

Item 11 [Basic]

A 78-year-old woman is evaluated in the emergency department 12 hours after onset of left-sided weakness and slurred speech. She has a history of hypertension and type 2 diabetes mellitus, both of which she tries to control with lifestyle modifications. She takes no medications.

On physical examination, blood pressure is 190/90 mm Hg, pulse rate is 68/min and regular, and respiration rate is 16/min. Cardiopulmonary and abdominal examinations are unremarkable. Neurologic examination reveals facial weakness on the left side, severe dysarthria, left-sided hemiplegia, left-sided sensory loss, and normal mental status.

A noncontrast computed tomographic scan of the head shows a faint hypodensity in the right posterior limb of the internal capsule. An electrocardiogram shows normal sinus rhythm with no ischemic changes. A chest radiograph is normal.

Which of the following is the most appropriate immediate treatment of this patient's elevated blood pressure?

(A) Intravenous hydralazine
(B) Oral labetalol
(C) Oral nitroglycerin
(D) No treatment is required

Item 12 [Basic]

A 75-year-old woman is evaluated for a 60-minute episode of right arm weakness and dysarthria. The symptoms have not recurred. She has hypertension and type 2 diabetes mellitus. Medications are aspirin, metoprolol, enalapril, and metformin.

On physical examination, blood pressure is 156/94 mm Hg, pulse rate is 62/min and regular, and respiration rate is 16/min. No carotid bruits are noted. Neurologic examination findings are normal.

Results of laboratory studies obtained 3 weeks ago show a hemoglobin A_{1c} value of 7.1% and a serum low-density lipoprotein cholesterol level of 68 mg/dL (1.76 mmol/L).

Which of the following is the most appropriate next step in management?

(A) Addition of clopidogrel
(B) Immediate hospital admission
(C) Outpatient magnetic resonance imaging of the brain
(D) 24-Hour electrocardiographic monitoring

Item 13 [Advanced]

An 86-year-old woman is evaluated in the emergency department 60 minutes after onset of difficulty speaking and right arm weakness. The patient has a history of hypertension for which she takes amlodipine. She has no history of previous stroke or gastrointestinal or genitourinary bleeding and no recent surgical procedures.

On physical examination, blood pressure is 170/100 mm Hg and pulse rate is 86/min and irregular. Neurologic examination shows global aphasia, right hemiparesis, left gaze preference, and a right visual field cut.

Results of laboratory studies show an international normalized ratio of 1.1, a platelet count of 180,000/µL (180×10^9/L), and a random plasma glucose level of 120 mg/dL (6.7 mmol/L).

A computed tomographic scan of the head without contrast shows no acute infarct or hemorrhage.

Which of the following is the most appropriate next step in treatment?

(A) High-dose aspirin
(B) Intravenous heparin
(C) Intravenous recombinant tissue plasminogen activator
(D) Labetalol

Item 14 [Advanced]

A 56-year-old woman is evaluated in the emergency department for sudden onset of a severe, intractable, generalized headache that began 36 hours ago and has not responded to over-the-counter medications. The patient has a history of hypertension treated with lifestyle modifications. She has a 30-pack-year history of smoking.

On physical examination, blood pressure is 148/68 mm Hg, pulse rate is 96/min and regular, and respiration rate is 16/min. Nuchal rigidity is noted. Ophthalmoscopic examination does not show papilledema. The remainder of her physical and neurologic examination is normal.

Results of laboratory studies are notable for a platelet count of 190,000/µL (190 × 10⁹/L), an international normalized ratio of 0.9, and a serum creatinine level of 0.9 mg/dL (79.6 µmol/L).

Computed tomography (CT) of the head without contrast is normal.

Which of the following is the most appropriate next diagnostic test?

(A) CT of the head with contrast
(B) Lumbar puncture
(C) Magnetic resonance angiography of the head and neck
(D) Magnetic resonance imaging of the brain

Item 15 [Basic]

A 67-year-old woman is evaluated during a routine examination. The patient has a history of moderate dementia. She is in good spirits and reports no problems. Her daughter, who accompanied her, has not noticed worsening in her memory loss or further decline in her ability to perform activities of daily living. The patient's only medication is donepezil. Her daughter would like advice about nonpharmacologic interventions to help keep her mother's disease stable.

Which of the following is the most appropriate additional nonpharmacologic management for this patient's dementia?

(A) Acupuncture
(B) Cognitive stimulation
(C) Reminiscence therapy
(D) Vitamin E

Item 16 [Advanced]

A 59-year-old man is evaluated for a 5-year history of memory difficulty. The history is provided by his wife. She states that he has become apathetic and depressed, has lost language skills, and no longer participates in activities he previously enjoyed. His behavior is often inappropriate, and neighbors have occasionally complained that he urinates in the front yard. He has developed repetitive compulsive behaviors such as repeatedly shuffling cards for hours and can no longer make simple decisions.

On physical examination, vital signs are normal. The patient's general appearance is disheveled and unkempt. There is a loss of verbal fluency. Mental status examination shows prominent memory loss and difficulty drawing a complex figure.

Which of the following is the most likely diagnosis?

(A) Alzheimer disease
(B) Creutzfeldt-Jakob disease
(C) Dementia with Lewy bodies
(D) Frontotemporal dementia

Item 17 [Advanced]

A 76-year-old woman is evaluated for progressive memory loss and increasing difficulty with activities of daily living (ADLs). The patient now relies entirely on her caregiver for all ADLs. According to the caregiver, these symptoms have progressed over the past 4 to 5 years. Three years ago, the patient was diagnosed with Alzheimer disease, and donepezil was begun at that time. She discontinued the donepezil because of nausea and vomiting. Her only other medical problem is hypertension that is treated with lisinopril.

On physical examination, vital signs are normal. Her level of alertness, speech, and gait are normal. The patient's caregiver reports no apparent change in mood. The patient scores 21/30 on the Mini–Mental State Examination.

Which of the following is the most appropriate next step in treatment?

(A) Lorazepam
(B) Memantine
(C) Sertraline
(D) Quetiapine

Item 18 [Basic]

A 68-year-old man is evaluated for memory loss. He teaches history at a local university, supervises graduate students, and writes chapters of textbooks. He reports occasionally having difficulty remembering the names of his students and colleagues, forgetting telephone numbers, and often misplacing his glasses. The patient has not experienced confusion and has no history of depression, hallucinations, or head trauma. He drives, manages his own finances, and is fully independent. Medical history is unremarkable, and he takes no medications.

On physical examination, the patient appears anxious. Vital signs are normal, as are other findings from the general physical examination. He scores 29/30 on the Mini–Mental State Examination.

Which of the following is the most appropriate next step in management?

(A) Daily low-dose aspirin
(B) Magnetic resonance imaging of the brain
(C) Trial of donepezil
(D) Clinical follow-up

Item 19 [Basic]

A 75-year-old man is evaluated because of memory loss. His son accompanies him to the office. The patient lives independently, but family members have noted declining memory over the past year. He has stopped cleaning his home, has forgotten to pay utility bills, and recently had a minor motor vehicle accident. He has a history of hypertension and hyperlipidemia for which he takes lisinopril and simvastatin. The patient's wife died 1 year ago.

On physical examination, he is cooperative and in no distress. Blood pressure is 120/70 mm Hg and pulse rate is 70/min. The remainder of the examination, including a detailed neurologic examination, is normal.

Which of the following is the most appropriate next step in the evaluation of this patient's memory loss?

(A) Cognitive function screening test
(B) Lumbar puncture
(C) Magnetic resonance imaging of the head
(D) Metabolic panel
(E) Toxicology screen

Item 20 [Advanced]

A 75-year-old woman undergoes surgical repair of a fractured hip. Two days postoperatively, she develops increasing confusion and agitation. The patient has periods of relatively clear thinking but at other times becomes agitated or drowsy and does not respond to questions. Before admission, she was living independently at home since the death of her husband 3 years ago and has maintained full activities of daily living. She has never exhibited signs of dementia. She does not smoke or drink alcoholic beverages.

On physical examination, vital signs are normal. General examination findings are unremarkable. She has some difficulty cooperating during the examination. Speech and language are normal, but she is not oriented to place or time and exhibits occasional perseveration. Neurologic examination findings are otherwise nonfocal.

Results of routine laboratory studies, including urinalysis, are normal.

A chest radiograph is normal.

Which of the following is the most likely diagnosis?

(A) Delirium
(B) Dementia
(C) Herpes simplex encephalitis
(D) Stroke

Item 21 [Basic]

An 80-year old woman is admitted to the hospital with pneumonia. In the emergency department, oxygen by nasal cannula was started, appropriate antibiotics were initiated, and a urinary catheter was placed. Medical history is significant for dementia, and the patient resides in a memory care unit at an extended-care facility.

On physical examination, temperature is 38.3°C (101.0°F), blood pressure is 140/88 mm Hg, pulse rate is 100/min, and respiration rate is 16/min. The lung examination reveals crackles at the right base. The remainder of the general examination is normal. Moderate cognitive impairment is noted, but there is no inattention or evidence of focal neurologic deficits.

She is provided access to her glasses and hearing aid, and a clock and night light are in place in her room.

Which of the following additional steps should be taken to prevent delirium in this patient?

(A) Administer a benzodiazepine for sleep
(B) Administer low-dose haloperidol twice daily
(C) Provide safety checks every 4 hours throughout the night
(D) Remove the urinary catheter

Item 22 [Basic]

A 58-year-old woman is evaluated for a 7-week history of tingling pain involving the first, second, and third digits of the left hand. The pain is worse at night and radiates into the thenar eminence but does not radiate into the proximal forearm. Medical history is significant for hypothyroidism. Her only current medication is levothyroxine.

On physical examination, the patient reports pain with plantar flexion at the wrist with the elbow extended. She also reports pain with percussion over the median nerve at the level of the wrist. There is no thenar or hypothenar eminence atrophy. Strength is 5/5 with thumb opposition. A completed hand diagram demonstrating the location of the patient's paresthesia is shown.

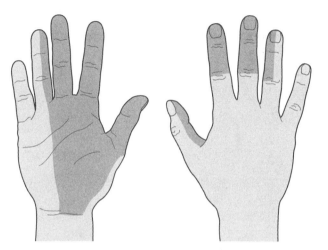

In addition to avoidance of repetitive wrist motions, which of the following is the most appropriate initial treatment?

(A) Local glucocorticoid injection
(B) Ibuprofen
(C) Surgical intervention
(D) Wrist splinting

Item 23 [Basic]

A 27-year-old woman is evaluated in the emergency department. Four hours ago, she awoke with drooping of the left face, inability to close the left eye, mild numbness and tingling of the left cheek, dizziness, nausea, a mild headache, a dry mouth, and increased sensitivity to noise. Two weeks ago, she had a flulike illness with rhinorrhea, a sore throat, and a cough that resolved spontaneously. She has a history of uncomplicated migraine for which she takes acetaminophen as needed.

On physical examination, vital signs are normal. No lesions of the skin or mucous membranes are noted. Neurologic examination reveals severe weakness of the left upper and lower facial muscles and an inability to close the left eye completely. Sensory examination shows that facial sensation is normal bilaterally. The remainder of the neurologic examination is unremarkable.

Which of the following is the most appropriate treatment?

(A) Acyclovir
(B) Intravenous methylprednisolone
(C) Prednisone
(D) Sumatriptan

Item 24 [Basic]

A 62-year-old man is evaluated for a 6-month history of burning and stabbing pain in both feet that is worse in the toes. The pain is more severe at night and is partially relieved when he walks or massages his feet. The patient has a 15-year history of poorly controlled type 2 diabetes mellitus. Medications are metformin and glipizide. He does not smoke or drink alcoholic beverages.

On physical examination, vital signs are normal. Body mass index is 32. Both feet are exquisitely sensitive to touch. Pulses are easily palpated in both feet. No fasciculations, muscle weakness, foot ulcers, or foot deformities are noted. Monofilament testing reveals insensate feet bilaterally. Ankle reflexes are absent bilaterally.

Results of laboratory studies show a hemoglobin A_{1c} value of 9.2%.

In addition to improving glycemic control, which of the following is the most appropriate next step in management?

(A) Gabapentin
(B) Nerve conduction studies
(C) Oxycodone
(D) Sural nerve biopsy

Item 25 [Advanced]

A 52-year-old woman is evaluated for a 2-year history of burning feet. Symptoms are constant and are worse at night. Medical history is significant for hypertension treated with lisinopril. There is no known family history of peripheral neuropathy.

On physical examination, the patient is afebrile; blood pressure is 134/88 mm Hg, pulse rate is 66/min, respiration rate is 12/min, and Body mass index is 28. Neurologic examination shows diminished pinprick and temperature sensation on the dorsal and plantar surfaces of both feet. Cranial nerve examination and testing of manual muscle strength, deep tendon reflexes, proprioception, and coordination reveal no abnormalities.

Laboratory studies show a fasting plasma glucose level of 102 mg/dL (5.7 mmol/L). Results of a complete blood count, vitamin B12 measurement, and serum protein electrophoresis are all normal.

Which of the following is the most appropriate next diagnostic test?

(A) Cerebrospinal fluid examination
(B) Genetic testing for hereditary motor sensory polyneuropathy (Charcot-Marie-Tooth)
(C) Glucose tolerance testing
(D) Skin biopsy

Item 26 [Advanced]

A 50-year-old woman is evaluated because of involuntary, uncomfortable movements in her neck. The symptoms developed 4 months after beginning treatment with ziprasidone, a D_2 dopamine receptor antagonist being used to treat her atypical depression. Ziprasidone was discontinued 2 months ago, but her neck movements have persisted. She has never had these symptoms before. The patient states that standing and emotional stress make the movements more severe and more painful. Her medical history is significant only for depression, and she takes no other medications. There is no family history of abnormal movements of this type.

On physical examination, vital signs are normal. Involuntary head tilting to the right due to tonic contraction of the cervical musculature is present. There are no other neuromuscular abnormalities, and the remainder of the examination is unremarkable.

Which of the following is the most appropriate treatment?

(A) Cervical muscle release procedure
(B) Deep brain stimulation
(C) Diphenhydramine
(D) Propranolol

Item 27 [Basic]

A 47-year-old man is evaluated for tremor. Over the past year he has noticed shaking in his hands, particularly with activities such as reading a newspaper. His wife has also noticed slight, occasional movement of his head up and down when he is sitting. Although these symptoms have not caused him to discontinue or modify his daily activities, he is concerned that they may be due to Parkinson disease, which he believes his father had. He notes that the shaking usually gets better in the evening when he has a glass of wine, which he has started to drink on a nightly basis. He reports no falls or apparent postural changes. Medical history is otherwise unremarkable, and he takes no medications.

On physical examination, vital signs are normal. Neurologic examination is significant only for a mild, bilateral, symmetric tremor that occurs with the arms extended and with finger-to-nose testing.

Which of the following is the most appropriate next step in management?

(A) An anticholinergic agent
(B) A dopamine agonist
(C) Deep brain stimulation
(D) Lifestyle modifications

Item 28 [Basic]

A 63-year-old woman is evaluated for a tremor in her left hand. She has increasing difficulty performing fine motor activities with this hand, although she thinks that the tremor is less severe when the hand is in use. Medical history is unremarkable, there is no family history of any neurologic disorders, and she takes no medications.

On physical examination, vital signs are normal. General examination is normal, although the patient does show a paucity of facial expression. On neurologic examination, cranial nerve function is normal. Motor strength is normal, but there is mild left upper extremity rigidity and a low-frequency resting tremor of the left hand. Deep tendon reflexes and sensory examinations are normal, and there is no gait abnormality.

Which of the following is the most likely diagnosis?

(A) Cervical dystonia
(B) Essential tremor
(C) Huntington disease
(D) Parkinson disease

Item 29 [Basic]

An 84-year-old man is evaluated in the emergency department because of abnormal behavior noted by his family. The patient was eating dinner when he suddenly dropped his fork and stared blankly around the room. This was followed by shaking of his left arm that lasted approximately 1 minute. He did not lose consciousness but did not respond when family members spoke to him. Afterwards, he voraciously ate a large amount of food but remained confused for about 30 minutes until returning to normal awareness. Medical history is significant for hypertension. There is no history of head trauma, stroke, or seizures. His only medication is lisinopril.

On physical examination, the patient is alert and oriented, although he does not remember the event. Vital signs are normal, and examination findings, including neurologic examination, are normal.

Results of laboratory studies, including a complete blood count, comprehensive metabolic panel, and urinalysis, are normal. An electrocardiogram shows normal sinus rhythm and no acute changes.

Which of the following is the most appropriate next step in management?

(A) Echocardiogram
(B) Lumbar puncture
(C) MRI of the brain
(D) Psychiatric evaluation

Item 30 [Advanced]

A 35-year-old woman is evaluated 30 minutes after having a generalized tonic-clonic seizure witnessed by her husband who brought her to the emergency department. The seizure lasted approximately 2 minutes during which the patient was incontinent of urine. She has not regained consciousness. She had two more generalized tonic-clonic seizures while being transported to the hospital. Medical history is significant for focal seizures. Her only medication is levetiracetam, which she takes intermittently.

On physical examination, temperature is 37.9°C (100.2°F), blood pressure is 114/78 mm Hg, pulse rate is 105/min, and respiration rate is 18/min. Oxygen saturation is 96% (ambient air). The patient is obtunded with a positive gag reflex. Before a full examination is completed, she exhibits more generalized tonic-clonic convulsive activity.

In addition to supportive and safety measures, which of the following is the most appropriate immediate treatment for this patient?

(A) Fosphenytoin
(B) Levetiracetam
(C) Lorazepam
(D) Phenobarbital
(E) Valproate

Item 31 [Advanced]

An 18-year-old man is evaluated following a single generalized tonic-clonic seizure. The patient is a college student. The seizure began when he was asleep in his dormitory and resolved uneventfully. He has no history of head trauma, meningitis, or prior seizure and no family history of epilepsy. He takes no medications and prefers to avoid taking medications if possible.

Physical examination findings, including neurologic examination, are normal.

Results of laboratory studies, including a complete blood count, serum electrolyte panel, and urine toxicology screen, are also normal.

MRI of the brain and an electroencephalogram show no abnormalities.

Which of the following is the most appropriate treatment recommendation for this patient?

(A) Carbamazepine
(B) Epilepsy surgery evaluation
(C) Phenytoin
(D) Clinical follow-up

Item 32 [Basic]

A 65-year-old man is evaluated for possible seizures. He describes three similar "spells" over the past month of which he recalls a feeling of déjà vu followed by a loss of awareness. He says that family members who witnessed these episodes have described him as being unresponsive during each episode, recounting that he stares and repetitively smacks his lips for about a minute, followed by a few minutes of confusion and garbled speech before he returns to normal awareness. He has no significant personal or family medical history and takes no medications.

Physical examination findings, including neurologic examination, are normal.

An MRI of the brain is unremarkable and an electroencephalogram is normal.

Which of the following is the most likely diagnosis?

(A) Absence seizure
(B) Focal seizure with dyscognitive features (complex partial seizure)
(C) Focal seizure without dyscognitive features (simple partial seizure)
(D) Generalized tonic-clonic seizure
(E) Myoclonic seizure

Item 33 [Basic]

A 35-year-old man is evaluated in the emergency department for rapidly progressive weakness in both legs. He first noted numbness and tingling in his legs 1 week ago following an acute diarrheal illness and now has severe lower extremity weakness. The patient has no history of recent travel or trauma, was previously healthy, and takes no medications. He does not drink alcoholic beverages, use illicit drugs, or smoke cigarettes.

On physical examination, vital signs are normal. BMI is 22. He cannot walk without assistance. There is normal sensation in the feet and absent ankle and knee deep tendon reflexes. There is weakness of abduction and flexion of the upper extremities and diminished biceps deep tendon reflexes.

Cerebrospinal fluid analysis shows a normal cell count and increased protein.

Which of the following in the most likely diagnosis?

(A) Amyotrophic lateral sclerosis
(B) Guillain-Barré syndrome
(C) Multiple sclerosis
(D) Spinal cord compression

Item 34 [Advanced]

A 30-year-old woman is evaluated for difficulty chewing and swallowing food. Chewing becomes especially difficult after a prolonged effort but improves following rest. She also notes that her speech becomes slurred and sometimes nasal by the end of the day. She is unable to whistle or blow up a balloon. The patient frequently develops a droopy left eyelid and double vision by late morning, which disappear following a night's rest. She has no other medical problems and takes no medications.

On physical examination, vital signs are normal. Pupils are regular and reactive but ptosis of the left eyelid is noted. The patient is unable to keep the upper eyelids closed against efforts to raise them. She has a "snarly" expression when asked to smile. Deep tendon reflexes and sensory examination are normal.

Which of the following studies is most likely to establish the diagnosis?

(A) Acetylcholine receptor antibody assay
(B) MRI of the brain
(C) Muscle biopsy
(D) Nerve biopsy
(E) Serum creatine kinase measurement

Item 35 [Basic]

A 28-year-old woman is evaluated for a 1-day history of lower extremity weakness and blurred vision. She recalls an episode of "double vision" 1 year ago that resolved over several days. Her current symptoms include blurriness in her left eye and weakness in her right leg. Medical history is otherwise unremarkable. She does not smoke or drink alcoholic beverages and takes no illicit drugs or prescription or over-the-counter medications.

On physical examination, vital signs are normal. There is pallor of the left optic disc with measured visual acuity of 20/80. Muscle testing shows 4/5 strength in the right quadriceps muscle group. Deep tendon reflexes are normal. The remainder of the examination, including neurologic examination, is normal.

Which of the following is the most likely diagnosis?

(A) Amyotrophic lateral sclerosis
(B) Guillain-Barré syndrome
(C) Lambert-Eaton myasthenic syndrome
(D) Multiple sclerosis
(E) Myasthenia gravis

Item 36 [Advanced]

A 25-year-old woman is evaluated in the office for a 1-week history of numbness of the left leg. She also had a 2-week history of diplopia and vertigo 1 year ago; an MRI obtained at that time showed nonspecific periventricular white matter changes but was otherwise unremarkable. There is no family history of neurologic problems. She takes no medications.

On physical examination, vital signs are normal. Cardiopulmonary examination is unremarkable. Neurologic examination is significant for an extensor plantar response on the left. There is mild loss of vibratory sense in both feet with a patchy, reduced pain sensation throughout the left lower extremity.

Laboratory studies including a comprehensive metabolic profile and complete blood count are normal.

A repeat MRI of the brain shows periventricular white matter lesions unchanged from the previous examination. MRIs of the cervical spine and thoracic spine show no abnormalities.

Which of the following is the most appropriate next step in diagnosis?

(A) Antimyelin antibodies
(B) Electronystagmography
(C) Lumbar puncture
(D) Magnetic resonance angiography

Section 8

Neurology

Answers and Critiques

Item 1 **Answer: C**

Educational Objective: *Manage a tension-type headache.*

This patient should begin taking ibuprofen for his tension-type headache. Episodic tension-type headache is defined as episodes of recurrent nondisabling headache lasting 30 minutes to 7 days. Often recognized as a featureless headache, it is characterized by bilateral, steady, mild-to-moderate intensity discomfort that is unaffected by physical activity. Whereas migraine is characterized primarily by the positive features of photophobia and/or phonophobia, nausea and/or vomiting, and pain worsening with activity, tension-type headache is characterized by the absence of these features. Aspirin and acetaminophen are more effective than placebo in treating these headaches, but comparative studies suggest superior benefit from the nonsteroidal anti-inflammatory drugs (NSAIDs) ibuprofen and naproxen.

Although tricyclic antidepressants, such as amitriptyline, are commonly used for prophylaxis for tension-type headache, the relatively low headache frequency in this patient does not justify daily pharmacotherapy.

Muscle relaxants, such as cyclobenzaprine, have no role in the management of tension-type headache. Similarly, benzodiazepines, which depress the central nervous system, have not been shown to be effective.

In the absence of any cervical root or spinal cord findings on examination, magnetic resonance imagin of the cervical spine is unnecessary.

No evidence supports recommending physical therapy for patients with tension-type headache.

KEY POINT

NSAIDs are the preferred therapy for tension-type headache.

Bibliography

Freitag F. Managing and treating tension-type headache. Med Clin North Am. 2013;97: 281-92. [PMID: 23419626]

Item 2 **Answer: D**

Educational Objective: *Treat migraine with aura.*

This patient should next receive a triptan medication such as sumatriptan for acute migraine treatment. Her headache is characteristic of migraine with aura and meets the diagnostic criteria of exhibiting at least two of four pain features (unilateral location, pulsatile nature, moderate to severe intensity, and aggravation by routine activity) and at least one of two associated features (nausea or photophobia/phonophobia). The once or twice yearly visual symptoms meet symptomatic and duration criteria for typical aura and do not have any characteristics suggestive of a transient ischemic attack. Nonsteroidal anti-inflammatory drugs have been unsuccessful for this patient, and evidence-based guidelines suggest advancing to a triptan medication for acute treatment. The use of an acute migraine medication is appropriate when administration is strictly limited to fewer than 10 days per month to avoid the potential development of medication overuse headache.

No evidence supports the use of butalbital with acetaminophen and caffeine as acute migraine therapy. In addition, butalbital poses a drug-dependency risk. Therefore, this drug regimen should not be considered a first- or second-line therapy for this patient.

Dihydroergotamine is an α-adrenergic blocker that can be administered by intravenous, intramuscular, intranasal, and subcutaneous routes. It is typically used as an alternative to treatment with a triptan for acute migraine and is often used for intractable migraine headaches. Dihydroergotamine should not be used concurrently with a triptan and is contraindicated in patients with coronary artery disease and pregnant women.

Although propranolol is an effective agent for preventing migraine, daily prophylactic medication is not needed in this patient who has only one to two headache attacks per month, for a maximum of 4 days per month.

KEY POINT

Therapy with a triptan is appropriate to treat acute exacerbations of migraine with aura.

Bibliography

McGregor EA. In the clinic. Migraine. Ann Intern Med. 2013;159:ITC5 1-16; quiz ITC5 16. [PMID: 24189604]

Item 3 **Answer: B**

Educational Objective: *Treat migraine without aura.*

This patient should receive propranolol as a preventive medication for his increasingly frequent headache attacks. He has no "red flags" potentially indicating a secondary headache including dizziness, lack of coordination, tingling, awakening from sleep due to headache, focal neurologic findings, papilledema, fever, neck stiffness, meningeal signs, tenderness or diminished pulse over the temporal artery, diastolic blood pressure >120 mm Hg, or decreased visual acuity. Additionally, given his history of headaches dating back to childhood, a primary headache syndrome is clearly present. These attacks meet criteria for migraine without aura (unilateral, pulsating headache lasting 4-72 hours that is accompanied by photophobia, phonophobia, and nausea) and may be distinguished from cluster headache by their episode duration (>3 hours) and from tension-type headache by their severe intensity and association with nausea, photophobia, and phonophobia. Approximately 38% of patients with migraine need preventive treatment, but preventive medications are prescribed to only 3% to 13% of these patients. The major medications shown to be effective for migraine prevention include β-blockers (such as propranolol, metoprolol, or timolol), tricyclic antidepressants (such as amitriptyline), and anticonvulsants (such as valproate, topiramate, or gabapentin).

No significant evidence supports the use of fluoxetine or other selective serotonin reuptake inhibitors in the prevention of migraine.

Verapamil is an effective agent for preventing cluster headache. Evidence of its effectiveness in preventing migraine, however, is quite limited.

Although data support the use of several nutritional supplements, such as magnesium and riboflavin, in migraine prevention, no evidence supports the use of vitamin D in this context.

KEY POINT

Preventive therapy for migraine may be indicated for patients who have frequent disabling headaches (usually ≥2 headaches per week) or who experience poor relief from acute therapies; effective medications include β-blockers, tricyclic antidepressants, and anticonvulsants.

Bibliography

Silberstein SD. Preventive migraine treatment. Neurol Clin. 2009;27:429-43. [PMID: 19289224]

Item 4   Answer: D

Educational Objective: *Diagnose a secondary headache.*

This patient may have a secondary headache syndrome and should undergo an magnetic resonance imaging (MRI) of the brain. Secondary headache disorders are characterized by unstable or progressive temporal patterns and usually raise a "red flag" of concern during the history or physical examination. These clinical indicators include awakening from sleep due to headache; focal neurologic findings; more general neurologic findings such as dizziness, lack of coordination, or tingling; fever; neck stiffness or meningeal signs; tenderness or diminished pulse over the temporal artery; diastolic blood pressure >120 mm Hg; or papilledema or decreased visual acuity. This patient has a long-standing history of migraine with aura, but the headache pattern has become more frequent over the past 3 months, and the new neurologic symptom of visual blurring has developed. Although this change may represent a superimposition of medication overuse headache syndrome, the presence of an intracranial mass lesion must be excluded with neuroimaging. MRI of the brain is preferable to computed tomography of the head in the evaluation of subacute or chronic headache because of improved sensitivity resulting from superior anatomic resolution.

Medication overuse headache, previously known as "rebound" headache, may be a contributing factor in the transformation of episodic migraine into a pattern of chronic daily headache. Because the presence of daily visual blurring would not be explained by analgesic overuse, however, the analgesic does not have to be discontinued, and the neuroimaging study remains the management step of first choice.

Although there is little evidence supporting the use of one triptan over another and switching between different agents may be appropriate based on delivery route, preference, and cost, tolerance to triptans does not generally occur. Therefore, this patient's change in headache pattern and symptoms would not likely be explained by her triptan treatment, and evaluation for another cause should be pursued.

This patient has no indications of meningitis, such as acute onset, fever, and neck stiffness, which would warrant a lumbar puncture as the initial diagnostic test. Additionally, before a lumbar puncture can be safely performed, an intracranial mass lesion must be excluded with brain neuroimaging.

KEY POINT

In a patient with a headache of an unstable or progressive temporal pattern that raises a "red flag" of concern during the history or physical examination, MRI of the brain is appropriate to exclude an intracranial mass lesion.

Bibliography

DeLuca GC, Bartleson JD. When and how to investigate the patient with headache. Semin Neurol. 2010;30:131-44. [PMID: 20352583]

Item 5   Answer: A

Educational Objective: *Treat* Listeria monocytogenes *meningitis.*

This patient has *Listeria monocytogenes* meningitis, and her antibiotic regimen should be changed to intravenous ampicillin (or penicillin G). In patients who are allergic to penicillin, trimethoprim-sulfamethoxazole is an alternative agent.

Adult patients with bacterial meningitis typically present with fever, headache, nuchal rigidity, and signs of cerebral dysfunction, although an insidious onset with lethargy or obtundation and variable signs of meningeal irritation may be present in elderly patients, especially in those with diabetes mellitus or cardiopulmonary disease. The diagnosis of acute bacterial meningitis is established by cerebrospinal fluid (CSF) analysis. Once acute bacterial meningitis is suspected, blood cultures must be obtained, and a lumbar puncture must be performed immediately to determine whether the CSF findings are consistent with the clinical diagnosis. Computed tomography of the head should be performed before lumbar puncture in patients who are immunocompromised, have a history of central nervous system disease, present with new-onset seizures, or have an abnormal level of consciousness, focal neurologic deficit, or papilledema to evaluate for causes of increased intracranial pressure that might lead to complications due to the procedure. Once CSF analysis is performed, targeted antimicrobial therapy can be initiated in patients with a positive Gram stain result.

That this patient has *L. monocytogenes* meningitis is suggested by the identification of Gram-positive bacilli in the CSF fluid. Ampicillin is included in empiric therapy for bacterial meningitis in patients who are at risk for developing invasive infections with this Gram-positive bacillus. *L. monocytogenes* meningitis develops most frequently in neonates, older adults (>50 years of age), and those who are immunocompromised (diabetes mellitus, liver or kidney disease, collagen vascular disorders, disorders of iron overload, HIV infection, transplant recipients, and patients taking anti-tumor necrosis factor α agents such as infliximab and etanercept), although cases have been reported in patients with no underlying disorders.

Ceftriaxone is not effective against *L. monocytogenes*.

Vancomycin is also not indicated, as treatment failures have been reported with the use of vancomycin in these infections.

KEY POINT

Treatment for *Listeria monocytogenes*-associated meningitis is ampicillin (or penicillin G).

Bibliography

van de Beek D, Brouwer MC, Thwaites GE, Tunkel AR. Advances in treatment of bacterial meningitis. Lancet. 2012;380:1693-702. [PMID: 23141618]

Item 6 Answer: B

Educational Objective: *Diagnose herpes simplex encephalitis.*

Cerebrospinal fluid (CSF) polymerase chain reaction (PCR) assay for herpes simplex virus should be done next. Encephalitis is defined by the presence of an inflammatory process in the brain associated with clinical evidence of neurologic dysfunction. Herpes simplex virus is one of the most common causes of identified sporadic encephalitis worldwide, accounting for 5% to 10% of cases. Clinical features of herpes simplex encephalitis include fever, hemicranial headache, language and behavioral abnormalities, memory impairment, cranial nerve deficits, and seizures.

The development of nucleic acid amplification tests, such as polymerase chain reaction (PCR), has markedly increased the ability to diagnose central nervous system viral infections, especially those caused by the herpesviruses. The usefulness of PCR assays on CSF for the diagnosis of herpes simplex encephalitis has been reliably demonstrated, with sensitivities of 96% to 98% and specificities of 95% to 99%, making PCR the best rapidly available diagnostic test in this setting.

Before development of PCR assays, brain biopsy was the only definitive way to establish the diagnosis of herpes simplex encephalitis, but this procedure is associated with intracranial hemorrhage and brain edema at the biopsy site. Currently, brain biopsy has a limited role in the etiologic diagnosis of encephalitis and should be considered only in patients who continue to deteriorate neurologically despite treatment with acyclovir, which suggests an alternative diagnosis.

Electroencephalography (EEG) is nonspecific for diagnosing herpes simplex encephalitis, although in more than 80% of patients, EEG findings show a temporal focus demonstrating periodic lateralizing epileptiform discharges.

In patients with herpes simplex encephalitis, T1-weighted magnetic resonance imaging (MRI) of the brain may identify edema and hemorrhage in the temporal lobes and hypodense areas and nonhomogeneous contrast enhancement. Bilateral temporal lobe involvement is nearly always pathognomonic for herpes simplex encephalitis but is a late development. Although MRI is useful for detecting the early changes of encephalitis, it also does not necessarily assist in determining a specific cause or in guiding therapy.

KEY POINT

Cerebrospinal fluid polymerase chain reaction assay is the most sensitive and specific test for the diagnosis of herpes simplex encephalitis.

Bibliography
Sabah M, Mulcahy J, Zeman A. Herpes simplex encephalitis. BMJ. 2012;344:e3166. [PMID: 22674925]

Item 7 Answer: D

Educational Objective: *Treat a patient with pneumococcal meningitis.*

Vancomycin and ceftriaxone are indicated for this patient, who most likely has acute bacterial meningitis. Cerebrospinal fluid analysis was consistent with this diagnosis, and Gram stain revealed gram-positive diplococci, suggesting that *Streptococcus pneumoniae* is the bacterial pathogen. Pending in vitro susceptibility testing of the isolated microorganism, the patient should be presumed to have pneumococcal meningitis caused by a pathogen that is resistant to peni-

cillin G. The combination of vancomycin and a third-generation cephalosporin (either ceftriaxone or cefotaxime) is therefore recommended because these agents have been shown to be synergistic in killing resistant pneumococi in experimental animal models of pneumococcal meningitis. Once results of in vitro susceptibility testing are available, antimicrobial therapy can be modified for optimal treatment.

The other antimicrobial combinations listed have not shown efficacy in the treatment of pneumococcal meningitis caused by highly penicillin-resistant strains.

KEY POINT

The recommended empiric therapy for pneumococcal meningitis is vancomycin plus a third-generation cephalosporin (either ceftriaxone or cefotaxime).

Bibliography
Brouwer MC, Tunkel AR, van de Beek D. Epidemiology, diagnosis, and antimicrobial treatment of acute bacterial meningitis. Clin Microbiol Rev. 2010;23:467-92. [PMID: 20610819]

Item 8 Answer: C

Educational Objective: *Diagnose aseptic meningitis.*

This patient's clinical illness and cerebrospinal fluid (CSF) findings are most consistent with aseptic meningitis, likely caused by herpes simplex virus (HSV). Aseptic meningitis is defined as meningeal inflammation without a known bacterial or fungal cause. Most cases are caused by viruses, although aseptic meningitis may also be associated with difficult-to-identify infectious agents, inflammation triggered by medications, malignancy, and other systemic inflammatory conditions. Although HSV-1 is typically associated with encephalitis, overt viral meningitis is much more common with HSV-2. The genital lesions of HSV-2 usually precede or accompany the onset of meningitis.

Typical CSF findings of acute bacterial meningitis include a leukocyte count of 1000 to 5000/µL ($1.0\text{-}5.0 \times 10^9$/L), a predominance of neutrophils, a glucose level of less than or equal to 40 mg/dL (2.2 mmol/L), a CSF-to-plasma glucose ratio of less than or equal to 0.4, and Gram stain positivity of 60% to 90%. This patient's CSF findings are inconsistent with acute bacterial meningitis.

Acute HIV infection associated with systemic symptoms is known as acute retroviral syndrome. It may present with fatigue, fever, pharyngitis, and lymphadenopathy. A small percentage of patients may have central nervous system involvement, including meningitis. The rash associated with acute HIV infection tends to be a diffuse, maculopapular eruption across the chest, back, face, and upper extremities; it may affect the palms and soles and is generally not painful or pruritic. Although this patient should be considered at risk for acute HIV infection, her presentation is less consistent with this diagnosis.

The differential diagnosis of HSV aseptic meningitis includes other illnesses with concurrent genital or perineal ulcerations and central nervous system involvement. These include other viral causes, collagen vascular diseases, inflammatory bowel disease, porphyria, and Behçet disease. Although relatively rare in the United States, Behçet disease is associated with recurrent painful oral and genital aphthous ulcerations, skin lesions, and uveitis, with neurologic manifestations in up to 25% of patients. When Behçet disease causes aseptic meningitis, the level of CSF pleocytosis is usually less than 100 cells/µL (0.10×10^9/L). Additionally, the lack of history or findings consistent with this uncommon condition makes this an unlikely diagnosis in this patient.

Aseptic meningitis is commonly associated with genital infection caused by herpes simplex virus 2 and is characterized by recurrent episodes of fever, headache, vomiting, and photosensitivity.

Bibliography

Putz K, Hayani K, Zar FA. Meningitis. Prim Care. 2013;40:707-26. [PMID: 23958365]

Item 9   Answer: C
Educational Objective: *Evaluate acute stroke*

Obtaining a noncontrast CT of the head to exclude hemorrhagic stroke is the most appropriate next step in the management of this patient. She has already undergone appropriate laboratory studies for evaluation of acute stroke. Determination of the plasma glucose level is a critical component of the acute stroke evaluation to exclude other conditions that may mimic stroke and to identify hyperglycemia, which is associated with poor outcome after stroke. Other laboratory studies required acutely include a complete blood count, basic metabolic panel, measurement of the serum troponin level, and a coagulation profile. An electrocardiogram is needed to rule out acute myocardial infarction and evaluate for atrial fibrillation.

Hemorrhagic stroke cannot be reliably distinguished from ischemic stroke on clinical grounds alone. Modern neuroimaging studies are necessary to identify the brain territory involved in a stroke and understand the pathophysiology involved. In the acute setting, CT of the head without contrast is the initial test of choice to confirm or exclude hemorrhagic stroke, and should be performed without significant delay as the results are needed to make treatment decisions, particularly related to thrombolytic therapy which should be administered as soon as possible once a patient is determined to be an appropriate candidate. Administering thrombolytic therapy before excluding a hemorrhagic stroke would be inappropriate.

CT of the head without contrast will easily rule out intracerebral hemorrhage, the principal initial criterion for excluding thrombolysis. Subtle signs of early infarction can sometimes be seen on a head CT scan, but many patients with acute ischemic stroke have normal results on this imaging study. MRI of the brain is the subsequent test of choice and can identify acute and subacute ischemia, hemorrhage, nonvascular lesions, or another underlying cause.

The treatment of blood pressure in the acute setting depends on whether the patient will be treated with intravenous tissue plasminogen activator (rtPA). In patients who are candidates for this agent, blood pressure should be less than 185/110 mm Hg, which can be achieved by the continuous infusion of labetalol or nicardipine. After rtPA infusion, blood pressure should be targeted to less than 180/105 mm Hg; labetalol or nicardipine is again appropriate for patients whose blood pressure exceeds these limits. Because this patient's blood pressure does not exceed these limits, she does not require intravenous labetalol.

In the acute setting, CT of the head without contrast is the initial test of choice to confirm or exclude hemorrhagic stroke.

Bibliography

Jauch EC, Saver JL, Adams HP Jr, et al. Guidelines for the early management of patients with acute ischemic stroke: a guideline for healthcare professionals from the American Heart Association/American Stroke Association. Stroke. 2013 Mar;44(3): 870-947. [PMID: 23370205]

Item 10   Answer: A
Educational Objective: *Treat acute ischemic stroke.*

The most appropriate therapy for this patient with a rapidly resolving acute stroke is antiplatelet therapy with aspirin. Antithrombotic agents remain the most commonly used drugs for acute stroke treatment. Two large clinical trials showed a benefit of treatment with aspirin compared with placebo in short-term mortality and recurrent stroke risk when administered within 48 hours of ischemic stroke onset. Aspirin plus extended-release dipyridamole has also been shown to be effective in acute stroke therapy. Clopridogrel is a reasonable alternative to aspirin in intolerant patients. One of these agents should be used in all patients with a transient ischemic attack (TIA) or stroke.

Neither dabigatran nor warfarin is appropriate for this patient. Warfarin may be considered for patients with high-risk cardioembolic causes of stroke and TIA (atrial fibrillation, left atrial appendage thrombus, left ventricular thrombus, and dilated cardiomyopathy with a significant reduction in ejection fraction). The direct thrombin inhibitor dabigatran can be considered as an alternative to warfarin in eligible patients with nonvalvular atrial fibrillation and stroke. Defer anticoagulation for 48 to 96 hours after established stroke if dabigatran is to be used

Heparins (such as low-molecular-weight enoxaparin) and related agents are not effective in reducing mortality or recurrent stroke in patients with either cardioembolic or noncardioembolic stroke. Heparin may be considered in the acute setting for patients with stroke caused by atrial fibrillation after cardiac surgery, for patients with a mechanical heart valve, or for those with cervicocephalic arterial dissections, none of which are present in this patient. Caution is warranted in administering heparin to patients with large cerebral infarcts because of the risk of hemorrhagic conversion of the ischemic stroke.

The effectiveness of thrombolysis with recombinant tissue plasminogen activator (rtPA) administered within 3 hours of development of acute ischemic stroke was examined in the National Institute of Neurological Disorders and Stroke trial. Compared with a placebo infusion, rtPA infusion was associated with improved functional outcomes at 3 months but not with earlier neurologic improvement or lower mortality. National guidelines recommend that treatment be initiated within 1 hour of arrival at the emergency department and within 3 hours of symptom onset. More recent evidence has shown a benefit of rtPA up to 4.5 hours after stroke onset, although exclusion criteria (age greater than 80 years, severe stroke, diabetes mellitus with a previous infarct, and any anticoagulant use) are more restrictive than for treatment 3 hours or less from onset. This patient's symptoms of stroke began 5 hours ago, and she is therefore not eligible for thrombolytic therapy.

Aspirin reduces short-term mortality and recurrent stroke risk when administered within 48 hours of ischemic stroke onset.

Bibliography

van der Worp HB, van Gijn J. Clinical practice. Acute ischemic stroke. N Engl J Med. 2007;357:572-9. [PMID: 17687132]

Item 11   Answer: D

Educational Objective: *Manage hypertension in the acute setting of ischemic stroke.*

This patient does not require treatment of her elevated blood pressure (190/90 mm Hg) at this time. Because her initial evaluation occurred 12 hours after her acute ischemic stroke, she is not a candidate for intravenous recombinant tissue plasminogen activator (rtPA). The American Heart Association guidelines support allowing blood pressures of up to 220/120 mm Hg in patients with ischemic stroke who are ineligible for rtPA treatment, unless evidence of end-organ damage (active ischemic coronary disease, heart failure, aortic dissection, hypertensive encephalopathy, acute kidney failure, or preeclampsia/eclampsia) exists. Treatment with antihypertensive agents in the acute setting may lead to neurologic worsening due to a decline in cerebral perfusion in the area of the tissue at risk (penumbra). In the recently completed Scandinavian Candesartan Acute Stroke Trial (SCAST), treatment with candesartan was associated with a trend toward poorer outcomes, primarily because of worsening neurologic status. The blood pressure target of less than 220/120 mm Hg is maintained until hospital discharge to home or a rehabilitation facility, at which time patients can begin or resume taking antihypertensive medication.

Intravenous hydralazine, a medication used to rapidly reduce blood pressure, is inappropriate because this patient does not require immediate treatment for hypertension.

Labetalol and nitroglycerin are similarly inappropriate because of their antihypertensive effect. Additionally, because this patient is at high risk for aspiration, oral medications should not be administered until a formal dysphagia screen is performed.

KEY POINT

Patients with ischemic stroke who are ineligible to receive recombinant tissue plasminogen activator and have no evidence of end-organ damage should not be treated for elevated blood pressure of up to 220/120 mm Hg.

Bibliography

Jauch EC, Saver JL, Adams HP Jr, et al. Guidelines for the early management of patients with acute ischemic stroke: a guideline for healthcare professionals from the American Heart Association/American Stroke Association. Stroke. 2013;44:870-947. [PMID: 23370205]

Item 12   Answer: B

Educational Objective: *Manage a transient ischemic attack.*

This patient most likely has had a transient ischemic attack (TIA) and should be admitted to the hospital immediately. Several clinical scoring systems are available to help guide management of TIA, including the ABCD[2] score. This score assigns one point for an Age of 60 years or greater, one point for a Blood pressure of 140/90 mm Hg or greater, two points for the Clinical symptom of hemiparesis, two points for Duration of 60 minutes or greater, and one point for the presence of Diabetes mellitus). Her score is 7, which indicates a 2-day stroke risk of 8.1%. The American Heart Association guidelines recommend hospital admission for all patients with probable TIAs whose ABCD[2] scores are 3 or greater. A noninvasive stroke evaluation can be completed more quickly in the hospital, with a particular focus on excluding cerebral infarction as a cause of symptoms and diagnosing the presence of intracardiac thrombi and extracranial internal carotid artery stenosis.

No evidence supports the combination of aspirin and clopidogrel for stroke prevention, and the use of the two agents in patients with TIA remains investigational. The combination of aspirin and clopidogrel was associated with a reduction in the risk of recurrent stroke or myocardial infarction in a major study, but the benefit was offset by a significant increase in the risk of intracerebral hemorrhage.

MRI may ultimately be indicated in this patient to rule out ischemic stroke and, in combination with magnetic resonance angiography, to evaluate the cause of the patient's TIA. However, MRI is often not readily available and, in any case, would not influence the decision to hospitalize the patient.

Although 24-hour electrocardiographic monitoring may be indicated for the evaluation of paroxysmal atrial fibrillation, the immediate next step is to admit this patient to the hospital for observation and to complete a stroke evaluation and monitor for recurrence of the TIA.

KEY POINT

All patients with probable transient ischemic attacks whose ABCD[2] scores (based on Age, Blood pressure, Clinical symptoms, Duration, and presence of Diabetes mellitus) are 3 or greater should be admitted to the hospital for evaluation.

Bibliography

Giles MF, Rothwell PM. Transient ischaemic attack: clinical relevance, risk prediction and urgency of secondary prevention. Curr Opin Neurol. 2009 Feb;22(1):46-53. [PMID: 19155761]

Item 13   Answer: C

Educational Objective: *Treat acute ischemic stroke with thrombolysis.*

This patient should receive intravenous recombinant tissue plasminogen activator (rtPA). She is evaluated only 60 minutes after onset of an acute ischemic stroke, which is well within the window for administration of thrombolysis, and has a measurable deficit on neurologic examination. She does not meet any of the exclusion criteria that would prevent thrombolytic treatment: her international normalized ratio and platelet count are within recommended limits, her blood pressure is less than 185/110 mm Hg, and an imaging study shows no hemorrhage. The National Institute of Neurological Disorders and Stroke rtPA trial showed that patients who received intravenous rtPA within 3 hours of stroke onset had a greater likelihood of clinical improvement at 3 months than did those who received placebo. The trial had no upper limit of neurologic deficit or age. Additionally, there is evidence of benefit of rtPA up to 4.5 hours after stroke onset, although exclusion criteria (age greater than 80 years, severe stroke, diabetes mellitus with a previous infarct, and any anticoagulant use) are more restrictive than for treatment 3 hours or less from onset.

High-dose (325-mg) aspirin is appropriate for patients who are not eligible for intravenous rtPA. However, in patients who have received intravenous rtPA, antiplatelet agents, including aspirin, must be withheld for at least 24 hours.

Intravenous heparin does not reduce the risk of recurrent embolic stroke or mortality in patients with stroke except in patients who have atrial fibrillation and thus is an incorrect therapeutic choice for this patient.

Administering labetalol to lower this patient's blood pressure is also inappropriate. For an uncomplicated ischemic stroke in patients without concurrent acute coronary artery disease or heart failure, antihypertensive medications should be withheld unless the blood pressure is greater than 220/120 mm Hg. If the patient is eligible for thrombolysis, blood pressure must be lowered and stabilized below 185/110 mm Hg before thrombolytic therapy is started. Because this patient's blood pressure (170/100 mm Hg) is less than these limits, an antihypertensive medication, such as labetalol, is not required. After thrombolysis, the target blood pressure is less than 180/105 mm Hg for at least 24 hours.

KEY POINT

Intravenous recombinant tissue plasminogen activator should be administered to a patient with ischemic stroke if it can be given within 3 hours of stroke onset and the patient meets the guideline criteria.

Bibliography

Wardlaw JM, Koumellis P, Liu M. Thrombolysis (different doses, routes of administration and agents) for acute ischaemic stroke. Cochrane Database Syst Rev. 2013; CD000514. [PMID: 23728633]

Item 14   Answer: B

Educational Objective: *Evaluate suspected subarachnoid hemorrhage.*

This patient should have a lumbar puncture. At presentation, she has the sudden onset of a severe headache, which is most concerning for subarachnoid hemorrhage. In a minority of patients with a small amount of blood in the subarachnoid space, computed tomography (CT) of the head may initially be normal. When this occurs, a lumbar puncture is required to detect erythrocytes or xanthochromia (a yellowish discoloration caused by the breakdown of erythrocytes) in the cerebrospinal fluid (CSF). Because xanthochromia may not develop for 6 hours or longer after the initial event, the presence of erythrocytes in the CSF should prompt consideration of a subarachnoid hemorrhage. A lumbar puncture is also helpful for excluding other diagnoses, such as meningitis, and for measuring the CSF opening pressure.

Because the initial CT of the head without contrast was normal, CT with contrast is unlikely to show a mass lesion sufficient in size to cause headache. CT angiography or venography may eventually be used to rule out aneurysms or dural sinus thrombosis, but subarachnoid hemorrhage first needs to be ruled out in the acute setting.

Although magnetic resonance angiography (MRA) eventually may be necessary to exclude dissection or aneurysms as the cause of this patient's symptoms, it is inappropriate at this time. Unless the presence of a subarachnoid hemorrhage is first established, an aneurysm detected on MRA or other vascular imaging studies may be an incidental finding that does not require surgical intervention.

The effectiveness of magnetic resonance imaging (MRI) for diagnosing subarachnoid hemorrhage remains under investigation. Additionally, MRI is time consuming and may not adequately differentiate subarachnoid hemorrhage from other diagnoses. Unlike CSF analysis, MRI does not afford the additional benefit of measuring the CSF opening pressure.

Of note, clinical examination findings, including those from funduscopy, have insufficient sensitivity and specificity to establish the diagnosis of subarachnoid hemorrhage.

KEY POINT

In a patient with a suspected subarachnoid hemorrhage and normal CT scan of the head, a lumbar puncture is the most appropriate next step in evaluation.

Bibliography

Perry JJ, Spacek A, Forbes M, et al. Is the combination of negative computed tomography result and negative lumbar puncture result sufficient to rule out subarachnoid hemorrhage? Ann Emerg Med. 2008;51:707-13. [PMID: 18191293]

Item 15   Answer: B

Educational Objective: *Treat dementia with cognitive stimulation.*

Patients with dementia should be encouraged to work on cognitive tasks. A 2012 Cochrane review evaluated the benefit of cognitive stimulation on the cognition of patients with dementia. Cognitive stimulation included a range of activities designed to stimulate thinking, concentration, and memory. Cognitive stimulation was associated with improved cognitive function immediately after treatment. Quality of life also improved, but there was no impact on mood, overall functional level, or caregiver outcomes.

Acupuncture does not seem to improve cognition in patients with dementia. A 2009 systematic review identified three randomized controlled trials, two of which examined the effect of acupuncture on cognition and found no benefit compared with drug therapy.

A review of controlled trials of reminiscence therapy, the use of written or oral life histories to improve psychological well-being, found insufficient evidence to recommend the efficacy of this intervention to improve cognition in patients with dementia.

The antioxidant vitamin E may reduce the rate of institutionalization for patients with Alzheimer disease, although the effect is modest and no improvement on cognitive scores was found. However, a meta-analysis found an increase in all-cause mortality in patients taking high-dose vitamin E compared with controls, and this intervention is therefore not recommended.

KEY POINT

In patients with dementia, cognitive stimulation is associated with improved cognitive function and quality of life immediately after treatment but had no impact on mood, overall functional level, or caregiver outcomes.

Bibliography

Woods B, Aguirre E, Spector AE, Orrell M. Cognitive stimulation to improve cognitive functioning in people with dementia. Cochrane Database Syst Rev. 2012; CD005562. [PMID: 22336813]

Item 16   Answer: D

Educational Objective: *Diagnose frontotemporal dementia*

The most likely diagnosis is frontotemporal dementia, which is a progressive neuropsychiatric disorder characterized by early behavioral and personality changes that range from apathy to social disinhibition. Patients may fail to change their clothes, brush their teeth, pursue their former interests, or initiate many of their previous activities that constituted a normal day. They may fixate, in a seemingly idiosyncratic fashion, on a particular activity, such as going to the bathroom, sorting through a wallet, hoarding magazines, or watching television. Some patients have greater disinhibition and emotional lability (crying or laughing inappropriately). Magnetic resonance imaging of the brain shows disproportionate atrophy of the frontal and anterior temporal regions.

The onset of Alzheimer disease is insidious. Persistent forgetfulness is the hallmark of Alzheimer disease. As the disease progresses, memories are lost and problems with word-finding ability become apparent. The ability to perform complex mental operations, such as reading or calculating, or to execute multistep tasks, such as planning a meal or shopping, declines. Visuospatial impairment and apraxia develop, with patients losing the ability to dress themselves, perform complex motor actions, or use tools, such as a television remote control or a telephone.

Creutzfeldt-Jakob disease (CJD) is the most common of the human prion diseases, with an annual worldwide incidence of less than 1 in 1,000,000 persons. The main clinical features of CJD are dementia that progresses rapidly over months and startle myoclonus, although the latter may not be present early in the illness. Other prominent features include visual or cerebellar disturbance, pyramidal/extrapyramidal dysfunction, and akinetic mutism.

Dementia with Lewy bodies is accompanied by parkinsonism, visual hallucinations, and fluctuating symptoms, none of which this patient has. The characteristic cognitive profile of dementia in patients with dementia with Lewy bodies includes impaired learning and attention, psychomotor slowing, constructional apraxia, and more profound visuospatial impairment but less memory impairment than in similarly staged patients with Alzheimer disease.

KEY POINT

Frontotemporal dementia is a progressive neuropsychiatric condition characterized by early behavioral and personality changes that range from apathy to social disinhibition.

Bibliography

Blass DM, Rabins PV. In the clinic. Dementia. Ann Intern Med. 2008;148:ITC4-1-ITC4-16. [PMID: 18378944]

Item 17   Answer: B
Educational Objective: *Treat Alzheimer disease.*

The most appropriate next step in treatment is a trial of memantine. This patient has Alzheimer disease that is moderately advanced and now has difficulties with basic activities of daily living. The N-methyl-D-aspartate receptor antagonist memantine is the only drug approved by the Food and Drug Administration as first-line treatment of moderate to advanced Alzheimer disease. Memantine has been shown to improve cognition and global assessment of dementia, but although the changes have been statistically significant, the clinical effect is not always evident. Memantine may improve quality-of-life measures, but these findings are not robust. Although evidence is limited, there is some suggestion that the stepped approach of adding memantine to a regimen that includes a cholinesterase inhibitor (such as donepezil) results in a modest additional benefit compared with substituting memantine for the cholinesterase inhibitor. This patient did not tolerate donepezil, but could be tried on a different cholinesterase inhibitor at a low dose. If the patient tolerates the cholinesterase inhibitor, memantine could be added to the regimen as well.

Benzodiazepines, such as lorazepam, are used to treat anxiety and some sleep disorders. However, their use is limited in patients with dementia because of lack of efficacy and risks of causing delirium, and they should generally be avoided.

Quetiapine is an antipsychotic medication, and sertraline is an antidepressant agent. Although both drugs can be used in treating patients with Alzheimer disease, their use is limited to the treatment of the behavioral symptoms of psychosis and depression, respec-

tively, neither of which this patient has at this time. The effectiveness of antipsychotic medications on behavioral problems is limited, and their use is associated with an increased risk of death in patients with dementia.

KEY POINT

The N-methyl-D-aspartate receptor antagonist memantine is approved by the Food and Drug Administration as first-line treatment of moderate to advanced Alzheimer disease.

Bibliography

Blass DM, Rabins PV. In the clinic. Dementia. Ann Intern Med. 2008;148:ITC4-1-ITC4-16. [PMID: 18378944]

Item 18   Answer: D
Educational Objective: *Manage age-related memory loss.*

This patient should be followed clinically for evidence of progressive cognitive deficits. There are universal age-related declines in cognition that chiefly affect memory, learning, and problem solving beginning around age 40 years, and these changes may be noticeable to patients. Distinguishing normal changes associated with age from more significant cognitive impairments may be challenging. This patient's symptoms of memory impairment are primarily related to short-term memory (recall of names, numbers, faces, and the location of placed objects). However, in other cognitive domains, he continues to function at a high level, with no evidence of deterioration from his previous performance and no impairment in social or occupational function. There is no suggestion that his perceived memory loss is progressive, and his score on cognitive screening testing does not meet clinical criteria for dementia. Memory loss that does not interfere significantly with a patient's social or occupational function does not require immediate evaluation or treatment, although clinical follow-up for evidence of progressive change is appropriate.

Mild cognitive impairment (MCI) describes a loss of cognitive ability that exceeds the expected age-related memory loss but does not interfere significantly with daily activities. The boundary between MCI and dementia is unclear, although 10% to 15% of patients with MCI will meet the criteria for dementia within 1 year. Accurately detecting MCI can be challenging, and in some patients with atypical features or in whom the degree of cognitive functional decline is unclear, formal neuropsychological testing can more fully reveal a patient's cognitive deficits and abilities. However, no neuroprotective interventions have been shown to prevent the progression from MCI to dementia in these patients.

Although a daily aspirin may be helpful in the primary prevention of cardiovascular disease in high-risk patients, there is no evidence that aspirin decreases the risk of cognitive decline, and it is not recommended for prophylaxis.

If this patient had evidence of dementia or a history of head trauma, magnetic resonance imaging of the brain (or computed tomography of the head) would be appropriate. However, an imaging study serves no purpose in patients with age-related memory loss or MCI.

Donepezil is a cholinesterase inhibitor that has been shown to improve the cognitive function of patients with mild, moderate, and even severe dementia due to Alzheimer disease. The drug has no role in preventing or treating age-related memory loss or in preventing the progression from MCI to dementia.

Memory loss that does not interfere significantly with patients' social or occupational function does not indicate dementia, and such patients may be appropriately followed without immediate evaluation or treatment.

Bibliography

Petersen RC. Clinical practice. Mild cognitive impairment. N Engl J Med. 2011;364: 2227-34. [PMID: 21651394]

Item 19   Answer: A

Educational Objective: *Evaluate suspected dementia.*

The next step in the evaluation of this patient is to perform a cognitive function screening test. Multiple validated instruments are available that may be administered in the office or at the bedside that help identify cognitive deficits and estimate their severity. Two commonly used tests are the Mini-Mental State Examination (MMSE) and the Montreal Cognitive Assessment (MoCA). Both tests may be administered in approximately 10 minutes, report scores on a 30-point scale, and have excellent sensitivity and specificity for dementia. This patient's progressive loss of memory and cognitive function are consistent with a diagnosis of dementia, and testing would be helpful in confirming and gauging the degree of severity of the cognitive deficits suggested by his recent history. The social history is significant for the timing of symptom recognition. With the death of his wife, the patient lost his primary caregiver, who may have been compensating for his cognitive deficits.

The U.S. Preventive Services Task Force has concluded that there is insufficient evidence to recommend routine screening for dementia in older adults, primarily because the early diagnosis of cognitive deficits does not appear to alter outcomes. However, in patients presenting with evidence of clinically significant cognitive impairment, testing to establish the diagnosis and guide therapy is indicated, as in this patient.

The other tests listed in the options may help determine the cause of dementia after the diagnosis is established. Lumbar puncture and electroencephalography, although not part of the routine evaluation of patients with dementia, may help establish a diagnosis in some patients. For example, in patients with clouding of consciousness or delirium, the lumbar puncture would be helpful in identifying meningitis.

The results of a basic metabolic panel may help distinguish some of the reversible causes of memory loss, including metabolic abnormalities, infection, and endocrinopathies.

Numerous expert consensus statements recommend that neuroimaging (magnetic resonance imaging of the brain or computed tomography of the head) be done in patients with dementia to detect clinical findings not suspected from the history and physical examination. However, the benefit of detecting these unsuspected lesions is not always clear.

Toxicology screening should be directed by clinical clues in the history or physical examination and is not part of the routine evaluation of patients with possible dementia.

Validated office or bedside screening tests for cognitive function are useful for evaluating the presence of dementia in patients presenting with evidence of cognitive impairment.

Bibliography

Blass DM, Rabins PV. In the clinic. Dementia. Ann Intern Med. 2008;148:ITC4-1-ITC4-16. [PMID: 18378944]

Item 20   Answer: A

Educational Objective: *Diagnose delirium in an older patient after surgery.*

This patient has classic signs and symptoms of delirium, which is a syndrome characterized by altered mental status with a wide range of potential neuropsychiatric manifestations. The clinical hallmark is inattention and a fluctuating course. Delirium is the most common complication in older hospitalized patients, in whom it is especially common after surgery (up to 50% of postoperative patients in some studies). Delirium may be caused by almost any medical or surgical condition, intoxication, or medication (or withdrawal from that medication). Primary considerations include medication toxicity, central nervous system infection (meningitis or encephalitis), alcohol withdrawal, thiamine deficiency, folate deficiency, hepatic encephalopathy, and seizures.

Although a potentially reversible condition, delirium is associated with significant morbidity and mortality. Delirium is an independent risk factor for death, need for institutionalization, and development of dementia. Unfortunately, management of delirium has not been shown to improve long-term mortality or reduce the need for institutional care.

A diagnosis of dementia cannot be established in this patient because she has no history of cognitive impairment and her current mental status changes developed abruptly after surgery. The presence of a fluctuating level of consciousness is also atypical for dementia.

Clinical features of herpes simplex encephalitis include fever, headache, confusion, cranial nerve deficits, and seizures. Although this patient has some of these findings, the lack of fever and focal findings on neurologic examination argue strongly against a diagnosis of herpes simplex encephalitis.

Stroke is unlikely in this patient because mental status changes in isolation, without any focal or localizing findings on the neurologic examination, are not typical of stroke.

Delirium in older patients is an independent risk factor for increased mortality, institutionalization, and development of dementia.

Bibliography

Witlox J, Eurelings LS, de Jonghe JF, et al. Delirium in elderly patients and the risk of postdischarge mortality, institutionalization, and dementia: a meta-analysis. JAMA. 2010;304:443-51. [PMID: 20664045]

Item 21   Answer: D

Educational Objective: *Prevent delirium in a hospitalized patient at high risk.*

Elderly patients with a history of dementia are at very high risk for developing delirium during a hospitalization. Delirium is an acute state of confusion that may manifest as a reduced level of consciousness, cognitive abnormalities, perceptual disturbances, or emotional disturbances. Prevention involves addressing medical and environmental issues. Urinary catheters are associated with an increased risk of delirium. In the absence of a medical indication for a catheter (relieve urinary retention, monitor fluid status in acutely ill patients when this directly impacts medical treatment, manage patients with stage 3 or 4 pressure ulcers on the buttocks), the catheter should be removed.

Benzodiazepines and anticholinergic medications have sedating effects but can cause delirium in elderly patients. They should generally be avoided unless a specific indication is present, such as benzodiazepines for alcohol withdrawal or diphenhydramine for an allergic reaction. Alternative nonpharmacologic methods for relaxation include music, massage, and meditation.

In appropriately selected patients with severe delirium, low-dose haloperidol or another antipsychotic agent may lessen the severity and duration of delirium, but these drugs are not indicated for the prevention of this disorder. The use of antipsychotic medications in elderly patients with dementia is associated with an increased risk of death, primarily due to infection such as pneumonia.

A normal sleep-wake cycle should be maintained as much as possible, minimizing interruptions or unnecessary testing during the night, and keeping a light on and increasing stimulation during the day. Unless medically necessary, routine safety checks throughout the night are therefore not indicated.

KEY POINT

Access to hearing aids, glasses, and canes and removal of unnecessary restraints and urinary catheters are basic procedures to reduce the risk of delirium in hospitalized patients at risk for developing this disorder.

Bibliography

Downing LJ, Caprio TV, Lyness JM. Geriatric psychiatry review: differential diagnosis and treatment of the 3 D's - delirium, dementia, and depression. Curr Psychiatry Rep. 2013;15:365. [PMID: 23636988]

Item 22   Answer: D
Educational Objective: *Treat carpal tunnel syndrome.*

This patient has carpal tunnel syndrome, and the most appropriate initial treatment, in addition to the avoidance of repetitive wrist motions, is wrist splinting. Wrist splinting is most effective when done in the neutral position compared with 20 degrees of extension, and full-time splinting appears to be superior to nocturnal splinting, although nocturnal splinting is more convenient for patients.

Local glucocorticoid injections have been shown to provide short-term (up to 3 months) pain relief, although the effect does not appear to be durable. Contraindications to local glucocorticoid injections include thenar weakness and atrophy and profound sensory loss.

Owing to possible adverse effects, drug therapy should be reserved for patients in whom wrist splinting has failed. Although nonsteroidal anti-inflammatory drugs, such as ibuprofen, are frequently used as first-line therapy, evidence of their effectiveness is lacking.

Surgical intervention should be reserved for patients in whom both nonpharmacologic and pharmacologic conservative therapies have failed or patients who have progressive sensory or motor deficits and moderate to severe findings on electrodiagnostic studies.

KEY POINT

Initial therapy for carpal tunnel syndrome is wrist splinting and avoidance of repetitive wrist motions.

Bibliography

Jarvik JG, Comstock BA, Kliot M, et al. Surgery versus non-surgical therapy for carpal tunnel syndrome: a randomised parallel-group trial. Lancet. 2009;374:1074-81. [PMID: 19782873]

Item 23   Answer: C
Educational Objective: *Treat acute Bell palsy.*

This patient has the acute onset of Bell palsy and should receive prednisone. Mounting evidence implicates an inflammatory/infectious cause of Bell palsy that is most likely due to human herpesvirus 1 infection of the facial nerve. However, Bell palsy is not considered contagious. Cranial nerve VII innervates all muscles of facial expression. Therefore, any cause of a complete facial neuropathy will impair the entire hemiface, including the forehead corrugator muscles that are typically spared by cerebral lesions. Bell palsy should not be confused with Bell phenomenon, which describes the reflexive rolling upwards of the globe during eye closure. When a normal person is asked to close the eyes, forced eyelid opening will reveal this phenomenon, as will the presence of selective paralysis of the orbicularis oculi muscles due to a facial neuropathy. Facial neuropathies will otherwise spare the extraocular muscles that govern globe movement. Patients with Bell palsy may also report dry mouth, hyperacusis, impaired taste, and pain and numbness near the ear. Abrupt onset of symptoms building over 1 to 2 days is typical. Because Bell palsy is a diagnosis of exclusion, every effort must be made to exclude other identifiable causes of facial paralysis, such as Lyme disease, HIV infection, acute and chronic otitis media, cholesteatoma, and multiple sclerosis. Patients with other common causes of acute peripheral facial paralysis will often have findings on history or physical examination that suggest the correct diagnosis. The most appropriate treatment of Bell palsy is prednisone, 40 mg/d, preferably administered within the first 72 hours.

The use of antiherpesvirus agents, such as acyclovir, as monotherapy for Bell palsy has not been shown to be helpful, although a prodromal viral illness can sometimes precede Bell palsy, as it did in this patient.

High-dose intravenous glucocorticoids, such as methylprednisolone, can be used in the treatment of acute exacerbations of multiple sclerosis but are not indicated in the treatment of Bell palsy. This patient is less likely to have multiple sclerosis than isolated Bell palsy because this is her first episode of a neurologic deficit, and most of the neurologic examination is unremarkable.

This patient's headache is relatively mild, and sumatriptan is therefore not indicated. Migraine, when complicated, can result in facial weakness, but this does not occur in a Bell palsy distribution. In Bell palsy, both the upper and lower facial muscles are affected (lower motoneuron cranial nerve VII weakness). In migraine-associated weakness (upper motoneuron cranial nerve VII weakness), the lower facial muscles are weak, but the upper facial muscles are spared.

KEY POINT

The most appropriate treatment of Bell palsy is prednisone, preferably administered within the first 72 hours of development.

Bibliography

Thaera GM, Wellik KE, Barrs DM, et al. Are corticosteroid and antiviral treatments effective for Bell palsy? A critically appraised topic. Neurologist. 2010;16:138-40. [PMID: 20220455]

Item 24   Answer: A

Educational Objective: *Treat diabetic neuropathy.*

This patient should be treated with gabapentin. He has diabetic neuropathy, which involves injury to sensory, motor, and autonomic nerves. Loss of sensation in the distal extremities, typically beginning in the feet and toes and eventually developing a "stocking-glove" distribution associated with paresthesia or painful dysesthesia, is the most common presentation of this condition. Loss of sensation in the lower extremities plays a major part in the development of foot ulcerations, which can lead to limb loss. No definitive treatment for diabetic neuropathy exists other than to improve glycemic control. Pharmacologic therapy, however, may help alleviate symptoms. Treatment options consist of various antiseizure medications (gabapentin, phenytoin, carbamazepine), tricyclic antidepressants (amitriptyline, desipramine), and partial serotonin and norepinephrine reuptake inhibitors (duloxetine). Topical application of capsaicin cream is also appropriate. Some patients also experience acute pain after a period of poor glycemic control; improvement can occur if excellent glycemic control (hemoglobin A_{1c} level <7.0%) is established and maintained for several months.

Nerve conduction studies might show marked slowing of nerve conduction, and a sural nerve biopsy would confirm the presence of segmental demyelination. These diagnostic tests, however, are unnecessary in a patient in whom the diagnosis of acute painful diabetic neuropathy is so likely, given his compatible history and physical examination findings.

Starting a potentially addictive and dangerous drug (such as oxycodone), especially when used for prolonged periods, is inappropriate therapy for a condition that may well be self-limiting.

KEY POINT

Pharmacologic therapy for painful diabetic neuropathy may include anticonvulsant therapy, tricyclic antidepressants, partial serotonin and norepinephrine reuptake inhibitors, and topical capsaicin.

Bibliography

Hovaguimian A, Gibbons CH. Clinical approach to the treatment of painful diabetic neuropathy. Ther Adv Endocrinol Metab. 2011;2:27-38. [PMID: 21709806]

Item 25   Answer: C

Educational Objective: *Test for diabetes mellitus and impaired glucose tolerance in a patient with suspected small-fiber peripheral neuropathy.*

A glucose tolerance test to detect diabetes mellitus or impaired glucose tolerance is the most appropriate next diagnostic study for this patient. The patient's history of burning feet, in conjunction with neurologic examination findings showing only distal sensory loss with normal reflexes and muscle strength, is suggestive of early diabetic neuropathy, which is a primarily axonal, symmetric sensory polyneuropathy that may have only minimal findings (such as a mild reduction in sensory nerve action potentials on nerve conduction testing) early in the course of the disease. Diabetic neuropathy typically initially affects the distal lower extremities due to the length of these nerve fibers. Over time, the sensory loss ascends, with symptoms appearing in the hands when the lower extremity sensory loss reaches the mid-calf level; this is termed the "stocking-glove" pattern. Motor involvement follows the same pattern, but occurs only in severe cases after sensory changes are present. Almost 20% of patients have some evidence of nerve dysfunction when their diabetes is diagnosed, indicating that nerve damage can occur before true diabetes is present, such as with impaired fasting glucose. In this patient with evidence of possible diabetic neuropathy and mildly elevated fasting blood glucose, further testing for abnormal glucose metabolism is warranted. A 2-hour glucose tolerance test can be used to detect diabetes in patients with a normal or near-normal fasting plasma glucose level; approximately 30% of patients with normal fasting plasma glucose levels will have an oral glucose tolerance test diagnostic for diabetes. A result of 140 mg/dL to 199 mg/dL (7.8 mmol/L to 11.0 mmol/L) from this test establishes a diagnosis of impaired glucose tolerance, and a result of 200 mg/dL (11.1 mg/dL) or greater is diagnostic of diabetes.

An examination of cerebrospinal fluid (CSF) obtained on lumbar puncture is not indicated in this patient. CSF studies should be considered in patients with acute or rapidly progressive neuropathy or polyradiculoneuropathy and in patients with severe weakness, sensory loss, or absent deep tendon reflexes. In patients with Guillain-Barré syndrome or chronic inflammatory polyradiculoneuropathy, CSF examination typically shows a normal cell count with elevated CSF protein level (albuminocytologic dissociation). CSF testing in such patients also helps to exclude infectious disorders, such as West Nile virus, HIV, and polyradiculoneuropathy caused by cytomegalovirus, which can present similarly.

Given the symptom of burning feet and the absence of foot deformities (high arches, hammertoes) or abnormalities on strength and reflex testing, hereditary motor sensory polyneuropathy (Charcot-Marie-Tooth) disease is not likely. Although it is a common cause of peripheral neuropathy, patients with this disorder typically do not have neuropathic pain, and many patients also do not have sensory symptoms, despite having sensory loss on examination. Many patients in whom hereditary motor sensory polyneuropathy is ultimately diagnosed are unaware of a family history of peripheral neuropathy, so the lack of family history in this patient does not necessarily exclude the diagnosis. Genetic testing is commercially available for many of the different forms of this disease, but genetic testing should be considered only in those patients with a known family history or in those with long-standing neuropathic symptoms and high arches and hammertoes on examination.

A skin biopsy may be helpful in diagnosing patients with polyneuropathy of unclear etiology to assess the status of small nerve fibers in the dermis, and is particularly useful in patients without a likely cause and normal nerve conduction studies. This test would not be indicated in this patient prior to testing for abnormalities in glucose metabolism or further evaluation for the causes of her neuropathy.

KEY POINT

A history of burning or lancinating distal extremity pain and examination findings showing only sensory loss suggest a small-fiber peripheral neuropathy, which is most frequently associated with diabetes mellitus and impaired glucose tolerance.

Bibliography

Papanas N, Ziegler D. Polyneuropathy in impaired glucose tolerance: is postprandial hyperglycemia the main culprit? A mini-review. Gerontology. 2013;59:193-8. [PMID: 23207896]

Item 26   Answer: C

Educational Objective: *Treat drug-induced dystonic reaction.*

Treatment with an anticholinergic medication, such as diphenhydramine, is the most appropriate next step in therapy. Typical and atypical antipsychotic drugs (also known as neuroleptics) such as ziprasidone, as well as antiemetic and serotoninergic medications, can cause dystonic reactions that develop rapidly or sometimes occur after weeks, months, or years. Dystonic reactions generally consist of intermittent spasmodic or sustained involuntary muscle contractions. The first step in treatment is withdrawal of the offending agent, which can sometimes resolve the dystonic reaction. However, additional treatment may be needed. Treatment options include anticholinergic agents, benzodiazepines, botulinum injections, NSAIDs, and muscle relaxants.

More invasive therapies such as surgery (for example, to restructure the sternocleidomastoid muscle) or deep brain stimulation are considered only if conservative treatment fails and significant dystonia continues.

Propranolol is not known to be an effective medication for treatment of drug-induced dystonic reactions.

KEY POINT

Initial treatment of drug-induced dystonic reactions is conservative, starting with withdrawal of the offending agent and then with drug therapy such as benzodiazepines or anticholinergic agents or botulinum injections.

Bibliography
Kutlu A, Dündar S, Altun NS, Budak F. Ziprasidone induced tardive cervical dystonia. Psychopharmacol Bull. 2009;42(4):64-8. [PMID: 20581794]

Item 27   Answer: D

Educational Objective: *Differentiate essential tremor from Parkinson disease.*

Recommending lifestyle modifications would be the most appropriate next step in management. The most likely diagnosis in this younger (<50 years of age) patient with a symmetric action/postural movement disorder is essential tremor. This is likely to have been inherited from a parent in an autosomal dominant fashion. Lifestyle changes, such as getting enough sleep and reduction of caffeine, can be helpful. Essential tremor characteristically improves with alcohol intake, and patients with essential tremor are at increased risk of alcohol misuse because of this. If lifestyle modifications do not adequately control essential tremor symptoms, medications, including β-blockers (such as propranolol) and anticonvulsants (such as primidone), are usually effective.

Although used more frequently for the treatment of refractory Parkinson disease, deep brain stimulation may be helpful in patients with severe essential tremor when other treatments have not been effective, but would not be an appropriate first-line treatment.

Parkinson disease is considerably less common than essential tremor and would be more likely to induce an asymmetric resting tremor (although essential tremor may be somewhat asymmetric early in its course before becoming more symmetric). Patients with Parkinson disease may also have other associated symptoms and signs such as postural changes and non-motor changes, including the potential for neuropsychiatric problems such as depression and memory loss. Bradykinesia (slower movements, including a slow shuffling gait)

and cogwheel rigidity are typically present on examination. Additionally, Parkinson disease would be less likely to affect an individual less than 50 years of age. Because this patient does not have a clinical picture consistent with Parkinson syndrome, treatment with a dopamine agonist would not be appropriate.

Anticholinergic agents are not known to be effective for treatment of essential tremor and would not be helpful in this patient.

KEY POINT

Essential tremor is characterized by a postural or action tremor that is symmetric, whereas Parkinson disease usually involves an asymmetric resting tremor.

Bibliography
Elble RJ. What is essential tremor? Curr Neurol Neurosci Rep. 2013 Jun;13(6):353. [PMID: 23591755]

Item 28   Answer: D

Educational Objective: *Diagnose Parkinson disease.*

The most likely diagnosis in this patient is Parkinson disease. Parkinson disease is a clinical diagnosis based on any combination of five cardinal features: (1) tremor in a limb at rest, (2) rigidity, (3) bradykinesia, (4) loss of postural reflexes, and (5) gait freezing. The manifestations of Parkinson disease vary from a barely perceptible tremor to severe, generalized akinetic-rigid parkinsonism. A tremor at rest is perhaps the most obvious feature of Parkinson disease and is a common presenting symptom. The tremor at rest readily disappears when sustaining a posture or during manual activities, in contrast to an essential tremor, which is an action tremor. Bradykinesia is manifested by paucity of spontaneous movement with severely affected patients sitting unnaturally still and demonstrating a lack of facial expressiveness ("facial masking"). In addition to whole-body slowness and impairment in fine motor movements, other consequences of advanced bradykinesia include drooling of saliva due to a lack of spontaneous swallowing, soft monotonous speech, micrographia (small, cramped handwriting), reduced arm swing when walking, and a short, shuffling gait. Sustained response to levodopa therapy is expected in patients with Parkinson disease and helps confirm the clinical diagnosis. Features suggesting an alternative condition include symmetric symptoms or signs, early falls, rapid progression, poor or waning response to levodopa, dementia, early autonomic failure, and ataxia.

The patient's findings are not compatible with cervical dystonia, essential tremor, or Huntington disease. Cervical dystonia, formerly known as torticollis, is a focal dystonia that involves the cervical musculature and causes abnormal postures of the head, neck, and shoulders. Quick, nonrhythmic, repetitive movements can also occur and can be mistaken for tremor.

Essential tremor is characterized by an upper extremity high-frequency tremor, which is present with both limb movement and sustained posture of the involved extremities and is absent at rest. The tremor is characteristically bilateral, but mild to moderate asymmetry may be present. Essential tremors typically improve with alcohol and worsen with stress. Tremor amplitude over time generally increases and can be so severe as to interfere with writing, drinking, and other activities requiring smooth, coordinated upper limb movements.

Huntington disease is an hereditary, progressive, neurodegenerative disorder characterized by increasingly severe motor impairment, cognitive decline, and psychiatric symptoms. In addition to chorea, other motor symptoms include ataxia, dystonia, slurred speech, impaired swallowing, and myoclonus. Various psychiatric symptoms, such as dysphoria, agitation, irritability, anxiety, apathy, disinhibition, delusions, and hallucinations, commonly occur.

> **KEY POINT**
>
> The diagnosis of Parkinson disease is based on a cardinal set of clinical features, including resting tremor, bradykinesia, rigidity, and postural instability.

Bibliography

Jankovic, J. (2013). Medical treatment of dystonia. Mov. Disord. 2013 Jun 15;28(7): 1001–12. [PMID: 23893456]

Item 29   Answer: C

Educational Objective: *Evaluate a first episode of seizure.*

This patient should be evaluated with an MRI of the brain. His history of an episode of blank stare, shaking left upper extremity, and abnormal complex behavior in the form of eating a large amount of food is concerning for a focal seizure with dyscognitive features (complex partial seizure). This is supported by the patient's inability to remember the episode. Imaging of the brain may reveal a structural abnormality, such as a previous subclinical stroke, that may be a focus of seizure activity. As his laboratory evaluation did not reveal any evidence of metabolic disturbance, the next steps in the evaluation of a first seizure include imaging of the brain and an electroencephalogram. MRI is preferred as an imaging modality because of its increased sensitivity compared with CT for detecting the types of structural lesions associated with seizure activity.

Echocardiography is not indicated in the routine evaluation of new or suspected seizure activity. Although seizure activity is sometimes mistaken for syncope, this patient remained conscious throughout the episode, excluding syncope. He also experienced confusion following the episode, which is also not characteristic for syncope. Additionally, echocardiography for evaluation of syncope is indicated only if structural heart disease is suspected.

A lumbar puncture is not indicated for this patient who has no evidence of infection based on the history and physical examination findings. He has not had photophobia, neck stiffness, fever, or persistent altered mental status to suggest meningitis or encephalitis.

Pseudoseizures can mimic true seizures. However, a complete seizure evaluation must be done before considering psychiatric evaluation for this diagnosis. Pseudoseizures can typically only be proved with video encephalography during an episode. Evaluation for metabolic or structural causes with laboratory and imaging studies is performed first.

> **KEY POINT**
>
> Patients presenting with a first seizure should undergo evaluation for a structural cause with brain imaging if no metabolic abnormalities are found.

Bibliography

Krumholz, A., S. Wiebe, G. Gronseth, et al. Practice Parameter: evaluating an apparent inprovoked first seizure in adults (an evidence-based review): Report of the Quality Standards Subcommittee of the American Academy of Neurology and the American Epilepsy Society." Neurology. 2007 Nov 20;69(21):1996–2007. [PMID: 18025394]

Item 30   Answer: C

Educational Objective: *Manage status epilepticus.*

This patient should be given lorazepam for treatment of status epilepticus. Status epilepticus is a condition in which a patient experiences a continuous generalized seizure or rapidly repeating seizures between which the patient does not regain consciousness that last more than 30 minutes, as occurred in this patient. Intravenous benzodiazepines are fast-acting, potent antiseizure medications and can terminate seizure activity within 2 to 3 minutes. Lorazepam or diazepam may be used, but lorazepam is preferred owing to its longer duration of action (12 to 24 hours) compared with diazepam (15 to 30 minutes).

Fosphenytoin (a water-soluble prodrug of phenytoin) or phenytoin is also given to patients in status epilepticus, following the administration of an intravenous benzodiazepine. Phenytoin has been shown to be effective as an initial therapy for status epilepticus as well as for maintaining a prolonged antiepileptic effect. However, it can take 10 minutes or longer to reach a therapeutic level at maximal infusion rates. Additionally, hypotension (28% to 50% of patients) and cardiac arrhythmias (2% of patients) are potential complications of rapid infusion and therefore limit the speed of administration. Consequently, administration of intravenous benzodiazepines is the preferred first-line treatment.

Levetiracetam is a relatively new antiepileptic agent with few side effects. However, its efficacy in the treatment of status epilepticus is limited, and its use for this indication is not currently recommended. There is no current evidence to suggest that levetiracetam would be more effective than a benzodiazepine as a first-line treatment option.

Phenobarbital is used for patients with status epilepticus only if initial treatment with benzodiazepines and fosphenytoin fails to terminate seizure activity. Phenobarbital causes significant depression of respiration and blood pressure, as well as strong sedation. Its use often requires intubation and mechanical ventilation and administration of vasopressors to support the patient until seizure activity ceases.

Valproate has been shown to be an effective alternative to phenytoin as a second-line drug in status epilepticus. However, similarly to phenytoin, limitations on infusion rate and time to therapeutic levels preclude it from use as a first-line treatment. Valproate also should be avoided in women of childbearing age, if possible.

Status epilepticus is a medical emergency and is associated with a significant increased risk of mortality, which is due in part to the metabolic stress of repeated muscular convulsions.

> **KEY POINT**
>
> Intravenous lorazepam is the first-line treatment for status epilepticus.

Bibliography

Nair PP, Kalita J, Misra UK. Status epilepticus: why, what, and how. J Postgrad Med. 2011 Jul-Sep;57(3):242–52. [PMID: 21941070]

Item 31   Answer: D

Educational Objective: *Manage a single unprovoked seizure.*

Clinical observation without antiepileptic drug therapy is reasonable for this patient. After a single unprovoked seizure, the risk of recurrence in patients without risk factors is estimated to be approximately 25%. The risk of recurrence is greatest in patients who have status epilepticus on presentation, an identifiable underlying neurologic cause, or abnormal results on an electroencephalogram (EEG). Patients with a partial seizure who are age 65 years or older or who have a family history of epilepsy may also be in a higher-risk category. The appropriate recommendation for this young patient, who has experienced a single idiopathic seizure but has no personal or family history of epilepsy, no identified neurologic cause of his seizure, and normal results on an EEG, and does not prefer treatment, is that no medication be started. As with all medical treatment recommendations, patient preference must be taken into account, and some patients in the low-risk group may elect to start therapy after a single seizure, particularly if they have a high-risk occupation. If a second seizure occurs, the recurrence risk is greater than 60%, and antiepileptic medical therapy should be recommended at that time.

Since this patient prefers not to start drug therapy at this time, neither carbamazepine nor phenytoin is indicated.

Epilepsy surgery is reserved for patients who have disabling seizures that cannot be controlled with medication. Such surgery is not indicated for this patient, who had a single seizure that resolved uneventfully.

Of note, driver's license privileges are restricted in every state in the United States for persons who have experienced a seizure. Specific restrictions vary by state, with typical requirements of a seizure-free period of 3 to 12 months in order to again operate a motor vehicle; a few states make exceptions for a single seizure. Reinstatement of driving privileges depends on demonstrating freedom from seizures for the specified period and having a reasonable expectation of future seizure control. Initiation of antiepileptic medication is not required by law.

KEY POINT

Unless special circumstances exist, not starting antiepileptic drug therapy in a patient with a single unprovoked seizure is a reasonable treatment option.

Bibliography
Seneviratne U. Management of the first seizure: an evidence based approach. Postgrad Med J. 2009 Dec;85(1010):667-73. [PMID: 20075405]

Item 32   Answer: B

Educational Objective: *Diagnose focal seizure with dyscognitive features (complex partial seizure).*

This patient's "spells" are most likely focal seizures with dyscognitive features (complex partial seizures). The incidence of seizures is greatest in infants and older adults, with half of new-onset seizures presenting in persons older than 65 years. The latter reflects the increased prevalence of underlying brain diseases–particularly cerebrovascular disease, neurodegenerative conditions (such as Alzheimer disease), and brain tumors– that increase seizure risk in this segment of the population.

Seizures are classified as focal or generalized on the basis of the areas of the brain involved at onset. Seizures that present in adulthood are usually focal in onset; focal seizures in which the patient maintains full awareness are termed focal seizures without dyscognitive features (simple partial seizures), whereas those involving an alteration of consciousness, as in this patient, are classified as focal seizures with dyscognitive features (complex partial seizures). The most common site of onset for partial seizures is the temporal lobe. As described by this patient, temporal lobe events often begin with an aura of déjà vu, a rising epigastric sensation, or autonomic disturbances. Although automatisms, such as lip smacking, are occasionally reported in absence seizures, these features are atypical in absence seizures and are more suggestive of partial complex seizures. In this patient, his age of onset, duration of the event (several minutes), presence of oral automatisms, and reported postictal confusion and speech impairment all suggest a partial complex seizure.

Absence, generalized tonic–clonic, and myoclonic seizures are all manifestations of generalized epilepsy and are correlated with generalized epileptiform discharges on an electroencephalogram. Absence seizures are characterized by brief periods of staring and unresponsiveness, typically lasting seconds, with an immediate return to normal awareness. Absence seizures usually present in childhood. The duration of this patient's episodes, his confusion before returning to normal awareness, and his age argue against absence seizure being the diagnosis.

Generalized tonic–clonic (grand mal) seizures are characterized by stiffening of the trunk and extremities followed by generalized symmetric jerking. Such features were not reported by this patient.

Myoclonic seizures consist of brief, shock–like muscle jerks without loss of awareness. These features are not consistent with the history that this patient provides.

KEY POINT

Seizures that present in adulthood are usually focal in onset; focal seizures that involve altered awareness are classified as focal seizures with dyscognitive features (complex partial seizures), whereas seizures in which full awareness is maintained are termed focal seizures without dyscognitive features (simple partial seizures).

Bibliography
Berg AT, Berkovic SF, Brodie MJ, et al. Revised terminology and concepts for organization of seizures and epilepsies: report of the ILAE Commission on Classification and Terminology, 2005-2009. Epilepsia. 2010 Apr;51(4):676-85. [PMID: 20196795]

Item 33   Answer: B

Educational Objective: *Diagnose Guillain-Barré syndrome.*

The most likely diagnosis is Guillain-Barré syndrome (GBS), which is the most common cause of acute diffuse neuromuscular paralysis. GBS results from immune-mediated attacks on peripheral nerve myelin or axonal components. Patients initially experience rapid onset of symmetric weakness of the upper and lower limbs over days to weeks, generally in the setting of a recent infection (particularly *Campylobacter jejuni* infection), trauma, or surgery. Although many patients describe paresthesias or neuropathic pain in the hands and feet, objective sensory loss is usually mild or absent. Low back pain, presumably due to inflammatory demyelination at the spinal nerve root level, is often mistaken for compressive lumbosacral radiculopathy. Neurologic examination typically reveals weakness and decreased or absent deep tendon reflexes. Cerebrospinal fluid (CSF) analysis usually shows a normal cell count and an increased protein level (albuminocytologic dissociation) in 80% to 90% of patients; CSF glucose levels are normal.

Amyotrophic lateral sclerosis (ALS) is an incurable progressive neurodegenerative disease of unknown cause that results in muscle paralysis and death from respiratory failure, usually within 3 to 5 years of symptom onset. Common upper motoneuron features are spasticity, hyperreflexia, and pathologic reflexes, including extensor plantar responses. Typical lower motoneuron features are muscle weakness, atrophy, fasciculations, and cramps. The time course of this patient's symptoms and physical examination findings are not compatible with ALS.

Multiple sclerosis (MS) can present with a variety of symptoms, including a more slowly progressive myelopathy characterized by sensory or motor symptoms below an involved spinal level. Paralysis is typically flaccid in the early stage and progresses to become spastic at a later stage. However, this patient's rapid progression of primarily motor findings without sensory symptoms with involvement of the upper and lower extremities following an apparent triggering infection makes this an unlikely clinical presentation of MS.

Neck or back pain is often the initial symptom of spinal cord compression, followed rapidly by weakness, sensory changes, and bowel or bladder dysfunction. This young patient's rapidly progressive pain and weakness in the absence of trauma or a history of cancer make spinal cord compression unlikely.

KEY POINT

Patients with Guillain-Barré syndrome initially experience rapid onset of symmetric weakness of the upper and lower limbs over days to weeks, generally in the setting of a recent infection (particularly *Campylobacter jejuni* infection), trauma, or surgery.

Bibliography

Yuki N, Hartung HP. Guillain-Barré syndrome. N Engl J Med. 2012 Jun 14;366(24): 2294-304. [PMID: 22694000]

Item 34   Answer: A
Educational Objective: *Diagnose myasthenia gravis.*

Measurement of acetylcholine receptor antibodies and a repetitive nerve stimulation study are most likely to establish the diagnosis. This patient has myasthenia gravis caused by an autoantibody that blocks postsynaptic neuromuscular junctions. A generalized form and a less common ocular/oculobulbar form exist. The classic clinical feature of this disorder is fluctuating, fatigable muscle weakness that worsens with activity and improves with rest. All voluntary muscles can be affected, especially the ocular and bulbar muscles. Approximately 50% of patients initially have diplopia or ptosis. Bulbar symptoms, including slurred speech, dysphagia, nasal regurgitation of liquids, and fatigue while chewing, are presenting features in approximately 15% of these patients. Most patients have identifiable autoantibodies directed against the postsynaptic acetylcholine receptor or against muscle-specific tyrosine kinase (MuSK) receptors. Electromyography (EMG) testing, including single-fiber EMG, has a 97% to 99% sensitivity for diagnosis but lacks specificity. Serum thyroid-stimulating hormone levels should also be measured because of the association of myasthenia gravis with autoimmune thyroid disorders. Once the diagnosis is confirmed, a CT scan of the

chest should be performed to exclude a thymoma, which is present in up to 15% of patients.

Since myasthenia gravis is a disorder of the neuromuscular junction, MRI of the brain, muscle biopsy, nerve biopsy. and serum creatine kinase measurement are unlikely to be helpful in establishing the diagnosis.

KEY POINT

The classic clinical feature of myasthenia gravis is fluctuating, fatigable muscle weakness that worsens with activity and improves with rest.

Bibliography

Spillane J, Higham E, Kullmann DM. Myasthenia gravis. BMJ. 2012 Dec 21;345:e8497. [PMID: 23261848]

Item 35   Answer: D
Educational Objective: *Diagnose multiple sclerosis.*

This patient most likely has a relapse of multiple sclerosis (MS). She has a history of a previous episode consistent with intranuclear ophthalmoplegia and now presents with acute blurred vision with evidence of optic neuritis and focal muscle weakness, common presentations for MS flares. Internuclear ophthalmoplegia is a specific gaze abnormality characterized by impaired horizontal eye movement with weak adduction of the affected eye and abduction nystagmus of the contralateral eye. MS is an autoimmune disorder in which lymphocytes cross the blood-brain barrier and target myelin antigens, leading to inflammation and demyelination with neuroaxonal injury and neurodegenerative changes. Pathologic changes in nerve axons include accumulation of amyloid precursor proteins during acute stages of illness. The lesions are seen as plaques located primarily in the white matter on MRI.

Amyotrophic lateral sclerosis (ALS) is a devastating neurodenegerative disorder that affects the motor system at all levels. Although most patients with ALS tend to be older, it may affect individuals as early as the third decade. However, unlike this patient, most patients with ALS present with upper and lower extremity weakness and eventual development of dysarthria and dysphagia. Physical examination findings include fasciculations and profound wasting with hyperreflexia. The course is fulminant with eventual respiratory failure and frequent aspiration.

Guillain-Barré syndrome (GBS) has a dramatic presentation with areflexic paralysis and is a neurologic emergency. Patients with GBS typically present with paresthesias and weakness and pain in the extremities with paralysis and loss of reflexes. Two thirds of patients have a history of either respiratory tract infection or diarrhea that is believed to induce the formation of autoantibodies that target peripheral nerves. Inflammatory infiltrates cause areas of segmental demyelination that leads to subsequent polyneuropathy. This patient's clinical presentation is not consistent with GBS.

Lambert-Eaton myasthenic syndrome (LEMS) is an autoimmune neuromuscular disease that is classically associated with small cell lung cancer. The underlying pathologic mechanism involves autoantibodies that target voltage-gated calcium channels in the neuromuscular junction. Immune reactions on the tumor's surface trigger autoantibody production and release. Patients with LEMS commonly present with proximal muscle weakness, autonomic symptoms, and loss of reflexes, all of which are not present in this patient.

In myasthenia gravis, patients have IgG antibodies against acetylcholine receptors on the postsynaptic motor endplate that impede neuromuscular transmission. Fifty percent of patients present with ptosis or diplopia, although optic neuritis does not occur as is present in this patient. Limb weakness tends to be proximal, affects the arms more than the legs, and is generally symmetric, unlike in this patient with focal right proximal leg weakness. Muscle bulk and reflexes are normal, and sensation remains intact.

KEY POINT

The diagnosis of multiple sclerosis is based on clinical findings along with classic lesions seen on MRI that result from inflammation and axonal injury with resultant demyelination.

Bibliography

Frohman E, Racke M, Raine C. Multiple sclerosis - the plaque and its pathogenesis. N Engl J Med. 2006 Mar 2;354(9):942-55. [PMID: 16510748]

Item 36   Answer: C

Educational Objective: *Evaluate suspected multiple sclerosis.*

A lumbar puncture would be the most appropriate next diagnostic step for this patient. There is a high clinical suspicion for multiple sclerosis (MS) because of the patient's age, her prior transient neurologic symptoms, the abnormal findings on neurologic examination, and the periventricular white matter lesion seen on two MRIs of the brain. However, these imaging and examination results are insufficient to confirm that multiple regions of the central nervous system are affected at different times (dissemination in time and space), which is one of the diagnostic criteria of MS. Up to 85% of patients with MS have an abnormal finding on cerebrospinal fluid analysis, such as the presence of oligoclonal bands or elevation of the IgG index. Therefore, lumbar puncture is the most appropriate next step in diagnosis. Confirmation of the diagnosis of MS at this stage would allow intervention with immunomodulatory therapy and result in a lower risk of both future relapses and accumulation of neurologic impairment.

Antimyelin antibodies are antibodies to myelin oligodendrocyte glycoprotein and myelin basic protein and have been evaluated as potential markers of MS disease activity. However, studies have not documented effectiveness of their use in the diagnosis of MS. They would therefore not be indicated as a next diagnostic step in this patient.

In the assessment of vestibular function, electronystagmography (ENG) uses electrodes to record eye movements to help discriminate between central and peripheral causes of vertigo. However, this patient's current leg numbness, history of diplopia and vertigo, and findings of an extensor plantar response, a loss of vibratory sense, and reduced pain sensation of the leg point to a process not confined to vestibular function but associated with manifestations that are separate in both time (two neurologic events over 2 years) and space (different parts of the central nervous system). This is most compatible with MS. Furthermore, in a patient without symptoms of vertigo, the ENG is likely to be normal.

Similarly, magnetic resonance angiography, a noninvasive imaging technique used to detect vascular lesions, is unlikely to be helpful in this patient with probable MS.

KEY POINT

Cerebrospinal fluid analysis is useful when the clinical setting is suspicious for multiple sclerosis but neuroimaging is inconclusive.

Bibliography

Harrison DM. Multiple sclerosis. Ann Intern Med. 2014;160:ITC4-2-ITC4-18. [PMID: 24763702]

Section 9

Oncology

Questions

Item 1 [Basic]

A 62-year-old man is evaluated for a persistent cough of 9 months' duration and a 4.5-kg (10-lb) unintentional weight loss over the past 6 weeks. The patient has a 30-pack-year history of smoking cigarettes and continues to smoke.

On physical examination, his vital signs are normal. His body mass index is 24. There are decreased breath sounds and dullness to percussion at the right base. The remainder of the physical examination is normal.

Chest radiography confirms a right pleural effusion. Chest computed tomography (CT) confirms a right pleural effusion and a 2.1-cm spiculated nodule in the right middle lobe.

Which of the following is the most appropriate next diagnostic test?

(A)   CT-guided biopsy of the lung nodule
(B)   Integrated whole body PET-CT scan
(C)   Magnetic resonance imaging of the brain
(D)   Radiographic bone survey
(E)   Thoracentesis and pleural fluid cytology

Item 2 [Basic]

A 65-year-old woman seeks consultation in the office regarding lung cancer screening. She has a 40-pack-year history of cigarette smoking and continues to smoke. Her only active medical problem is chronic obstructive pulmonary disease treated with daily tiotropium inhaler and an albuterol inhaler as needed.

On physical examination, her vital signs are normal. Breath sounds are distant with occasional wheezing. The remainder of the physical examination is normal.

Which of the following screening tests can be recommended?

(A)   Annual chest radiography
(B)   Annual sputum for cytology
(C)   Combination annual chest radiography and sputum for cytology
(D)   Low-dose spiral chest computed tomography

Item 3 [Basic]

A 62-year-old man is evaluated following the incidental discovery of a 3-mm left lower lobe lung nodule on a recent computed tomography (CT) scan of the abdomen performed to evaluate for kidney stones. He has never smoked and has an otherwise unremarkable medical history. He takes no medications.

On physical examination, his vital signs are normal. The physical examination is unremarkable.

A dedicated CT of the chest shows only the 3-mm left lower lobe nodule and is otherwise normal. There are no other chest images available for comparison.

Which of the following is the most appropriate next step in management of this patient?

(A)   CT of the chest in 3 months
(B)   CT of the chest in 6 months
(C)   CT of the chest in 12 months
(D)   No follow-up imaging

Item 4 [Advanced]

A 55-year-old woman is evaluated for a cough, weakness, and fatigue of 4 weeks' duration. She has a 40-pack-year history of cigarette smoking.

On physical examination, her temperature is normal, blood pressure is 136/78 mm Hg, and pulse rate is 68 beats/min. No palpable lymphadenopathy is noted. The cardiopulmonary and neurologic examinations are normal.

A chest radiograph demonstrates a 5-cm left upper lobe pulmonary mass. A subsequent computed tomography (CT) scan shows the mass but no evident mediastinal lymphadenopathy. A positron emission tomography (PET) scan displays radiographic uptake in the mass but no disease elsewhere. A CT-guided biopsy demonstrates squamous cell carcinoma.

Which of the following is the most appropriate treatment?

(A)   Combination chemotherapy and radiation
(B)   Radiation
(C)   Surgery and adjuvant chemotherapy
(D)   Systemic chemotherapy

Item 5 [Advanced]

A 63-year-old man is evaluated for fatigue and a persistent cough of 7 weeks' duration. He has a 60-pack-year smoking history.

On physical examination, his vital signs and physical examination are normal.

A chest radiograph reveals a right hilar mass. A computed tomography (CT) scan of the thorax confirms the presence of a right perihilar mass and enlarged hilar and mediastinal lymph nodes.

An endobronchial mass is identified by bronchoscopy; brushings and biopsy reveal small cell lung cancer. A CT scan of the chest and abdomen is negative. A bone scan and magnetic resonance imaging of the brain are negative.

Which of the following is the most appropriate next step in the management of this patient?

(A) Chemotherapy with adjunctive radiation therapy

(B) Mediastinoscopy

(C) Radiation therapy

(D) Resection for cure

Item 6 [Advanced]

A 47-year-old premenopausal woman is evaluated after undergoing a wide excisional biopsy (lumpectomy) of her left breast after an abnormal screening mammogram. Pathology revealed an estrogen-receptor positive and progesterone-receptor-positive 1.4-cm intra-ductal carcinoma. There is no evidence of invasion, and biopsy spec-imen margins are free of cancer. The patient is otherwise well and takes no medications. There is no family history of breast or ovarian cancer.

Other than a well-healing biopsy scar, physical examination is nor-mal.

Which of the following is the most appropriate treatment for this patient?

(A) Adjuvant chemotherapy

(B) Aromatase inhibitor therapy

(C) Bilateral prophylactic mastectomy

(D) Radiation therapy to the left breast and tamoxifen therapy

Item 7 [Advanced]

A 23-year-old woman with a family history of cancer is evaluated for breast cancer risk. Her mother developed invasive breast cancer at age 47 years, and a maternal aunt died from ovarian cancer at age 52 years. The patient has no medical problems and takes no medications. She has never participated in a breast cancer screening program.

Physical examination, including breast and pelvic examination, are normal.

Which of the following is the most appropriate management for this patient?

(A) Annual mammography starting at age 50 years

(B) Tamoxifen therapy

(C) Prophylactic bilateral mastectomy and salpingo-oophorectomy

(D) Use a familial risk assessment tool to assess need for counsel-ing and testing

Item 8 [Basic]

A 46-year-old woman is evaluated for a painless lump she noticed in her left breast 2 weeks ago. She is premenopausal, and her last menstrual period was 1 week ago. Her mother had breast cancer diagnosed at age 55 years. Her medical history is unremarkable, and she takes no medications.

On physical examination, her vital signs are normal. There is a 1.0-cm firm, discrete, mobile mass in the upper outer quadrant of the right breast. There are no other breast abnormalities noted and no left axillary lymphadenopathy. The remainder of the physical exam-ination is normal.

A bilateral mammogram does not reveal any suspicious lesion in either breast.

Which of the following is the most appropriate management option for this patient?

(A) Aspiration or biopsy

(B) Clinical reevaluation in 1 month

(C) Magnetic resonance imaging of both breasts

(D) Repeat mammography in 6 months

Item 9 [Basic]

A 57-year-old woman is being evaluated after a recent diagnosis of invasive ductal adenocarcinoma of the right breast after detection of a mass on screening mammography. She has no family history of breast or ovarian cancer. Her medical history is otherwise unre-markable, and she takes no medications.

On physical examination, her vital signs are normal. No other breast abnormalities are noted, and there is no right axillary lympha-denopathy detected.

The patient undergoes tumor resection and a sentinel lymph node biopsy of the right axilla. A 1.2-cm invasive ductal adenocarcinoma with clear margins is confirmed, with no lymph node metastases. A complete blood count, metabolic profile, liver chemistry tests, and chest radiography are normal.

Which of the following will be most helpful in directing the approach to management of this patient?

(A) Full right axillary lymph node dissection

(B) Genetic testing for the *BRCA1/2* mutation

(C) Tumor estrogen and progesterone receptor assay

(D) Whole-body positron emission tomography

Item 10 [Basic]

A 55-year-old postmenopausal woman is evaluated for discussion of therapy after a recent diagnosis of breast cancer. She is post-menopausal, and a screening mammogram revealed a new 1.5-cm area of microcalcification in the left breast without any associated mass. She underwent a stereotactic biopsy that showed a moderate-ly differentiated estrogen receptor–negative, progesterone recep-tor–negative, and *HER2*-negative infiltrating ductal carcinoma. Her medical history is otherwise negative, and she takes no medications.

On physical examination, her vital signs are normal. There is mild ecchymosis at the site of the breast biopsy but no other palpable masses or detectable left axillary lymphadenopathy.

Which of the following is the most appropriate next step in man-agement?

(A) Left lumpectomy and tamoxifen

(B) Left lumpectomy followed by breast irradiation

(C) Left lumpectomy with sentinel lymph node biopsy and tamoxifen

(D) Left lumpectomy with sentinel lymph node biopsy followed by breast irradiation

Item 11 [Basic]

A 55-year-old woman is evaluated in the office during a routine examination. She has no medical problems and takes no medications. Her family history is unremarkable.

Physical examination is normal. The patient is sent home with a guaiac fecal occult blood test. The following week, six samples (two each from three separate stools) are analyzed. One of six stool samples tests positive for occult blood.

Which of the following is the most appropriate management of this patient?

(A) Colonoscopy now
(B) Repeat fecal occult blood testing now
(C) Repeat fecal occult blood testing in 1 year
(D) Obtain a carcinoembryonic antigen assay now

Item 12 [Advanced]

A 37-year-old woman is evaluated in the office during a routine visit. She has no medical problems and is taking only an oral contraceptive medication. Her family history reveals that her father was diagnosed with colorectal cancer at 47 years of age.

On physical examination, her vital signs and physical examination are normal.

Which of the following is the best colorectal screening recommendation for this patient?

(A) Initiate colonoscopy screening at age 40 years.
(B) Initiate colonoscopy screening at age 47 years.
(C) Initiate colonoscopy screening at age 50 years.
(D) Schedule a colonoscopy now.

Item 13 [Basic]

A 57-year-old man is evaluated after a recent diagnosis of stage III colon cancer. Three weeks ago, he underwent a hemicolectomy with removal of all evidence of tumor. His postoperative recovery has been uneventful. He has no symptoms.

On physical examination, his vital signs are normal. Abdominal examination reveals a well-healing surgical scar and is otherwise unremarkable.

Which of the following is the most appropriate next step in this patient's treatment?

(A) Adjuvant chemotherapy
(B) Combined adjuvant chemotherapy and radiation therapy
(C) Radiation therapy
(D) Observation

Item 14 [Advanced]

A 68-year-old woman underwent a right hemicolectomy 2 years ago for stage III colon cancer. She received 6 months of adjuvant chemotherapy after surgery. On a recent routine follow-up visit, a serum carcinoembryonic antigen level was found to be elevated to 43 ng/mL (upper limit of normal, 5 ng/mL). She has no other medical issues and takes no medications.

On physical examination, her vital signs are normal. Her abdomen is soft with no distention or masses, the liver edge is palpable just below the right costal margin, and bowel sounds are normal. No supraclavicular lymph nodes are palpable.

Computed tomography (CT) scans of the chest, abdomen, and pelvis demonstrate a single, 1.5-cm-diameter hypodense lesion in the right lobe of the liver. No other abnormalities are seen on the scan.

Which of the following is the most appropriate management?

(A) CT-guided fine-needle aspiration of the liver lesion
(B) Hepatic arterial embolization
(C) Palliative systemic chemotherapy
(D) Radiation therapy to the liver
(E) Right hepatectomy

Item 15 [Basic]

A 35-year-old woman is evaluated during a routine office visit. The results of her last Papanicolaou (Pap) smear and HIV test done 3 years ago were normal. She has no medical problems and takes no medications

On physical examination, her vital signs and physical examination findings are normal. A Pap smear and human papillomavirus (HPV) DNA testing are performed. A week later, her Pap smear results are reported as atypical squamous cells of undetermined significance (ASC-US), and her HPV DNA test result is positive.

Which of the following is the most appropriate management strategy?

(A) Perform colposcopy now.
(B) Repeat the HPV DNA test in 12 months.
(C) Repeat the Pap smear and HPV DNA test in 12 months.
(D) Repeat the Pap smear and HPV DNA test in 36 months.
(E) Repeat the Pap smear in 6 months.

Item 16 [Basic]

A 32-year-old woman is evaluated during a routine office visit. She has been receiving her Pap smears every 3 years, and the results have all been normal. Her last Pap smear was 3 years ago.

On physical examination, her vital signs and pelvic examination findings are normal. A human papillomavirus (HPV) DNA test is obtained. One week later, her cervical cytology results are reported as normal, and her HPV DNA test result is negative.

When should the Pap smear be repeated?

(A) 1 year
(B) 3 years
(C) 5 years
(D) 10 years

Item 17 [Basic]

A 47-year-old woman is seen for a routine follow-up visit. She feels well and has no current complaints. Her medical history is significant for a complete vaginal hysterectomy 1 year ago that was performed because of pelvic pain because of several large leiomyomas. Before the surgery, she received cervical Papanicolaou (Pap) tests every 3 years since around age 25 years, and all results had been normal. She takes no medications and does not smoke.

On physical examination, her vital signs are normal. Her general medical examination findings are unremarkable.

Which of the following is the most appropriate recommendation for Pap testing in this patient?

(A) Every 3 years, indefinitely
(B) Every 5 years, indefinitely
(C) Every 3 years until age 65 years
(D) Every 5 years until age 65 years
(E) Discontinue Pap smears

Item 18 [Basic]

A 52-year-old man requests prostate cancer screening during a routine office visit. He feels well, with no weight loss, fatigue, bone pain, or urinary symptoms. He has no other medical problems.

After a discussion of risks and benefits, he desires prostate screening with a digital rectal examination that reveals a nontender normal-sized prostate with a firm peripheral nodule.

A prostate-specific antigen (PSA) level is 3.8 ng/mL.

Which of the following is the most appropriate next step in management?

(A) Computed tomography of abdomen and pelvis
(B) Transrectal prostate biopsy
(C) Repeat PSA level in 8 weeks
(D) No further evaluation or therapy is needed

Item 19 [Basic]

A 68-year-old man is evaluated in the emergency department for nontraumatic low-back pain and left leg numbness of 1 day's duration. He has no weakness or bowel or bladder incontinence. He has a past medical history of prostate cancer treated with external-beam radiation 8 years ago.

On physical examination, his vital signs are normal. There is tenderness around the L4 vertebra. Deep tendon reflexes are normal. There is no weakness or saddle anesthesia.

Prostate-specific antigen (PSA) level is 50 ng/mL. His last PSA measurement 6 months ago was 1 ng/mL.

Magnetic resonance imaging of the spine reveals an osteoblastic metastasis at L4 with nerve root impingement.

In addition to intravenous glucocorticoids and external-beam radiation to the lumbar spine, which of the following is the most appropriate next step in management?

(A) 5-α reductase inhibitor
(B) Androgen deprivation
(C) Chemotherapy
(D) Diethylstilbestrol
(E) No further therapy

Item 20 [Advanced]

An 86-year-old man is evaluated after a recent diagnosis of prostate cancer. He developed significant urinary hesitancy, and a prostate examination showed an enlarged prostate with a right-sided nodule. A subsequent biopsy revealed adenocarcinoma with a Gleason score of 6. He reports no bone pain, weight loss, fever, chest pain, or shortness of breath. His medical history is notable for hypertension and type 2 diabetes mellitus for which he takes antihypertensive and diabetic medications.

On physical examination, his vital signs are normal. No lymphadenopathy is noted. His lungs are clear to auscultation, and his abdomen is soft, with normal bowel sounds. Except for his prostate findings, the remainder of his physical examination is unremarkable.

Prostate-specific antigen level is 6.4 ng/mL (6.4 µg/L).

Which of the following is the most appropriate management?

(A) Androgen deprivation therapy
(B) Radiation therapy
(C) Radical prostatectomy
(D) Observation

Item 21 [Advanced]

A 67-year-old man is evaluated during a 3-month follow-up examination for stage II Gleason grade 7 prostate cancer treated with external-beam radiation therapy. He reports feeling well except for mild fatigue. Urine function is normal.

On physical examination, his blood pressure is 142/70 mm Hg, pulse rate is 72 beats/min, and respiration rate is 14 breaths/min. No lymphadenopathy is noted. The cardiopulmonary examination is normal. Bowel sounds are normal and active. The prostate is firm but without nodules.

Laboratory studies, including a complete blood count and serum chemistries, are normal. Prostate-specific antigen (PSA) level is 0.1 ng/mL (0.1 µg/L).

Which of the following is the most appropriate management?

(A) Adjuvant androgen deprivation therapy
(B) Adjuvant chemotherapy
(C) Annual prostate ultrasonography for 5 years
(D) PSA measurement every 6 to 12 months

Item 22 [Basic]

A 75-year-old man is evaluated for a nodular lesion on the anterior portion of his left ear. He reports that the lesion has been slowly enlarging over the past year and spontaneously bleeds. It is not painful and does not itch.

On physical examination, his vital signs are normal. The skin lesion is shown (Plate 22). No other skin lesions or lymphadenopathy noted.

Which of the following is the most likely diagnosis?

(A) Basal cell carcinoma
(B) Keratoacanthoma
(C) Melanoma
(D) Sebaceous hyperplasia
(E) Squamous cell carcinoma

Item 23 [Advanced]

A 45-year-old woman is evaluated for a pigmented area on her toe. She reports that the dark area has been there for several months. There is no history of trauma, and the lesion is not painful.

On physical examination, the vital signs are normal. The skin lesion is shown (Plate 23).

Which of the following is the most likely diagnosis?

(A) Acral lentiginous melanoma
(B) Lentigo maligna melanoma
(C) Nodular melanoma
(D) Superficial spreading melanoma

Item 24 [Advanced]

A 65-year-old man presents with an asymptomatic large brown patch on his cheek. It has been present for many years and is enlarging slowly. The patient is a retired farmer and received a significant amount of sun exposure over the course of his life. The lesion is shown (Plate 24).

Which of the following is the most likely diagnosis?

(A) Actinic purpura
(B) Lentigo maligna
(C) Pigmented actinic keratosis
(D) Seborrheic keratosis
(E) Solar lentigo

Item 25 [Basic]

A 58-year-old man is evaluated in the office for an enlarging dark mole on his back. One of its borders bleeds occasionally. He feels well and has no history of rash, trauma to that area, or skin cancer. The skin examination findings are shown (Plate 25).

Which of the following is the most appropriate next step in management?

(A) Excisional biopsy
(B) Liquid nitrogen (cryotherapy)
(C) Punch biopsy
(D) Superficial shave biopsy

Item 26 [Basic]

A 57-year-old man is evaluated for a sore on the lip of 3 months' duration. The patient is a former smoker who quit 10 years ago. Skin findings are shown (Plate 26).

Which of the following is the most likely diagnosis?

(A) Actinic cheilitis
(B) Herpes simplex infection
(C) Lichen planus
(D) Squamous cell carcinoma

Item 27 [Basic]

A 19-year-old female college student presents to your clinic with complaints of a 10-lb unintentional weight loss, intermittent fevers, dry cough, and dyspnea on exertion. She is no longer able to run or jog because of shortness of breath and fatigue. Her symptoms began 6 months ago but have worsened over the past 3 months.

On physical examination, her vital signs are normal. She has fullness in the supraclavicular regions and palpable, nontender lymphadenopathy in the bilateral low cervical lymph nodes chains. The rest of her examination findings are unremarkable.

Laboratory studies are significant for a leukocyte count of 9500/µL with a normal differential, a hemoglobin level of 10 g/dL with a mean corpuscular volume of 85 fL, and a platelet count of 173,800/µL.

A left cervical lymph node excisional biopsy shows scattered, very large cells with abundant pale cytoplasm and two or more oval lobulated nuclei containing large nucleoli, with a surrounding mixture of inflammatory cells and bands of fibrosis.

Which of the following is the most likely diagnosis?

(A) Cat scratch disease
(B) Chronic lymphocytic leukemia
(C) Hodgkin lymphoma
(D) Infectious mononucleosis

Item 28 [Advanced]

A 29-year-old man has a 3-week history of a growing mass in the right supraclavicular region. He has not had fever, night sweats, or weight loss. The patient is otherwise healthy.

On physical examination, his temperature is 37.1°C (98.7°F), blood pressure is 118/72 mm Hg, pulse rate is 84 beats/min, and respiration rate is 16 beats/min. A 4-cm mass is present in the right supraclavicular region. The rest of the physical examination findings are normal.

Laboratory studies reveal a normal complete blood count, liver chemistry studies, and tests of kidney function. A positron emission tomography/computed tomography scan shows only the right supraclavicular mass. The results of a lymph node biopsy are consistent with large B-cell lymphoma. A bone marrow biopsy is negative.

Which of the following is the most appropriate treatment?

(A) Chemotherapy and rituximab
(B) Chemotherapy and rituximab followed by radiation therapy
(C) Radiation therapy
(D) Rituximab

Item 29 [Basic]

A 70-year-old woman undergoes a routine examination. She is asymptomatic and is not taking any medications.

On physical examination, her vital signs are normal. Multiple areas of palpable, small, nontender lymphadenopathy are noted in the cervical, axillary, and inguinal areas; these were not present on a previous examination 3 years ago. The rest of the physical examination findings are unremarkable.

Laboratory studies:

Hemoglobin	12.5 g/dL (125 g/L)
Leukocyte count	65,000/µl (65 × 10⁹/L), with 30% neutrophils and 70% lymphocytes
Platelet count	190,000/µL (190 × 10⁹/L)

Review of the peripheral blood smear reveals numerous small lymphoid cells.

Which of the following will provide the most prognostic information in the diagnostic evaluation?

(A) Bone marrow biopsy and aspirate
(B) Computed tomography of the chest, abdomen, and pelvis
(C) Flow cytometry
(D) Positron emission tomography

Item 30 [Advanced]

A 63-year-old man is evaluated in the emergency department for facial swelling and mild dyspnea. He reports no headache, change in vision, or chest pain. He has a 40-pack-year history of tobacco use.

On physical examination, his temperature is 37.0°C (98.6°F), blood pressure is 150/95 mm Hg, pulse rate is 100 beats/min, and respiration rate is 18 breaths/min. Oxygen saturation is 95% with the patient breathing ambient air. He has facial plethora and bilateral jugular venous distention. Wheezing is noted in the left upper lung field, but the lungs are otherwise clear. Cardiac examination findings are normal. There is no peripheral edema and no lymphadenopathy in the head or neck.

Chest radiograph reveals a widened mediastinum and a left upper lobe infiltrate. A computed tomography scan of the chest demonstrates a left upper lobe mass with impingement on the superior vena cava and mediastinal lymphadenopathy.

Which of the following is the most appropriate next step in management?

(A) Chemotherapy
(B) Combination chemotherapy and radiation therapy
(C) Glucocorticoids
(D) Mediastinoscopy and biopsy
(E) Radiation therapy

Item 31 [Basic]

A 64-year-old man is evaluated for a 1-month history of progressive midback pain and a 2-week history of lower extremity weakness. His medical history is significant for asymptomatic multiple myeloma that has been followed with periodic examinations and laboratory studies; his last assessment was 3 months ago and was stable.

On physical examination, his vital signs are normal. He has point tenderness over the T10 and T11 vertebral bodies, decreased lower extremity muscle strength (3⁺ of 5⁺), increased reflexes isolated to both lower extremities, and bilateral extensor plantar reflexes. The remainder of the physical examination is unremarkable.

Laboratory studies are significant for a hemoglobin level of 6.5 g/dL (65 g/L) and calcium of 13 g/dL (130 g/L)

Magnetic resonance imaging of the thoracic and lumbar spine shows a vertebral body mass with extension into the epidural space (T12) and compression of the spinal cord.

Which of the following is the most appropriate next step in management?

(A) Biopsy of the epidural mass
(B) Glucocorticoids followed by radiation therapy
(C) Chemotherapy
(D) Radiation therapy

Item 32 [Basic]

A 26-year-old man is evaluated for a 2-week history of fever, rapidly enlarging lymph nodes in the head and neck, and abdominal distention.

On physical examination, his temperature is 39.0°C (102.4°F), blood pressure is 90/60 mm Hg, pulse rate is 115 beats/min, and respiration rate is 24 breaths/min. He has massive cervical and axillary lymphadenopathy. On abdominal examination, his spleen is palpable 8 cm below the left costal margin and a firm intraabdominal mass is noted.

Laboratory studies:

Hemoglobin	10.5 g/dL (105 g/L)
Leukocyte count	65,000/µL (65 × 10⁹/L) with 35% neutrophils and 65% atypical lymphocytes
Platelet count	90,000/µL (90 × 10⁹/L)
Creatinine	2.8 mg/dL (336 µmol/L)
Lactate dehydrogenase	12,000 units/L
Phosphorus	9.9 mg/dL (3.20 mmol/L)
Potassium	5.0 meq/L (5.0 mmol/L)
Uric acid	18.6 mg/dL (1.10 mmol/L)

A biopsy of a cervical lymph node confirms Burkitt lymphoma.

Which of the following is the most appropriate immediate next step in treatment?

(A) Combination chemotherapy
(B) Glucocorticoid therapy
(C) Intravenous normal saline and rasburicase
(D) Radiation therapy

Item 33 [Advanced]

A 46-year-old woman is evaluated for the recent onset of headaches that are most intense on waking in the morning and are not relieved by analgesics. She has no nausea or vomiting but notes some difficulty with fine motor skills when using her right hand. The patient was diagnosed with breast cancer and was treated with local treatment and chemotherapy 2 years ago.

On physical examination, her temperature is 37.0°C (98.6°F), blood pressure is 140/95 mm Hg, pulse rate is 90 beats/min, and respiration rate is 12 breaths/min. Funduscopic examination reveals papilledema. She has reduced strength (4/5+) in her right hand. The reminder of the examination is unremarkable.

Computed tomography of the head reveals two separate masses, both involving the left temporal lobe, with associated edema, as well as blastic lesions involving the skull.

Which of the following is the most appropriate management?

(A) Chemotherapy

(B) Intravenous dexamethasone and radiation therapy

(C) Lumbar puncture

(D) Resection of the masses

Oncology
Answers and Critiques

Item 1 **Answer: E**
Educational Objective: *Diagnose lung cancer.*

The most appropriate next diagnostic test is thoracentesis and pleural fluid cytology. Lung cancer is usually discovered during the evaluation of symptoms. By the time cancer causes symptoms, approximately three of four lung cancers are advanced. To limit unnecessary invasive testing, the diagnosis and staging of lung cancer are best done simultaneously. When advanced disease is suggested by computed tomography (CT) or positron emission tomography–CT (PET-CT), the diagnosis and staging are best accomplished with a single invasive test, usually of the location that would confirm the most advanced stage. For example, in a patient with a 4-cm lung mass and mediastinal lymphadenopathy on CT, biopsy should start with the mediastinal nodes to establish a diagnosis and a more advanced stage than would be established with a needle biopsy of the mass. In this patient's situation, a positive pleural fluid cytology report would both diagnose and stage the lung cancer as advanced.

PET scanning and integrated PET-CT are valuable tools in the evaluation of non–small cell lung cancer (NSCLC). Randomized controlled trials have shown the cost effectiveness of adding PET-CT to preoperative staging. Approximately one in five patients thought to have resectable disease before PET-CT will have evidence of mediastinal or distant spread, and unnecessary surgery can be avoided. PET-CT is most often pursued in the preoperative staging of NSCLC; however, it is frequently also used by oncologists for treatment planning in nonresectable disease, and it may be helpful in determining limited versus extensive disease in small cell lung cancer. PET-CT is recommended after histologic (tissue) confirmation of diagnosis is achieved.

Magnetic resonance imaging (MRI) of the brain would be appropriate in the case of new headaches, visual changes, or unsteadiness but not as an initial test in patients without neurologic symptoms. New sites of bone pain should be imaged, but a routine radiologic survey of bone in the absence of symptoms is not indicated. The patient does not have neurologic symptoms to warrant an MRI of the brain. CT-guided biopsy of the lung nodule would lead to tissue diagnosis but does not address the need for staging.

KEY POINT

Lung cancer staging is best accomplished by the least invasive procedure that could confirm the most advanced stage via histologic (tissue) diagnosis.

Bibliography
Detterbeck FC, Lewis SZ, Diekemper R, et al. Executive summary: diagnosis and management of lung cancer, 3rd ed: American College of Chest Physicians evidence-based clinical practice guidelines. Chest 2013;143(suppl):7S–37S. [PMID: 23649434]

Item 2 **Answer: D**
Educational Objective: *Screen for lung cancer.*

Low-dose spiral computed tomography (CT) scan is a recommended lung cancer screening strategy. An effective cancer screening program demonstrates a benefit in reducing mortality. Prior studies evaluating chest radiographs and sputum cytology in cigarette smokers were not able to demonstrate improvements in lung cancer mortality. However, a recent study evaluating low-dose spiral CT scans has shown such a benefit, leading to advocacy to begin lung cancer screening in appropriate populations. The National Lung Screening Trial evaluated low-dose CT scans or chest radiographs in current or prior smokers with a minimum 30-pack-year smoking history. Participants were screened yearly for 3 years and followed for an additional 5 years. More than 53,000 men and women participated in this study, which showed a statistically significant 20% reduction in lung cancer mortality and all cause mortality with screening by low-dose spiral CT. The U.S. Preventive Services Task Force now recommends low-dose spiral chest CT scans to screen for early stage lung cancer in current or former smokers. Individuals to be considered for screening are those age 55 to 79 years who have a 30-pack-year or greater smoking history either as current smokers or as former smokers who have quit within the past 15 years. Harms of screening included radiation exposure, overdiagnosis, and a high rate of false-positive findings that typically were resolved with further imaging or biopsy. Smoking cessation was not affected by screening. Incidental findings were common.

Neither annual chest radiography nor annual sputum cytology nor a combination of annual radiography and sputum cytology has been shown to decrease lung cancer–related mortality or overall mortality.

KEY POINT

The U.S. Preventive Services Task Force recommends lung cancer screening with low-dose spiral chest CT scans for individuals age 55 to 79 years who have a 30-pack-year or greater smoking history either as current smokers or as former smokers who have quit within the past 15 years.

Bibliography
Humphrey LL, Deffebach M, Pappas M, et al. Screening for lung cancer with low-dose computed tomography: a systematic review to update the U.S. Preventive Services Task Force recommendation. Ann Intern Med. 2013;159:411-20. [PMID: 23897166]

Item 3 **Answer: D**
Educational Objective: *Manage a small pulmonary nodule in a patient at risk for lung cancer.*

No additional imaging is required in this patient. The Fleischner Society and the American College of Chest Physicians guidelines recommend that no follow-up is necessary for nodules that are smaller than 4 mm in never-smokers with no other known risk factors for malignancy (history of a first-degree relative with lung cancer or significant radon or asbestos exposure). For those with nodules smaller than 4 mm but who are current or former smokers or have other risk factors, follow-up computed tomography (CT) at 12 months is recommended; if the nodule is unchanged at that point, no further follow-up is required. Studies evaluating the risk for lung cancer in patients at risk show that nodules of this size have a risk of malignancy of less than 1%. Nodules 4 mm or larger should be further evaluated according to the recommendations in the guidelines. A new nodule larger than 8 mm for which there are no old images should be considered for biopsy or should be imaged at 3, 9, and 24 months if unchanged in size at each imaging step regardless of risk factors. For nodules between these sizes, the frequency of imaging is based on the patient's risk factors for lung cancer. Review of previous chest imaging studies is important in the evaluation of nodules to determine whether a nodule is stable, becoming larger, or shrinking. In addition to previous chest radiographs and chest CT scans, abdominal imaging (which shows the lower aspect of the chest) and CT scans done to assess the coronary arteries (which show the lungs) should be reviewed. A solid nodule that is stable on chest radiograph or CT scan for 2 years is considered benign. Growth of a nodule is a strong indicator that it may be malignant.

Repeat imaging in very-low-risk patients is not recommended because of the low risk of malignancy and to avoid unnecessary radiation exposure.

KEY POINT

In patients who have never smoked, a pulmonary nodule that is smaller than 4 mm does not require follow-up imaging.

Bibliography
Gould MK, Fletcher J, Iannettoni MD, et al; American College of Chest Physicians. Evaluation of patients with pulmonary nodules: when is it lung cancer? ACCP evidence-based clinical practice guidelines (2nd edition). Chest. 2007;132(3 suppl):108S-30S. [PMID: 17873164]

Item 4   Answer: C

Educational Objective: *Treat a patient with early-stage non-small cell lung cancer.*

The most appropriate treatment for this patient is surgery and adjuvant chemotherapy. This patient with a 5-cm lung mass and no apparent spread of disease has early-stage non–small cell lung cancer (NSCLC). A solitary tumor without regional (peribronchial or hilar) or mediastinal lymph node involvement is classified as stage I. For patients with early-stage (stages I and II) disease, the most appropriate treatment is surgery. Patients with stage I NSCLC have the most favorable prognosis, but only 60% of these patients are cured after surgery. Stage I is subdivided into stage IA, consisting of tumors less than 3 cm in greatest diameter, and stage IB, including all larger tumors. Currently, the benefits of adjuvant chemotherapy have not been demonstrated for patients with better prognosis, stage IA disease. However, in patients with stage IB NSCLC, which this patient has, improvements in overall survival have been seen, and adjuvant chemotherapy should be considered after surgical resection.

Chemotherapy plus radiation is indicated for locally advanced tumors (i.e., stage III disease characterized by mediastinal lymph node involvement) and is not appropriate therapy for patients with earlier stage disease such as this patient.

Radiation therapy is rarely used as the sole treatment for lung cancer. In patients with early-stage disease, it may add to morbidity without improving chances of cure. In patients with advanced dis-

ease, radiation therapy alone is not as effective as chemotherapy in prolonging survival and disease-free remission.

Chemotherapy is used as palliative therapy in advanced-stage disease, not in those with early-stage disease. Chemotherapy alone in patients with early disease does not offer the best chance of cure compared with surgery and adjuvant chemotherapy.

KEY POINT

For patients with early-stage (stage I and II) NSCLC, the most appropriate treatment is surgery; adjuvant chemotherapy is appropriate for patients with stage IB NSCLC.

Bibliography
Gewanter RM, Rosenzweig KE, Chang JY, et al. ACR Appropriateness criteria: nonsurgical treatment for non-small-cell lung cancer: good performance status/definitive intent. Curr Probl Cancer. 2010;34:228-49. [PMID: 20541060]

Item 5   Answer: A

Educational Objective: *Manage a patient with limited-stage small cell lung cancer.*

The most appropriate management of this patient with small cell lung cancer (SCLC) is radiation and chemotherapy. Patients with SCLC rarely present with disease that is sufficiently localized to allow for surgical resection, so the TNM (tumor, node, metastasis) system is generally not used in these patients. Instead, the Veterans Administration Lung Study Group staging system is typically used, which classifies disease as limited or extensive. The definition of limited-stage disease consists of disease limited to one hemithorax, with hilar and mediastinal lymphadenopathy that can be encompassed within one tolerable radiotherapy portal. Extensive-stage disease consists of any disease that exceeds those boundaries. If disease is confined to the chest (i.e., limited stage) as in this patient, then chemotherapy is initiated with the addition of radiation to the chest concurrent with the first or second cycle of chemotherapy. In this setting, radiation decreases rates of a local recurrence and increases median survival. Routine use of chest radiotherapy in extensive-stage disease does not prolong survival. Also, if a significant response is evident, prophylactic brain radiation is administered after the chemotherapy is complete. If advanced-stage disease is identified, chemotherapy alone is recommended.

Mediastinoscopy is indicated in patients with non-small cell lung cancer if there is mediastinal lymph node involvement (stage III disease) to assess for the presence or absence of cancer and the patient's suitability for surgical cure. It is not typically used in patients with SCLC.

Radiation is used only as an adjunct to systemic chemotherapy and is not appropriate as single-modality therapy.

SCLC is an aggressive form of lung cancer that tends to disseminate early in the vast majority of patients. Patients rarely have disease that is localized enough to allow for surgical resection; therefore, surgical referral for cure in patients with SCLC is not typically recommended. SCLC is not treated by surgical resection unless it is found incidentally.

KEY POINT

Patients with limited-stage small cell lung cancer are treated with combination chemotherapy and radiation therapy.

Bibliography
Stinchcombe TE, Gore EM. Limited-stage small cell lung cancer: current chemoradiotherapy treatment paradigms. Oncologist. 2010;15:187-95. [PMID: 20145192]

Item 6   Answer: D

Educational Objective: *Treat carcinoma in situ breast cancer.*

Local therapy for patients with ductal carcinoma in situ (DCIS) consists of breast-conserving treatment (lumpectomy plus radiation therapy) or mastectomy. These lesions are identified mostly through mammography, but some can present as palpable masses. After adequate local therapy for hormone receptor–positive DCIS, the standard of care is to discuss the use of tamoxifen for 5 years to reduce both the risk of recurrence and the development of a new primary tumor in the ipsilateral or contralateral breast. After wide local excision alone, the risk of recurrence is 25%. The risk of recurrence is 13% with excision and radiotherapy and 8% with excision together with radiotherapy and tamoxifen therapy.

There are no data on the use of aromatase inhibitors in patients with DCIS. In addition, aromatase inhibitors are contraindicated in premenopausal women because they are ineffective in inhibiting ovarian production of estrogen.

There is also currently no role for adjuvant chemotherapy, trastuzumab, or raloxifene as standard therapy for DCIS. Bilateral prophylactic mastectomy may be considered as a preventive option for women with a significantly high risk of developing breast cancer, particularly in women with a documented family history of multiple cases of premenopausal or bilateral cancer with or without ovarian cancer or an inherited genetic predisposition such as carrying the *BRCA1* or *BRCA2* gene mutation or carrying a p53 gene mutation (Li-Fraumeni syndrome).

KEY POINT

Local therapy for patients with DCIS consists of breast-conserving treatment (lumpectomy plus radiation therapy) or mastectomy followed by tamoxifen therapy for 5 years.

Bibliography

Boxer MM, Delaney GP, Chua BH. A review of the management of ductal carcinoma in situ following breast conserving surgery. Breast. 2013;22:1019-25. [PMID: 24070852]

Item 7   Answer: D

Educational Objective: *Screen for* BRCA *mutations.*

A familial risk stratification tools should be used to determine the need for in-depth genetic counseling in this patient with at least 1 family member with breast, ovarian, or other type of *BRCA*-related cancer. These instruments include the Ontario Family History Assessment Tool, Manchester Scoring System, Referral Screening Tool, Pedigree Assessment Tool, and the FHS-7 instrument.

The U.S. Preventive Services Task Force (USPSTF) has identified several family history risk factors associated with increased likelihood of having a BRCA1/2 mutation:

· Breast cancer diagnosis before age 50 years
· Bilateral breast cancerFamily history of breast and ovarian cancer
· Presence of breast cancer in ≥1 male family member
· Multiple cases of breast cancer in the family
· One or more family members with 2 primary types of BRCA-related cancer
· Ashkenazi Jewish ethnicity

These screening tools are easy to administer in clinical settings and are equally effective in eliciting information about these factors that are associated with increased likelihood of *BRCA* mutations; if identified as being at increased risk, referral for formal genetic counseling and possible *BRCA1/BRCA2* gene mutation testing is indicated.

Annual mammography beginning at age 50 years is a recommended screening strategy for average-risk women. This strategy is inadequate for this patient who may be at high risk for both breast and ovarian cancer, which should be determined by further assessment.

In women at high risk for breast cancer as determine by the Gail model (minimum absolute risk of 1.67% over 5 years), a 49% reduction in invasive breast cancer was noted in the women who took tamoxifen. This decrease in the incidence of invasive breast cancer has not yet translated into a survival advantage. However, despite this apparent benefit in some women, the benefits of tamoxifen therapy are not well defined for prophylactic use in carriers of *BRCA1/BRCA2* mutations.

Prophylactic bilateral mastectomy in high-risk patients decreases the risk of invasive breast cancer by greater than 90%. Prophylactic salpingo-oophorectomy decreases the risk of primary ovarian cancer by greater than 95% and, in premenopausal women, decreases the risk of invasive breast cancer by 50%. The decision regarding use of prophylactic surgery to reduce breast cancer risk should be made only after extensive discussion with women considering this procedure. Prophylactic surgery would only be discussed if she was found to have the *BRCA* mutation.

KEY POINT

The need for genetic counseling and possible testing for *BRCA1/BRCA2* gene mutations should be assessed using a risk stratification instrument in patients with at least 1 family member with breast, ovarian, or other type of *BRCA*-related cancer.

Bibliography

Moyer VA; U.S. Preventive Services Task Force. Risk Assessment, Genetic Counseling, and Genetic Testing for BRCA-Related Cancer in Women: U.S. Preventive Services Task Force Recommendation Statement. Ann Intern Med. 2014;160: 271-82. [PMID: 24366376]

Item 8   Answer: A

Educational Objective: *Manage a breast mass with aspiration or biopsy.*

The most appropriate management option is fine-needle aspiration (FNA) or biopsy of the breast mass. All patients with a breast mass should undergo triple assessment: palpation, mammography with or without ultrasonography, and surgical evaluation for biopsy. Mammograms may be normal in 10% to 15% of patients with breast lumps, some of which may be cancerous. After performance of bilateral diagnostic mammography, the initial focus of the workup of a dominant breast mass is to distinguish a simple cyst from a solid mass by FNA or ultrasonography. If the fluid from FNA is bloody, the fluid should undergo cytologic evaluation. Women with simple cysts should undergo a breast examination 4 to 6 weeks after cyst aspiration to evaluate for cyst recurrence or a residual lump. A solid mass requires a tissue diagnosis by fine-needle aspiration biopsy (FNAB), core-needle biopsy, or excisional biopsy. Patients with benign FNAB or core-needle biopsy results and negative mammogram results require close clinical follow-up of the breast abnormality.

Because she has a discrete mass that may represent breast cancer despite the normal mammographic findings, it is inappropriate to observe the patient without further workup or to repeat mammography later. Even if ultrasound results are negative, the patient requires tissue sampling.

The role of breast magnetic resonance imaging (MRI) for screening high-risk patients is currently being defined. Because it is able to define soft tissue abnormalities more effectively than mammography, it has a developing role in evaluating patients in whom other imaging modalities may be less effective. However, it is not indicated for routine evaluation of breast abnormalities. In this patient, a breast MRI would not obviate the need for FNA or FNAB and is much more expensive than ultrasonography.

KEY POINT

A patient with a breast mass requires aspiration or biopsy regardless of mammography results.

Bibliography

Smetherman DH. Screening, imaging, and image-guided biopsy techniques for breast cancer. Surg Clin North Am. 2013;93:309-27. [PMID: 23464688]

Item 9   Answer: C

Educational Objective: *Evaluate a patient with early-stage breast cancer for tumor estrogen- and progesterone-receptor status.*

The next step is a tumor estrogen-receptor (ER) and progesterone-receptor (PR) assay. This patient has early-stage breast cancer (stage I) based on the tumor size (<2 cm), the absence of lymph node involvement, and no evidence of metastatic disease. Assaying her tumor for expression of ER and PR positivity would be most helpful in directing the approach to management of this patient. This information helps determine the optimal systemic treatment, and this evaluative step should be performed in all cases of primary breast cancer. Endocrine therapy (eg, tamoxifen, aromatase inhibitors) is beneficial only in patients with ER- or PR-positive tumors. Patients whose tumors are hormone receptor negative are refractory to endocrine treatment and should receive chemotherapy instead. Additionally, most tumors are now assayed for human epidermal growth factor receptors (HER). HERs are a family of membrane-bound proteins with tyrosine kinase activity that act as epidermal growth factors. Overexpression of HER2 occurs in up to 40% of breast cancers and is associated with a poorer prognosis. It, however, allows for targeted adjuvant therapy to be used in cases when it is detected.

In patients with early-stage breast cancer, the routine evaluation is limited to a thorough history and physical examination, diagnostic mammography, chest radiography, and routine blood tests (including liver chemistry tests). The use of additional imaging studies or blood tests is not warranted in the absence of specific symptoms because they may lead to the detection of abnormalities of no significance (a false-positive test result).

In early-stage disease, the positive predictive value of abnormal findings of whole-body positron emission tomography is approximately 1%; therefore, this type of imaging modality is not recommended.

The absence of metastases in a sentinel axillary lymph node has a high negative predictive value, obviating the need for a complete axillary lymph node dissection with its associated morbidity.

About 5% of breast cancer cases are attributable to rare, high-penetrance mutations in a few specific genes; mutations in *BRCA1* and *BRCA2* account for up to 50% of all cases of hereditary and familial breast cancer. This proportion is higher in patients with breast cancer at a younger age of onset and in families with multiple breast or ovarian cancer cases. Testing for the *BRCA1* or *BRCA2* gene in this patient would not be indicated without a more compelling family history of disease.

KEY POINT

Assay for expression of estrogen and progesterone receptors is crucial in determining the optimal systemic treatment for breast cancer and should be performed in all patients with primary breast cancer.

Bibliography

Burstein HJ, Prestrud AA, Seidenfeld J, et al. American Society of Clinical Oncology clinical practice guideline: update on adjuvant endocrine therapy for women with hormone receptor-positive breast cancer. J Clin Oncol. 2010;28:3784-96. [PMID: 20625130]

Item 10   Answer: D

Educational Objective: *Treat a patient with breast cancer and a small focal tumor with lumpectomy, sentinel node dissection, and radiation.*

This patient should undergo breast lumpectomy plus sentinel lymph node biopsy followed by radiation therapy. This approach, involving removal of the primary tumor (lumpectomy) plus radiation therapy to the remainder of the ipsilateral breast, is known as "breast-conserving therapy." Breast-conserving therapy is generally indicated for patients with focal disease and small tumors for which conservation will offer a good cosmetic result. The survival rate for women undergoing breast-conserving therapy is equivalent to that for those who undergo removal of the entire breast (mastectomy), with breast-conserving therapy resulting in less morbidity than mastectomy. Radiation therapy is coupled with lumpectomy because of the high risk for local recurrence for lumpectomy alone. In addition, sentinel lymph node biopsy is an accurate method for screening the axillary lymph nodes for metastases in women with small breast tumors. Sentinel lymph node biopsy has replaced full axillary lymph node dissection for the staging of disease in many women with early-stage, clinically lymph node–negative breast cancer.

The first draining (or sentinel) lymph node is identified by injecting dye and radioactive colloid into the tumor site. If the sentinel lymph node does not contain metastases, it is unlikely that more distal axillary lymph nodes will contain metastases; consequently, no further surgery is indicated in this setting, and the toxicity from a full axillary lymph node dissection is avoided. However, if the sentinel lymph node shows metastatic involvement, then axillary lymph node dissection is performed to determine the number of involved lymph nodes.

Selective estrogen receptor modulators such as tamoxifen are not indicated in patients with estrogen receptor–negative tumors.

KEY POINT

Lumpectomy with sentinel lymph node biopsy followed by breast irradiation is the appropriate management of women with small, focal breast cancer.

Bibliography

Buchholz TA. Radiation therapy for early-stage breast cancer after breast-conserving surgery. N Engl J Med. 2009;360:63-70. [PMID: 19118305]

Item 11   Answer: A

Educational Objective: *Diagnose colorectal cancer.*

This patient should have colonoscopy now. Guaiac fecal occult blood test (gFOBT) uses a reagent that changes color in the presence of peroxidase, which is found in human blood, animal blood, and other dietary sources. Proper test performance typically requires the collection of two samples from three consecutive stools (six samples total). Samples can be obtained at home and mailed in to a clinical laboratory for processing and analysis. Randomized, controlled trials have shown statistically significant reductions in colorectal cancer incidence (17% to 20%) and mortality (15% to 33%) with regular gFOBT screening. Limitations of gFOBT screening are low sensitivity for advanced adenomas (11% to 41%), diet and medication interactions that may produce false-positive or false-negative results, the need for annual testing if the result is negative, and the need for appropriate diagnostic follow-up if the test result is positive to achieve maximum benefit. For any single positive screening gFOBT result, colonoscopy is the indicated diagnostic test. Current recommendations from the U.S. Multi-Society Task Force on Colorectal Cancer specify that a high-sensitivity gFOBT be used if this colorectal cancer screening option is pursued.

Carcinoembryonic antigen (CEA) is an oncofetal protein that is elevated in patients with colorectal cancer and other cancers. CEA is an insensitive marker for colorectal cancer and is not a recommended screening or case finding tool. CEA measurement is a useful test in patients with established colorectal cancer because the level of CEA correlates with cancer burden and prognosis. CEA levels that fail to drop after surgical resection of colorectal cancer predicts the presence of residual disease.

KEY POINT

For any single positive screening gFOBT result, colonoscopy is the indicated diagnostic test.

Bibliography

Levin B, Lieberman DA, McFarland B, et al. American Cancer Society Colorectal Cancer Advisory Group; US Multi-Society Task Force; American College of Radiology Colon Cancer Committee. Screening and surveillance for the early detection of colorectal cancer and adenomatous polyps, 2008: a joint guideline from the American Cancer Society, the US Multi-Society Task Force on Colorectal Cancer, and the American College of Radiology. CA Cancer J Clin. 2008;58:130-60. [PMID: 18322143]

Item 12   Answer: D

Educational Objective: *Screen for colorectal cancer in a high-risk patient.*

This patient should be referred for colonoscopy now. Colorectal cancer screening guidelines are available for patients at increased risk owing to chronic inflammatory bowel disease, nonsyndromic family history, or a hereditary cancer syndrome. The U.S. Multi-Society Task Force on Colorectal Cancer and others recommend colonoscopic screening for patients with a first-degree relative with colorectal neoplasia (advanced adenoma characterized by size 1 cm or greater or high-grade dysplasia, or villous elements) at age younger than 60 years or two or more first-degree relatives with colorectal cancer diagnosed at any age. For these individuals, colonoscopy screening should begin at age 40 years or age 10 years before youngest age at colorectal neoplasia or colorectal cancer diagnosis in the family, whichever is younger. Any approved colorectal cancer screening modality is recommended for patients with a first-degree relative with colorectal neoplasia diagnosed after age 60 years or with more than two second-degree relatives with colorectal cancer diagnosed at any age. Because this patient's father was diagnosed with colorectal cancer at the age of 37 years, colorectal cancer screening with colonoscopy should be initiated at age 37 years. As the patient is 37 years old, colonoscopy should be scheduled now.

KEY POINT

The U.S. Multi-Society Task Force on Colorectal Cancer recommends colonoscopic screening for patients with a first-degree relative with colorectal neoplasia at age younger than 60 years or two or more first-degree relatives with colorectal cancer diagnosed at any age.

Bibliography

Levin B, Lieberman DA, McFarland B, et al. American Cancer Society Colorectal Cancer Advisory Group; US Multi-Society Task Force; American College of Radiology Colon Cancer Committee. Screening and surveillance for the early detection of colorectal cancer and adenomatous polyps, 2008: a joint guideline from the American Cancer Society, the US Multi-Society Task Force on Colorectal Cancer, and the American College of Radiology. CA Cancer J Clin. 2008;58:130-60. [PMID: 18322143]

Item 13   Answer: A

Educational Objective: *Treat a patient with stage III colon cancer.*

The most appropriate treatment of this patient's stage III colon cancer (tumor involving regional lymph nodes) is adjuvant chemotherapy. The purpose of adjuvant treatment in colorectal cancer is to eradicate possible micrometastatic disease after removal of the primary tumor. Stage III colon cancer has an approximate 30% to 60% chance of cure with surgical resection alone. Adjuvant chemotherapy for colon cancer reduces recurrence rates and increases the likelihood for cure by an additional 7% to 15%. First-line agents for stage III colorectal cancer include 5-fluorouracil and leucovorin for 6 months; oral capecitabine for 24 weeks; or 5-fluorouracil, leucovorin, and oxaliplatin for 24 weeks.

Postoperative radiation therapy is not routinely indicated for completely resected colon cancer. However, because of the anatomical location of rectal cancer and the difficulty in obtaining adequate tumor-free margins, local recurrence rates tend to be high. Therefore, neoadjuvant (given before surgical treatment) chemoradiotherapy is indicated in patients with locally advanced rectal cancer, in addition to postoperative adjuvant therapy. However, radiation therapy or combined radiation and chemotherapy is not indicated in most cases of rectal cancer.

Clinical observation after resection of stage III colon cancer is not appropriate given the improved outcomes associated with postoperative chemotherapy.

KEY POINT

Adjuvant chemotherapy for stage III colon cancer reduces recurrence rates and increases the likelihood for disease-free survival.

Bibliography

Stein A, Hiemer S, Schmoll HJ. Adjuvant therapy for early colon cancer: current status. Drugs. 2011;71:2257-75. [PMID: 22085384]

Item 14   Answer: E

Educational Objective: *Manage oligometastatic colorectal cancer.*

This patient has a potential for curative resection and should undergo a right hepatectomy if no other sites of disease are identified during exploratory surgery. She has a limited number of metastatic foci of cancer confined to one organ, or oligometastatic disease.

A fine-needle aspiration is not indicated because the results of this invasive procedure will not change management. The clinical presentation is suggestive enough of metastatic disease in the liver that a negative needle aspiration will not sufficiently exclude the presence of cancer, and a definitive resection will still be required. Thus, in the setting of what appears to be resectable disease, a needle aspiration or biopsy should not be done.

Hepatic arterial embolization is a procedure used in the palliation of hepatocellular or neuroendocrine tumors; however, the procedure is not indicated in colorectal cancer, and because it is not curative, it would not be an appropriate consideration in a patient whose disease might be curable with surgery.

Radiation therapy is rarely used for treatment of liver metastases and does not have the potential to be curative. Because this patient may have curable disease, noncurative treatment such as palliative chemotherapy is not appropriate.

KEY POINT

Surgical resection of a few isolated metastatic lesions may be curative for patients with colorectal cancer.

Bibliography

House MG, Ito H, Gönen M, et al. Survival after hepatic resection for metastatic colorectal cancer: trends in outcomes for 1,600 patients during two decades at a single institution. J Am Coll Surg. 2010;210:744-55. [PMID: 20421043]

Item 15　　　Answer:　A

Educational Objective:　*Manage atypical squamous cells of undetermined significance (ASC-US).*

The most appropriate management of this patient is referral for colposcopy. The colposcope is a low-powered magnification device that permits the identification of mucosal abnormalities characteristic of dysplasia or invasive cancer and guides selection of tissue for biopsy.

Screening with conventional cervical cytology (Pap smear) results in a 95% decrease in mortality from cervical cancer. Owing to poor specificity, screening with HPV DNA testing alone is not recommended, although clinicians can consider using HPV DNA testing along with cervical cytology in women age 30 years and older to help guide further investigation and decrease the frequency of testing to every 5 years.

If cervical cytology is interpreted as unsatisfactory, the test should be immediately repeated. When interpreted as ASC-US, acceptable options include referring for colposcopy, obtaining HPV DNA testing, and then referring for colposcopy if positive or repeating the Pap smear in 6 to 12 months. With any other abnormal result, the patient should be referred for colposcopy. Because this patient has the finding of ASC-US and the HPV DNA test result is positive, the most appropriate action is to refer her for colposcopy.

KEY POINT

When cervical cytology (Pap test) is interpreted as ASC-US, acceptable options include referring for colposcopy, obtaining with HPV DNA testing and then referring for colposcopy if positive or repeating the Pap smear in 6 to 12 months.

Bibliography

Moyer VA; U.S. Preventive Services Task Force. Screening for cervical cancer: U.S. Preventive Services Task Force recommendation statement. Ann Intern Med. 2012;156:880-91. [PMID: 22711081]

Item 16　　　Answer:　C

Educational Objective:　*Screen for cervical cancer in women older than the age of 30 years.*

The American Cancer Society and the U.S. Preventive Services Task Force recommend screening with cervical cytology (Papanicolaou smear) alone beginning at age 21 years and repeating every 3 years if previous tests have been normal. These societies also recommend that physicians may consider obtaining cervical cytology and HPV DNA testing every 5 years in women ages 30 through 65 years. Screening can be discontinued in women 65 years and older if there have been no recent abnormal test results. These screening recommendations apply only to women who are not at high risk for cervical cancer and have had previous normal test results. High-risk conditions include a history of in utero diethylstilbestrol exposure, any immunocompromise, and HIV positivity. The American Congress of Obstetricians and Gynecologists has slightly different recommendations for cervical cancer screening. Cervical cytology is recommended every 2 years for women ages 21 through 29 years and cervical cytology alone for women ages 30 through 65 years. Screening is discontinued at age 65 to 70 years if the previous three cervical cytology test results were normal.

KEY POINT

Physicians may consider screening for cervical cancer by obtaining cervical cytology and HPV DNA testing every 5 years in women ages 30 through 65 years who are not at high risk for cervical cancer and have had previous normal test results.

Bibliography

Moyer VA; U.S. Preventive Services Task Force. Screening for cervical cancer: U.S. Preventive Services Task Force recommendation statement. Ann Intern Med. 2012;156:880-91. [PMID: 22711081]

Item 17　　　Answer:　E

Educational Objective:　*Discontinue screening for cervical cancer in patients who have had a hysterectomy for benign disease.*

Discontinuing routine cervical cancer screening is the most appropriate recommendation in this patient who has had a hysterectomy for benign disease. Studies of Papanicolaou smear testing in women who have had their cervixes removed for nonmalignant causes show extremely low rates of cancer detection, and estimates of the positive predictive value of an abnormal vaginal smear in this setting approach zero. Because of this, there is no proven benefit to screening these women; vaginal hysterectomy for benign disease is not associated with an increased risk of vaginal malignancy. Therefore, the U.S. Preventive Service Task Force recommends cervical cancer screening only for women who are sexually active and have a cervix.

KEY POINT

In asymptomatic women who have had a vaginal hysterectomy for benign disease, there is no proven benefit to routine Pap testing to detect cancer.

Bibliography

Stokes-Lampard H, Wilson S, Waddell C, Ryan A, Holder R, Kehoe S. Vaginal vault smears after hysterectomy for reasons other than malignancy: a systematic review of the literature. BJOG. 2006;113:1354-65. [PMID: 17081187]

Item 18   Answer: B

Educational Objective: *Diagnose prostate cancer.*

The most appropriate next step in management is a transrectal prostate biopsy. Although most prostate cancers discovered through screening are nonpalpable, a small number are discovered by digital rectal examination. Prostate cancers discovered on digital rectal examination are often higher clinical stage than those found using prostate-specific antigen (PSA) testing alone. Although a PSA level less than 4 ng/mL is usually considered normal, PSA blood testing has only modest sensitivity (38%–81%), and a low PSA does not exclude prostate cancer. If abnormalities are found on digital rectal examination, transrectal ultrasonography should be done to evaluate the anterior and medial portions of the prostate that are difficult to assess by physical examination. Transrectal biopsy of the prostate is the definitive diagnostic study and should be done in all patients with asymmetric induration or nodularity.

In the setting of a palpable prostate nodule, the pretest probability of prostate cancer is so high that a normal PSA level has a high likelihood of being a false-negative test result. Waiting 8 weeks to repeat the test in this situation is not appropriate. Patients with prostatitis or genitourinary surgery may have a transient increase in PSA. In these patients, an elevated PSA level should be followed up approximately 8 weeks later to exclude a false-positive reading.

After a diagnosis of prostate cancer is made, additional studies such as a bone scan or computed tomography (CT) scan of the abdomen and pelvis should be considered in patients with signs or symptoms suggestive of distant spread of the malignancy. A diagnosis of prostate cancer has not been established and the patient is asymptomatic; a CT scan at this time is not appropriate.

KEY POINT

Palpable prostate nodules require further evaluation for possible prostate cancer regardless of PSA level.

Bibliography

Hoffman RM. Clinical practice. Screening for prostate cancer. N Engl J Med. 2011;365:2013. [PMID: 22029754]

Item 19   Answer: B

Educational Objective: *Treat prostate cancer with androgen deprivation therapy.*

The most appropriate next step in management is androgen deprivation therapy (ADT). This patient has recurrence of prostate cancer 8 years after treatment for localized prostate cancer. The mainstay of treatment for local treatment failure is ADT. Such therapy is usually provided with gonadotropin-releasing hormone (GnRH) agonist, or less commonly, surgical orchiectomy. Use of GnRH agonists (chemical castration) is as effective as bilateral orchiectomy (surgical castration) in treating patients with metastatic disease. Chemical castration is often preferred psychologically and is reversible after discontinuation of therapy but requires repeated intramuscular or subcutaneous administration of hormonal agonists over long periods of time. GnRH agonists act by disrupting the pituitary–testes axis, thereby decreasing testosterone levels. Oral antiandrogens such as bicalutamide, flutamide, and nilutamide act by blocking the androgen receptors on cancer cells. In patients electing for "chemical castration," there is often a transient surge of testosterone, which can cause transient growth in prostate metastasis; thus, androgen recep-

tor blockers are typically used as part of initial therapy. In this patient with a lumbar spinal metastasis, such therapy would be indicated.

5-α reductase inhibitors are primarily used to treat benign prostatic hypertrophy. They have been studied for chemoprophylaxis for prostate cancer but have not been shown to improve mortality rates. They have no role in the treatment of metastatic prostate cancer.

Chemotherapy can be used for metastatic prostate cancer that progresses despite ADT. However, most metastatic prostate cancer is initially androgen sensitive, and systemic chemotherapy is used later in the treatment of metastatic prostate cancer than other cancers. In this case, ADT should be attempted first.

Watchful waiting is often performed in patients with local, asymptomatic prostate cancer. This treatment strategy capitalizes on the relatively slow growth and metastatic potential of most prostate cancers and recognizes that many patients with prostate cancer die from competing causes. However, after symptoms manifest, some therapy is typically warranted, especially relatively well tolerated treatment such as ADT.

KEY POINT

ADT is the treatment of choice for metastatic prostate cancer.

Bibliography

Loblaw DA, Virgo KS, Nam R, et al. American Society of Clinical Oncology. Initial hormonal management of androgen-sensitive metastatic, recurrent, or progressive prostate cancer: 2006 update of an American Society of Clinical Oncology practice guideline. J Clin Oncol. 2007;25:1596-605. [PMID: 17404365]

Item 20   Answer: D

Educational Objective: *Manage low-risk prostate cancer in an elderly patient.*

The most appropriate management is observation. This elderly patient has low-risk, stage I prostate cancer based on his clinical stage, low prostate-specific antigen level, and low Gleason score. Patients with newly diagnosed prostate cancer have several options for treatment. Treatment is tailored to an individual patient's estimated risk of progression or recurrence, as well as the patient's age and overall health. This patient with low-risk disease and a relatively short life expectancy (likely <10 years) would be best managed with observation.

Androgen deprivation therapy is generally reserved for patients with metastatic, hormone-sensitive cancer and in selected patients with more localized but high-risk disease, neither of which are present in this patient.

Radiation therapy and radical prostatectomy are appropriate treatment considerations for patients with low-risk, localized disease but a longer (>10 years) life expectancy. This patient's age and underlying medical problems make him a poor candidate for these more aggressive treatments and their associated potential adverse effects.

KEY POINT

Patients with low-risk prostate cancer and a short life expectancy are optimally managed with observation.

Bibliography

Mohler J, Bahnson RR, Boston B, et al. NCCN clinical practice guidelines in oncology: prostate cancer. J Natl Compr Canc Netw. 2010;8:162-200. [PMID: 20141676]

Item 21   Answer: D

Educational Objective: *Manage prostate cancer follow-up.*

The most appropriate management is prostate-specific antigen (PSA) measurement every 6 to 12 months. This patient has average-risk prostate cancer based on his clinical stage of II and good response to radiation therapy. After initial treatment, patients should be followed with periodic serum PSA measurement on at least an annual basis. As many as 75% of recurrences are discovered by the fifth year of follow-up. A rising PSA level indicates biochemical recurrence, and estimates of survival can be made from the time of completion of treatment to the rise in the PSA, the rate of that rise, and the initial Gleason score. Although recurrent disease after definitive therapy of early-stage prostate cancer is incurable, significant palliation can be achieved with hormone deprivation therapy and chemotherapy.

Androgen deprivation (hormonal) therapy is recommended only for patients with high-risk or advanced localized disease and in those with metastatic disease. Because this patient has average-risk localized disease without evidence of metastasis, androgen deprivation therapy is not indicated.

Chemotherapy in prostate cancer is indicated only in patients with hormone-refractory metastatic disease. There is no evidence of benefit from chemotherapy in patients without metastatic prostate cancer.

Serial radiographic examinations are not recommended in the adjuvant setting for monitoring patients with prostate cancer.

KEY POINT

Patients with average-risk prostate cancer who achieve remission after radiation therapy should receive follow-up with serial digital rectal examinations and serum PSA measurement every 6 to 12 months.

Bibliography

Mohler J, Bahnson RR, Boston B, et al. NCCN clinical practice guidelines in oncology: prostate cancer. J Natl Compr Canc Netw. 2010;8:162-200. [PMID: 20141676]

Item 22   Answer: A

Educational Objective: *Diagnose basal cell carcinoma.*

This lesion is most consistent with basal cell carcinoma (BCC). BCC classically presents as a pink, pearly or translucent, dome-shaped papule with telangiectatic vessels. As the lesion grows, the central area often ulcerates, resulting in its characteristic rolled edge. The most readily recognized clue to the diagnosis of a BCC is a changing skin lesion, including ulceration or erosion that spontaneously bleeds. BCC rarely metastasizes, but its growth and treatment can be sources of morbidity.

Keratoacanthomas are red, volcano-like nodules with a prominent central keratin plug. They are considered to be a subtype of well-differentiated squamous cell carcinoma. They grow rapidly and may reach a size of several centimeters within a few weeks. Classic keratoacanthomas eventually stabilize in size and may spontaneously regress without treatment.

Melanoma is classically a pigmented macule or plaque that is asymmetric and has irregular, notched, scalloped, or poorly defined borders. The lesion usually has shades of brown, tan, red, white, blue-black, or combinations thereof. Rarely, melanomas are not pigmented (amelanotic), can mimic BCC, and can be nonspecific in appearance.

Sebaceous hyperplasia results from enlargement of the sebaceous oil glands, producing single or multiple small umbilicated pink or yellowish papules on the face. Although harmless, these papules can be mistaken for BCCs. The main distinguishing features are the pink or yellowish color, the absence of telangiectasias, and the absence of translucency ("pearliness") that is seen in BCCs.

Squamous cell carcinoma presents as a firm, isolated, flesh-colored, pink or red ulcerated keratotic macule, papule, or nodule commonly found on the scalp, neck, pinna, or lip. The thickness of the lesion is an important prognostic indicator. Squamous cell cancer metastases occur in 1% to 5% of cases and are associated with a poor prognosis.

KEY POINT

BCCs are characterized as pink, pearly or translucent nodules with telangiectases with the central area often ulcerating, resulting in its characteristic rolled border.

Bibliography

Madan V, Lear JT, Szeimies RM. Non-melanoma skin cancer. Lancet. 2010;375:673-85. [PMID: 20171403]

Item 23   Answer: A

Educational Objective: *Diagnose acral melanoma.*

This lesion is most consistent with acral lentiginous melanoma. Acral lentiginous melanoma can present in a variety of ways, including as a longitudinal dark pigmented streak on a fingernail or toenail, dark pigmentation of a proximal nail fold, and dark pigmented patches on the palms or soles. This variant of melanoma is the most common type among Asian and dark-skinned people. Acral lentiginous melanomas account for only 5% of melanoma cases.

Lentigo maligna melanoma presents initially as a freckle-like, tan-brown patch. When confined to the epidermis, the lesion is called lentigo maligna type. The lesion may be present for many years before it expands and becomes more variegated in color. When it invades the dermis, it becomes melanoma. It most often arises in sun-damaged areas (face, upper trunk) in older people. Lentigo maligna melanoma accounts for approximately 10% of melanoma cases.

Nodular melanoma presents as a dark blue or black "berry-like" lesion that expands vertically (penetrating skin). It most commonly arises from normal skin and is most often found in people age 60 years or older. Nodular melanoma accounts for approximately 15% of melanoma cases.

Superficial spreading melanoma presents as a variably pigmented plaque with an irregular border and expanding diameter ranging from a few millimeters to several centimeters. It can occur at any age and anywhere on the body, although it is most commonly seen on the back in men and on the legs in women. Most superficial spreading melanomas appear to arise de novo. Superficial spreading melanoma accounts for approximately 70% of melanoma cases.

KEY POINT

Acral lentiginous melanoma presents as an unevenly darkly pigmented patch that most often arises on the palmar, plantar, or subungual surfaces.

Bibliography

Thompson JF, Scolyer RA, Kefford RF. Cutaneous melanoma. Lancet. 2005;365:687-701. [PMID: 15721476]

Item 24   Answer: B

Educational Objective: *Diagnose lentigo maligna.*

This patient has lentigo maligna, which is a slow-growing type of melanoma most commonly seen on the face of older fair-skinned persons who have received a substantial amount of cumulative sun exposure with resultant evidence of sun damage. It has a prolonged radial growth phase and can be present for many years before developing an invasive component (vertical growth phase). Once it becomes invasive, the staging and prognosis are identical to those of other types of melanoma.

Actinic purpuras are well-demarcated, smooth, reddish-violet patches that occur in elderly patients with significantly sun-damaged skin; they are indicative of skin fragility. They invariably arise from trauma, although often the inciting event is so mild as to escape notice. They typically occur on the dorsal arms and pretibial lower legs; patients on anticoagulant agents often have prominent lesions. They may heal with postinflammatory hyperpigmentation, which can sometimes mimic lentigo maligna.

Actinic keratoses (AKs) are premalignant (squamous cell precursor) lesions that occur in sun-damaged areas. They may occasionally be pigmented and be mistaken for the more serious lentigo maligna. Pigmented AKs behave in a manner identical to typical AKs.

Seborrheic keratoses are brown, scaly, waxy papules and plaques that occur in older persons. Although benign, they may sometimes be difficult to differentiate definitively from melanoma, and thus atypical lesions are often biopsied.

Solar lentigines are brown macules and patches that occur in elderly fair-skinned persons in sun-damaged areas. Although benign, they may occasionally be difficult to distinguish from lentigo maligna. Useful discriminating characteristics include more homogeneous pigmentation and lighter color; in equivocal cases, a biopsy is indicated.

KEY POINT

Lentigo maligna is a slow-growing melanoma most commonly seen on sun-exposed skin of older fair-skinned persons.

Bibliography

Smalberger GJ, Siegel DM, Khachemoune A. Lentigo maligna. Dermatol Ther. 2008;21: 439-46. PMID: 19076621

Item 25   Answer: A

Educational Objective: *Diagnose melanoma.*

This lesion is a nodular melanoma, and the preferred method to confirm the diagnosis is excisional biopsy. Fully excising the lesion allows for both assessment of the degree of cytologic atypia and the depth of invasion (termed the Breslow depth), which is the most significant prognostic feature of melanomas and is used to guide therapy. Melanomas account for 5% of skin cancers but are responsible for most deaths from skin cancer because of their propensity to metastasize. Clinical features that help distinguish melanomas from other pigmented lesions may be remembered by the ABCD mnemonic: asymmetry (inability to draw a line down the middle to produce two mirror images), border that is irregular, scalloped, or poorly circumscribed, color (more than one color in the same lesion or very dark, black, occasionally white, red, or blue), and diameter ≥6 mm (the size of a pencil eraser).

Destruction of suspicious lesions could not only result in the spread of malignant cells and significantly alter the prognosis, but it also makes it impossible to diagnose or stage the lesion and thereby select the correct treatment. Therefore, cryotherapy with liquid nitrogen or destruction with electrodessication would not be appropriate in this patient.

Although a punch biopsy of a portion of the lesion is sometimes performed when an excisional biopsy is not feasible, this runs the risk of underestimating both the degree of cytologic atypia and the depth because of sampling error and thus is less desirable than an excisional biopsy.

A broad, shallow shave biopsy in this situation runs the risk of transecting the base of the lesion, thus making accurate determination of the depth (and hence appropriate management) difficult.

KEY POINT

Lesions suspicious for melanoma require an excisional biopsy.

Bibliography

Tsao H, Atkins MB, Sober AJ. Management of cutaneous melanoma. N Engl J Med. 2004;351:998-1012. [PMID: 15342808]

Item 26   Answer: D

Educational Objective: *Diagnose squamous cell carcinoma.*

This patient has squamous cell carcinoma (SCC), which is the most common type of malignancy on the lips and oral cavity. Risk factors include smoking and alcohol consumption; for lesions that occur on the lips, sun exposure is an additional risk factor. SCCs generally consist of red plaques or nodules that may be covered with scale, crust, and erosions. Biopsy establishes the diagnosis and should be performed as quickly as possible to avoid treatment delays because lesions arising in these areas are often particularly aggressive.

Actinic cheilitis is a chronic erythema and scaling of the lower lip caused by extensive sun damage. It is a precancerous condition, and SCCs may arise within the affected area. Actinic cheilitis appears as a rash rather than a tumor; however, any bulky area should be biopsied to rule out SCC. Actinic cheilitis is often treated with cryotherapy, topical 5-fluorouracil, or laser ablation to reduce the risk of malignant transformation.

Herpes simplex infection (herpes labialis, "cold sores") are commonly found on and around the vermilion lips. Patients often experience a prodrome consisting of tingling or tenderness before the onset of vesicles. After the vesicles arise, they rupture to form erosions that are covered by crusts. Resolution occurs within 2 weeks. Recurrences are common.

Lichen planus can affect the lips and buccal mucosa and occasionally may ulcerate; furthermore, SCCs may arise within them. The characteristic feature is Wickham striae, which is a white lacy rash found on the buccal mucosa. Areas of lichen planus are shallow and lack the tangible substance of the lesion that is shown. They also lack scale and crust. Any suspicious lesion arising within an area of lichen planus should be biopsied, however, to rule out an evolving SCC.

KEY POINT

SCC, the most common type of oral malignancy, generally consists of red plaques or nodules that may be covered with scale, crust, and erosions.

Bibliography

Mirowski GW, Schlosser BJ. The diagnosis and treatment of oral mucosal lesions. Dermatol Ther. 2010;23:207-8. [PMID: 20597939]

Item 27   Answer: C

Educational Objective: *Diagnose classical Hodgkin lymphoma.*

The patient has classical Hodgkin lymphoma (HL). Classical HL is a B cell–derived malignancy, and the malignant cell of origin is the Reed-Sternberg cell. The cellular makeup of HL is unique in that the tumor tissue is composed of a minority of the malignant Reed-Sternberg cells are surrounded by many inflammatory cells. Weight loss, fever, and night sweats are often referred to as "B" symptoms based on the Ann Arbor classification system for lymphomas that adds the suffix B to a stage if systemic symptoms are present. B symptoms are frequently seen in patients with HL. Cough and dyspnea on exertion are generally caused by an anterior mediastinal mass, a common finding in classical HL.

Infectious mononucleosis is caused by the Epstein-Barr virus and is characterized by fever, pharyngitis, and lymphadenopathy. Most symptoms resolve within 1 month, although fatigue may persist for longer. Lymphadenopathy is usually tender, and the complete blood count is often notable for atypical lymphocytosis.

Chronic lymphocytic leukemia, sometimes referred to as small lymphocytic lymphoma, usually presents with painless lymphadenopathy or asymptomatic lymphocytosis, often found incidentally. On biopsy, the abundant malignant cells appear as small, mature-appearing lymphocytes.

Cat scratch disease is an infectious disease caused by *Bartonella henselae* and is associated with cat and flea exposure. It is characterized by regional, self-limited lymphadenopathy. A cutaneous lesion is often seen at the site of inoculation of the infectious organism, and this lesion can persist from 1 to 3 weeks. The enlarged lymph nodes are tender and associated with overlying erythema.

KEY POINT

The Reed-Sternberg cell is the malignant cell of origin of classical HL.

Bibliography

Ansell SM. Hodgkin lymphoma: 2012 update on diagnosis, risk stratification, and management. Am J Hematol. 2012;87:1096-103. [PMID: 23151980]

Item 28   Answer: B

Educational Objective: *Understand the appropriate treatment of early-stage, aggressive, diffuse large B-cell non-Hodgkin lymphoma.*

This patient has early-stage, diffuse, large B-cell non-Hodgkin lymphoma (NHL), which can be aggressive, but may be curable. Five-year overall survival rate ranges from 30% to 50% for all stages, although early-stage, low-risk patients such as this one may have overall survival rates up to 90%. Treatment for all patients with large B-cell NHL includes chemotherapy (usually cyclophosphamide, doxorubicin, vincristine, and prednisone with rituximab [R-CHOP]) and immunotherapy with rituximab. Radiation therapy is used after a shorter course of chemoimmunotherapy in patients with localized or bulky disease, such as this patient. Using the combination of abbreviated chemoimmunotherapy and radiation minimizes exposure to a longer course of chemotherapy if used alone and has been shown to have equivalent survival with less toxicity.

Radiation therapy alone is not indicated because the relapse rate is at least 50% when only irradiation is used.

Treatment of this aggressive lymphoma in a young man without comorbidities is associated with a cure rate of at least 75%. Therefore, observation is inappropriate.

The addition of the monoclonal antibody rituximab to combination chemotherapy has been the first major therapeutic advance for patients with diffuse large B-cell lymphoma in more than 20 years, improving the cure rate by 10% to 15%. However, rituximab alone is associated with a 30% response rate but no chance of cure.

KEY POINT

Treatment of early-stage, diffuse, large B-cell NHL with an abbreviated course of chemotherapy followed by involved-field radiation therapy is associated with excellent long-term survival and decreased toxicity.

Bibliography

Zelenetz AD, Advani RH, Buadi F, et al. Non-Hodgkin's lymphoma. Clinical practice guidelines in oncology. J Natl Compr Canc Netw. 2006;4:258-310. [PMID: 16507273]

Item 29   Answer: C

Educational Objective: *Evaluate a patient with newly diagnosed chronic lymphocytic leukemia.*

The most appropriate next step in the evaluation of this patient is flow cytometry of the peripheral blood. She has a clinical picture consistent with chronic lymphocytic leukemia (CLL), which is diagnosed by an absolute increase in mature lymphocytes (>5000/µL [5×10^9/L]) in the absence of an acute viral illness or other trigger of reactive lymphocytosis and demonstration of clonality of the circulating B-lymphocytes on flow cytometry. Immunophenotyping will show a monoclonal proliferation of mature B lymphocytes expressing CD19, CD20, and CD5. CLL is the most common form of lymphoid malignancy of all the hematologic neoplasms, and its incidence increases with age. Most patients are asymptomatic and present with early-stage disease discovered incidentally during routine laboratory testing. The natural history of CLL is highly variable. Patients are stratified into risk groups based on presenting features. This risk stratification constitutes the staging criteria, which include the presence of lymphadenopathy, hepatosplenomegaly, anemia, or thrombocytopenia (excluding immune thrombocytopenic purpura). This patient has stage I disease (lymphocytosis and lymphadenopathy without splenomegaly or other organomegaly). Further prognostic information, such as the β_2-microglobulin level, heavy gene mutational status, and cytogenetics, may provide prognostic information to guide longer term management decisions.

Bone marrow biopsy is not required for the diagnosis of CLL; flow cytometry on a peripheral blood sample is adequate.

Computed tomography scans would not provide additional prognostic information that will help guide therapy in an asymptomatic patient with CLL.

Positron emission tomography (PET) scanning has a limited role in CLL and should be reserved for patients in whom a transformation to aggressive lymphoma is suspected. In patients with suspected transformed lymphoma, the detection of foci of intense uptake on PET scanning supports the diagnosis.

KEY POINT

In patients with CLL, the β_2-microglobulin level, heavy gene mutational status, and cytogenetics provide independent prognostic information on appropriate follow-up monitoring and time to initiate treatment.

Bibliography

Gribben JG, O'Brien S. Update on therapy of chronic lymphocytic leukemia. J Clin Oncol. 2011;29:544-50. [PMID: 21220603]

Item 30 Answer: D

Educational Objective: *Manage a patient with superior vena cava syndrome.*

The most appropriate management of this patient is mediastinoscopy and biopsy. Superior vena cava (SVC) syndrome is most commonly caused by lung cancer but can also be caused by lymphoma, including Hodgkin lymphoma, and mediastinal germ cell tumors. SVC syndrome is the initial manifestation in approximately 60% of patients with previously undiagnosed malignancy, and its onset is insidious. Common symptoms and findings include progressive dyspnea, facial swelling, cough, distention of the neck and chest veins, facial edema, cyanosis, facial plethora, and upper extremity edema. Common radiographic findings include mediastinal widening and pleural effusion.

The appropriate immediate management of patients with SVC syndrome depends on the histopathology; therefore, it is necessary to first obtain a tissue diagnosis. In the absence of more accessible sites such as peripheral lymphadenopathy, mediastinoscopy and biopsy has a high likelihood of providing adequate tissue for a diagnosis and is associated with a low incidence of complications (5%). The goal of treatment, which can usually be delayed while a tissue diagnosis is obtained, is to reduce symptoms and treat the underlying malignancy.

Oral glucocorticoids might be effective for treating lymphoma or Hodgkin lymphoma but would not be appropriate for lung cancer.

Although radiation therapy alone would be appropriate for treating non–small cell lung cancer and chemotherapy alone would be appropriate for small cell lung cancer, a histologic diagnosis must first be established before a treatment regimen can be selected. Similarly, combination chemotherapy and radiation may be appropriate in some cases; however, whether combination therapy is appropriate cannot be determined until a tissue diagnosis is made.

KEY POINT

A tissue diagnosis should be obtained before a therapeutic intervention is initiated in patients with superior vena cava syndrome.

Bibliography

Wan JF, Bezjak A. Superior vena cava syndrome. Hematol Oncol Clin North Am. 2010;24:501-13. [PMID: 20488350]

Item 31 Answer: B

Educational Objective: *Manage spinal cord compression.*

The most appropriate management of this patient is corticosteroids followed by radiation therapy. This patient has magnetic resonance imaging-confirmed spinal compression characterized by midback pain and physical findings of lower extremity hyperreflexia and weakness. Spinal cord compression occurs in 5% to 10% of patients with cancer and is one of this disease's most debilitating complications. To avoid progressive neurologic deterioration and reverse the lower extremity weakness, immediate corticosteroid therapy followed by radiation therapy is indicated. His known multiple myeloma with corresponding anemia and hypercalcemia suggest progression of his disease with a plasma cell tumor as the cause of his spinal cord compression. Glucocorticoid therapy is the initial treatment in most cases of malignant spinal cord compression as they decrease inflammation and reduce the mass effect of many tumors. In this case, glucocorticoid therapy has the added benefit of directly treating the hypercalcemia and plasma cell myeloma. Glucocorticoid treatment is then followed with more definitive therapy, usually radiation; neurosurgical intervention may be indicated in extreme situations.

Biopsy of the epidural mass is not necessary because of the patient's known likely causative disease and could delay initiation of corticosteroids and radiation therapy.

Definitive treatment with chemotherapy or an immunomodulator such as lenalidomide is appropriate but would not have the required immediate effect of corticosteroids and radiation therapy in preventing progressive neurologic damage.

Radiation therapy alone would not address the swelling associated with spinal cord compression nor the hypercalcemia or underlying systemic plasma cell myeloma.

KEY POINT

Spinal cord compression is a medical emergency requiring immediate treatment to reduce swelling and avoid progression or permanent spinal cord injury.

Bibliography

Taylor JW, Schiff D. Metastatic epidural spinal cord compression. Semin Neurol. 2010;30:245-53. [PMID: 20577931]

Item 32 Answer: C

Educational Objective: *Treat a patient with tumor lysis syndrome.*

This patient has tumor lysis syndrome (TLS) and requires immediate treatment with aggressive hydration with normal saline and rasburicase. TLS is a life-threatening complication that occurs most often in patients with malignancies associated with rapid cell turnover (leukemia, Burkitt lymphoma) or in patients with bulky disease and high leukocyte counts associated with rapid and significant sensitivity to chemotherapeutic agents (large cell lymphoma, chronic lymphocytic leukemia). The manifestations of TLS include hyperkalemia, hyperuricemia, hyperphosphatemia, hypocalcemia, acute kidney injury, and disseminated intravascular coagulation. In this case, any further acceleration of tumor cell turnover resulting from institution of immediate chemotherapy occurring before the patient's current metabolic condition is addressed would be potentially life threatening. In patients at risk for TLS, prophylactic treatment with aggressive hydration with diuresis and allopurinol is indicated. Allopurinol prevents further formation of uric acid, and rasburicase, a recombinant urate oxidase, can break down existing uric acid and actively reduce serum levels. Because this patient's uric acid level is significantly elevated, rasburicase would be preferred therapy. If his kidney injury progresses or lysis-associated electrolyte abnormalities cannot be managed with hydration and supportive care, hemodialysis may be needed. After the patient's life-threatening metabolic condition is stabilized, therapy for his malignancy can be instituted.

Besides hemodialysis, aggressive hydration with normal saline and rasburicase, any form of therapy, including corticosteroids, would accelerate this patient's TLS; consequently, immediate antineoplastic therapy and glucocorticoids are contraindicated.

Radiation therapy has no role in the treatment of Burkitt lymphoma, and, in any event, treatment of the patient's TLS takes precedence.

KEY POINT

Prophylactic treatment of TLS consists of aggressive hydration with diuresis and use of allopurinol and rasburicase, and when necessary, hemodialysis before initiation of antineoplastic therapy.

Bibliography

Abu-Alfa AK, Younes A. Tumor lysis syndrome and acute kidney injury: evaluation, prevention, and management. Am J Kidney Dis. 2010;55(5 suppl 3):S1-S13; quiz S14-S149. [PMID: 20420966]

Item 33   Answer: B

Educational Objective: *Manage brain metastasis and increased intracranial pressure in a patient with breast cancer.*

The most appropriate management of this patient is glucocorticoids (eg, dexamethasone) and radiation therapy. Increased intracranial pressure (ICP) results from mass effect and is common in patients with intracerebral tumors, particularly tumors caused by metastatic breast cancer, lung cancer, and melanoma. Headache is the most common symptom of increased ICP and is often severe and persistent despite analgesia and is of maximum intensity in the morning on awakening. Although a severe morning headache may occur as a sign of increased ICP, nonspecific headaches, cognitive changes, focal neurologic findings, and seizures may all be manifestations. Funduscopic examination may reveal papilledema. Brain metastasis associated with increased ICP is a medical emergency that requires immediate administration of parenteral glucocorticoids and surgical resection or radiation therapy to avoid progressive neurologic deficits. Glucocorticoids decrease the edema usually associated with metastases and decreases the intracranial mass effect. Radiation provides more definitive treatment, which is important given the potential consequences of enlarging intracranial mass lesions. In this case, the patient's breast cancer has recurred is suggested by the multiple blastic bone lesions seen on computed tomography.

Combination chemotherapy may eventually be appropriate management; however, such therapy is not appropriate initially because of the need for immediate treatment with corticosteroids and radiation therapy to prevent later consequences from increased ICP and brain metastases, including brainstem herniation, permanent neurologic dysfunction, and death. In addition, chemotherapeutic agents have limited efficacy in treating brain metastases.

ICP caused by mass effect is an absolute contraindication for lumbar puncture because the procedure may precipitate catastrophic brainstem herniation.

Surgery to remove the lesions is less desirable because more than one mass is present, and the patient has evidence of systemic breast cancer, which eventually will require systemic treatment with chemotherapy.

KEY POINT

Immediate corticosteroid administration and early initiation of radiation therapy are indicated to treat brain metastasis and increased ICP.

Bibliography

Khasraw M, Posner JB. Neurological complications of systemic cancer. Lancet Neurol. 2010;9:1214-1227. [PMID: 21087743]

Section 10

Pulmonary Medicine

Questions

Item 1 [Basic]

A 58-year-old man is evaluated because of insidious onset of slowly progressive dyspnea over the last 3 years. At this point, he must stop to rest when walking 1 block. Previously, he walked 1 to 2 miles daily without difficulty. He has no cough, chest pain, or orthopnea. He has no other medical problems.

On physical examination, vital signs are normal. Body mass index is 35. Oxygen saturation is 93% breathing ambient air. Dry crackles are noted on auscultation. Cardiac examination shows a parasternal heave and persistent splitting of S_2.

Chest radiograph shows diffuse reticular infiltrates that are most prominent in the upper lung zones.

Spirometry shows forced expiratory volume in 1 second (FEV_1) that is 60% of predicted and an FEV_1/forced vital capacity ratio of 80%. Total lung capacity is 70% of expected. Diffusing capacity of carbon monoxide is 45% of expected.

Which of the following is the most likely diagnosis?

(A) Diffuse parenchymal lung disease
(B) Heart failure
(C) Obesity hypoventilation syndrome
(D) Obstructive airways disease
(E) Respiratory muscle weakness

Item 2 [Basic]

A 30-year-old man is evaluated for chronic cough that has lasted nearly 1 year. He recalls that the cough began after a "bad cold." He was treated with a course of a macrolide antibiotic without significant improvement. The cough is nonproductive, is most noticeable at night and on cold days, and sometimes occurs after exercise. He has no postnasal drip, nasal congestion, or heartburn. He does not smoke. He has no history of occupational or other exposures. Medical history is otherwise unremarkable except for gastroesophageal reflux for which he takes a daily proton pump inhibitor.

On physical examination, vital signs are normal. The oropharynx is normal, without postnasal drip. Findings on pulmonary examination are normal. Spirometry shows forced expiratory volume in 1 second (FEV_1) of 90% of predicted and an FEV_1/forced vital capacity ratio of 80%. Chest radiograph is normal.

Which of the following is the most appropriate diagnostic test to perform next?

(A) Bronchial challenge test
(B) Bronchoscopy
(C) Chest computed tomography
(D) Pertussis culture

Item 3 [Advanced]

A 63-year-old man is evaluated for progressive dyspnea on exertion for the last several months. He can walk two to three blocks on a flat surface but becomes short of breath when going upstairs or uphill. He has a 10-pack-year history of smoking but quit 20 years ago. He takes no medications.

On physical examination, vital signs are normal except for a respiration rate of 22/min. No jugular venous distention is noted. Pulmonary examination shows reduced breath sounds at the lung bases. Findings on cardiac examination are normal. There is no leg edema.

Pulmonary function tests show forced expiratory volume in 1 second (FEV_1) of 75% of predicted, forced vital capacity (FVC) of 68% of predicted with no change after administration of a bronchodilator, total lung capacity of 68% of predicted, and residual volume of 125% of predicted. The FEV_1/FVC ratio is 82%. Chest radiograph shows low lung volumes with suggested bibasilar atelectasis.

Which of the following is the most likely diagnosis?

(A) Chronic obstructive pulmonary disease
(B) Heart failure
(C) Interstitial lung disease
(D) Respiratory muscle weakness

Item 4 [Basic]

A 36-year-old woman is evaluated because of shortness of breath. She describes her symptoms as "difficulty getting air" both at rest and with exertion. Onset of symptoms has been gradually progressive over the last 6 months. She has no cough or wheezing. Medical history is significant for severe injuries sustained in a motor vehicle accident 2 years ago. She had multiple head and chest injuries requiring prolonged mechanical ventilation and multiple corrective surgeries. She has recovered completely and now feels well. She takes no medications.

On physical examination, vital signs are normal. Oxygen saturation is 99% on ambient air. The oropharynx is patent, and she has no stridor. The chest shows multiple well-healed surgical incisions; respiratory effort and chest excursion are normal. The lungs are clear to auscultation. The remainder of the examination is unremarkable.

Which of the following is the most appropriate next diagnostic step?

(A) Chest computed tomography
(B) Flow-volume pulmonary function testing
(C) Plain chest radiograph
(D) Ventilation-perfusion scan

Item 5 [Advanced]

A 66-year-old man is admitted to the hospital with a 2-month history of progressive dyspnea and worsening pedal edema. Medical history is significant for coronary artery bypass surgery 3 years ago. He has a 10-year history of hypertension. Medications are metoprolol, atorvastatin, and aspirin.

On physical examination, temperature is normal, blood pressure is 118/64 mm Hg, pulse rate is 120/min, and respiration rate is 26/min. Jugular venous distention that increases with inspiration is noted. Cardiac examination shows no murmur, rub, or gallop. Pulsus paradoxus of 5 mm Hg is present. Lungs are clear to auscultation. Hepatojugular reflux is present. Pedal edema of 2+ is noted.

Electrocardiogram shows sinus rhythm with increased voltage in the precordial leads. Echocardiogram shows a normal left ventricular ejection fraction, restrictive left ventricular filling, increased ventricular wall thickness, biatrial enlargement, a small pericardial effusion, and abnormal diastolic to-and-fro ventricular septal motion. Chest radiograph shows no infiltrates.

Which of the following is the most likely cause of this patient's dyspnea?

(A) Cardiac tamponade
(B) Constrictive pericarditis
(C) Restrictive cardiomyopathy
(D) Severe tricuspid regurgitation

Item 6 [Basic]

A 50-year-old man is evaluated in the emergency department for a 3-day history of dyspnea, fever, productive cough, and left-sided pleuritic chest pain. He has been in good health previously and takes no medications.

On examination, temperature is 39°C (102.2°F), blood pressure is 140/80 mm Hg, pulse rate is 105/min, respiration rate is 22/min, and oxygen saturation is 94% on ambient air. Pulmonary examination shows crackles on the left side.

Chest radiograph shows a patchy left lower lobe infiltrate with blunting of the costophrenic angle. Left lateral decubitus film shows free-flowing fluid that layers out to 8 mm.

Treatment with empiric oral antibiotics is initiated for community-acquired pneumonia.

Which of the following is the most appropriate next step in management of the pleural effusion?

(A) Chest computed tomography
(B) Furosemide
(C) Thoracentesis
(D) Observation

Item 7 [Advanced]

A 74-year-old man is evaluated because of progressive dyspnea, productive cough, and left-sided chest pain of 10 days' duration. He also reports fever and chills. The medical history includes heart failure. Medications are aspirin, carvedilol, enalapril, and furosemide.

On physical examination, temperature is 39°C (102.2°F), blood pressure is 144/88 mm Hg, pulse rate is 102/min, respiration rate is

28/min, and oxygen saturation is 90% on ambient air. Pulmonary examination shows dullness to percussion and decreased breath sounds over the left posterior thorax. Cardiac examination shows a grade 2/6 holosystolic murmur and a fourth heart sound.

Serum glucose level is 110 mg/dL (6.11 mmol/L), serum lactate dehydrogenase level is 250 units/L, and serum protein level is 5.8 g/dL (58 g/L).

Chest radiograph shows a moderate left-sided effusion. Thoracentesis yields 500 mL of cloudy-appearing pleural fluid.

Pleural fluid analysis:

Blood cell count	Erythrocyte count, 1/µL; leukocyte count, 8900/µL (8.90 × 10⁹/L) with 10% lymphocytes and 85% neutrophils
Total protein	3.5 g/dL (35 g/L)
Lactate dehydrogenase	160 units/L
Glucose	25 mg/dL (1.39 mmol/L)
pH	7.10

Which of the following is the most likely cause of the effusion?

(A) Bacterial pneumonia
(B) Heart failure
(C) Malignancy
(D) Tuberculosis

Item 8 [Advanced]

A 78-year-old man was admitted to the hospital 4 days ago because of dyspnea. He has a history of heart failure.

On physical examination at admission, he was afebrile, blood pressure was 150/88 mm Hg, pulse rate was 108/min, and respiration rate was 22/min. Jugular venous distention was present, there were bibasilar crackles and dullness to percussion at both lung bases, and there was 2+ lower extremity edema. Chest radiograph showed cardiomegaly, vascular congestion, and moderate bilateral pleural effusions. He was treated with furosemide but continued to have shortness of breath. Thoracentesis was performed on hospital day 3 for further relief of dyspnea.

Pleural fluid analysis shows a pleural fluid–serum lactate dehydrogenase (LDH) ratio of .52, a pleural fluid LDH level of 46% of the upper limit of the normal level, and a pleural fluid–serum total protein ratio of 0.45. Results of pleural fluid cultures and cytology are pending.

Which of the following is the most likely cause of this patient's pleural effusions?

(A) Heart failure
(B) Malignancy
(C) Pneumonia
(D) Pulmonary embolism

Item 9 [Basic]

A 54-year-old woman is evaluated in the emergency department because of a 7-day history of cough and dyspnea. She had fatigue at the onset of symptoms. She reports feeling feverish, with nonproductive cough and progressive shortness of breath. Medical history is otherwise unremarkable. She takes no medications.

On physical examination, temperature is 37.9°C (100.3°F), blood pressure is 105/70 mm Hg, pulse rate is 106/min, and respiration rate is 32/min. Oxygen saturation is 92% on ambient air. Lung examination shows dullness to percussion, decreased tactile fremitus, and decreased breath sounds at the right base. The remainder of the findings on physical examination are unremarkable.

Which of the following is the most likely diagnosis?

(A) Heart failure
(B) Lobar consolidation
(C) Pleural effusion
(D) Pneumothorax

Item 10 [Basic]

A 26-year-old man is evaluated because of a 6-month history of chest tightness, cough, and shortness of breath that occur after running. He has no symptoms while running. His symptoms usually start a few minutes after he finishes running and continue for the next 30 minutes. Symptoms are worse when he runs in cold weather. He has no other medical problems and takes no medications.

On physical examination, temperature is 36.5°C (97.7°F), blood pressure is 120/70 mm Hg, pulse rate is 65/min, respiration rate is 14/min, and oxygen saturation is 98% on ambient air. Body mass index is 21. Pulmonary examination shows good air movement without wheezing.

Office spirometry is normal. After an exercise challenge test, Forced expiratory volume in 1 second decreased by 15% from the baseline measurement obtained before exercise.

Which of the following is the most appropriate treatment for this patient?

(A) Inhaled glucocorticoid before exercise
(B) Inhaled long-acting β_2-agonist daily
(C) Inhaled short-acting β_2-agonist before exercise
(D) Oral leukotriene receptor agonist daily

Item 11 [Basic]

A 55-year-old woman is evaluated because of a recent increase in symptoms of asthma characterized by daily cough and dyspnea. She reports waking up two to three nights per week with her typical asthma symptoms. She has no postnasal drip, nasal discharge, fever, or heartburn. Her medications are medium-dose inhaled corticosteroids and albuterol as needed. She demonstrates proper use of her metered-dose inhalers.

On physical examination, she appears comfortable and is in no respiratory distress. Pulse rate is 76/min, and respiration rate is 18/min. Pulmonary examination shows bilateral wheezing. The remainder of the findings on examination are normal.

Which of the following is the most appropriate treatment?

(A) Add a long-acting β_2-agonist inhaler
(B) Add an ipratropium metered-dose inhaler
(C) Double the dose of inhaled corticosteroids
(D) Start a 10-day course of a macrolide antibiotic

Item 12 [Basic]

A 24-year-old woman is evaluated because of worsening symptoms of asthma. She uses an as-needed albuterol inhaler two to three times per week and has been waking at night at least once a week with

asthma symptoms that require use of the inhaler. She is still able to perform most of her daily activities, including regular exercise, if she uses albuterol for prevention. She is allergic to house dust mites, ragweed, grass, trees, and cats.

On physical examination, vital signs are normal. Pulmonary examination is normal with no wheezing. Spirometry shows forced expiratory volume in 1 second (FEV$_1$) of 85% of predicted and an FEV$_1$/forced vital capacity ratio of 80% of predicted.

Which of the following is the most appropriate treatment?

(A) Add a long-acting β_2-agonist
(B) Add a long-acting β_2-agonist and a low-dose inhaled glucocorticoid
(C) Add a low-dose inhaled glucocorticoid
(D) Advise scheduled use of albuterol
(E) Refer for allergen immunotherapy

Item 13 [Advanced]

A 24-year-old woman is evaluated because of chronic cough that began after a respiratory tract infection 7 months ago. She notices that exposure to cold air and exercise, such as running, are likely to induce cough and wheezing. On rare occasions she is awakened at night with cough. She does not smoke, has no travel history, works as an accountant, and is not exposed to animals. She has no personal or family history of allergy or asthma. She otherwise feels well and takes no medications.

On physical examination, vital signs are normal. Upper airway examination is normal, and lungs are clear to auscultation. The remainder of the examination is normal.

Chest radiography is normal. On office spirometry, forced expiratory volume in 1 second (FEV$_1$) is 85% of predicted and FVC is 85% of predicted. The FEV$_1$/forced vital capacity (FVC) ratio is 76%. The flow-volume loop is normal. Pulmonary function testing shows total lung capacity of 105% of predicted. After the patient inhaled methacholine, there was a 20% drop in FEV$_1$ and FVC.

Which of the following is the most likely diagnosis?

(A) Asthma
(B) Cystic fibrosis
(C) Idiopathic pulmonary fibrosis
(D) Vocal cord dysfunction

Item 14 [Advanced]

A 28-year-old woman is evaluated because of symptoms of asthma that have worsened since she became pregnant 2 months ago. She has frequent daytime symptoms and increased nighttime awakening because of the symptoms. She has used her albuterol inhaler several times per week to achieve symptomatic relief. History includes mild persistent asthma that was well controlled before her pregnancy with an as-needed short-acting β_2-agonist and medium-dose inhaled glucocorticoids.

On physical examination, vital signs are normal. The lungs are clear. Cardiac examination shows normal S_1 and S_2 with no gallops or murmurs. No leg edema is noted.

Spirometry shows forced expiratory volume in 1 second (FEV₁) of 85% of predicted and an FEV₁/forced vital capacity ratio of 78%. Laboratory studies show a hemoglobin level of 11.5 g/dL (115 g/L).

Which of the following is the most appropriate next step in management?

(A) Add a long-acting β₂-agonist
(B) Add theophylline
(C) Double the dose of inhaled glucocorticoid
(D) Obtain a bronchial challenge test

Item 15 [Advanced]

A 36-year-old man is evaluated because of progressive shortness of breath over the last 3 years. He has episodic wheezing and decreased exercise capacity when he climbs stairs or walks quickly. He has a 10-pack-year history of smoking, but has not used tobacco for the past 5 years.

His father is 60 years old and has severe emphysema.

On physical examination, vital signs are normal. Oxygen saturation is 95% on ambient air. Body mass index is 22. There is wheezing in the posterior and lower lung fields. The remainder of the findings on physical examination are normal.

Chest radiograph is shown.

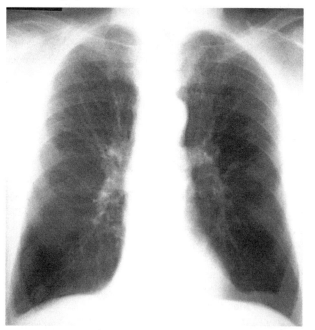

Spirometry shows Forced expiratory volume in 1 second (FEV₁) of 53% of predicted and an FEV₁/forced vital capacity ratio of 64%. Diffusing capacity of carbon monoxide is 67% of predicted. A six-minute walking test shows no significant oxygen desaturation while breathing ambient air.

In addition to smoking cessation, which of the following is the most appropriate next step in management?

(A) α₁-Antitrypsin level measurement
(B) Chest computed tomography
(C) Inhaled glucocorticoid treatment
(D) Oxygen therapy

Item 16 [Basic]

A 66-year-old man is evaluated because of slowly progressive shortness of breath and productive cough. He has a 5-year history of chronic obstructive pulmonary disease. He has a 55-pack-year smoking history, but stopped tobacco use 4 years ago. Medications are inhaled salbutamol and inhaled ipratropium. He uses inhaled albuterol as rescue medication. The patient continues to experience limiting dyspnea with activities of daily living. He demonstrates excellent inhaler technique. He reports no change in the color or volume of his sputum and does not have fever or chills.

On physical examination, temperature is 37.5°C (99.5°F), blood pressure is 128/76 mm Hg, pulse rate is 94/min, respiration rate is 20/min, and oxygen saturation is 82% on ambient air. Body mass index is 20. Heart sounds are distant, and breath sounds are diminished bilaterally and associated with a prolonged expiratory phase.

Spirometry shows Forced expiratory volume in 1 second (FEV₁) of 40% of predicted and an FEV₁/forced vital capacity ratio of 45%. Chest radiograph shows hyperinflation.

Which of the following interventions is most likely to prolong the patient's survival?

(A) Continuous oxygen therapy
(B) Inhaled glucocorticoid therapy
(C) Long-term antibiotic therapy
(D) Pulmonary rehabilitation

Item 17 [Basic]

A 72-year-old man is evaluated for follow-up after his first exacerbation of moderate chronic obstructive pulmonary disease. The dose of prednisone was tapered, and treatment was stopped 1 week ago. He is afebrile and his cough has decreased. He still has dyspnea despite adherence to the treatment regimen. Medical history is otherwise unremarkable. He has a 45-pack-year smoking history but stopped 6 months ago. Medications are tiotropium, a salmeterol dry powder inhaler, and an albuterol metered-dose inhaler as needed. He uses albuterol up to six times daily.

On physical examination, vital signs are normal. Pulmonary examination shows occasional expiratory wheezes. Oxygen saturation is 94% on ambient air.

Which of the following is the most appropriate next step in management?

(A) Add a fluticasone inhaler
(B) Add oxygen therapy
(C) Check the patient's inhaler technique
(D) Resume treatment with prednisone

Item 18 [Basic]

A 48-year-old man is evaluated because of a 1-year history of cough. He has no shortness of breath, heartburn, or change in appetite or weight. He has a 35-pack-year history of smoking. He has no seasonal allergies. The medical history is significant for hypertension. His only medication is losartan.

On physical examination, vital signs are normal. Pulmonary examination shows normal breath sounds that are equal bilaterally without wheezing. No nasal polyps are noted. Findings on abdominal examination are unremarkable. There is no cyanosis, clubbing, or edema. Pulmonary function tests show forced expiratory volume in 1 second (FEV_1) of 75% of predicted and an FEV_1/forced vital capacity (FVC) ratio of 63%. After administration of a bronchodilator, there is no significant change in the FEV_1/FVC ratio and FEV_1 is 83% of predicted. Chest radiograph shows no masses, and normal lung markings are seen.

Which of the following is the most likely cause of this patient's cough?

(A) Asthma
(B) Chronic obstructive pulmonary disease
(C) Gastroesophageal reflux disease
(D) Losartan use

Item 19 [Advanced]

A 72-year-old woman is evaluated for follow-up because of exacerbation of COPD. She has severe COPD without resting hypoxemia. The patient presented 1 week ago with fever, productive cough, and mild dyspnea over her baseline. Use of an albuterol inhaler was increased to six times daily, and a β-lactam/β-lactamase inhibitor and glucocorticoid taper were started. On follow-up today, she is fatigued and dyspneic relative to baseline. The medical history is otherwise unremarkable. Medications are tiotropium, fluticasone-salmeterol, and albuterol.

On physical examination, temperature is 37.8°C (100.0°F), blood pressure is 130/85 mm Hg, pulse rate is 95/min and regular, and respiration rate is 28/min. She is dyspneic at rest. Pulmonary examination shows bilateral expiratory wheezing. Oxygen saturation is 86% on ambient air and 92% on 2 L oxygen via nasal cannula.

Chest radiograph shows no infiltrate and no cardiomegaly.

Which of the following is the most appropriate next step in management?

(A) Add home oxygen treatment
(B) Admit to the hospital
(C) Expand the antibiotic spectrum
(D) Prolong the glucocorticoid taper

Item 20 [Advanced]

A 56-year-old man is evaluated in the emergency department because of a 3-day history of increasing dyspnea, fever, and cough with purulent sputum. He has severe chronic obstructive pulmonary disease with a history of exacerbations requiring hospitalization. Medications are ipratropium, salmeterol-fluticasone, and albuterol.

On physical examination, temperature is 38.0°C (100.4°F), blood pressure is 134/84 mm Hg, pulse rate is 88/min, and respiration rate is 30/min. He is awake and alert but is dyspneic and uses the accessory muscles to breathe. Pulmonary examination shows bilateral expiratory wheezes but no crackles.

An arterial blood gas study performed while breathing 2 L of oxygen via nasal cannula shows pH of 7.31, P_{CO_2} of 53 mm Hg (7.0 kPa), and P_{O_2} of 55 mm Hg (7.3 kPa). Oxygen saturation is 89%. Chest radiograph shows hyperinflation but no infiltrates.

In addition to antibiotics, glucocorticoids, and bronchodilators, which of the following is the most appropriate management?

(A) Continuous positive airway pressure
(B) Increase in nasal oxygen
(C) Intubation and mechanical ventilation
(D) Noninvasive positive pressure ventilation

Item 21 [Basic]

A 43-year-old man is evaluated because of a 3-year history of excessive sleepiness. He sleeps 8 hours nightly but never seems to wake refreshed. He reports that his wife complains about his snoring. She also notes that he appears to stop breathing suddenly for several seconds many times during the night. He resumes breathing with a loud gasp and snort. He falls asleep easily during the day, particularly in meetings or while reading. He has a history of hypertension and prediabetes. He has a 15-pack-year history of smoking but has not used tobacco for the past 8 years. He does not use alcohol. Medications are chlorthalidone and lisinopril. He works as an accountant and is generally sedentary.

On physical examination, vital signs are normal. Body mass index is 39. Other than obesity, the remainder of the findings on physical examination are normal.

Which of the following is most directly responsible for the patient's symptoms?

(A) History of smoking
(B) Hypertension
(C) Sedentary life style
(D) Weight

Item 22 [Basic]

A 61-year-old woman is evaluated because of excessive daytime sleepiness of 7 months' duration. She falls asleep while watching television or reading and recently fell asleep during church and during a conversation. She has no respiratory symptoms. Her only other medical problem is hypertension. Her only medication is amlodipine. Her husband states that she snores loudly during the night. She does not drink alcohol, smoke cigarettes, or use sedating drugs.

On physical examination, vital signs are normal. Body mass index is 37. Oxygen saturation is 96% on ambient air. The patient has a low-hanging soft palate and tongue and tonsils. Other than obesity, the remainder of the findings on physical examination are normal.

Results of complete blood count, electrocardiography, and chest radiograph are normal. The thyroid-stimulating hormone level and resting arterial blood gas results are normal.

Which of the following is most likely to establish the diagnosis?

(A) Chest computed tomography
(B) Overnight pulse oximetry
(C) Polysomnography
(D) Pulmonary function testing

Item 23 [Advanced]

A 58-year-old man is evaluated because of a 3-month history of loud snoring and "gasping" during sleep. He also frequently falls asleep in a chair while reading in the evening. His medical history is otherwise unremarkable.

On physical examination, temperature is 37.4°C (99.3°F), blood pressure is 130/82 mm Hg, pulse rate is 80/min, and respiration rate is 14/min. Body mass index is 34. Neck circumference is 45.7 cm (18.0 in), and a low-lying soft palate is noted. Polysomnography shows severe obstructive sleep apnea, with an apnea-hypopnea index of 42/h.

Which of the following is the most appropriate next step in treatment?

(A) Continuous positive airway pressure
(B) Nocturnal oxygen therapy
(C) Oral appliance
(D) Upper airway surgery

Item 24 [Basic]

A 32-year-old woman is evaluated because of slowly progressive dyspnea. For the last 6 months she has experienced progressive exertional dyspnea, exertional chest pressure, and dry cough. She is now short of breath when climbing one flight of stairs. She has no fever or weight loss. She reports one episode of a painful raised erythematous lesion on the anterior right shin accompanied by fever and ankle pain 6 months ago that resolved spontaneously after 3 weeks. She does not smoke.

On physical examination, she is afebrile, blood pressure is 120/70 mm Hg, pulse rate is 90/min, and respiration rate is 20/min. Body mass index is 23. Skin appears normal. Results of cardiopulmonary examination are normal.

Pulmonary function tests show Forced expiratory volume in 1 second (FEV$_1$) of 75% of predicted, forced vital capacity (FVC) of 88%, total lung capacity of 78% of predicted, and residual volume of 70% of predicted. The FEV$_1$/FVC ratio is 68%.

Chest radiograph is shown.

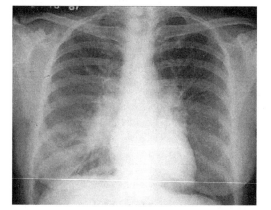

Which of the following is the most likely diagnosis?

(A) Chronic hypersensitivity pneumonitis
(B) Lymphangioleiomyomatosis
(C) Respiratory bronchiolitis-associated interstitial lung disease
(D) Sarcoidosis

Item 25 [Basic]

A 65-year-old man is evaluated because of a 4-month history of gradually progressive shortness of breath. Initially, symptoms were present only with exertion but now are present at rest. He also has an occasionally productive cough. He has a 30-pack-year history of smoking and quit 10 years ago. His occupation history includes extensive and unprotected exposure to asbestos 20 years ago.

On physical examination, he is afebrile, blood pressure is 136/88 mm Hg, pulse rate is 100/min, respiration rate is 24/min, and oxygen saturation on ambient air is 89% and drops to 86% with exercise. There is clubbing of the fingers. Pulmonary examination shows fine inspiratory crackles bilaterally in the posterior lung zones.

Chest radiograph shows linear opacities in the lung bases bilaterally and linear calcifications along the diaphragm. There is no lymphadenopathy. High-resolution chest computed tomographic scan shows basilar interstitial fibrosis, fine and course honeycombing, traction bronchiectasis, increased interlobular septal thickening in the subpleural regions, and diaphragmatic plaques with calcification.

Pulmonary function testing shows a predominantly restrictive disease pattern.

Which of the following diagnostic tests should be done next?

(A) Antinuclear antibody, rheumatoid factor, and erythrocyte sedimentation rate
(B) Open lung biopsy
(C) Transbronchial lung biopsy
(D) No further testing

Item 26 [Advanced]

A 32-year-old man is evaluated because of severe dyspnea and dry cough. He has an 8-week history of increasing shortness of breath without fever or chills. He was treated for presumed pneumonia with

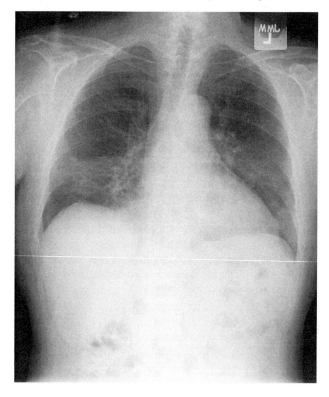

azithromycin when his symptoms began. However, the symptoms have continued to worsen. His medical history is otherwise unremarkable. He has never smoked, and he takes no medications.

On physical examination, temperature is normal, blood pressure is 135/85 mm Hg, pulse rate is 105/min, and respiration rate is 28/min. Oxygen saturation is 88% on ambient air. There is no jugular venous distention. Pulmonary examination shows bilateral crackles in the midlung zones. Findings on cardiac examination are normal. There is no peripheral edema and no rash or joint swelling.

Chest radiograph is shown.

Which of the following is the most likely diagnosis?

(A) Chronic pulmonary embolism
(B) Community-acquired pneumonia
(C) Cryptogenic organizing pneumonia
(D) Idiopathic pulmonary fibrosis

Item 27 [Advanced]

A 75-year-old man is evaluated because of a 12-month history of cough and dyspnea. He reports no other symptoms or medical problems and takes no medications. He has a 40-pack-year history of smoking and does not currently smoke. He is a retired carpenter. He has no pets and no known environmental exposures other than wood dust.

On physical examination, blood pressure is 135/75 mm Hg, pulse rate is 88/min, and respiration rate is 24/min. Oxygen saturation is 88% on ambient air. There is no jugular venous distention. Findings on cardiac examination are normal. Pulmonary examination shows inspiratory crackles at the lung bases bilaterally. Digital clubbing is present.

Pulmonary function testing shows decreased forced expiratory volume in 1 second (FEV_1), decreased forced vital capacity (FVC), a normal FEV_1/FVC ratio, and decreased Diffusing capacity of carbon monoxide.

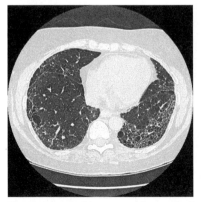

Chest computed tomographic scan is shown.

Which of the following is the most likely diagnosis?

(A) Chronic obstructive pulmonary disease
(B) Heart failure
(C) Hypersensitivity pneumonitis
(D) Idiopathic pulmonary fibrosis

Item 28 [Basic]

A 63-year-old woman is evaluated in the emergency department because of sudden onset of anterior chest pain and shortness of breath. The pain is sharp, is worse with inspiration, and does not radiate. She cannot walk more than a few steps without dyspnea. The medical history is significant for lung cancer that was diagnosed 2 weeks ago. She is undergoing radiation therapy. She has not been hospitalized recently. She has no cough, fever, chills, or hemoptysis. She has a 35-pack-year history of smoking and stopped smoking 3 months ago.

On physical examination, she is afebrile, blood pressure is 110/70 mm Hg, pulse rate is 115/min, respiration rate is 22/min, and oxygen saturation is 84% on ambient air. Findings on cardiopulmonary examination are normal. The extremities are normal, without pain or edema.

The electrocardiogram shows sinus tachycardia with ST-segment depression in leads V_3 to V_6, unchanged from 2 months ago. The initial troponin I level is 0.1 ng/mL (0.1 µg/L). Chest radiograph shows a right hilar mass that is unchanged from 2 weeks ago.

Which of the following diagnostic tests should be performed next?

(A) Cardiac catheterization
(B) Chest computed tomographic angiography
(C) D-Dimer assay
(D) Dobutamine echocardiographic stress test
(E) Transthoracic echocardiogram

Item 29 [Basic]

A 54-year-old man is evaluated in the emergency department for a 1-hour history of chest pain and shortness of breath. He had been hospitalized 1 week ago for a colectomy for colon cancer. His medical history is otherwise significant for hypertension complicated by hypertensive nephropathy. His medications include amlodipine, ramipril, and as-needed acetaminophen for postoperative pain.

On physical examination, temperature is 37.5°C (100°F), blood pressure is 110/60 mm Hg, heart rate is 115/min, and respiration rate is 24/min. Oxygen saturation is 89% with the patient breathing ambient air and 97% on oxygen, 4 L/min by nasal cannula. The lungs are clear. Cardiac examination shows tachycardia but is otherwise normal. There is a surgical incision in the left lower quadrant that is healing well. The remainder of the examination is unremarkable.

Chest radiograph is negative for infiltrates, widened mediastinum, and pneumothorax. Serum creatinine concentration is 2.1 mg/dL (185.6 µmol/L).

Empiric intravenous unfractionated heparin therapy is begun.

Which of the following is the most appropriate study to confirm the diagnosis in this patient?

(A) CT angiography
(B) D-dimer assay
(C) Lower extremity Doppler ultrasonography
(D) Ventilation-perfusion scanning

Item 30 [Basic]

A 42-year-old man is evaluated in the hospital for dyspnea and pleuritic chest pain. The patient was involved in a motor vehicle accident 3 weeks ago in which he sustained multiple lacerations and a fracture of his right femur. Medical history is otherwise unremarkable and he takes no medications.

Physical examination shows a temperature of 38.1°C (100.6°F), blood pressure of 130/78 mm Hg, pulse rate of 110/min, and respiration rate of 22/min. Oxygen saturation is 87% breathing ambient air and 92% on 2 L/min of oxygen by nasal cannula. The lungs are clear and the cardiac examination is significant only for tachycardia. There is a cast in place on the right lower extremity, and there are scattered healing lacerations present. The remainder of the examination is unremarkable.

Chest radiograph shows no abnormalities. A complete metabolic profile, including measures of kidney function, is normal. Contrast-enhanced CT scan shows pulmonary emboli in the arteries perfusing the lingula and the posterior basal segment of the left lower lobe.

Which of the following is the most appropriate treatment for this patient?

(A) Inferior vena cava filter
(B) Intravenous unfractionated heparin
(C) Intravenous tissue plasminogen activator
(D) Surgical embolectomy

Item 31 [Advanced]

A 33-year-old woman is evaluated for a 2-year history of progressive dyspnea on exertion accompanied by weakness and fatigue. There is no seasonal variation to her symptoms. She reports no history of nocturnal awakening, snoring, or daytime somnolence. She does not have dizziness or syncope. Her medical history is otherwise normal, and she takes no medications.

On physical examination, the patient is afebrile. Blood pressure 115/75 mm Hg, pulse rate is 108/min and regular, and respiration rate is 18/min. BMI is 21. The neck veins are distended. The lungs are clear. Cardiac examination shows regular tachycardia and a prominent pulmonic component of S_2. There is edema of the legs bilaterally to the level of the knees.

Laboratory studies, including a complete blood count, serum chemistries, and thyroid and coagulation studies, are normal. Antinuclear antibody, rheumatoid factor, and ANCA studies are negative. Chest radiograph reveals prominent central pulmonary arteries, clear lungs, and normal heart size. Pulmonary function tests reveal a mildly decreased DLCO without evidence of airway obstruction or decreased lung volumes. Electrocardiogram shows right axis deviation. Transthoracic echocardiogram shows normal left ventricular size and function, a dilated right ventricle, and an estimated right ventricular systolic pressure of 40 mm Hg. Ventilation-perfusion scan is normal.

Which of the following is the most appropriate diagnostic test to perform next?

(A) High-resolution CT scan
(B) Pulmonary angiography
(C) Right heart catheterization
(D) Sleep study
(E) Transesophageal echocardiography

Section 10

Pulmonary Medicine
Answers and Critiques

Item 1   **Answer: A**
Educational Objective: *Diagnose restrictive lung disease.*

The most likely diagnosis is diffuse parenchymal lung disease. Pulmonary function tests are used to evaluate patients with pulmonary symptoms (most frequently dyspnea). They provide information on the degree of impairment and the potential causes. These tests are typically performed in patients with known lung disease or unexplained pulmonary symptoms. They are also used to establish a baseline in patients who are starting a job or a treatment that may cause lung dysfunction. This patient has a reduced forced expiratory volume in 1 second (FEV_1) but a normal FEV_1/forced vital capacity (FCV) ratio. This finding is compatible with restrictive lung disease rather than obstructive lung disease. The low total lung capacity is further evidence of a restrictive impairment. Restriction can be secondary to diffuse parenchymal lung disease, such as pulmonary fibrosis; in such patients, diffusing capacity of carbon monoxide (D_{LCO}) is also reduced, as it is in this patient. D_{LCO} measures the ability of the lungs to transfer gas across the alveolar-capillary membrane. There are several causes of reduced diffusing capacity of carbon monoxide (D_{LCO}), including loss of surface for gas exchange (emphysema), diffuse parenchymal lung disease, and parenchymal infiltration (diffuse pneumonia). The crackles noted on pulmonary examination and the diffuse reticular infiltrate shown on chest radiograph pinpoint the lung as the cause of the restrictive abnormality. The chronic and slow progression of the symptoms and absence of fever argue against pneumonia.

Chest restriction may also result from respiratory muscle weakness as a result of neuromuscular disease and obesity. However, in these cases, the results of pulmonary examination, chest radiograph, and D_{LCO} are normal. Although heart failure can be associated with pulmonary crackles, it is not associated with a restrictive spirometry pattern, decreased total lung capacity, or low D_{LCO}.

KEY POINT

Restrictive lung disease is characterized by a reduced FEV_1, normal FEV_1/FVC ratio, and reduced total lung capacity and D_{LCO}.

Bibliography

Pellegrino R, Viegi G, Brusasco V, et al. Interpretative strategies for lung function tests. Eur Respir J. 2005;26:948-68. [PMID: 16264058]

Item 2   **Answer: A**
Educational Objective: *Diagnose cough-variant asthma.*

The most appropriate diagnostic test is a bronchial challenge test. This patient has chronic cough. Asthma, postnasal drip, and gastroesophageal reflux are the most common diagnoses for patients with chronic cough and normal findings on chest radiograph. This patient has episodic cough triggered by cold air and hyperventilation. The symptoms are suggestive of cough-variant asthma. Negative findings on bronchial challenge testing in such a patient can exclude asthma,

and positive findings suggest cough-variant asthma. Such testing is indicated when asthma is suspected even though routine spirometry shows no evidence of bronchospasm. Patients with underlying asthma typically have bronchial hyperresponsiveness and have an exaggerated response to agents that promote bronchoconstriction. Diagnostic criteria are based on the degree of airway obstruction triggered by inhalation of these medications relative to baseline. The diagnosis of cough-variant asthma should be confirmed with clinical response to usual asthma therapy.

Although it is important to consider pertussis in patients with acute or subacute cough, this patient has had cough for nearly 1 year and has no recent symptoms to suggest acute infection. Furthermore, he has already received a course of antibiotics with a drug that should have been effective against *Bordetella pertussis*.

Bronchoscopy should be reserved for patients with abnormal findings on chest radiograph and those who are at increased risk for lung cancer (eg, long-standing history of smoking, older age).

Chest computed tomography in a young nonsmoker with a clear chest radiograph would be unlikely to provide any useful information. Therefore, it is not indicated.

KEY POINT

Bronchial challenge testing in patients with suspected cough-variant asthma can exclude asthma if results are negative and suggest cough-variant asthma if results are positive.

Bibliography

Dicpinigaitis PV. Chronic cough due to asthma: ACCP evidence-based clinical practice guidelines. Chest. 2006;129(1 suppl):75S-9S. [PMID: 16428696]

Item 3   **Answer: D**
Educational Objective: *Diagnose respiratory muscle weakness.*

The most likely diagnosis is respiratory muscle weakness. This patient has progressive dyspnea without other associated respiratory symptoms. Pulmonary function tests show a restrictive pattern without evidence of obstruction and with increased residual volume, which is typical for a patient with respiratory muscle weakness. Residual volume is increased because of the patient's inability to exhale fully. This patient should undergo further evaluation, with measurement of respiratory muscle forces and a detailed neurologic assessment. It is important to recognize that dyspnea (as a result of respiratory muscle weakness) can be the presenting symptom for patients with neuromuscular disease.

Patients with chronic obstructive pulmonary disease would have increased residual volume, but total lung capacity would be increased at the same time. Chest radiograph shows low lung volume, which is more consistent with respiratory muscle weakness.

Heart failure should be considered in patients with this type of presentation. However, there are no findings to suggest heart failure in this patient. There is no jugular venous distention or edema, and findings on cardiac examination are normal.

Interstitial lung disease is associated with a reduction in both total lung capacity and residual volume.

KEY POINT

Respiratory muscle weakness as a result of neuromuscular disease is characterized by reduced total lung capacity and increased residual volume because of the patient's inability to exhale fully.

Bibliography

Ambrosino N, Carpenè N, Gherardi M. Chronic respiratory care for neuromuscular diseases in adults. Eur Respir J. 2009;34:444-51. [PMID: 19648521]

Item 4   Answer: B

Educational Objective: *Suspect tracheomalacia as a cause of chronic dyspnea in a patient with a history of multiple intubations.*

The patient should undergo pulmonary function testing with flow-volume measurements. The clinical history is highly suggestive of tracheomalacia or tracheal stenosis. These complications may be seen in patients who have had endotracheal intubation, particularly when intubation has been repeated or prolonged. Injury to the trachea from chronic trauma caused by an endotracheal tube may result in inflammation, scarring, and fibrosis or loss of integrity of the tracheal structures, leading to airway narrowing and clinical symptoms. Normal findings on physical examination and absence of stridor do not exclude this condition. Tracheomalacia and tracheal stenosis are best diagnosed on pulmonary function testing, where a characteristic flattening of the curve is observed on flow-volume measurements.

Chest radiograph generally is not useful in diagnosing tracheal pathology. The patient's history is not suggestive of thromboembolic disease; therefore, a ventilation-perfusion scan would not be diagnostically helpful. Although chest computed tomography may show evidence of tracheal pathology, pulmonary function testing is needed to determine the clinical significance of any observed radiographic abnormalities as a potential cause of the patient's symptoms.

KEY POINT

In a patient with a history of intubation and mechanical ventilation who presents with chronic dyspnea, pulmonary function testing with flow-volume measurements should be obtained to diagnose tracheal pathology.

Bibliography

Nesek-Adam V, Mrsic' V, Oberhofer D, et al. Post-intubation long-segment tracheal stenosis of the posterior wall: a case report and review of the literature. J Anesth. 2010;24:621-5. [PMID: 20454809]

Item 5   Answer: B

Educational Objective: *Diagnose constrictive pericarditis.*

This patient most likely has constrictive pericarditis as a cause of his dyspnea and lower extremity edema. He has evidence of elevated right ventricular heart pressure on examination (jugular venous distention, hepatojugular reflux, pedal edema), with no evidence of left-sided heart failure. The finding of Kussmaul sign (jugular vein engorgement with inspiration) raises clinical suspicion for constrictive pericarditis. Constrictive pericarditis is evident on the basis of

echocardiographic findings of restrictive filling and ventricular interdependence (ie, diastolic filling of one ventricular chamber that impedes that of the other, as may be manifested by a to-and-fro diastolic motion of the ventricular septum). Cardiac computed tomography or cardiac magnetic resonance imaging would likely show pericardial thickening, further supporting this diagnosis. Constrictive pericarditis is a recognized potential complication after coronary artery bypass surgery.

Restrictive cardiomyopathy as a result of infiltrative disease (eg, cardiac amyloidosis) could result in dyspnea, right-sided heart failure, restrictive ventricular filling, and increased wall thickness. However, left ventricular hypertrophy and ventricular interdependence would be unusual findings in cardiac amyloidosis.

Although cardiac tamponade could account for dyspnea and jugular venous distention, it is an unlikely diagnosis in this patient. Pulsus paradoxus greater than 10 mm Hg, a typical finding in cardiac tamponade, is absent in this patient.

Severe tricuspid regurgitation could account for dyspnea and pedal edema and the findings of elevated right ventricular pressure on physical examination, as seen in this patient. Although a holosystolic murmur is commonly heard, a murmur may be absent with severe tricuspid regurgitation. However, tricuspid regurgitation would be evident on echocardiography.

KEY POINT

Dyspnea, pedal edema, clear lung fields, and jugular vein engorgement with inspiration raise clinical suspicion for constrictive pericarditis.

Bibliography

Imazio M. Contemporary management of pericardial diseases. Curr Opin Cardiol. 2012;27:308-17. [PMID: 22450720]

Item 6   Answer: D

Educational Objective: *Diagnose uncomplicated parapneumonic pleural effusion.*

The most appropriate management is clinical observation. This patient has a diagnosis of community-acquired pneumonia, and the pleural effusion is likely parapneumonic. A parapneumonic effusion is a noninfected effusion occurring in the pleural space adjacent to the site of bacterial pneumonia. These types of effusions occur in up to 50% of patients who are admitted to the hospital with bacterial pneumonia. Most parapneumonic effusions are small and clinically insignificant, and they resolve without specific therapy. However, approximately 10% become complicated or progress to empyema. In the setting of a small, free-flowing pleural effusion, it is appropriate to treat the underlying cause. The presence of loculated (non-free-flowing) fluid predicts a poor response to treatment with antibiotics alone.

Thoracentesis is not necessary in patients who have small pleural effusions (<1 cm between the lung and chest wall on lateral chest radiograph) associated with heart failure, pneumonia, or heart surgery. Unexplained effusions larger than 1 cm should be aspirated. The use of diuretics is not recommended in the absence of volume overload. Obtaining a computed tomographic (CT) scan of the chest is unlikely to add more information or affect management. CT scan also exposes the patient to unnecessary radiation and increases medical costs.

Thoracentesis or other imaging is not necessary in patients who have small pleural effusions (<1 cm between the lung and chest wall on lateral chest radiography) associated with heart failure, pneumonia, or heart surgery.

Bibliography

Wrightson JM, Davies RJ. The approach to the patient with a parapneumonic effusion. Semin Respir Crit Care Med. 2010;31:706-15. [PMID: 21213202]

Item 7   Answer: A

Educational Objective: *Diagnose an empyema.*

The patient has an empyema (pus in the pleural space) most likely secondary to bacterial pneumonia. The laboratory findings are consistent with an exudative effusion. Two criteria are most frequently used to determine whether pleural fluid is transudative or exudative. These are pleural fluid total protein–serum total protein ratio greater than 0.5 and pleural fluid lactate dehydrogenase level greater than two thirds of the upper limit of normal (or pleural fluid–serum lactate dehydrogenase ratio >0.6). If either of these criteria is met, the fluid is almost always an exudate. If neither criterion is met, the fluid is almost always a transudate. Pleural fluid leukocyte count greater than 10,000/µL (10.0 × 10⁹/L) implies infection. Transudative processes typically have a leukocyte count of less than 1000/µL (1.0 × 10⁹/L). A predominance of neutrophils suggests acute inflammation or infection. A pleural fluid glucose level of less than 60 mg/dL is most commonly caused by tuberculosis, parapneumonic effusion, malignant effusion, or rheumatoid disease. A pleural fluid pH of less than 7.2 is seen in complicated parapneumonic effusions (eg, empyema), esophageal rupture, rheumatoid and tuberculous pleuritis, malignant pleural disease, systemic acidosis, paragonimiasis, lupus pleuritis, or urinothorax. The predominance of neutrophils in the pleural fluid and the low level of glucose in the pleural fluid suggest either a parapneumonic effusion or empyema. Normal pleural fluid pH is 7.60 to 7.66. The very low pleural fluid pH of less than 7.20 supports an infectious cause. Bacterial Gram staining and culture can be used to confirm a diagnosis of empyema.

Heart failure is more likely to present as a bilateral transudative pleural effusion. Malignancy presents as an exudative effusion with a predominance of lymphocytes. Low glucose and pH values are seen in fewer than 10% of patients and often denote a poor prognosis. Tuberculous effusion is associated with an exudate effusion with a lymphocytic predominance.

Two criteria are most frequently used to determine whether pleural fluid is transudative or exudative: a pleural fluid total protein-serum total protein ratio greater than 0.5 and a pleural fluid lactate dehydrogenase level greater than two thirds of the upper limit of normal (or a pleural fluid–serum lactate dehydrogenase ratio >0.6).

Bibliography

Light RW. Clinical practice. Pleural effusion. N Engl J Med. 2002;346:1971-7. [PMID: 12075059]

Item 8   Answer: A

Educational Objective: *Diagnose pleural effusion caused by heart failure.*

The most likely cause of this patient's pleural effusions is heart failure. The patient presents with classic findings of decompensated heart failure. The findings of pleural fluid analysis are consistent with a transudate, with a pleural fluid–serum lactate dehydrogenase (LDH) ratio of less than 0.6, a pleural fluid LDH level that is less than two thirds of the upper limit of the normal level, and a pleural fluid–serum total protein ratio of less than 0.5. Pleural fluid studies help to differentiate transudative effusions from exudative effusions. These categories help to guide therapy. In this patient, pleural fluid analysis confirms that the effusions are likely caused by heart failure and are not related to an alternative diagnosis.

Pleural effusions caused by malignancy tend to be unilateral, with exudative chemical characteristics, and up to two thirds are predominantly lymphocytes. The effusions in this patient are most consistent with transudate, in which case the lymphocyte predominance is of no clinical significance.

Pneumonia is associated with an exudative pleural effusion, which is not present in this patient. In addition, the absence of fever decreases the probability of a parapneumonic effusion. Although the results of pleural fluid analysis may increase or decrease the posttest probability that the effusions are exudative, borderline test results do not affect the low clinical suspicion for this finding.

Pleural effusions caused by pulmonary embolims are small and unilateral, with 86% causing only blunting of the costophrenic angle. Pleural fluid analysis is not helpful in establishing the diagnosis; however, the findings are almost always consistent with an exudative process.

Heart failure is the most common cause of transudative effusion, as suggested by a pleural fluid-serum lactate dehydrogenase ratio of less than 0.6, a pleural fluid lactate dehydrogenase level that is less than two thirds of the upper limit of the normal level, and a pleural fluid-serum total protein ratio of less than 0.5.

Bibliography

Light RW. Clinical practice. Pleural effusion. N Engl J Med. 2002;346:1971-7. [PMID: 12075059]

Item 9   Answer: C

Educational Objective: *Diagnose pleural effusion.*

The most likely diagnosis is a pleural effusion secondary to right lower lobe pneumonia with a parapneumonic effusion. Significant fluid accumulation in the pleural space blocks transmission of sound between the lung and the chest wall, causing dullness to percussion on examination. On auscultation, the most common findings are decreased to absent breath sounds over the effusion because of the separation of aerated lung from the chest wall. Tactile (vocal) fremitus is caused by transmission of sound from the central airway to the chest wall, usually as a result of consolidated lung that more effectively propagates sound through the lung to the chest wall. The finding of diminished fremitus in this patient suggests that there is no lobar consolidation. The patient's history, with recent onset of fever, cough, and shortness of breath, makes a pneumonia-related parapneumonic effusion without underlying lung consolidation likely.

Heart failure is one of the most common causes of pleural effusion. However, the effusions are most commonly bilateral and are usually accompanied by other evidence of heart failure (eg, jugular venous distention, third heart sound, and lower extremity edema). These are not present in this patient.

Patients with lobar consolidation typically have dullness to percussion, crackles, bronchial breath sounds, and increased tactile fremitus. Decreased fremitus is seen in patients with an isolated pleural effusion.

Pneumothorax should be considered in any patient who has sudden onset of pleuritic chest pain and dyspnea. Physical examination may show decreased breath sounds and hyperresonance to percussion rather than dullness to percussion on the affected side.

KEY POINT

A large pleural effusion is associated with dullness to percussion and absent or decreased tactile (vocal) fremitus and breath sounds over the affected area.

Bibliography

Wong CL, Holroyd-Leduc J, Straus SE. Does this patient have a pleural effusion? JAMA. 2009;301:309-17. [PMID: 19155458]

Item 10   Answer: C

Educational Objective: *Treat exercise-induced bronchospasm.*

The most appropriate treatment for this patient is an inhaled short-acting β_2-agonist before exercise. Exercise-induced bronchoconstriction (EIB) is common in patients with asthma, and some patients only experience symptoms after exercise. EIB is diagnosed by measuring Forced expiratory volume in 1 second (FEV_1) before and after exercise. A decrease in FEV_1 of greater than 10% within 30 minutes of exercise is diagnostic of EIB. First-line therapy is administration of an inhaled short-acting β_2-agonist 15 to 20 minutes before exercise. These agents work by stimulating airway β_2 receptors, resulting in muscle relaxation and bronchodilation. When given before exercise, in approximately 80% of patients, these drugs are usually effective for 2 to 4 hours in protecting against bronchoconstriction. Nonpharmacologic approaches to prevent EIB include gradual warm-up before intense exercise, using a mask over the nose and mouth during cold weather, and avoiding high-intensity intermittent exercise.

The use of an inhaled glucocorticoid immediately before exercise is not effective in preventing EIB. Leukotriene-modifying drugs can also be used to prevent EIB. However, they are not as effective as inhaled short-acting β_2-agonists. Inhaled long-acting β_2-agonists are not used as monotherapy for asthma. These drugs control asthma symptoms but provide no anti-inflammatory effects. Therefore, single-agent treatment of asthma with long-acting β_2-agonists can mask worsening of airway inflammation and lead to increased risk of asthma-related complications, including death.

KEY POINT

First-line therapy for exercise-induced asthma is administration of an inhaled short-acting β_2-agonist 15 to 20 minutes before exercise.

Bibliography

Parsons JP, Hallstrand TS, Mastronarde JG, et al. An official American Thoracic Society clinical practice guideline: exercise-induced bronchoconstriction. Am J Respir Crit Care Med. 2013;187:1016-27. [PMID: 23634861]

Item 11   Answer: A

Educational Objective: *Treat inadequately controlled asthma.*

The most appropriate treatment is to add a long-acting β_2-agonist inhaler. This patient was doing well until the recent exacerbation of asthma. Her asthma is now classified as moderate persistent, based on the National Asthma Education and Prevention Program guidelines (daily symptoms of asthma and nocturnal awakenings more than once per week). Symptoms are not well controlled on a moderate dose of inhaled corticosteroids. The guidelines recommend the addition of a long-acting β_2-agonist in this case. This treatment has been shown to lead to greater improvement in asthma control compared with doubling the dose of inhaled corticosteroids. The systemic side effects of inhaled corticosteroids are relatively uncommon but occur in patients who are receiving high-dose therapy (particularly long-term, high-dose therapy). These effects include adrenal suppression, glaucoma, cataracts, osteopenia, and thinning of the skin. Therefore, the lowest dose that provides disease control should always be used. Finally, treatment of asthma with a metered-dose inhaler with various agents is essential. Patients should be shown the proper technique for using inhalers, and those with poorly controlled disease should be evaluated for proper inhaler technique.

Ipratropium enhances the bronchodilator effect of β_2-agonists when given for acute exacerbations of asthma. However, its use for long-term control of asthma generally is not recommended. Recent studies showed that the addition of a long-acting anticholinergic drug (tiotropium) was equivalent to the addition of a long-acting β_2-agonist in patients with asthma whose symptoms were inadequately controlled with inhaled corticosteroids alone.

Although macrolide antibiotics are beneficial in treating atypical respiratory tract infections (which can be associated with exacerbations of asthma and asthma-like symptoms), their routine use in the treatment of asthma is not recommended and has not been shown to improve asthma control.

KEY POINT

Guidelines recommend the addition of a long-acting β_2-agonist to medium-dose corticosteroids in patients with moderate persistent asthma. This treatment has proved to lead to greater improvement in asthma control compared with doubling the dose of inhaled corticosteroids.

Bibliography

National Asthma Education and Prevention Program. Expert Panel Report 3. Guidelines for the Diagnosis and Management of Asthma. www.nhlbi.nih.gov/guidelines/asthma/asthsumm.pdf

Item 12   Answer: C

Educational Objective: *Treat mild persistent asthma.*

The most appropriate treatment is to add a low-dose inhaled glucocorticoid. This patient has mild persistent asthma. She has symptoms more than 2 days per week but not daily, and she wakes up once a week but not nightly. The preferred therapy for this patient is a low-dose inhaled glucocorticoid added to an as-needed short-acting β_2-agonist. Alternatives to inhaled glucocorticoids include a leukotriene receptor antagonist and theophylline.

Adding a long-acting β_2-agonist is not recommended for patients with asthma who are not already receiving inhaled glucocorticoid therapy.

Providing a combination of long-acting β_2-agonist and inhaled corticosteroid therapy is not indicated. Based on the National Asthma Education and Prevention Program guidelines and a Food and Drug Administration black box warning, treatment with inhaled glucocorticoids should be started first. Long-acting β_2-agonists should be added only if medium-dose inhaled glucocorticoid therapy does not control symptoms.

Scheduled use of albuterol is not recommended because it can mask ongoing airway inflammation and the need to provide anti-inflammatory therapy with inhaled glucocorticoids.

Allergen immunotherapy is an option for some patients. However, its benefits are mostly for those with allergic rhinitis. It would not be recommended for patients with mild persistent asthma.

KEY POINT

The preferred therapy for mild persistent asthma is a low-dose inhaled glucocorticoid added to an as-needed short-acting β_2-agonist.

Bibliography

National Asthma Education and Prevention Program. Expert Panel Report 3. Guidelines for the Diagnosis and Management of Asthma. www.nhlbi.nih.gov/guidelines/asthma/asthsumm.pdf

Item 13   Answer: A

Educational Objective: *Diagnose cough variant asthma.*

The most likely diagnosis is asthma. The patient's history is suspicious for reactive airway disease with onset after a respiratory tract infection, symptoms of cough and wheezing when exposed to cold air or after exercise, and occasional nighttime symptoms. Findings on initial spirometry were normal. In patients who have symptoms suggestive of asthma but normal findings on spirometry, bronchoprovocation with methacholine can help to establish the presence of airway hyperresponsiveness. Methacholine is administered by inhalation in increasing concentrations through a nebulizer. Cigarette smoking, chronic obstructive pulmonary disease, allergic rhinitis, and recent viral respiratory tract infection can lead to increased airway hyperresponsiveness and a positive result on methacholine challenge test. Therefore, a positive test should be correlated with other features of asthma before a clinical diagnosis can be established. The most appropriate use of this test is to exclude asthma in patients with normal findings on spirometry and methacholine challenge and symptoms consistent with, but not typical of, asthma.

Nearly 10% of patients who are diagnosed with cystic fibrosis are older than 18 years of age. In cystic fibrosis lung disease, chest radiograph typically shows hyperinflation and accentuated bronchovascular markings, appearing first in the upper lobes, followed by bronchiectasis and cyst formation. Pulmonary function testing shows an obstructive pattern. This patient has no findings consistent with cystic fibrosis.

The hallmark of idiopathic pulmonary fibrosis is the finding of peripheral- and basal-predominant disease on computed tomography in a patient with progressive pulmonary symptoms associated with restrictive lung physiology. This picture is not compatible with the patient's presentation.

When patients with asthma present with prominent wheezing that is more notable during inspiration (stridor), vocal cord dysfunction (VCD) should be suspected. Abrupt onset and termination of the episode is characteristic of VCD and is atypical for asthma. Flow-volume loops show inspiratory flow cutoff and preserved expiratory flow, in contrast to what is seen in asthma. In the absence of concomitant asthma, patients with VCD have negative findings on methacholine challenge test.

KEY POINT

In patients who have symptoms suggestive of asthma but normal findings on spirometry, bronchoprovocation with methacholine can help to establish the presence of airway hyperresponsiveness.

Bibliography

Cockcroft DW. Direct challenge tests: Airway hyperresponsiveness in asthma: its measurement and clinical significance. Chest. 2010;138(2 suppl):18S-24S. [PMID: 20668014]

Item 14   Answer: A

Educational Objective: *Manage asthma during pregnancy.*

The most appropriate next step in management is to add a long-acting β_2-agonist and continue the use of inhaled glucocorticoids. Approximately one third of patients with asthma experience worsening of symptoms during pregnancy. Although this patient previously had good control of symptoms while taking medium-dose inhaled glucocorticoids, the same regimen is not providing adequate control at this point. The recommendation for step-up therapy in pregnant patients is similar to that for nonpregnant patients. The understanding is that it is safer for pregnant women to be exposed to asthma medications with limited human safety data than it is for them to experience ongoing symptoms and exacerbations of asthma. Long-acting β_2-agonists are classified as pregnancy category C drugs, meaning that some safety data are lacking but the potential benefit of the drug may justify the potential risk. Therefore, the addition of a long-acting β_2-agonist is recommended when symptoms are not controlled with medium-dose inhaled glucocorticoids. The addition of this medication results in better asthma control compared with doubling the dose of inhaled glucocorticoids. This recommendation is based on studies of nonpregnant patients. Large-scale studies of pregnant patients have not been performed.

Theophylline is also classified as a pregnancy category C drug. Theophylline provides an alternative to step-up therapy with a long-acting β_2-agonist. However, because the metabolism of the drug is altered during pregnancy, more frequent monitoring of serum levels and for evidence of toxicity is required. Therefore, a long-acting β_2-agonist is preferred over theophylline.

A bronchial challenge test (methacholine or mannitol) can be performed to evaluate patients whose symptoms are not clearly consistent with asthma. However, methacholine challenge is contraindicated during pregnancy. Mannitol is listed as a pregnancy category C drug; adequate information is not available on its safety during pregnancy. Furthermore, bronchial challenge is not likely to provide clinically useful information.

KEY POINT

In pregnant patients with asthma, the addition of a long-acting β_2-agonist is recommended when symptoms are not controlled with medium-dose inhaled glucocorticoids.

Bibliography

Schatz M, Dombrowski MP. Clinical practice. Asthma in pregnancy. N Engl J Med. 2009;360:1862-9. [PMID: 19403904]

Item 15   Answer: A

Educational Objective: *Diagnose α$_1$-antitrypsin deficiency.*

The most appropriate next step in management is to measure the α$_1$-antitrypsin level. Chronic obstructive pulmonary disease (COPD) is affected by multiple genes. The best-documented genetic influence is hereditary deficiency of α$_1$-antitrypsin (a circulating inhibitor of serine protease). Deficiency should be considered in patients who are diagnosed with COPD at a young age (younger than 45 years), in nonsmokers, in patients with predominantly basilar lung disease, and in patients with concurrent liver disease. Other genes, including those for α$_1$-antichymotrypsin, α$_2$-macroglobulin, vitamin D–binding protein, and blood group antigens, also have been associated with the development of COPD. The patient's young age, the severity of disease, and the finding of radiolucency (absence of lung markings) in the lung bases on chest radiograph are all consistent with the diagnosis of α$_1$-antitrypsin deficiency. Measuring the α$_1$-antitrypsin level is the most appropriate next step in management.

A computed tomographic (CT) scan exposes the patient to significantly higher doses of radiation than a chest radiograph. The effective dose for a CT scan is approximately 40 times that of a chest radiograph. The benefit of CT scan in clinical evaluation should be weighed against the risk associated with radiation exposure, especially in younger patients who are more vulnerable to radiation-induced malignancy. However, the risk is usually acceptable when a CT scan is the most appropriate test. Chest CT scan is unlikely to provide additional information that will improve the management of this patient, and it will not establish the diagnosis of α$_1$-antitrypsin deficiency.

The effectiveness of an inhaled glucocorticoid as monotherapy for COPD has not been established. Therefore, this treatment is not recommended. Long-acting β-agonist and anticholinergic agent monotherapy is recommended, primarily for patients with FEV$_1$ of less than 60% of predicted. This treatment has been shown to reduce the number of exacerbations and improve quality of life. An inhaled glucocorticoid may be considered as an adjunctive treatment to long-acting bronchodilators in patients whose symptoms remain poorly controlled.

Oxygen therapy is a major component of treatment for patients with very severe COPD. It is indicated for patients who have resting hypoxemia, defined as an arterial Po$_2$ of 55 mm Hg or less or arterial oxygen saturation of 88% or less. Although resting oxygen saturation may not meet those criteria, some patients may still benefit from supplemental oxygen if desaturation occurs during exercise or at night while they are sleeping. However, this patient does not have a clear indication for oxygen therapy.

KEY POINT

α$_1$-Antitrypsin deficiency should be considered in patients who are diagnosed with COPD at a young age (younger than 45 years), nonsmokers, patients with predominantly basilar lung disease, and patients with concurrent liver disease.

Bibliography

Brode SK, Ling SC, Chapman KR. Alpha-1 antitrypsin deficiency: a commonly overlooked cause of lung disease. CMAJ. 2012;184:1365-71. [PMID: 22761482]

Item 16   Answer: A

Educational Objective: *Treat hypoxic respiratory failure with continuous oxygen therapy.*

Oxygen therapy is a major component of treatment for patients with very severe chronic obstructive pulmonary disease (COPD). This treatment is indicated for patients who have resting hypoxemia, defined as arterial Po$_2$ of 55 mm Hg or less or arterial oxygen saturation of 88% or less. In patients who qualify for continuous therapy because of resting hypoxemia, oxygen treatment should be administered for at least 15 h/day. The use of long-term oxygen therapy in patients with chronic respiratory failure improves survival and has a beneficial effect on hemodynamics, hematologic characteristics, exercise capacity, and mental status.

Antibiotic therapy is most beneficial in treating infectious exacerbations of COPD that are characterized by increases in dyspnea and sputum volume and purulence. Antibiotics in this setting improve airflow and reduce the mortality rate and the rate of treatment failure, especially in patients who have more severe exacerbations. Although there is some evidence of their effectiveness, more definitive data are awaited on the long-term use of prophylactic antibiotics to prevent exacerbations. There is no evidence that long-term antibiotic therapy prolongs survival.

An inhaled glucocorticoid is widely prescribed for COPD and is frequently added to treatment with long-acting bronchodilators when patients remain symptomatic or have repeated exacerbations. In some patients with severe COPD and inadequately controlled symptoms, the combination of a long-acting β$_2$-agonist, a long-acting anticholinergic agent, and an inhaled glucocorticoid is used. There is some evidence that triple therapy may be beneficial, but the efficacy and safety of this intervention have not been definitively proved. There is no evidence that inhaled glucocorticoid therapy alone or in combination prolongs survival.

Pulmonary rehabilitation can be considered for all symptomatic patients with forced expiratory volume in 1 second of less than 50% of predicted. When added to other forms of therapy, pulmonary rehabilitation reduces the perceived intensity of breathlessness, decreases dyspnea and fatigue, increases participation in daily activities, improves quality of life (including a reduction of anxiety and depression associated with COPD), and reduces the number of hospitalizations and the length of stay. Pulmonary rehabilitation, although indicated in this patient, does not improve survival.

KEY POINT

The use of long-term oxygen therapy in patients with chronic respiratory failure improves survival as well as hemodynamics, hematologic characteristics, exercise capacity, and mental status.

Bibliography

American College of Physicians; American College of Chest Physicians; American Thoracic Society; European Respiratory Society. Diagnosis and management of stable chronic obstructive pulmonary disease: a clinical practice guideline update from the American College of Physicians, American College of Chest Physicians, American Thoracic Society, and European Respiratory Society. Ann Intern Med. 2011;155:179-91. [PMID: 21810710]

Item 17   Answer: C

Educational Objective: *Manage lack of response to appropriate therapy for chronic obstructive pulmonary disease (COPD) by checking the patient's inhaler technique.*

The most appropriate next step in management is to check the patient's inhaler technique. This patient has moderate (stage 2) COPD and is on an appropriate medication regimen that includes a long-acting anticholinergic agent and a long-acting β_2-agonist. The patient is adherent to this regimen. The most appropriate next step is to check his inhaler technique. Inhaler therapy is very important in the treatment of COPD. Several drug- and patient-dependent factors, including age, eyesight, finger dexterity, degree of lung function, cognitive function, breathing pattern, inhaler technique, drug formulation, and device-related variables, affect the distribution of the drug and clinical outcomes. Patient-dependent factors also change over time. It is very important to ensure that the inhaler technique is correct.

Adding an inhaled glucocorticoid is not an appropriate option before the inhaler technique is assessed.

Oxygen therapy is a major component of treatment for patients with very severe COPD. It is usually prescribed for patients who have arterial P_{O_2} of 55 mm Hg (7.3 kPa) or less or oxygen saturation of 88% or less with or without hypercapnia. It is also prescribed for those with arterial P_{O_2} of 56 to 59 mm Hg (7.4-7.8 kPa) or oxygen saturation of less than 89% with one or more of the following: pulmonary hypertension, evidence of cor pulmonale or edema as a result of right-sided heart failure, or hematocrit greater than 56%. This patient has none of these indications for oxygen therapy.

Resuming treatment with prednisone is not appropriate at this time because this patient was treated adequately with a short course of a systemic glucocorticoid. Long-term use of glucocorticoids is not recommended because there is no evidence of benefit and these drugs have many side effects.

KEY POINT

If a patient is not responding to appropriate therapy for COPD, the inhaler technique should be assessed before therapy is adjusted.

Bibliography

Fromer L, Goodwin E, Walsh J. Customizing inhaled therapy to meet the needs of COPD patients. Postgrad Med. 2010;122:83-93. [PMID: 20203459]

Item 18   Answer: B

Educational Objective: *Diagnose chronic obstructive pulmonary disease (COPD).*

The most likely cause of this patient's cough is COPD. The post-bronchodilator forced expiratory volume in 1 second (FEV_1)/forced vital capacity (FVC) ratio of less than 70% confirms airflow limitation and a diagnosis of COPD. The relatively preserved FEV_1 suggests that the COPD is mild. COPD should be considered in any patient older than 40 years of age who has dyspnea, chronic cough or sputum production, or a history of risk factors (eg, exposure to tobacco smoke, dust, chemicals, outdoor air pollution, or biomass smoke). Spirometry is the gold standard for diagnosing COPD and monitoring its progress. It should be performed to confirm the diagnosis and exclude other diseases. The American College of Physicians and Global Initiative for Chronic Obstructive Lung Disease (GOLD) guidelines require an FEV_1/FVC ratio of less than 70% of predicted to establish the diagnosis of COPD. The GOLD guidelines use the degree of airflow obstruction as measured by FEV_1 to further describe the level of disease. Level 1 (mild) COPD is characterized by FEV_1 of 80% or greater of predicted. Level 2 (moderate) COPD is characterized by FEV_1 of 50% to 79% of predicted. Level 3 (severe) COPD is characterized by FEV_1 of 30% to 49% of predicted. Level 4 (very severe) COPD is characterized by FEV_1 of less than 30% of predicted.

Although asthma may present with cough, asthma is unlikely in this patient because of the lack of atopy and history of respiratory symptoms as a child. There are no other clinical findings consistent with bronchospasm.

Gastroesophageal reflux disease may cause cough. However, COPD is the more likely cause of cough in this patient who does not have heartburn, has a history of smoking, and shows airflow obstruction on pulmonary function testing.

Although angiotensin-converting enzyme inhibitors may be associated with cough, angiotensin receptor blockers (eg, losartan) are less likely to cause cough and would not be an expected cause of this patient's cough, given the other clinical findings.

KEY POINT

Spirometry is essential for diagnosing COPD and assessing its severity. A post-bronchodilator FEV_1/FVC ratio of less than 70% confirms airflow limitation.

Bibliography

Global Strategy for the Diagnosis, Management and Prevention of COPD, Global Initiative for Chronic Obstructive Lung Disease (GOLD) 2014. www.goldcopd.org

Item 19   Answer: B

Educational Objective: *Manage an acute exacerbation of chronic obstructive pulmonary disease (COPD).*

The most appropriate next step in management is hospital admission. Many exacerbations of COPD can be managed with in-home treatment. However, hospital admission should be considered in patients with severe disease, advanced age, significant comorbidities, a marked increase in intensity of symptoms, newly occurring arrhythmias, diagnostic uncertainty, insufficient home support, onset of new physical signs, or poor response to initial medical management, as in this patient. This patient has not responded to appropriate outpatient treatment and now has a mild oxygen requirement. She should be admitted to the hospital for more aggressive treatment with inhaled bronchodilators, continuous oxygen therapy, pulmonary toilet, antibiotics, glucocorticoids, and monitoring for potential complications.

Home oxygen treatment is frequently used in patients with COPD. However, this patient's new resting hypoxia suggests lack of improvement or worsening of the current exacerbation. Therefore, providing home oxygen treatment alone would not be appropriate as a next therapeutic step.

This patient has purulent sputum, an increase in sputum volume, and worsening dyspnea. Therefore, antibiotic treatment is appropriate. The initial antibiotic choice was appropriate, but empiric expansion of antibiotic coverage is not indicated in the absence of additional risk factors.

Glucocorticoids have been shown to be effective in treating acute exacerbations of COPD. Although the ideal dose and duration of therapy are not well defined, prolonging the treatment course alone in a patient who is not responding to treatment would not be appropriate.

Patients who have exacerbations of COPD should be admitted to the hospital if they have underlying severe COPD and advanced age, significant comorbidities, a marked increase in the intensity of symptoms, newly occurring arrhythmias, diagnostic uncertainty, insufficient home support, or onset of new physical signs, or if they do not respond to initial medical management.

Bibliography

Global Strategy for the Diagnosis, Management and Prevention of COPD, Global Initiative for Chronic Obstructive Lung Disease (GOLD) 2014. www.goldcopd.org

Item 20   Answer: D

Educational Objective: *Manage an exacerbation of chronic obstructive pulmonary disease (COPD) with noninvasive positive pressure ventilation.*

The most appropriate additional management is noninvasive positive pressure ventilation (NPPV). This patient's acute exacerbation of COPD warrants a trial of NPPV. This treatment reduces the mortality rate, the need for intubation, and the length of hospital stay, and also improves respiratory acidosis and decreases the respiration rate and the severity of breathlessness in patients who are candidates for therapy. Patients with moderate to severe dyspnea, moderate to severe acidosis (pH <7.35) or hypercapnia, and respiration rate greater than 25/min benefit from NPPV. Exclusion criteria for NPPV are respiratory arrest, cardiovascular instability (hypotension, arrhythmias, and myocardial infarction), change in mental status, uncooperativeness, high aspiration risk, viscous or copious secretions, recent facial or gastroesophageal surgery, craniofacial trauma, fixed nasopharyngeal abnormalities, burns, and extreme obesity. Severe acidosis (pH <7.25) and respiration rate greater than 35/min are indications for intubation rather than NPPV. Intubation is also indicated in patients who do not benefit from an initial trial of NPPV.

Positive airway pressure is the treatment of choice for most patients with obstructive sleep apnea. Continuous positive airway pressure (CPAP), which provides a constant fixed-level pressure throughout the respiratory cycle, is used for most patients. However, CPAP does not provide ventilatory support and would not be helpful in treating hypoxic ventilatory failure, as in this patient.

Increasing the administration of oxygen alone is not an appropriate treatment option because the patient's oxygen saturation is adequate. Oxygen therapy is indicated for patients who have hypoxemia, arterial P_{O_2} of less than 55 mm Hg (7.3 kPa), or oxygen saturation of 88% or less.

In patients with exacerbation of COPD characterized by acute hypercapnic respiratory failure, noninvasive positive pressure ventilation reduces the mortality rate, the need for intubation, and the length of hospital stay.

Bibliography

Khilnani GC, Banga A. Noninvasive ventilation in patients with chronic obstructive airway disease. Int J Chron Obstruct Pulmon Dis. 2008;3:351-7. [PMID: 18990962]

Item 21   Answer: D

Educational Objective: *Identify obesity as a risk factor for obstructive sleep apnea.*

The patient's obesity is the factor most responsible for his symptoms. It is likely that this patient has obstructive sleep apnea (OSA). Loud

snoring, gasping, and pauses in breathing are commonly observed by a bed partner in patients with OSA. Subjective symptoms include frequent awakenings, snorting, and nonrestorative sleep. The most important risk factor for OSA is obesity, particularly in patients with prominent distribution of adipose tissue in the trunk and neck. Most patients with OSA are obese, and obesity significantly increases the risk of OSA in middle-aged adults. Weight loss is recommended as the initial therapy for OSA. Less important risk factors include male sex, postmenopausal state, family history of OSA, and race. Some possible mechanisms by which obesity can cause OSA include increased upper airway fat deposition, leading to a decrease in airway size and muscle tone as well as reduced lung volume. Central obesity (larger waist-hip ratio) is more important than general obesity. Other risk factors for OSA are larger neck circumference (>17 inches in men; >16 inches in women), nasal narrowing or congestion, large tongue, low-lying soft palate, enlarged tonsils and adenoids, abnormalities of the face or jaw that contribute to airway narrowing, use of muscle relaxants, smoking and alcohol use, and primary medical disorders (acromegaly, androgen therapy, neuromuscular disorders, and stroke).

Hypertension, a previous history of smoking, and a sedentary lifestyle are not independent risk factors for OSA.

Objective testing is required for a diagnosis of OSA. The current gold standard is polysomnography.

The most important risk factor for obstructive sleep apnea is obesity, particularly in patients with prominent distribution of adipose tissue in the trunk and neck.

Bibliography

Qaseem A, Holty JE, Owens DK, Dallas P, Starkey M, Shekelle P; for the Clinical Guidelines Committee of the American College of Physicians. Management of Obstructive Sleep Apnea in Adults: A Clinical Practice Guideline From the American College of Physicians. Ann Intern Med. 2013;159:471-83. [PMID:24061345]

Item 22   Answer: C

Educational Objective: *Diagnose obstructive sleep apnea.*

The most appropriate test to perform for this patient is polysomnography (PSG) to assess for obstructive sleep apnea (OSA). PSG is the gold standard for diagnosis of OSA. This patient has several risk factors for OSA, including her age, weight, and postmenopausal status. The symptom of daytime sleepiness is concerning, and a complete sleep history should be obtained to assess the patient's amount and quality of sleep. In some patients, a validated sleep questionnaire, such as the Epworth Sleepiness Scale, can be considered to obtain information about how sleepy the patient gets during the day and support a decision for further testing with PSG. During PSG monitoring, upper airway events are classified as apneas (characterized by complete cessation of airflow) or hypopneas (reductions in airflow), collectively known as disordered breathing events. The apnea-hypopnea index (AHI) is the number of disordered breathing events per hour of sleep and is the standard for measuring the severity of OSA. An AHI of 5 to 15 indicates mild OSA; an AHI of more than 30 indicates severe OSA.

Chest computed tomography is unlikely to be helpful in a patient without pulmonary symptoms and with normal findings on chest radiograph. Pulmonary function tests are generally performed for patients with pulmonary symptoms, including dyspnea and wheezing. These symptoms are absent in this patient. In addition, the patient has normal arterial blood gas findings, reducing the likelihood that significant pulmonary disease accounts for the symptoms. Overnight pulse oximetry is an inadequate test to diagnose OSA because of its lack of sensitivity and specificity.

KEY POINT

Polysomnography is the test of choice for the diagnosis of obstructive sleep apnea.

Bibliography

Qaseem A, Holty JE, Owens DK, Dallas P, Starkey M, Shekelle P; for the Clinical Guidelines Committee of the American College of Physicians. Management of Obstructive Sleep Apnea in Adults: A Clinical Practice Guideline From the American College of Physicians. Ann Intern Med. 2013;159:471-83. [PMID:24061345]

Item 23   Answer: A

Educational Objective: *Treat obstructive sleep apnea (OSA) with continuous positive airway pressure.*

The most appropriate next step in treatment is continuous positive airway pressure (CPAP). OSA is defined by upper airway narrowing or collapse that results in cessation (apnea) or reduction (hypopnea) in airflow despite ongoing efforts to breathe. The severity of OSA is commonly measured using the apnea-hypopnea index (AHI), which is the sum of instances of apnea and hypopnea per hour of sleep. An AHI of 5 to 15 indicates mild OSA, an AHI of 16 to 30 indicates moderate OSA, and an AHI of more than 30 indicates severe OSA. It is estimated that 24% of men aged 30 to 60 years and 9% of similarly aged women have OSA (AHI of ≥5/hour). CPAP should be considered first-line therapy in any patient who has OSA and associated symptoms, particularly excessive daytime sleepiness. Optimal positive airway pressure therapy may have salutary effects on cardiovascular diseases that are associated with OSA. Suboptimal adherence to CPAP and bilevel positive airway pressure devices is common in clinical practice, and rates of discontinuation are high. Therefore, objective monitoring of use of these devices and periodic follow-up are important to ensure adherence.

Nocturnal oxygen therapy alone is inadequate to prevent complications associated with OSA because it does not correct upper airway obstruction, which is the primary cause of oxygen desaturation.

Oral devices may be considered for patients who cannot tolerate or are unwilling to use CPAP therapy but should be reserved for patients with mild to moderate OSA.

Surgery may be indicated for patients with specific underlying surgically correctable craniofacial or upper airway abnormalities that contribute to OSA. These abnormalities include nasal polyps, nasal septal deviation, tonsillar enlargement, and retrognathia. However, CPAP may still be required following surgery for some of these patients as these procedures may not adequately treat their OSA. Upper airway surgery may be considered in some patients with OSA to improve the effectiveness of CPAP or in those unable to tolerate other therapeutic modalities.

KEY POINT

Continuous positive airway pressure is first-line therapy in patients with obstructive sleep apnea and associated symptoms, particularly excessive daytime sleepiness.

Bibliography

Epstein LJ, Kristo D, Strollo PJ Jr, et al. Clinical guideline for the evaluation, management and long-term care of obstructive sleep apnea in adults. J Clin Sleep Med. 2009;5:263-76. [PMID: 19960649]

Item 24   Answer: D

Educational Objective: *Diagnose pulmonary sarcoidosis.*

The most likely diagnosis is pulmonary sarcoidosis. Sarcoidosis presents with varying time courses, ranging from acute disease with erythema nodosum, fever, arthralgia, and hilar lymphadenopathy (Löfgren syndrome), to a more indolent course. Ninety percent of patients have pulmonary involvement. The patient's chest radiograph shows interstitial lung changes and hilar lymphadenopathy. Pulmonary function tests often show restriction, but obstruction can be seen as well. Sarcoidosis is a diagnosis of exclusion based on multisystem involvement and histologic evidence of noncaseating granulomas when all other causes have been excluded. Most patients require tissue diagnosis, but some cases do not warrant histologic confirmation. These include classic clinical presentations of known sarcoid syndromes, such as Löfgren syndrome and Heerfordt syndrome (uveitis, parotid gland enlargement, and fever). This patient's previous episode of Löfgren syndrome establishes the diagnosis of sarcoidosis and excludes lymphangioleiomyomatosis, chronic hypersensitivity pneumonitis, and respiratory bronchiolitis-associated interstitial lung disease as diagnostic possibilities.

Lymphangioleiomyomatosis is a rare cystic lung disease that occurs sporadically in women of childbearing age or in association with tuberous sclerosis. Although the disease is rare, a diagnosis of emphysema, spontaneous pneumothorax, or chylothorax in a young woman with dyspnea and a chest radiograph that shows hyperinflation should prompt consideration of this condition.

Chronic hypersensitivity pneumonitis is caused by repeated inhalation of finely dispersed antigens. Subacute and chronic forms typically occur with chronic low-level exposure to an inhaled antigen. Patients typically present with dyspnea, cough, fatigue, anorexia, malaise, and weight loss. Pulmonary function testing may show obstructive and restrictive defects. Hilar adenopathy, as seen in this patient, is not consistent with chronic hypersensitivity pneumonitis.

Respiratory bronchiolitis-associated interstitial lung disease is a micronodular disease that causes mild symptoms and typically presents in active smokers with subacute progressive cough and dyspnea. Pulmonary function tests may show an obstructive pattern, but in patients with milder disease, pulmonary function tests can show a restrictive, normal, or obstructive pattern. This patient is a nonsmoker, making respiratory bronchiolitis-associated interstitial lung disease unlikely.

KEY POINT

Sarcoidosis presents with varying time courses, ranging from acute disease, with erythema nodosum, fever, arthralgia, and hilar lymphadenopathy (Löfgren syndrome), to a more indolent course.

Bibliography

Israel-Biet D, Valeyre D. Diagnosis of pulmonary sarcoidosis. Curr Opin Pulm Med. 2013;19:510-5. [PMID:23880701]

Item 25   Answer: D

Educational Objective: *Diagnose pulmonary asbestosis*

No further testing is required. The diagnosis is asbestosis. Between 1940 and 1979, approximately 20 million workers in the United States were exposed to asbestos. Because of the latency of asbestos-related disease (15-35 years), this exposure will remain a concern in the United States well into the current century. The construction, automotive servicing, and shipbuilding industries are most commonly affected. Pleural plaques are the most common radiographic finding in patients exposed to asbestos. Ninety percent of asbestos-induced pleural abnormalities are caused by pleural plaques (well-circumscribed lesions) and diffuse pleural thickening. The diagnosis of asbestosis is based on two essential findings: a convincing history of asbestos exposure with an appropriately long latent period and definite evidence of interstitial fibrosis. This patient meets both criteria, and there is no clinical evidence suggesting an alternative diagnosis.

Biopsy to confirm the diagnosis of asbestosis typically is not necessary but should be considered in certain cases, such as when the history of asbestos exposure is questionable, when the latent period between exposure and symptoms is atypical (too long or too short), when there is a reasonable alternative diagnosis under consideration, or when the patient is experiencing an accelerated course of disease. When biopsy is needed, open surgical biopsy is preferred to transbronchial biopsy to allow an adequate specimen to be obtained.

Serologic tests, such as antinuclear antibody test, rheumatoid factor, and erythrocyte sedimentation rate, occasionally are helpful in the diagnosis of interstitial lung disease. However, the results of these tests may be positive in patients with asbestosis. In the absence of findings suggesting another diagnosis, these tests are unlikely to be helpful.

KEY POINT

The diagnosis of asbestosis is based on two essential findings: a convincing history of asbestos exposure with an appropriately long latent period and definite evidence of interstitial fibrosis.

Bibliography

Lazarus A, Massoumi A, Hostler J, Hostler DC. Asbestos-related pleuropulmonary diseases: benign and malignant. Postgrad Med. 2012;124:116-30. [PMID: 22691906]

Item 26   Answer: C
Educational Objective: *Diagnose cryptogenic organizing pneumonia.*

The most likely diagnosis in this patient is cryptogenic organizing pneumonia (COP). The chest radiograph shows bilateral diffuse alveolar opacities in the presence of normal lung volume. In the appropriate clinical setting, this finding is most consistent with bronchiolitis obliterans organizing pneumonia (BOOP). COP is the idiopathic form of BOOP. Patients with COP often present with signs and symptoms consistent with community-acquired pneumonia and may be treated at least once with antibiotics for this presumed diagnosis. However, a subacute process that develops in a patient who does not benefit from treatment suggests a noninfectious diffuse parenchymal lung disease. Many underlying conditions, including certain infectious diseases, collagen vascular diseases, and drug-induced reactions, are associated with the histopathologic features of BOOP and respond best to specific treatment of the primary disease process. Most patients have symptoms for less than 3 months, and very few have symptoms for more than 6 months. Prognosis is typically favorable, with a good response to systemic glucocorticoids.

Subacute or chronic pulmonary emboli may present with progressive dyspnea and hypoxia over weeks to months without systemic symptoms, such as fever or chills. However, this patient has no clear risk factors for hypercoagulability. Results of chest imaging in patients with chronic pulmonary emboli are often normal or show minimal parenchymal findings, unlike the findings in this patient.

Idiopathic pulmonary fibrosis (IPF) typically follows a prolonged course, with evidence of respiratory symptoms and radiographic findings that progress slowly over months or years. Radiographic findings in COP are also distinct from those in IPF. A dominant alveolar opacification process is typically present in patients with COP. The opacities are almost always bilateral and show varied distribution. One of the key radiographic features of COP is the tendency for opacities to "migrate," or involve different areas of the lung on serial examinations. Although the radiographic findings of IPF are varied, it has a dominant interstitial (reticular) pattern, with or without opacities.

KEY POINT

Cryptogenic organizing pneumonia presents with cough and other symptoms that suggest community-acquired pneumonia. The diagnosis should be considered when symptoms and clinical findings persist despite one or more courses of antibiotics.

Bibliography

Drakopanagiotakis F, Paschalaki K, Abu-Hijleh M, et al. Cryptogenic and secondary organizing pneumonia: clinical presentation, radiographic findings, treatment response, and prognosis. Chest. 2011;139:893-900. [PMID: 20724743]

Item 27   Answer: D
Educational Objective: *Diagnose idiopathic pulmonary fibrosis.*

The most likely diagnosis is idiopathic pulmonary fibrosis (IPF), a diffuse parenchymal lung disease. Patients typically present with progressive dyspnea of greater than 6 months' duration and a dry, hacking cough. Digital clubbing is present in 30% of patients. In addition, this patient has several risk factors for IPF, including a history of smoking, previous work as a carpenter (with extensive organic dust exposure), and age (the prevalence of IPF increases with age). Computed tomographic (CT) scan shows the classic findings of IPF, including basal and peripheral disease with septal thickening, evidence of honeycomb changes, traction bronchiectasis, and no evidence of ground-glass opacities or nodules.

This patient does not have chronic obstructive pulmonary disease (COPD) because spirometry shows a normal forced expiratory volume in 1 second/forced vital capacity ratio. Physical examination also shows inspiratory crackles, which are not characteristic of COPD. This finding, in conjunction with the CT findings, excludes COPD as a likely diagnosis.

Heart failure is typically associated with orthopnea, paroxysmal nocturnal dyspnea, or lower extremity edema, none of which are present in this patient. There is no third heart sound or jugular venous distention on examination. Additionally, honeycomb changes on CT scan are not a finding of pulmonary edema.

Hypersensitivity pneumonitis is an allergic, inflammatory lung disease that is also called extrinsic allergic alveolitis. It results from exposure to airborne allergens that cause cell-mediated immunologic sensitization. Most patients who are exposed to an inhalational antigen have symptoms within 4 to 12 hours. This patient's 12-month history of progressive dyspnea and cough and lack of history of exposure are not compatible with this diagnosis.

KEY POINT

Idiopathic pulmonary fibrosis is characterized by progressive dyspnea and cough persisting for more than 6 months in addition to dry inspiratory crackles. Classic findings on CT scan are basal and peripheral disease with evidence of honeycomb changes but without ground-glass opacities or nodules.

Bibliography

Raghu G, Collard HR, Egan JJ, et al. An official ATS/ERS/JRS/ALAT statement: idiopathic pulmonary fibrosis: evidence-based guidelines for diagnosis and management. Am J Respir Crit Care Med. 2011;183:788-824. [PMID: 21471066]

Item 28   **Answer: B**

Educational Objective: *Diagnose pulmonary embolism.*

Chest computed tomographic angiography should be ordered next. Diagnosis of pulmonary embolism (PE) is complicated by its variable clinical presentation and the lack of sensitivity and specificity of symptoms and signs. Well-validated clinical risk prediction scores, such as the Wells score or the revised Geneva score, can generate a pretest probability of PE. Assessment of pretest probability (low, intermediate, or high) and hemodynamic status is essential to guide additional cost-effective evaluation and may aid in the interpretation of subsequent tests. Using the Wells criteria, the patient has 5.5 points and an intermediate probability of PE. For patients with moderate or high probability of PE, diagnostic imaging is the next diagnostic step.

D-Dimer assay is helpful in assessing clinically stable patients who have a low pretest likelihood of PE. In this setting, a negative test result indicates a low likelihood of PE and deep venous thrombosis. In this case, no further testing is indicated. In patients with intermediate or high pretest probability of PE, however, a negative D-dimer test result is not sufficient to exclude PE.

The characterization of chest pain is helpful in distinguishing chest pain from an ischemic cardiac etiology from other causes, such as pulmonary embolism. Pain that radiates to both shoulders, which is not present in this patient, is suggestive of an ischemic cardiac cause with a positive likelihood ratio (LR[+]) of 9.7. Conversely, pain that is pleuritic in nature (sharp and stabbing and associated with inspiration) as experienced by this patient has a negative likelihood ratio (LR[-]) of 0.3. Coupled with an electrocardiogram that shows no evidence of ischemic changes and an initial troponin level that is normal, the probability of ischemic heart disease as a cause of her symptoms is lowered significantly, although not eliminated. However, this patient's overall clinical presentation is most compatible with PE. Therefore, coronary catheterization, echocardiography, and pharmacologic stress testing are not indicated as the first diagnostic tests.

KEY POINT

Well-validated clinical risk prediction scores, such as the Wells or revised Geneva scores, can generate a pretest probability for pulmonary embolism.

Bibliography

Agnelli G, Becattini C. Acute pulmonary embolism. N Engl J Med. 2010;363:266-74. [PMID: 20592294]

Item 29   **Answer: D**

Educational Objective: *Evaluate acute pulmonary embolism in a patient with kidney failure.*

A ventilation-perfusion scan is the most appropriate study to confirm the suspected diagnosis of pulmonary embolism in this patient with kidney failure. Both CT angiography and ventilation-perfusion scans are able to reliably diagnose larger pulmonary emboli, although each study does this in a different way. Ventilation-perfusion scans detect abnormalities of blood flow in comparison to the pattern of ventilation, with areas of mismatch between perfusion and ventilation being evidence of vascular occlusion due to a pulmonary embolus. CT angiography works by detecting irregularities in the pulmonary vasculature caused by thrombosis following administration of contrast media. Because some pulmonary conditions other than pulmonary embolism may alter pulmonary blood flow and result in indeterminant ventilation-perfusion scans, CT angiography is the more frequently used study for detecting pulmonary embolism. However, CT angiography involves administration of a significant dose of potentially nephrotoxic contrast media, which is contraindicated in this patient with kidney failure. Ventilation-perfusion scanning does not use nephrotoxic agents, and would therefore be the most appropriate study to confirm pulmonary embolism in this patient.

The pretest probability of pulmonary embolism is very high in this patient based on his recent hospitalization and surgery, active cancer, symptoms of chest pain and dyspnea, hypoxia with a normal chest radiograph, and no other likely explanation for his findings. His Wells score for assessing the probability of pulmonary embolism is >6, placing him in the high-risk category. D-dimer testing is indicated for clinical decision making only in patients in whom there is a low probability of pulmonary embolism; a negative D-dimer in this patient would not be sufficient to exclude a pulmonary embolism given his high likelihood of disease, and a positive test would not contribute significantly to further diagnostic evaluation.

Lower extremity ultrasonography may disclose deep venous thrombosis in a percentage of patients presenting with symptoms of pulmonary embolism that may reflect a source of thrombosis. However, the yield is generally low and a negative study would not rule out the diagnosis of pulmonary embolism, making ventilation-perfusion scanning a much more accurate study in this patient.

KEY POINT

Ventilation-perfusion scanning is an option for evaluating for suspected pulmonary embolism, and is the indicated study in patients with kidney failure and a contraindication to contrast-enhanced CT angiography.

Bibliography

Mos IC, Klok FA, Kroft LJ, et al. Imaging tests in the diagnosis of pulmonary embolism. Semin Respir Crit Care Med. 2012;33:138-43. [PMID: 22648485]

Item 30   **Answer: B**

Educational Objective: *Treat pulmonary embolism.*

The patient has an acute pulmonary embolism and intravenous unfractionated heparin is appropriate initial therapy. In the absence of contraindications, the patient should be treated initially with intravenous or subcutaneous unfractionated heparin, low-molecular-weight heparin, or fondaparinux. Most patients with pulmonary embolism are treated in the hospital, although carefully selected, stable patients may be candidates for outpatient treatment. Following initial therapy, patients are usually transitioned to warfarin for long-term therapy, with factor Xa and direct thrombin inhibitors being increasingly-available options for this purpose.

Placement of an inferior vena cava filter might be considered in a patient with a contraindication to anticoagulation, the onset of clinically important bleeding during anticoagulation, or recurrent pulmonary embolism despite adequate anticoagulation. However, this patient has no clear contraindication to anticoagulation and no other indication for inferior vena cava filter placement.

Thrombolytic agents, such as tissue plasminogen activator, are not used for treatment of hemodynamically stable patients with pulmonary embolism due to the high risk of bleeding and typically good outcomes with anticoagulation alone. Patients with massive or hemodynamically unstable pulmonary embolism, however, have a high mortality rate, and thrombolytic agents are sometimes used in these patients to attempt to decrease the clot burden, although the effectiveness of this therapy on overall outcomes. Thrombolytic therapy would therefore not be an appropriate treatment in this hemodynamically stable patient without evidence of massive thromboembolic disease.

Acute pulmonary embolectomy is rarely warranted because medical therapy is usually successful, appropriate patient selection is difficult, and the results of acute embolectomy have been equivocal. However, embolectomy may be considered for a confirmed, massive embolism that fails to respond promptly to medical therapy. Embolectomy would not be indicated in this otherwise stable patient.

KEY POINT

Unfractionated heparin, low-molecular-weight heparin, or fondaparinux is indicated for initial therapy for acute pulmonary embolism.

Bibliography

Kearon C, Akl EA, Comerota AJ, et al; American College of Chest Physicians. Antithrombotic therapy for VTE disease: Antithrombotic Therapy and Prevention of Thrombosis, 9th ed: American College of Chest Physicians Evidence-Based Clinical Practice Guidelines. Chest. 2012;141(2 Suppl):e419S-94S. Erratum in: Chest. 2012;142:1698-1704. [PMID: 22315268]

Item 31   Answer: C

Educational Objective: *Diagnose pulmonary arterial hypertension.*

The most appropriate diagnostic test in this patient is right heart catheterization for suspected pulmonary arterial hypertension. Her presentation is consistent with pulmonary hypertension, including dyspnea on exertion and evidence of elevated right-sided pressures indicated by jugular venous distension, a prominent pulmonic component of S_2, and lower extremity edema. Because of her otherwise negative medical history and evaluation, this patient's pulmonary arterial hypertension is suggestive of the idiopathic variety. This diagnosis can only be confirmed by right heart catheterization. Moreover, assessment of responsiveness to vasodilator agents can be tested during the procedure, providing information that may be essential to management.

This patient's clear lung fields, symptoms out of proportion to her stable pulmonary function tests, and normal clear chest radiograph are evidence against an interstitial lung process as the cause of her symptoms. Therefore, a high-resolution CT scan would likely not be of diagnostic benefit.

Although chronic thromboemboli could be responsible for this patient's clinical presentation, the negative ventilation-perfusion scan makes this diagnosis extremely unlikely. In patients with pulmonary hypertension due to chronic thromboemboli, ventilation-perfusion lung scans are typically quite abnormal with major lobar and segmental mismatched perfusion defects. A normal study therefore suggests strongly against thromboembolic disease as a cause of her pulmonary hypertension, and a CT angiogram to evaluate this possibility further is not indciated.

This patient is unlikely to have obstructive sleep apnea as a cause for her underlying pulmonary hypertension given her negative history of snoring or daytime somnolence and her normal BMI. Because of the low pretest probability for obstructive sleep apnea, a sleep study would be a low-yield test.

Transesophageal echocardiography is not indicated because it is unlikely to add appreciable new information to the recent transthoracic study.

KEY POINT

Right heart catheterization is essential to confirm the diagnosis of pulmonary hypertension by direct measurement of mean pulmonary artery pressure.

Bibliography

Forfia PR, Trow TK. Diagnosis of pulmonary arterial hypertension. Clin Chest Med. 2013;34:665-81. [PMID: 24267297]

Section 11

Rheumatology

Questions

Item 1 [Basic]

A 52-year-old man is evaluated for a 3-month history of fatigue and pain of the hands and knees. The pain has progressively worsened and is accompanied by 1 hour of morning stiffness. He takes ibuprofen as needed, which provides minimal pain relief.

On physical examination, vital signs are normal. Synovitis of the proximal interphalangeal joints, elbows, left knee, and ankles is noted.

Radiographs of the hands and knees are normal. Aspiration of the left knee reveals a synovial fluid leukocyte count of 12,000/µL (12 × 10⁹/L).

Which of the following is the most likely diagnosis?

(A) Fibromyalgia
(B) Osteoarthritis
(C) Polymyalgia rheumatica
(D) Rheumatoid arthritis

Item 2 [Basic]

A 65-year-old man is evaluated for a 3-week history of nonradiating left hip pain that worsens with walking or lying on his left side. He reports no locking symptoms or paresthesia. His only medication is ibuprofen as needed, which provides partial pain relief.

On physical examination, vital signs are normal. Full range of motion of the left hip is present. There is tenderness over the lateral aspect of the hip with direct palpation. Results of a straight-leg-raising test are normal, and reflexes are normal.

Which of the following is the most likely diagnosis?

(A) Iliotibial band syndrome
(B) Lumbar radiculopathy
(C) Osteoarthritis of the hip
(D) Trochanteric bursitis

Item 3 [Advanced]

A 26-year-old man is hospitalized for a 2-month history of daily spiking fever, diffuse joint pain, myalgia, intermittent rash, and a 9-kg (20-lb) weight loss.

On physical examination, temperature is 38.4°C (101.2°F), blood pressure is 126/68 mm Hg, pulse rate is 92/min, and respiration rate is 16/min. There are enlarged cervical lymph nodes. A salmon-colored rash is noted on the trunk and proximal extremities. Abdominal examination discloses hepatomegaly. Musculoskeletal examination reveals tenderness of the wrists, knees, and ankles without swelling; there is decreased range of motion of the wrists.

Laboratory studies:

Hemoglobin	9.8 g/dL (98 g/L)
Leukocyte count	21,000/µL (21 × 10⁹/L)
Platelet count	560,000/µL (560 × 10⁹/L)
Erythrocyte sedimentation rate	102 mm/h
Aspartate aminotransferase	56 U/L (0.94 µkat/L)
Alanine aminotransferase	63 U/L (1.05 µkat/L)
Ferritin	5250 ng/mL (5250 µg/L)

Computed tomography of the chest, abdomen, and pelvis reveals diffuse lymphadenopathy. Bone marrow biopsy results are normal. Blood cultures are negative.

Which of the following is the most likely diagnosis?

(A) Adult-onset Still disease
(B) Lymphoma
(C) Parvovirus B19 infection
(D) Systemic lupus erythematosus

Item 4 [Basic]

A 31-year-old woman is evaluated for a 4-week history of left anterior knee pain. The pain developed insidiously and has progressively worsened, especially with prolonged sitting and walking up and down stairs. There is no morning stiffness. The patient has no history of trauma. She is taking acetaminophen as needed for the pain.

On physical examination, vital signs are normal. The pain is reproduced by applying pressure to the surface of the patella with the knee in extension and moving the patella both laterally and medially. There is no effusion, swelling, or warmth. Range of motion of the knee is normal, without crepitus or pain.

Which of the following is the most likely diagnosis?

(A) Osteoarthritis of the knee
(B) Patellofemoral pain syndrome
(C) Pes anserine bursitis
(D) Prepatellar bursitis

Item 5 [Basic]

A 35-year-old woman is evaluated for a 1-week history of right knee pain that began when she jumped from a 4-foot height and twisted her knee. At the time she felt a popping sensation; her knee became swollen over the next several hours. She has continued to have moderate pain, particularly when walking up or down stairs. There is no locking or "giving way" of the knee. She reports no previous knee injury.

On physical examination, vital signs are normal. The right knee has a minimal effusion. There is full range of motion. The medial aspect of the joint line is tender to palpation. Maximally flexing the hip and knee and applying abduction (valgus) force to the knee while externally rotating the foot and passively extending the knee (McMurray test) results in a palpable snap.

Which of the following is the most likely diagnosis?

(A) Anserine bursitis
(B) Anterior cruciate ligament tear
(C) Meniscal tear
(D) Patellofemoral pain syndrome

Item 6 [Advanced]

A 38-year-old woman is evaluated for left knee pain that has been present for the past 3 weeks. Before onset, she had been preparing for a 5-kilometer race by running approximately 2 miles each day, 6 days each week, for the past 6 months. Walking up stairs makes the pain worse; she also notes pain at night. She has never had this pain before.

On physical examination, vital signs are normal. There is tenderness to palpation located near the anteromedial aspect of the proximal tibia. A small amount of swelling is present at the insertion of the medial hamstring muscle. There is no medial or lateral joint line tenderness.

Which of the following is the most likely diagnosis?

(A) Iliotibial band syndrome
(B) Patellofemoral pain syndrome
(C) Pes anserine bursitis
(D) Prepatellar bursitis

Item 7 [Basic]

A 42-year-old woman is evaluated for a 10-day history of posterior and superior right shoulder pain that becomes worse with overhead activities. The patient recently painted her basement ceiling but reports no history of trauma. She has no arm weakness or paresthesia. She has been taking ibuprofen as needed for pain relief.

On physical examination, vital signs are normal. There is no shoulder asymmetry and no tenderness to palpation of bony structures or soft-tissue structures. There is full range of motion (other than with internal rotation, which is limited by pain), and strength is 5/5 throughout the right arm, with sensation intact. She is able to slowly lower her extended arm from over her head to her side (negative drop-arm test). Pain occurs with abduction of the right arm between 60 and 120 degrees.

Which of the following is the most likely diagnosis?

(A) Acromioclavicular joint degeneration
(B) Adhesive capsulitis
(C) Rotator cuff impingement syndrome
(D) Rotator cuff tear

Item 8 [Advanced]

A 29-year-old man is evaluated for a 1-day history of left shoulder pain. He was throwing a football when the pain began. The pain is located over the left lateral deltoid muscle and is associated with weakness with arm abduction. The patient has no previous history of shoulder problems and no history of trauma. He has been taking ibuprofen as needed for pain.

On physical examination, temperature is normal, blood pressure is 126/80 mm Hg, and pulse rate is 96/min. There is pain in the left shoulder with active abduction beginning at approximately 60 degrees, and he has difficulty actively abducting the left arm beyond 60 degrees. The patient is unable to slowly lower his left arm to his waist (positive drop-arm test). Strength, other than during abduction, is intact.

Which of the following is the most appropriate next step in management?

(A) Magnetic resonance imaging of the left shoulder
(B) Nonsteroidal anti-inflammatory drug therapy
(C) Physical therapy
(D) Subacromial glucocorticoid injection

Item 9 [Advanced]

An 83-year-old man is evaluated for poorly controlled pain from osteoarthritis of the left knee. Osteoarthritis was diagnosed 15 years ago, and his pain had been controlled until recently with regular doses of acetaminophen. Over the past 8 weeks, acetaminophen has no longer provided relief. There is no history of trauma, and he does not have fever or chills. Medical history is significant for hypertension, chronic kidney disease, and a healed peptic ulcer. Medications are amlodipine and metoprolol.

On physical examination, vital signs are normal. Body mass index is 26. The left knee has a moderate-sized, ballottable effusion without overlying erythema or warmth. There is crepitus with knee flexion and extension. The remainder of the examination is unremarkable.

Which of the following is the most appropriate treatment?

(A) Arthrocentesis and intra-articular glucocorticoid injection
(B) Celecoxib
(C) Diclofenac
(D) Glucosamine sulfate and chondroitin

Item 10 [Advanced]

A 69-year-old woman is evaluated for pain in her thumbs for the past 3 months, with the right being worse than the left. She describes the pain as a dull ache at the base of her thumbs. The pain is most pronounced early in the morning, improves after she has been up and active for about 20 minutes, and recurs with repetitive use of her hands later in the day. She does not have swelling, fever, chills, or any other symptoms.

On physical examination, vital signs are normal. There is tenderness at the base of both thumbs to palpation. Her left thumb is shown (Plate 27).

Which of the following is the most likely diagnosis?

(A) de Quervain tenosynovitis

(B) Ganglion cyst

(C) Osteoarthritis

(D) Rheumatoid arthritis

Item 11 [Basic]

A 52-year-old man is evaluated for a 5-year history of gradually progressive left knee pain. The patient has 20 minutes of morning stiffness that recurs after prolonged inactivity. He has minimal to no pain at rest and no clicking or locking of the knee. Over the past several months, the pain has limited ambulation so that he can only walk a few blocks.

On physical examination, vital signs are normal. Body mass index is 25. The left knee has a small effusion without erythema or warmth. Range of motion of the knee elicits crepitus. There is medial joint line tenderness to palpation, bony hypertrophy, and a moderate varus deformity. There is no evidence of joint instability on stress testing.

Radiographs of the knee reveal bone-on-bone joint-space loss and numerous osteophytes.

Which of the following diagnostic studies should be done next?

(A) Computed tomography of the knee

(B) Diagnostic joint aspiration

(C) Magnetic resonance imaging of the knee

(D) No additional diagnostic testing

Item 12 [Advanced]

A 76-year-old woman is evaluated for a 3-month history of moderate left knee pain that worsens with ambulation. She reports minimal pain at rest and no nocturnal pain. There are no clicking or locking symptoms. She has tried naproxen and ibuprofen but developed dyspepsia; acetaminophen provides mild to moderate pain relief. Medical history is significant for hypertension. Medications are lisinopril and as-needed acetaminophen.

On physical examination, vital signs are normal. Body mass index is 32. Range of motion of the left knee elicits crepitus. There is a small effusion without erythema or warmth. Tenderness to palpation is present along the medial joint line. Testing for meniscal or ligamentous injury is negative.

Radiographs of the knee reveal medial tibiofemoral compartment joint-space narrowing and sclerosis; small medial osteophytes are present.

Which of the following is the most appropriate next step in management?

(A) Celecoxib

(B) Glucosamine sulfate

(C) Magnetic resonance imaging of the knee

(D) Weight loss and exercise

Item 13 [Basic]

A 38-year-old man is evaluated during a follow-up examination. An abnormal serum uric acid level of 7.9 mg/dL (0.47 mmol/L) was obtained at a health screening performed at his place of employment. All other measures from the comprehensive metabolic profile were normal. He drinks two alcoholic beverages each weekend and eats meat several times weekly. Medical history is otherwise unremarkable, and he takes no medications. Family history is notable for his father who has gout.

On physical examination, vital signs are normal. Body mass index is 24. The remainder of the examination is normal.

Which of the following is the most appropriate treatment at this time?

(A) Allopurinol

(B) Colchicine

(C) Hydrochlorothiazide

(D) Probenecid

(E) No treatment is required

Item 14 [Basic]

A 59-year-old man is evaluated for a 10-year history of gout. He is currently asymptomatic but has had four to five attacks per year over the past 3 years. The patient's only medication is ibuprofen as needed for gout attacks.

On physical examination, vital signs are normal. The general physical examination is normal. The joint examination is unremarkable, and no tophi are seen.

Results of laboratory studies, including complete blood count, metabolic profile, and liver chemistry tests, are normal; the erythrocyte sedimentation rate is 16 mm/h, and the serum uric acid level is 9.2 mg/dL (0.54 mmol/L).

Radiographs of the hands and feet are normal.

Which of the following is the most appropriate treatment to prevent further gout flares in this patient?

(A) Allopurinol

(B) Colchicine

(C) Colchicine and allopurinol

(D) Febuxostat

Item 15 [Advanced]

A 74-year-old woman is evaluated for a 2-year history of progressive pain of the fingers and knees, along with morning stiffness lasting 20 minutes. She has no other pertinent personal or family medical history. Her only medication is acetaminophen as needed for pain.

On physical examination, vital signs are normal. Musculoskeletal examination reveals tenderness, erythema, some soft-tissue swelling, and bony hypertrophy of the second and third metacarpophalangeal joints bilaterally. Bony hypertrophy and fluctuance of the knees are noted bilaterally.

Results of laboratory studies, including erythrocyte sedimentation rate, serum ferritin and serum iron levels, and transferrin saturation, are normal. Rheumatoid factor and anti–cyclic citrullinated peptide antibody assay are negative.

Radiographs of the hands reveal joint-space narrowing, particularly of the second and third metacarpophalangeal joints; osteophytes; subchondral sclerosis; and linear calcification of the cartilage. Radiographs of the knees show diffuse joint-space narrowing with osteophytes and cartilaginous calcification.

Which of the following is the most likely diagnosis?

(A) Calcium pyrophosphate dihydrate deposition disease
(B) Hemochromatosis
(C) Osteoarthritis
(D) Rheumatoid arthritis

Item 16 [Basic]

A 30-year-old woman is evaluated in the emergency department for a 2-day history of fever and progressive swelling and pain of the right knee. The patient fell 2 weeks ago and abraded both knees. She later developed cellulitis over the left knee and was treated with a first-generation cephalosporin for 7 days with resolution of the infection. She is otherwise healthy and takes no medications.

On physical examination, temperature is 38.1°C (100.5°F); other vital signs are normal. Healing abrasions are noted on the anterior surfaces of both knees; there are no rashes or other skin lesions. The right knee is swollen, erythematous, warm, and exquisitely tender with markedly diminished range of motion but no instability.

Radiographs of the right knee reveal soft-tissue swelling and a large effusion but no bony changes.

Which of the following is the most likely diagnosis?

(A) Acute gouty arthritis
(B) Anterior cruciate ligament tear
(C) Lyme arthritis
(D) *Staphylococcus aureus* infection

Item 17 [Advanced]

A 77-year-old woman is evaluated in follow-up for a prosthetic joint infection. Three years ago, she underwent right total knee replacement to treat osteoarthritis. Three days ago she developed right knee pain and swelling around the knee, and a low-grade fever. A synovial fluid aspirate was obtained and sent for culture, and empiric intravenous vancomycin was started. Her culture grew methicillin-sensitive *Staphylococcus aureus*.

On physical examination today, temperature is 38.0°C (100.4°F); other vital signs are normal. There is a well-healed surgical scar overlying the right knee. The knee is slightly warm with pain on passive range of motion.

Laboratory studies are significant for a leukocyte count of 13,000/µL (13×10⁹/L), with 88% neutrophils, and an erythrocyte sedimentation rate of 88 mm/h.

Radiographs of the right knee show prosthetic loosening and periprosthetic lucency of the femur.

In addition to switching to intravenous nafcillin, which of the following is the most appropriate next step in management?

(A) Add rifampin
(B) Add vancomycin
(C) Schedule surgical removal of the prosthetic joint
(D) Surgical debridement of the prosthetic joint

Item 18 [Basic]

A 24-year-old woman is evaluated in the emergency department for a 5-day history of fever and right knee pain. Over the past 2 days, the left ankle and right wrist have also become painful and swollen. The patient was previously well and has no history of trauma. Her only medication is an oral contraceptive.

On physical examination, temperature is 38.4°C (101.2°F); other vital signs are normal. The right wrist is swollen, erythematous, warm, and painful. The dorsum of the right hand is swollen, erythematous, and warm with tenderness to direct palpation and minimal ability to move the fingers. The right knee is tender to palpation with a moderate effusion. The left ankle is tender, and the dorsum of the foot is swollen and tender. Findings on examination of the skin are shown (Plate 28).

Arthrocentesis of the knee shows a synovial fluid leukocyte count of 14,400/µL (14.4×10⁹/L), with 85% neutrophils. The synovial fluid is negative for crystals, and Gram stain and cultures are negative.

Which of the following is the most likely diagnosis?

(A) Disseminated gonococcal infection
(B) Gout
(C) Rheumatoid arthritis
(D) Staphylococcal arthritis

Item 19 [Basic]

A 49-year-old woman is evaluated for a 3-month history of progressive joint pain. She has bilateral hand, knee, and foot pain associated with 90 minutes of morning stiffness. Over the last 6 weeks, she has noted swelling in her hands. She now has functional limitations due to her disease. She cannot turn a door knob or open jars or walk more than 2 blocks because of pain. Ibuprofen provides minimal relief. She otherwise is well and takes no additional medications.

On physical examination, vital signs are normal. Musculoskeletal examination reveals tenderness and swelling of the first and second metacarpophalangeal and proximal interphalangeal joints and tenderness and swelling of the metatarsophalangeal joints and ankles. Her knees are noticeably swollen but without a clear effusion, and tender to palpation. The remainder of the examination is unremarkable.

Laboratory studies:

Erythrocyte sedimentation rate	58 mm/h
Rheumatoid factor	48 U/mL (40 kU/L)
Anti–cyclic citrullinated peptide antibodies	Positive
Parvovirus B19 IgM antibody	Negative

Hand radiographs show soft-tissue swelling without bone erosions or periarticular osteopenia.

Which of the following is the most appropriate therapy?

(A) Hydroxychloroquine
(B) Infliximab
(C) Methotrexate
(D) Sulfasalazine

Item 20 [Basic]

A 65-year-old woman is evaluated for a 7-month history of hand, wrist, and knee pain. The joint pain is associated with morning stiffness that improves after 2 hours of activity. Naproxen provides some relief. The patient has had no recent illnesses, has no other medical problems, and takes no additional medications.

On physical examination, vital signs are normal. Bogginess is noted when palpating the metacarpophalangeal and proximal interphalangeal joints of the second through fifth digits of each hand. There is tenderness to palpation over the wrists. A right knee effusion with mild overlying erythema is present. A smaller knee effusion is present on the left. The patient has pain with range of motion in her fingers, wrists, right knee, and left shoulder. She has full range of motion of her back without any midline tenderness on palpation.

Aspiration of the right knee reveals a synovial fluid leukocyte count of 10,500/µL (10.5×10^9/L).

Which of the following is the most likely diagnosis?

(A) Ankylosing spondylitis
(B) Chronic gouty arthritis
(C) Osteoarthritis
(D) Rheumatoid arthritis

Item 21 [Advanced]

A 29-year-old woman is evaluated during a routine examination. She seeks advice about reducing her risk of developing rheumatoid arthritis because her mother was recently diagnosed with this disorder. The patient is asymptomatic. She has a 10-pack-year history of smoking and consumes six alcoholic beverages per week, usually on weekends. She is sedentary and overweight. Her only medication is an oral contraceptive.

On physical examination, vital signs are normal. Body mass index is 29. There is no synovitis or bony abnormalities. The remainder of the examination is normal.

Which of the following lifestyle modifications is most likely to reduce this patient's risk of developing rheumatoid arthritis?

(A) Alcohol cessation
(B) Discontinuation of oral contraceptives
(C) Increased physical activity
(D) Smoking cessation
(E) Weight loss

Item 22 [Basic]

A 52-year-old man is evaluated for an 8-week history of bilateral hand pain. He also has 2 hours of morning stiffness of the hands that improves with activity. The patient has no pertinent personal or family medical history. He takes no medications.

On physical examination, vital signs are normal. Synovitis is noted at the metacarpophalangeal joints of the second through fifth digits bilaterally with swelling, tenderness, and pain on range of motion. The remainder of the examination is normal.

Laboratory studies are significant for a mild normochromic, normocytic anemia and erythrocyte sedimentation rate of 100 mm/h; rheumatoid factor is negative, and liver chemistry tests are normal.

Radiographs of the hands are normal.

Which of the following antibody assays would be most helpful in establishing this patient's diagnosis?

(A) Anti-cyclic citrullinated peptide antibodies
(B) Antimitochondrial antibodies
(C) Antineutrophil cytoplasmic antibodies
(D) Antinuclear antibodies

Item 23 [Advanced]

A 33-year-old woman is evaluated during a follow-up examination. Rheumatoid arthritis was diagnosed 3 months ago, and methotrexate was begun at that time. The patient also takes ibuprofen and acetaminophen. Despite this treatment, she still has 2 to 3 hours of morning stiffness daily and wakes frequently during the night with pain and stiffness.

On physical examination, vital signs are normal. The neck and shoulders are stiff but have full range of motion. The wrists and metacarpophalangeal and metatarsophalangeal joints are tender bilaterally, and there is synovitis of the wrists. The left knee has a small effusion.

Laboratory studies show a hemoglobin level of 12.2 g/dL (122 g/L), platelet count of 460,000/µL (460×10^9/L), and erythrocyte sedimentation rate of 45 mm/h.

Radiographs of the hands show periarticular osteopenia and erosion of the right ulnar styloid.

Which of the following is the most appropriate next step in this patient's treatment?

(A) Add etanercept
(B) Add hydroxychloroquine
(C) Add cyclophosphamide
(D) Discontinue methotrexate; begin sulfasalazine

Item 24 [Basic]

A 52-year-old woman is evaluated for a 3-month history of fatigue, a photosensitive rash on her face, and hand pain accompanied by morning stiffness. She has no other pertinent personal or family medical history and takes no medications.

On physical examination, vital signs are normal. There is a 5-mm shallow ulcer on the hard palate. There is an erythematous rash across the cheeks and bridge of the nose. Tenderness of the metacarpophalangeal and proximal interphalangeal joints is noted; there is no swelling. The remainder of the examination is normal.

Initial laboratory studies, including complete blood count, erythrocyte sedimentation rate, and urinalysis, are normal. Antinuclear antibody assay results are positive with a titer of 1:160.

Which of the following tests is most specific for confirming this patient's diagnosis?

(A) Anti–double-stranded DNA antibodies

(B) Anti-Ro/SSA and anti-La/SSB antibodies

(C) Anti-U1-ribonucleoprotein antibodies

(D) Antiproteinase-3 antibodies

Item 25 [Basic]

A 25-year-old woman is evaluated during a follow-up examination. The patient was first seen 3 months ago because of fatigue, a malar rash, and arthralgia. After laboratory confirmation of systemic lupus erythematosus, she was treated with hydroxychloroquine and a 1-month course of low-dose prednisone. She reports some improvement, although fatigue and joint pain continue.

On physical examination, temperature is 36.4°C (97.6°F), blood pressure is 148/95 mm Hg, pulse rate is 84/min, and respiration rate is 18/min. The facial rash has resolved, the joint examination is normal, and there is trace bipedal edema. The remainder of the examination is unremarkable.

Laboratory studies are significant for a serum creatinine level of 1.0 mg/dL (88.4 µmol/L) and a urinalysis showing 2+ protein; 3+ blood; 5-10 leukocytes/high-power field (hpf), 15-20 erythrocytes/hpf, and 1 erythrocyte cast/hpf. Serum complement levels (C3 and C4) are decreased.

Which of the following is the most appropriate next step in this patient's treatment?

(A) High-dose prednisone

(B) Ibuprofen

(C) Lisinopril

(D) Low-dose prednisone

Item 26 [Advanced]

A 20-year-old man is evaluated for a 6-month history of low back pain accompanied by prolonged morning stiffness. His symptoms improve over the course of the day, but he is now unable to play recreational soccer. Rest and physical therapy have not improved his symptoms. Use of acetaminophen or ibuprofen provides only partial relief. He has no other pertinent medical history and takes no additional medications.

On physical examination, vital signs are normal. There is loss of normal lumbar lordosis, and flexion of the lumbar spine is decreased. The low back and pelvis are tender to palpation. Pain increases when the patient crosses his legs. Reflexes and muscle strength are intact.

Radiographs of the lumbar spine and sacroiliac joints are normal.

Which of the following studies is most likely to establish the diagnosis in this patient?

(A) Bone scan

(B) Computed tomography CT of the sacroiliac joints

(C) Magnetic resonance imaging (MRI) of the lumbar spine

(D) MRI of the sacroiliac joints

Item 27 [Basic]

A 24-year-old woman is evaluated for a 3-week history of pain and swelling of the right knee and left ankle. The patient also reports mild burning with urination. She has no history of tick exposure, skin rash, diarrhea, or abdominal pain. She has not been sexually active in the past month. She takes no medications.

On physical examination, vital signs are normal. Musculoskeletal examination shows swelling, tenderness, warmth, pain on range of motion, and an effusion of the right knee; the left ankle is also swollen and tender.

Serologic studies for Lyme disease are negative. Urinalysis reveals 18 leukocytes/high-power field and 2+ leukocyte esterase but is otherwise normal.

Aspiration of the right knee shows a synovial fluid leukocyte count of 7500/µL (7.5×10^9/L) and negative Gram stain. Synovial fluid culture results are pending.

Which of the following is the most appropriate next step in management?

(A) Antinuclear antibody testing

(B) Rheumatoid factor testing

(C) Synovial fluid testing for Lyme disease

(D) Testing for *Chlamydia trachomatis* infection

Item 28 [Advanced]

A 24-year-old man is evaluated for worsening low back pain of 6 months' duration. He notes severe back stiffness on awakening in the morning or after prolonged sitting that seems to improve with activity. He otherwise feels well and has no other symptoms. Medical history is significant for Crohn disease diagnosed 4 years ago that has been well controlled with daily mesalamine.

On physical examination, vital signs, including temperature, are normal. Cutaneous examination, including the nails and oral mucosa, is normal. There is no evidence of conjunctivitis or iritis. Musculoskeletal examination reveals moderate tenderness to palpation over the low back, with decreased ability to flex at the waist. The remainder of the examination is unremarkable.

Laboratory studies include a normal hemoglobin level and leukocyte count and negative rheumatoid factor.

Which of the following is the most likely diagnosis?

(A) Enteropathic arthritis

(B) Psoriatic arthritis

(C) Reactive arthritis

(D) Rheumatoid arthritis

Item 29 [Advanced]

A 42-year-old man is evaluated for a 1-month history of a painful, swollen right finger and a swollen left toe. He has no other symptoms and generally feels well. He has not noticed a skin rash. Medical history is unremarkable, and his only medication is as-needed ibuprofen for his joint pain.

On physical examination, vital signs are normal. The right third distal interphalangeal joint is swollen, with localized tenderness to palpation and pain with active and passive range of motion. The appearance of the nails is shown (Plate 29). Examination of the left second toe shows fusiform swelling and mild diffuse tenderness with decreased active and passive range of motion. There is onycholysis of several toenails, including the left second toenail. The remainder of the examination is normal.

Which of the following is the most likely diagnosis?

(A) Lyme arthritis
(B) Osteoarthritis
(C) Psoriatic arthritis
(D) Rheumatoid arthritis

Item 30 [Basic]

A 46-year-old woman is evaluated for pain and color changes in her fingers and hands. She has had these symptoms for several years, but they have worsened since her diagnosis of limited systemic sclerosis 1 year ago. She notes that her symptoms occur mostly with exposure to cold (such as taking items out of a freezer or when not wearing gloves outside in the winter). She also believes that stress may make her symptoms worse. During an episode, her fingers turn white and become very painful, then blue, and over 15 to 20 minutes become red with eventual resolution of her pain. Her episodes are worsening despite her efforts to avoid cold exposure and minimize stress. Medical history is significant only for gastroesophageal reflux disease and her only medication is omeprazole.

On physical examination, she is afebrile, blood pressure is 122/68 mm Hg, and pulse rate is 82/min. Examination of the hands shows sclerodactyly but with evidence of normal perfusion. The radial and ulnar pulses are normal bilaterally. The remainder of her examination is unremarkable.

Which of the following is the most appropriate additional treatment for this patient?

(A) Amlodipine
(B) Isosorbide dinitrate
(C) Metoprolol
(D) Prednisone

Item 31 [Advanced]

A 60-year-old man is evaluated for an 8-month history of progressive, generalized weakness and difficulty rising from a chair. He reports occasional fever and muscle aches. Medical history is otherwise unremarkable. He does not smoke and drinks 1 to 2 alcoholic beverages daily. He takes no medications.

On physical examination, temperature is 37.4°C (99.3°F), blood pressure is 128/76 mm Hg, pulse rate is 72/min, and respiration rate is 18/min. No rash is present. Bilateral proximal upper and lower extremity weakness is noted with mild tenderness of the large muscle groups to palpation. Distal muscle strength is normal.

Laboratory studies reveal an erythrocyte sedimentation rate of 56 mm/h and a serum creatine kinase level of 1100 U/L.

Electromyogram shows muscle irritability without evidence of neuropathy. A proximal thigh muscle biopsy reveals pronounced lymphocytic infiltration of the muscle fascicles; there is no evidence of perivascular infiltration or filamentous particles in the sarcoplasm.

Which of the following is the most likely diagnosis?

(A) Alcohol-related myopathy
(B) Dermatomyositis
(C) Inclusion body myositis
(D) Polymyositis

Item 32 [Advanced]

A 38-year-old woman is evaluated for a gritty, burning sensation in her eyes that worsens over the course of the day. Her eyes are often dry, especially on windy days. She also reports a dry mouth with difficulty salivating at times. She has no other symptoms.

On physical examination, vital signs are normal. The conjunctivae are irritated. Visual acuity and funduscopic examination are normal. Decreased tear production is documented with the Schirmer test. The remainder of the examination is normal.

Laboratory studies are significant for a positive antinuclear antibody assay, rheumatoid factor, and anti-Ro/SSA and anti-La/SSB titers.

Which of the following is the most likely diagnosis?

(A) Lacrimal gland dysfunction
(B) Primary Sjögren syndrome
(C) Rheumatoid arthritis
(D) Systemic lupus erythematosus

Item 33 [Basic]

A 34-year-old woman is evaluated during a follow-up examination. Fibromyalgia was diagnosed 1 year ago. At that time, she received intensive education about her condition, and an aerobic exercise program was prescribed. Pregabalin was also initiated but was discontinued when she developed hives. She continues to have fatigue, widespread pain, and difficulty sleeping. She currently takes an over-the-counter nonsteroidal anti-inflammatory drug intermittently without relief of pain.

On physical examination, vital signs are normal. Musculoskeletal examination reveals multiple tender points but no synovitis or muscle weakness. Screening for mood disorders is negative. The remainder of the examination is normal.

Repeat laboratory studies since her initial diagnosis, including erythrocyte sedimentation rate and serum thyroid-stimulating hormone level, are normal.

Which of the following is the most appropriate class of pharmacologic treatment for this patient?

(A) Glucocorticoids
(B) Long-acting opioids
(C) Selective serotonin reuptake inhibitors
(D) Serotonin-norepinephrine reuptake inhibitors

Item 34 [Basic]

A 58-year-old man is evaluated for a 6-week history of pain and stiffness of the shoulders and hips. His symptoms are worse in the morning, and he notes significant discomfort when putting on his clothes. Over the past 2 weeks, he has developed fever, a 2.2-kg (5-lb) weight loss, and headache. The patient is otherwise well and takes no medications.

On physical examination, temperature is 38.6°C (101.5°F), blood pressure is 140/70 mm Hg, pulse rate is 100/min and regular, and respiration rate is 16/min. There is mild tenderness of the scalp to palpation. Musculoskeletal examination reveals mild pain and limitation at the extremes of shoulder and hip rotation bilaterally. Neurologic examination is unremarkable.

Laboratory studies are significant for a hematocrit of 32%, an erythrocyte sedimentation rate of 103 mm/h, and normal kidney function tests and urinalysis.

Which of the following is the most appropriate next step in management?

(A) Dilated ophthalmologic examination
(B) Magnetic resonance imaging (MRI) of the brain
(C) MRI of the shoulder and hip joints
(D) Temporal artery biopsy

Item 35 [Basic]

A 58-year-old woman is evaluated for a 3-month history of a nonproductive cough and hoarseness and a 3-week history of worsening shortness of breath. She is otherwise well and takes no medications.

On physical examination, temperature is 37.7°C (99.8°F), blood pressure is 160/105 mm Hg, pulse rate is 100/min, and respiration rate is 18/min. Oral mucous membranes are normal. There is scattered lymphadenopathy and mild tenderness to palpation over the anterior aspect of the neck. Diffuse crackles are auscultated. The remainder of the examination is unremarkable.

Laboratory studies are significant for a hematocrit of 32% and serum creatinine level of 1.6 mg/dL (141.4 µmol/L). A urinalysis shows 2+ protein, 10-15 erythrocytes/high-power field (hpf), 0-5 leukocytes/hpf, and erythrocyte casts.

A chest radiograph reveals right upper and lower lobe pulmonary infiltrates with several cavitary lesions.

Which of the following is the most likely diagnosis?

(A) Granulomatosis with polyangiitis
(B) Sarcoidosis
(C) Sjögren syndrome
(D) Tuberculosis

Item 36 [Advanced]

A 62-year-old man is evaluated for a 2-week history of purpuric lesions on the lower extremities. He is otherwise well and takes no medications.

On physical examination, temperature is 37.2°C (99.0°F), blood pressure is 160/100 mm Hg, pulse rate is 88/min, and respiration rate is 12/min. The mucous membranes are normal. Tender, nonblanching, purpuric papules are present on the feet and distal lower extremities. There is 1+ bilateral tibial and pedal edema. No joint swelling is noted.

Laboratory studies:

Hematocrit	28%
Leukocyte count	9500/µL (9.5 × 10⁹/L) with a normal differential
Creatinine	1.9 mg/dL (168 µmol/L)
Urinalysis	2+ protein, 15-20 erythrocytes/high-power field (hpf), 0-5 leukocytes/hpf

A skin biopsy shows a leukocytoclastic vasculitis with deposits of IgA.

Which of the following is the most likely diagnosis?

(A) Churg-Strauss syndrome
(B) Henoch-Schönlein purpura
(C) Microscopic polyangiitis
(D) Polyarteritis nodosa

Item 37 [Basic]

A 47-year-old man is evaluated for a 3-week history of paresthesia of the left leg and a 6-month history of a nonproductive cough. He also has allergic rhinitis and a history of asthma. Medications are fluticasone and inhaled albuterol as needed.

On physical examination, temperature is 37.1°C (98.8°F), blood pressure is 150/100 mm Hg, pulse rate is 100/min, and respiration rate is 18/min. There is no rash, and ocular, nasal, and oral mucous membranes are normal. Examination of the lungs reveals scattered expiratory rhonchi. There is weakness of eversion of the left foot.

Laboratory studies:

Leukocyte count	12,500/µL (12.5 × 10⁹/L) with 44% neutrophils, 32% eosinophils, 15 lymphocytes, and 9% monocytes
Creatinine	1.8 mg/dL (159.1 µmol/L)
Perinuclear antineutrophil cytoplasmic antibody	Positive
Urinalysis	1+ protein, 5-10 erythrocytes/high-power field (hpf), 0-5 leukocytes/hpf

A chest radiograph reveals scattered bilateral nodular pulmonary infiltrates.

Which of the following is the most likely diagnosis?

(A) Churg-Strauss syndrome
(B) Granulomatosis with polyangiitis
(C) Microscopic polyangiitis
(D) Polyarteritis nodosa

Item 38 [Advanced]

A 75-year-old woman is evaluated for a sudden loss of vision in the left eye that began 30 minutes ago. She has a 2-week history of fatigue, malaise, and pain in the shoulders, neck, hips, and lower back. She also has a 5-day history of mild bitemporal headache.

On physical examination, temperature is 37.3°C (99.1°F), blood pressure is 140/85 mm Hg, pulse rate is 72/min, and respiration rate is 16/min. BMI is 31. The left temporal artery is tender. Funduscopic examination reveals a pale, swollen optic disc. Range of motion of the shoulders and hips elicits moderate pain. The remainder of the examination is unremarkable.

Laboratory studies are significant for a hemoglobin of 9.9 g/dL (99 g/L), leukocyte count of 7300/µL (7.3 × 10⁹/L), platelet count of 456,000/µL (456 × 10⁹/L), and erythrocyte sedimentation rate of 116 mm/h.

Which of the following is the most appropriate next step in this patient's management?

(A) Brain MRI
(B) High-dose intravenous methylprednisolone
(C) Low-dose oral prednisone
(D) Temporal artery biopsy

Section 11

Rheumatology
Answers and Critiques

Item 1   **Answer: D**

Educational Objective: *Distinguish between inflammatory and noninflammatory arthritis.*

The presence of symmetric swelling of the proximal interphalangeal joints, elbows, and ankles in this patient is strongly suggestive of an inflammatory arthritis, most likely rheumatoid arthritis. Rheumatoid arthritis can affect most joints; however, the lumbar spine, thoracic spine. and distal interphalangeal joints are spared. Rheumatoid arthritis typically results in prolonged morning stiffness and inflammatory joint fluid, as noted in this patient.

Fibromyalgia is characterized by chronic widespread musculoskeletal pain for at least 3 months and is more common in female patients. The physical examination in patients with fibromyalgia usually is normal except for widespread pain and tenderness. Active synovitis is not consistent with a diagnosis of fibromyalgia.

Osteoarthritis can affect the hips, knees, lumbar and cervical spine, and proximal and distal interphalangeal joints; however, involvement typically is asymmetric, and the pain does not begin in multiple joints abruptly and simultaneously, as noted in this patient.

Polymyalgia rheumatica is characterized by aching in the shoulders, neck, and hip girdle region, as well as fatigue and malaise that develop over weeks to months. This patient's symptoms and the objective findings of synovitis are not consistent with polymyalgia rheumatica.

> **KEY POINT**
>
> Morning stiffness lasting more than 1 hour and a synovial fluid leukocyte count greater than 5000/µL (5.0×10^9/L) are associated with inflammatory arthritis.

Bibliography

Huizinga TW, Pincus T. In the clinic. Rheumatoid arthritis. Ann Intern Med. 2010;153: ITC1-1-ITC1-15; quiz ITC1-16. [PMID: 20621898]

Item 2   **Answer: D**

Educational Objective: *Diagnose trochanteric bursitis.*

This patient most likely has trochanteric bursitis, a common cause of lateral hip pain. A bursa is a connective tissue sac with a potential space that facilitates smooth movement of one tissue over another. Bursitis results when a bursa becomes inflamed (usually from trauma or an overuse syndrome) or infected, and the examination typically reveals pain and tenderness over the greater trochanter. Patients describe pain when lying on their side or swinging their leg into a car. Although bursae may be near or overlie a joint, it is important to differentiate pain arising from bursae and other non-joint structures from disorders in the joint. Although patients may indicate that they believe they are having pain in the joint, nonarticular pain is often worse with active range of motion and is localized away from the joint on palpation.

Iliotibial band syndrome most commonly occurs in young athletes such as runners or cyclists. This condition also can cause lateral hip pain; however, patients often describe pain that radiates down the outside of the leg. Patients with iliotibial band syndrome exhibit pain to palpation along the band down to the knee. Stretching of the iliotibial band by adducting the knee often reproduces the pain. In contrast, patients with trochanteric bursitis have more localized pain on examination.

Lumbar radiculopathy can cause pain localized to the lateral hip; however, the area is not generally tender, and straight-leg-raising test results are often positive. Lumbar radiculopathy can also result in paresthesia and weakness of the leg. Pain is often felt while sitting but is not generally exacerbated by walking.

Hip joint pathology (osteoarthritis and synovitis) often causes groin or gluteal muscle pain, and passive range of motion elicits pain in these areas. Patients often demonstrate guarding or reduced range of motion.

> **KEY POINT**
>
> Trochanteric bursitis can be confirmed in patients in whom active hip abduction intensifies the pain or in those in whom the examination reveals pain and tenderness over the bursa.

Bibliography

Strauss EJ, Nho SJ, Kelly BT. Greater trochanteric pain syndrome. Sports Med Arthrosc. 2010;18:113-9. [PMID: 20473130]

Item 3   **Answer: A**

Educational Objective: *Diagnose adult-onset Still disease.*

This patient most likely has adult-onset Still disease (AOSD), a systemic inflammatory disorder characterized by quotidian (daily) fever, evanescent rash, arthritis, and multisystem involvement. Diagnosis is based on the typical clinical presentation and exclusion of infection and malignancy, particularly leukemia and lymphoma. Laboratory abnormalities in patients with AOSD include leukocytosis, anemia, thrombocytosis, elevated erythrocyte sedimentation rate, elevated serum ferritin level (≥1000 ng/mL [1000 µg/L]), and abnormal liver chemistry tests; antinuclear antibody titer and rheumatoid factor typically are negative.

Lymphadenopathy and fever may suggest lymphoma; however, the constellation of other signs and symptoms in this patient, as well as the negative bone marrow biopsy results, suggests AOSD. Furthermore, elevated serum ferritin levels are not associated with lymphoma or leukemia.

Patients with parvovirus B19 infection have arthritis and rash lasting days to weeks, often after a flu-like illness. Spiking fevers, lymphadenopathy, and an elevated leukocyte count and serum ferritin level are not associated findings.

Fever, arthritis, and lymphadenopathy occur in patients with systemic lupus erythematosus (SLE), but the presence of elevated (rather than decreased) leukocyte and platelet counts and the markedly elevated serum ferritin level point toward a diagnosis of AOSD. An evanescent, salmon-colored rash also is not associated with SLE.

KEY POINT

Adult-onset Still disease is a systemic inflammatory disorder characterized by quotidian (daily) fever, an evanescent salmon-colored rash, arthritis, multisystem involvement, and markedly elevated serum ferritin levels.

Bibliography

Efthimiou P, Paik PK, Bielory L. Diagnosis and management of adult onset Still's disease. Ann Rheum Dis. 2006;65:564-72. [PMID: 16219707]

Item 4   Answer: B
Educational Objective: *Diagnose patellofemoral pain syndrome.*

This patient most likely has patellofemoral pain syndrome, the most common cause of knee pain in patients younger than age 45 years. Patellofemoral pain syndrome is a clinical diagnosis, and additional diagnostic testing such as radiography is not necessary. Patellofemoral pain syndrome is more common in women and is characterized by anterior knee pain that is made worse with prolonged sitting and with going up and down stairs. The pain is reproduced by applying pressure to the patella with the knee in extension and moving the patella both medially and laterally (patellofemoral compression test).

According to the American College of Rheumatology's clinical criteria, osteoarthritis of the knee can be diagnosed if knee pain is accompanied by at least three of the following features: age greater than 50 years, morning stiffness lasting less than 30 minutes, crepitus, bone tenderness, bone enlargement, and no palpable warmth. These criteria are 95% sensitive and 69% specific for a diagnosis of osteoarthritis but have not been validated for use in clinical practice. Crepitus of the knee is common in patients with osteoarthritis between the patella and the femur. Passive range of motion of the knee often elicits pain at the extremes of flexion and extension. Palpation of the knee discloses only mild tenderness. This patient has no clinical evidence of knee osteoarthritis.

Pes anserine bursitis characteristically produces pain that is located near the anteromedial aspect of the proximal tibia. On examination, tenderness is elicited at the level of the tibial tuberosity (approximately 3.8 cm [1.5 in] below the level of the medial joint line). Swelling may be present at the insertion of the medial hamstring muscles. This patient's presentation is not consistent with pes anserine bursitis.

Prepatellar bursitis is often caused by recurrent trauma, such as repeated kneeling ("housemaid's knee") but can also be caused by infection or gout. Although the pain is located anteriorly, examination reveals swelling, tenderness to palpation (usually localized near the lower pole of the patella), and erythema, all of which are lacking in this patient.

KEY POINT

Patellofemoral pain syndrome is more common in women and is characterized by anterior knee pain that is made worse with prolonged sitting and with going up and down stairs.

Bibliography

Collado H, Fredericson M. Patellofemoral pain syndrome. Clin Sports Med. 2010;29: 379-98. [PMID: 20610028]

Item 5   Answer: C
Educational Objective: *Diagnose a meniscal tear.*

The patient's history is suspicious for a meniscal tear. Patients typically describe a twisting injury with the foot in a weight-bearing position, in which a popping or tearing sensation is often felt, followed by severe pain. Swelling occurs over several hours, in contrast to ligamentous injuries, in which swelling is immediate. Patients with meniscal tears may report a clicking or locking of the knee secondary to loose cartilage in the knee but often have pain only on walking, particularly going up or down stairs. Although no clinical maneuver is able to definitively diagnose or exclude a meniscal tear, pain along the joint line is 76% sensitive for a meniscal tear, and an audible pop or snap on the McMurray test is 97% specific for such a tear.

Anserine bursitis is characterized by pain and tenderness over the anteromedial aspect of the lower leg below the joint line of the knee. The location of this patient's pain and her abnormal physical examination findings do not support the diagnosis of anserine bursitis.

Ligamentous damage, such as an anterior cruciate ligament tear, usually occurs as a result of forceful stress or direct blows to the knee while the extremity is bearing weight. Excessive medial rotation with a planted foot stresses the anterior cruciate ligament. A popping or tearing sensation is frequently reported in patients with ligamentous damage. This patient's physical examination findings, particularly the result of the McMurray test, support a diagnosis of a meniscal, rather than a ligamentous, injury.

Patellofemoral pain syndrome is the most common cause of chronic knee pain in active adults, particularly women, younger than age 45 years. The exacerbation of the pain by going down steps and the development of knee stiffness and pain at rest when the knee is flexed for an extended period of time are clues to the diagnosis. Reproducing the pain by firmly moving the patella along the femur confirms the diagnosis. This patient's history and physical examination findings are consistent with acute injury to the meniscus rather than the patellofemoral pain syndrome.

KEY POINT

Pain along the joint line is 76% sensitive for a meniscal tear, and an audible pop or snap on the McMurray test is 97% specific for such a tear.

Bibliography

Schraeder TL, Terek RM, Smith CC. Clinical evaluation of the knee. N Engl J Med. 2010;363:e5. [PMID: 20660399]

Item 6   Answer: C
Educational Objective: *Diagnose pes anserine bursitis.*

This patient most likely has pes anserine bursitis. Although pes anserine bursitis most commonly occurs in patients with medial compartment osteoarthritis, it also occurs in the setting of overuse, as in this patient. The pain is typically located along the anteromedial aspect of the proximal tibia distal to the joint line of the knee. Pain is worse with climbing stairs and frequently worsens at night.

Iliotibial band syndrome is a common cause of knife-like lateral knee pain that occurs with vigorous flexion-extension activities of the knee, such as running. It is treated conservatively with rest and stretching exercises. This patient's presentation is not consistent with iliotibial band syndrome, as her pain is located medially. Also, the pain with iliotibial band syndrome is characteristically worsened with walking both up and down stairs, which this patient does not report.

The most common cause of knee pain in persons younger than age 45 years, especially in women, is the patellofemoral pain syndrome. The pain is peripatellar and exacerbated by overuse (such as running), descending stairs, or prolonged sitting. On examination, pain can often be elicited by applying pressure on the patella (the patellofemoral compression test).

Patients with prepatellar bursitis present with pain in the anterior aspect of the knee. On examination, swelling and tenderness to palpation are frequently present near the lower pole of the patella.

KEY POINT

The pain of pes anserine bursitis is typically located along the anteromedial aspect of the proximal tibia distal to the joint line of the knee and characteristically worsens with stair climbing and at night.

Bibliography
Schraeder TL, Terek RM, Smith CC. Clinical evaluation of the knee. Engl J Med. 2010; 363:e5. [PMID: 20660399]

Item 7   Answer: C
Educational Objective: *Diagnose rotator cuff impingement syndrome.*

This patient most likely has rotator cuff impingement syndrome caused by underlying tendinitis. She presents with pain in her shoulder that began after performing the repetitive overhead motion of painting, and her pain is most pronounced with abduction of her arm. On examination, her pain occurs between 60 and 120 degrees of abduction, which supports the diagnosis of rotator cuff tendinitis. Rotator cuff tendonitis is often caused by an impingement syndrome in which the greater tuberosity of the humerus pushes against the coraco-humeral ligament, trapping the intervening structures and causing inflammation. This syndrome may be identified by the Hawkins test in which the patient is examined with the arm at 90° and the elbow flexed to 90°, supported by the examiner to ensure maximal relaxation. The examiner then stabilizes the elbow with their outside hand and with the other holds the patient's arm just proximal to the wrist. The arm is then quickly internally rotated. This test has a sensitivity for detecting impingement of >90%, although it has a significantly lower specificity. Treatment is typically with physical therapy and specific exercises.

Acromioclavicular joint degeneration is typically associated with trauma (in younger patients) or osteoarthritis (in older patients). Palpable osteophytes may be present, and radiographs, if obtained, may show degenerative changes. Acromioclavicular joint degeneration characteristically presents with pain that occurs with shoulder adduction and abduction above 120 degrees. This diagnosis is unlikely in this patient given that she has no history of trauma and that there is no acromioclavicular joint tenderness on examination.

Adhesive capsulitis is caused by thickening of the capsule surrounding the glenohumeral joint. Adhesive capsulitis is characterized by loss of both passive and active range of motion in multiple planes and patient-reported stiffness, which are not present in this patient. Also, pain is typically slow in onset and is located near the insertion of the deltoid muscle.

Rotator cuff tears are usually accompanied by weakness and loss of function. Examination findings include supraspinatus muscle weakness, weakness with external rotation, and a positive drop-arm test. The absence of weakness and the negative drop-arm test argue against the presence of a rotator cuff tear in this patient.

KEY POINT

Rotator cuff impingement syndrome due to underlying tendinitis is a common cause of nontraumatic shoulder pain; characteristic findings are pain with arm abduction and a positive Hawkins test.

Bibliography
House J, Mooradian A. Evaluation and management of shoulder pain in primary care clinics. South Med J. 2010;103:1129-35. [PMID: 20890250]

Item 8   Answer: A
Educational Objective: *Manage a suspected rotator cuff tear.*

This patient most likely has a complete left supraspinatus rotator cuff tear and should undergo magnetic resonance imaging (MRI) of the left shoulder to confirm the diagnosis. The diagnosis is suggested by his difficulty abducting the left arm and the positive drop-arm test. The drop-arm test can be performed by the examiner passively abducting the patient's arm and then having the patient slowly lower the arm to the waist. When a complete supraspinatus tear is present, the patient's arm often drops to the waist. Although imaging is not necessary in most patients with uncomplicated shoulder pain, because of this patient's high likelihood of having a complete supraspinatus tear based on history and examination findings, it is appropriate to obtain an MRI to confirm the diagnosis. MRI has a high sensitivity (98%) and specificity (79%) in the diagnosis of rotator cuff tears. Shoulder ultrasonography is another diagnostic option for rotator cuff tears in centers where it is available. Not all rotator cuff tears require surgical intervention and many respond to conservative therapy; however, establishing the diagnosis and obtaining more detailed anatomic information are necessary in deciding whether surgery is indicated.

Medication with an a nonsteroidal anti-inflammatory drug may be part of the initial treatment plan, but a confirmed diagnosis is necessary to make definitive treatment decisions.

Although referral to physical therapy is appropriate for patients with suspected or confirmed incomplete rotator cuff tears, it would not be the appropriate first step for this patient with a suspected complete tear who is young and has no medical comorbidities.

A subacromial glucocorticoid injection is not the most appropriate option in this patient with a suspected complete supraspinatus rotator cuff tear. Subacromial glucocorticoid injections have been shown to provide pain relief that lasts up to 9 months in patients with rotator cuff tendinitis or an impingement syndrome, but a significant tear may require surgical intervention, and this should be determined as an initial step in management.

KEY POINT

Imaging studies are appropriate to further evaluate a likely rotator cuff tear as suggested by the history and physical examination findings.

Bibliography
Seida JC, LeBlanc C, Schouten JR, et al. Systematic review: nonoperative and operative treatments for rotator cuff tears. Ann Intern Med. 2010;153:246-55. [PMID: 20621893]

Item 9   Answer: A

Educational Objective: *Treat osteoarthritis of the knee.*

The most appropriate treatment at this time is to perform arthrocentesis followed by an intra-articular glucocorticoid injection. In patients with osteoarthritis in whom a single joint or several joints cause pain that is disproportionate to pain in other joints and limits function, intra-articular glucocorticoids may be effective in providing pain relief and improving function. The degree and duration of pain relief vary by patient; furthermore, there is no good method for identifying who might respond well to this therapy. Successful injections provide pain relief for an average of 3 months. Risks of injection, including pain, bleeding, and infection, should be discussed with the patient before the injection. Potential long-term risks from repeated injections may occur, including atrophy of the cartilage. Therefore, the general recommendation calls for no more than three injections per year in a single joint. Rare adverse effects include fat atrophy and depigmentation of the skin. Intra-articular injection may be particularly useful in patients who obtain no relief from acetaminophen and have contraindications to the use of nonsteroidal anti-inflammatory drugs (NSAIDs), such as this patient who has chronic kidney disease, hypertension and a history of peptic ulcer disease.

Diclofenac is an NSAID and should be avoided in this patient for multiple reasons, including his history of advanced chronic kidney disease, hypertension and distant history of peptic ulcer disease. In younger patients without these comorbidities, NSAIDs are reasonable second-line treatment if acetaminophen has failed to provide relief.

Celecoxib is a cyclooxygenase-2–specific inhibitor. Although celecoxib may decrease the risk of gastrointestinal side effects, it has similar effects on the kidney and blood pressure as nonselective NSAIDs and should therefore be avoided in this patient.

A 2010 meta-analysis of the effects of glucosamine sulfate, chondroitin, and the combination of glucosamine sulfate and chondroitin concluded that these drugs alone or in combination were no more effective than placebo in controlling knee or hip pain due to osteoarthritis.

KEY POINT

In patients with osteoarthritis in whom a single joint or several joints cause pain that is disproportionate to pain in other joints and limits function, intra-articular glucocorticoid injections may be effective in providing pain relief and improving function.

Bibliography

Hochberg MC, Altman RD, April KT, et al.; American College of Rheumatology. American College of Rheumatology 2012 recommendations for the use of nonpharmacologic and pharmacologic therapies in osteoarthritis of the hand, hip, and knee. Arthritis Care Res (Hoboken). 2012;64:465-74. [PMID: 22563589]

Item 10   Answer: C

Educational Objective: *Diagnose osteoarthritis.*

The most likely diagnosis is osteoarthritis. Osteoarthritis is the most common form of arthritis, and the incidence increases with age. Common sites of osteoarthritis in the hand include the first carpometacarpal joint (base of the thumb), as well as the distal and proximal interphalangeal joints. Involvement of the carpometacarpal joint leads to "squaring" of the contour of the joint, as seen in the image. Systemic symptoms are generally absent in patients with osteoarthritis. Typically, these patients have morning joint stiffness that persists

for less than 30 minutes, whereas patients with inflammatory arthritis generally have a longer duration of morning stiffness.

de Quervain tenosynovitis is caused by inflammation of the abductor pollicis longus and extensor pollicis brevis tendons in the thumb. It is usually associated with repetitive use of the thumb but can also be associated with other conditions, including pregnancy, rheumatoid arthritis, and calcium apatite deposition disease. The typical presentation is of pain on the radial aspect of the wrist that occurs when the thumb is used to pinch or grasp. Examination findings include localized tenderness over the distal portion of the radial styloid process and pain with resisted thumb abduction and extension. The patient's findings are not consistent with de Quervain tenosynovitis.

Ganglion cysts, swellings that overlie either joints or tendons most typically on the dorsal surface, develop as a result of chronic irritation of the wrist. If the cyst is not painful, no intervention is required. A ganglion cyst would not explain this patient's symptoms at the base of the thumb or the squaring of the first carpometacarpal joint.

Rheumatoid arthritis is an inflammatory arthritis that typically causes a symmetric, inflammatory arthritis often involving the proximal interphalangeal joints and the metacarpophalangeal joints. Although rheumatoid arthritis is more common in women than in men, patients tend to have a younger age of presentation than the patient described here and should have a longer duration of morning stiffness, as well as objective signs of inflammation (synovitis, swollen joints), findings that are absent in this patient. Squaring of the first carpometacarpal joint is not characteristic of rheumatoid arthritis.

KEY POINT

Pain, stiffness, and squaring of the first carpometacarpal joint (base of the thumb) are common manifestations of osteoarthritis of the hand.

Bibliography

Abhishek A, Doherty M. Diagnosis and clinical presentation of osteoarthritis. Rheum Dis Clin North Am. 2013;39:45-66. [PMID: 23312410]

Item 11   Answer: D

Educational Objective: *Manage advanced knee osteoarthritis.*

No additional diagnostic testing is indicated for this patient who has osteoarthritis, which is a clinical diagnosis. According to the American College of Rheumatology's clinical criteria, knee osteoarthritis can be diagnosed if knee pain is accompanied by at least three of the following features: age greater than 50 years, stiffness lasting less than 30 minutes, crepitus, bone tenderness, bone enlargement, and no palpable warmth. These criteria are 95% sensitive and 69% specific for diagnosis. Additional diagnostic testing is not appropriate because it has no impact on the management of advanced disease.

Computed tomography (CT) of the knee is very sensitive for detecting pathologic findings in bone and can be used to look for evidence of an occult fracture, osteomyelitis, or bone erosions. However, none of these are suspected in this patient.

Small- to moderate-sized effusions can occur in patients with osteoarthritis, and the fluid is typically noninflammatory. Joint aspiration in this patient without evidence of joint inflammation and evident osteoarthritis is not useful diagnostically but is often done in the context of intra-articular glucocorticoid injections.

Magnetic resonance imaging (MRI) is useful to evaluate soft-tissue structures in the knee such as meniscal tears. Patients with meniscal tears may report a clicking or locking of the knee secondary to loose cartilage but often have pain only on walking, particularly going up or down stairs. Patients with degenerative arthritis often have MRI findings that indicate meniscal tears. These tears are part of the degenerative process but do not impact management; arthroscopic knee surgery for patients with osteoarthritis provides no clinical benefit. The one exception may be in patients with meniscal tears that result in a free flap or loose body, producing painful locking of the joint. These findings are not present in this patient.

KEY POINT

Osteoarthritis is diagnosed clinically and does not require advanced imaging studies to establish the diagnosis.

Bibliography

Hunter DJ. In the clinic. Osteoarthritis. Ann Intern Med. 2007;147:ITC8-1–ITC8-16. [PMID: 17679702]

Item 12   Answer: D

Educational Objective: *Manage knee osteoarthritis.*

Weight loss and exercise are indicated for this patient with knee osteoarthritis. Her knee pain, which is worse with weight bearing, is suggestive of tibiofemoral osteoarthritis, a diagnosis supported by the presence of medial joint line tenderness and radiographic findings of medial tibiofemoral compartment joint-space narrowing. The strongest risk factors for osteoarthritis are advancing age, obesity, female sex, joint injury (caused by occupation, repetitive use, or actual trauma), and genetic factors. Obesity, in particular, is the most important modifiable risk factor for knee osteoarthritis. Several trials have demonstrated that weight loss and/or exercise programs can provide relief of pain and improved function comparable to the benefits of nonsteroidal anti-inflammatory drug (NSAID) use. In long-term studies, sustained weight loss of approximately 6.8 kg (15 lb) has resulted in symptomatic relief.

Celecoxib, a cyclooxygenase-2 (COX-2)–specific inhibitor, has a lower risk of causing gastrointestinal ulcers than nonselective NSAIDs but can still cause dyspepsia, which occurred in this patient after taking naproxen and ibuprofen. COX-2 inhibitors are not more effective than nonselective NSAIDs, are significantly more expensive, and are associated with an increased risk for adverse cardiovascular events. Therefore, celecoxib would not be a preferred treatment for this patient.

Although glucosamine sulfate is commonly used in the management of osteoarthritis, multiple studies have failed to document its effectiveness in reducing pain or affecting the course of the disease.

Magnetic resonance imaging of the knee is indicated to evaluate possible meniscal or other ligamentous injuries, none of which is suggested by this patient's history (no knee locking or "giving way") or examination findings (negative examination for tendinous or ligamentous injury).

KEY POINT

Obesity is the most important modifiable risk factor for knee osteoarthritis, and weight loss and exercise are recommended to reduce pain and improve function.

Bibliography

Messier SP. Diet and exercise for obese adults with knee osteoarthritis. Clin Geriatr Med. 2010;26:461-77. [PMID: 20699166]

Item 13   Answer: E

Educational Objective: *Treat a patient with asymptomatic hyperuricemia.*

No treatment is required for this patient with asymptomatic hyperuricemia. This condition is characterized by a moderately elevated serum uric acid level without evidence of symptoms of gout. Patients with asymptomatic hyperuricemia have an increased risk for gout over the long term but a low likelihood of a gout attack in the short term; thus, a pharmacologic intervention at this time is not indicated. Although studies suggest that hyperuricemia may contribute to several comorbidities (hypertension, kidney disease, cardiovascular disease), there is not yet consensus that these risks are sufficient to independently warrant chronic urate-lowering therapy. In patients with asymptomatic hyperuricemia, dietary and lifestyle considerations are always worth reviewing. Decreasing consumption of high-purine foods (particularly meat and seafood), alcohol, and high-fructose foods may lower serum uric acid concentrations. An increase in dairy consumption, as well as weight loss (if indicated), may also help lower serum uric acid concentrations. In making recommendations for lifestyle changes, the ability of the patient to comply should always be taken into account.

Allopurinol is an effective urate-lowering agent used to treat symptomatic hyperuricemia. Colchicine is an anti-inflammatory agent that can treat or prevent gout attacks. Probenecid is a uricosuric drug that is also used to treat symptomatic hyperuricemia. All of these agents may be helpful in treating patients with gout; however, based on this patient's findings, none of these treatment options is warranted at this time.

The diuretic hydrochlorothiazide is used to treat hypertension and promotes increases in serum uric acid concentration by inhibiting kidney urate excretion; this patient does not have hypertension, and such a strategy would increase his risk of future gout attacks while providing no specific benefit. In patients who are taking thiazide diuretics and require urate lowering, switching to an alternative antihypertensive agent that does not raise the serum uric acid concentration is a reasonable intervention.

KEY POINT

Treatment is not indicated for patients with asymptomatic hyperuricemia.

Bibliography

Roddy E, Doherty M. Treatment of hyperuricaemia and gout. Clin Med. 2013;13:400-3. [PMID: 23908515]

Item 14   Answer: C

Educational Objective: *Manage gout with urate-lowering agents.*

This patient should be started on allopurinol and colchicine. He has frequent, symptomatic gout attacks, and treatment with urate-lowering therapy such as allopurinol is indicated. Gout manifests as acute, intermittent attacks of severe pain, redness, and swelling of a joint accompanied by intracellular urate crystals seen on polarized light microscopy of the synovial fluid. For acute gout attacks, nonsteroidal anti-inflammatory drugs, glucocorticoids, and colchicine are appropriate management strategies; choice of treatment is based on relative efficacy and, most importantly, the side-effect profiles of the agents and the risk of toxicity in the individual patient.

Because gout is associated with hyperuricemia, patients with recurrent episodes (≥2 attacks in 1 year) usually benefit from urate-lowering therapy to prevent both future attacks and occult urate deposition. However, the addition of urate-lowering therapy transiently increases the risk for acute gout attacks for at least 3 to 6 months; accordingly, prophylaxis with an anti-inflammatory agent such as colchicine, at least during that period, is indicated concurrent with urate-lowering therapy.

Along with this treatment regimen, management of risk factors can help to lower serum uric acid concentrations, including reducing dietary purine and fructose and increasing dairy intake (within the limits of individual tolerance), weight loss if indicated, and reducing alcohol consumption. Medications that raise serum uric acid levels, including thiazide diuretics and low-dose salicylates, should be discontinued if alternative therapy is appropriate.

Use of either allopurinol or febuxostat would be appropriate but only in the setting of concurrent prophylaxis. The dose of both febuxostat and allopurinol should be adjusted to achieve a serum uric acid level ≤6.0 mg/dL (0.35 mmol/L), rather than a fixed dose. The relative effectiveness of these two agents is not well established; febuxostat is more potent on a per-mole basis but is also more expensive than allopurinol.

Treatment with colchicine alone might lower the risk of gout attacks in this patient but would not address the underlying problem of urate deposition, which would likely worsen progressively over time.

KEY POINT

Colchicine or another anti-inflammatory agent is indicated concurrent with initiation of urate-lowering agents in patients with frequently recurring gout attacks.

Bibliography

Yang LP. Oral colchicine in the treatment and prophylaxis of gout. Drugs. 2010;70: 1603-13. [PMID: 20687623]

Item 15   Answer: A

Educational Objective: *Diagnose chronic calcium pyrophosphate dihydrate deposition disease.*

This patient has chronic calcium pyrophosphate dihydrate (CPPD) deposition disease, sometimes referred to as calcium pyrophosphate arthropathy. CPPD deposition disease is a clinical diagnosis made by observing typical osteoarthritis features along with radiographic evidence of calcium deposition in the cartilage (chondrocalcinosis) in locations atypical for osteoarthritis, such as the metacarpophalangeal joints. A chronic inflammatory condition may result, leading to progressive joint destruction. This patient has polyarthritis with radiologic findings that resemble osteoarthritis (subchondral sclerosis and osteophytes); however, involvement includes the second and third metacarpophalangeal joints, which are not typically involved in osteoarthritis. There also is evidence of calcium deposition in the cartilage of the affected joints. This constellation of findings is pathognomonic for CPPD deposition disease. Although this patient has not had acute gout-like attacks, termed pseudogout, an acute inflammatory arthritis may be caused by calcium pyrophosphate crystals in the joints.

Hemochromatosis may overlap with CPPD deposition disease and can cause osteoarthritis-like arthritis in atypical joints. However, this patient has no evidence of iron overload (normal serum ferritin, iron, and transferrin saturation values) that is characteristic of hemochromatosis.

Although this patient has radiographic findings consistent with osteoarthritis, the involvement of metacarpophalangeal joints and the presence of chondrocalcinosis are not typical for this disorder.

This patient's findings, including involvement of only the second and third metacarpophalangeal joints; limited morning stiffness and soft-tissue swelling; negative rheumatoid factor and anti–cyclic citrullinated peptide antibody assay results; and no marginal erosions or periarticular osteopenia, do not support a diagnosis of rheumatoid arthritis.

KEY POINT

Calcium pyrophosphate dihydrate deposition disease is characterized by osteoarthritis-like arthritis in atypical joints, such as the metacarpophalangeal joints, along with the presence of chondrocalcinosis.

Bibliography

Zhang W, Doherty M, Bardin T, et al. European League Against Rheumatism recommendations for calcium pyrophosphate deposition. Part I: terminology and diagnosis. Ann Rheum Dis. 2011;70:563-70. [PMID: 21216817]

Item 16   Answer: D

Educational Objective: *Diagnose infectious arthritis due to* Staphylococcus aureus.

This patient has *Staphylococcus aureus* infection. Gram-positive microorganisms are the most frequent causes of infectious arthritis, with *S. aureus* being the most common. These infections typically are monoarticular, affect the large joints (particularly the knee), and have a rapid onset (hours or 1 to 2 days). This otherwise healthy patient has an acute arthritis following a skin break with cellulitis over the knee, consistent with hematogenous spread of a skin-derived infection. The presence of fever, along with a markedly swollen and inflamed joint, is consistent with *S. aureus* infection.

Acute gouty arthritis typically is monoarticular and frequently involves the knee; however, gout is exceedingly rare in healthy premenopausal women.

Anterior cruciate ligament tear can cause acute swelling, but the joint is usually less inflamed, and this condition is not associated with fever. This patient's knee was not injured after her fall, making this diagnosis unlikely. In addition, an anterior cruciate ligament tear causes anterior instability (assessed using the anterior drawer and Lachman tests), whereas this patient's knee remained stable.

Although chronic Lyme arthritis can manifest as monoarticular arthritis of the lower extremity, the onset is typically gradual, rather than acute, and is not associated with fever.

KEY POINT

Infectious arthritis caused by gram-positive microorganisms is typically monoarticular and affects the large joints, particularly the knee, with a rapid onset of development (hours or 1 to 2 days).

Bibliography

Mathews CJ, Weston VC, Jones A, et al. Bacterial septic arthritis in adults. Lancet. 2010;375:846-55. [PMID: 20206778]

Item 17   Answer: C

Educational Objective: *Treat a patient with a prosthetic joint infection.*

This patient has a prosthetic knee joint infection caused by methicillin-sensitive *Staphylococcus aureus* and requires surgical removal of the prosthesis. This patient's findings, including joint pain and elevated leukocyte count, elevated erythrocyte sedimentation rate (ESR), along with positive synovial fluid cultures, prosthetic loosening, and periprosthetic bone erosion, are consistent with prosthetic joint infection.

Prosthetic joints may become infected late after implantation (>3 months to years) via hematogenous spread of microorganisms or a delayed response to low-intensity pathogens. The joint may be swollen and inflamed or only painful. Leukocyte counts may be only modestly elevated; inflammatory markers such as the ESR or C-reactive protein (CRP) are usually elevated. Radiographs may reveal erosion or loosening around the implantation site. Diagnosis requires synovial fluid aspiration or open debridement, along with Gram stain and cultures. Treatment of prosthetic joint infection typically involves removal of the infected prosthesis, and is required for late infection or with infection-related dysfunction of the prosthesis, such as loosening. After removal, an antibiotic spacer is often inserted, and long-term (weeks to months) antibiotic therapy is initiated. Reimplantation can only be considered after complete resolution of the infection.

Surgical debridement alone with a prolonged course of antibiotics may be curative in some selected cases of early prosthetic joint infection. However, dysfunction of the prosthesis and late presentation, both features in this patient, make this approach inappropriate.

Some evidence suggests that adding rifampin to treatment with sensitive antibiotics may improve outcomes in patients with methicillin-sensitive *S. aureus* prosthetic joint infection who undergo early extensive surgical debridement in an attempt to preserve the prosthesis. However, this patient is not a candidate for this approach, and rifampin is therefore not indicated.

Intravenous vancomycin is useful for treating infection with methicillin-resistant *S. aureus* and was a reasonable initial choice for antibiotic therapy pending culture results. However, this patient has methicillin-sensitive *S. aueus* infection, which should respond to nafcillin or oxacillin along with joint removal, and no additional benefit from vancomycin would be expected. Additionally, except in specific cases, there is no evidence that dual antibiotic therapy is more effective than treatment with a single antibiotic agent to which the infecting organism is sensitive.

KEY POINT

Treatment of delayed-onset prosthetic joint infection typically involves removal of the infected prosthesis.

Bibliography

Del Pozo JL, Patel R. Clinical practice. Infection associated with prosthetic joints. N Engl J Med. 2009;361:787-94. [PMID: 19692690]

Item 18   Answer: A

Educational Objective: *Diagnose disseminated gonococcal infection.*

This patient has disseminated gonococcal infection with associated gonococcal arthritis. This form of infectious arthritis most commonly occurs in young, sexually active adults, particularly women. Disseminated gonococcemia is characterized by a prodrome of tenosynovitis, migratory or additive polyarthralgia, and cutaneous lesions that progress from papules or macules to pustules. Fever and rigors are common. As in this patient, subsequent frank arthritis can develop, affecting large and medium-sized joints and accompanied by tendinitis and papulopustular skin lesions. The leukocyte count is typically less than that of other types of bacterial arthritis, and Gram stain and culture results are usually negative.

Gout also may be highly inflammatory and polyarticular; however, it rarely occurs in premenopausal women, who typically have lower serum uric acid levels. Furthermore, the first attack of gout is rarely polyarticular, does not typically affect the wrists, usually involves the first metatarsophalangeal joint, and is not associated with papulopustular skin lesions.

Rheumatoid arthritis also is a systemic polyarticular disease. However, onset is typically more gradual; arthritic changes characteristically involve the proximal small joints of the hands; tendinitis is not present; and papulopustular skin lesions do not occur. Fever is not a common feature of rheumatoid arthritis.

Staphylococcal arthritis is the most common form of infectious arthritis and can damage joints rapidly. It is more common in children, older patients, and those with previously damaged joints, unlike this 24-year-old patient with no history of, or risk factors for, staphylococcal infection. Staphylococcal arthritis is usually monoarticular, does not cause tenosynovitis, and is not accompanied by systemic skin findings such as the classic papulopustular skin lesions of disseminated gonococcal infection.

KEY POINT

Gonococcal arthritis, which develops in association with a systemic gonococcal infection, typically begins as migratory or polyarticular disease and can affect large and medium-sized joints; other findings are tendinitis and papulopustular skin lesions.

Bibliography

Garcia-De La Torre I, Nava Zavala A. Gonococcal and nongonococcal arthritis. Rheum Dis Clin North Am. 2009;35:63-73. [PMID: 19480997]

Item 19   Answer: C

Educational Objective: *Treat rheumatoid arthritis.*

Methotrexate is indicated for this patient with early rheumatoid arthritis. She has synovitis; symmetric distribution of arthritis involving small joints of hands, feet, and ankles; an elevated erythrocyte sedimentation rate; and positive rheumatoid factor and anti–cyclic citrullinated peptide (anti-CCP) antibodies, which support the diagnosis of rheumatoid arthritis. Experts recommend that patients begin disease-modifying antirheumatic drugs (DMARDs) within 3 months of the onset of rheumatoid arthritis. The earlier that DMARDs are instituted, the more likely that damage from this condition will be limited. The initial choice of a DMARD is based on the severity of the inflammatory disease, the rate of disease progression, whether erosive disease is seen on radiographs, and whether a patient has anti-CCP antibody positivity. Use of methotrexate may benefit patients with early mild to moderate rheumatoid arthritis, but its use is imperative in patients with rapid disease progression or functional limitations. In the absence of contraindications, methotrexate should be instituted immediately in patients with erosive disease documented at disease onset. This agent can be used a monotherapy in patients with early disease, as it is highly effective, is well tolerated, is associated with high rates of adherence, and has a relatively low cost compared with other DMARDs.

Monotherapy with hydroxychloroquine or sulfasalazine or combination therapy with these agents is indicated to treat early, mild, and nonerosive disease. Hydroxychloroquine alone has not been shown to retard radiographic progression of rheumatoid arthritis and therefore should be used only in patients whose disease has remained nonerosive for several years. Sulfasalazine is an aspirin-like agent that is often used in combination with methotrexate or another nonbiologic DMARD when there is an inadequate response to therapy. Sulfasalazine is not indicated initially in this patient who has not had a trial of methotrexate therapy alone.

Infliximab is a tumor necrosis factor α inhibitor that is often used when patients do not respond to methotrexate or if they have advanced disease and a poor prognosis, such as early erosive disease.

KEY POINT

Methotrexate may benefit patients with early mild to moderate rheumatoid arthritis, but its use is imperative in patients who have rheumatoid arthritis associated with rapid disease progression or functional limitations

Bibliography

Huizinga TW, Pincus T. In the clinic. Rheumatoid arthritis. Ann Intern Med. 2010;153: ITC1-1-ITC1-15; quiz ITC1-16. [PMID: 20621898]

Item 20   Answer: D
Educational Objective: *Diagnose rheumatoid arthritis.*

The most likely diagnosis is rheumatoid arthritis. Morning stiffness lasting more than 60 minutes and a synovial fluid leukocyte count greater than 5000/μL (5×10^9/L) are typical of an inflammatory arthritis. Most patients with rheumatoid arthritis have a symmetric polyarthritis involving small, medium, and large joints. The wrists, the metacarpophalangeal and proximal interphalangeal joints of the hands, and the metatarsophalangeal joints of the feet are almost always affected. Early in the disease course, the oligoarthritis may be asymmetric in some joints but becomes symmetric as the disease progresses. Typically, the distal interphalangeal joints and lumbar spine are spared.

Ankylosing spondylitis is a spondyloarthritis that begins in the sacroiliac joints and lumbar spine and progresses cranially over time. There is a male predominance, and patients are typically between 20 and 30 years of age at presentation. Patients with inflammatory back pain and synovitis of peripheral joints should be evaluated for spondyloarthropathy.

Acute gout typically develops over hours and often starts at night. Early in the disease course, acute gouty attacks occur in single joints, typically the first metatarsophalangeal joint of the foot. Gouty attacks can occur in any joint and are associated with erythema, swelling, and pain of the affected joint. Patients may experience a low-grade fever. Patients with gout whose high serum uric acid levels go

unmanaged are at risk for developing tophi, which are urate crystal deposits that are often surrounded by local inflammation. Patients with long-standing gout and established tophaceous disease typically have increased frequency of acute gouty attacks and may experience smoldering chronic arthritis. This patient has no characteristics of acute, tophaceous, or chronic gouty arthritis.

Osteoarthritis often affects the first metacarpophalangeal joint and the proximal and distal interphalangeal joints, knees, lumbar and cervical spine, and hips. Joint involvement tends to be asymmetric. Morning stiffness associated with noninflammatory osteoarthritis typically lasts less than 30 minutes. This patient's morning stiffness exceeds 60 minutes.

KEY POINT

Morning stiffness lasting more than 60 minutes and a synovial fluid leukocyte count greater than 5000/μL (5×10^9/L) are associated with inflammatory arthritis, such as rheumatoid arthritis.

Bibliography

Huizinga TW, Pincus T. In the clinic. Rheumatoid arthritis. Ann Intern Med. 2010;153: ITC1-1-ITC1-15; quiz ITC1-16. [PMID: 20621898]

Item 21   Answer: D
Educational Objective: *Recognize the risk factors for rheumatoid arthritis.*

Smoking is associated with an increased risk of developing rheumatoid arthritis, and cessation is therefore recommended for this and other health reasons. Hereditary factors convey susceptibility for developing rheumatoid arthritis, and changes in environmental factors seem to modify this risk. The duration and intensity of smoking correlate with the risk of developing rheumatoid arthritis. Users of smokeless tobacco do not have an increased risk of developing this disorder, suggesting that it is not simply an effect of nicotine. Smoking cessation is associated with a decline in the risk of developing rheumatoid arthritis, although this benefit is not immediate.

Alcohol use is not associated with an increased risk of rheumatoid arthritis. This patient may be advised to moderate her consumption of alcohol, but it will not alter her risk of developing this disorder.

Hormonal factors may play a role in developing rheumatoid arthritis. The risk is higher in women, but is not as high in women who have had children. Breastfeeding is associated with a decreased risk of developing rheumatoid arthritis and may account for some or all of the protective effect of parity. The risk of rheumatoid arthritis is inversely associated with duration of lifetime breastfeeding. Use of oral contraceptives may also be protective. In one study, use of oral contraceptives for 7 or more years was associated with a decreased risk of rheumatoid arthritis. Discontinuing oral contraceptives in this patient may be associated with increased risk or no change in her risk but not with a decreased risk of rheumatoid arthritis.

Obesity and sedentary lifestyle are associated with a number of health risks but have not been clearly linked to the development of rheumatoid arthritis. In patients with rheumatoid arthritis, range-of-motion exercises help preserve joint motion; in patients with osteoarthritis, aerobic exercise helps maintain muscle strength, joint stability, and physical performance, and weight reduction reduces stress on weight-bearing joints.

KEY POINT

Smoking is associated with an increased risk of developing rheumatoid arthritis, and smoking cessation is recommended for this and other health reasons.

Bibliography

Costenbader KH, Feskanich D, Mandl LA, Karlson EW. Smoking intensity, duration and cessation, and the risk of rheumatoid arthritis in women. Am J Med. 2006;119: 503.e1-e9. [PMID: 16750964]

Item 22   Answer: A

Educational Objective: *Diagnose rheumatoid arthritis.*

An anti–cyclic citrullinated peptide (anti-CCP) antibody assay is warranted for this patient in whom rheumatoid arthritis is suspected. Anti-CCP antibodies are present in approximately 40% to 60% of patients with early rheumatoid arthritis, including some patients with a negative rheumatoid factor. These antibodies are 95% specific for rheumatoid arthritis. The presence of higher titers of either rheumatoid factor or anti-CCP antibodies or the presence of both increases the likelihood of disease. Although this patient's rheumatoid factor is negative, rheumatoid arthritis remains a significant concern because he has synovitis of eight small joints and morning stiffness lasting more than 1 hour, common symptoms of rheumatoid arthritis. Additionally, he has evidence of systemic inflammation with an elevated erythrocyte sedimentation rate and mild anemia. Therefore, an anti-CCP antibody assay is appropriate to determine whether this patient's symptoms are caused by rheumatoid arthritis.

Antimitochondrial antibodies are present in patients with autoimmune hepatitis. Patients with this disease can develop arthralgia and arthritis similar to findings in this patient; however, he does not have liver chemistry test abnormalities that are characteristic of autoimmune hepatitis.

Antineutrophil cytoplasmic antibodies are typically associated with vasculitis such as granulomatosis with polyangiitis (formerly known as Wegener granulomatosis), microscopic polyangiitis, Churg-Strauss syndrome, anti–glomerular basement membrane antibody disease, and drug-induced vasculitis. Arthritis and arthralgia can be associated with these syndromes; however, the presence of these vascular inflammatory disorders would be unusual in the absence of other systemic involvement.

Assay for antinuclear antibodies (ANA) can be clinically useful when there is clinical suspicion for autoimmune conditions associated with these antibodies, such as systemic lupus erythematosus (SLE). Patients with SLE may present with arthritis, but SLE is less likely than rheumatoid arthritis in the patient described here. SLE typically occurs in women of childbearing age and is associated with additional clinical and/or laboratory abnormalities rather than with isolated arthritis. ANA are present in some patients with rheumatoid arthritis but are not specific for this disorder.

KEY POINT

Anti-cyclic citrullinated peptide antibodies are a highly specific marker for rheumatoid arthritis.

Bibliography

Whiting PF, Smidt N, Sterne JA, et al. Systematic review: accuracy of anti-citrullinated peptide antibodies for diagnosing rheumatoid arthritis. Ann Intern Med. 2010; 152:456-64; W155-66. [PMID: 20368651]

Item 23   Answer: A

Educational Objective: *Treat persistent, aggressive rheumatoid arthritis.*

This patient has early, aggressive rheumatoid arthritis, and the addition of etanercept is indicated. Methotrexate is the most commonly used and safest among the more effective disease-modifying antirheumatic drugs (DMARDs), has the greatest potential for modifying disease compared with hydroxychloroquine and sulfasalazine, and is central to most treatments for rheumatoid arthritis. Despite treatment with methotrexate, this patient has persistent morning stiffness, numerous tender and swollen joints, and an elevated erythrocyte sedimentation rate.

When adequate disease control is not achieved with one or more oral DMARDs, biologic therapy is indicated. The preferred initial biologic agent is a tumor necrosis factor α (TNF-α) inhibitor such as etanercept, which is usually added to baseline methotrexate therapy. Use of a TNF-α inhibitor in addition to methotrexate is significantly more effective in controlling joint damage and improving function compared with single-agent therapy with either medication alone. Screening for tuberculosis is indicated before beginning therapy with any biologic agent, and patients who test positive for latent tuberculosis should be treated with isoniazid before beginning this therapy.

Hydroxychloroquine is an effective agent in the treatment of early, mild, and nonerosive rheumatoid arthritis but most likely would not be beneficial in a patient with aggressive disease, functional limitations, and radiographic evidence of joint erosion. Even the addition of hydroxychloroquine to methotrexate is unlikely to be as helpful for treating erosive rheumatoid arthritis as is the combination of methotrexate and a TNF-α inhibitor.

Cyclophosphamide is not indicated for the treatment of active rheumatoid arthritis except in patients with rheumatoid vasculitis in whom major organ function is compromised. This patient does not have manifestations consistent with rheumatoid vasculitis, such as cutaneous ulcers and mononeuritis multiplex.

Sulfasalazine is often administered in combination with methotrexate and/or hydroxychloroquine in the treatment of early rheumatoid arthritis. Single-agent therapy with sulfasalazine also may be used when there are contraindications to the use of methotrexate. However, sulfasalazine is less effective than methotrexate in the treatment of rheumatoid arthritis and is not likely to benefit this patient if substituted for methotrexate.

KEY POINT

When adequate control of rheumatoid arthritis is not achieved with one or more oral disease-modifying antirheumatic drugs (DMARDs), the addition of biologic therapy with a tumor necrosis factor α inhibitor is usually indicated.

Bibliography

Singh JA, Furst DE, Bharat A, et al. 2012 update of the 2008 American College of Rheumatology recommendations for the use of disease-modifying antirheumatic drugs and biologic agents in the treatment of rheumatoid arthritis. Arthritis Care Res (Hoboken). 2012;64:625-39. [PMID: 22473917]

Item 24   Answer: A

Educational Objective: *Diagnose systemic lupus erythematosus.*

An anti–double-stranded DNA (anti-dsDNA) antibody assay has the greatest specificity for confirming a diagnosis in this patient, who has manifestations of systemic lupus erythematosus (SLE). She meets criteria for SLE because of the presence of positive antinuclear antibodies (ANA), along with arthritis, an oral ulcer, and photosensitive rash. Patients with a high pretest probability of SLE and positive ANA assay (usually a titer ≥1:160) should undergo confirmatory testing using a more specific autoantibody study with either an anti-dsDNA antibody assay or an anti-Smith antibody assay. Anti-dsDNA antibodies are present in approximately 50% to 70% of patients with SLE and generally are not found in those with other autoimmune diseases. The presence of anti-dsDNA antibodies is correlated with kidney disease in patients with SLE, and rising titers may precede disease flare. Anti-Smith antibodies, which are present in approximately 30% of patients with SLE, are also very specific for the disease. Patients with a new diagnosis of SLE should also undergo screening for anticardiolipin antibodies and the lupus anticoagulant.

Anti-Ro/SSA and anti-La/SSB antibodies are present in 10% to 60% of patients with SLE; however, these antibodies are less specific than anti-dsDNA antibodies because they can also be present in patients with rheumatoid arthritis, systemic sclerosis, and Sjögren syndrome.

Anti-U1-ribonucleoprotein (RNP) antibodies are found in patients with mixed connective tissue disease, which is characterized by features of systemic sclerosis, polymyositis, and SLE. The diagnosis requires the presence of high-titer RNP antibodies, generally in the absence of other autoantibodies. Positive RNP antibodies are also found in 30% to 40% of patients with SLE, but the test is less sensitive and specific than anti-dsDNA antibody testing. The presence of antiproteinase-3 antibodies, which produces a c-ANCA pattern on immunofluorescence testing, is suggestive of granulomatosis with polyangiitis (formerly known as Wegener granulomatosis), a necrotizing vasculitis that typically affects the respiratory tract and kidneys. This test is not indicated, because this patient does not have findings consistent with granulomatosis with polyangiitis.

KEY POINT

Anti–double-stranded DNA antibodies are present in approximately 50% to 70% of patients with systemic lupus erythematosus and are very specific for the disease.

Bibliography
D'Cruz DP, Khamashta MA, Hughes GR. Systemic lupus erythematosus. Lancet. 2007; 369:587-96. [PMID: 17307106]

Item 25   Answer: A
Educational Objective: *Treat suspected lupus glomerulonephritis.*

This patient should be treated with high-dose glucocorticoid therapy such as prednisone. Her hypertension, ankle edema, hematuria, proteinuria, and erythrocyte casts on urinalysis are highly suggestive of lupus nephritis despite the absence of kidney insufficiency. To prevent irreversible kidney damage, early treatment with a high-dose glucocorticoid is indicated for patients whose condition raises strong suspicion for lupus nephritis. Whether kidney biopsy is necessary in order to establish a diagnosis remains uncertain, and treatment with high-dose glucocorticoids would not significantly alter subsequent biopsy results if a decision is made to pursue biopsy.

Ibuprofen may help to control this patient's arthralgia. However, nonsteroidal anti-inflammatory drugs can significantly worsen kidney function in patients with lupus nephritis and are therefore contraindicated in this patient population.

Initiation of antihypertensive therapy, such as lisinopril, would benefit this patient but is not the most appropriate next step in the management of her condition; treatment of her nephritis takes precedence and may itself help to control her hypertension. Angiotensin-converting enzyme inhibitors such as lisinopril are the antihypertensive drugs of choice in patients with lupus nephritis because these agents help to control proteinuria.

Low-dose prednisone may help to alleviate this patient's arthralgia and rash but would not treat her lupus nephritis.

KEY POINT

Early treatment with high-dose glucocorticoids is indicated for patients with systemic lupus erythematosus and findings strongly suspicious for lupus nephritis.

Bibliography
Sprangers B, Monahan M, Appel GB. Diagnosis and treatment of lupus nephritis flares -an update. Nat Rev Nephrol. 2012;8:709-17. [PMID: 23147758]

Item 26   Answer: D
Educational Objective: *Diagnose ankylosing spondylitis.*

This patient most likely has ankylosing spondylitis, and magnetic resonance imaging (MRI) of the sacroiliac joints is most likely to establish the diagnosis. Radiographic evidence of sacroiliitis is required for definitive diagnosis and is the most consistent finding associated with this condition. Onset of ankylosing spondylitis usually occurs in the teenage years or 20s and manifests as persistent pain and morning stiffness involving the low back that is alleviated with activity. This condition also may be associated with tenderness of the pelvis.

Typically, the earliest radiographic changes involve the sacroiliac joints, but these changes may not be visible during the first few years from onset; therefore, this patient's normal radiographs of the sacroiliac joints do not exclude sacroiliitis. MRI findings of the sacroiliac joints can include bone marrow edema, synovitis, and erosions. Bone marrow edema is the earliest finding and can precede the development of erosions. MRI, especially with gadolinium enhancement, is considered a sensitive method for detecting early erosive inflammatory changes in the sacroiliac joints and spine and can assess sites of active disease and response to effective therapy.

A bone scan can demonstrate increased radionuclide uptake of the sacroiliac joints in patients with ankylosing spondylitis but is less sensitive and specific than MRI for establishing the diagnosis.

Computed tomography is the most sensitive modality available to demonstrate bone changes such as erosions; however, it cannot detect early changes such as bone marrow edema that precede erosive change in patients with ankylosing spondylitis.

Sacroiliac joint MRI is more sensitive than lumbar spine MRI in diagnosing early ankylosing spondylitis. Although changes in the lumbar spine can be detected on MRI, they are usually preceded by changes in the sacroiliac joints. Therefore, if imaging of the lumbar spine is negative, subsequent imaging of the sacroiliac joints would still be necessary to exclude ankylosing spondylitis.

KEY POINT

MRI is considered the most sensitive imaging study for detecting early erosive inflammatory changes in the sacroiliac joints indicative of ankylosing spondylitis when radiographs are normal.

Bibliography

Chary-Valckenaere I, d'Agostino MA, Loeuille D. Role for imaging studies in anky-losing spondylitis. Joint Bone Spine. 2011;78:138–43. [PMID: 20851029]

Item 27   Answer: D

Educational Objective: *Diagnose reactive arthritis.*

This patient should have urine nucleic acid amplification testing for *Chlamydia trachomatis* infection. She has acute arthritis of the right knee, enthesitis of the left ankle, and urethritis, all of which can occur with disseminated gonorrheal infection. However, in the absence of any recent history of sexual activity, these findings are more suggestive of reactive arthritis that can develop after *C. trachomatis* infection. Reactive arthritis occurs in both men and women, and enthesitis and oligoarthritis are common. The classic triad of arthritis, urethritis, and conjunctivitis occurs in only about one third of patients. Symptoms typically develop 2 to 4 weeks after an infection.

Classic pathogens associated with reactive arthritis include *C. trachomatis* as well as several enteric pathogens. *C. trachomatis* infection may be asymptomatic, and examination of a urine sample can establish the diagnosis. If infection is present, antibiotic treatment is warranted, and sexual partners should also be counseled and treated. However, nonsteroidal anti-inflammatory drugs are first-line therapy for musculoskeletal symptoms, as antibiotics do not effectively treat the reactive arthritis.

Antinuclear antibody testing can be helpful in the diagnosis of systemic lupus erythematosus (SLE). Although arthritis and pyuria can occur in SLE, the pyuria typically results from glomerulonephritis and is therefore not associated with the lower urinary tract symptoms of frequency and urgency. The patient does not have any other symptoms or signs of SLE.

Rheumatoid factor is present in approximately 70% of patients with rheumatoid arthritis. This disorder typically presents with a symmetric, small joint polyarthritis and does not explain this patient's urinary symptoms and pyuria.

This patient's negative Lyme disease serology results indicate that she does not have Lyme arthritis, and testing the synovial fluid for *Borrelia burgdorferi* infection is not needed. In patients with Lyme arthritis, testing by polymerase chain reaction (PCR) can detect *B. burgdorferi* DNA in synovial fluid. However, synovial fluid PCR testing has not been validated for wide use.

KEY POINT

Detection of pathogens such as *Chlamydia trachomatis* in patients with arthritis, urethritis, conjunctivitis, and/or enthesitis supports a diagnosis of reactive arthritis.

Bibliography

Morris D, Inman RD. Reactive arthritis: developments and challenges in diagnosis and treatment. Curr Rheumatol Rep. 2012;14:390–4. [PMID: 22821199]

Item 28   Answer: A

Educational Objective: *Diagnose Crohn disease–related arthritis.*

This patient most likely has Crohn disease–related arthritis, which is a form of enteropathic arthritis (arthritic conditions associated with gastrointestinal disease). Up to 20% of patients with Crohn disease or ulcerative colitis develop inflammatory joint disease. Polyarthritis that resembles seronegative rheumatoid arthritis develops in 20% of these patients, whereas 10% to 15% of these patients develop spondylitis and sacroiliitis. The risk for inflammatory joint disease associated with Crohn disease or ulcerative colitis increases in patients with more advanced colonic conditions and additional concomitant extraintestinal manifestations, including abscesses, erythema nodosum, uveitis, and pyoderma gangrenosum. Peripheral arthritis associated with inflammatory bowel disease (IBD) is often classified as one of two types. In type I arthropathy, the peripheral arthritis tends to be acute, affects only a few joints, tends to occur early in the course of IBD, may worsen with flares of IBD, and is often self-limited. In type II arthropathy, more joints tend to be involved and symptoms may be migratory. Joint pain is usually not related to IBD activity, and symptoms may wax and wane over years. In patients with arthritis sensitive to flares of IBD, treating the underlying gastrointestinal disease is indicated. Additional treatment for sacroiliitis and peripheral joint disease is otherwise symptomatic.

Psoriatic arthritis is a systemic chronic inflammatory arthritis associated with numerous clinical manifestations, including joint pain that appears similar to rheumatoid arthritis. Cutaneous involvement may be limited to nail pitting and commonly precedes joint inflammation, although 15% of patients develop joint inflammation first. However, there is no clear relationship to IBD, and this patient's lack of cutaneous findings makes psoriatic arthritis unlikely.

Reactive arthritis is characterized by the presence of inflammatory arthritis that manifests within 2 months of an episode of bacterial gastroenteritis or nongonococcal urethritis or cervicitis in a genetically predisposed patient. Reactive arthritis was previously called Reiter syndrome, which referred to the coincidence of arthritis, conjunctivitis, and urethritis (or cervicitis). However, only about one third of patients have all three symptoms. Reactive arthritis usually affects the peripheral joints, often in the lower extremities, although inflammatory back pain also may be present. This patient has no history of a previous infection or findings typical of reactive arthritis.

Rheumatoid arthritis is a symmetric polyarthritis that involves the small joints of the hands and feet as well as other joints throughout the body and is a consideration in the differential diagnosis of this patient. However, rheumatoid arthritis does not have an association with IBD, and this patient's symptoms in the context of his Crohn disease make enteropathic arthritis a much more likely diagnosis.

KEY POINT

Arthritis is a recognized extraintestinal manifestation of several gastrointestinal diseases, including inflammatory bowel disease.

Bibliography

Lakatos PL, Lakatos L, Kiss LS, et al. Treatment of extraintestinal manifestations in inflammatory bowel disease. Digestion. 2012;86 Suppl 1:28–35. [PMID: 23051724]

Item 29   Answer: C

Educational Objective: *Diagnose psoriatic arthritis.*

This patient has psoriatic arthritis, a systemic chronic inflammatory arthritis associated with numerous clinical manifestations. Typically, psoriasis predates the arthritis by years, whereas arthritis develops before skin disease in 15% of patients. Although there is a poor correlation between the severity of skin and joint disease, there is a good correlation between the severity of nail disease and the severity of both skin and joint disease. Psoriatic findings may also be limited to nail pitting and onycholysis. There are five patterns of joint involvement in psoriatic arthritis: involvement of the distal interphalangeal joints; asymmetric oligoarthritis; symmetric polyarthritis (similar to that of rheumatoid arthritis); arthritis mutilans (extensive osteolysis of the digits with striking deformity); and spondylitis. Characteristic features of psoriatic arthritis include enthesitis (inflammation of sites where tendons or ligaments insert into bone), dactylitis (inflammation of an entire digit), and tenosynovitis (inflammation of the synovial sheath surrounding a tendon). This patient has findings characteristic of psoriatic arthritis, including inflammation of a distal interphalangeal joint and dactylitis of a toe. He also has nail changes, including pitting and onycholysis.

Lyme arthritis typically involves medium- or large-sized joints rather than distal interphalangeal joints and does not typically cause tenosynovitis. Furthermore, this disorder does not cause nail changes, as seen in this patient.

Osteoarthritis can involve the distal interphalangeal joints but does not cause dactylitis or nail changes.

Rheumatoid arthritis can initially present with an asymmetric pattern, although it classically takes on a symmetric distribution with time. In contrast to this patient, patients with rheumatoid arthritis typically have sparing of the distal interphalangeal joints and preferential involvement of the proximal interphalangeal joints and metacarpophalangeal joints. In addition, rheumatoid arthritis also does not cause nail changes.

KEY POINT

Psoriatic arthritis is associated with various patterns of joint involvement, most notably distal interphalangeal joint involvement, and is characterized by enthesitis, dactylitis, tenosynovitis, and cutaneous involvement such as nail pitting.

Bibliography

Mease P. Psoriatic arthritis and spondyloarthritis assessment and management update. Curr Opin Rheumatol. 2013;25:287-96. [PMID: 23492739]

Item 30   Answer: A

Educational Objective: *Treat Raynaud phenomenon associated with systemic sclerosis.*

This patient has Raynaud phenomenon, which is present in more than 95% of patients with systemic sclerosis and is particularly likely to develop in patients with limited cutaneous disease. The most appropriate treatment for this patient is a long-acting dihydropyridine calcium channel blocker such as amlodipine.

Systemic sclerosis is classified according to the degree of skin involvement. Systemic sclerosis with limited cutaneous involvement, or CREST syndrome (calcinosis, Raynaud phenomenon, esophageal dysmotility, sclerodactyly, and telangiectasia), manifests as skin thickening distal to the elbows and knees. Conversely, systemic sclerosis with diffuse cutaneous involvement is associated with skin thickening proximal to the elbows and knees. Diffuse and limited cutaneous systemic sclerosis may affect the face.

Raynaud phenomenon is an abnormal vascular response to cold exposure or stress and usually involves the extremities. Although Raynaud phenomenon may occur in the absence of another disorder (primary Raynaud phenomenon), it frequently accompanies connective tissue diseases in which there are believed to be microvascular changes that alter normal vasoconstrictor activity. Episodes commonly involve an initial onset of vasoconstriction lasting for 15 to 20 minutes with ischemia (white phase) or cyanosis (blue phase), with erythema (red phase) developing with reperfusion.

In patients with Raynaud phenomenon, cigarette smoking is contraindicated and avoidance of cold is recommended; pharmacologic therapy is warranted for patients in whom these interventions do not provide sufficient relief. Dihydropyridine calcium channel blockers such as amlodipine have been shown to reduce the frequency and severity of attacks in patients with both primary and secondary Raynaud phenomenon, and these agents are frequently used as first-line treatment in this condition. Antiplatelet agents, such as aspirin and dipyridamole, also are used. The phosphodiesterase type 5 inhibitor sildenafil reduces the development of digital ulcers. Surgical revascularization, sympathetic nerve blockade or sympathectomy, prostacyclin analogues, or endothelin antagonists may be indicated in severe, refractory cases.

Topical nitrates applied to the finger webs are often used in the treatment of Raynaud phenomenon but are usually used as second-line therapy. Oral therapy with nitroglycerin is less effective and less well tolerated than amlodipine and is not indicated as a first-line drug for this condition.

Raynaud phenomenon is caused by microvascular involvement in patients with systemic sclerosis and is characterized by intimal proliferation and progressive luminal obliteration, as well as digital spasm. This process does not respond to anti-inflammatory agents; therefore, prednisone is not indicated in the treatment of Raynaud phenomenon.

β-Blockers such as metoprolol are not indicated in the treatment of Raynaud phenomenon and may actually worsen symptoms by preventing β-adrenergic-mediated vasodilation.

KEY POINT

Use of a dihydropyridine calcium channel blocker is warranted in patients with Raynaud phenomenon in whom cold avoidance does not provide sufficient relief.

Bibliography

Herrick AL. Management of Raynaud's phenomenon and digital ischemia. Curr Rheumatol Rep. 2013;15:303. [PMID: 23292819]

Item 31   Answer: D

Educational Objective: *Diagnose polymyositis.*

This patient most likely has polymyositis, a disorder characterized by acute or subacute onset of proximal muscle weakness without rash or distal muscle involvement. Electromyography (EMG) cannot reliably distinguish polymyositis from other forms of inflammatory myopathy. Muscle biopsy is the gold standard for diagnosing the idiopathic inflammatory myopathies. The muscle biopsy is usually not obtained on the same side as the EMG because the EMG can disrupt muscle architecture, cause local inflammation, and affect biopsy results. Biopsy characterization of the infiltration pattern and cell markers allows for the diagnosis of polymyositis, dermatomyositis, or inclusion body myositis. Muscle biopsy results from a patient with polymyositis characteristically show CD8-positive T-cell infiltration within the muscle fascicles, often with invasion of intact major histocompatibility complex–expressing muscle fibers. This pattern is seen in this patient and is often accompanied by evidence of muscle fiber necrosis and regeneration.

Patients with chronic alcohol-related myopathy may present with diffuse, often proximal muscle weakness that develops over weeks or months. However, this disorder tends to occur in patients with very high levels of chronic alcohol use, involves only a mild elevation of muscle enzymes, and is not associated with evidence of inflammation on muscle biopsy, as seen in this patient. Dermatomyositis is characterized by myopathic symptoms similar to those in polymyositis but is also associated with a typical rash (heliotrope rash on the upper eyelids and periorbital area, photosensitive rashes involving the shoulders, neck, and anterior chest) and Gottron papules (hyperkeratotic red papules and plaques over bony prominences). Biopsy results differ from those in polymyositis and are notable for CD4-positive T cells around the muscle fascicles and in the perimysial areas.

Inclusion body myositis usually affects older persons, has an insidious course, and is characterized by proximal and distal muscle weakness. Typical biopsy results are similar to those of polymyositis but also include characteristic filamentous particles in the sarcoplasm, termed inclusion bodies, which are not present in this patient.

KEY POINT

Muscle biopsy is the gold standard for diagnosing the idiopathic inflammatory myopathies.

Bibliography

Chahin N, Engel A. Correlation of muscle biopsy, clinical course, and outcome in PM and sporadic IBM. Neurology. 2008;70:418-24. [PMID: 17881720]

Item 32   Answer: B

Educational Objective: *Diagnose primary Sjögren syndrome.*

This patient has primary Sjögren syndrome. Sjögren syndrome is characterized by sicca syndrome, which causes xerophthalmia (dry eyes), and xerostomia (dry mouth). The absence of oral mucosal moisture often causes difficulty with mastication and swallowing and increases the risk for dental caries and periodontal disease. Vaginal dryness and parotid gland enlargement are frequently present, and mild fatigue and arthralgia are common. Abnormal findings on the Schirmer test, which measures moisture under the lower eyelids, are consistent with Sjögren syndrome. Approximately 50% of patients with this syndrome are antinuclear antibody positive and 60% to 75% of patients with primary Sjögren syndrome are anti-Ro/SSA antibody positive, and approximately 40% of these patients are anti-La/SSB antibody positive. In addition, 60% to 80% of patients with this condition have rheumatoid factor positivity. The presence of xerophthalmia and xerostomia accompanied by anti-Ro/SSA and anti-La/SSB antibody positivity and abnormal findings on the Schirmer test have a 94% sensitivity and specificity for diagnosing primary Sjögren syndrome. Other systemic features of Sjögren syndrome are uncommon but may include an inflammatory polyarthritis, cutaneous vasculitis, peripheral neuropathy, interstitial nephritis, and interstitial lung disease.

Lacrimal gland dysfunction is a common cause of dry eyes that may be age-related or due to obstruction of the lacrimal gland. However, given this patient's age and the presence of a dry mouth and anti-Ro/SSA and anti-La/SSB positivity, lacrimal gland dysfunction would not be adequate to explain her clinical picture.

Both rheumatoid arthritis and systemic lupus erythematosus (SLE) can be associated with Sjögren syndrome, in which case multiple systemic symptoms and findings such as joint involvement, pleuritis, cerebritis, lung dysfunction, and skin changes may all occur. Despite this patient's positive antinuclear antibody and rheumatoid factor test results, her lack of systemic symptoms and normal physical examination findings (except for xerophthalmia and xerostomia) argue against rheumatoid arthritis or SLE as a cause of secondary Sjögren syndrome.

KEY POINT

The presence of xerophthalmia and xerostomia accompanied by anti-Ro/SSA and anti-La/SSB antibody positivity and abnormal findings on the Schirmer test have a 94% sensitivity and specificity for the diagnosis of primary Sjögren syndrome.

Bibliography

Latkany R. Dry eyes: etiology and management. Curr Opin Ophthalmol. 2008;19:287-91. [PMID: 18545008]

Item 33   Answer: D

Educational Objective: *Manage fibromyalgia in a patient without depression.*

Treatment with a serotonin-norepinephrine reuptake inhibitor (SNRI) is appropriate for this patient with fibromyalgia. Fibromyalgia is characterized by widespread pain and tenderness of at least 3 months' duration. Other manifestations include fatigue, sleep disturbance, mood disorder, and cognitive dysfunction. Nonpharmacologic therapy is the cornerstone of fibromyalgia treatment and should be initiated in all patients. Regular aerobic exercise has been shown to be effective in this setting. Although high-impact aerobic exercises frequently are poorly tolerated, walking and/or water aerobics are often better accepted. Cognitive behavioral therapy has been shown to be beneficial but may not be as readily available to some patients. This patient has a 1-year history of widespread pain and tenderness along with fatigue and difficulty sleeping, features consistent with fibromyalgia. She tried pregabalin, which was discontinued because of an allergic reaction; therefore, treatment with an SNRI is warranted. Duloxetine and milnacipran are SNRIs approved by the Food and Drug Administration (FDA) to treat fibromyalgia with or without mood disorder and are as effective as pregabalin.

Fibromyalgia is not an inflammatory condition and therefore does not respond well to either glucocorticoids or nonsteroidal anti-inflammatory drugs (NSAIDs). Use of anti-inflammatory medications is not only ineffective, but in the case of glucocorticoids, exposes the patient to possible serious side effects. NSAIDs can help control pain caused by conditions such as osteoarthritis but are not effective as monotherapy for fibromyalgia symptoms; however, NSAIDs can be useful when combined with centrally acting drugs such as duloxetine or milnacipran in patients with resistant symptoms. This patient does not have evidence of another source of pain that requires treatment with NSAIDs and has not yet had a trial of a centrally acting medication.

Opioid medications have not been shown to be effective in treating fibromyalgia and also carry the significant risk of side effects and dependency. They should therefore not be used in treating patients with this disorder.

Data on the use of selective serotonin reuptake inhibitors in patients with fibromyalgia are conflicting, and none of these agents is currently FDA approved for this condition. Neurotransmitters other than serotonin may be important in fibromyalgia.

The serotonin-norepinephrine reuptake inhibitors duloxetine and milnacipran are FDA approved to treat patients who have fibromyalgia with or without associated depression.

Bibliography

Fitzcharles MA, Ste-Marie PA, Pereira JX; Canadian Fibromyalgia Guidelines Committee. Fibromyalgia: evolving concepts over the past 2 decades. CMAJ. 2013;185: E645-51. [PMID: 23649418]

Item 34   Answer: D
Educational Objective: *Diagnose giant cell arteritis.*

This patient, who has symptoms and signs of both polymyalgia rheumatica (PMR) and giant cell arteritis (GCA), should undergo a temporal artery biopsy. PMR is a condition closely related to GCA that presents with hip and shoulder girdle stiffness and pain and elevated inflammatory markers. Although PMR may occur independently from GCA and is not considered a vasculitis, it shares many features with GCA, including the same inflammatory cytokines and associations with age, ethnicity, and HLA class II alleles. GCA may be present in 15% to 30% of patients with PMR. Patients with only PMR do not have the classic findings of GCA such as temporal artery tenderness, headache, jaw pain, vision loss, or noncranial ischemia (such as arm claudication). In the absence of symptoms or clinical findings consistent with GCA, a trial of glucocorticoid therapy is indicated, as PMR typically responds dramatically to this therapy. However, this patient has headache and scalp tenderness in addition to PMR symptoms, suggesting the possibility of GCA. Therefore, a temporal artery biopsy is indicated.

Visual manifestations such as amaurosis fugax and anterior ischemic optic neuropathy due to vascular occlusion are the most feared complications of GCA. However, a dilated ophthalmologic examination may be normal in patients with GCA and would not provide adequate diagnostic information to guide therapy.

Although patients with suspected GCA may have headache and scalp tenderness, standard magnetic resonance imaging (MRI) brain imaging is not able to detect the vascular lesions associated with vasculitis and would not provide adequate diagnostic information. Magnetic resonance angiography may be abnormal in patients with GCA, but also does not provide enough information to establish the diagnosis and guide therapy.

MRI of the shoulder and hip joints may show evidence of inflammation of the periarticular structures in patients with PMR, but these findings are not required for diagnosis of this condition.

Temporal artery biopsy is the diagnostic procedure of choice in patients with suspected giant cell arteritis.

Bibliography

Waldman CW, Waldman SD, Waldman RA. Giant cell arteritis. Med Clin North Am. 2013;97:329-35. [PMID: 23419630]

Item 35   Answer: A
Educational Objective: *Diagnose granulomatosis with polyangiitis.*

This patient most likely has granulomatosis with polyangiitis (formerly known as Wegener granulomatosis), a systemic necrotizing vasculitis that predominantly affects the upper and lower respiratory tract and kidneys. More than 70% of patients have upper airway manifestations such as sinusitis. Orbital, nasal, inner ear, and laryngotracheal inflammation may also occur. Pulmonary manifestations include cough, hemoptysis, and pleurisy. Characteristic radiographic findings include multifocal pulmonary infiltrates or nodules, some of which may cavitate. Pauci-immune glomerulonephritis occurs in up to 80% of patients. Although glomerulonephritis may be the presenting manifestation, it is most often preceded by respiratory tract manifestations.

Sarcoidosis may cause inflammatory lesions of the orbits and trachea as well as nodular pulmonary infiltrates (necrotizing sarcoid granulomatosis) and an interstitial nephritis but not associated with significant glomerular disease.

Patients with Sjögren syndrome may have salivary gland enlargement and pulmonary infiltrates; however, significant tracheal inflammation and nodular or cavitary lung lesions are rare. Sjögren syndrome may cause an interstitial nephritis but is not associated with significant glomerular disease.

Tuberculosis may cause cavitary pulmonary lesions, but would not account for the glomerulopathy in this patient.

Granulomatosis with polyangiitis (formerly known as Wegener granulomatosis) is a systemic necrotizing vasculitis that predominantly affects the upper and lower respiratory tract and kidneys.

Bibliography

Holle JU, Laudien M, Gross WL. Clinical manifestations and treatment of Wegener's granulomatosis. Rheum Dis Clin North Am. 2010;36:507-26. [PMID: 20688247]

Item 36   Answer: B
Educational Objective: *Diagnose Henoch-Schönlein purpura.*

This patient has clinical features most consistent with Henoch-Schönlein purpura (HSP), a syndrome that most commonly occurs in children but can affect adults with greater severity. Characteristic features are a purpuric rash predominantly affecting the distal lower extremities, arthritis, abdominal pain, and hematuria. Skin biopsy specimens reveal the presence of leukocytoclastic vasculitis with deposits of IgA. Kidney biopsies obtained in patients with persistent hematuria and proteinuria or kidney disease following an attack of HSP reveal glomerulonephritis with IgA deposition consistent with lesions seen in IgA nephropathy. Kidney disease may be aggressive in some patients, with transition to diffuse proliferative glomerulonephritis. In men over the age of 50 years, HSP has been reported to occur in association with solid tumors or the myelodysplastic syndrome.

Churg-Strauss syndrome is a vasculitis that typically occurs in patients with a history of asthma. Common associated laboratory findings include peripheral eosinophilia and the presence of perinuclear antineutrophil cytoplasmic antibody (pANCA).

Microscopic polyangiitis typically involves small arterioles and may be associated with glomerulonephritis and purpuric skin lesions; however, immune deposits in the skin are not characteristic of this disorder, and most patients have a positive p-ANCA titer.

Polyarteritis nodosa is a small- to medium-vessel vasculitis that may be associated with renal artery involvement and hypertension. Purpura with skin biopsy findings of immune deposits is not a characteristic cutaneous feature.

KEY POINT

Onset of Henoch-Schönlein purpura may occur in adults and can be associated with solid tumors or the myelodysplastic syndrome.

Bibliography

Roberts PF, Waller TA, Brinker TM, et al. Henoch-Schönlein purpura: a review article. South Med J. 2007;100:821-4. [PMID: 17713309]

Item 37   Answer: A

Educational Objective: *Diagnose Churg-Strauss syndrome.*

This patient most likely has Churg-Strauss syndrome, a form of systemic vasculitis that most often occurs in the setting of antecedent asthma, allergic rhinitis, or sinusitis. Patients typically have eosinophilia, migratory pulmonary infiltrates, purpuric skin rash, and mononeuritis multiplex; fever, arthralgia, and myalgia also are common presenting features. Up to 40% of patients have perinuclear antineutrophil cytoplasmic antibody (p-ANCA) positivity with specificity for antimyeloperoxidase antibodies. Patients with p-ANCA positivity are more likely to have glomerulonephritis, alveolar hemorrhage, mononeuritis multiplex, and purpura.

Granulomatosis with polyangiitis (formerly known as Wegener granulomatosis) is a necrotizing vasculitis that typically affects the respiratory tract and kidneys. Radiographs show pulmonary infiltrates or nodules that are often cavitary, as well as pulmonary hemorrhage.

Microscopic polyangiitis is a necrotizing vasculitis that typically involves the kidneys and lungs. Patients frequently present with rapidly progressive glomerulonephritis; 50% of patients have pulmonary involvement that usually manifests as pulmonary hemorrhage. Fever, arthralgia, purpura, and mononeuritis multiplex can also occur.

Microscopic polyangiitis or granulomatosis with polyangiitis could account for the lung and kidney lesions in this patient; however, his findings of profound eosinophilia and antecedent allergic rhinitis, as well as his history of reactive airways disease, are more suggestive of Churg-Strauss syndrome.

Patients with polyarteritis nodosa typically present with fever, abdominal pain, arthralgia, and weight loss that develop over days to months. Two thirds of these patients have mononeuritis multiplex, and one third have hypertension and cutaneous involvement, including nodules, ulcers, purpura, and livedo reticularis (testicular pain also occurs in about one third of male patients). However, lung involvement is uncommon and ANCA test results typically are negative.

KEY POINT

Churg-Strauss syndrome is characterized by eosinophilia, migratory pulmonary infiltrates, purpuric skin rash, and mononeuritis multiplex in the setting of antecedent asthma, allergic rhinitis, or sinusitis.

Bibliography

Baldini C, Talarico R, Della Rossa A, Bombardieri S. Clinical manifestations and treatment of Churg-Strauss syndrome. Rheum Dis Clin North Am. 2010;36:527-43. [PMID: 20688248]

Item 38   Answer: B

Educational Objective: *Manage giant cell arteritis.*

Immediate high-dose intravenous methylprednisolone is indicated for this patient. The patient's headache, temporal artery tenderness, fever, and mild anemia are strongly suggestive of giant cell arteritis (GCA), and her pain in the shoulder and hip girdle accompanied by a significant elevation in the erythrocyte sedimentation rate is consistent with polymyalgia rheumatica, which is present in approximately a third of patients with GCA. Patients with GCA are usually treated with high-dose glucocorticoids, such as 1 mg/kg/d of prednisone. In some patients with GCA, however, anterior ischemic optic neuropathy may cause acute and complete visual loss with funduscopic examination revealing a pale, swollen optic nerve. Rarely, patients with GCA regain vision if treated immediately with high dose ("pulse") intravenous glucocorticoid such as methylprednisolone (1 g/d or 100 mg every 8 hours for 3 days) followed by oral prednisone (1 to 2 mg/kg/d). More importantly, this aggressive regimen helps to prevent blindness in the contralateral eye. Therefore, although temporal artery biopsy is the gold standard for diagnosing GCA, diagnostic testing should not precede treatment in patients whose clinical presentation is suspicious for this condition.

Low-dose oral prednisone is appropriate therapy for isolated polymyalgia rheumatic but does not sufficiently treat GCA. It would therefore not be appropriate treatment for a patient with suspected giant cell arteritis with visual loss.

A process in the brain is unlikely to cause monocular visual loss, and patients with GCA typically have normal findings on brain MRI. Therefore, this study would most likely be unhelpful in this patient.

In patients whose condition raises a strong suspicion of GCA, temporal artery biopsy should be performed after corticosteroid therapy is begun. Corticosteroid therapy will not affect the results of temporal artery biopsy as long as biopsy is performed within 4 weeks of initiating this therapy; positive biopsy results have been seen as late as 6 weeks after institution of high-dose glucocorticoid therapy, but the yield of biopsy is higher when this study is performed sooner.

KEY POINT

In patients whose clinical presentation is suspicious for giant cell arteritis, glucocorticoid therapy should be instituted immediately before diagnostic testing is performed.

Bibliography

Waldman CW, Waldman SD, Waldman RA. Giant cell arteritis. Med Clin North Am. 2013;97:329-35. [PMID: 23419630]

Laboratory Values
IM Essentials

U.S. traditional units are followed in parentheses by equivalent values expressed in S.I. units.

Hematology

Absolute neutrophil count
  Male — 1780-5380/µL (1.78-5.38 × 109/L)
  Female — 1560-6130/µL (1.56-6.13 × 109/L)
Activated partial thromboplastin time — 25-35 s
Bleeding time — less than 10 min
Erythrocyte count — 4.2-5.9 x 10^6/µL (4.2-5.9 × 10^{12}/L)
Erythrocyte sedimentation rate
  Male — 0-15 mm/h
  Female — 0-20 mm/h
Erythropoietin — less than 30 mU/mL (30 units/L)
D-Dimer — less than 0.5 µg/mL (0.5 mg/L)
Ferritin, serum — 15-200 ng/mL (15-200 µg/L)
Haptoglobin, serum — 50-150 mg/dL (500-1500 mg/L)
Hematocrit
  Male — 41%-51%
  Female — 36%-47%
Hemoglobin, blood
  Male — 14-17 g/dL (140-170 g/L)
  Female — 12-16 g/dL (120-160 g/L)
Leukocyte alkaline phosphatase — 15-40 mg of phosphorus liberated/h per 10^{10} cells; score = 13-130/100 polymorphonuclear neutrophils and band forms
Leukocyte count — 4000-10,000/µL (4.0-10 x 10^9/L)
Mean corpuscular hemoglobin — 28-32 pg
Mean corpuscular hemoglobin concentration — 32-36 g/dL (320-360 g/L)
Mean corpuscular volume — 80-100 fL
Platelet count — 150,000-350,000/µL (150-350 × 10^9/L)
Prothrombin time — 11-13 s
Reticulocyte count — 0.5%-1.5% of erythrocytes; absolute: 23,000-90,000/µL (23-90 x 10^9/L)

Blood, Plasma, and Serum Chemistry Studies

Albumin, serum — 3.5-5.5 g/dL (35-55 g/L)
Alkaline phosphatase, serum — 36-92 units/L
α-Fetoprotein, serum — 0-20 ng/mL (0-20 µg/L)
Aminotransferase, alanine (ALT) — 0-35 units/L
Aminotransferase, aspartate (AST) — 0-35 units/L
Ammonia, plasma — 40-80 µg/dL (23-47 µmol/L)
Amylase, serum — 0-130 units/L
Bicarbonate, serum — 23-28 meq/L (23-28 mmol/L)
Bilirubin, serum
  Total — 0.3-1.2 mg/dL (5.1-20.5 µmol/L)
  Direct — 0-0.3 mg/dL (0-5.1 µmol/L)
Blood gases, arterial (ambient air)
  pH — 7.38-7.44
  Pco_2 — 35-45 mm Hg (4.7-6.0 kPa)
  Po_2 — 80-100 mm Hg (10.6-13.3 kPa)
  Oxygen saturation — 95% or greater
Blood urea nitrogen — 8-20 mg/dL (2.9-7.1 mmol/L)
C-reactive protein — 0.0-0.8 mg/dL (0.0-8.0 mg/L)
Calcium, serum — 9-10.5 mg/dL (2.2-2.6 mmol/L)
Carbon dioxide, serum — See Bicarbonate
Chloride, serum — 98-106 meq/L (98-106 mmol/L)
Cholesterol, plasma
  Total — 150-199 mg/dL (3.88-5.15 mmol/L), desirable
  Low-density lipoprotein (LDL) — less than or equal to 130 mg/dL (3.36 mmol/L), desirable
  High-density lipoprotein (HDL) — greater than or equal to 40 mg/dL (1.04 mmol/L), desirable
Complement, serum
  C3 — 55-120 mg/dL (550-1200 mg/L)
  Total (CH$_{50}$) — 37-55 units/mL (37-55 kU/L)
Creatine kinase, serum — 30-170 units/L
Creatinine, serum — 0.7-1.3 mg/dL (61.9-115 µmol/L)
Electrolytes, serum
  Sodium — 136-145 meq/L (136-145 mmol/L)
  Potassium — 3.5-5.0 meq/L (3.5-5.0 mmol/L)
  Chloride — 98-106 meq/L (98-106 mmol/L)
  Bicarbonate — 23-28 meq/L (23-28 mmol/L)
Fibrinogen, plasma — 150-350 mg/dL (1.5-3.5 g/L)
Folate, red cell — 160-855 ng/mL (362-1937 nmol/L)
Folate, serum — 2.5-20 ng/mL (5.7-45.3 nmol/L)
Glucose, plasma — fasting, 70-100 mg/dL (3.9-5.6 mmol/L)
γ-Glutamyltransferase, serum — 0-30 units/L
Homocysteine, plasma
  Male — 0.54-2.16 mg/L (4-16 µmol/L)
  Female — 0.41-1.89 mg/L (3-14 µmol/L)
Immunoglobulins
  Globulins, total — 2.5-3.5 g/dL (25-35 g/L)
    IgG — 640-1430 mg/dL (6.4-14.3 g/L)
    IgA — 70-300 mg/dL (0.7-3.0 g/L)
    IgM — 20-140 mg/dL (0.2-1.4 g/L)
    IgD — less than 8 mg/dL (80 mg/L)
    IgE — 0.01-0.04 mg/dL (0.1-0.4 mg/L)
Iron studies
  Ferritin, serum — 15-200 ng/mL (15-200 µg/L)
  Iron, serum — 60-160 µg/dL (11-29 µmol/L)
  Iron-binding capacity, total, serum — 250-460 µg/dL (45-82 µmol/L)
  Transferrin saturation — 20%-50%
Lactate dehydrogenase, serum — 60-100 units/L
Lactic acid, venous blood — 6-16 mg/dL (0.67-1.8 mmol/L)
Lipase, serum — less than 95 units/L
Magnesium, serum — 1.5-2.4 mg/dL (0.62-0.99 mmol/L)
Methylmalonic acid, serum — 150-370 nmol/L
Osmolality, plasma — 275-295 mosm/kg H_2O
Phosphatase, alkaline, serum — 36-92 units/L
Phosphorus, serum — 3-4.5 mg/dL (0.97-1.45 mmol/L)
Potassium, serum — 3.5-5.0 meq/L (3.5-5.0 mmol/L)
Prostate-specific antigen, serum - less than 4 ng/mL (4 µg/L)
Protein, serum
  Total — 6.0-7.8 g/dL (60-78 g/L)
  Albumin — 3.5-5.5 g/dL (35-55 g/L)
  Globulins, total — 2.5-3.5 g/dL (25-35 g/L)
Rheumatoid factor — less than 40 units/mL (40 kU/L)
Sodium, serum — 136-145 meq/L (136-145 mmol/L)
Transferrin saturation — 20%-50%
Triglycerides — less than 150 mg/dL (1.69 mmol/L), desirable
Troponins, serum
  Troponin I — 0-0.5 ng/mL (0-0.5 µg/L)
  Troponin T — 0-0.10 ng/mL (0-0.10 µg/L)
Urea nitrogen, blood — 8-20 mg/dL (2.9-7.1 mmol/L)
Uric acid, serum — 2.5-8 mg/dL (0.15-0.47 mmol/L)
Vitamin B$_{12}$, serum — 200-800 pg/mL (148-590 pmol/L)

Endocrine

Adrenocorticotropic hormone (ACTH), serum — 9-52 pg/mL (2-11 pmol/L)

Aldosterone, serum

Supine — 2-5 ng/dL (55-138 pmol/L)

Standing — 7-20 ng/dL (194-554 pmol/L)

Aldosterone, urine — 5-19 µg/24 h (13.9-52.6 nmol/24 h)

Catecholamines

Epinephrine, plasma (supine) — less than 75 ng/L (410 pmol/L)

Norepinephrine, plasma (supine) — 50-440 ng/L (296-2600 pmol/L)

Catecholamines, 24-hour, urine — less than 100 µg/m^2 per 24 h (591 nmol/m^2 per 24 h)

Cortisol, free, urine - less than 50 µg/24 h (138 nmol/24 h)

Dehydroepiandrosterone sulfate (DHEA), plasma

Male — 1.3-5.5 µg/mL (3.5-14.9 µmol/L)

Female — 0.6-3.3 µg/mL (1.6-8.9 µmol/L)

Epinephrine, plasma (supine) — less than 75 ng/L (410 pmol/L)

Estradiol, serum

Male — 10-30 pg/mL (37-110 pmol/L);

Female — day 1-10, 14-27 pg/mL (50-100 pmol/L); day 11-20, 14-54 pg/mL (50-200 pmol/L); day 21-30, 19-41 pg/mL (70-150 pmol/L)

Follicle-stimulating hormone, serum

Male (adult) — 5-15 mU/mL (5-15 units/L)

Female — follicular or luteal phase, 5-20 mU/mL (5-20 units/L); mid-cycle peak, 30-50 mU/mL (30-50 units/L); postmenopausal, greater than 35 mU/mL (35 units/L)

Growth hormone, plasma — after oral glucose: less than 2 ng/mL (2 µg/L); response to provocative stimuli: greater than 7 ng/mL (7 µg/L)

Luteinizing hormone, serum

Male — 3-15 mU/mL (3-15 units/L)

Female — follicular or luteal phase, 5-22 mU/mL (5-22 units/L); midcycle peak, 30-250 mU/mL (30-250 units/L); postmenopausal, greater than 30 mU/mL (30 units/L)

Metanephrine, urine — less than 1.2 mg/24 h (6.1 mmol/24 h)

Norepinephrine, plasma (supine) — 50-440 ng/L (296-2600 pmol/L)

Parathyroid hormone, serum — 10-65 pg/mL (10-65 ng/L)

Progesterone, blood

Male (adult) — 0.27-0.9 ng/mL (0.9-2.9 nmol/L)

Female — follicular phase, 0.33-1.20 ng/mL (1.0-3.8 nmol/L); luteal phase, 0.72-17.8 ng/mL (2.3-56.6 nmol/L);

postmenopausal, less than 0.2-1 ng/mL (0.6-3.18 nmol/L);

oral contraceptives, 0.34-0.92 ng/mL (1.1-2.9 nmol/L)

Prolactin, serum

Male — less than 15 ng/mL (15 µg/L)

Female — less than 20 ng/mL (20 µg/L)

Testosterone, serum

Male (adult) — 300-1200 ng/dL (10-42 nmol/L)

Female — 20-75 ng/dL (0.7-2.6 nmol/L)

Thyroid function tests

Thyroid iodine (^{131}I) uptake — 10%-30% of administered dose at 24 h

Thyroid-stimulating hormone (TSH) — 0.5-5.0 µU/mL (0.5-5.0 mU/L)

Thyroxine (T$_4$), serum

Total — 5-12 µg/dL (64-155 nmol/L)

Free — 0.9-2.4 ng/dL (12-31 pmol/L)

Free T$_4$ index — 4-11

Triiodothyronine, free (T$_3$) — 3.6-5.6 ng/L (5.6-8.6 pmol/L)

Triiodothyronine, resin (T$_3$) — 25%-35%

Triiodothyronine, serum (T$_3$) — 70-195 ng/dL (1.1-3.0 nmol/L)

Vanillylmandelic acid, urine — less than 8 mg/24 h (40.4 µmol/24 h)

Vitamin D

1,25-dihydroxy, serum — 25-65 pg/mL (60-156 pmol/L)

25-hydroxy, serum — 25-80 ng/mL (62-200 nmol/L)

Urine

Albumin–creatinine ratio — less than 30 mg/g

Calcium — 100-300 mg/24 h (2.5-7.5 mmol/24 h) on unrestricted diet

Creatinine — 15-25 mg/kg per 24 h (133-221 mmol/kg per 24 h)

Glomerular filtration rate (GFR)

Normal

Male — 130 mL/min/1.73 m^2

Female — 120 mL/min/1.73 m^2

Stages of Chronic Kidney Disease

Stage 1 — greater than or equal to 90 mL/min/1.73 m^2

Stage 2 — 60-89 mL/min/1.73 m^2

Stage 3 — 30-59 mL/min/1.73 m^2

Stage 4 — 15-29 mL/min/1.73 m^2

Stage 5 — less than 15 mL/min/1.73 m^2

5-Hydroxyindoleacetic acid (5-HIAA) — 2-9 mg/24 h (10.4-46.8 µmol/24 h)

Protein–creatinine ratio - less than or equal to 150 mg/g

Sodium — 100-260 meq/24 h (100-260 mmol/24 h) (varies with intake)

Uric acid — 250-750 mg/24 h (1.48-4.43 mmol/24 h) (varies with diet)

Gastrointestinal

Gastrin, serum — 0-180 pg/mL (0-180 ng/L)

Stool fat — less than 5 g/d on a 100-g fat diet

Stool weight — less than 200 g/d

Pulmonary

Forced expiratory volume in 1 second (FEV$_1$) — greater than 80% of predicted

Forced vital capacity (FVC) — greater than 80% of predicted

FEV$_1$/FVC — greater than 75%

Cerebrospinal Fluid

Cell count — 0-5/µL (0-5 x 10^6/L)

Glucose — 40-80 mg/dL (2.2-4.4 mmol/L); less than 40% of simultaneous plasma concentration is abnormal

Pressure (opening) — 70-200 mm H$_2$O

Protein — 15-60 mg/dL (150-600 mg/L)

Hemodynamic Measurements

Cardiac index — 2.5-4.2 L/min/m^2

Left ventricular ejection fraction — greater than 55%

Pressures

Pulmonary artery

Systolic — 20-25 mm Hg

Diastolic — 5-10 mm Hg

Mean — 9-16 mm Hg

Pulmonary capillary wedge — 6-12 mm Hg

Right atrium — mean 0-5 mm Hg

Right ventricle

Systolic — 20-25 mm Hg

Diastolic — 0-5 mm Hg

American College of Physicians

190 N. Independence Mall West, Philadelphia, PA 19106-1572

This page intentionally left blank.

This page intentionally left blank.

This page intentionally left blank.

This page intentionally left blank.

Color Plates

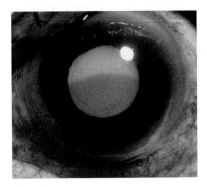

Plate 1
General Internal Medicine, Item 71

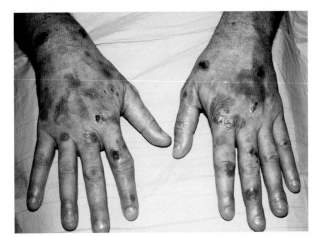

Plate 3
General Internal Medicine, Item 87

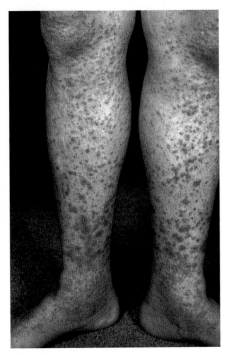

Plate 2
General Internal Medicine, Item 86

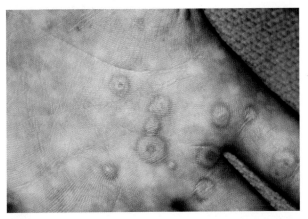

Plate 4
General Internal Medicine, Item 88

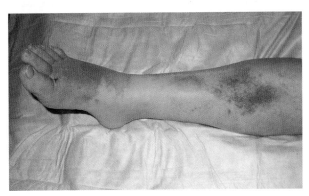

Plate 5
General Internal Medicine, Item 89

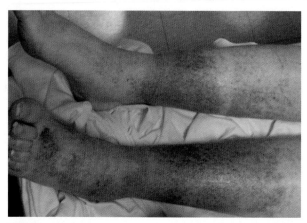

Plate 6
General Internal Medicine, Item 90

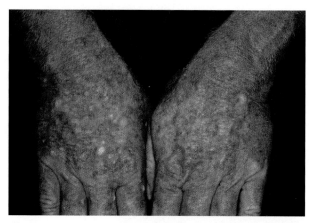

Plate 8
General Internal Medicine, Item 93

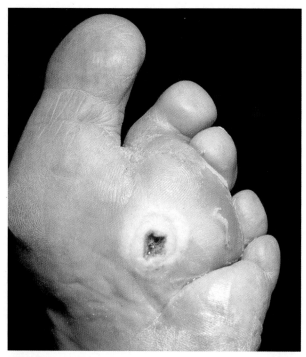

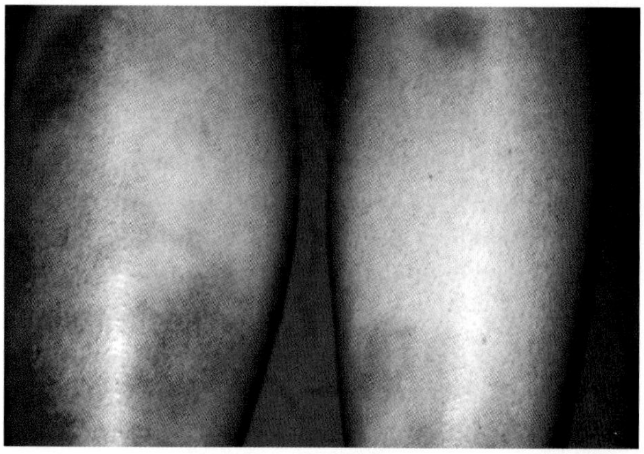

Plate 7
General Internal Medicine, Item 91

Plate 9
General Internal Medicine, Item 94

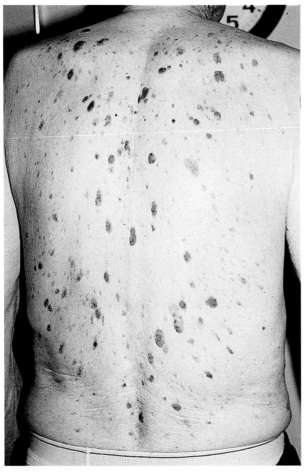

Plate 10
General Internal Medicine, Item 95

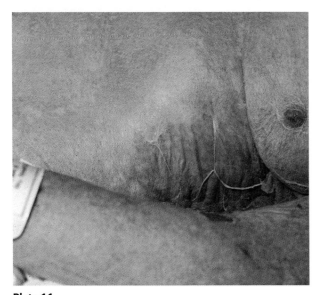

Plate 11
General Internal Medicine, Item 96

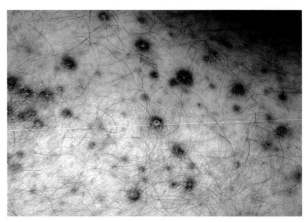

Plate 12
General Internal Medicine, Item 98

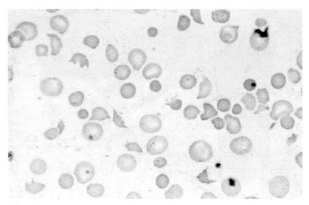

Plate 13
Hematology, Item 13

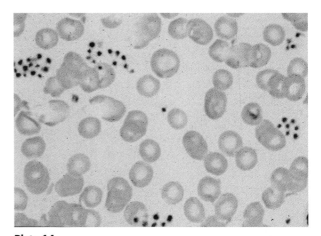

Plate 14
Hematology, Item 14

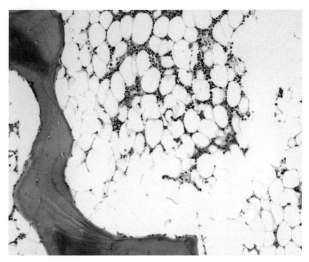

Plate 15
Hematology, Item 18

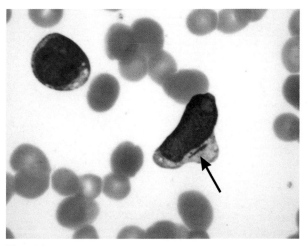

Plate 16
Hematology, Item 20

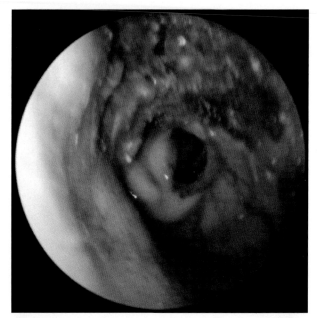

Plate 17
Infectious Disease Medicine, Item 6

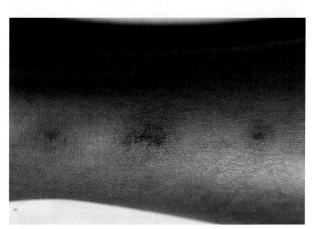

Plate 18
Infectious Disease Medicine, Item 31

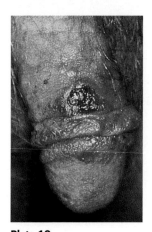

Plate 19
Infectious Disease Medicine, Item 33

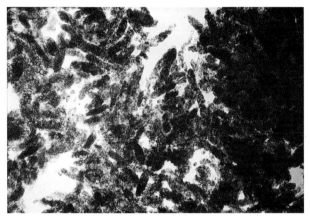

Plate 20
Nephrology, Item 25

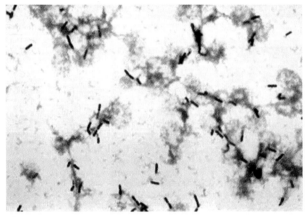

Plate 21
Neurology, Item 5

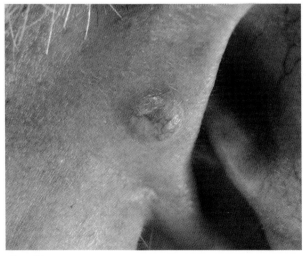

Plate 22
Oncology, Item 22

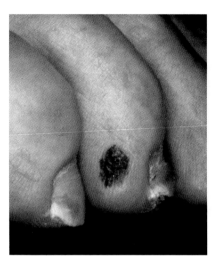

Plate 23
Oncology, Item 23

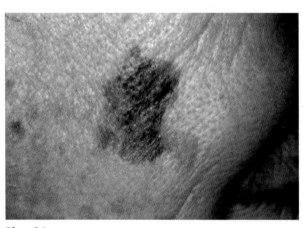

Plate 24
Oncology, Item 24

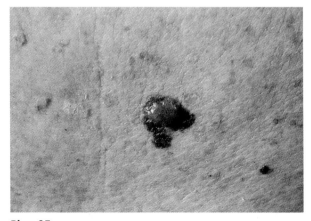

Plate 25
Oncology, Item 25

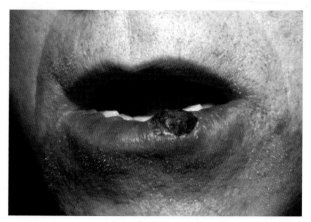

Plate 26
Oncology, Item 26

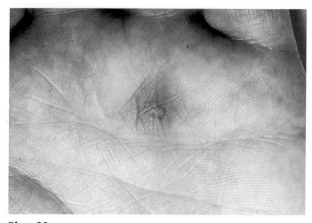

Plate 28
Rheumatology, Item 18

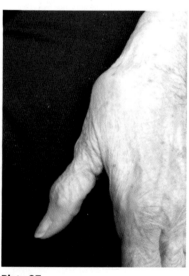

Plate 27
Rheumatology, Item 10

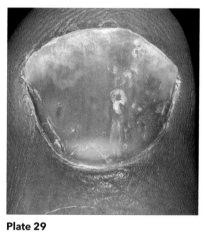

Plate 29
Rheumatology, Item 29